Land Records
of
Wicomico County Maryland

1666–1810

by

Ruth T. Dryden

HERITAGE BOOKS
2011

HERITAGE BOOKS
AN IMPRINT OF HERITAGE BOOKS, INC.

Books, CDs, and more—Worldwide

For our listing of thousands of titles see our website at
www.HeritageBooks.com

Published 2011 by
HERITAGE BOOKS, INC.
Publishing Division
100 Railroad Ave. #104
Westminster, Maryland 21157

Originally published 1992

All rights reserved. No part of this book may be reproduced or transmitted in any form or by any means, electronic or mechanical, including photocopying, recording or by any information storage and retrieval system without written permission from the author, except for the inclusion of brief quotations in a review.

International Standard Book Numbers
Paperbound: 978-0-7884-5271-0
Clothbound: 978-0-7884-8596-1

Dedicated to my family

Susan D. Morgan

L. Thomas Morgan

Matthew T. Morgan

Mark A. Morgan

Michael T. Morgan

Melissa S. Morgan

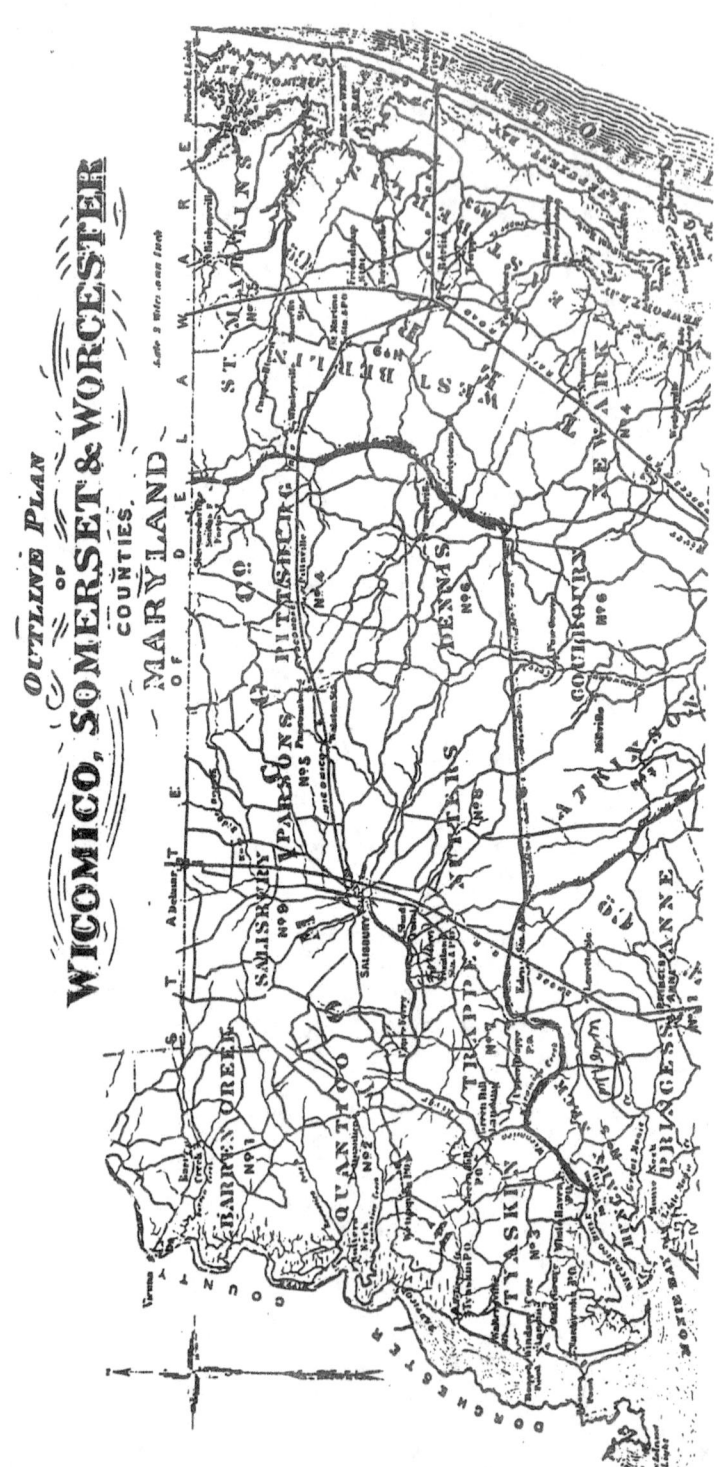

NOTES ON USING THIS BOOK

Wicomico County Maryland was formed in 1867, taken from the northern section of Somerset County and the north west part of Worcester County. Since I had no maps to indicate the exact location of these lands I have had to make some assumptions as to their locations from descriptions as found in the deeds. The lands that were in Worcester County were sometimes difficult to identify so the ommissions determined by the reader will be found in the forthcomming book on Worcester County lands.

All land records are in Capital letters and in alphabetical order. Where "no name" or "unnamed" is used there could be a question as to the verification of this deed. These are my determination as to which lands were exchanged so beware of these entries.

Widows were entitled to one third of their husbands estates. This was called Dower Rights and are indicated when she relinquished her claim on land sold. She is usually referred to as the relic of her husband.

Variations in the spelling of a name are due to the original deed or patent, i.e. Benson could be Benston, McReady could be McCready, McGrath is also Magraugh.

When the land is sold for 5 shillings, it is usually to a relative, daughter, brother, nephew, since this is a token payment. The term, no acreage, means that the land was described in the deed but the exact number of acres sold was not included. One moity is one half of the land. In 1780 the Maryland Assemby passed an act stating "All property within the State belonging to British subjects (Torys) shall be seized and hereby confiscated to the use of the State."

In the year 1767 there was an adjustment of the Maryland and Delaware boundaries which put some of these lands in the state of Delaware, as noted by the warrants within this book.

The index omits titles such as Jr., Sr., Esq. Rev. & Col.since these titles vary and the same person could have any or all of these.

The land sometimes passed from one generation to another and there is no deed or will to indicate this. It descends by law to the eldest son. If there are no sons, to a brother or nephew, or occasionally to daughters and their husbands or dower rights to the widow's second husband.

Note that the names of lands when patented can be a clue to the origin of the patentee such as BELFAST, also in Ireland. The name can be also an indication of the owners personality, MISORY, HARD FORTUNE, LUCK, MISTAKE, or a description of the land itself such as FLATLAND and MEADOW.

Notes in parenthesis are mine.

LIST OF ABBREVIATIONS

exec= Executor of the will
adm.=administrator of the estate
Dorc.Co.= Dorcester County Maryland
Acco.Co.Va.= Accomack County Virginia
Som.Co.Md. = Somerset County Maryland
Worc.Co.= Worcester County Maryland
etc= and so forth

d/o= daughter of   w/o= wife of   s/o= son of
Del.=state of Delaware
mtg.= mortgage
aka= also known as or alias.
Q.V. = Questionable verification.

SOURCES

Deed books of Somerset County Maryland to 1810
Will books of Somerset County and Worcester Co.Md abstracted by Dryden
Deed books of Worcester County Maryland to 1810
Marylander Calendar of Wills by Baldwin
Old Somerset on the Eastern Shore of Maryland by Torrence
1783 tax lists abstracted by Dryden
1666-1723 Rent Rolls abstracted by Dryden
Federal Census Records.
Card Index, patent files, Hall of Records, Annapolis, Maryland.
1877 Atlas of Eastern Shore Maryland.

AARONS FOLLY

Patented Somerset County in 1739 by Aaron Lynn for 150 acres.
24 June 1749 Aaron Lynn sold to Robert Swan of Annapolis 150 acres.

ABERDEEN

Patented in 1759 by Andrew Smith for 50 acres.
29 Oct.1772 Andrew Smith son of Andrew with wife Elizabeth Smith sold to Jacob Parker 50 acres.
1783 tax lists Jacob Parker 50 acres in Wic.100 Worcester County.

ABERGAVENY

Patented on 10 May 1675 for 100 acres by Roger Phillips in Nanticoke 100 on the south side of Quantico Creek.
8 Jan 1677 Roger Phillips and wife Dorothy Phillips sold 100 acres to Samuel Jackson.
1687 Samuel Jackson willed to son Jonathan 200 acres (includes 100 acres of CHANCE)
Rent Rolls 1666-1723 Possessed by Jonathan Jackson
1738 Jonathan Jackson and wife Rachel Jackson sold for 5 shillings to Thomas Jackson 100 acres of CHANCE being part of two tracts SMALL LOTT & ABERGAVENY.
14 Jan 1745 Thomas Jackson, wife Sarah Jackson sold to John Leatherbury of Acco. Co. Va. part CHANCE, part of two tracts 100 acres.
12 Aug.1808 James Anderson sold 40 acres SMALL LOTT to Henry Crawford adjacent ABERGAVENY.

ABERGELDIE

Patented in 1794 by Salathiel Griffith
1795 Salathiel Griffith willed to son Martin Griffith.

ABORIGINES NEGLECT

Patented in 1834 by Gideon Badley

ABRAHAMS LOT

Patented in 1714 by Thomas Highway for 250 acres.
Resurvey 1735 by Henry Toadvine for 250 acres.
31 July 1736 Henry Toadvine sold 1/2 to John Christopher Jr. for 5 shillings, 125 acres.
1748 John Christopher willed planatation, unnamed to son John.
1756 Henry Toadvine willed to grandson Ezekiel Toadvine s/o Joshua Toadvine 125 acres.
5 Aug.1767 Ezekiel Toadvine sold 125 acres to James Cathell Jr.
14 Mar.1771 James Cathell Jr. with wife Elizabeth Cathell sold 125 acres to James Niven.
9 Mar.1765 John Christopher sold 125 acres to Stephen Horsey.
1783 tax - Stephen Horsey 125 acres, Worc.Co. Wic. 100
2 May 1778 William McBryde executor of James Niven deceased sold to Stephen Livingston 125 acres.

1788 Stephen Horsey willed to grandson George Livingston (he married Sarah Horsey)
1747 George Livingston willed part to wife Susan Livingston and after death to son Samuel Livingston.
Repantented in 1863 by John White, 3 acres, 2 perches 28 rods.

ACCOMODATION

Patented in 1813 by Reuben Davis

ACWORTHS CHANCE

Patented in 1759 by James Acworth for 30 acres in Rewastico
20 June 1769 James Acworth sold to William Acworth 30 acres.
1783 tax- Train Acworth 30 acres.

ACWORTHS CHOICE

Patented on 16 Feb.1664 by Richard Acworth for 100 acres on the east side of Barren Creek.
Rent Rolls 1666-1723 - Possessed by James Weatherly (he married Ann Acworth widow of Richard Acworth)
1727 Richard Acworth willed to three sons, Charles Acworth, Thomas Acworth and Richard Acworth.
25 Sep.1759 Charles Acworth sold to Mary Harris part of ACWORTHS DELIGHT, & ACWORTHS CHOICE 75 acres and part of THE RIDGES.
23 Nov.1769 Charles Acworth gave to brother James Acworth (son of Thomas Acworth) 450 acres of ACWORTHS DELIGHT, ACWORTHS CHICE, HOGG QUARTER, THE RIDGES & part of MARISH POINT.
20 June 1769 James Acworth sold to Richard Acworth 180 acres, this includes 10 acres of ACWORTHS CHOICE.
6 April 1774 John Weatherly and Joshua Weatherly sold 62 acres to William Acworth for 5 shillings.

ACWORTHS CONTRIVANCE

Patented on 26 Feb 1674 by Richard Acworth for 100 acres on the south side of the Nanticoke River on the north side of a fresh water run.
Rent Rolls 1666-1723 Possessed by James Weatherly (Richard Acworth married Ann Manlove, she married 2nd. James Weatherly) Richard Acworth died in 1675 and willed lands (unnamed)to his children.
10 Oct. 1758 Joseph Weatherly and Elijah Weatherly sold 41 acres to John Weatherly with tract ADDITION.
3 June 1769 John Weatherly sold to McKimmey Porter 13 3/4 acres with FATHERS DELIGHT, LAST CHOICE.
1770 John Weatherly sold to Richard Waller his rights to ACWORTHS CONTRIVANCE, ADDITION, LAST CHOICE and saw mill adjacent.
3 Aug.1771 Richard Waller and John Weatherly sold to William Winder Sr. 20 acres (with ADDITION resurveyed to PARTNERSHIP.)
23 Nov.1779 Charles Weatherly, James Weatherly, John Weatherly and Jesse Weatherly sold to William Winder, with ADDITION alias PARTNERSHIP and LAST CHOICE and PREVENTION.
23 Nov.1779 Richard Acworth sold to William Winder part, no acres given with SONS CHOICE & ACWORTHS DELIGHT.

1783 tax- McKimmey Porter 13 1/2 acres
1783 tax- James Weatherly 35 acres
1783 tax- William Winder 33 acres
1790 will McKimmey Porter, to son Levi Porter, FATHERS DELIGHT, LAST CHOICE & WEATHERLYS CONTRIVANCE.
11 June 1810 Levi Porter, wife Hetty Porter sold to Joshua Brattan lands devised by father McKimmey Porter, no name or acres.

ACWORTHS DELIGHT

Patented on 20 November 1672 by Richard Acworth for 100 acres in Nanticoke 100, Rewastico District.
5 Nov.1688 Richard Acworth patented 500 acres of the same, probably a resurvey.
Rent Rolls 1666-1723 Possessed by the heirs of Thomas Acworth
1727 will Richard Acworth, to sons Charles Acworth and Thomas Acworth.
2 March 1736 Charles Acworth sold to Joseph Tully 50 acres, on Barren Creek.
2 Jan.1747 Charles Acworth and wife Elizabeth Acworth sold to Joseph Tully 42 acres, a total of 92 acres formerly sold but not recorded.
1 March 1755 Thomas Acworth sold 50 acres to James Acworth.
1 March 1755 Thomas Acworth and Charles Acworth sold to Richard Acworth, blacksmith 100 acres of HOGG QUARTER & ACWORTHS DELIGHT.
25 March 1757 Joseph Tully, with wife Sarah Tully sold to Stephen Stevens 92 acres.
12 Aug.1758 Stephen Stevens sold to Stephen Parramore 92 acres.
1 July 1759 Charles Acworth sold 89 acres to Joseph Alpha.
1759 Thomas Acworth willed to sons James Acworth and Richard Acworth.
25 Sep.1759 Charles Acworth sold to Mary Harris part of ACWORTHS DELIGHT & ACWORTHS CHOICE 75 acres and part of THE RIDGES.
25 Sep.1759 Charles Acworth sold 75 acres to James West.
23 Nov.1759 Charles Acworth gave to James Acworth son of Thomas Acworth deceased, brother of Charles,ACWORTHS DELIGHT, ACWORTHS CHOICE, HOGG QUARTER, THE RIDGES and pt. MARISH POINT   450 acres.
7 Aug.1761 Stephen Parramore, wife Mary Parramore sold to John Carmichael 92 acres.
6 July 1765 Thomas Acworth sold to Ephraim King, 50 acres.
20 June 1769 James Acworth sold to William Acworth 180 acres of ACWORTHS DELIGHT, CHOICE, HOGG QUARTER, THE RIDGES, MARISH POINT, etc.
20 June 1769 James Acworth sold to brother Richard Acworth 100 acres of HOGG QUARTER, ACWORTHS DELIGHT, THE RIDGES.
4 July 1769 James Acworth with wife Mary Acworth and William Acworth sold to Beauchamp Hull 30 acres.
6 Apr.1774 John Weatherly and Joshua Weatherly sold to William Acworth for 5 shillings, no acres mentioned.
23 Nov.1779 Richard Acworth sold part to William Winder.
1783 tax- Richard Acworth, 100 acres- Rewastico
1783 tax- Train Acworth 60 acres
1783 tax- Joseph Alpha 89 acres
1783 tax- John Grumble 93 acres
1783 tax- Beauchamp Hull 36 acres
1783 tax- Mary Harris 75 acres
1783 tax- William Kennerly 100 acres
1783 tax- James West 75 acres
29 June 1787 John Carmichael son of John,sold to James Walter 92

acres.
21 May 1790 Richard Acworth, wife Elizabeth Acworth sold to James Walter 30 1/2 acres.
22 July 1791 Richard Acworth, wife Elizabeth Acworth sold to James Walter 46 3/4 acres.
29 Aug.1794 Constant Weatherly sold to Levin Carmichael all his rights.
28 April 1797 Robert Venables Sr. and wife Amelia Venables sold to Mary C. Dashiell wife of Robert Dashiell.(land William Acworth father of Amelia Venables and Mary Dashiell possessed, all except 10 acres.)
1797 will Robert Venables, to wife Amelia Venables.
28 Apr.1797 Robert Dashiell Jr.,wife Mary Dashiell sold to Amelia Venables w/o Robert Venables 148 acres, at Barren Creek with tract UNITED STATES.
3 Dec.1795 Richard Acworth mortgaged to Robert Venables.
7 Dec.1804 Levin Carmichael, Hetty Russell, Samuel Green and wife Rachel Green sold all rights to James Walter.
1789 Joseph Alpha willed lands to wife Mary Alpha (unnamed)
8 April 1805 Elijah Reed of Worc.Co. heir at law of Obediah Reed and Zachariah Reed deceased, sold to William Winder his great uncle, all interest he has in SONS CHOICE, WEATHERLYS CONTRIVANCE, ACWORTHS DELIGHT. Zachariah Reed died possessed and it descended to the only son of Obediah Reed, who went to New York in 1777 and supposed to have died the year of 1778 and never has been heard from since. He died without issue or brothers or sisters. Oldest brother of Zachariah Reed was John Reed who went to Worcester County and died ther leaving, eldest son Jacob who died in 1773 and afsd Obediah Reed (Had son John) and son Elijah and two daughters. John Reed son of Jacob was living in 1778 and it was supposed that afsd. Obediah was heir at law but he died in 1792 without issue.29 March 1806 Henry Davis and wife Martha Davis and Adam Brattan with wife Elizabeth Brattan sold to Elijah Reed brother of Martha and Elizabeth.
8 Apr.1806 Elijah Reed of Worc. Co. heir of Obediah Reed, sold to John Nelson of Somerset Co. As Obediah Reed inherited from his father. He died without issue and no descendents from brother or sister. It descended to John Reed eldest brother of Elijah and eldest son of Jacob Reed who was the eldest son of John Reed grandfather to first named John Reed who was the eldest brother to Zachariah Reed father of Obediah. First named John Reed son of Jacob, died without issue so descended to eldest brother afsd Elijah Reed.

ACWORTHS FOLLY

Patented on 18 Feb. 1664 by Richard Acworth for 300 acres in Nanticoke 100.
14 Sep.1695 James Weatherly sold 108 acres to Robert Bowditch.
Rent Rolls 1666-1723 possessed by James Weatherly
1710/15 Robert Bowditch gave to wife Ann Bowditch and then to daughters Joanna Bowditch and Rebecca Clark and heirs (unnamed land)
18 Feb 1751 triparte deed- Levin Hitch son of Rebecca Hitch formerly Rebecca Clark, and Mary Storey of Dorcester Co. spinster only surviving daughters of Joanna Storey formerly Joanna Clark, sold to Robert Twilley and John Kellum the younger 108 acres.
18 Nov.1756 James Weatherly and John Weatherly sold for 10 shillings to Joseph Weatherly 50 acres plus 10 more(division line between Elijah

Weatherly and Richard Weatherly two of his sons- this deed is not clear.)
1783 tax- Constantine Weatherly 10 acres- Rewastico 100
1783 tax- James Weatherly 27 acres
1783 tax- John Weatherly 158 acres.
1789 will John Weatherly, to son William Weatherly lands (description) at division line of James Weatherly on Rewastico Creek, no name.
9 Dec.1803 Priscilla Kennedy sold to John Kellum 160 acres.

ACWORTHS OLD AGE

Patented in 1797 by Richard Acworth in Barren Creek for 825 3/4 acres.
1789 Richard Acworth willed to son Richard.
1797 Robert Venables willed to wife Amelia Venables, part.

ACWORTHS PURCHASE

Patented on 19 Feb.1664 by Richard Acworth for 300 acres in Nanticoke 100 at Barren Creek.
Rent Rolls 1666-1723 possessed by James Weatherly, 300 acres.
Richard Acworth willed to son Henry Acworth and at his death to his eldest brother Richard Acworth.
1715 will Henry Acworth, to sons John Acworth, Samuel Acworth and Henry Acworth, 300 acres.
12 March 1724 Richard Acworth of barren Creek sold to John Acworth and Samuel Acworth sons of Henry Acworth of Richard in accordance to his fathers wishes 300 acres.
1761 Samuel Acworth willed to son Ephraim Acworth ADDITION TO ACWORTHS PURCHASE.
1783 tax- Sarah Acworth 200 acres
1783 tax- Stephen Stevens 100 acres.
14 June 1808 Samuel Acworth, and wife Kittury Acworth of Kent Co. Del. sold 25 acres to Joshua Donoho of Somerset Co.
1816 Joshua Donoho gave to son Filmurroh Donoho and Joshua Donoho.
1856 Robert Dorman willed to wife Catherine Dorman ACWORTHS PURCHASE, purchased of Ralph Lowe that Lowe purchased of William D. Donoho and wife.

ACWORTHS SECURITY

Patented in 1796 by James Acworth for 12 3/4 acres.

ADAMS ADVENTURE

Patented on 16 Jan.1767 by Adam Christopher for 38 acres.
1783 tax- Adam Christopher- Wicomico 100, Worcester Co.
1796 Adam Christopher willed lands to sons Eben Christopher, Tubman Christopher and George Christopher, unnamed.

ADAMS CHOICE

Patented on 1 Sep.1688 by Sumner Adams for 180 acres in Nanticoke 100.
1686 Sumner Adams, will, this land not mentioned
Rent Rolls 1666-1723 possessed vide Capt. John McClester account, in a point between the Nanticok and Wicomico Rivers.
26 Apr.1743 Samuel McClester sold for 5 shillings to brother George

McClester 180 acres. that John McClester father, bought of Sumner Adams and his wife Ann Adams.
1783 tax- John Sterling 20 acres
1783 tax- Mary Smith 160 acres
28 June 1790 John Sterling, wife Rachel Sterling sold to Jesse Hughes and wife Sarah Hughes, with ADVENTURE & POINT MARISH.

ADAMS CHOICE

Patented in 1782 by Alexander Chain for 52 acres, patented Wicomico Co.
24 Oct.1795 Isaiah Chain and Sarah Chain sold 52 acres to George Marshall.

ADAMS FOLLY

Patented on 23 Feb.1761 by Thomas Collier for 9 acres in Deep Creek.

ADAMS GOOD LUCK

This is part of GURNSEY

ADAMS PURCHASE

Patented in 1732 by Alexander Adams for 18 acres.
28 Oct.1765 Rev. Alexander Adams gave to son Andrew Adams 18 acres with SMITHS ADVENTURE, between the branches of the Wicomico River.
1783 tax- Andrew Adams
1817 Andrew Adams wiled to nephew Andrew Adams son of nephew John Adams.

ADAMS VEXATION

Patented in 1742 by John Noble for 83 acres.
1781 will John Noble, dwelling plantation (unnamed) to son Thomas Noble.

ADDITONS DESIRE

Patented in 1748 by Jacob Addison for 100 acres in Parsons Neck.
31 Oct.1757 Jacob Addison of Sussex Co. Delaware sold to Arthur Johnson 100 acres.

ADDITION

Surveyed by Richard Keen and assigned to Thomas Walker who patented in 1681 for 100 acres.
26 July 1735 Thomas Walker son of Thomas sold to Levin Gale ADDITION & LAST PURCHASE.
11742 Levin Gale willed to brother Matthias Gale, land near White Haven Town, unnamed.

ADDITION

Patented on 29 Nov.1685 by Thomas Gordon for 250 acres in Wicomico 100 acres.
2 Feb.1750 Thomas Gordon of Sussex Co.Del. sold to Charles Perry of Sussex Co. Del. 550 acres of ADDITION (250 acres) and CARLISLE.

This land was probably resurveyed into Sussex Co. Delaware.

ADDITION

Patented in 1688 by James Weatherly for 450 acres.
18 Nov.1756 James Weatherly and John Weatherly sold for 10 shillings 15 acres to Joseph Weatherly.
18 Oct.1758 Joseph Weatherly and Elijah Weatherly sold 173 1/2 acres to James Weatherly.
21 Dec.1758 Elijah Weatherly and James Weatherly and John Weatherly sold 108 acres to Joseph Weatherly. These entries are probably division of lands.
10 Oct.1758 Joseph Weatherly and Elijah Weatherly sold to John Weatherly 83 3/4 acres with ACWORTHS CONTRIVANCE, now called PARTNERSHIP
1763 resurveyed to PARTNERSHIP 527 1/2 acres.
1764 Joseph Weatherly willed to James Weatherly, Charles Weatherly and Jesse Weatherly ADDITION I conveyed to their father James Weatherly now called PARTNERSHIP.

ADDITION

Patented on 8 April 1703 by Phillip Ascue for 50 acres on the south side of Wicomico Ck, south west side of Cowasick Creek.
Rent Rolls 1666-1723 possessed by Phillip Ascue.
3 July 1708 Phillip Ascue and wife Grace Ascue sold to Thomas Benson.
14 April 1721 Thomas Benson sold 50 acres to Edward Hertz late of the island of Bermuda.

ADDITION

Patented 27 Sep.1704 by Robert Givans for 100 acres in Nanticoke 100.
Rent Rolls 1666-1723 possesed by Robert Givans
1735 Robert Givans willed to son Robert 100 acres.
1 May 1770 William Givans of Boston, New England, sold to Ephraim King 100 acres with LYONS LOTT in Rewastico.
1783 tax - Samuel King 50 acres- Rewastico 100
4 Jan 1790 Samuel King sold 50 acres to William Winder that father Ephraim King bought of William Givans with LYONS LOTT.
1808 William Winder willed all lands, unnamed, to son William Henry Winder.

ADDITION

Patented on 9 Sep. 1713 by Alexander Carlylse for 100 acres on the north side of a branch of the Quantico River.
Rent Rolls 1666-1723 possessed by Alexander Carlylse.
18 March 1773 Adam Carlylse late of North Britain, now of Brampton of Cumberland, Great Britain, eldest son of Alexander Carlylse sold to Richard Dickenson of Somerset County Md. 100 acres. He appointed Charles Little, attorney of Alexandria Virginia to convey same.

ADDITION

Patented on 10 Sep.1722 by James Train for 30 acres on the south side

of the Nanticoke River.
Rent Rolls 1666-1723 possessed by James Train.
3 March 1764 Isaac Hardy of Worcester County heir of James Hardy and Eliza Train Hardy sold to Matthew Dorman ADDITION, COMPLETE, TRAINS LOTT, PASTURAGE.
1783 tax- William Dorman (s/o Matthew Dorman) 30 acres, Rewastico 100.

ADDITION

Patented on 2 March 1723 by Joseph McClester for 713 acres on the south side of Quantico Creek.
Rent Rolls 1666-1723 possessed by Joseph McClester.
18 Oct 1728 Joseph McClester sold to Betty Gale widow 713 acres.
13 July 1729 confirmed same as above.
14 May 1772 Joshua Sturgis of Worc.Co. sold to Peter Peterson and George Taylor , merchants, ADDITION part in Worc.Co. and part in Som.Co. except 200 acres sold to William Sturgis conveyed to Joshua Sturgis by Nathaniel Ramsey, commissioner to sell confiscated real estate 209 1/2 acres.
17 Dec.1791 Peter Peterson and George Taylor sold 209 1/2 acres to Thomas Johnson.
1783 tax- Levin Gale Jr. 500 acres Wic.100 (resurvey)
1783 tax- Levin Gale Sr. 1130 acres Wic.100 (resurvey)
15 Nov.1793 George Purnell, sheriff sold to Purnell Johnson, lands of Joshua Sturgis who died. Land in the hads of John Sturgis Jr.,Joshua Sturgis and William Sturgis, 100 acres given to son Joshua Sturgis.
15 Nov.1793 Purnell Johnson sold to William Sturgis son of Joshua 200 acres.
8 June 1798 Purnell Johnson with wife Amelia Johnson,sold to Joshua Sturgis 209 1/2 acres land of Thomas Johnson.

ADDITION

Patented in 1730 by William Wallace for 180 acres.

ADDITION

Patented in 1738 by Henry Lowe for 18 acres.

ADDITION

Patented in 1738 by Thomas Gillis for 52 acres.
1783 tax- John Fowler, 52 acres in Rewastico 100.

ADDITION

Patented in 1742 by Charles Dashiell for 47 acres.

ADDITION

Patented in 1743 by George Dashiell for 54 acres
1809 George Dashiell willed lands to wife Betty Dashiell, after her death to grandson George son of William Dashiell, unnamed.

ADDITION

Patented in 174- by Day Givans for 384 acres.
11 Jan 1755 Day Givans sold to Joseph Collins 135 acres, part.
1767 Joseph Collins willed to daughter Margaret Collins 135 acres(he called it ADVENTURE)

ADDITION

Patented on 20 Aug.1747 by James O'Neal for 50 acres in Parsons Neck on the north side of Broad Creek.
10 Mar.1769 Thomas O'Neal sold to John Collins of Somerset Co. 50 acres.

ADDITION

Patented on 19 Aug.1750 by Thomas Johnson for 100 acres

ADDITION

Patented in 1755 by Thomas Acworth for 116 acres
1759 Thomas Acworth willed to sons Charles Acworth and Train Acworth.

ADDITION

Patented in 1759 by Samuel Acworth for 50 acres.
16 Dec.1780 Ephraim Acworth son of Samuel sold to Thomas Bedsworth 50 acres on the north side of Rewastico Creek.
1783 tax- Thomas Bedsworth, Rewastico 100
1785 will Thomas Bedsworth, to wife Susanna Bedsworth, dwelling plantation where I live, then to son William Bedsworth, unanmed land.

ADDITION

Patented 1763 by Charles Hayman for 13 1/2 acres.
1774 will Charles Hayman, to son Revel Hayman
1796 Revel Hayman willed to wife Sarah Hayman, lands, after her death to son William Brown Hayman, unnamed lands.

ADDITION

Patented on 28 Sep.1763 by Daniel Melson for 50 acres in Wicomico forest.

ADDITION

Patented in 1765 by William Turner Wooten (certificate was issued to Richard Wooten) for 210 acres.

ADDITION

Patented in 1765 by Thomas Rencher for 66 acres.
1783 tax- Thomas Rencher 66 acres in Wicomico 100.
1806 Thomas Rencher willed lands to sons John Rencher, Thomas Rencher and William Rencher, unnamed land.

ADDITION

Patented in 1770 by Levin Gunby for 31 1/2 acres.
28 Oct.1806 Tubman Lowe, trustee to sell the real estate of Levin Gunby sold to Kirk Gunby 31 1/2 acres with STANFORDS FINDING & THOMAS CONCLUSION.

ADDITION

Patented in 1773 by William McClemmy for 7 acres in Rewastico 100.
1783 tax- William McClemmy.

ADDITION

Patented in 1782 by William Winder for 31 3/4 acres.
1808 William Winder willed all lands (unnamed) to son William Henry Winder.

ADDITION

Patented in 1783 by Joshua Sturgis for 409 1/2 acres at the head of the Wicomico River purchased of the comissioners to sell British property.
1786 Joshua Sturgis willed lands to sons John Sturgis, William Sturgis and Joshua Sturgis, unnamed.
4 Nov.1790 Joshua Sturgis sold to his son William Sturgis 200 acres.

ADDITION

Patented in 1784 by George Disharoon for 22 1/2 acres.
19 March 1796 Stephen Disharoon son of George sold to Cyrus Sharp 11 1/2 acres with SHAVE THE BALD FRIAR, & GOOD INTENTION.
1802 Cyrus Charp willed lands, unnamed, to brothers William Sharp and Daniel Sharp.
31 May 1810 Daniel Sharp, wife Rebecca Sharp, sold to James Bennett.

ADDITION

Patented in 1791 by John Sterling for 34 1/2 acres.

ADDITION

Patented in 1796 by William Hitch for 14 1/2 acres (certificated issued to Joshua Hitch)
15 June 1799 William Hitch and John Hitch with wife Jean Hitch, sons of Joshua Hitch sold 14 1/2 acres to Thomas Humphries Jr.

ADDITION

Patented in 1814 by William Pollitt for 1 1/2 acres.

ADDITION

Patented in 1817 by Isaac Leonard for 5 1/2 acres.
He is living in 1850 in the Salisibury District HH#182.

ADDITION

Patented in 1820 to George P. Jones for 23 acres.

ADDITION

Patented in 1848 by Valentine Insley for 77 1/2 acres.
1850 living in Tyaskin Wicomico Co. HH 956.

ADDITION TO NEIGHBORS TO NEIGHBORS LOTT

Patented in 1796 by Charles Nicholson for 126 1/2 acres.

ADDITION TO PARRIES CHOICE

Patented in 1799 by George Waller for 34 3/4 acres.

ADVENTURE

Patented on 20 Feb.1762 by John Davis for 45 acres
1783 tax- John Davis, Wic.100 Worc.Co. 45 acres.
1789 John Davis willed to son Daniel Davis 45 acres.

ADVENTURE

Patented on 5 May 1706 by Richard Crockett in the fork made by Crocketts Creek on the south side of Shields Creek, 70 acres.
Rent Rolls 1666-1723 possessed by the widow Lowe.
1726/8 Charles Crockett did not name lands in his will.

ADVENTURE

Surveyed in 1772 by Smullen Layfield for 84 acres from Wicomico Manor.
31 May 1783 Clement Holliday and Nathaniel Ramsey comissioners to sell ADVENTURE sold 84 acres to Smullen Layfield.
1 Aug. 1807 Aaron Mezick, John Mezick, and Sarah Banks sold to Peter Dashiell 84 acres on Tony Tank Creek per deed to Smullen Layfield.
Resurveyd to JINNY DANG THE WEAVER.

ADVENTURE

Patented on 2 Nov.1664 to William Thomas of Northumberland Co. Va. for 100 acres.
25 Sep.1673 William Thomas of Va. sold to Sumner Adams of Va. 100 acres.
Rent Rolls 1666-1723 Possessed by Sumner Adams in the right of the heir of Capt. John McClester.
21 Aug.1736 Morgan Adams of Dorc. Co. sold to John McClester, patented William Thomas of Va. that was made over to Sumner Adams deceased.
Morgan Adams eldest son of Sumner.

6 April 1743 Samuel McClester son of John McClester gave 100 acres to brother George McClester.
28 June 1790 John Sterling and wife Rachel Sterling sold 100 acres to Jesse Hughes and wife Sarah Hughes with ADAMS CHANCE, POINT PATIENCE. 100 acres FLETCHERS ADDTIONAL PURCHASE is part of ADVENTURE per patents.

AGHEULOWE (AKALOW)

Patented on 21 Oct.1686 by James McWilliams for 100 acres on the south side of the Nanticoke River.
Rent Rolls 1666-1723 possessed by James Givans.
1723 James Givans of Rewastico willed to son George Givans and part to daughter Margaret Givans.
15 Nov.1742 George Givans sold to John Gale land from father part of LARGY & AKALOW 100 acres.
1771 John Kellum willed to son Edward Kellum.
14 April 1774 Edward Kellum, wife Priscilla Kellum, sold to Thomas Bedsworth and Thomas Russell Jr. (land James Givan left to daughter Margaret Givans that James Givans bought of James McWilliams 100 acres with LARGEE given Margaret by father. She conveyed to John Kellum who willed to son Edward.
20 Feb.1779 John Gale Sr. sold to George Gale Sr. 220 acres of LARGEY & AKELOW
17 June 1783 George Gale son of George sold to James Phillips 148 1/2 acres of LARGEE & AKALOW.
17 June 1783 George Gale son of George sold to Cornelius Ready 148 1/2 acres of LARGEE & AKELOW.
1783 tax- Thomas Russell   (with LARGEE)
1783 tax- John Nelson   "   "
1783 tax- Cornelius Ready   "   "
1783 tax- Thomas Bedsworth   "   "
13 June 1791 Henry Acworth, executor of Isaac Giles sold to William Bedsworth 148 1/2 acres of LARGEE & AKALOW.
1790 Isaac Giles willed lands to be sold, no names.
1 March 1805 Levi Russell sold to Charles Rhoads AKELOW, LARGEE & RUSSELLS HARD BARGAIN, except 1/2 of graveyard, no acres mentioned.

AIRES PURCHASE

Patented in 1751 by Jacob Aires for 323 acres.
Tax lists 1788- George Aires 269 1/2 acres
3 May 1800 Charles Willin sold to George Willin 3 1/2 acres.
1818 George Aires willed to wife Betty Aires.

A JOKE

Patented in 1792 by Henry Cordrey 92 acres.
1797 Henry Cordrey willed to son Covington Cordrey lands unnamed.

AKAM

Patented in 1737 by Levin Gale for 2162 acres.
19 Aug.1742 Daniel Cordrey and wife Rachel Cordrey sold to Levin Gale all interest in tract belonging to Levin Gale AKAM 200 acres called

JONES HOLE & SUNKEN GROUND.(note-Nicholas Evans gave to daughter Rachel Collier part ONES HOLE & SUNKEN GROUND. She married first George Betts Collier and second Daniel Cordrey.)
1742 Levin Gale willed land devised by Col. Evans to daughter Rachel now wife of Daniel Cordrey.
15 July 1743 Levin Gale sold to Day Scott 48 acres not to include Green Hill Church or churchyard.
5 Feb.1744 George Gale and Matthias Gale sold to James Robertson rector of Coventry Parish all that Levin Gale willed to George Gale and Matthias Gale to sell except 48 acres that was conveyed to Capt. Day Scott.
9 Feb.1752 Day Scott sold to Joseph Ennals of Dorc.Co.Md. 648 acres of SUNKEN GROUND,JONES HOLE, LAST CHOICE, DUNKINHALL.
6 Dec.1755 Joseph Ennals conveyed back to Day Scott the same.
17 July 1771 Alexander Robertson sold 543 acres to Levin Gale Esq.
1783 tax- Alexander Robertson 878 1/2 acres, Nanticoke 100.
1783 tax- George Gale of Levin Gale 543 acres, Nanticoke 100.
11 May 1784 Moses Parks and wife Elizabeth Parks of Worc.Co. sold to Alexander Robertson of Som. Co. their claim. Elizabeth Parks was a lineal descendant and heir of James Jones formerly of Som.Co. and native of the Kingdom of Great Britain- conveyed by George Gale and Matthias Gale executors of Col.Levin Gale deceased to James Robertson father of Alexander Robertson.
11 May 1784 Moses Parks and Elizabeth Parks his wife sold part to Levin Gale, no acreage mentioned.
21 Dec.1785 Alexander Robertson sold to James Robertson, all.
23 Feb.1793 George Robertson gave to Alexander Robertson all.
28 May 1793 Alexander Robertson sold to George Robertson all.
1798 Alexander Robertson willed to sons James Robertson and George Robertson all the lands they already have, no names.
25 June 1796 James Gale of Baltimore Town,son of Levin Gale, sold to Alexander Stewart 655 acres.
1850 John B. Slemons willed to three children Albert Slemons, Clara Slemons and Francis Marion Slemons AKAM purchased from James Robertson (to be sold and money divided)

ALDERBURY

Patented on 14 May 1688 by Thomas Cox for 550 acres on the south side of the main branch of Rokiawalkin River. (Wicomico River)
Rent Rolls 1666-1723 possessed by Thomas Cox.
13 July 1724 Thomas Cox Sr. sold to Ebenezer Handy 100 acres out of ALDERBURY & WILTON, resurveyed to HANDYS BEGINNING.
1 Sep.1752 Lewis Disharoon of Worc.Co. who was the son of John Disharoon deceased who was the eldest son of Lewis and Jane Disharoon who was the daughter of Thomas Cox, sold to John Handy of Wor.Co. son of Ebenezer Handy and to Benjamin Handy 220 acres.
10 Dec.1752 Benjamin Handy sold 220 acres to Mary Williams of Som.Co. spinster.
1754 Mary Williams willed to son Levin Williams 220 acres bought of Benjamin Handy, no name.
10 Apr.1754 Benjamin Handy and Lydia Wright (dau/o Thomas Cox) sold to Mary Williams 200 acres.
10 Apr.1754 Benjamin Handy and Lydia Wright sold to George Smith 120 acres.

1783 tax- Charles Harris 200 acres.
1783 tax- James Brewington (with WILTON 130 acres)
1783 tax- Ebenezer Handy 61 acres.
12 Aug.1795 George Smith son of Andrew Smith sold to Seth Smith and Isaac Vinson 150 acres.
1 Nov.1805 Robert Lemon and wife Nancy Lemon sold to Isaac Vinson 63 acres.
1 Nov.1806 Robert Lemon with wife Nancy Lemon sold to William Smith 150 acres.
5 Mar.1808 John Bounds with wife Nancy Bounds of Dorcester County sold to Isaac Vinson 5 3/4a. MILL SUPPORT adjacent ALDERBURY

ALDERMANBURY

Patented on 14 May 1688 by Thomas Cox for 172 acres on the south side of the Rokiawalkin.
Rent Rolls 1666-1723 possessed by Thomas Cox.
8 March 1750 Lewis Disharoon, merchant, sold to George Smith Jr. 50 acres that Thomas Cox gave to daughter Jane Disharoon and her husband Lewis, grandmother and grandfather to afsd.
6 April 1751 Lydia Wright sold to son Jeremiah Wright 380 acres of WILTON & ALDERMANBURY bequeathed by her father Thomas Cox.
5 June 1751 Lewis Disharoon sold to Benjamin Handy 150 acres.
20 Sep.1752 Lydia Wright widow of Jeremiah Wright and son Jeremiah Wright sold to Lewis Disharoon 170 acres (an agreement that Lewis will pay John Handy money owed him)
1 Apr.1757 John Handy sold to Samuel Brereton for 5 shilings 215 acres of WILTON AND ALDERMANBURY
13 May 1763 Hill Cox sold to George Parker Sr. 100 acres, 28 acres of PLUMPTONS SALT ASH & 72 acres of ALDERBERRY
14 Sep.1764 Hill Cox of Worc.Co. sold this part of ALDERMANBURY to George Parker.
1765 George Parker Sr. of Worc.Co.willed to wife Sarah Parker 100 acres conveyed by Hill Cox, unnamed, after her death to son John Parker
2 Oct.1784 John Parker Sr. of Sussex Co.Delaware with wife Sarah Parker sold to Elisha Parker of Worc.County Md. 16 acres
2 Oct.1784 Elisha Parker Sr. sold to Elisha Parker Jr. 183 acres, no name.
2 Oct.1784 Elisha Parker sold to Henry Turner 70 1/4 acres, no name.
2 Oct.1784 Elisha Parker sold to John Parker 146 3/4 acres no name.
5 July 1788 Levi King, as Power of Attorney for John Parker son of George, and Jacob Parker son of John of Sussex Co.Del., sold to George Parker son of Elisha 110 acres of ALDERBURY, WILTON,PARKERS CHANCE.
20 Mar.1788 Joshua Townsend, sheriff sold to John Biglands per judgement against James Brereton 37 acres.
12 June 1794 John Biglands sold to Solomon Layfield 37 acres
29 Apr.1806 William Brewington Jr. sold to Thomas Layfield 7 acres 17 1/2 perches and 9 acres and 15 perches.

ALGAHS BEGINNING

Patented in 1745 by Algah Johnson for 86 1/2 acres in Somerset Co.Md.

ALGATE

Patented on 12 Nov.1688 by Edward Wright for 150 acres in the woods from the main branch of Barren Creek.
11 March 1720 Edward Wright of Dorc.Co. sold to Thomas Wood of the same.
14 Apr.1733 Thomas Wood sold to John Cope 150 acres.
1 March 1755 John Cope Sr. sold to James Brown.
18 Feb.1768 James Brown, shipwright, and wife Sarah Brown of Dor.Co. sold to Joseph Venables of Som.Co. 150 acres with part of BROWNS PRIVILDEDGE on road from Vienna Ferry to Barren Ck. Mill.
1783 tax- Joseph Venables 150 acres at REWASTICO
1788 Joseph Venables willed to be sold.
9 Nov.1799 William Russum executor, sold to Joshua Bennett Jr. of Sussex Co.Del.that Joseph Venables devised to be sold if Samuel Venables his grandson died without issue, 322 acres of ALGATE & LEBANON.
1819/21 William Russum willed to son Joseph Russum
1831 will of Eli Bennett, to brothers Turpin Bennett and Levin Bennett.
1833 Turpin Bennett willed to brothers Eli Bennett and Levin Bennett of Joshua Bennett.

ALISONS DELIGHT

Patented in 1852 for 20 7/8 acres by Jehu Parsons.
(see SAILORS DELIGHT)

AMBITION

Patented on 28 Feb.1761 by Joseph Marshall for 9 acres near the Nanticoke River.

AMITY

Patented in 1822 by William Whittington for 33 1/4 acres.

ANDERSONS CHANCE

Patented in 1764 by John Anderson for 3 1/2 acres.
1783 tax- John Anderson 3 1/2 acres in Rewastico.

ANDERSONS GRIEF

Patented in 1770 by Matthew Miles
1783 tax- Benjamin Atkinson 15 acres in Rewastico.
5 June 1786 James Makmorie Jones sold to Sarah Marshall Skinner daughter of Benjamin Atkinson 15 3/4 acres, on road at Quantico Mill that bounds MARYS CHOICE.

ANDERSONS INDUSTRY

Patented in 1790 by James Anderson for 114 1/4 acres.

ANDERSONS INVENTION

Patented on 3 Sep.1682 by Cornelius Anderson for 200 acres on the south side of the Rokiawalkin River.
Rent Rolls 1666-1723 Cornelius Anderson deserted this county long since and the land was assigned to Daniel Haste and now possessed by Benjamin Wailes and Robert Dashiell, each 100 acres.
1701 will Daniel Haste, 100 acres each to sons-in-law Robert Dashiell and Benjamin Wailes.
1718 Robert Dashiell (married Sarah Haste) made a will, this land not mentioned
1726/9 Benjamin Wailes (married Elizabeth Haste) made a will, this land not mentioned.
24 May 1743 Capell King and wife Sarah King sold to William Ellis 200 acres for 5 shillings as Daniel Haste left to daughters Elizabeth and Sarah Haste. Capell King married Sarah Haste.
1782 William Ellis willed to daughter Ann Ellis 100 acres and dau. Sarah Ellis 100 acres.
18 June 1796 James Ritchie sold to Samuel Price and Sarah Price.
18 June 1796 Samuel Price and wife Sarah sold to James Ritchie, devised by William Ellis to Sarah Price.
4 July 1796 Samuel Price, wife Sarah Price sold to Rachel Marshall and Betsy Marshall d/o George 109 1/4 acres.
2 July 1803 James Ritchie sold to Charles Winright part sold in 1743 by Capell King.
2 July 1803 Charles Winright and wife Sarah Winright(d/o William Ellis) sold to James Ritchie.
7 March 1807 Charles Winright and wife Sarah Winright sold 20 acres to James Bennett.
12 Sep.1807 Charles Winright, wife Sarah, sold 11 1/2 acres to James Bennett.

ANDERSONS LONG RUN

Patented in 1776 by James Anderson for 58 acres.
9 Nov.1793 James Anderson, John Anderson and Joshua Anderson sold 68 acres to Isaac Anderson with COME BY CHANCE.

ANDERSONS LOTT

Patented in 1788 by James Anderson for 11 3/4 acres

ANGHALOE

Patented in 1724/5 by James Caldwell and John Williams for 29 acres.

ANNAN

Patented on 21 Sep.1796 from TAYLORS CHANCE by Bartholomew Taylor for 148 1/2 acres
21 Sep.1796 Bartholomew Taylor sold to Isaac Kinney.
18 March 1796 Bartholomew Taylor sold 22 3/4 acres to Jacob Wright
1796/7 Jacob Wright willed to sons Joseph Wright and Benjamin Wright tract of Bartholomew Taylor, no name.
13 Oct.1804 Isaac Kinney, wife Milly Kinney, sold to Jesse Bradley 130

acres AKA TAYLORS CHANCE.

ANNIE

Patented in 1882 by Train A. Bounds for 43 acres.

ANNS SURVEY

Patented in 1770 by John Henry Carey for 15 acres.
(he was a Maryland Loyalist who went to New Brunswick Nova Scotia by 1775)

ANYTHING

Patented in 1732 by William Ralph for 50 acres.
8 June 1734 William Ralph and wife Sarah Ralph sold to Edward Collins 50 acres at the head of Barren Creek.
22 April 1755 Joseph Calloway sold to Henry Lowe, part two tracts 196 acres of CORKLAND & ANYTHING PURCHASED by Joseph Calloway of Edward Collins
1761 Henry Lowe willed to Richard Biglands land purchased from Joseph Calloway
20 Feb.1762 John Collins sold to Samuel Collins 50 acres purchased of William Ralph
13 June 1768 Samuel Collins sold to John Twilley 50 acres.
14 May 1768 Henry Lowe son of Henry sold to John Moore (per indenture) 50 acres
23 Aug.1770 John Twilley sold to John Nelms 50 acres.
1804 Will of John Moore, property to be sold for benefit of family, no name.

ANYTHING

10 Nov.1696 William Whittington assigned to James Dashiell Jr.
Patented on 21 Oct.1696 by James Dashiell for 137 acres on the south side of the Nanticoke River.
Rent Rolls 1666-1723 possessed by James Dashiell
1708/9 James Dashiell son of James willed to son Christopher Dashiell.
15 Aug.1748 John Nicholson and wife Mary Nicholson of Som.Co. and William Owens and wife Elizabeth Owens of Worc.Co. sold to Joseph Bounds 137 acres that became by will of James Dashiell the right of Christopher Dashiell who died before he conveyed to Mary Dashiell and Elizabeth Dashiell his heirs (adj. John Bounds plantation in Quantico)
1748 Joseph Bounds and wife Tabitha Bounds gave to Sophia Richardson.
15 Feb.1768 Jehu Bounds sold 59 1/2 acres to William Stewart.
1783 tax- Richardson Donoho 68 1/2 acres
1783 tax- William Stewart 1 acre
7 April 1785 William Stewart sold to John Stewart 49 1/4 acres.
1808 William Stewart willed to nephew Alexander Stewart.
10 Oct.1809 Robert Stewart of Baltimore sold to Alexander Stewart of Somerset County.
2 Nov.1809 John Stewart, James Evans and wife Elizabeth Evans (formerly Elizabeth Stewart) Nancy Stewart and Matty Stewart sold to Alexander Stewart, their interest.

ANYTHING

Patented on 15 May 1702 by Robert Caldwell for 100 acres near Rokiawalkin River
Rent Rolls 1666-1723 possessed by Robert Caldwell
1723 John Caldwell Jr. and Margaret Caldwell gave to John Caldwell, friend and kinsman.
1759 Joshua Caldwell willed tract surveyed for Robert Caldwell ANYTHING to be sold.
19 Aug.1762 Littleton Dennis and Joseph Scroggin administrators of the will of Joshua Caldwell sold to Robertson Lingo 100 acres.
19 Aug.1766 Robertson Lingo of Worc.Co. sold to Joseph Scroggin of Som.Co. 100 acres.
1772 Joseph Scroggin willed 100 acres to son Samuel Scroggin
1783 tax- John Scroggin 100 acres- Rewastico
1783 tax- John Scroggin 50 acres ADDITION TO ANYTHING
1790 ADDITION patented by John Scroggin for 42 acres.
16 May 1785 Samuel Scroggin sold 100 acres to John Scroggin
13 June 1789 John Scroggin and wife Eunice Scroggin sold to Eli Vinson 30 acres of HARD TO COME AT & ADDITION TO ANYTHING.
8 Oct.1790 John Scroggin and wife Eunice Scroggin sold 42 acres to Joseph Scroggin of HARD TO COME AT & ANYTHING.
10 April 1792 Eli Vinson and wife Ann Vinson sold 27 1/4 acres to James Selby
1793 Joseph Scroggin willed to brother Phillip Jenkins Scroggin ADDITION TO ANYTHING.
19 Jan 1793 Joseph Scroggin and wife Betsey Scroggin sold to Eli Vinson 28 acres.
20 July 1794 Eli Vinson sold to James Selby son of Ezekiel Selby of Worc.Co. 80 acres of HARD TO COME AT & ADDITION TO ANYTHING.
3 Dec.1794 Phillip Scroggin and wife Polly Scroggin sold to John Dashiell 224 1/2 acres of ANYTHING, STAINS, HARD TO COME AT.
17 Sep.1804 James Selby and wife Mary Selby sold to Eli Vinson.
16 Oct.1804 Eli Vinson and wife Ann Vinson sold to Benjamin Waller part to settle division lines.
16 Oct.1804 Benjamin Waller son of Richard Waller and wife Mary Whittington Waller sold to John Dashiell, part of ADDN.TO ANYTHING.
1 March 1808 John Dashiell sold to Eli Vinson 18 1/4 acres of VENTURE, BALLY BUGIN & ANYTHING.

ARABIA

Patented on 14 June 1726 by Henry Toadvine for 200 acres.
6 Dec.1742 Henry Toadvine and wife Alice Toadvine sold to Nathaniel Willis 75 acres on the east side of the main branch of the Wicomico River.
6 Dec.1742 Henry Toadvine and wife Alice Toadvine sold to Robertson Lingo 125 acres.
7 May 1768 Benjamin Willis sold to Elijah Shockley, mtg.
4 Mar.1771 John Willis with wife Betty Willis and Benjamin Willis sons of Nathaniel Willis sold to Joseph Dashiell 75 acres.
1772 will of Robertson Lingo, to son Smith Lingo.
1783 tax- Nathaniel Whaley 75 acres- Wic.100 Worc.Co.
1783 tax- Col. Joseph Dashiell 75 acres
4 Sep.1789 Smith Lingo of Sussex Co. Delaware sold to James Perdue,

his interest.
25 July 1796 Thomas Harwood of Annapolis sold to Joshua Johnson and Isaac Hearn 75 acres.

ARABIA

Patented in 1794 for James Bennett
1801 James Bennett willed 100 acre (unnamed) to son William Bennett

ARABIA

Patented in 1841 by George D. Scott for 5 acres.

ATKINSONS VENTURE

Patented in 1761 by Isaac Atkinson for 155 acres
1783 tax- Elizabeth Atkinson (wid/o Isaac) 155 acres, Nanticoke 100.

AVALON

Patented in 1758 for William J. Leonard for 369 acres.

A VEIN OF THE LAST CONCLUSION

Patented in 1791 by David Dutton for 62 3/4 acres.

ATTAPKEWANT

Patented on 12 Aug.1665 by Stephen Horsey on the east side of the Nanticoke River at the mouth of Wetepkwant Creek.
20 Dec.1688 Stephen Horsey sold to Thomas Davis (carpenter)
6 March 1776 Sussex Co. Delaware warrants, John Jessup at head of Nanticoke River, originally patented in Maryland.

ATTAWATTAQUAQUO

Patented on 2 June 1682 by William Stevens who assigned to Charles Nutter for 1200 acres at the head of the Nanticoke
Rent Rolls 1666-1723 400 acres apportains to the orphans of John Nutter at Delaware Bay and 800 acres to Charles Nutter.
1702 3/ Christopher Nutter willed to son Charles Nutter and William Nutter 800 acres and to son John Nutter 400 acres.
9 Nov.1756 Ann Handy gave to son Thomas Handy, lands between Quantico Creek and Manumsco Creek where she then lived in Nutters Neck.
Christopher Nutter willed to sons Christopher and William Nutter lands and Ann the daughter of Christopher who married and had issue Thomas Handy. Ann was the only daughter of Christopher Nutter the younger who died intestate.(land unnamed.)
23 Feb.1773 Thomas Handy and wife Sarah Handy sold to Ephraim King the above land.
1777 Ephraim King willed to son Samuel land on east side of Quantico Creek (unnamed) if no issue to Levin Gale.
1787 Samuel King willed to wife Mary King lands where I live and lands my father Ephraim King purchased of my half brother Thomas Handy in Nutters Neck.

26 Feb.1776 400 acres resurveyed to Sussex Co. Del. Mary Nutter.

AUSTINS SECURITY

29 May 1783 Nathaniel Ramsey commissioner tp sell confiscated property sold to Elijah Austin 104 1/2 acres was part of Wicomico Manor.
1783 tax- Elijah Austin 60 1/2 acres, Wicomico 100
16 Jan 1801 Robert Nairn and wife Polly Nairn of Wor.Co. sold to William Pollitt 1/3rd part of 104 acres patented in Som.Co. and Worc.Co.and 1/3rd part of HUNGER & THIRST in Worc.Co.
9 July 1809 William Pollitt sold 1/3rd part to James Toadvine as Elijah Austin died leaving daughters Nancy Austin, Polly Austin and Prissy Austin. Polly Austin married Robert Nairn.
1822 James Toadvine willed to son Anthony Roach Toadvine land bought of William Pollitt, no name.

AUGHTY NAUGHTY

Patented in 1795 by William Russum
19 Aug.1797 William Russum sold 66 acres to Ephraim Badley
1799 Ephraim Badley willed to daughter Milly Badley 60 acres bought from William Russum.
1821 William Russum willed to sons William and Robert Russum.

AVERYS POLICY

Patented on 31 March 1666 by John Avery for 300 acres.
26 Nov.1667 John Avery and wife Sarah Avery sold to William Green of Calvert County Md.
Rent Rolls 1666-1723 on the north side of Cuttamachico at an oak dividing from the land of Thomas Cottingman. The land including a resurvey for 480 acres by William Elgate, a special warrent dated 25 Sep.1704.
1725 William Elgate willed to daughter Ann Hall 260 acres and balance to daughter Cathrine Driskell.
1738 William Elgate willed 480 acres to wife Sarah Elgate and daughters Sarah Elgate, Hannah Elgate, Rebecca Elgate, Ann Elgate and Catherine Elgate (includes ELGATES LOTTand JESHIMINE)
1 Aug.1737 William Elgate and wife Catherine Elgate gave to Catherine Driskell wife of Moses 1/3 part, 150 acres.
1 Aug.1737 William Elgate and wife Catherine Elgate gave to daughter Rebecca Evans 150 acres.
1 March 1738 William Elgate gave to Ann Hall wife of Thomas Hall 1/3 part of AVERYS POLICY & MUNSLEY.(resurveyed 168a. to HALLS ADVENTURE in 1743)
13 Nov.1747 Moses Driskell and wife Catherine Driskell, Ann Hall and Rebecca Evans of Worc.Co. sold to William Murray 45 acres of MUNSLEY & AVERYS POLICY, that William Elgate sold part to maintain himself in old age to George Gale who disposed to William Murray but never conveyed.
6 Apr.1790 William Driskell of Worc.Co. sold to William McBryde his rights to 150 acres of MUMSLEY & AVERYS POLICY that William Elgate willed to daughter Catherine Driskell who was the mother of above William Driskell.
7 July 1810 Sarah McBryde sold to John Rider.

7 July 1810 John Rider sold to Sarah McBryde, probably a settlement of boundaries..

AYDELOTTES BEAVER DAM

Patented in 1747 by Joshua Mitchell for 150 acres.
1783 tax- John Mitchell 125 acres in Acquango 100
26 Aug.1787 Col. Joshua Mitchell sold to John Pope Mitchell.
1806 John Mitchell willed to son Rufus Mitchell.
1830 Jonathan Fooks willed 6 1/3rd acres to daughter Henrietta Byrd.

BACON QUARTER

Patented on 13 Nov.1685 by Peter Parsons for 200 acres at the head of the Wicomico River.
1686/7 Peter Parsons willed to son Peter Parsons
1709 Peter Parsons Jr. died intestate.
Rent Rolls 1666-1723 possessed by George Badley 200 acres.
1776 John Badley gave to son John Badley 1/2 and to son Dean Badley 1/2.
Repatented on 11 Feb.1765 by George Smith for 596 acres.
5 Aug.1772 George Smith Sr. sold to George Smith, blacksmith 100 acres.
1773 second patent by George Smith for 1626 acres.
13 July 1775 George Smith Sr. sold to son George Smith Jr, blacksmith 200 acres.
5 Apr.1774 George Smith sold to ELisha Parker 35 acres
5 Apr.1774 George Smith Sr. sold to Jacob Parker 342 acres
5 Apr.1774 George Smith Sr. sold to son Levin Smith 365 acres
5 Apr.1774 George Smith Sr. sold to Solomon Smith 112 acres, 400 acres and 22 acres.
1775 George Smith, wife Patience Smith willed to son Benjamin Smith 100 acres and remaining lands to be sold to pay debts and the balance to be equally devided between sons George Smith and Benjamin Smith.
1782 Dean Badley gave to son Ephraim Badley
1783 Tax - Matthias Coston (married Abigail Parsons daughter of John Parsons) in Rewastico 100.
1783 tax- George Smith 100 acres- Wic.100 Worc.Co.
1783 tax- Benjamin Smith 150 acres.
1783 tax- Archibald Smith 100 acres
1783 tax- Levin Smith 150 acres
1783 tax- Samuel Shockley 134 acres
1783 tax- Jacob Parker 342 acres
1783 tax- Elisha Parker 430 acres
13 Mar.1785 Jacob Parker sold to William Beauchamp and wife Nancy Beauchamp part.
12 Jan.1786 Archibald Smith with wife Mary Smith sold to John Anderson 137 acres, property of George Smith.
29 Aug.1789 George Smith, blacksmith sold to Jonathan Parsons and Elijah Shockley 27 acres.
22 Oct 1789 John Anderson sold 100 acres to Thomas Caton with GREENS RECANTATION
10 Aug.1790 Elijah Shockley sold to Jonathan Parsons 27 acres.

9 Oct.1790 Jacob Parker and Mary Parker and George Smith sold to Peter Gordy Hearn 350 acres.
20 Oct.1790 Jacob Parker Sr. with wife Mary Parker sold to Nathan Gordy 150 acres.
25 Apr.1791 John Anderson sold to Robert Lemon 137 acres.
1 Dec 1791 Elijah Hearn sold to George Parker 150 acres.
13 Jan.1792 Boaz Walston sold to Elizabeth Trader 14 1/2 acres
3 Oct.1795 Henry Turner with wife Abigail Turner sold to Elijah Parker 81 /12 acres of BACON QUARTER & BUCK RANGE.
21 Nov.1795 Archibald Smith now of Georgia, son of George Smith sold to Robert Lemon 84 acres, 53 acres.
23 pr.1799 Zadock Sturgis, sheriff sold to Jonathan Parsons 37 3/4 acres at public sale conveyed by George Smith to son George.
1 Oct 1803 Elijah Smith with wife Sally Smith sold to Archibald Smith 14 1/4.
20 Dec.1806 Purnell Trader sold rights to Joshua Trader.
4 Aug.1807 Aaron Mezick sonstable of Wic. 100, sold to Levin Parsons per judgement against George Smith, part.
2 July 1808 Jonathan Parsons Sr. with wife Leah Parsons sold to Archibald Smith 37 1/4 acres.
2 July 1808 Elijah Smith Sr. son of Benjamin Smith with wife Sally Smith sold to Archibald Smith
24 Sep.1808 Joshua Trader sold to George Parker 12 acres.
27 Mar.1810 Levin Derrickson, sheriff sold to Henry Parsons per judgement against Levin Parsons son of Jonathan Parsons.
1837 Peter G. Hearn willed to daughter Tabitha Hearn and son Peter Hearn (could be other land)

BAD LUCK

Patented in 1785 for John Scroggin for 95 1/4 acres.
Aug.1790 John Scroggin sold to John Dashiell son of Jesse Dashiell 142 acres at Rewastico.
7 Aug.1790 John Scroggin,wife Eunice Scroggin sold to John Dashiell 245 acres of FAIRFIELDS, BAD LUCK (except 9 acres deeded Elijah Hearn and burying ground)
3 Oct.1794 John Dashiell of Jesse Dashiell sold to Benjamin Jones 245 acres of FAIRFIELD & BAD LUCK for 5 shillings.
9 May 1795 Benjamin Jones sold to John Dashiell, same as above, a settlement of lines.

BADLEYS BEGINNING

Patented in 1851 to Azariah Badley and John W. Badley, certificate by Elijah Badley for 1 acre.

BADLEYS CHOICE

Patented in 1755 for 50 acres by Samuel Badley
22 Feb.1772 Samuel Badley sold to Thomas Badley 50 acres.

BADLEYS DELIGHT

Patented in 1794 by Gideon Badley.

This land was resurveyed to Sussex Co.Delaware.
1799 Ephraim Badley, willed to brother William Badley 50 acres of BADLEYS DELIGHT in Delaware and to brother John Badley 45 acres of the same.

BADLEYS INTENT

Patented in 1760 by William Badley for 49 acres.
1778 William Badley willed to son Eli Badley 49 acres.
2 April 1776 Sussex Co. Del. land warrants, William Badley.

BADLEYS LOOKOUT

Patented in 1822 by Severn Badley for 122 1/2 acres.

BADLEYS LOTT

Patented in 1799 by James Badley for 10 3/4 acres.

BAILEYS CHANCE

Patented in 1742 by George Bayley.
12 Aug.1776 Robins Bayley, heir of George Bayley and Isaiah Bayley deceased sold to Benjamin Bayley with GLOSTER, BAILYS CRAFT, STRIFE, patented by father George Bayley.
5 Dec.1795 Boardvine Bayley sold to Obed Bayley 3 acres with END OF STRIFE.

BAILEYS CHANCE

Patented in 1762 by Samuel Jackson Bayley for 730 acres.
17 Nov.1762 Samuel Jackson Bayley sold to Ezekiel James 50 acres
17 Nov.1762 Samuel Jackson Bayley sold to George Culver 64 acres
14 July 1763 Samuel Jackson Bayley sold to William Records 50 acres
18 Feb.1764 Samuel Jackson Bayley sold 72 acres to George Wailes.
19 Oct.1764 Samuel Bayley sold to Stephen Bayley 150 acres.
25 Oct.1765 Samuel Jackson Bayley and wife Sarah Bayley sold for 5 shillings to Davis Bayley 100 acres with tract PLEASURE.
21 March 1770 George Culver sold to John Winright 64 acres.
17 Oct.1772 John Winright sold to Isaac Phillips 64 acres.
23 Oct.1772 Samuel Jackson Bayley, with wife Leah Bayley sold 50 acres to George Wailes for 5 shillings.
5 Jan 1775 Ezekiel Jones of Dorc.Co. sold to Joshua Phillips of Som. Co.Md. 50 acres.
1788 George Wailes willed to son John Irving Wailes 122 1/2 acres conveyed me by Jackson Bayley.
2 May 1776 Sussex Co.Del. land Warrents BAILEYS CHANCE patented in Som.Co.by Joshua Phillips (son of Isaac Phillips)

BAILEYS CRAFT

Patented in 1774 by Isaiah Bayley 40 1/2 acres.
12 Aug.1776 Robins Bayley heir of George Bayley and Isaiah Bayley deceased sold to Benjamin Bayley in consideration of money to be paid to Robins after death of his mother Newton Bayley, 40 1/2 acres.

BAILEYS DISCOVERY

Patented in 1791 by Obed Bayley for 91 1/2 acres.
5 Dec.1795 Obed Bayley sold to Boadvine Bayley 5 acres of SAND HILL & BAILEYS DISCOVERY.

BAILEYS GRAB

Patented in 1798 by Obed Bayley

BAILEYS SUPPORT

Patented in 1797 by Elias Bayley for 8 7/8 acres.

BAILEYS GOOD LUCK

Patented in 1836 by Benjamin Bayley for 17 1/8 acres
1837 Benjamin Bayley willed to wife Polly Bayley and children, no land mentioned.

BAKERS FOLLY

Ptented on 10 June 1689 by Isaac Baker for 150 acres on the south side of the Nanticoke
Rent Rolls 1666-1723 Isaac Baker died at Delaware Bay and no one possesses.
20 Nov.1723 James Baker of Dorc.Co. sold to Thomas Huffington 150 acres.1 March 1755 Thomas Huffington sold 50 acres to Richard Huffington
1 March 1755 Thomas Huffington sold 25 acres to George Brown.
1759 Thomas Huffington willed to son Thomas, dwelling plantation.
17 Nov.1762 Richard Huffington sold 50 acres to Charles Marine.
19 Nov.1762 Richard Huffington sold 75 acres to Charles Marine.
1766 William Marine willed to sons Charles Marine and Zorobable Marine.
15 Nov.1777 Zorobable Marine and wife Mary Marine of Dorc.Co. and Charles Marine with wife Ann Marine of Sussex Co. Del. sold to Lazarus Huffington part on the east side of the Nanticoke River on the north side of Plumb Creek 50 acres and another part of same 75 acres.
9 March 1786 Thomas Huffington and wife Mary Huffington sold to James Dean, merchant, devised to Thomas by his fathers will, 25 acres.
1783 tax- Lazarus Huffington 125 acres- Rewastico 100
12 March 1789 James Dean sold 20 acres to Hugh Allen of Virginia.

BALLEY BUGGIN

Patented on 16 May 1688 by John Caldwell for 200 acres on the north side of the head of Wicomico River.
Rent Rolls 1666-1723 possessed by John Caldwell
Resurveyed 10 Aug.1713 for 190 acres John Caldwell
1723 John Caldwell Jr. and wife Margaret Caldwell gave to friend and kinsman John Caldwell, where Margaret Caldwell now lives, 190 acres.
22 Nov.1750 Joshua Caldwell sold to Robert Jenkins Henry and John Henry of Worc.Co. 190 acres.
23 June 1758 Robert Jenkins Henry and John Henry of Worc.Co. sold to Thomas Savage 190 acres with MAIDEN HEAD.

12 Dec 1758 Thomas Savage sold to Jonathan Bounds 190 acres with CALDWELLS CHANCE.
1758 Joshua Caldwell son of John Caldwell willed to Thomas Savage.
14 Nov.1764 Jonathan Bounds gave to son Richard Stevens Bounds 190 acres.
9 Sep.1797 Eli Vinson sold to Eli Vinson Jr.
13 Oct.1804 Eli Vinson and wife Comfort Vinson sold to Henry White of Worc.Co. 324 1/2 acres of BALLY BUGGIN, TRIFALDI, CALDWELLS CHANCE, SNOW HILL,etc.
16 Oct 1804 Eli Vinson and wife Comfort Vinson sold to Benjamin Waller 12 acres.
16 Oct.1804 Benjamin Waller son of Richard Waller, with wife Mary Whittington Waller sold to John Dashiell 92 1/2 acres of ADDN. TO ANYTHING, BALLY BUGGIN, HARD TO COME AT, etc.
8 Aug.1806 Henry White with wife Catherine White sold to Benjamin White 152 acres of VICTORY OF WISDOM OVER HAYNIES ADVERSARY, BALLEY BUGGIN, ADDITION TO WILLIAMS GREEN.
1815 John Dashiell willed to son George Dashiell near William Hearn and Elihu Jackson.
1 March 1808 John Dashiell sold to Eli Vinson 18 1/4 acres of VENTURE, BALLEY BUGGIN & ANYTHING.

BALLY SHANNEY

Patented in 1734 by Henry Spear for 100 acres.
1758 Henry Spear willed 100 acres to son Andrew Spear.
15 March 1759 Henry Spear sold to Andrew Spear.
10 March 1770 Andrew Spear and wife Betty Spear sold to Charles Davis (at Barren Creek) with POOR CHOICE, adjacent. 100 acres.
18 July 1773 Charles Davis sold 100 acres to Ahab Costin
11 March 1775 Ahab Costin sold 90 acres to William Mills
1818 William Mills willed to son Selby Mills 50 acres.
(note: 1850 census shows Selby Mills in Salisbury district)

BAMAGIE

Patented in 1793 for 9 1/4 acres by Ezekiel Green
24 July 1795 Ezekiel Green of Sussex Co.Del. sold to James Badley 9 1/4 acres.

BARBERS ADDITION

Patented on 17 April 1673 by Robert Hardy for 50 acres on the north side of the Wicomico River.
1678 Robert Hardy willed to son James Hardy 350 acres (includes BARBERS REST.)
Rent Rolls 1666-1723 Possessed by James Harding son of Robert Harding 50 acres.
1722/7 Robert Hardy gave to son James Hardy 50 acres.
1722/26 James Hardy willed to son James Hardy BARBERS REST & ADDITION.
12 Feb.1728/9 James Hardy and wife Elizabeth Hardy sold to Christopher Piper and his wife Rachel Piper ADDITION & BARBERS REST.
1756 will James Hardy, to son Isaac Hardy, now dwelling plantation and land to son William Hardy, unnamed.
19 Feb.1762 George Hardy sold to Thomas Irving BARBERS ADDITION

devised by Robert Hardy great grandfather of George who devised to son James Hardy grandfather of George Hardy.
1770 Ezekiel James will shows he possessed JAMES DEBATE formerly BARBERS ADDITION.
1783 tax- George James 50 acres. Nanticoke 100

BARBERS REST

Patented on 6 April 1666 for 300 acres by Robert Hardy.
1678 will Robert Hardy, to son James Hardy
Rent Rolls 1666-1723 James Hardy son of Robert Hardy 300 acres.
1722/27 James Hardy willed to son James.
12 Feb 1728/9 James Hardy and wife Elizabeth Hardy sold to Christopher Piper and wife Rachel Piper
25 Sep.1752 George Hardy sold to Charles Hardy 150 acres that Robert Hardy left to son James Hardy who willed to eldest sons Robert and James. Robert Hardy the younger died without devising his part so fell to his eldest son George afsd.
9 June 1753 Charles Hardy sold to Samuel Hardy.
1756 James Hardy willed to sons Isaac Hardy and William Hardy, lands unnamed.
19 Feb.1762 George Hardy sold to Thomas Irving
5 Aug.1762 Christopher Piper sold 42 acres to Ezekiel James with WHAT YOU PLEASE & DEAR LOTT.
1770 Ezekiel James willed lands to daughter Unice James.
6 July 1787 John Hardy and wife Mary Hardy sold for 5 shillings 65 acres to George James.
1783 tax- John Hardy 150 acres. Nanticoke 100
1783 tax- George James 77 acres.
1809 George James willed to son Thomas James 65 acres bought of John Hardy, unnamed.
2 Dec 1809 Francis James sold to John Chattam Jr. 521 acres of BARBERS REST & JAMES DEBATE as Dr. Ezekiel James willed to daughter Unice James, dwelling plantation. Issue of Unice is Francis James.
2 Dec 1809 John Chattam sold to Francis James, same as above.

BARKLEYS LOTT

Patented in 1750 by John Barkley for 101 acres
ADDITION patented in 1758 105 acres by John Barkley
11 June 1759 Aylworth Barkley and wife Nancy Barkley sold to Teague Dickerson, tailor, that John Barkley willed on the north side of the Wicomico River at Broad Creek, called ADDITION 205 acres on bounder of BARKLEYS LOTT.
1764 Teague Dickerson of Stepney Parish gave to son Levi Dickerson land on Broad Creek.
10 Aug.1784 Isaac Dickerson son of Levi Dickerson sold to Thomas Smith 205 acres with pt. ST.ALBANS that Aylworth Barkley sold to Teague Dickerson who gave to his son Levi Dickerson.

BARREN NECK

Patented on 23 Oct.1695 for 100 acres by Edmund Huggins on the east most side of Wetepquant Creek.
Rent Rolls 1666-1723 possessed by Edmund Huggins.

15 Dec.1740 Daniel Cunningham sold to Joseph Bounds 100 acres taken up by Edmund Huggins.
1748 Joseph Bounds willed to son William 100 acres bought of John Cooper.
17 June 1760 William Bounds sold to William Warner of Acco.Co.Va.
22 June 1769 William Bounds sold to William Warner of Acco.Co.Va. 100 acres that father Joseph Bounds willed to William Bounds.
4 Dec.1784 Isaac Warner of Acco.Co.Va. sold to Richardson Donoho 100 acres.

BARREN FIELD

Patented on 10 Oct.1713 by Alexander Adams for 75 acres.
1740 ADDITION patented by Alexander Adams for 118 acres.
1769 Alexander Adams willed to grandson Alexander son of Samuel Adams in Worc.Co.

BARREN QUARTER

Patented on 14 Dec.1696 for 250 acres by Edward Wright on the north side of a creek issuing out of the south side of the Nanticoke, called Barren Creek.
Rent Rolls 1666-1723 possessed by Edward Wright
5 June 1711 Edward Wright sold 35 acres to Richard Jefferson
6 July 1723 Peter Freeney and wife Elizabeth Freeney sold 250 acres to John Huffington.
1783 tax- Jonathan Huffington 15 acres.
1783 tax- Joseph Hust(resurvey pt. to ILL NEIGHBORHOOD)
26 Nov.1801 Jonathan Huffington sold 100 acres to William Russum of BARREN QUARTER, ILL NEIGHBORHOOD & MORRIS DELIGHT.
1821 William Russum willed to sons William and Robert Russum.

BARTHOLOMEWS FIRST ATTEMPT

Patented in 1783 by Bartholomew Slattery for 290 acres.
29 Mar.1782 Bartholomew Slattery sold to Truitt Brittingham 31 acres.
1783 tax - Truitt Brittingham 31 acres, Acquango 100 Worc.Co.
1783 tax - Bartholomew Slattery 259 acres.
16 May 1783 Truitt Brittingham sold to Jarman Brittingham 31 acres.
9 Jan.1790 Jarman Brittingham sold to Benjamin Truitt 31 acres.
1802 Bartholomew Slattery willed to son William Slattery 124 acres unnamed land and land also to son John Slattery.
1845 Thomas Littleton willed to son Minos Covington Littleton and to daughter Charlotte Gault wife of David Gault, part.

BASHAN

Patented on 24 April 1684 by George Layfield for 300 acres 6 miles from north east branch of Nanticoke River.
Rent Rolls 1666-1723 appertains to Samuel Layfield heir of George.
4 May 1723 Thomas Layfield and wife Catherine Layfield sold 300 acres to Adam Muir
19 March 1724 Adam Muir sold 300 acres to John Newbold and Francis Newbold
17 June 1735 John Newbold and wife Rachel Newbold sold to John Willey

150 acres
17 Nov.1762 John Alexander with wife Elizabeth Alexander sold to Samuel Jones 150 acres with CHARLES ADVANTAGE.

BASS LEGG

Patented on 1 Oct.1683 for 150 acres by Francis Jenkins
Rent Rolls 166-1723 possessed by Col. Francis Jenkins
1705 Francis Jenkins sold to Phillip Gravener
1783 tax- Louder Gravener 100 acres- Rewastico
1783 tax- Mary Gravener 50 acres
16 Apr 1783 Louder Gravener sold to William Phillips of Delaware, on road from Gillis Ferry to Vienna.
13 Feb.1786 Louder Gravener sold to William Phillips 77 3/4 acres at Barren Creek.(Mary Gravener widow of William Gravener releases her dower right.)

BASSETTS HOG QUARTER

Patented on 22 Sep.1763 by William Bassett for 40 acres.
1796 William Bassett willed to daughter Martha Duncan 40 acres.

BATCHELORS ADDITION

Patented in 1747 for 18 acres by Christopher Piper.

BATCHELORS ADVENTURE

Patented on 5 Oct.1674 for 200 acres by Robert Collier who assigned to Isaac Foxcroft.
Rent Rolls 1666-1723 Apportains to the widow Waters widow of Sampson Waters in Boston New England. Capt. James Dashiell manages.(James Dashiell married 1689 Mary Waters daughter of Sampson Waters and Rebecca Foxcroft daughter of Isaac Foxcroft)
2 March 1717 Obediah Wakefield and John Wakefield both of Boston Mass. sold to Peter Bowden son of John Bowden, late of Northampton Co.Va. 1/2 of BATCHELLORS ADVENTURE pat. by Isaac Foxcroft with JESHIMON, CONVENT GARDEN, THE SUPPLY, BENTLEY.
19 Nov.1738 John Perkinson of Bridge Town in Barbadoes, merchant heir of Daniel Perkinson late of said island sold to Capell King several tracts of land between the Nanticoke River and Quantico Creek the whole 1750 acres that Simon Waters of New England alienated to John Parkinson the Elder.
23 Aug.1739 Peter Bowdoin and wife Susannah Bowdoin of Northampton Co.Va. sold to Capell King 1 moity of 1750 acres where Joseph McClester lives, no name.

BATCHELLORS CHANCE

Patented in 1729 by Walter Darby for 50 acres.
1762 will of Walter Darby, to wife Sarah Darby and after death to sons Thomas Darby and William Darby.
1783 tax- Sarah Darby 50 acres, Rewastico 100
13 Aug.1793 Ralph Moore and wife Mary Moore (Mary Darby) sold to Levin Bennett 50 acres

12 Sep 1800 Levin Bennett and wife Elizabeth Bennett sold to Lewis Graham 79 5/8 acres of BATCHELLORS CHANCE & DARBYS ADDITION.
13 June 1805 Lewis Graham with wife Sarah Graham sold to Joshua Bennett Jr. 79 5/8 acres of above.

BATCHELLORS CHOICE

Patented in 1763 by John Huffington Jr. for 22 3/4 acres.
21 Oct.1780 John Phillips sold to Benjamin Darby for 5 shillings 22 1/2 acres
1783 tax- Benjamin Darby 22 1/2 acres, Rewastico 100

BATCHELLORS CHOICE

Patented in 1796 by Benjamin Johnson for 30 1/2 acres.
29 May 1798 Benjamin Johnson sold to Elijah Christopher 30 1/2 acres.

BATCHELLORS CHOICE

see GETHESEME

BATCHELLORS CHOICE

Patented on 1 Aug.1704 by John Wilson, probably a resurvey of WILSONS LOTT on the west side of Barren Creek.
Rent Rolls 1666-1723 John Wilson
1752 will John Wilson, to cousin Mary Wilson Taylor 100 acres of WILSONS LOTT left her by my fathers will.
25 March 1765 James Taylor of Acco.Co.Va. sold to Nathan Culver of Som. Co.Md. 100 acres. As Thomas Wilson patented and it became the right of John Wilson who willed to Mary Wilson Taylor the late wife of said James Taylor. She died without issue and land descended to James Taylor as heir of Mary Wilson Taylor.

BATCHELLORS CONTRIVANCE

Patented on 1 June 1683 by James Wyeth and Marmaduke Mister for 150 acres in Nanticoke 100.
Rent Rolls 1666-1723 Both persons have deceased the county long since and said to be dead. No heirs appear or rent ever paid.
15 April 1725 Charles Mister son of Marmaduke Mister, planter sold to James Makemorie 150 acres assigned to Marmaduke Mister.
1738 James Makemorie willed to daughter Mary Makemorie land bought of Charles Mister.

BATCHELORS DELIGHT

Patented on 8 June 1683 by James Wyeth and Marmaduke Mister for 250 acres.
16 April 1725 Charles Mister son of Marmaduke Mister sold to James Makemorie.
1738 James Makemorie willed to grandson James Makemorie 250 acres, unnamed.

BATCHELORS DENN

Patented in 1801 by Mary Nairn Ann Austin and Priscilla Austin
3 May 1803 Robert Nairn and wife Mary Nairn of Worc.Co. sold to William Pollitt 10 3/4 acres.
1814 William Pollitt willed to nephew James Morris land bought of Robert Nairn, unnamed.

BATCHELORS FOLLY

Patented in 1764 to Joseph Collins for 409 acres.
16 April 1770 John Collins eldest son of Joseph deceased sold to John Kellum of Somerset Co.
1771 John Kellum willed to son Edward Kellum the plantation where I live, unnamed.
8 April 1776 Edward Kellum sold to Frederick Hill 204 acres that John Kellum willed to Edward Kellum.
1783 tax- Angelo Huffington (escheat) 238 acres- Rewastico
1783 tax- Richard James (Escheat) 204 acres
1783 tax- Francis Lank 106 1/2 acres.
26 Nov.1782 Clement Holliday and Nathaniel Ramsey of the commission to sell confiscated property sold 106 1/4 acres of BATCHELORS FOLLY in Wicomico Manor.
21 March 1788 Stephen Bayley of Sussex Co.Delaware am bound to Elias Bayley of Somerset Co. to make over BATCHELLORS FOLLY 100 acres to Elias Bayley.
13 March 1802 Joseph Gillis, Levin Bennett and Lewis Graham sold to Benjamin Melson 205 1/2 acres.
9 Jan 1802 John Kellum sold to Joseph Gillis, Levin Bennett and Levin Graham rights 204 1/2 acres.

BATCHELLORS FOLLY

Patented in 1772 by Alexander Porter for 89 3/4 acres.

BATCHELORS INVENTION

Patented on 8 June 1683 by James Wyeth and Marmaduke Mister.
15 April 1725 Charles Mister son of Marmaduke sold to James Makemorie with BATCHELLORS CONTRIVANCE & BATCHELORS DELIGHT.
1738 James Makemorie willed lands to grandsons James Makemorie, James Makemorie Jones. This land not named.

BATCHELLORS LOTT

Patented on 12 Sep.1759 for 50 acres by John Hearn in Wicomico forest.
5 Feb. 1767 John Hearn with wife Elizabeth Hearn sold to George Davis 50 acres
24 Mar.1774 George Davis sold to Elijah Smith 50 acres.
14 May 1783 Elijah Smith sold to James Ward of Sussex Co. Delaware 50 acres.
8 Sep.1794 James Ward with wife Frances Ward sold to Nathan Gordy 50 acres

BATCHELLORS LOTT

Patented on 5 Feb.1761 by Isaac Phillips for 50 acres.

BATCHELLORS LOTT

Patented in 1795 by William Pollitt for 187 acres.
24 Oct.1795 William Pollitt sold to Samuel Pollitt 20 acres

BATCHELLORS PROSPECT

Patented in 1807 by John Saints for 260 acres.

BATCHELORS PURCHASE

Patented in 1755 by James Acworth for 50 acres.
23 May 1769 James Acworth and wife Mary Acworth sold to John Phillips 50 acres on the south side of Barren Creek, north side of Wicomico River.
5 Dec.1772 John Phillips sold to John Sterling son of Aaron Sterling, 50 acres.

BATCHELORS PURCHASE

Patented in 1764 by James Acworth for 425 acres.
This could be a resurvey of the previous entry.

BEACH AND PINE

Patented in 1687 by John Dorman (certificate in name of Edward Howard) for 100 acres.
1719 Thomas Tull (wife Elizabeth Tull) willed to son Solomon Tull 100 acres.
1 April 1742 William Wharton and wife Mary Wharton sold to Edward Rook 70 acres, on the south side of Back Creek purchased from Solomon Tull and wife Elizabeth Tull, 50 acres of BEACH & PINE, 20 acres WILSONS PINE LOTT.

BEACH ISLAND

Patented in 1794 for William Parsons, 337 2/4 acres.
17 April 1794 William Parsons sold to George Smith 111 acres.
9 Sep.1800 William Parsons with wife Priscilla Parsons sold to George Smith 111 acres.
9 Sep.1800 George Smith with wife Mary Smith sold to David Smith Walston 111 acres.

BEAKS

see WESTERN FIELDS

BEAR GARDEN

Patented in 1713 Wrixam White, 100 acres.

BEARDS ADVANTAGE

Patented in 1744 to Lewis Beard for 50 acres.
22 March 1759 John Beard son of Lewis Beard, of Dorc. Co. sold to

George Dashiell 25 acres that his brother Lewis Beard gave him by will.
1783 tax- William Ellingsworth 25 acres(married Rachel Beard in 1750) Nanticoke 100.
3 March 1796 James Beard of Sussex Co.Del. sold to John Jones of Benjamin Jones 25 1/2 acres.

BEARDS BALANCE

Patented in 1747 by William Haynie

BEAUCHAMPS ADDITION

Patented in 1760 by Marcy Beauchamp for 414 1/2 acres.

BEAUCHAMPS CHOICE

Patented on 4 July 1760 by Edmund Beauchamp for 27 acres.

BEAUCHAMPS GAIN

Patented in 1748 by Edmund Beauchamp for 258 acres.

BEAVER DAMS

Patented on 15 Sep.1725 by Patrick Causey for 50 acres.
10 Aug.1744 Patrick Causey Sr. and wife Isabel Causey sold to Richardson Lingo 50 acres with PAGELE aka NEW HOLLAND (signed Patrick Kersey)
7 March 1755 Robinson Lingo with wife Ann Lingo sold to John Perdue 50 acres with EAGLES POINT on the north side of the head of the Wicomico River.
Part resurveyed 1773 to EAGLE POINT ADDITION
27 Oct.1782 John Perdue gave to son James Perdue 1/2 acre
1783 tax- John Perdue
25 Jan.1796 I John Perdue am bound to James Perdue for part of BEAVER DAMS and ADDITION TO EAGLE POINT, END OF STRIFE. (wife Sabrough Fooks Perdue)
1796 James Perdue willed to sons James W.B. Perdue, John K.H. Perdue and Elijah S.W. Perdue, all lands I possess.
12 Aug.1809 John K.H. Perdue sold rights to Jonathan S. Parsons

BECKMAN

Patented on 20 Nov.1681 by Andrew Jones on the south side of Wetipquin Creek for 150 acres.
23 April 1677 Leonard Jones assigned to James Dashiell 150 acres.
10 April 1678 James Dashiell assigned to Andrew Jones who surveyed it. 150 acres.
6 Jan 1681/2 Andrew Jones sold to James Dashiell.
1697 James Dashiell willed to son Thomas Dashiell 150 acres.
Rent Rolls 1666-1723 possessed by Thomas Dashiell.
1755 Thomas Dashiell willed to son Henry 150 acres.

14 March 1801 Josiah Sterling, wife Matilda Sterling sold to Thomas Dashiell of Thomas 340 or 350 acres of CANNONS PEACE, COME BY CHANCE, BECKMAN.
1827 James Walter willed to son Littleton Robertson Walter. Sarah Walter wife of James Walter.

BEDFORD

Patented on 4 April 1680 by William Stevens and assigned to James Weatherly for 500 acres at the head of Barren Creek.
Rent Rolls 1666-1723 James Weatherly possessed.
1736 Gabriel Cooper willed to sons Samuel Cooper, Gabriel Cooper, Isaac Cooper and Thomas Cooper, purchased of James Weatherly.
23 Jan 1745 Isaac Cooper son of Gabriel, and wife Isabel Cooper sold to Aaron Aires of Acco.Co.Va. 100 acres
8 March 1755 Samuel Cooper son of Gabriel Cooper sold to William Cooper 50 acres
1 March 1755 Aaron Aires sold to John Finch 100 acres.
1758 John Finch willed lands to wife Margaret Finch and then to sons John Finch and James Finch, unnamed.
10 April 1756 Thomas Cooper sold to Edward McDaniel 134 acres.
1760 Samuel Cooper willed to son Samuel Cooper
10 May 1761 Levin Cooper sold to Samuel Cooper Jr. 50 acres that he received by the death of his brother William Cooper that father Samuel Cooper conveyed to William Cooper.
27 May 1765 Edward McDaniel sold to James McDaniel 134 acres.
1766 Thomas Cooper willed plantation to son Abraham Cooper.
7 Jan 1768 John Finch son of John, and wife Elizabeth Finch sold to Henry Cordrey 100 acres.
1 Nov.1771 Henry Cordrey and Elizabeth Cordrey sold to Isaac Cooper 80 1/2 acres where Isaac Cooper formerly lived.
19 April 1779 John Cooper sold to James Tully 100 acres that Henry Cordrey sold to Isaac Cooper father of John Cooper.
1783 tax- John Cooper 83 acres Rewastico
1783 tax- Samuel Cooper 70 acres
1783 tax- Abraham Cooper 50 acres (resurvey to ADDITION)
1783 tax- Thomas Cooper 80 acres (with ADDITION 50 acres)
1783 tax- James McDaniel 134 1/2 acres (a resurvey)
1783 tax- James Tully 18 acres.
9 Aug.1788 James Tully and wife Anna Tully sold to John Grumble 100 acres.
21 May 1791 Abraham Cooper, wife Nancy Cooper of Sussex Co.Del. sold to Benjamin Venables of Somerset Co.125 1/2 acres of BEDFORD & HARDSHIP.
6 April 1799 Samuel Cooper, attorney for Levin Cooper of Shelby Co. Ky. and John Grumble of Sussex Co.Del for property of Samuel Cooper deceased.
26 March 1803 Samuel Cooper son of Levin Cooper, of Shelby Co.Ky. sold to Jonathan Waller of Sussex Co.Del. (no acres given)
21 Nov.1807 Benjamin Venables sold to Joseph Venables 125 1/2 acres of BEDFORD & HARDSHIP.

BEE HILL

Patented on 1 Apr.1763 by John Rayne for 50 acres.

8 Jan.1782 John Rayne sold to Caleb Rayne 50 acres
1783 tax - John Rayne 50 acres, Acquango 100, Worc.Co.
15 Jan.1803 Caleb Rayne sold to John Brittingham, 7 acres of GREENLAND and BEE HILL.
6 April 1803 Caleb Rayne sold part to John Brittingham.

BEGINNING

see WILSONS DISCOVERY(Delight)
see PASTURAGE

BELGRADE

Patented in 1800 to John Jones for 280 1/2 acres.

BELL AIR

Patented in 1800 to George Aires for 315 1/2 acres, a resurvey.
1818 will George Aires, to son Isaac Aires part and part to wife Betsy Aires, purchased from Littleton Aires and Matthias Hopkins.

BELLAIN

A resurvey of HORSEYS BAILYWICK by Robert Ridgley of 450 acres.
Patented on 26 Nov.1675 with 200 more acres, for 600 acres by Robert Ridgley. Sometimes spelled BELEAN,BELIAN, BELEAN
1680/81 Robert Ridgley of St.Inigoes, St. Marys Co. Md. willed to son Robert 600 acres of BELLAIN in Somerset County Maryland.
1701/2 Robert Ridgley of St. Mary's County willed the land in Somerset County to be sold.
13 March 1718 George Hutchins sold to Thomas Handy 280 acres.
13 March 1719 Samuel Handy willed 280 acres to son Thomas Handy.
31 July 1722 George Hutchins and wife Margaret Hutchins sold 3 1/2 acres to Thomas Humphries Jr. that Robert Ridgley willed to be sold. His wife Elizabeth Ridgley now married to William Goldsmith with Thomas Beale and John Baker sold all rights to George Hutchins.
3 July 1725 George Hutchins sold to John Handy 320 acres.
13 March 1748 George Tucker of Bermuda and wife Mary Tucker sold to John Seon of Somerset County as Thomas Handy died intestate and his daughter Mary Handy married George Tucker of Bermuda.
3 Feb.1752 Ezekiel Humphries son of Thomas Humphries and Mary Humphries, sold to Abraham Dean 3 1/2 acres part inherited from his father 1/2 acre and 3 acres from brother Joseph Humphries.
31 March 1753 Abraham Dean mortgaged to Henry Waggaman called THE COLLAR.
1755 part resurveyed 363 1/2 acre to BELLAIN by John Handy.
22 Feb 1755 Abraham Dean sold to Henry Lowe 3 1/2 acres mortgaged to Henry Waggaman, now redeemed.
2 Jan 1756 Henry Waggaman sold to Henry Lowe, 3 acres and 1 acre and 3 acres.
10 June 1763 Thomas Seon of the Isle of Bermuda, mariner sold to Nehemiah King 280 acres.
1766 Nehemiah King willed to son Levin King parcel bought of Thomas Seon on the Wicomico River.
19 June 1782 Henry Lowe, wife Esther Lowe, sold to George Waggaman part called THE COLLAR 3 1/2 acres, except 40 ft. where Abraham Dean

and family are burried.
1783 tax- Levin King 280 acres.
18 Sep.1792 Nehemiah King sold 42 acres for 10 shillings to Esme Bayley.
1798 James Moore willed to wife Mary Moore BELANE with saw and grist mill on Rockawalkin Branch.
20 July 1804 Benjamin Moore s/o James Moore sold to Elijah Humphries 1/4th pt. of mills and lands on Rokiawalkin Branch at Terrapin Town purchased by James Moore deceased. no name or acreage given.

BELLAIN

Patented in 1755 to John Handy for 363 1/2 acres, partial resurvey of original tract BELLAIN.
1755 Samuel Handy gave to John Handy a part, no acres given.
1756 Capt. John Handy, willed land on Wicomico River to son Levin Handy, unnamed.
1783 tax- Levin Handy 363 1/2 acres Rewastico, a resurvey of BELLEAN, WHAT YOU PLEASE & CHERVELEY.
14 Mar.1800 Ephraim K. Wilson executor of the will of Levin Handy sold to George Richardson Nasango mills and lands 2/3rds part, no name.
17 Feb.1810 Thomas J. Winder, wife Harriett Winder sold to William Hopkins 252 acres of BELLAIN,CHEVERLY,CALCUTTA, LOTT that Levin Handy father of Harriett had and moity of 10 acres entered for a water mill.

BELLS FIRST CHOICE

Patented on 16 June 1695 by John Bell for 200 aces on the north side of the Wicomico River.
Rent Rolls 1666-1723 John Bell moved southward. William Keen assumed to pay the rent.
Nov.1755 Newell Bell son of Isaac Bell sold 200 acres to Benjamin Venables son of Joseph Venables (confirmation of sale)
4 Oct.1758 Benjamin Venables and wife Ann Venables sold to Thomas Fletcher 200 acres.
March 1760 deposition of Benjamin Venables says that William Venables exchanged with Samuel Caldwell for 25 acres SECURITY and mills before the sale of Benjamin Venables to Thomas Fletcher.

BELLS CONCLUSION

Patented in 1802 by Ezekiel Bell for 283 acres.
1809 Ezekiel Bell willed to son Peter Bell 183 acres
1837 Peter Bell willed to all children unnamed.

BELLS GARDEN

see OUTLETT

BELLS HOOK

Patented in 1794 by Ebenezer C. Waller for 3 1/2 acres.

BELLVILLE

Patented in 1818 by John H. Bell and Anna M. Bell and Arminta Cottman probably a resurvey of land James Cottman willed in 1816 to daughters on the south side of Wicomico Creek, Anna M. Bell and Arminta Cottman.

BELLY AKE

Patented in 1798 by Robert Dashiell for 28 3/4 acres.

BELVEDER

Patented on 11 Oct.1804 by George D. Atkinson 310 3/4 acres.
2 Jan 1802 George D. Atkinson sold 6 acres to John Robertson (adj. SLIPE & MOREFIELDS)
7 Sep.1805 George D. Atkinson sold to Hambleton Wainright 8 1/2 acrs in Muddy Hole.
20 Feb.1807 George D. Atkinson sold to Stephen Wainright 68 1/4 acres on Shiles creek.
24 Nov.1807 George D. Atkinson sold 12 1/2 acres to Elias Robertson.
1836 Stephen Wainright willed 205 acres to son Stephen.

BENJAMINS ADDITION

Patented on 22 July 1760 by Benjamin Hearn for 40 acres.
Resurveyed in 1775 by Benjamin Hearn for 377 acres.

BENJAMINS CHOICE

Patented on 5 Oct.1760 by Benjamin Perdue for 22 1/2 acres.
4 June 1770 Benjamin Perdue sold to James Perdue of John Perdue 22 1/2 acres.
1783 tax- James Perdue of John 22 1/2 acres Wic.100 Worc.Co.

BENJAMINS GOOD SUCESS

Patented on 8 Sep.1723 by Benjamin Easum at the mouth of the east side of the Nanticoke River.
Rent Rolls 1666-1723 Benjamin Easum
1783 tax- Henry Nichols 16 acres. Nanticoke 100

BENJAMINS SECURITY

Patented on 19 May 1759 by John Maglamery for 81 acres.
15 Feb.1765 John Maglamery of North Carolina sold to William Parsons, in Wicomico Forrest. 81 acres.
1783 tax- William Parsons 81 acres Wic.100 Worc.Co.
1792 William Parsons willed to son William Parsons
2 Jan.1809 Samuel Parsons son of William sold to William Parsons son of William.

BENNETTS ADDITION

Patented in 1857 by Levin Bennett for 215 acres
1850 he lived in Barrren Creek area.

BENNETTS ADVENTURE

Patented on 7 June 1665 by Richard Bennett Esq. of Nasamond Co.Va. for 2500 acres.

15 March 1674 Richard Bennett willed to grandchildren Elizabeth Ann Scarborough and Bennett Scarborough and any other of my daughters children.
Rent Rolls 1666-1723 Apportains to the children of Charles Scarborough in Virginia who married Elizabeth Bennett daughter of Richard Bennett. 1701/2 Charles Scarborough of Acco.Co.Va. willed to son Bennett Scarborough his share of 250 acres in Wic. Co.Md. and to dau. Ann Parker wife of George Parker 1/2 of the same land.
2 Oct.1721 Bennett Scarborough sold to George Dashiell 2500 acres. This deed was signed by Bennett Scarborough son of Charles Scarborough, Henry Scarborough and Winifred Scarborough, Mary Leatherbury daughter of Charles Scarborough,John Bagwell and Tabitha Bagwell daughter of Charles, William Black and wife Sarah Black d/o Charles, Scarborough Drummond widow of Richard Drummond heir of deceased daughter of Charles, and George Parker son and heir of Ann Scarborough daughter of Charles Scarborough.
10 Oct.1734 George Dashiell resurveyed to DASHIELLS LOTT 1740 acres.

BENNETTS BEGINNING

Patented in 1735 by Elisha Bennett for 13 1/2 acres

BENNETTS HARD BARGAIN

Patented in 1851 by Jonathan N. Bennett for 61 3/4 acres.

BENNETTS HOOK

Patented on 3 May 1805 by James Bennett
14 Feb.1810 James Bennett sold 9 1/4 acres to Samuel Williams Jr.
1834 Samuel Williams willed that son Samuel sell all lands, unnamed.

BENNETTS PURCHASE

Patented in 1792 by James Bennett for 57 acres.

BENNETTS VENTURE

Patented in 1760 by Edward Bennett Jr. for 50 acres.

BENSONS LOTT

Patented in 1725 by Thomas Benson for 50 acres.

BENTLEY

Patented on 2 April 1672 by Thomas Walker for 300 acres on the south most side of Quantico Creek..
Rent Rolls 1666-1723 Apportains to the widow of Sampson Waters in Boston, New England but managed by James Dashiell.
24 Sep.1675 Thomas Walker sold to Isaiah Showcraft of Northampton Co. Virginia.
2 March 1717 Obediah Wakefield and John Wakefield both of Boston in Suffolk Co. Mass. sold to Peter Bowdoin son of John Bowdoin late of Northampton Co. Va. 1/2 of 875 acres JESHIMON, BATCHELLORS ADVENTURE,

BERNTLEY,COVENT GARDEN and THE SUPPLY in Nanticoke, Somerset Co.Md.
22 Aug.1739 Peter Bowdoin with wife Susanna Bowdoin of Northampton
Co.Va. sold to Capell King, 1 moity of 1750 acres, unnamed.

BERKS

Patented 3 Oct.1677 by John White for 150 acres who assigned to
Benjamin Cottman.
Rent Rolls 1666-1723 Possessed by the heirs of Benjamin Cottman or
Benjamin Nesham in the right who married the widow.
1708 Benjamin Nesham willed to wife her dower rights, unnamed.

BERWICK

Patented in 1792 by Levin Follin for 149 1/2 acres in Rewastico 100a.

BETSYS BLESSING

Patented in 1793 by John Biggans for 3 3/4 acres.

BETTER THAN IT PROMISES
see HORSEYS BALYWICK

BETSEYS GIFT

Patented by Phillip Covington in 1795 for 406 1/2 acres a resurvey
from DUDLEY
Repatented in 1774 for 387 acres by Priscilla Nicholson and Robert
Graham (certificate of John Nicholson.
1783 tax- Phillip Covington 387 acres in Nanticoke 100
1 Nov.1790 Robert Graham and wife Elizabeth Graham sold to Phillip
Covington and Priscilla Covington 387 acres (exchange of land)
1 Nov 1791 Phillip Covington and wife Priscilla Covington and Robert
Graham and wife Elizabeth Graham sold to Daniel Walter all land that
Robert Walter father of Daniel Walter bought of John Nicholson in
1755. 21 acres.
1 Sep.1802 George D. Walter sold to Phillip Covington for 10 shillings
part from Phillip Covington.
1 Sep.1802 Phillip Covington and wife Priscilla Covington sold to
George D. Walker.
21 Aug.1809 George D. Walter sold to James Ritchie 7 acres of DUDLEY

BETTS PRIVILEDGE

Patented in 1666 to Francis Betts son of George Betts
Repatented in 1742 by Levin Nicholson for 50 acres.
18 May 1773 Phillip Jones and wife Mary Jones sold to Phillip Graham
50 acres as Mary wife of Phillip has one moiety.
1 Nov.1790 Phillip Covington and wife Priscilla Covington sold to
Robert Graham 50 acres with WESTLOW LNECK.
12 July 1791 Sarah Graham executrix of Phillip Graham sold to John
Gale her 1/3rd part.
25 Jan.1794 Robert Graham of Worc.Co. sold to Edward Austin of Som.
Co. 280 acres of WESTLOCK & BETTS PRIVILEDGE.
4 Mar.1794 Edward Austin traded John Gale 33 /23 acres for GALES
UNION.

BETTY MARGERY

Patented on 20 Dec.1717 by Robert Hastings for 50 acres on the southmost branch of Little Creek.
Rent Rolls 1666-1723 possessed by Robert Hastings
11 March 1757 Robert Hastings sold to John Hastings.

BETSYS CHOICE

Patented on 29 Oct.1679 by John Richardson for 200 acres in Rewastico.
7 March 1681 John Richardson and wife Elizabeth Richardson sold to John Wood of Talbot County Md.
Rent Rolls 1666-1723 possessed by John Wood who ran away or deserted the county and since dead. No heir appearing.
12 Apr.1723 William Wood son of John Wood who died intestate, of Talbot Co. sold to Edward Serman of Som. Co.Md. 200 acres.
2 May 1737 Edward Serman, Isaac Serman, and Edward Serman grandson of Edward by his son Edward deceased that Edward Serman made over to Isaac and Edward his grandson.(division of lands) Jane Serman widow of Edward Jr. agrees.(Serman spelled Sherman and Sirman in same document.)
24 Feb 1770 Edward Serman and wife Isbell Serman and Isaac Serman sold to Benjamin Mitchell 50 acres for 10 shillings.
24 Feb.1770 Edward Serman and wife Isbell Serman and Isaac Serman sold to Michael White 50 acres for 10 shillings.
1782 Michael White willed to son George White.
1783 tax- Priscilla White widow of William White, 50 acres.
11 Oct.1794 Joseph Mitchell, wife Mary Mitchell sold to James Bennett 50 acres.

BETTYS CHOICE

Patented in 1748 by Robert Collier for 100 acres in Nanticoke 100.
1783 Tax- Robert Collier 100 acres.
1789 will of Robert Collier, to son Douty Collier and daughter Nelly Dashiell wife of William Dashiell, lands, unnamed.

BETTYS ENLARGEMENT

Patented on 20 Nov.1685 by Lewis Beard (wife Rebecca Beard) for 100 acres in Nanticoke 100.
Rent Rolls 1666-1723 possessed by Peter Douty for Beard's orphans.
1734 I Lewis Beard Sr. son of Lewis, for love give to son Lewis Jr. 130 acres out of FISHERMANS QUARTER & BETTYS ENLARGEMENT.
28 Oct.1752 John Beard eldest son of Lewis Beard and wife Rachel Beard sold to Samuel Fluellin all that is not contained in the conveyance of Lewis Beard to his son Lewis of 135 acres with FISHERMANS QUArter, and except the graveyard 1/4th acre, and also part 5 1/2 acres of RECOVERY.
1766 Samuel Fluellin willed to son Samuel Fluellin land bought of John Beard, unnamed.
17 May 1771 Samuel Fluellin sold to Ephraim King 130 acres of FISHERMANS QUARTER, BETTYS ENLARGEMENT and part of RECOVERY.

1777 Ephraim King willed to Richard Crockett Fluellin and Samuel Fluellin land their father Samuel bought of John Beard, unnamed.
1783 tax- William Ellingsworth (married Rachel Beard)
27 May 1792 Samuel Fluellin son of Samuel sold to James Winright with FISHERMANS QUARTER, CALLOWAYS ADDITION.
24 Dec.1793 Jarvis Beard sold to James Mezick 130 acres of FISHERMANS QUARTER & BETTYS ENLARGEMENT.
3 Aug.1799 Samuel Fluellin sold to Covington Cordrey TURNSTILE aka FISHERMANS QUARTER & BETTYS ENLARGEMENT, with CALLOWAYS ADDITION, 100 acres.
1795 James Winright willed to wife Eleanor Winright and daughters Nancy Winright and Jane Winright lands, unanmed. After deaths to grandson Levi Selby son of Henry Selby and Rebecca Selby.

BETTYS ESTATE

Patented by Levin Wright in 1760 for 50 acres.
1775 Levin Wright willed to daughter Easter Wright 50 acres where William Wright now lives.
1783 tax- William Tully 50 acres, Rewastico 100.

BETTYS LOTT

Patented by Richard Samuels for 50 acres in Stepney Parish
8 Aug.1722 Richard Samuels and wife Ann Samuels sold to Stephen Hopkins and wife Elizabeth Hopkins 60 acres. (Elizabeth Hopkins was a daughter of Richard Samuels.)
9 April 1774 Elizabeth Hopkins sold to Richard Hopkins son of Stephen Hopkins 60 acres.

BEVERLY

Patented on 13 May 1689 by Edward Gold for 200 acres in a fork of a branch of Barren Creek.
Rent Rolls 1666-1723 possessed by the orphans of Robert Downs.
2 April 1731 Robert Downs and wife Ann Downs sold to John Jones 50 acres sold by Edward Gold to Robert Downs.
18 Feb.1737/8 Robert Downs and wife Ann Downs, sold 150 acres to John Culver.
1755 John Culver of Stepney Parish willed to sons Moses Culver and Aaron Culver land and dwelling plantation, unnamed.
17 March 1746/7 John Jones sold to William Phillips 50 acres.
20 Jan.1755 John Culver and wife Mary Culver sold to William Phillips 57 1/4 acres.

BEVERLY

This 500 acres is part of DOUBLE PURCHASE.
1744 John Rousbey of Calvert Co.Md. willed to daughter Ann Lloyd wife of Edward Lloyd, BEVERLY in Som.Co.Md.

BEWDLY

Patented on 24 June 1676 by Leonard Jones 600 acres and assigned to

James Dashiell.
Rent Rolls 1666-1723 possessed by James Dashiell 600 acres.
1708/9 James Dashiell willed 600 acres to son George Dashiell.
6 Dec.1729 Thomas Dashiell and wife Elizabeth Dashiell, George Dashiell and wife Priscilla Dashiell, George Downs and wife Mary Downs deeded to Joseph McClester and Isabel McClester his wife.
8 Dec.1737 Joseph McClester and wife Isabel McClester deeded to George Dashiell son of Isabel her rights.
(note James Dashiell married 2nd Isabel Mitchell daughter of George Mitchell. She married 2nd. after 1708 Joseph McClester.)
27 Jan.1755 George Dashiell and wife Rebecca Dashiell deeded to Joshua Jackson 100 acres now called JACKSONS PURCHASE.
1764 Joshua Jackson does not mention lands in his wife. (wife Sarah Jackson)
21 Oct.1766 George Dashiell and wife Rebecca Dashiell sold 250 acres to John North with LITTLEWORTH.
21 Oct.1766 John North and wife Esther North sold to John Daugherty 104 acres of the 300 acres George Dashiell deeded him.
20 July 1784 John North sold to Joseph Austin 39 acres of BEWDLY & LITTLEWORTH.
1783 Tax- William Brinkley 33 1/2 acres
1783 Tax- Alice Jackson 66 3/4 acres
1783 Tax- John Libby 35 acres
1783 Tax- John North 50 acres
1783 Tax- Thomas Stevens 20 acres
14 July 1785 Esther North and John North sold to John Libby 35 acres.
25 Oct.1786 Esther North and John North sold to James Mezick 21 acres.
17 March 1795 James Mezick and wife Bridget Mezick sold to John Daugherty 21 acres.
9 June 1798 George Austin sold to Thomas Jones of James Jones, 39 acres.
6 Jan 1798 John Libby sold 35 acres to Thomas Dunn.
16 Feb.1799 Edward North and Levin Thomas sold to Ebenezer Collier, their interest.
19 June 1799 Ebenezer Collier sold to Richard Dunn 21 1/2 acres of BEWDLY & LITTLEWORTH.
3 Aug.1799 George Dashiell Walter sold to Richard Dunn 23 1/4 acres of BEWDLY & SHADWELL.
16 Mar.1804 Thomas Jones of James Jones, wife Nelly Jones sold to Richard Dunn 39 acres.
9 Nov.1805 Ebenezer Collier sold to Levin Horner 26 2/4 acres and 15 poles.
1831 SECOND ADDITION TO BEWDLY patented by George Walter for 420 3/4 acres.

BILL JOHNSONS HARRY

Patented by George Farlow in 1842 for 15 acres in Pittsburgh District
1850 George Farlow in the 4th district Worc.Co.Md.

BIRKHEADS CHANCE

Patented by William Birkhead in 1813 for 78 1/2 acres

1850 William Birkhead in the Salisbury District.

BITE THE BITER

Patented in 1807 by Sampson Parker

BLACK BRIER

Patented in 1784 by Benjamin Johnson for 189 acres.

BLACK MARSH

Patented by Joseph Weatherly in 1762 for 15 acres.
1764 Joseph Weatherly willed to son Joshua, marsh on Nanticoke River, unnamed. (he is under 18)
6 Apr.1774 John Weatherly and Joshua Weatherly sold 15 acres to William Acworth with WEATHERLYS ADDN. MARISH POINT, etc.
1783 Tax- Train Acworth 15 acres, Rewastico 100.

BLACK SOILE

Patented by William Jones in 1746 for 100 acres.
1783 Tax- Thomas Humphries 50 acres, Rewastico

BLACKWATER

Patented on 15 June 1679 by William Elgate for 25 acres on the north side of the Wicomico River.
Rent Rolls 1666-1723 possessed by Joseph Venables who purchased it.
15 Sep.1753 Benjamin Venables, Elgate Hitch, Thomas Bird, Ann Hall, Rebecca Evans, Moses Driskell sold 25 acres to Jonathan Stott.
10 Feb.1762 Jonathan Stott sold 25 acres to Christopher Piper with DEAR LOTT, WHAT YOU PLEASE, WORST IS PAST.
13 Jan. 1767 Christopher Piper sold to Esme Bayley of Worc. Co. 25 acres.
1783 tax- Esme Bayley 25 acres, Rewastico 100.

BLACKWATER BRANCH

see ORPHANS LOTT

BLIZARDS CHANCE

Patented in 1741 by Richard Blizard for 50 acres.

BOARD TREE SWAMP

Patented in 1774 by William McBryde for 232 acres.
1783 Tax- William McBryde 232 acres in Wic.100 Worc.Co.
1832 Elizabeth McBryde willed to nephew John B. Slemons.
1850 John B. Slemons willed all lands to be sold to the benefit of three children, Albert Slemons, Clara E. Slemons and Francis Marion Slemons.

BOADWINS LUCK

Patented in 1807 by Boadvine Bayley for 15 1/2 acres.

(THE) BOOT

Patented in 1802 by Joshua Morris for 2 1/2 acres.

BOOT AND A HALF

Patented in 1793 by John Robertson for 179 1/2 acres.
17 Jan 1794 John Robertson sold 13 3/4 acres to James Dean Badley.
14 Feb.1794 John Robertson sold 4 3/4 acres to Emanuel Walker of Sussex Co. Delaware.
1799 John Robertson willed to grandson Joshua Robertson balance of BOOT and 1/2 to son Eli Robertson.

BOOTHS PURCHASE

see CHANCE (1677)

BOSTON

Patented in 1762 by Richard Tully for 18 acres.

BOTANNY BAY

Patented in 1808 by Sandy Robertson for 43 acres.

BOTTLE RIDGE

Patented in 1732 by Daniel Davis for 50 acres.
1747 Daniel Davis willed to son William Davis 50 acres.
1767 William Davis willed to son Spencer Davis
1783 Tax- Patience Davis 50 acres Wic.100, Worc.Co.
1809 Spencer Davis willed to sons Levin Davis, Spencer Davis and William Davis.

BOTTOM ON THE NECK

Patented in 1734 by Christopher Nutter for 143 1/2 acres.
6 March 1752 George Hardy and wife Sarah Hardy formerly relic of Christopher Nutter sold to John Handy with NUTTERS ADVENTURE, NUTTERS CONTRIVANCE, MIDDLE TRACT, BOTTOM, ROSS, DELIGHT, etc.
1783 Tax- Thomas Whalen 105 acres
1783 Tax- Samuel King, Rewastico 100
29 May 1793 Charles Nutter to William Nutter, division of lands.
27 Aug.1806 Henry E. Bayley, wife Sarah Bayley sold to Charles Nutter.
1813 Charles Nutter willed Quantico lands to son Christopher Columbus Nutter, unnamed.

BOTTOM OF THE NECK

Patented in 1735 by William Kibble for 198 acres.
18 Feb.1737 William Kibble and John Kibble sold to George Dashiell 80

acres that he resurveyed and called RIVER LANDING.
1748 will George Dashiell, to son Joseph 80 acres.
27 April 1765 Joseph Dashiell son of George Dashiell, of Worc.Co. sold to John Newman of Som.Co. 80 acres.
1783 Tax- Sarah Newman 80 acres.

BOUNDS ADDITION

19 Aug.1740 Robert Givans sold to Jacob Bounds part of WHITE OAK SWAMP now called BOUNDS ADDITION on the south side of Nanticoke River at head of Broad Breek 23 acres.
1773 will Jacob Bounds, lands(unnamed) to son Jesse Bounds.
This land is probably now in Sussex Co.Delaware.

BOUNDS CHANCE

Patented in 1741 by Jacob Bounds for 50 acres.
1773 Jacob Bounds willed lands to son Jesse Bounds.

BOUNDS CHANCE

Patented on 17 April 1761 by Jonathan Bounds for 274 1/4 acres in a fork of the Wicomico River and Wicomico Creek.
1741 Jonathan Bounds willed to son James Bounds 174 1/2 acres.
22 March 1752 Levin Dashiell and wife Bridget Dashiell sold to Isaac Dashiell 80 acres with MEECHES HOPE, MITCHELLS IMPROVEMENT, and two other tracts that was sold by Jonathan Bounds to John Collins, CHANCE & 100 acres of marsh.
1783 Tax- Matilda Bounds 257 1/2 acres, Wicomico 100.
13 Jan.1801 William Bounds of James Bounds, with wife Magaret Bounds sold to George Fooks 244 3/4 acres patented Jonathan Bounds at Cowesick Creek being original bounds of BOUNDS LOTT.
(this land was part of STEVENS CONQUEST.)

BOUNDS LOTT

Patented in 1735 by Jonathan Bounds for 300 acres
6 Oct 1741 James Bounds of Dorcester Co.Md. sold to Daniel Kelly of Som. Co. 50 acres near the nead of Nanticoke river, near land of Samuel Griffith adj. GOLDEN GROVE on the west side of the northeast fork. This land was probably in Dorcester County.

BOUNDS NEGLECT

Patented in 1860 by George W. Bounds for 8 acres.

BOUNDS SITUATION

Patented in 1803 by James Bounds for 164 1/4 acres.

BOWER HILL

Patented in 1800 by William Winder for 1146 acres.
28 Feb.1806 William Winder sold 43 acres to William Bounds of James Bounds on the south side of Rewastico Creek.

8 Nov.1806 William Winder sold all to Edward Austin.
2 Nov.1807 Edward Austin sold to James McCree 20 1/2 acres.
18 Dec.1807 John Taylor of Ezekiel Taylor sold to John Messick of Benjamin Messick 6 acres.
19 Dec.1817 Matthias Whittington sold to William Bounds of James Bounds, 56 acres of BOWER HILL & GIVANS SECURITY
31 Oct.1818 Edward Austin sold part to William Bounds.
26 Feb.1825 William Bounds sold to John Bounds 265 3/4 acres of BOWER HILL & GIVANS SECURITY.

BRANDY RIDGE

Patented in 1750 by Peter Gordy for 50 acres
1772 Peter Gordy willed to son Peter 25 acres and to son John Gordy 25 acres
27 Apr.1797 Peter Gordy, Elisha Parker with wife Eleanor Parker, Samuel Parker with wife Hetty Parker, Benjamin Hearn son of Samuel Hearn and William Hearn of Sussex Co. Delaware with wife Polly Hearn sold all rights to William Gordy.
9 Nov.1809 William Gordy with wife Eliza Gordy sold to Betty Gordy.

BRATTANS BEGINNING

Patented in 1834 by Jesse Brattan for 72 3/4 acres.

BREADYS CHANCE

Patented by Rebecca Bready in 1744 for 171 acres.
18 March 1752 Rebecca Evans formerly Rebecca Bready sold 171 acres to John Handy and Isaac Handy (agreement)
10 March 1770 Samuel Carter and wife Unice Carter and Sophia Bready alias Sophia Wright sold 158 acres to Ezekiel Bell.

BREWINGTONS NEGLECT

Patented in 1831 by Levin D. Collier for 6 1/2 acres.
(1850 Levin D. Collier in Salisbury District)

BRIER GROVE

Patented in 1786 by Benjamin Johnson for 36 acres.

BRIMELOU

see SUFFOLK (pat Thomas Walker)

BRITTAIN

Patented on 15 April 1695 by Michael Disharoon for 100 acres 1 mile from south side of Wicomico River.
1690 Michael Disharoon willed 100 acres to son Michael.
Rent Rolls 1666-1723 possessed by Michael Disharoon s/o Michael.
24 May 1743 Michael Disharoon sold to John Haywood 50 acres.
15 March 1755 Michael Disharoon Jr. sold to John Hilman 50 acres.

1744 John Haywood willed 50 acres to son David Haywood.
2 April 1767 David Howard, wife Eleanor Howard sold to Robert Banks 50 acres with HOWARDS DISCOVERY.
1769 will Robert Banks, to son Henry Banks.
13 May 1775 Joshua Hilman sold 50 acres to Levin Dashiell.
1783 Tax- Henry Banks 50 acres. Wicomico 100.
21 Aug.1793 Joshua Hilman sold 100 acres to William Hilman of BRITTAIN & LAST CHOICE.
1820 William Hilman willed to sons George Hilman and William Hilman BRITTAIN or LAST CHOICE bought of the trustee of Samuel Hilman of Worc.Co.Md.

BRITTINGHAMS FORTUNE

Patented in 1785 by Truitt Brittingham for 20 acres.
16 May 1783 Truitt Brittingham sold to Jarman Brittingham 20 acres.
9 Jan.1790 Jarman Brittingham sold to Benjamin Truitt 20 acres.

BROTHERS AGREEMENT

Patented on 25 Nov.1685 by James Knox for 500 acres.
13 March 1687 Ephraim Wilson sold 500 acres to James Knox
Rent Rolls 1666-1723 belongs to James Knox who denys payment of rent.
17 Mar.1763 John Elzey Sr., Jonathan Vaughn and William Douglas and David McMurke and Persisor Frazier sold to Christopher Marshall of Philadelphia Pa. and John Chamberlain of Aston in Chester Co. Pa. 500 acres.
6 June 1763 Joseph Boyce, Jonathan Vaughn, William Douglas, John Chamberlain of Chester Co. Pa. David McMurke, Persisor Frazier to Christopher Marshall of City of Philadelphia 5 acres., no name of land.
10 Jan 1806 William Stewart, shipwright eldest son of Patrick Stewart, sold to George Adams of Sussex Co.Del.in trade for 500 acres in Virginia: in Nanticoke River in Sussex Co.Del. formerly Worc.Co.Md.

BROTHERS CARE

Patented in 1771 by William Stewart for 53 1/2 acres.
1783 tax- William Stewart 53 1/2 acres, Nanticoke 100.
10 Oct.1809 Robert Stewart of Baltimore sold to Alexander Stewart of Somerset Co.
2 Nov.1809 John Stewart, James Evans and wife Elizabeth Evans, formerly Elizabeth Stewart, Nancy Stewart, Matty Stewart sold to Alexander Stewart.

BROTHERS GOOD WILL

Patented on 1 April 1762 by John Christopher for 50 acres.
9 Mar.1765 John Christopher sold to Stephen Horsey of Somerset Co. 125 acres, 1/2 of ABRAHAMS LOTT and 50 acres of BROTHERS GOOD WILL.
1783 Tax- Stephen Horsey, 50 acres, Wic.100 Worc.Co.
1788 Stephen Horsey willed to grandson George Livingston
20 March 1789 George Livingston sold to Todd Livingston for 5 shillings 50 acres.
20 Jan.1792 Todd Livingston sold to Thomas Fooks 50 acres.

BROWNS BEGINNING

Patented in 1763 by William Brown Jr. for 50 acres, Rewastico 100.
A second patent in 1774 by Robert Brown for 27 acres.
1785 Robert Brown willed to sons Robert Brown, Thomas Brown plantation and lands in Vienna Marsh, no name.
1783 Tax- Robert Brown 27 acres.
29 April 1790 John Brown mortgaged to Lewis Daltrieu on south side of Barren Ck.
7 June 1793 Lewis Daltrieu sold to John Hopkins tract Robert Brown devised to son Robert, no name.
24 Oct.1793 Robert Brown son of Robert sold to Lewis Daltrieu, merchant, tract from father Robert who willed to him if brother Thomas Brown dies before age 21, no name.
24 Sep.1806 Robert Brown son of Robert, in Ohio Co. Virginia sold to James Huffington and John Huffington Jr. planters of same county, land Robert Brown devised to son Thomas 1/2 of his land.

BROWNS CONCLUSION

Patented in 1792 by Robert Brown and Thomas Brown for 269 3/4 acres a resurvey of WHICH YOU PLEASE.

BROWNS PRIVILEDGE

Patented 1764 by James Brown for 50 acres.
18 Feb.1768 James Brown, shipwright and wife Sarah Brown of Dorc.Co. sold 33 acres to Joseph Venables of Somerset County with ALGATE.
1783 tax- Joseph Venables 33 1/2 acres in Rewastico 100
1788 will Joseph Venables, to Benjamin Venables and Richard Venables sons of William Venables.

BROWNS SETTLEMENT

Patented in 1864 by John W. Brown in Barren Creek for 132 1/2 acres.

BUCK HILL

Patented on 4 Aug.1751 by Jacob Spear for 37 acres.
26 Jan 1770 Jacob Spear and wife Elizabeth Spear sold to Capt. Charles Dashiell 37 acres.
20 Jan 1773 ADDITION TO BUCK HILL patented Charles Dashiell for 206 1/2 acres.
1783 tax- Charles Dashiell, Rewastico 100.
1800 Charles Dashiell willed to grandsons Charles Dashiell and George Dashiell 150 acres part of resurvey.
2 May 1809 Chapman Dashiell sold to Peter Bell 40 acres.

BUCK RANGE

Patented in 1740 by Joseph Morgan for 50 acres.

BUCK RIDGE

Patented in 1751 by William Laws for 153 acres

1751 ADDITION TO BUCK RIDGE 199 1/2 acres by William Laws.

BUCK RIDGE

Patented on 9 Dec.1757 by Andrew Smith son of Andrew for 50 acres on a branch of the Wicomico River, in Wicomico forrest.
3 Dec.1774 Andrew Smith with wife Elizabeth Smith sold to Elijah Hearn
1783 tax - Elijah Hearn 50 acres
1 Dec.1791 Elijah Hearn sold to George Parker 50 acres
24 Sep.1808 George Parker sold part to Joshua Trader.

BUCK RIDGE

Patented on 26 Nov.1762 by Jeremiah Nelms for 108 acres in Wicomico forrest.
19 June 1772 Jeremiah Nelms of North Carolina sold to John Nelms of Somerset County 108 acres.

BUCKINGHAM

Patented in 1803 by Thomas Dashiell for 152 1/4 acres
1783 tax- Mary Dashiell 100 acre, Nanticoke 100
1783 Tax- Jane Dashiell 50 acres.

BURBAGES MISTAKE

Patented in 1787 by Jesse Jones for 64 3/4 acres.

BUSH FIELD

Patented in 1794 by William Winder for 88 1/2 acres.

BUSH RIDGE

Patented in 1775 by Joshua Freeney for 10 acres.
1783 Tax- Joshua Freeney Wic.100 Worc.Co.
1822 Joshua Freeney willed land in Som.Co. to son John Freeney (unnamed.)

BUSHEY NECK

Patented on 22 Sep.1758 by David Smith for 150 acres.
1846 Isaiah Smith willed to daughters Mandy Smith and Lovey Smith 150 acres, farm in BUSH NECK adjacent Nathaniel Gunby.

BUSHEY RIDGE

Patented in 1824 by William Parsons for 8 acres.
1839 William Parsons willed to wife Molly Parsons and son Benjamin Parsons, lands(unnamed,)

BUSHY RIDGE

Patented in 1767 by David Wilson for 50 acres.
1772 will of David Wilson living at head of Barren Creek, to son John

Wilson and son Ephraim Wilson lands, unnamed.
15 Dec.1792 Ephraim Wilson sold 22 acres to Arthur Dashiell.
1802 Arthur Dashiell willed lands to son Matthias Dashiell.

BUTTER FLYE

Patented in 1759 by Robert Walter for 5 acres.
1783 tax- Robert Walter Sr. 5 acres, Nanticoke 100.

BURKHEADS DISCOVERY

Patented in 1848 by William Birkhead in Salsibury District for 21 3/4 acres.

BURNT MARSH

Patented in 1742 by Jeremiah Townsend for 395 acres.
1743 Jeremiah Townsend willed 445 acres to son Brickhouse Townsend.
1783 Tax- Luke Townsend 200 acres, Wicomico 100
26 April 1790 Luke Townsend sold to William Riley Evans of Delaware 50 acres.
15 Nov.1805 Lemuel Evans power of attorney for William Riley Evans of Sussex Co.Del. sold to John Townsend of Worcester County Md.

BURTONS CHOICE

Patented in 1740 by Robert Parsons for 100 acres.

BUTTOCKING RIDGE

Patented in 1769 by Francis Chattam for 100 acres.
1773 Francis Chattam willed to son John Chattam. To David Polk part of resurvey on BUTTOCKING RIDGE 121 acres.
1778 David Polk willed to son Josiah Polk.
1783 Tax- John Chattam 151 acres, Wic.Co.100 Worc.Co.
1784 Josiah Polk willed to brother James Polk, purchased of John Chattam and to brother William Polk land from my father, unnamed.
24 Dec.1790 Esme Bayley Esq. and wife Sinah Bayley sold to Josiah Bayley son of Esme, as Josiah Polk deceased and brother of Sinah willed to his sister one moity of mills and lands on the Nanticoke River during life and then to her sons. Same deed 21 May 1794, unnamed land.
1795 James Polk willed, that devised me by brother Josiah Polk to be sold.
2 Jan 1796 William Polk sold to Esme Bayley per will of James Polk.
2 Jan 1796 Esme Bayly sold to William Polk same as above.
14 July 1801 deed of bargain- William Polk Esq. sold to William H. Winder and Gertrude Winder for affection during their lifetime part of James Polks estate purchased at public sale.
3 May 1803 William H. Winder and wife Gertrude Winder of Baltimore City sold to Robert Dashiell and Peter Dashiell of Somerset Co. all interest.

BYRDS CONCLUSION

Patented in 1821 by Thomas Byrd for 559 acres.

1821 Thomas Byrd willed to son John Byrd.

CABIN RIDGE

Patented in 1759 by Peter Parsons for 15 acres. He added on same date 50 acres.
1762 will Peter Parsons, to son Porter Parsons 15 acres and 50 acres to son John Parsons.
1783 Tax- Martha Parsons (wife of Peter) 15 acres.
29 May 1793 John Parsons sold to Zachariah Parsons 15 acres

CAHOONS CHOICE

Patented in 1773 by Benjamin Cahoon for 50 acres in Wicomico Forest.
4 Dec.1773 Benjamin Cahoon with wife Lanta Cahoon sold to Joshua Holloway 50 acres.

CALCUTTA

Patented in 1754 by Henry Waggaman for 539 1/2 acres in Rewastico 100.
1759 Henry Waggaman willed to son Henry.
10 Nov.1781 Henry Waggaman sold to George Waggaman
1783 Tax- George Waggaman 505 acres.
12 Sep.1808 Daniel Ballard, Esq. sheriff, sold to Josiah Bayley of Dorc.Co., per judgement against Henry Waggaman.
12 Apr.1808 Josiah Bayley and wife Ann Bayley of Dorc.Co. sold to John Rider.
11 Jan 1809 Henry Waggaman and wife Sarah Waggaman of Worc.Co. sold to John Rider of Som.Co. as George Waggaman died intestate and Henry was entitled to 1/3rd part. William Elliott Waggaman to 1/3rd part, Harriett Dickenson of Dorc.Co. 1/6th part, John W. Footman of Charlestown SC entitled to 1/6th part as coheirs. 496 acres.
7 July 1810 Sarah McBryde sold to John Rider part of AVERS POLICY, CALCUTTA & MUMSLEY.
7 July 1810 John Rider sold to Sarah McBryde, same as above, probably a settlement of boundaries.
17 Feb.1810 Thomas J. Winder and wife Harriett Winder sold to William Hopkins BELEAN,CHEVERLY,CALCUTTA, LOTT that Levin Handy father of Harriett had.
1820 William Hopkins willed lands unnamed, to mother Eleanor Hopkins and sister Margaret Leatherbury.

(The) CALDER

Patented in 1755 by Joseph Weatherly for 100 acres in Rewastico 100a.
1764 Joseph Weatherly willed to son John Weatherly lands unnamed, and to son Constantine Weatherly.
1789 John Weatherly willed to brother Constantine Weatherly.
1783 tax- Constantine Weatherly 70 acres, Rewastico 100a.
16 Sep.1791 Constantine Weatherly and wife Elizabeth Weatherly, ship carpenter sold to William Winder WEATHERLYS RIDGES, CALDER & CONSTANTINES DELIGHT.

CALDWELLS CHANCE

Patented on 10 July 1688 by John Caldwell for 27 acres.
Rent Rolls 1666-1723 possessed by John Caldwell
12 Dec.1758 Littleton Dennis, Joseph Scroggin executors of the will of Joshua Caldwell sold to Thomas Savage that Joshua willed to be sold.
12 Dec.1758 Thomas Savage sold to Jonathan Bounds 27 acres.
14 Nov.1764 Jonathan Bounds gave to son Richard Stevens Bounds.
1783 Tax- Elijah Vinson 27 acres.
13 Oct.1804 Eli Vinson Jr, wife Comfort Vinson sold to Henry White of Worc.Co.

CALDWELLS LOTT

Patented on 15 Sep.1704 by Robert Caldwell for 200 acres on the north side of Rewastico Glade.
Rent Rolls 1666-1723 possessed by Robert Caldwell
13 March 1727 John Caldwell Jr. and wife Rachel Caldwell and Margaret Caldwell his mother, sold 200 acres to Andrew Scott (heirs of Robert Caldwell)
27 Sep.1744 Robert Caldwell appointed Robert Givans attorney to sell all lands to Joseph Ennals of Dor.Co., several tracts DESART, CALDWELLS LOTT wherein he mill now stands on Little Creek taken up by John Caldwell father of Robert and all lands in Somerset County.
19 Dec.1733 Andrew Scott sold to Richard Wallace.
1763 Richard Wallace (wife Esther Wallace) willed to Hudson Lowe 100 acres he purchased of me on the south side of CALDWELLS LOTT.
13 July 1768 John Fletcher and wife Esther Fletcher sold to Hudson Lowe 100 acres (as Richard Wallace willed Esther Wallace, his then wife executrix with power to make over to Hudson Lowe.)
21 Dec.1779 Esther Fletcher sold 200 acres to Thomas Lank.
26 Oct.1785 Thomas Lank with wife Mary Lank sold to Hudson Lowe 33 3/4 acres..
26 Oct.1786 Thomas Lank with wife Mary Lank sold 33 /34 acres to Charles Dashiell.
1793 ADDITION patented by Hudson Lowe for 182 1/2 acres.
1800 Charles Dashiell willed to grandsons Charles and George Dashiell.
1802 will of Hudson Lowe, to son Levin Lowe CALDWELLS LOTT & ADDITION.

CALLOWAYS ADDITION

Patented in 1752 by John Beard for 25 acres.
27 May 1792 Samuel Fluellin sold to James Winright all land Samuel Flueullin father of Samuel bought of John Beard with FISHERMANS QUARTER, BETTYS ENLARGEMENT, CALLOWAYS ADDITION.
3 Aug.1799 Samuel Fluellin sold 100 acres to Covington Cordrey of TURNSTILE aka FISHERMANS QUARTER, BETTYS ENLARGEMENT & CALLOWAYS ADDITION.

CALLOWAYS DELIGHT

I found no patent for this land. It is now probably in Sussex Co.Del.
30 July 1769 John Stilley sold to John Cordrey 50 acres with STILLYS PRIVILDEGE near Broad Creek.
3 Oct.1772 John Stilley and wife Grace Stilley sold 123 acres to Ann

Moore for 5 shillings except 50 acres conveyed to John Cordrey.

CALLOWAYS FANCY

Patented in 1742 by Peter Calloway for 100 acres.
Resurveyed to CALLOWAYS NEGLECT. This certificate was voided.

CALLOWAYS FOLLY

Patented 10 June 1718 by John Calloway on the east side of the head of Little Creek for 50 acres.
Rent Rolls 1666-1723 possessed by John Calloway
27 Jan 1755 John Calloway gave 25 acres to son Ebenezer Calloway.
This land was probably resurveyed to Sussex Co.Delaware.

CALLOWAYS HARD FORTUNE

Patented in 1749 by Benjamin Calloway for 50 acres.

CALLOWAYS INVENTION

Patented on 29 Jan.1715 by Peter Calloway for 100 acres on the north east side of Little Creek out the Nanticoke River.
1738 Peter Calloway willed to son Thomas Calloway.
5 Nov.1742 Thomas Calloway sold to John Calloway 100 acres.
20 July 1771 John Calloway sold 100 acres to Peter Calloway
14 Apr.1775 Peter Calloway sold 100 acres to Caleb Balding.
26 Mar.1776 Sussex Co.Delaware warrants to Elijah Tilghman.

CALLOWAYS NEGLECT

Patented on 3 Aug.1759 by William Bevans for 222 acres.
13 Sep.1763 William Bevans sold to James Ward 50 acres
13 Sep.1763 William Bevans sold to Francis Ellis 62 acres.
17 March 1770 Francis Ellis with wife Amey Ellis sold to William Maddux 62 acres.
2 May 1776 Sussex Co.Delaware land warrents
2 March 1784 William Maddux of Little Creek 100, Sussex Co.Delaware sold to Aaron Gordy.

CALLOWAYS RIDGE

Patented in 1738 by George Dashiell for 50 acres.

CALLOWAYS VENTURE

Patented in 1765 by Samuel Calloway for 172 acres.
17 Jan.1755 John Calloway gave 25 acres to son Ebenezer Calloway
27 Jan.1755 John Calloway gave 25 acres to son Isaac Calloway
1 Sep.1760 Isaac Calloway sold to John Crouch 25 acres.
21 Aug.1766 Samuel Calloway sold to George Moore, blacksmith 172 acres.
6 Apr.1774 Robert Crouch sold part to William Polk 50 acres patented 18 March 1746 to John Calloway.
Evidently there was more than one patent by this name.

1776 Sussex Co. land warrants, CALLOWAYS ADVENTURE pat. Benjamin Calloway and on 8 March 1776 Sussex Co.Del. land warrents George Moore, CALLOWAYS ADVENTURE pat.Som.Co.Md. by Samuel Calloway.

CAMBRIDGE

Patented on 26 Nov.1672 by George Smith for 300 acres near the Nanticoke River.
Rent Rolls 1666-1723 possessed by Thomas Gordon 300 acres.
25 Nov.1779 Edward Kellum sold 105 acres to Charles Weatherly, shipwright.
26 Nov.1801 Charles Weatherly sold to William Russum with part of a marsh bought of Ezekiel Graham.
15 Jan.1802 Charles Weatherly sold to Jonathan Huffington 20 acres.
3 Aug.1802 Jonathan Huffington willed to wife Sarah Huffington and sons John Huffington, James Huffington and Jesse Huffington, lands unnamed.

CAMP

Patented on 10 April 1680 by Col. William Stevens for 300 acres.
Rent Rolls 1666-1723 possessed by Richard Wallace 150 acres & James Smith 150 acres.
1 June 1718 John Holder attorney of James Wallace sold to James Smith.
1718/23 James Smith willed all to sons David Smith and James Smith, no land mentioned.
23 Oct.1723 I James Wallace of Cecil Co. Md. make over to Richard Wallace of Somerset County Md.(bond)
3 Mar.1741 James Smith gave to son Moses Smith 100 acres at the south end being 1 moity bought of Robert Wallace and made over by James Wallace his son.
7 Sep.1744 Richard Wallace made over to son Thomas Wallace right to bond of James Wallace.
1754 Thomas Wallace willed 100 acres near GOLDEN QUARTER to daughters Agnes Wallace, Janet Donelson and Katherine Wallace, lands where I live, unnamed.
21 Apr.1794 Mary Smith of Sussex Co.Delaware sold to Jonathan Parsons of Worc.Co. Md. 300 acres
14 Sep.1789 Elizabeth Wallace of Dorc. Co.Md. sold to Moses Claywell Smith of Worc.Co. 150 acres.

CAMP NECK

Patented on 9 July 1721 by James Bouger for 50 acres in fork of the north main branch of Broad Creek.
31 May 1736 James Bouger and wife Mary Bouger sold to John Houston.
1783 tax- Jonathan Parsons 50 acres (CAMP) Wicomico 100
1808 Jonathan Parsons willed to son Jonathan Stevens Parsons.

CANADA

Patented in 1773 by Boaz Walston for 40 acres.
1783 Tax- Boaz Walston 40 acres Wic. 100 Worc.Co.

CANADA

Patented 1822 by Samuel Lecompte for 186 1/2 acres.

CANNADYS CHOICE

Patented in 1758 by Hugh Cannady for 50 acres.
15 Oct.1792 Hon. Alexander Contee Hanson, chancellor of State of Maryland sold to William McBryde 48 3/4 acres KENNEDYS CHOICE and 31 1/2 acres DOWGATE.
21 Aug.1793 William McBryde and wife Sarah McBryde sold 50 acres to Henry Banks.

CANNAAN

Patented on 6 May 1760 by David Smith for 100 acres in Wicomico Forest.
8 Nov.1769 Isaiah Smith sold 100 acres to Bathsheba Smith.
1783 Tax- Elijah Smith 200 acres, Wicomico 100
1783 Tax- Boaz Walston 75 acres
1805 Hezekiah Maddux of Worc.Co. willed to son Wilson Maddox
1820 SECOND ADDITION TO CANNAAN by John P. Gordy, 1861 acres.

CANNAAN

Patented on 26 Aug.1762 by John Hearn a resurvey from MARTINS CHOICE for 207 acres.
1769 John Hearn willed to sons John Hearn, Isaac Hearn, Peter Hearn to share 207 acres.
1790 ADDITION TO CANAAN patented by John Hearn for 233 acres.
29 May 1798 John Hearn with wife Betty Hearn sold to Isaac Hearn 1/2 acre.
29 May 1798 Peter Gordy Hearn son of John Hearn, with wife Lovey Hearn sold to Isaac Hearn rights.
4 Nov.1799 John Hearn and Elijah Smith of Sussex Co.Delaware sold to Hezekiah Maddux 50 acres CANNAAN and LIBERTY.
1806 John Hearn willed to son James Hearn, ADDITION 1/6th part.
10 Sep.1808 Isaac Hearn with wife Nancy Hearn sold to James Hearn 11 3/4 acres of ADDITION TO CANNAAN

CANNONS ADDITION

Patented in 1797 by Thomas Cannon for 36 acres
13 Nov.1798 Mary Cannon sold to Augustus Cannon
12 Apr.1799 Augustus Cannon sold all rights to William Polk
15 Jan 1801 Thomas Cannon sold to James Russell 36 1/4 acres.
11 Feb.1806 William Polk Esq. sold to Josiah Polk, lands bought of Augustus Cannon, unnamed.
7 Apr.1810 Josiah Polk and wife Rebecca Polk sold to Levin D. Jones.

CANNONS CHOICE

Patented on 8 April 1674 by Stephen Cannon for 300 acres and assigned to John Furrs on Wetipquin Creek.
Rent Rolls 1666-1723 since resurveyed for Peter Douty 188 acres and

Thomas Larramore for 182 acres.
1783 tax- Sarah Lawrence 9 1/4 acres
1783 Tax- Samuel Fluellin 5 acres.

CANNONS DISCOVERY

No patent found for this land. It is on the north east fork of the Nanticoke River.
2 Aug.1749 John Cannon of Dorc.Co. Md. sold to Joseph Cannon of Worc.Co. Md. 49 acres (Worc.Deeds)
2 Aug.1749 John Cannon of Dorc.Co. sold to Elijah Cannon 51 acrs.
James Cannon of Dorc. Co. willed to son Joseph. This is probably now part of Sussex Co. Delaware.

CANNONS GOOD LUCK

Patented in 1797 by Thomas Cannon for 68 1/2 acres.
7 Nov.1799 Thomas Cannon sold to Charles Rider 68 1/2 acres.
1801 Charles Rider willed to son James 68 acres.
13 Feb.1804 James Rider son of Charles Rider sold 68 acres to John Taylor.

CANNONS LOTT

Patented on 8 Sep.1681 by James Sangstor and assigned to Stephen Cannon on the south side of Wetipquin Creek for 100 acres.
Rent Rolls 1666-1723 possessed by Patrick Quatermas who lives in Dorcester County.
13 Oct.1721 Samuel Fluellin sold 50 acres to Richard Dunn
28 Dec.1749 Nicholas Dunn sold 50 acres to George Collier.
1774 George Collier Sr. willed 50 acres to son John Collier.
1783 tax- Ann Collier 50 acres
26 March 1793 Gillis Polk, surviving trustee of Ephraim King and Samuel Fluellin brother of Richard C. Fluellin sold to Isaac Atkinson son of Isaac.
22 Aug.1808 George Collier, wife Martha Collier sold to Matthias Dashiell Hopkins 50 acres.
5 Nov.1808 Matthias D. Hopkins and wife Eleanor Hopkins sold 50 acres to James Walter.
1827 James Walter, wife Sarah Walter, willed to daughter Ann Maria Dorothy Walter.

CANNONS PEACE

Patented on 14 Feb.1699 Stephen Cannon on west side of Wetipquin Creek for 100 acres.
Rent Rolls 1666-1723 possessed by Peter Body
26 Feb.1709 Peter Body sold to Thomas Dashiell 100 acres being his wife's share of her father Stephen Cannon's estate, unnamed.
14 March 1801 Josiah Sterling and wife Matilda Sterling sold to Thomas Dashiell son of Thomas 350 acres of CANNONS PEACE, COME BY CHANCE, BECKNAM.

CANNON SHOTT

Patented on 8 April 1674 by Stephen Cannon on south side of Wetipquin

Creek for 300 acres..
Rent Rolls 1666-1723 possessed by William Winright as marrying the cohier of Stephen Cannon.
14 Jan.1725 Francis Langeake and wife Judah Langeake sold to John Hopkins land that Stephen Cannon willed Judah Langeake parcel on Wetiquin Creek that bounds land Stephen Cannon gave to Mary Wainright and Jane Hopkins.
18 July 1737 George Langeake, bricklayer, and wife Mary Langeake sold to Solomon Winright 50 acres, unnamed land.
1752 John Hopkins willed to son Isaac Hopkins part where I live.
24 June 1759 John Hopkins sold to Isaac Hopkins 100 acres devised to Allie Cannon by her father Steven.
16 Aug.1769 James Wainright and wife Eleanor Wainright sold to Solomon Wainright part Stephen Cannon gave to daughter Mary grandmother of James afsd. (his father was Cannon Wainright)
22 March 1770 John Hopkins son of Levi Hopkins sold 100 acres to Isaac Hopkins part devised by John Hopkins his grandfather.
1783 Tax- Stephen Hopkins
1783 Tax- Isaac Hopkins
1783 Tax- Solomon Wainright
1783 Tax- George C. Hopkins, Nanticoke 100.

CANT GET NO MORE

Patented on 23 Feb.1770 by George Dashiell for 16 acres adjacent COME BY CHANCE on the north west side of Wicomico River.
1809 George Dashiell willed to wife Betty Dashiell and then to grandson George son of William Dashiell.

CAN'T TELL

Patented in 1735 by Rachel Cordrey wife of Daniel Cordrey for 91 acres.
14 June 1746 Rachel Cordrey widow and daughter of Col. Nicholas Evans gave to son Nicholas Evans Collier 91 acres.
1783 Tax- Nicholas Evans Collier 91 acres, Nanticoke 100.
1786 Nicholas Evans Collier, willed to son Nicholas Evans Collier. If no issue to daughters Rebecca Collier, Priscilla Collier, Elizabeth Collier and Mary Evans Collier.

CAREYS ADDITION

Patented on 31 July 1764 by Thomas Carey for 27 acres.

CAREYS ADVANCE

Patented in 1684 by Edward Carey for 50 acres.
Rent Rolls 1666-1723 possessed by Richard Carey
1722/3 Richard Carey willed to John McGrath.
1751 John McGrath willed lands to son Levin McGrath, no name.

CAREYS CHOICE

Patented in 1756 by Thomas Carey for 50 acres.
1783 Tax- Levin Carey of Thomas 50 acres Wic. 100, Worc.Co.

CAREYS CONCLUSION

Patented in 1784 by Levin Carey for 50 acres.
2 Aug.1801 Thomas Carey son of Levin sold to Benjamin Johnson
8 June 1802 Benjamin Johnson sold to Ambrose P. Dixon.

CAREYS DESIRE

Patented in 1770 by John Henry Carey (he was a Maryland Loyalist and went to Nova Scotia by 1775)

CAREYS HARDSHIP

Patented in 1784 by Hezekiah Carey for 144 1/2 acres.
1 Oct.1777 Hezekiah Carey sold to James Houston 72 1/2 acres.
1783 tax- Hezekiah Carey 69 acres Wic.100 Worc.Co.
15 Mar.1783 Dr. James Houston sold to Hezekiah Carey 72 1/2 acres.
24 May 1788 Robert Smyley and Hezekiah Carey sold to William Morris son of Thomas Morris 114 1/4 acres. Mortgaged to Robert Smyley.
3 Apr.1789 William Morris son of Thomas Morris with wife Catherine Morris sold to Luke Bowen son of John Bowen, 144 1/4 acres.
20 Oct.1794 Luke Bowen sold to Saul Shockley 96 1/2 acres
20 Oct.1794 Luke Bowen sold to Eli Showell 47 3/4 acres.
12 Mar.1806 Eli Showell with wife Sarah Showell sold rights to Hezekiah D. Shockley.

CARLISLE

Patented on 17 May 1689 by Thomas Gordon per Rent Rolls but not found in Wicomico or Worcester Counties. On the south side of the Nanticoke River.
2 Feb.1750 Thomas Gordon of Sussex Co.Delaware sold to Charles Perry of Sussex Co. ADDITION & CARLISLE the whole 550 acres.(so is probably wholly in Sussex Co.Del.)

CARMICHAELS MISFORTUNE

Patented in 1784 by Jacob Reed for 210 acres.

CARTERS LODGE

Patented on 14 May 1683 by George Carter for 350 acres.
Rent Rolls 1666-1723 apportions to George Trotter
1750 Phillip Quinton, wife Anslee Quinton, willed to wife and after death to son Dixon Quinton.
18 June 1759 James Reed and wife Mary Reed sold to William Donoho 40 acres of CARTERS LODGE and is called END OF STRIFE with part that was added. (part resurveyed in 1750 for 272 acres END OF STRIFE)

CASTLE FINE

Patented on 10 June 1689 by Phoenix Hall for 200 acres back in the woods near the head of Wicomico River.
Rent Rolls 1666-1723 possessed by Phoenix Hall 200 acres.
6 Aug.1762 Joshua Hall sold to Benjamin Handy CASTLE FINE 140 acres at the head of the Wicomico River.

Repatented in 1768 by Benjamin Handy for 407 acres, a resurvey of above land.
4 May 1769 John Hendy son of Benjamin, with wife Martha Handy sold 240 acres to John Nelms
6 May 1769 John Handy with wife Martha Handy sold to John Davis 52 acres.
1772 John Handy son of Benjamin willed CASTLE FINE or ADDITION TO CASTLE FINE to be sold.
1783 Tax- John Nelms 240 acres Wic.100
1783 Tax- John Davis 52 acres
11 June 1793 Dr.Haste Handy of Savannah Georgia sold to Francis Gurley 25 1/2 acres.
3 May 1794 Francis Gurley with wife Eleanor Gurley sold to Joshua Pollitt, 7 3/4 acres
1789 John Davis willed to son Stephen Davis 52 acres.
1810 will of John Nelms of Jamica, to neice Mrs. Ann Eliza Nelms.
1859 Jehu Parsons willed to daughter Juliet Amanda Toadvine wife of Purnell Toadvine, near Salisbury.

CASTLE HAVEN

Patented on 15 April 1673 by Henry Hayman for 200 acres on the south side of the Wicomico River. He sold to Cornelius Anderson who sold to Thomas Passwater.
Rent Rolls 1666-1723 possessed by Edward Ruttledge in right of Passwaters orphans 200 acres.
31 Aug 1733 Jonas Passwater son of Thomas Passwater of Kent Co.Del. sold 200 acres to Alexander Fullerton.
31 May 1762 Hiram Reddish of Worc.Co. sold to John Reddish of Som.Co. 40 acres where Elizabeth Reddish lived (she was the widow Elizabeth Johnson wife of Hiram Reddish)
21 Jan 1764 Alexander Fullerton sold 40 acres to John Reddish
23 April 1764 John Reddish sold 5 acres to Francis Chattam
1773 Francis Chattam willed to son John Chattam.
1783 Tax- John Chattam 50 acres
1783 Tax- John Reddish Sr. 35 acres
3 Nov 1806 Richard Ingersol and Richard Bennett sold to Benjamin Johnson Sr. of Worc.Co. all interest.
24 Sep.1808 John Reddish of Worc.Co. sold 40 acres to Benjamin Johnson
19 Aug.1809 John Reddish sold 40 acres to Benjamin Johnson.
1830 John Chattam willed plantation to son Josiah Chattam.

CASTOWAY (Cassoway)

Patented on 2 April 1680 by William Stevens who assigned to Thomas and Susanna Walker children of Thomas Walker and wife Jane Walker for 1100 acres.
Rent Rolls 1666-1723 possessed by Thomas Walker and Capt. Nicholas Evans who married Susanna Walker.
19 Nov.1755 John Richardson, mariner, and wife Mary Richardson sold 300 acres to John North received from her father Thomas Walker, part called RICHARDSONS ADDITON.
25 Sep.1756 Nehemiah Hearn and wife Betty Day Hearn sold to John Lowe

and Ralph Lowe part.
19 Aug.1760 Ralph Lowe and wife Ann Lowe sold to John Gupton 100 acres of CASSOWAY & WOODFIELD.
18 Nov.1762 Jane Lucas sold to John Fletcher her part 250 acres devised her by Thomas Walker.
18 Nov.1762 Rebecca Evans spinster, Sarah Richardson, Mary Richardson, Jane Lucas and Eleanor Walker sold 175 acres to Joshua Cottman for 10 shillings.
21 Jan 1769 Ralph Lowe and wife Ann Lowe, George Lowe and Robert Lowe sold 24 acres to Joshua Cottman.
2 Jan 1773 John Fletcher and wife Esther Fletcher sold 20 acres to George Fletcher purchased of Jane Lucas.
3 Sep.1778 Sarah Richardson widow of Benjamin Richardson gave to George Fletcher son of Sarah Fletcher all lands at head of Rewastico Creek, 250 acres that came to Sarah from her father Thomas Walker part of a tract assigned Thomas by William Stevens. no name.
1782 John North sold 300 acres to George Wilson.
1783 Tax- Esther Fletcher 76 1/2 acres
1783 Tax- Thomas Fletcher 153 1/2 acres
1783 Tax- Jeanne Gupton 43 1/2 acres
1783 Tax- George Fletcher 170 acres
1783 Tax- George Phillips 102 acres
1783 Tax- George Wilson 300 acres.
19 July 1785 Thomas Fletcher sold 30 acres to George Fletcher.
23 July 1785 George Fletcher, wife Mary Fletcher sold to George Wilson 300 acres, 20 acres of which Sarah Richardson his mother bought of John Fletcher and 30 acres which George Fletcher purchased of Thomas Fletcher.
29 Aug.1786 Benjamin Dashiell and wife Mary Dashiell of Baltimore Md. sold to Isaac Henry of Som. Co. part CASSOWAY & WOODFIELD now known as WOODFIELDS 121 1/4 acres.
1793 will of Thomas Fletcher 200 acres to son Clement Bell Fletcher.
7 Oct.1793 George Wilson gave to George Wilson Jr.
11 May 1799 Benjamin Cottman and wife Susannah Cottman sold to Horatio Stayton 50 acres that Thomas Walker devised to daughter Rebecca Walker and sold by her to Joshua Cottman.
12 Jan 1828 Sally McCready Stayton willed to Sally Ann Stayton Vance and Mary Storks Vance 1/2 tract left by father Horatio Stayton. If they die to heirs of Rosannah Vance w/o David Vance.
6 Feb.1801 Horatio Stayton and wife Mary Stayton sold to Isaac Henry 27 3/8 acres of RICHARDSONS GRIEF & CASSOWAY.
5 Sep.1809 George Wilson sold to Caleb Kennerly 600 acres with tr. purchased of Mr. Collins unnamed. 45 acres.

CATHELLS CHANCE

Patented on 14 March 1742 by James Cathell for 70 acres.
1772 will James Cathell, to son James 50 acres.
27 March 1780 Joshua Cathell of Delaware sold to Alexander Porter 70 acres.
27 Mar.1780 Joshua Cathell sold 70 acres to Alexander Porter.
1 Jan 1793 Betty Christopher sold 70 acres to David Cathell.
13 March 1796 Levin Pollitt, sheriff sold to David Cathell part with

JAMES ADDITION per judgement against from James Cathell son of James 70 acres.
2 Jan.1810 Levi Cathell son of David Cathell sold to David Cathell 100 acres.
17 June 1815 John Cathell and Nancy Cathell deeded to Matty Cathell part.
18 May 1824 Joshua Cathell sold to Levi Cathell Jr.

CATHELLS LOTT & ADDITION

Patented CATHELLS ADDITION, a resurvey for 50 acres by David Cathell
1764 David Cathell willed 150 acres to son Levi Cathell.
20 Aug.1831 Purnell Massey purchased 11 3/4 acres of CATHELLS ADDITION to CATHELLS LOTT.

CATHELLS LUCK

Patented in 1818 by Levi Cathell and wife for 62 3/4 acres
ADDITION TO patented in 1829 by Levi Cathell for 318 3/4 acres.

CATHELLS VENTURE

Patented on 10 April 1729 by James Cathell for 52 acres.
1764/7 David Cathell willed to son David Cathell.
1772 James Cathell willed 50 acres to grandson David Cathell son of David.
1783 Tax- David Cathell 50 acres , Wic.100 Worc.Co.

CAUDREYS GRIEF

Patented 1770 by William Tully for 7 acres.
21 Sep.1778 William Tully sold to William Turpin on the north side of Blackwater Branch
1783 Tax- William Turpin 7 acres, Rewastico 100.

CEDAR HAMMOCK

Patented in 1747 by Peter Presley
Patented in 1773 by Henry Lowes

CEDAR SWAMP

Patented in 1762 by James O'Neal for 50 acres.

CERTAINTY

Patented in 1793 by William Jones Sr. for 9 1/4 acres.

CHALETT

Patented on 4 Sep.1690 by John Caldwell for 380 acres.
8 Feb.1754 Joshua Caldwell sold 380 acres to Richard Waller.

CHAMBERS PURCHASE

Patented in 1772 by John Chambers for 185 1/2 acres.

1777 John Chambers willed to wife Rachel Chambers and daughters Mary
Chambers and Nancy Chambers.

CHANCE

see ABERGAVENY 100 acres.

CHANCE

Patented on 2 Oct.1677 by John White who assigned to Benjamin Cottman
for 500 acres.
12 Nov.1684 Benjamin Cottman and wife Mary Cottman sold 300 acres to
John Booth called BOOTHS PURCHASE.
13 Mar.1685 Benjamin Cottman and wife Mary sold to William Roldolphus
200 acres now called REMAINDER OF CHANCE.
Rent Rolls 1666-1723 possessed 300 acres by John Booth. 200 acres
belongs to William Roldolphus in Acco.Co.Va.
1698 John Booth willed to son John 300 acres.
10 Jan 1742 George Dashiell gave to son Clement Dashiell.
16 Feb.1743/4 George Booth sold to Benjamin Cottman of Philadelphia
Co.Pa. 60 acres, now possessed by Absalom Hobbs.
1756 Clement Dashiell willed to son Josiah Dashiell, part.
6 March 1749 William Booth sold to Benjamin Cottman Sr. 60 acres.
22 March 1756 Arnold Elzey and wife Margaret Elzey sold to Isaac
Dashiell 60 acres.
21 July 1757 Isaac Dashiell sold to Louther Dashiell 60 acres.
23 Aug.1764 Joseph Dashiell released to Charles Redding 50 acres with
30 acres of CONTENT.
1764 Louther Dashiell willed to son Louther part and to son Matthias
Dashiell part.
5 April 1768 Nicholas Thomas of Talbot Co. Attorney at Law sold to
George Hobbs 90 acres.
19 April 1768 George Hobbs and wife Ann Hobbs sold 100 acres to Ann
Dashiell.
1783 Matthias Dashiell willed to Robert Dashiell son of uncle George
Dashiell land, unamed.
19 Feb.1800 Dr. Robert Dashiell of Nasamond Co.Va. sold to William
Cottman son of Joseph Cottman of Som.Co. devised him by Matthias
Dashiell with DASHIELLS LOTT.
20 Feb.1800 William Cottman son of Joseph Cottman sold to Dr. Robert
Dashiell of Virginia, mortgage.
10 Dec.1801 Dr. Robert Dashiell with wife Sally Dashiell of Nasemond
Co.Va. released mortgage to William Cottman son of Joseph Cottman.
1805 William Cottman willed lands to be sold to pay debts.

CHANCE

Patented on 19 May 1683 by John Parremore for 300 acres.
9 Nov.1762 Matthew Parremore of Sussex Co.Del. sold 90 acres to Henry
Dashiell.
29 Oct.1762 Matthew Parremore sold 100 acres to Roger Nicholson of
Somerset County.
29 Oct.1762 Matthew Parremore sold 100 acres to James Twilley.
27 March 1769 James Twilley and wife Mary Twilley sold to George
Twilley CHANCE at Rewastico Creek, 100 acres with WOODSTOCK
1783 Tax- George Twilley 100 acres   Rewastico 100
1783 Tax- Roger Nicholson 100 acres   "   "

1790 Roger Nicholson willed to daughter Sarah Nicholson 100 acres.
22 Jan 1791 George Twilley traded 4 1/2 acres with Arthur Dashiell for LAST CHOICE.
12 April 1799 James H. West sold to John Harris 100 acres
1802 Arthur Dashiell willed to son Levin Dashiell.
12 April 1802 James H. West and wife Sarah West, John Harris Sr, William Harris with wife Alse Harris, of Solomon Harris sold to George Twilley that Roger Nicholson gave to daughter Sarah Nicholson who married James H. West, 100 acres.

CHANCE

Patented 1 Nov.1688 by James Weatherly for 300 acres who assigned to John Gillis.
1720 John Gillis willed to son Joseph Gillis 550 acres, unnamed.
23 March 1762 Joseph Gillis gave to son George Gillis 300 acres with MANLOVES ADVENTURE and OAK HALL.
1 Feb.1780 Ezekiel Jackson of Sussex Co.Del. sold to Joshua Humphries part of QUAIKSON NECK and 100 acres of CHANCE (c/b other land)
19 Jan 1793 Joshua Humphries with wife Sarah sold to John Smith 91 3/4 acres at Quaikson Neck.

CHANCE

Patented 17 May 1688 by John Lankford for 200 acres.
Rent Rolls 1666-1723 possessed by John Lankford 100 acres,
Thomas Lankford 100 acres, called GOOD WILL.
5 Nov.1726 John Lankford Jr. sold 100 acres to Thomas Dashiell
13 April 1731 John Lankford son of John sold to Thomas Lankford 100 acres called GOOD WILL.
25 Feb.1735 Thomas Dashiell sold upper part to William Wright 100 acres.
1755 Thomas Lankford (wife Judea Lankford) willed to son Thomas.
1757 Thomas Lankford Jr. mortgaged his right to Henry Lowe.
5 April 1757 Triparte agreement- Thomas Lankford to William Hayward and Henry Lowe CHANCE now called GOODWILL, part 100 acres with MORRIS LOTT that Thomas has a right from his father Thomas's will 30 acres.
13 Dec.1769 Henry Lowe sold 100 acres to James Jones, part called GOOD WILL for 5 shillings.
13 Dec.1769 James Makemorie Jones sold to William Rencher 88 1/4 acres of CHANCE called GOODWILL.
22 Nov 1771 Henry Lowe and wife Esther Lowe sold 100 acres to Josiah Polk for 5 shillings.
1783 Tax- William Rencher 88 acres.(GOOD WILL)
1783 Tax- John Anderson 100 acres.
17 June 1786 James Makemorie Jones and John Dorman sold 15 acres to Levin Winder with MORRIS LOTT.
14 Nov.1788 Stephen Wright sold 67 acres to Levin Winder adjacent MORRIS LOTT.
12 March 1789 Stephen Wright and John Anderson sold to Levin Winder 67 acres.
12 March 1789 Stephen Wright sold to John Anderson 2 acres adjacent St.GILES.
26 May 1791 John Anderson sold 20 acres to Lambert Hyland.
25 Jan.1800 Stephen Wright sold 24 3/4 acres to George Furbush.

25 July 1810 Levin D. Collier, Stephen Wright and Methia Wright sold 3 1/2 acres to Ephraim K. Harris with WESTON & SPRY.

CHANCE

Patented on 10 July 1695 by Thomas Horseman for 140 acres
5 Nov.1764 Henry Toadvine resurveyed to HENRYS CHANCE.

CHANCE

Patented in 1713 by William White for 120 acres.

CHANCE

Patented on 1 May 1707 by John Evans for 150 acres at LITTLE MONMOUTH.
25 June 1741 John Evans Sr. sold to son John Evans Jr. 150 acres with 337 acres of SECOND CHANCE.

CHANCE

Patented on 22 Oct.1722 by John Wooten for 50 acres.
Rent Rolls 1666-1723 possessed by John Wooten
26 Oct.1722 John Wooten gave to sister Culett Shearman wife of Thomas Shearman 50 acres.

CHANCE

Patented 25 Nov.1721 by John Reed for 20 acres.
Rent Rolls 1666-1723 possessed by John Reed
1745 John Reed willed lands to son Jacob Reed, unnamed.
1783 tax- Hezekiah Reed 27 acres. Nanticoke 100.
19 April 1798 James Reed with wife Betty Reed sold 21 3/4 acres to David Dutton with WESTON & HOG QUARTER.
1 Dec.1804 Belitha Wright and wife Mary Ann Wright (Mary Ann Dutton) sold to Stephen Wright lands purchased of James Reed, unnamed.
7 April 1810 Stephen Wright sold to Delaney Wright 101 acres of CHANCE, WESTON & HOG QUARTER.

CHANCE

Patented in 1724 by Samuel Miles for 30 acres.

CHANCE

Patented in 1728 by John Stevens for 32 acres.

CHANCE

Patented in 1732 by Samuel Fluellin for 25 acres.
1751 resurveyed by Samuel Fluellin with vacancy and called FLUELLINS SETTLEMENT, 137 acres.

CHANCE

Patented in 1737 by John Collins for 80 acres.

26 Dec.1729 John Collins, chairmaker sold 80 acres to Levin Dashiell at head of Wetipquin Creek.

CHANCE

Patented in 1741 by Charles Acworth for 100 acres.
6 Feb.1746 Charles Acworth sold to William Givans 100 acres now called GIVANS on the south side of Barren Creek.
1751 William Givans willed to father-in-law William Taylor 100 acres of dwelling plantation, unnamed. (wife Ann Givans)
17 Dec.1772 William Taylor sold to John Sterling son of Aaron Sterling 100 acres.

CHANCE

Patented on 26 Jan.1715 by Thomas Jones
Rent Rolls 1666-1723 possessed by Thomas Jones
Repatented on 8 Dec.1741 by Thomas Jones for 150 acres.
16 Mar.1746 Thomas Jones, late of Dorc.Co. now of Som.Co.,merchant, sold to Charles Bannister, shipwright 150a., on north side Deep Creek.

CHANCE

Patented in 1754 by Patience Records for 338 acres.

CHANCE

Patented in 1755 by Henry Toadvine for 140 acres.
7 March 1755 I Henry Toadvine give to son Henry 50 acres.

CHANCE

Patented in 1760 by John Carmichael for 20 acres.

CHANCE

Patented in 1760 by John Hitch for 50 acres.
8 April 1765 George Hitch of Dartmouth Mass son of John Hitch, sold to Joseph Hitch of Somerset County.
15 June 1799 William Hitch and John Hitch with wife Jean Hitch sons of Joshua Hitch sold 50 acres to Thomas Humphries.

CHANCE

Patented in 1760 to George Howard for 15 acres.

CHANCE

Patented in 1761 by Joshua Dickenson for 30 acres.

CHANCE

Patented in 1761 by Paris Chapman for 2 acres.
1794 will of Pearce Chapman, estate to son John Chapman, if he dies without issue to wife Rebecca Chapman.

20 March 1802 Joshua Morris of Worc.Co. sold to Eben Disharoon 2 acres with MORRIS CONCLUSION & DISHAROONS ADVENTURE.
1815 Ebenezer Disharoon willed to son Francis Disharoon 1 acre adj. Kirk Gunby that Gunby got from Joshua Morris.

CHANCE

Patented in 1762 by George Collier Hopkins and Winder Dashiell for 12 1/2 acres.
1783 Tax- John Dashiell 4 acres
1783 Tax- George C. Hopkins 2 1/2 acres.
8 Nov.1786 John Dashiell with wife Anney Dashiell of the late Winder Dashiell sold 12 1/2 acres to George Collier Hopkins

CHANCE

Patented in 1762 William Badley
1778 William Badley willed to son James Dean Badley
1783 Tax- Elizabeth Badley w/o William Badley, 8 1/2 acres, Rewastico.

CHANCE

Patented 1762 by Jacob Wright for 50 acres.
1783 Tax- Jacob Wright 50 acres. Rewastico 100.
1796 Jacob Wright willed 25 acres to sons Joseph Wright and to son Benjamin Wright.

CHANCE

Patented in 1763 to Robert Collier for 21 acres.
1783 Tax- Robert Collier Sr. 21 acres, Nanticoke 100.

CHANCE

Patented 1763 by Richard Acworth for 20 acres.

CHANCE

Patented in 1764 by Samuel Jackson for 127 1/2 acres.
1783 tax- Samuel Jackson, Nanticoke 100
1788 Samuel Jackson with wife Patience Jackson sold to James Anderson 35 acres of CHANCE with WARRINGTONS ADDITION
1789 Samuel Jackson willed to son Jonathan Jackson lands unnamed, and then to his son Henry Jackson.
27 Feb.1790 James Anderson sold to Douty Collier for 5 shillings 3 1/2 acres of CHANCE & ADDITION TO CHANCE, 1/3rd pt. WARRINGTONS ADDITION.
20 Dec.1805 Jonathan Jackson son of Samuel Jackson sold to James Anderson, with WARRINGTON.
1795 Douty Collier willed land purchased of James Anderson to be sold, CHANCE & ADDITION TO CHANCE.

CHANCE

Patented on 7 July 1766 by James Bounds for 10 1/4 acres
ADDITION TO CHANCE patented in 1775 by William Bounds for 279 1/2

acres.
20 Aug.1760 Nehemiah Crockett and wife Alice Crockett sold to William Bounds, joyner two tracts at head of Wetipquin alienated to John Collins by Jonathan Bounds relation, 80 acres.
10 Aug.1775 William Bounds sold to Phillip Graham 46 acres for 5 shillings ADDITION
10 Aug.1775 William Bounds sold to Robert Collier for 5 shillings 42 acres. ADDITION
1783 tax- Robert Collier 42 acres, Nanticoke 100.
1783 Tax- Matilda Bounds 10 acres.
1783 tax- William Bounds 191 1/2 acres ADDITION TO CHANCE
29 March 1784 Robert Collier sold to Joseph Wailes 42 acres in trade for JOSEPHS LOTT & DANIELS MISTAKE
1789 Robert Collier willed lands unnamed, to son Douty Collier.
1795 Douty Collier willed to son Esme Collier CHANCE & ADDITION TO CHANCE.
1 Oct.1799 William Bounds with wife Peggy Bounds sold to John Wroten 106 2/4 acres (no name) adj. TURKEY RIDGE & DASHIELLS LOTT.
13 Jan 1801 William Bounds Jr. son of James Bounds sold 9 acres to George Fooks granted to James Bounds except 3/4 of an acre of burying ground.
31 Aug.1804 Daniel Wailes sold 42 acres to William Dashiell.
18 Dec.1805 William Dashiell with wife Mary Dashiell and Douty Bounds mortgaged to William Harris 42 acres.
11 Oct.1806 Henry Boston and wife Nancy Boston, late Nancy Graham sold to John Graham all interest in ADDITION TO CHANCE, that Phillip Graham devised to sons John Graham and William Graham.
16 March 1806 Francis Collier and wife Betsy Collier, lately Betsy Graham sold their interest to John Graham.
13 Oct.1807 Ralph Milbourn with wife Sarah Milbourn lately Sarah Graham sold rights to John Graham ADDITION TO CHANCE.

CHANCE

Patented in 1769 by George Handy for 3/4 acre
1783 tax- Isaac Handy 1 1/2 acres in Rewastico 100.

CHANCE

Patented in 1774 by John Weatherly for 21 acres.
1783 Tax- John Weatherly 21 acres in Rewastico 100.

CHANCE

Patented in 1775 by John Davis for 30 acres.

CHANCE

Patented on 12 Dec.1785 by Robert Dashiell son of William Dashiell for 93 1/2 acres, bounds on Jones Creek.
1783 Tax- Levi Dashiell 90 acres Rewastico 100
1786 Levi Dashiell willed 90 acres to son Henry
11 May 1803 Henry Dashiell blacksmith, with wife Jane Dashiell sold to James Harris 97 1/4 acres unnamed as heir of brother Levi Dashiell.
11 Aug.1807 John Bloodsworth Jr. and Margaret Lucas Bloodsworth sold

to John H. Anderson land Robert Dashiell father of Margaret died seized and it descended to daughters Matilda Dashiell, Jane Dashiell and Margaret Dashiell, no name of land.

CHANCE

Patented in 1790 by John Evans for 17 1/2 acres

CHANCE

Patented by John Pope Mitchell in 1792 for 47 acres
1806 John Pope Mitchell willed to daughter Polly Mitchell small tract adjacent William Collier, unnamed.
8 Dec.1807 John Houston and wife Nancy Houston sold to John Rider lot in Salisbury called Chance conveyed by John Pope Mitchell to Nancy Kennedy now wife of John Houston on 25 May 1795.

CHANCE

Patented by Robert Collier in 1795 for 10 acres.

CHANCE

Patented in 1802 by Levin Irving and George Gillis and Sarah Gillis.

CHANCE

Patented in 1804 by James Bennett for 6 1/2 acres.

CHANCE FORK

Patented in 1671 by Richard Whitty for 500 acres.

CHANCERY

Patented on 15 March 1753 by Joseph Marshall for 205 acres.
Repatented in 1768 by John Calloway for 205 acres.
1770 John Calloway willed to son Ebenezer Calloway, dwelling plantation, unnamed.

CHARLES ADVANTAGE

No patented found in Wicomico. 16 Oct.1739 Charles Polk and wife Patience sold 40 acres to John Willey at head of Nanticoke River. 17 Nov.1762 John Alexander Willey with wife Elizabeth Willey sold to Samuel Jones all with BASHAW.

CHARLES LOTT

Patented in 1728 by Charles Polk for 100 acres.

CHARLES LOTT

Patented on Aug.1758 by Charles Duncan for 54 acres.
ADDITION patented in 1770 for 88 acres by Charles Duncan

ADDITION patented in 1777 by Charles Duncan for 54 acres.
19 April 1805 Richard Sampson and Seth Whaley sold to Levi Duncan 6 1/4 acres of ADDITION TO CHARLES LOTT

CHARLES PURCHASE

Patented on 9 Sep.1721 for 100 acres by Charles Polk.
21 Aug.1733 Charles Polk sold to Barnaby Fallon of Dorc.Co., on east side of the main branch of the Nanticoke River.
28 May 1736 Barnaby Fallon of Dorc.Co. sold to Samuel Jones of Dorc.Co. 100 acres.
13 June 1754 Jacob Jones of Dorc.Co.to John Laws of Worc.Co.pat. Charles Polk who conveyed to Samuel Jones father of Jacob afsd.
12 Aug.1776 Sussex Co.Delaware land warrants John Laws Jr.

CHARLESTON

Patented on 24 Sep.1745 by Major Dorman for 50 acres.
7 Jan 1758 Major Dorman sold 50 acres to George Vincent.
24 Feb.1770 George Vincent sold to Jacob Bell 50 acres with SECURITY & LAST CHOICE.
2 Aug.1777 Jacob Bell and wife Judah Bell sold to George Handy tract unnamed on road from Spring Hill Church to Salisbury 145 3/4 acres.
1783 tax- Levin Irving - Rewastico 100 50 3/4 acres.

CHELSEY

Patented on 29 Nov.1672 for 3050 acres by Charles Hutchins of Dorcester County Md. in Nanticoke 100, Quantico District.
Rent Rolls 1666-1723, possessed by Daniel McGunis 100 acres, John Tully 100 acres, Stephen Tully 150 acres.
1737 Stephen Tully willed to son Benjamin Tully 150 acres.
6 Aug.1743 John Tully sold to Christopher Piper 100 acres, that Charles Hutchison gave to John Tully who died intestate and became right of Edward Tully who died intestate and became right of John Tully afsd.
13 Feb.1747/8 Richard Tully and Daniel Goslee and Elizabeth McGunis sold 100 acres to George Bennett where Elizabeth lives alienated by John Tully and wife Mary Tully to Daniel McGunis on 7 June 1700.
19 March 1767 George Bennett sold 100 acres to Ephraim King.
16 May 1767 Matthew Piper s/o Christopher Piper sold to Henry Gale 100 acres. Probably a confirmation of early conveyance.
30 Nov.1770 Richard Tully sold 100 acres to John Hopkins
30 Nov.1770 Richard Tully sold to John Nelson 28 1/2 acres of CHELSEY & EGYPT.
13 Nov.1770 Richard Tully sold to John Nelson 76 acres with EGYPT & FAIRHAM.
23 Feb.1773 Ephraim King sold to Thomas Handy 100 acres except part where Henry Gale has a mill and mill pond; with MONMOUTH & SANKEYS ISLAND & WEATHERLYS MARSHES.
25 Oct.1775 Thomas Handy son of John Handy deceased sold to Ephraim King his interest.
1783 tax Henry Gale 125 acres, Rewastico 100.
1783 tax John Hopkins 100 acres.

1783 tax Matthew Kemp 20 acres
1783 tax John Nelson 28 1/2 acres
10 Nov.1782 Samuel King and wife Mary King sold to Matthew Kemp, a bond to make over CHELSEA & MONMOUTH that father willed to Elinor Kemp, if no issue to revert to the heirs of Matthew Kemp.
22 Apr.1785 Samuel King with wife Mary King sold 30 acres to Henry Gale.
23 Sep.1796 Samuel Wilson and wife Leah Littleton Wilson sold to Eleanor Nelson wife of John Nelson for 5 shillings all rights.
23 Sep.1796 George Gale of Cecil Co.Md. and Levin Gale with wife Leah Gale of Somerset Co. sold to Eleanor Nelson and John Nelson for 5 shillings all rights.
5 Nov.1796 Matthew Kemp, John Nelson wife wife Eleanor Nelson sold to Henry Crawford late of New Castle Co.Delaware but not of Somerset County 3 acres.
24 Jan 1798 Matthew Kemp with wife Rebecca Kemp and John Nelson with wife Eleanor Nelson sold 3 acres to Henry Crawford.
24 Jan.1798 Matthew Kemp sold to John Nelson, all interest.
22 Sep.1800 John Nelson and wife Eleanor gave to son Samuel Nelson part, lot #3 2 3/4 acres 12 poles.
4 Nov.1800 John Nelson and wife Eleanor Nelson gave to son Cyrus Nelson 1 acre.
22 Sep.1800 John Nelson, wife Eleanor Nelson gave to son Francis Nelson balance with part of MONMOUTH
22 Sep.1800 John Nelson with wife Eleanor Nelson gave to daughter Hetty Nelson 1 acre, 23 poles.
1832 Francis D. Nelson willed to son Horatio Nelson, home place, unnamed and land to daughter Almira Nelson.
11 Sep.1840 William W. Handy, trustee sold to Benjamin Dashiell
6 Nov.1840 Benjamin J. Dashiell deeded part to John F. Collier (now the village of QUANTICO.)
10 Feb.1841 Benjamin J. Dashiell sold to John W. Taylor, part.
4 Aug.1841 Benjamin J. Dashiell sold to Henry Kennerly, part.
11 Oct.1841 Benjamin J. Dashiell sold to William Giles, part.
14 May 1842 Benjamin J. Dashiell sold to James Jones, part.
10 Nov.1841 John Austin and wife Jane Austin sold to James Bounds parts of CHELSEA, MONMOUTH & DELIGHT, total 112 acres, formerly belonging to Francis D. Nelson and Henry Gale adjacent village of QUANTICO.

CHERRY GARDEN

Patented on 1 Oct.1763 by Thomas Wells for 43 acres.
3 Nov.1772 Thomas Wells sold to Elisha Vinson 43 acres.
1783 tax - Henry Spear, Acquanto 100

CHERRY HILL

Patented on 24 Aug.1788 for 7 acres by Capt. Robert Dashiell on south side of Wicomico River.
ADDITION, Patented in 1812 for 9 3/4 acres by Robert Dashiell
13 June 1805 Robert Dashiell and wife Isabella Dashiell sold to Dorcas Jones spinster, 1 acre.

CHERRY TREE ISLAND

Patented in 1760 by Joseph Weatherly and John Kellum for 41 acres in Rewastico 100.
1764 Joseph Weatherly willed to son Constantine Weatherly 1/2.
1771 John Kellum willed to son Edward Kellum.
1783 Edward Kellum willed to son John Kellum land and marsh, unnamed.
1783 tax William McBryde 13 2/3rds acres
1783 tax Isaac Horsey 13 2/3rds acres
1790 Isaac Horsey willed to son Isaac Horsey.

CHERVERLY

Patented on 12 June 1682 by Christopher Nutter for 100 acres who assigned to William Keen.
Rent Rolls 1666-1723, possessed by Pascoe Bartlett given him in consideration of the daughters marriage (he married a daughter of William Keen.)
25 Oct.1742 Thomas Bartlett sold to Christopher Piper 100 acres
11 Apr.1748 Christopher Piper sold to John Handy 100 acres.
1783 tax- Levin Handy s/o John, Rewastico 100
17 Feb.1810 Thomas J. Winder with wife Harriett Winder sold to William Hopkins 252 acres of BOLEAN, CHEVERLY, CALCUTTA, & LOTT that Levin Handy father of Harriett afsd. had.
Part resurveyed to BELLAIN by John Handy.

CHESTNUT HILL

Patented in 1773 by Thomas Pollitt for 30 acres.
1788 Thomas Pollitt willed to son William Pollitt.

CHESTNUT LOTT

Patented in 1802 by Peter Dashiell.
14 March 1807 deed of Bargain, Peter Dashiell sold to William Williams, part of TONYS PLANK resurveyed from Chestnut Lott 15 acres 6 perches, on n/s of Tony Tank Creek.
1808 resurveyed to TONYS PLANK.

CHESTNUT OAK RIDGE

Patented on 1 May 1740 by Charles Parsons for 100 acres.
2 Nov.1756 Charles Parsons sold to James Truitt, on the southast side of the Nanticoke River at head of Windescomb Neck, 50 acres.
2 Nov.1756 Charles Parsons sold to Riley Truitt son of Thomas Truitt 50 acres.
26 Jan.1770 Charles Parker sold to John Pepper 50 acres conveyed to Riley Truitt by Charles Parsons.
5 Nov.1772 John Pepper sold to William Wingate 50 acres.
1 May 1776 Sussex Co.Del. land warrants, pat. James Truitt.

CHESTNUT RIDGE

Patented in 1764 by Joseph Gillis for 18 acres.
1783 tax Joseph Gillis 18 acres, Rewastico 100.

1793 Joseph Gillis willed to son Littleton Gillis.
7 Nov.1803 Ezekiel Gillis with wife Ann Gillis sold to Edward Hull 18 acres.
15 May 1804 Robert Leatherbury Esq. sheriff, sold to the highest bidder Levin Farrington, per suit of Samuel Robinson against Ezekiel Gillis 120 acres of CHESTNUT RIDGE & MAIDENS LOTT.
15 May 1804 Levin Farrington sold the 120 acres to Edward Hull.

CHESTNUT RIDGE

Patented in 1772 by Smith Brewington for 73 acres.
1783 tax Smith Brewington 70 acres in Wic.100 Worc. Co.

CHOICE

Patented in 1734 by James Smith for 75 acres.
10 Aug.1737 James Smith Jr. sold to Andrew Smith 75 acres on a branch of the Wicomico River in Timothys Neck.
24 Apr.1761 resurveyed to GEORGES LOTT

CHOICE

Patented on 20 Dec.1741 by Charles Tindell for 100 acres.
1761 Charles Tindell willd 100 acres to son Elijah Tindell.
6 Nov.1770 Elijah Tindell sold to Samuel Tindell, 100 acres.

CHOICE

Patented on 16 May 1745 by Daniel Dakes for 100 acres on the east fork of the head of Wicomico River.
1768 Debt Books- belongs to heirs of Daniel Dakes
ADDITION TO CHOICE patented on 10 Nov.1770 for 46 acres. Warrant issued to Arthur Dykes and patented by his son Ephraim Dykes again on 17 March 1800.
1774 Debt Books Arthur Dykes 100 acres.
1814 Ephraim Dykes willed to son Arthur Dykes, dwelling plantation, unnamed.

CHOICE

Patented on 2 Aug.1762 by Samuel Parker son of Samuel, for 50 acres.
1795 Samuel Parker willed to father-in-law Thomas Bevans land unnamed.

CHOICE

Patented in 1772 by Robert Layfield for 80 1/2 acres.

CHOICE

Patented in 1793 by William White for 50 acres.
19 April 1800 William White sold to John White 50 acres.

CHRISTOPHERS LOT

Patented in 1761 by John Christopher for 50 acres at Cabin Branch in the woods from the Nanticoke River.

CLARKS MARSH

Patented for 50 acres by John Clark

CLARKS RECOVERY

Patented in 1741 by Edward Clark for 250 acres.

CLAYS ADVENTURE

Patented on 2 March 1694 by John Clay for 160 acres.
Rent Rolls 1666-1723 possessed by John Clay is dead and no heir appears.
1756 Henry Toadvine willed 160 acres to son Henry.
5 Mar.1763 resurveyed to FIRST VENTURE, near the head of the Wicomico River.

CLEAR OF CANNON SHOTT

Patented on 22 Oct.1696 by Samuel Fluellin for 50 acres.
Rent Rolls 1666-1723, possessed by widow Fluellin.
1705 Samuel Fluellin died at Tipquean per inventory.
1766 Samuel Fluellin Jr. gave to son Richard Fluellin plantation where I live 25 acres or 1/2 of tract and to son Samuel Fluellin 25 acres of balance bought of John Beard..
19 March 1770 Richard Crockett Fluellin son of Samuel Fluellin deceased sold 15 acres to Ephraim King.
15 Jan 1768 Richard Crockett Fluellin sold 11 acres to Solomon Winright.
15 Jan.1768 Samuel Fluellin sold 25 acres to Solomon Winright.
21 March 1771 Solomon Winright sold all to Ephraim King.
1777 Ephraim King willed to Richard Crockett Fluellin and Samuel Fluellin lands their father bought of John Beard that was conveyed me by Samuel Fluellin son of Samuel.
26 March 1793 Gillis Polk surviving trustee of Ephraim King, Samuel Fluellin brother of Richard Crockett Fluellin, sold to Isaac Atkinson son of Isaac with FLUELLINS SETTLEMENT, ADDN. TO COW RIDGE, TICKNELL, SECURITY, MILKMORE, SMALL CHANCE, etc.
25 March 1809 Isaac Atkinson with wife Priscilla Atkinson sold to James Walker at Tyaskin, 5 acres 1 rod.
25 March 1809 James Walker sold to Isaac Atkinson 10 acres 2 rods,14 perches, (trade of land)

CLIFTON

Patented in 1853 by Robert S. Todd for 314 acres.
1850 living in Salisbury district.

CLOULETT

Patented on 10 Sep.1688 by John Caldwell on the north side of Wicomico River, for 380 acres.
Rent Rolls 1666-1723, possessed by John Caldwell.
ADDITION TO CLOULETT   1758 pat. Eleanor T. Wailes 689 1/4 acres.
1783 tax Ebenezer Waller 280 acres- Rewastico 100
1784 Ebenezer Waller gave to son Ebenezer Cottman Waller.

17 Oct.1803 James Weatherly Waller sold to Ebenezer Cottman Waller for 5 shillings his interest.
19 Oct.1804 Ebenezer Cottman Waller with wife Nancy Waller sold to Thomas Humphries WALLERS MEADOW & CLOULETT.
19 Oct.1804 Ebenezer Cottman Waller with wife Nancy Waller sold 267 acres to John Dashiell CLOULETT & TIMBER GROVE.
27 Oct.1801 Esme Marshall Waller sold to Hetty Kellum, Henrietta Kellum, Patience Kellum and William Kellum 100 acres of CLOULETT, WILLIAMS GREEN & WALLERS CONCLUSION.

CLOSEFORK

Patented on 12 Oct.1671 by Richard Whitty for 500 acres on the Quantico branch of Nanticoke River.
1 Feb.1671 Richard Whitty sold to Thomas Brereton of Northumberland Co. Va. 500 acres.
9 Dec.1697 Henry Brereton sold to George Dashiell.
Rent Rolls 1666-1723, possessed by George Dashiell by the name of RECOVERY.

CLOVERFIELD

Patented in 1765 for 684 acres by Ephraim King
14 June 1771 Ephraim King sold to William Winder Jr. 50 acres.
ADDITION TO CLOVERFIELD patented to William Winder 36 1/2 acres.
1777 Ephraim King willed power to Levin Gale, Levin Wilson and William Winder, Gillis Polk to convey to John Piper land I took up from him, no name.
1787 Samuel King willed to Lucretia Jones lands devised by my father Ephraim King to her mother Elizabeth King, unnamed.
5 Oct.1778 Levin Gale, Levin Wilson, William Winder and Gillis Polk sold 100 acres to John Piper as Ephraim King willed.
1783 tax- Joseph Piper 66 1/3 acres
1783 tax- Agnes Piper 33 1/3 acres
1783 tax- George Phillips or Joseph Piper 66 1/2 acres.
1 Aug.1801 Charles Nutter and wife Louisa Nutter sold to William Bounds part on the south side of Rewastico Creek conveyed by David Wilson to Charles Nutter 482 2/8 acres with SLIPE, PASTURAGE & WEATHERLYS PURCHASE.
14 May 1801 John O. Twiford of Acco.Co.Va. with wife Anna Twiford sold to Levin Farrington of Somerset Co. 1 moity of 1/4th part lands of Joseph Piper deceased between Rewastico Creek and Memumsco Branch 300 acres, no name.
28 Feb.1806 William Bounds son of James Bounds sold to William Winder 47 acres.
23 April 1805 James Joseph Dashiell Gillis sold to Levin Farrington all property of John Piper, unnamed.

CLOVER GROUNDS

Patented by Alexander Adams in 1759.
1769 Alexander Adams willed to son Andrew Adams
1783 tax- Andrew Adams 45 1/2 acres in Wicomico 100.

COLD HARBOUR

Patented 5 Mar.1755 by Josiah Dashiell for 61 acres.
11 Feb.1764 Josiah Dashiell sold to Ezekiel Hilman.

COLD QUARTER

Patented by John Larramore in 1735 for 125 acres.
1738 John Larramore willed to son Levin Larramore all real estate (unnamed). If no issue to the poor of Stepney Parish.

COLD STREAM

Patented in 1793 by John Brown for 618 1/2 acres.

(The) COLLAR

see BELEAN- 3 1/2 acres.

COLLIERS CHANCE

Patented on 5 Sep.1758 by Thomas Collier for 5 acres.

COLLIERS CONTENTMENT

Patented on 7 July 1754 by John Collier for 100 acres
1767 resurveyed to MAIDENS LOTT at the Nanticoke River

COLLIERS DESIRE

Patented in 1737 by Thomas Collier for 50 acres.

COLLIERS ENLARGEMENT

Patented in 1732 by Robert Collier for 90 acres in Nanticoke 100.
21 Nov.1759 Robert Collier sold to George Collier 90 acres that father Robert Collier willed to him.
1774 George Collier willed to son George and to son Robert Collier 10 acres.
1783 tax - Robert Collier Jr. 18 acres.
16 March 1793 Ebenezer Collier sold to William Dashiell ands where Robert Collier died seized, no name or acreage.
22 Aug.1808 George Collier and wife Martha Collier sold to Matthias Dashiell Hopkins 70 acres.
5 Nov.1808 Matthias D. Hopkins with wife Eleanor Hopkins sold to James Walter 70 acres.

COLLIERS GOOD SUCESS

Patented on 15 Apr.1684 by Robert Collier for 320 acres
Rent Rolls 1666-1723, possessed by James Collier son of Robert.
1708 James Collier died. the widow Mary Collier married 2nd. Nehemiah Nicholson.
1733 George Betts Collier sold to brother John Nicholson GOOD SUCESS at Nanticoke point.
6 July 1784 Phillip Jones and wife Mary Jones sold to Phillip

Covington as John Nicholson resurveyed two tracts coontiguous COLLIERS GOOD SUCESS & DUDLEY and now called BETSYS GIFT 387 acres. He died intestate and left 3 daughters, Ann Nicholson who married William Graham and had Robert Graham and Mary Graham who married Phillip Jones, and Priscilla Graham who married Phillip Covington-(except 21 acres left by John Nicholson to Robert Walter) sold their share.
1795 resurveyed to BETSYS GIFT 406 1/2 acres.

COLLINS ADVENTURE

Patented on 19 Apr.1680 by Thomas Walker and assigned to George Collins for 500 acres in Nanticoke 100.
12 June 1683 George Collins and wife Rachel Collins sold to Nehemiah Covington.
14 May 1688 ADDITION TO COLLINS ADVENTURE patented to Nehemiah Covington for 420 acres.
Rent Rolls 1666-1723, possessed by Nehemiah Covington
1710/3 Nehemiah Covington gave to daughter Priscilla Covington 500a. COLLINS ADVENTURE (she married Robert King of Kingsland.)
He also willed ADDITION to daughter Elizabeth Wailes 420 acres.
4 May 1726 Benjamin Wailes and wife Elizabeth sold to Robert King 420 acres ADDITION TO COLLINS ADVENTURE.
22 Mar.1742 Robert King gave to Robert King Jr. 50 acres of COLLINS ADVENTURE & ADDITION TO.
22 Mar.1742 Col. Robert King gave to son Nehemiah King 50 acres.
5 Apr.1748 Robert King sold to James Bradley of Worc.Co. 159 acres of ADDITION TO COLLINS ADVENTURE.
23 Aug.1752 Robert King sold to Isaac Moore 150 acres of ADDITION.
27 Oct.1764 James Bradley sold to John Freeney of Worc.Co. 45 acres of ADDITION TO COLLINS ADVENTURE.
1767 Joseph Collins of Worc.Co. willed to son George Collins 116 acres and to daughter Margaret Collins 135 acres of ADVENTURE.
1773 Andrew Collins mentions 150 acres sold to William Bradley who married Elizabeth Collins.
1779 Charles Collins willed to son Charles 135 acres of COLLINS ADVENTURE.
21 June 1780 Nehemiah King son of Nehemiah of Robert King who married Priscilla Covington sold to Nathan Culver 500 acres with ADDITION TO COLLINS ADVENTURE except part sold by Robert King.
1783 tax - James Bradley 104 acres
1783 tax - Isaac Moore Sr. 150 acres.
1783 tax - Hudson Lowe 194 acres ADDITION.
1784 Isaac Moore willed to son Elijah Moore 150 acres taken out of COLLINS ADVENTURE.
16 May 1785 Robert Scroggin and Nathan Culver sold 81 acres of HAZZARD & ADDN. TO COLLINS ADVENTURE to Joshua Hastings of Sussex Co. Delaware.
28 Nov.1789 Nathan Culver sold to Elihu Jackson of Sussex Co. Del. 150 acres of COLLINS ADVENTURE & ADDITION.
12 May 1790 Nathan Culver sold to John Byrd 190 acres of COLLINS ADVENTURE & ADDITION TO COLLINS ADVENTURE.
1790 James Bradley willed to wife Ann Bradley 1/3rd and to Elizabeth Jackson 1/6th of lands and then to her son Ezekiel Jackson (unnamed land.)
28 Sep.1790 Robert Scroggin with wife Ann Scroggin daughter of Nathan

Culver deceased, sold to William McBryde 230 acres COLLINS ADVENTURE, ADDITION TO COLLINS ADVENTURE and ADDITION TO GOOD LUCK
25 Apr.1791 William McBryde with wife Sarah McBryde sold to Samuel Williams 230 acres, as above.
28 Oct.1794 Elijah Moore with wife Betsy Moore sold to George Parker 186 acres with HAZZARD & HAZZARD ADDITION.
1795 Jonathan Jackson and wife Elizabeth Jackson sold 23 1/2 acres to William Hastings of Sussex Co.Del. that she got from her father James Bradley.
5 Nov.1796 Elihu Jackson with wife Betty Jackson sold to George Parker 189 1/2 acres of COLLINS ADVENTURE & FOX HALL
29 Apr.1797 George Parker sold to John Byrd 189 1/2 acres afsd.
13 July1799 John Byrd sold 189 1/2 acres to Elihu Jackson of afsd.
14 Dec.1799 Sarah Bradley sold to Hezekiah Hastings 37 acres.
22 May 1808 John Byrd and wife Margaret Byrd sold to Elihu Jackson part COLLINS ADVENTURE & ADDN. 184 acres 67 perches.
18 Feb.1809 John Rider with wife Nelly Rider sold to John Freeney 179 acres of HAZZARD, ADDITION TO COLLINS ADVENTURE.
1811 Sarah Bradley willed to Thomas Humphries son of Thomas ADDITION TO COLLINS ADVENTURE.

COLLINS ADVICE

Patented in 1748 to Bowdin Robins for 100 acres.
1780 Bowdin Robins willed to grandson Thomas Robins Handy 100 acres.
24 Aug.1801 Comfort Handy daughter of William Handy, granddaughter of Bowdin Robins sold to David Walston 100 acres.

COLLINS AMBITION

Patented in 1739 by Joseph Bounds for 235 acres.
1735/5 tax lists- possessed by Joseph Bounds (on the west side of YEARS LAND.)

COLLINS CHANCE

Patented on 13 March 1753 by Timothy Collins for 40 acres.
10 Nov.1758 Timothy Collins of Sussex Co.Del. sold to John Morris of Worcester County 40 acres.
Repatented on 20 Nov.1762 by John Morris for 231 acres in Wicomico 100, Worc.Co.
1773 John Morris willed to sons John and Samuel Morris (aka MEASLEYS BEGINNING.)
21 Dec.1773 Samuel Morris sold to John Robins 132 acres
3 Dec.1779 John Robins with wife Elinor Robins sold to Jacob Morris 132 acres on road from Salisbury to Stevens Ferry.
21 Aug.1779 Thomas Carey with wife Mary sold to John Robins 1/3rd part.
1783 tax - Joshua Morris
1783 tax - Jacob Morris 132 acres
1783 tax - Mary Morris 62 acres
9 April 1792 Jacob Morris sold 26 acres to William Pollitt
15 June 1803 Jacob Morris sold to John Morris son of Joseph Morris, part.
13 Mar.1804 John Morris sold to Jacob Morris son of Joseph Morris part.

15 March 1806 Joshua Morris son of John Morris with wife Amelia Morris
sold part to William Pollitt
15 Mar.1806 William Pollitt Sr. sold to Jacob Morris 14 3/4 acres,
also called MIDDLE NECK.
Part probably resurveyed to MORRIS CONCLUSION

COLLINS DESIRE

Patented in 1754 by Roger Taylor for 155 acres.
5 Oct.1785 Alexander Taylor, Joshua Taylor and Thomas Taylor all of
Roger Taylor sold to Benjamin Shockley of Jonathan Shockley 155 acres
12 May 1789 Benjamin Shockley sold to Billy Fooks 62 acres.
7 Sep.1799 Charles Shockley sold to Betty Shockley interest of
Benjamin Shockley 1/6th part.
23 Jan.1808 Benjamin Shockley sold part to Billy Fooks.
1823 Billy Fooks willed to son Handy Fooks.

COLLINS FANCY

Patented in 1734 by Timothy Atkinson for 72 acres in Rewastico 100
1783 tax- William Goddard, 72 acres.

COLLINS LUCK

Patented on 5 Apr.1755 by Joseph Collins for 181 acres a resurvey from
INCLOSED.
9 Nov.1758 Joseph Collins sold to Robert Houston 17 acres.
9 Apr.1759 Joseph Collins with wife Sarah Collins sold to Thomas Copes
and wife Elizabeth Copes
1763 Thomas Copes with wife Elizabeth Copes sold to Joshua Hall and
William Hall 160 acres for 5 shillings. Elizabeth to retain her dower
1/3rd rights.
1767 Joseph Collins willed to daughter Margaret Collins.

COME BETWEEN

Patented in 1770 by Obediah Disharoon for 10 1/4 acres
1783 tax - Stephen Disharoon 20 1/4 acres

COME BY CHANCE

Patented in 1684 by Cornelius Anderson for 100 acres. He sold to
Nicholas Jones who sold to Thomas Young father of Mary Young.
10 March 1739 George Bayley and wife Mary Bayley (Mary daughter of
Thomas Young deceased) sold to Henry Lowe 100 acres on the north side
of the Wicomico River.

COME BY CHANCE

Patented 10 Dec.1713 by John Disharoon for 85 acres.
Rent Rolls 1666-1723, possessed by John Disharoon.
1754 John Disheroon willed to son John, 85 acres.
22 Feb 1772 George Disharoon of Worc.Co. and wife Tomlinson Disharoon
sold to Jonathan Stanford Jr. 2 acres.

1783 tax- George Disharoon 73 acres
17 Mar.1784 Jonathan Stanford sold to Francis Disharoon, on road from Salisbury to Princess Anne.
9 Jan.1796 Stephen Disharoon sold to Joshua Morris with Wicomico Manor

COME BY CHANCE

Patented in 1721 by Thomas Willin for 100 acres.

COME BY CHANCE

Patented on 2 April 1721 by Adam Hitch for 563 acres on the south side of the main branch of Cottingham Creek.
1 July 1721 Adam Hitch and wife Ann Hitch sold to Francis Langeake 300 acres with HIGH SUFFOLK
8 Feb.1721 Adam Hitch and wife Ann Hitch sold to John Caudrey Jr. 70 acres with 30 acres of HIGH SUFFOLK.
6 May 1728 Adam Hitch gave to son Samuel Hitch 212 acres of HIGH SUFFOLK & COME BY CHANCE.
1730 Adam Hitch willed to wife Mary Hitch 1/3rd plantation and part to son Elgate Hitch.
31 Jan.1746/7 Morgan Cordrey and John Cordrey sold to Dennis Dulaney, tailor 70 acres.
7 Sep. 1769 Triarte Agreement of Francis Lank to Joshua Polk and Robert Hitch 250 acres of COME BY CHANCE & HIGH SUFFOLD that Francis Lank devised to grandson Francis Lank son of George Lank.
5 Sep.1769 William Lank sold to Isaac Coulbourn and Joshua Hitch 150 acres of COME BY CHANCE & HIGH SUFFOLK that Francis Lank willed to grandson William Langeake son of Stephen Lank.
17 July 1770 Robert Hitch sold to Esme Bayley 250 acres of COME BY CHANCE & HIGH SUFFOLK. Mortgage.
25 July 1772 Francis Lank sold to Esme Bayley for 5 shillings land devised by Francis Lank the elder, unnamed.
21 Jan.1775 Isaac Hitch sold to William Handy HIGH SUFFOLK & COME BY CHANCE that Adam Hitch conveyed in 1728 to son Samuel Hitch. Isaac Hitch is grandson of Samuel Hitch.
21 Jan 1775 Eve Nichols widow of Richard Nichols, before her marriage to said Nichols was the widow of Robert Hitch who was son of Samuel Hitch deceased, sold all rights to William Handy.
1783 tax - Sarah Hitch, Rewastico 100
1783 tax - Joseph Smith
21 Apr. 1798 Esme Bayley sold to William Elgate Hitch 150 acres of COME BY CHANCE & HIGH SUFFOLK.
25 Nov. 1783 Esme Bayley and wife Sinah Bayley sold to Sarah Ellegood Hitch d/o Robert Hitch 100 acres for 5 shillings of HIGH SUFFOLK & COME BY CHANCE.
15 May 1793 William Elgate Hitch son of Joshua Hitch sold 100 acres to William Adams.
1767 Joseph Hitch resurveyed 134 acres COME BY CHANCE.
1797 Joshua Hitch resurveyed 134 acres to CULVERS FOLLY.
6 Sep.1806 Littleton Aires, wife Sarah E. Aires sold to Henry Dulaney 130 3/4 acres purchased by Robert Hitch from Esme Bailey.
18 Nov.1808 John Byrd and Margaret Byrd sold to William Smith Handy, her dower rights, she was Margaret Handy wife of William Handy father of William Smith Handy.

18 Nov.1808 William Smith Handy and wife Phoebe Handy sold to Thomas Hooper of Worc.Co. 425 acres of PEMBERTON, HIGH SUFFOLK & COME BY CHANCE.
28 Feb.1810 Henry Dulany sold to William Hearn 100 acres of COME BY CHANCE & HIGH SUFFOLK.

COME BY CHANCE

Patented in 1734 by Jacob Lingo for 50 acres.

COME BY CHANCE

Patented by William Polk and Thomas Pollitt.
1743 Thomas Pollitt willed to wife Sarah Pollitt
1784 tax- Josiah Polk 100 acres, in Wicomico 100.
1784 Josiah Polk willed to brother William Polk 100 acres.

COME BY CHANCE

Patented in 1748 by Michael Raglin for 100 acres.
16 Dec.1766 Michael Raglin gave to David Raglin son of Michael 100 acres.
28 Feb 1775 David Raglin and wife Elizabeth Raglin sold 100 acres to Levin Ballard.
14 June 1776 Levin Ballard and wife Elizabeth Ballard sold 100 acres to Jacob Morris part in Som.Co. and part in Worc.Co.
1783 tax - Jacob Morris 100 acres
15 June 1803 Jacob Morris sold to John Morris son of Joseph Morris part.
13 Mar.1804 John Morris sold to Jacob Morris son of Joseph Morris, part- probably a division of lines.

COME BY CHANCE

Patented in 1762 by William Anderson for 50 acres.
1772 William Anderson willed to mother Margaret Anderson and brothers Joshua Anderson, James Anderson and Isaac Anderson.
1783 tax- Margaret Anderson 20 acres Rewastico 100.
1783 tax- Robert Anderson (resurv. to LONGTON 47 acres.)
9 Nov.1793 James Anderson, John Anderson and Joshua Anderson sold to Isaac Anderson, with ANDERSONS LONG RUN.

COME BY CHANCE

Patented 1763 George Dashiell 22 1/2 acres.
1783 tax Joseph Dashiell 22 1/2 acres- Rewastico 100.
1809 George Dashiell willed to wife Betty Dashiell COME BY CHANCE and then to grandson George Dashiell son of William Dashiell.

COME BY CHANCE

Patented in 1764 by Douty Collier and George Collier for 100 acres.
1775 Douty Collier willed 50 acres to daughter Betty Collier.
1783 tax - Elizabeth Handy 50 acres- Nanticoke 100.
22 Aug.1808 George Collier and wife Martha Collier sold to Matthias

Dashiell Hopkins 100 acres.
5 Nov.1808 Matthias D. Hopkins, with wife Eleanor Hopkins sold to Levin Winright.

COME BY CHANCE

Patented 8 June 1770 by Thomas Dashiell for 12 acres from a warrent from Matthias Miles and assigned to Thomas Dashiell and repatented to 54 acres adjacent BECKMAN.
14 Mar.1801 Josiah Sterling, wife Matilda Sterling sold to Thomas Dashiell 340 or 350 acres of CANNONS PEACE, COME BY CHANCE & BECKMAN.

COME BY CHANCE

Patented in 1775 by William Round for 35 acres
14 Mar.1796 resurveyed for Arthur Dashiell for 24 acres.
1783 tax- Arthur Dashiell, 24 acres Rewastico 100.
1783 tax- Jane Dashiell 4 acres
1783 tax- Mary Dashiell 8 acres
1809 George Dashiell willed to wife Betty Dashiell with CAN'T GET NO MORE.

COME BY CHANCE

Patented in 1783 by Phillip Graham for 61 acres.
1787 Phillip Graham willed this to be sold.

COME NO NIGHER

Patented in 1770 by Constant Disharoon for 50 acres.
Another patent in 1773 for 118 acres by Waitman Disharoon.
1762 William Disharoon willed to wife Mary Disharoon and to son Levin Disharoon, 50 acres.
28 Nov.1774 Waitman Disharoon, inkeeper sold to James Disharoon 118 acres (came Joshua Disharoon on 30 June 1787 and made oath)
1783 tax - James Disharoon 118 acres.
1783 tax - Constant Disharoon 50 acres, Wicomico 100
1795 Constant Disharoon willed to daughter Milla Stanford 36 acres and to Grandson John Disharoon 14 acres. After her death to grandson Constant Disharoon Stanford.
1831 James Disharoon willed to son John Disharoon part.

COMFORTS DELIGHT

Patented in 1760 by Windom Scott 50 acres.
1772 Windom Scott willed to wife Comfort Scott 1/3rd of lands and to son Michael Scott dwelling plantation, unnamed.

COMMONS

Patented on 12 Aug.1704 to James Givans for 250 acres on the south side of Rewastico branch between Quantico and Rewastico being the second ground of a parcel called KINGSTON
Rent Rolls 1666-1723, possessed by James Givans
18 Aug.1740 James Givans sold to Abraham Taylor 50 acres.
5 Oct.1743 James Givans eldest son of James deceased sold 117 acres to

William Windsor, lower part not already sold to Daniel Rhoads, with part of LYONS LOTT.
4 Nov.1743 James Givans sold 83 acres to Daniel Tully.
8 Dec.1743 Benjamin Warrington sold to William Winder for 5 shillings all lands conveyed by James Givans to William Winder, part two tracts 117 acres COMMONS & 86 acres LYONS LOTT.
10 Nov.1743 James Givans sold to John Gale lands in Nanticoke 20 acres from father James at Williams last bounder- unnamed so could be WHITE MARSH DELIGHT or LYONS LOTT.
12 Feb.1768 Richard Tully and William Winder sold to Lazarus Huffington 83 acres at head of Quantico Creek.
12 Feb.1768 Richard Tully sold to William Winder, all except that sold to Lazarus Huffington, no acreage mentioned.
1783 tax- William Winder 117 acres, Rewastico 100.
1783 tax- Richard Acworth 182 3/4 acres(resurvey to LAST CONCLUSION.
1792 William Winder willed to son William Winder all lands, unnamed, between Quantico & Rewastico creeks.
1808 William Winder willed to son William Henry Winder all lands, unnamed.

COMPLEAT

Patented in 1725 by James Train for 25 acres
1756 James Hardy willed to son Isaac now dwelling plantation, unnamed.
3 March 1764 Isaac Hardy of Worc.Co. heir of James Hardy and Eliza Train Hardy sold to Matthew Dorman, his interest.
1783 tax - William Dorman 25 acres, Rewastico 100

CONCLUDED

Patented in 1789 by Isaac Horsey for 523 3/4 acres in Wicomico 100.
4 Dec.1806 Littleton Robins Jr. with wife Martha Robins, coheir of Isaac Horsey sold to Jordan Parsons 251 1/2 acres
4 Dec. 1806 Littleton Robins Jr. with wife Mary Robins sold to William Biglands 104 acres.

CONCLUSION

Patented in 1772 by John Nelms for 65 1/2 acres a survey from Wicomico Manor.
15 May 1783 Clement Holliday and Nathaniel Ramsey, comissioners to sell confiscated property sold to John Nelms in Wicomico Manor 65 1/2 acres.

CONCLUSION

Patented in 1783 by Esme Bayley for 239 acres.

CONCLUSION

Patented 27 July 1785 for 119 1/2 acres by John Dashiell, a resurvey of 102 acres WINDERS ADDITION, 6 1/2 acres DISCOVERY, 14 1/2a. WOLF TRAP RIDGE, on road from head of Wetepquin to Nanticoke Point.
6 March 1786 John Dashiell son of Winder, with Ann Dashiell his mother and Ann Dashiell his wife sold to Littleton Aires 13 1/2 acres.
27 June 1787 John Dashiell son of Winder Dashiell with wife Nancy

Dashiell and mother Ann Dashiell sold to Thomas Smith 164 acres of CONCLUSION & DISCOVERY.

CONCLUSION

Patented in 1773 by Elijah Shockley for 946 acres.
Repatented in 1774 by Elijah Shockley for 1192 acres.
8 Mar.1775 Elijah Shockley sold 43 1/4 acres to Elisha Pennewell
8 Mar.1775 Elijah Shockley sold to Samuel Shockley for 125 1/2 acres
8 Mar.1775 Elijah Shockley with wife Sarah Shockley sold to John Magee 116 acres.
23 Oct.1778 Capt. Elijah Shockley sold to Samuel Parker 124 acres
23 Oct.1778 Samuel Parker sold to Eli Showell 60 acres of WRIGHTS ENLARGEMENT & CONCLUSION
1 Apr.1780 Samuel Parker with wife Anne Parker sold to Elijah Shockley and Capt. James Perdue 122 1/2 acres of CONCLUSION & ENLARGEMENT.
15 May 1780 Elijah Shockley with wife Sarah Shockley sold to George Parsons 180 acres.
2 Oct.1782 Elijah Shockley sold to Samuel Magee 68 acres, nine miles from Salisbury in Wicomico Forrest.
1783 tax - Elijah Shockley 291 acres, Wic.100 Worc.
1783 tax - Saul Shockley 125 acres.
9 May 1783 Elisha Pennewell sold to Hezekiah Carey 43 3/4 acres.
25 Mar.1784 Samuel Magee sold to Betty Robinson 68 O acres.
8 March 1786 Elijah Shockley and James Perdue sold to Eli Showell 122 1/2 acres of CONCLUSION and ENLAGEMENT
19 May 1786 Hezekiah Carey sold to William Morris son of Thomas Morris 44 acres
22 Nov.1794 William Morris sold to Eli Showell 43 3/4 acres
22 Feb.1796 John Magee sold to Saul Shockley, part.
5 Feb.1798 John Magee sold to William White of Henry White 113 1/2 acres
15 Mar.1806 Cornelius Morris sold to Samuel Magee 45 and 28 acres
15 Mar.1806 William Pollitt with wife Sarah Pollitt sold to Joshua Morris part.
14 May 1809 Robert Nairn, sheriff sold to Joshua Johnson, Solomon Smith and William Richardson, per judgement against Elijah Shockley part of 946 acres called END OF STRIFE.

CONCLUSION

Patented in 1793 by Jonathan Fooks for 803 1/2 acres.

CONCLUSION

Patented in 1794 by William Morris for 113 1/2 acres
22 Nov.1794 William Morris sold to Eli Showell 108 and 5 3/4 acres
12 Mar.1806 Eli Showell of Kent Co. Delaware sold to Hezekiah D. Shockley of Maryland.

CONCLUSION

Patented on 8 Oct.1801 by Cornelius Morris for 147 1/2 acres.
29 Dec.1808 Cornelius Morris sold to William Laws 147 1/2 acres
7 Jan.1809 William Laws sold to son Elijah Laws 150 acres.

CONCLUSION

Patented in 1810 by Jonathan Noble for 65 acres.

CONFUSION

Patented 1792 by Thomas Cooper for 8 3/4 acres.
1796 Thomas Cooper willed lands to sons Samuel Cooper and Thomas Cooper, unnamed.

CONFUSION

Patented in 1763 by Nathan Culver for 27 1/2 acres.
25 Feb.1764 Nathan Culver sold to William Stephens 27 1/2 acres.
16 Dec.1759 William Stephens sold 27 1/2 acres to Henry Trader.
5 Apr.1771 Henry Armatrader and wife Agnes Armatrader sold 27 1/2 acres to William McClemmy.
17 Aug.1774 William McClemmy mortgaged to Zorobable King and Solomon Long lands purchased of Henry Trader and others with all goods and chattels, unnamed lands.
1783 tax- William McClemmy 27 1/2 acres
7 Apr.1792 John Leatherbury, sheriff sold to Joshua Hitch 25 1/4 acres as highest bidder, sold lands of William McClemmy.
17 Apr.1792 Joshua Hitch Jr. sold to Levin Irving 25 1/4 acres bought at public sale, lands of William McClemmy.
8 Sep.1792 Levin Irving sold to Thomas Byrd 35 1/4 acres of CONFUSION & MADDUX FANCY.
1800 James Smith willed to son John Smith CONFUSION on Rewastico Creek.

CONNECTCICUT

Patented in 1801 by Samuel Parker for 182 acres
1803 ADDITION TO CONNECTICUT patented for 319 acres by Samuel T. Parker.

CONSOLIDATION

Patented in 1855 by James Fooks and Ritchie Fooks for 660 1/2 acres.

CONSTANTINOPLE

Patented in 1736 by John Stilley for 50 acres.

CONSTANTINES DELIGHT

Patented in 1791 from WEATHERLYS RIDGE by Constantine Weatherly for 125 acres.
16 Sep.1791 Constantine Weatherly with wife Elizabeth Weatherly sold to William Winder with WEATHERLYS RIDGE & pt. CALDER.
1808 William Winder willed all lands unnamed to son William Henry Winder.

CONTENT

Patented in 1765 by William Layfield for 238 1/2 acres.

CONTENTION

Patented on 15 Aug.1688 by Thomas Ralph for 95 acres on Wicomico Creek.
Rent Rolls 1666-1723, possessed by Thomas Ralph
7 Apr.1742 Robert Laws and wife Jane Laws sold to George Dashiell 95 acres patented by Thomas Ralph who died intestate and left son Thomas Ralph who also died intestate and left a daughter Jane Ralph now wife of Robert Laws.
1748 George Dashiell willed to son Benjamin Dashiell 95 acres sold me by Robert Laws commonly called by us WOODS PASTURE.
11 Aug.1760 resurveyed 63 1/2 acres to STEVENS FOLLY by Joseph Dashiell.
23 Aug.1764 I Joseph Dashiell release to Charles Redding 30 acres with CHANGE.

CONTENTION

Patented in 1724 by Alexander Leckie and wife Ann Leckie for 556 acres.
1740 Alexander Leckie died, land not in will.
1734 Ann Leckie widow of Alexander willed to grandson Huett Nutter son of John Huett Nutter.
19 Apr.1736 John Huett Nutter eldest son of Ann Leckie who was Ann Huett and later Ann Nutter daughter of Rev. John Huett late of Stepney Parish, sold to Levin Gale.
16 Apr.1736 Alexander Leckie sold 550 acres to Levin Gale.
1775 resurvey by William Nutter 87 1/2 acres.
1783 tax - William Nutter Sr. 37 1/2 acres. Rewastico 100.
1783 William Nutter willed to wife Sarah Nutter, sons William Nutter, Charles Nutter, lands unnamed.
29 May 1793 Charles Nutter and William Nutter, agreement to division of lines NUTTERS CONTENTION,DORMANS DELIGHT,BOTTOM OF THE NECK & NUTTERS CONTRIVANCE, etc.
27 Aug.1806 Henry E. Bayley, wife Sarah Bayley (formerly Sarah Nutter) sold to Charles Nutter with DORMANS DELIGHT, NUTTERS ADVENTURE, etc.
1813 Charles Nutter willed to son Christopher Columbus Nutter, Quantico farm, unnamed land.

CONTENTION

Patented in 1751 by Thomas Gillis for 50 acres.

CONTENTMENT

Patented in 1783 by Esme Bayley for 200 acres.
1783 tax - Esme Bayley 200 acres- Rewastico (escheat of WHETTSTONE)

CONVENIENCE

Patented 10 May 1689 John Huett for 13 acres on s/s of Nanticoke River.
9 Sep.1740 John Huett Nutter sold to Joseph Records 13 acres on an island on s/s of Nanticoke River.
29 Jan 1744. Joseph Records of Dorchester Co.,wife Ann Records sold to

James Lucas of Worc.Co., mariner 13 acres.

CONVENIENCY

Patented on 24 Nov.1685 by John Huett for 400 acres in Nanticoke 100.
2 June 1740 John Huett Nutter sold to Alexander Richards 400 acres.
Repatented on 23 May 1748 by Alexander Richards for 492 acres.
22 Nov.1754 Alexander Richards sold to Stephen Mitchell 150 acres.
22 Nov.1754 Alexander Richards with wife Katherine Richards sold to Thomas Moore part. 96 acres.
4 Apr.1763 Caleb Balding sold to Daniel Kelly 150 acres.
17 Dec.1764 Alexander Records sold to Thomas Records 246 acres.
1768/71 Thomas Records, willed to wife Sarah Records and children Esther Tull, Mary Records, Anna Records, Archelus Records, Sarah Records, Lame Records, Euphrosina Records, Amelia Records, lands GOOD LUCK VENTURE, CONVENIENCY, FOX HALL.
1788 Stephen Mitchell willed lands to son Thomas Mitchell, unnamed.
21 Aug.1806 Thomas Byrd, Samuel Tull and wife Nancy Tull and Polly Byrd sold to James Wallace of Sussex Co.Delaware all rights to CONVIENCY in fork of Nanticoke River and Broad Creek, in Sussex Co.Delaware.

COOPERS CHOICE

Patented in 1758 by Silas Cooper for 21 acres, was part of COVINGTONS CHANCE
2 July 1775 William Ellingsworth sold to Henry Nicholson 21 acres on south side Nanticoke River, east side of Wetpquin Creek.
2 July 1796 Henry Nicholson with wife Elizabeth Nicholson sold to Levin Willis 20 acres.
2 July 1796 Levin Willis with wife Esther Willis gave to grandson Newton Willis Mezick son of Covington Mezick.

COOPERS DEPARTURE

Patented in 1805 by Isaac Cooper for 4 acres
16 Nov1807 Isaac Cooper sold to Charles Venables.

COOPERS LUCK

Patented in 1793 by Thomas Cooper for 17 acres.

COOPERS MISTAKE

Patented on 1 Oct.1695 by Samuel Fluellin for 100 acres and assigned to Thomas Larramore.
Rent Rolls 1666-1723, possessed by Thomas Larramore between Wicomico and Nanticoke Rivers.
1731 Thomas Larramore willed 100 acres to son John Larramore.
1738 John Larramore willed plantation to son Levin Larramore, unnamed land.
14 Aug.1750 triparte agreement- Levin Larramore sold to Benjamin Wailes 100 acres at the RIDGES near the head of Tyaskin Creek with 50 acres of TICKNELL adjacent. (Jacob Aires to sue Benjamin Wailes for lands.)

CORKLAND

Patented 1 May 1688 by Thomas Cox for 246 acres on branch of Barren Creek.
Rent Rolls 1666-1723, possessed by Peter Calloway
2 Mar.1725 Peter Calloway, carpenter, with wife Sarah Calloway sold 50 acres to Thomas Waller, carpenter.
1738/40 Peter Calloway willed to son John Calloway 50 acres, to son Joshua Calloway 50 acres and sons Benjamin Calloway and Joshua 63 acres each.
14 April 1750 Peter Calloway sold to Samuel Calloway 50 acres left by will to Joshua Calloway now deceased.
31 Mar.1750 Benjamin Calloway and wife Rachel Calloway sold 63 acres to Joseph Calloway.
31 March 1750 John Calloway with wife Priscilla Calloway sold to Joseph Calloway 50 acres.
22 Apr.1755 Joseph Calloway sold to Henry Lowe 196 acres with 55 acres ANYTHING.
27 Aug.1757 Thomas Waller sold to Richard Waller 50 acres of WHAT YOU PLEASE being part of 250 acres of CORKLAND.
1761 Will of Henry Lowe to Richard Bigland land bought of Joseph Calloway
14 May 1768 Henry Lowe sold to John Moore 196 acres.
14 May 1658 John Moore sold to David Pritchard 50 acres.
15 Oct.1768 Matthias Vinson and wife Mary Vinson and Isaac Vinson sold to George Handy.
29 July 1769 Isaac Vinson with wife Mary Vinson sold to Littleton Dennis of Worc.Co. and Josiah Polk and Gillis Polk 11 acres where they created a mill dam.
20 April 1772 David Pritchard sold 100 acres to George Handy, part conveyed by John Moore and part conveyed by James Finch.
23 Apr.1775 Susanna Dennis, executrix of Littleton Dennis of Worc.Co. sold her 1/3rds, 25 acres, to Josiah Polk with mills and PARTNERS GOOD LUCK, and water mill, saw mill and bottling mill that he had in partnership with Gillis Polk & Josiah Polk.
1782 George Handy willed to son Isaac Handy land bought of Matthias Vinson
1783 tax - Josiah Polk & Gillis Polk 16 acres- Rewastico 100
1783 tax - Isaac Vinson 100 acres.
1783 tax - Isaac Handy 100 acres.
1805 Isaac Vincent willed to wife Mary Vincent.
1808 Mary Vincent willed to Samuel Moore 100 acres.
12 Aug.1809 Elijah Vinson sold to Samuel Moore of Sussex Co.Del. 100 acres.
12 Aug.1809 Samuel Moore of Sussex Co.Del. sold to Elijah Vinson 55 1/2 acres, trade of boundaries.
4 Sep.1809 Elijah Vinson with wife Bridget Vinson sold to Isaac Denson 55 1/2 acres.
4 Sep.1809 Isaac Vinson sold to Whitty Cox 12 1/4 acres.
26 Sep.1810 William Handy and Edward G. Handy of Washington DC sold to Spencer Todd 40 acres of NEWHAVEN,CORKLAND, SMALL LOTT, HANDYS CARE. (trustees to sell RE of Isaac Handy)
22 Sep.1810 William Handy and Edward G. Handy sold to Peter Dashiell land between CORKLAND & EXPENSE 43 5/8 acres.
26 Sep.1810 William Handy and Edward G. Handy sold to Thomas Bird 312

acres of NEW HAVEN, CORKLAND, HANDYS CARE.
24 Sep.1811 Robert Dashiell sold to Jehu Bounds that Dashiell purchased of the trustees to sell the real estate of Isaac Handy.
15 Apr.1813 Jehu Bounds and wife Nancy Bounds sold part to David Howard, no acreage mentioned.
1822 Thomas Byrd willed part to son Benjamin H. Byrd.
1826 Whitty Cox willed 40 acres to son Southy Cox.

CORDRYS BEGINNING

Patented on 4 June 1721 by John Cordrey for 100 acres in Nanticoke 100.
1721 John Cordrey willed to son Jacob Cordrey 100 acres.
28 March 1745 Jacob Cordrey sold to Robert Graham 100 acres.
1755 Robert Graham willed lands unnamed to son John Graham.
17 Aug.1744 Phillip Graham quitclaimed to David Williams part in trade for LAST CHOICE.
1787 Phillip Graham willed all lands in Wicomico to son John Graham and William Graham, that James Beard rents.
1783 tax- James Beard 100 acres
14 Mar.1806 Francis Collier, wife Betsy C. Collier (late Betsy Graham daughter of Phillip Graham) sold to John Graham, devised by Phillip to sons John Graham and William Graham.
13 Oct.1807 Ralph Milbourn with wife Sarah Milbourn (late Sarah Graham) sold all rights for 10 shillings to John Graham.

CORBY

12 Jan.1747 Capt. Day Scott sold to Edward Corby 100 acres taken out of LAST CHOICE, called CORBY.
1748 David Corby willed to wife Sarah Ann Corby 100 acres.
22 Jan 1755 Covington Mezick and wife Sarah Ann sold to Nicholas Evans Collier, 100 acres.
1786 Nicholas Evans Collier willed to son Nicholas E. Collier land that was part of land belonging to Day Scott and partially now in the heirs of David Williams.
1768 Thomas Williams willed to grandson David Williams lands bought of Major Day Scott on Wicomico River, unnamed.
1780 David Williams willed to son Thomas Williams, if he die to daughters Betty Williams and Amelia Williams (under 16) lands on Wicomico River.

CORDWINDERS HALL

Patented in 1760 by Joseph Leonard for 27 acres.
1767 Joseph Leonard willed to son Joseph Leonard.
1774 Joseph Leonard repatented for 184 acres.
1783 tax - Joseph Leonard, 18 1/4 acres, Wicomico 100.
1808 George Parsons willed 180 acres to son Jordan Parsons.

CORDWINDERS LOTT

Patented in 1763 by Thomas Cox for 50 acres in Wicomico 100a.
3 Dec.1774 Thomas Cox sold to Moses Cox 50 acres, on the south

side of the Wic. River adj. COX'S ADVANCE & PLUMPTON SALTASH.
5 Apr.1779 Moses Cox of Sussex Co.Delaware sold to Archibald Smith of Somerset Co. for 5 shillings 50 acres.
1783 tax - Archibald Smith 25 acres
1783 tax - John Smith 25 acres
1793 John Smith willed to Joshua Smith son of brother Archibald Smith.
23 Nov 1797 Archibald Smith with wife Esther Smith sold 50 acres to John Byrd.
10 May 1806 John Byrd with wife Margaret Byrd sold to Thomas Byrd

CORK

Patented in 1702 by Dennis Driskell for 100 acres.
1721 Dennis Diskell willed to son James Driskell.

CORN HILL

Patented on 10 Mar.1761 by William Driskell for 51 acres in Wicomico 100, Worcester Co.
4 Nov.1772 William Driskell sold to Shardrack Driskell 51 acres
31 May 1773 Shadrack Driskell sold to Solomon Givans 51 acres.
1783 tax - Spencer Harris 51 acres & Solomon Givans 51 acres.
12 May 1788 Solomon Gibbons sold to Jethro Morris son of Thomas Morris all rights.
16 Sep.1801 Thomas Burbage sold to Jethro Morris, for docking.

CORN HILL

Patented in 1804 by William Russum for 277 1/2 acres.
1821 William Russum willed to son Joseph Russum.

COVENT GARDEN

Patented on 12 May 1676 by Robert Collier for 200 acres a little southward of Quantico Ck.
5 Dec.1682 Robert Collier and wife Elizabeth Collier sold 200 acres to Isaac ? of Northampton Co.Virginia.
NO
Rent Rolls 1666-1723, possessed by to widow of Sampson Waters in Boston New England, Management of the escheat Robert Dashiell.
2 Mar.1717 Obediah Wakefield and John Wakefield of Boston Mass. sold to Peter Bowdoin son of John Bowdoin late, of Northampton Co. Va. 1/2 of JESHEMIN, BATCHLORS ADVENTURE, COVENT GARDEN & THE SUPPLY pat. Robert Collier in Nanticoke.
23 Aug.1739 Peter Bowdoin with wife Susanna Bowdoin of Northampton Co.Va. sold to Capell King 1 moity of 1750 acres at Quantico Creek, no name.

COSTONS ENTRY

Patented 1771 Jacob Coston for 7 acres.

COSTLY

Patented in 1760 by Elgate Bird for 3 acres.

COTTMANS SLIPE

Patented in 1795 by William Cottman for 10 1/2 acres.

COVINGTONS CHANCE

Patented in 1761 by Covington Mezick for 133 3/4 acres.
27 April 1775 Elihu Mezick and brother Jacob Mezick sold to William Donoho 33 3/4 acres.
22 Apr. 1785 James Mezick and wife Elizabeth Mezick of Dorc.Co. Md. sold 133 3/4 acres to Solomon McKimmey of Som. Co.
26 Mar.1789 Solomon McKimmey and wife Sarah McKimmey sold to Elihu Mezick 133 3/4 acres.
2 July 1796 Elihu Mezick and wife Leah Mezick and John Mezick and Daniel Mezick sold to Levi Willis 75 3/4 acres part called COOPERS CHANCE, formerly prop. of Silas Cooper.
1809 Levin Willis willed lands unnamed to the children of Covington Mezick
1828 Covington Mezick willed to son Levin W. Mezick tract SPIE being part of COVINGTONS CHANCE & STRIFE.

COVINGTONS CHOICE

Patented 28 Oct.1678 by Thomas Covington for 300 acres in Rewastico 100
Rent Rolls 1666-1723, possessed by Samuel Covington
1703/4 Samuel Covington willed 100 acres each to sons Isaac Covington, Abraham Covington & Thomas Covington.
13 May 1757 John Covington sold to Dockter Harny (negro) 150 acres. (Isaac Covington hold remaining 150 acres)
1 Sep.1764 Isaac Covington sold 47 acres to Daniel Maddox
14 May 1768 Isaac Covington sold to John Nelms part, 111 acres of COVINGTONS CHOICE, WHITEFILED.
1783 tax - Edward Ellis 109 1/2 acres
1783 tax - Samuel Game 55 acres
1783 tax - John Maddux 35 acres
1783 tax - Betty Maddux 47 1/2 acres
1 Apr.1784 Daniel Game sold 150 acres to John Nelms.
15 Oct.1784 Daniel Game sold to John Maddux 35 acres.

COVINGTONS CHOICE

Patented on 19 Nov.1757 for 60 acres by John Covington
8 Apr.1763 John Covington sold to George Smith 60 acres
12 Jan.1771 George Smith Sr. sold to Levin Ruark 60 acres.
3 May 1763 part resurveyed to SMITHS DEFENSE
1783 tax - Jeremiah Game 60 acres, Wic.100.

COVINGTONS HABITATION

Patented 1752 by Covington Mezick for 100 acres.

COW BRIDGE

Patented 1718 by Thomas Carey for 100 acres.

1760 John Morris willed to son William Morris and to sons Joseph Morris and Joshua Morris (of Worcester County)

COW HOUSE RIDGE

Patented in 1759 by Job Truitt for 40 acres
1762 resurveyed to HARDSHIP

COW QUARTER

Patented 1746 by Thomas Acworth for 50 acres.

COW QUARTER

Patented 1728 by William Twiford for 5 acres.
1783 ADDITION TO pat. John Twiford for 275 1/2 acres.
28 June 1802 Dennis Morris and Ann Starling Morris of Sussex Co.Del. sold to Bartholomew Twiford of Dorc.Co. land entitled to as heirs of Sally Twiford and parcel left by will of John Twiford to daughter Sally Twiford WALKERS LOTT & TWIFORDS BEGINNING alias ADDITION TO COW QUARTER.

COW RIDGE

Patented 1748 by Samuel Fluellin for 100 acres.
1766 ADDITION TO COW RIDGE pat. Samuel Fluellin for 237 1/2 acres.
1766 Samuel Fluellin willed to son John Fluellin
19 Mar.1770 Richard Crockett Fluellin son of Samuel sold to Ephraim King 846 acres with FLUELLINS SETTLEMENT that Samuel Fluellin devised to son John for lifetime ADDITION TO COW RIDGE & COW RIDGE. John Fluellin died without issue.
1777 Ephraim King willed to Richard Crockett Fluellin and Samuel Fluellin lands their father Samuel bought of John Beard which was conveyed to me by Samuel Fluellin son of Samuel, not named.
1783 tax - Abendego Green 237 acres. Nanticoke 100.
26 Mar.1793 Gillis Polk surviving trustee of Ephraim King and Samuel Fluellin brother of Richard C. Fluellin sold to Isaac Atkinson son of Isaac, CLEAR OF CANNON SHOTT, FLEULLINS SETTLEMENT, ADDITION TO COW RIDGE, etc.
Nov.1806 Isaac Dickerson with wife Rebecca Dickerson sold to William Winright Dickerson COW RIDGE possessed by William Winright deceased.

COWES SIX

This is part of tract FAIRFILEDS.
1713 Richard Stevens willed to daughter Sarah Bounds 300 acres and then to her son Jonathan Bounds
1741 Jonathan Bounds resurveyed to BOUNDS CHANCE.
1 Jan 1725 Isaac Stevens and wife Ann Stevens sold to George Dashiell, whereas Richard Stevens willed 1713 to son Isaac Stevens 1/2 of great marsh belonging to 300 acres of COWES SIX.

COXES ADVICE

Patented 16 Aug.1740 by Alexander Argo for 200 acres at head of Wicomico River.
10 Oct.1752 Alexander Argo of Sussex Co.Del. sold 200 acres to Thomas Gillis.
17 Mar.1763 Thomas Gillis sold to Hiram Reddish of Worc.Co. 200 acres part in Somerset Co. and part in Worc.Co. at head of Rokiawalkin River.
17 Feb.1770 Hiram Reddish with wife Elizabeth Reddish sold 200 acres to John Nelms.
1783 tax- John Nelms 150 acres Wic. 100, Worc.Co.
1794 John Nelms willed lands to wife Nancy Nelms until children become of age and to son Noah Nelms dwelling plantation unnamed.

COXES ADVICE

Patented 1758 Joseph Leonard 50 acres.
1767 Joseph Leonard willed 50 acres to son Joseph Leonard.
1783 tax - Joseph Leonard, 50 acres, Wicomico 100.

COXES CHOICE

Patented 1 May 1683 by Anthony Underwood for 200 acres.
5 May 1685 Anthony Underwood with wife Martha Underwood sold to Henry Smith 200 acres.
Rent Rolls 1666-1723, Captain Henry Smith the last possessed who died.
1715 John Smith of Sussex Co.Del. grandson of Henry Smith sold his grandfathers land in Som.Co.Md.
Resurveyed in 1748 by Alexander Argo 200 acres to COXES ADVICE.

COXES CHOICE

Patented 1 Dec.1681 by Cornelius Johnson for 300 acres.
10 June 1690 William Jones exec. of Cornelius Johnson sold to John Frizzell.
6 Nov.1702 John Frizzell gave to Edward Wooten his son-in-law 300 acres.
20 March 1726 Edward Wooten and wife Sarah Wooten sold to COXES CHOICE to John Magee.
1728/9 John Magee willed to sons George Magee, John Magee and Peter Magee.
8 March 1753 George Magee with wife Sarah Magee sold 100 acres to John Sturgis.
3 Aug.1756 Peter Magee sold to William Winder 200 acres.
9 June 1768 John Sturgis Jr. sold to Alexander Thomas Russell 100 acres.
2 Sep.1774 Alexander Thomas Russell sold to Price Russell 100 acres.
9 May 1778 Josiah Russell of Frederick Co., Price Russell with wife Anne Russell of Som.Co. sold to William Hopewell of Worcester County Maryland.
1783 tax - Joshua Sturgis Jr. 100 acres, Wic.100 Worc.Co.
29 Nov.1783 William Winder sold to Richard Mills 36 acres

25 May 1790 Richard Mills sold to Jesse Fooks 36 acres
1792 William Winder willed to son William Winder land between Rewastico branchs at Quantico, unnamed.
22 Feb.1796 John Magee sold to Elijah Shockley all rights
11 Oct.1800 Jesse Fooks sold to Rachel Fooks 36 acres
1802 Joshua Sturgis willed to son Joshua lands unnamed.

COXES DELIGHT

Patented on 26 Sep.1760 by John Cox for 60 acres.
1 May 1788 Thomas Cox Sr. sold to Jonathan Fooks 60 acres.

COX'S DISCOVERY

Patented on 15 May 1688 by Edward Day for 745 acres
Rent Rolls 1666-1723, belongs to heirs of Edward Day but widow refuses payment of rent.
2 July 1737 Day Scott and wife Alice sold to Dudson Bacon 100 acres at Little Creek out of the Nanticoke River pat. Edward Day and Day Scott heir at law.
2 July 1737 Day Scott and wife Alice Scott sold 500 acres to William Vaughn.
5 Nov.1740 Day Scott and wife Alice Scott sold to Dudson Bacon 145 acres.
5 Nov.1740 Day Scott and wife Alice Scott sold to John Rhoads blacksmith 100 acres called RHODES LOTT out of COXES DISCOVERY.
1742 William Vaughn willed to daughter Elizabeth Bacon and to son Ephraim Vaughn 100 acres bought of Dudson Bacon and to son Jethro 150 acres of dwelling plantation, unnamed.
19 Nov.1745 Jethro Vaughn sold to William Moore 100 acres.
10 June 1750 deposition of John Goddard age 60. About 6 or 7 years ago Dudson Bacon sold 100 acres to Robert Caldwell who sold to George Booth and said Bacon held 45 acres more than sold.
10 June 1750 John Williams deposition age 48. That 7 years ago John Williams drew a bond for making over 100 acres between Dudson Bacon and Robert Caldwell.
25 Feb.1769 Thomas Kennerly sold to Ephraim Vaughn pt. called RHOADES LOTT conveyed to Kennerly by John Rhoads.
1773 Ephraim Vaughn willed 150 acres left me by father William Vaughn, my now dwelling plantation and to son John Vaughn 100 acres bought of Thomas Kennerly.
12 Oct.1775 James Taylor of Caroline Co. Va. sold to William Vaughn of Som.Co. his rights.
12 Oct.1775 James Taylor of Caroline Co.Va. sold part to Jethro Vaughn.
12 Oct.1775 James Taylor of same, sold part to George Booth of Som.Co.
1775 William Vaughn of Sussex Co.Del. willed to sons Nathaniel Vaughn, William Vaughn and Ephraim Vaughn.
8 March 1776 Sussex Co.Delaware warrants William Vaughn.

COXES FOLLY

Patented in 1775 by Thomas Cox Jr. for 7 acres.
1797 Thomas Cox willed lands to sons Aaron Cox and John Cox, unnamed.

COX'S FORK

Patented on 16 Dec.1681 for Thomas Cox at the head of the Rokiawalkin River for 300 acres.
Rent Rolls 1666-1723, possessed by John Holder 150 acres and John Disharoon for 150 acres.
1716/7 John Holder willed to sons John and Joseph Holder
10 Apr. 1726 John Disharoon and wife Margaret Disharoon and John Stevens of Sussex Co. Del.with wife Frances Stevens sold to William Oliphant 150 acres that Thomas Cox with wife Rebecca Cox sold to John Stevens. The land descended to his son John Stevens.
9 Nov.1729 John Holder of Dorc.Co.Md. sold to Ebenezer Handy 75 acres.
15 Mar.1736 I Ebenezer Handy mortgage to John Trehearn 75 acres of COX's FORK and 65 acres of HOLDER CHANCE.
1767 John Handy of Worc.Co. sold to John Leonard of Worc.Co. 75 acres.
1767 Joseph Leonard willed to son John Leonard 75 acres.
1776 Matthew Oliphant willed to son Matthew Oliphant 80 acres and balance to son James Oliphant.
1783 tax - John Leonard 70 acres
1783 tax - John Maddux
1783 tax - Thomas Cox Sr. 8 1/4 acres.
1783 tax - Isaiah Wright 80 acres
21 Apr.1787 James Hill sold to James Fletcher, estate of John Leonard. He married Leah Leonard who had administration of her husband's estate.
20 March 1792 Joseph Holder sold pt. to John Holbrook.
10 Nov.1792 James Oliphant of Worc.Co. sold to Edmond Northern Nelms 80 acres.
26 Apr.1794 John Holbrook sold to Joseph Leonard part purchased of John Holder.
13 Aug.1804 John Bounds and wife Nancy Bounds (late Nancy Nutter) sold to Joseph Leonard 57 acres.

COX'S MISTAKE

Patented in 1744 by Daniel Jones for 52 acres.
1758 Daniel Jones willed to wife Elizabeth Jones 1/2 of Dwelling planation and to son Daniel Jones the same.
1783 Daniel Jones with wife Martha Jones willed plantation where I live to brother James Jones.

COX'S NEGLECT

Patented in 1773 by George Cox for 65 1/2 acres.
23 Apr.1796 John Biglands sold to William Daley 50 acres
16 Mar.1799 William Daley with wife Keziah Daley sold to Samuel T. Parker.
21 Feb.1794 Joshua Townsend, sheriff sold to John Biglands, plaintiff against William Dymock 50 acres.
21 Dec.1805 William Daley sold to Thomas Layfield 32 acres
29 Apr.1806 Thomas Layfield sold to William Brewington Jr. 17 acres and 8 perches.

COX'S PERFORMANCE

Patented on 16 Oct.1696 by John Windsor for 1000 acres in a fork of the branches of Broad Creek.
Rent Rolls 1666-1723, possessed by John Windsor
20 July 1722 John Windsor gave to son Henry Windsor 250 acres.
1730 John Windsor willed to son John 250 acres and to John Windsor son of James Windsor 250 acres and to John son of Lazarus Windsor 150 acres.
5 June 1738 Henry Windsor and wife Ann Windsor sold to Henry Lowe 250 acres.
17 Mar.1739 John Windsor sold to Robert Jenkins Henry 150 acres devised to John by his grandfather John Windsor.
1754 John Windsor willed to brother James Windsor 100 acres that fell to me as heir of John Windsor Jr. and to daughter Mary Windsor dwelling plantation willed me by John Windsor Sr. 150 acres.
29 July 1755 James Windsor sold to Joseph Marshall 100 acres.
7 June 1758 John Windsor, mariner sold to Levin Vaughn, wheelwright 150 acres.
1761 Henry Lowe willed to niece Ann Waters plantation purchased of Henry Windsor on Broad Creek.
24 Mar.1761 triparte agreement John Windsor and James Windsor to Levin Vaughn and Joseph Collins. James Windsor had 100 acres and John 250 acres.
17 Aug.1763 Joseph Marshall sold to John Houston 100 acres.
26 Oct.1764 Joseph Collins sold to Levin Vaughn, millright 100 acres.
5 Apr.1765 Joseph Collins sold to John Collins 250 acres.
1 Oct.1765 Henry Lowe sold to John Windsor 250 acres.
1768 John Houston willed to son John (wife Rhoda Houston) 250 acres.
6 April 1776 Land Warrants to Sussex Co.Delaware 200 acres by John Collins.

CROCKETTS PETITION

Patented to Richard Crockett for 25 acres.
14 Apr.1743 Richard Crockett of Som.Co. with wife Elizabeth Crockett sold to Adam Muir of Dorc.Co. 3 tracts on the south east side of the Nanticoke River s/s of Gravely Branch adj. THOMAS LOTT belonging to Thomas Brown, with PINEY MARSH & DELIGHT.

CRONEYS FOLLY

Patented 20 Dec.1741 James Croney for 196 acres.
3 June 1765 Margaret Croney of Northampton Co. Va. and Nathaniel Waller Jr. of Somerset Co. sold to David Polk of Dorc.Co.Md. that James Croney willed to be sold, formerly Dorcester Co. but now Worc.Co. 196 acres.

CROOKED CHANCE

Patented in 1773 by Levin Fletcher for 183 acres in Rewastico a resurvey of DONEGALL

14 Nov.1772 Levin Fletcher and Charles Davis sold to David Dutton free mulatto, part POOR CHANCE & 10 acres of CROOKED CHANCE.
1783 tax - David Dutton 50 acres.
1783 tax - Levin Fletcher 133 acres.
1 Oct. 1791 Levin Fletcher sold 11 acres to David Dutton for 5 shillings.
19 Nov.1791 Levin Fletcher Sr. and wife Betty Fletcher sold to Arthur Dashiell 183 acres except 61 acres sold to David Dutton, with tr. DONEGALL.
19 Dec.1805 Arthur Dashiell with wife Esther Dashiell sold to James Donoho, with WOOLF PITT RIDGE.

CROOKED LANE

No Patent found.
3 Sep.1762 John Alexander Willey sold 206 acres to Kirk Gunby
4 Nov.1762 John Alexander Willey sold to Southy King balance 57 acres.
1775 Kirk Gunby willed to grandson Stephen Gunby son of David Gunby where they now dwell after his mother's death. To daughter-in-law Elizabeth Gunby widow of David, in Sussex Co.Del.
1783 tax - Levin Gunby 31 acres, Wicomico 100.

CROOKED RIDGE

Patented in 1749 by John Parremore for 50 acres.
20 Apr.1765 John Parremore sold to John Quartermus 50 acres.

CROSS

Patented on 16 June 1695 by John Ricketts for 150 acres in the woods, from the south side of Nanticoke on south side of Quantico Creek.
Rent Rolls 1666-1723, possessed by John Ricketts
22 Jan 1738 John Records sold 150 acres to Robert Mears.
17 Mar.1740 Robert Mears and wife Sarah Mears sold 150 acres to William Moore Jr.
Resurveyed in 1756 for 266 acres by John Moore
1783 tax - William Moore 200 acres- resurveyed to WOODYARD
1783 tax - James Moore 50 acres -resurveyed Rewastico 100.
1766 all resurveyed to WOODYARD- 350 acres.

CROUCHES DESIRE

Patented on 24 May 1689 by Robert Crouch for 100 acres on the south side of the Wicomico River.
1711 Robert Crouch willed lands to wife Mary Crouch 100 acres, unnamed.
21 Aug.1739 Ann Crouch sold 100 acres to Jarvis Jenkins.
10 Mar.1755 I Jarvis Jenkins give to son Joseph Jenkins 50 acres.
3 Mar.1755 I Jarvis Jenkins give to son John Jenkins 50 acres.
1783 tax - John Jenkins 50 acres
1783 tax - James Bennett 50 acres.
4 Nov.1795 John Jenkins with wife Rachel Jenkins sold all rights to James Bennett.

7 July 1801 Leah Jenkins, Sinah Gray, Levinah Serman sold to James Bennett 50 acres, of land owned by Joseph Jenkins husband of Leah Jenkins and father of Sinah Gray and Levinah Serman.

CROWN POINT

Patented on 7 Feb.1763 by Outten Truitt for 48 acres.
1768 William Whittington willed land of Outten Truitt CROWN POINT, to cousin Nancy Harris.
1793 Daniel Fooks willed 48 acres to son Thomas Fooks
10 June 1795 Nancy Martin of Northampton Co.Virginia and William Whittington son of William sold to Thomas Fooks and rest of the children of Daniel Fooks 48 acres
8 Dec.1809 Billy Fooks, Jonathan Fooks and James Fooks sold all rights to Thomas Fooks.
1830 Jonathan Fooks of Daniel Fooks, willed to son James Minos Fooks 6 1/2 acres.

CROWS HARBOUR

Patented in 1845 by George Farlow

CRUSTY

Patented in 1767 by Josiah Polk
1784 Josiah Polk willed to brother William Polk.

CUBYS CHANCE

Patented on 23 March 1748 for 50 acres by Thomas Cuby Lankford in Rewastico 100.
Resurveyed in 1767 by same for 88 1/4 acres.
31 Dec.1768 Benjamin Lankford sold to George Wilson 16 acres, on road from Spring Hill Chapel to Wicomico River.
1774 ADDITION TO patented by Benjamin Lankford for 158 1/2 acres.
1783 tax - Benjamin Lankford 100 acres- resurvey
1783 tax - Mary Lankford (with Saw Mill Supply 40 acres)
1789 Benjamin Lankford willed to daughter Sarah Lankford 50 acres of ADDITION TO CUBYS CHANCE and balance to son Thomas Lankford.
20 Feb.1805 Thomas Lankford sold 54 acres of ADDITION to Joseph Jackson
20 Feb. 1805 Thomas Lankford, shoemaker sold to Joshua Nicholson 50 acres of JACKSONS BEGINNING & ADDN. TO CUBYS CHANCE.
1805 Joseph Jackson willed estate to wife Elizabeth Jackson and after death to Thomas Nicholson son of Jonathan Nicholson, no name of land.
29 Jan.1808 Thomas Lankford, eldest son of Benjamin Lankford sold 12 acres to George Wilson Jr.

CUCKOLDS DELIGHT

Patented 25 May 1688 by Robert Sudler for 500 acres on south side of Wicomico River.
1692 Robert Sudler sold to Robert Peyton
Rent Rolls 1666-1723, possessed by Major Peytons heirs in Glocester Co. Virginia.

CULVERS FOLLY

Patented in 1797 by William Hitch for 150 acres in Rewastico 100.
15 June 1799 William Hitch and John Hitch with wife Jean Hitch sons of Joshua Hitch sold to Thomas Humphries Jr. COME BY CHANCE 134 acres and since resurveyed by William Hitch to CULVERS FOLLY.

CULVERS PUZZLE

Patented in 1791 by Thomas Culver for 4 acres.

CUT CLOSE

Patented in 1822 by John Wright for 15 1/2 acres
1850 John Wright living in Barren Creek

CYPRESS GROVE

Patented in 1763 by George Smith for 10 acres.
12 Mar.1771 George Smith Sr. of Worc.Co. sold 10 acres to John Nelms of Som. Co. on s/side of a fork of the Wicomico River 1/4 mile above Salisbury town.

CYPRESS NECK

Patented in 1775 by Elijah Laws for 200 acres.

CYPRESS SWAMP

Patented by Robert Givans for 342 acres on s/s Nanticoke River.
1735 Robert Givans willed to son George Givans upper part and part to son Thomas Givans 72 acres and part to son George Givans and to son Day Givans.
6 Nov.1745 George Givans sold to Jonathan Bell Sr. of Northampton Co.Va. 154 acres, 107 acres of CYPRESS SWAMP and 47 acres of OUTLETT called BELLS GARDEN.
24 July 1747 Robert Givans gave bond to George Givans to makeover two tracts that fell him by the death of brother Thomas Givans 80 acres left Thomas by father Robert Givans.
25 July 1755 Day Givans sold to James Hardy 53 acres.
1756 James Hardy willed to wife Susanna Hardy 1/3rd estate and to son Isaac Hardy, dwelling plantation, unnamed.

DAKES FOLLY

Patented in 1748 by William Farlow for 50 acres.

DALFORFO

Patented on 20 Apr.1715 by Alexander Adams for 195 acres.
1 Oct.1752 Alexander Adams sold to son George Adams, in Deep Creek on south side of Nanticoke River, with FRIENDS DENIAL.

DANBURY

Patented on 4 Feb.1673 by Samuel Jackson for 300 acres.
1678 Samuel Jackson willed lands, unnamed, to sons Samuel and Daniel Jackson.
19 Oct.1749 Thomas Jackson sold to Thomas Gillis 300 acres patented by Samuel Jackson grandfather of Thomas.

DANGERFIELD

Patented 1790 by James Moore for 143 3/4 acres.

DANIELS ADVENTURE

Patented on 2 Apr.1666 by Daniel Haste for 300 acres.
30 Dec.1668 Daniel Haste sold to Richard Stevens 300 acres.
10 Apr.1680 Richard Stevens with wife Abigail Stevens sold to Richard Hull of Northumberland Co.Va.
Rent Rolls 1666-1723, belongs to orphans of Richard Hull in Virginia.
10 Nov.1739 Richard Hull of Northumberland Co.Va. s/o Richard Hull who was the son of Richard, and wife Elizabeth Hull sold to Alexander Leckie 300 acres.
1740 Alexander Leckie willed 50 acres to Thomas Jones and Susan Jones, LECKIES ADVENTURE, formerly DANIELS ADVENTURE.
16 Dec.1752 Thomas Jones and wife Susannah Jones sold 10 acres to Charles Hardy devised by Alexander Leckie and since devised to Jones by Ann Gillis formerly Ann Leckie widow.
9 June 1743 Charles Hardy sold to Samuel Hardy part.
1748 Ann Gillis willed to son Nicholas Evans and to son-in-law Thomas Jones and wife Susannah Jones 1/2 lands devised me by husband Alexander Leckie. no name.
20 Sep. 1753 I Thomas Gillis certify that the will of deceased wife Ann Gillis who devised DANIELS ADVENTURE to Thomas and Susannah Jones and Nicholas Evans equally.
14 July 1767 Nicholas Evans and wife Prisa Evans sold 150 acres to Thomas Irving.
1 Sep.1768 Thomas Irving and wife Sarah Irving sold to Matthias Cannon and wife 200 acres.
1783 tax - John Hardy 150 acres, Nanticoke 100
1783 tax - Thomas Irving of Pr. Anne 150 acres.
1783 tax - Matthew Cannon 20 acres.
1784 Thomas Irving gave to son Joseph Irving 1/2 of tract.
1785 will of Matthias Cannon, to son Thomas Cannon 20 acres bought of Thomas Irving.
14 Sep.1789 Joseph Irving son of Joseph sold to Levin Irving part,(no acreage given).
19 Jan.1799 Levin Irving son of Thomas Irving, with wife Leah Irving sold pt. to William Mezick.
18 June 1802 Mary Cannon sold all interest to Thomas Cannon.
1807 Thomas Cannon willed to son Matthew Cannon lands entailed by my father, unnamed.
1818 William Mezick willed to daughter Martha Washington Handy Mezick (wife Eleanor Mezick.)

DANIELS CHANCE

Patented in 1744 by Daniel McIntyre for 79 acres in Nanticoke 100.
21 Oct 1752 Daniel McIntyre and wife Elizabeth McIntyre sold to Robert Willin 39 1/2 acres.
1783 tax - William McIntyre 30 1/2 acres
1783 tax - Levin Willin 39 1/4 acres
12 Nov.1785 John McIntyre sold all rights to George Aires that Daniel McIntyre his father willed to him.
20 June 1796 Charles Willin with wife Eleanor Willin, Robert Willin and Ann Willin sold to George Aires 31 acres.
22 Apr.1799 Charles Willin sold 16 1/2 and 4 acres to George Aires.

DANIELS DISCOVERY

Patented 1760 by James Weatherly for 16 acres.
17 Apr.1775 James Weatherly sold to Daniel Rhoads 16 acres.
1780 Daniel Rhoads willed lands unnamed to son Jacob Rhoads.
1783 tax - John Brumble,8 acres, Rewastico 100.

DANIELS DISCOVERY

Patented in 1767 by Daniel McIntyre for 7 acres.
1773 Daniel McIntyre willed to wife Elizabeth McIntyre and after death to son William McIntyre.
1783 tax - Betty McIntyre 7 acres, Nanticoke 100.

DANIELS FOLLY

Patented in 1787 by Daniel Waller for 20 1/2 acres.

DANIELS HOPE

Patented in 1754 by Daniel McIntyre for 80 acres in Nanticoke 100.
24 July 1765 Daniel McIntyre sold 42 3/4 acres to Jacob Aires.
1783 tax - Littleton Aires 42 1/2 acres
1783 tax - William McIntyre 37 acres
1773 will Daniel McIntyre, to son John balance of lands, unnamed.
12 Nov.1785 John McIntyre sold to George Aires all rights that his father Daniel McIntyre willed.

DANIELS MISTAKE RECTIFIED

Patented in 1755 by Daniel Wailes for 408 acres in Nanticoke 100.
1783 tax - Joseph Wailes 207 acres
1783 tax - Betty Wailes 201 acres.
29 March 1784 Joseph Wailes sold to Robert Collier Sr. 57 1/2 acres of JOSEPHS LOTT & DANIELS MISTAKE (trade for ADDITION TO CHANCE)
31 Aug.1804 Daniel Wailes sold to William Dashiell 3 3/4 acres
31 Aug.1804 Daniel Wailes sold to William Dashiell 10 1/2 acres.
18 Nov.1808 Daniel Wailes with wife Betsy Wailes sold 320 acres to George Wilson.
1824 George Wilson willed lands to son James Wilson, unnamed.

DANIELS PRIVILEDGE

Patented in 1750 for Daniel McIntyre for 58 acres in Nanticoke 100.
21 Oct.1762 Daniel McIntyre sold 23 acres to Robert Willin
1783 tax - William McIntyre 35 acres
1783 tax - Robert Willin 23 acres
12 Nov.1785 John McIntyre son of Daniel sold to George Aires.
20 June 1786 Charles Willin with wife Elinor Willin, Robert Willin and Ann Willin sold to George Aires.

DARBY

Patented on 3 March 1680 by William Stevens for 350 acres who assigned to Thomas Wilson on the south side of the main branch of Barren Creek. Rent Rolls 1666-1723, possessed by Thomas Wilson
1732/9 Thomas Wilson will, lands not mentioned he had sons John Wilson and Thomas Wilson, deceased.
1752 John Wilson willed to youngest son James Wilson 1/2 and to son David Wilson 1/2.
17 Mar.1752 triparte agreement John Wilson son of Thomas Wilson sold to John Huffington and John Kellum (prob.mortgage.)
17 Aug.1753 John Wilson sold 175 acres to James Wilson
17 Aug.1753 John Wilson sold 175 acres to David Wilson
18 Feb.1768 James Wilson and wife Elizabeth Wilson sold 66 acres to David Wilson
1772 David Wilson living at head of Barren Creek willed to son John Wilson dwelling plantation. If no heirs to daughters Elizabeth Wilson and Denny Wilson. To son Ephraim Wilson 1/2 of lands. (unnamed)
1783 tax - Ephraim Wilson 100 acres- Rewastico 100
1783 tax - James Wilson 109 acres
1783 tax - John Wilson 100 acres
6 June 1796 James Wilson Sr. of Barren Creek and Samuel Wilson son of James sold 110 acres to Isaac Henry.
8 June 1798 Isaac Henry sold to David Wilson son of James Wilson, part.
8 June 1798 Isaac Henry and James Wilson with wife Elizabeth Wilson sold 70 acres to Arthur Dashiell, on road from Spring Hall to Barren Creek.
1802 Arthur Dashiell willed to son Thomas Dashiell
17 July 1808 David Wilson released to Thomas Dashiell 10 acres that Arthur Dashiell willed to Thomas Dashiell.

DARBYS ADDITION

Patented in 1756 by Walter Darby for 146 acres.
1762 Walter Darby willed to wife Sarah Darby and after death to sons Thomas Darby and William Darby.
1783 tax - Sarah Darby 146 acres- Rewastico 100
1 June 1793 Ralph Moore with with wife Mary Moore (was Mary Darby) sold to Edward Bennett of Sussex Co.Del. 94 acres.
13 Aug. 1793 Ralph Moore with wife Mary Moore sold to Levin Bennett 44 acres.
8 Nov.1793 Sarah Darby, Elizabeth Bennett and Levin Bennett sold 100 acres to John Bennett of Sussex Co.Delaware.
1 Sep.1797 Levin Bennett sold to Ann Robertson, William Robertson,

Samuel Robertson, Elendor Robertson and James Robertson 14 1/2 acres.
12 Sep.1800 Levin Bennett and wife Elizabeth Bennett sold to Lewis Graham 78 5/8 acres of BATCHELLORS CHANCE & DARBYS ADDN.
26 Aug.1803 Edward Bennett of Sussex Co.Del. sold to John Phillips of Somerset Co. 94 acres 26 perches.
13 June 1805 Lewis Graham with wife Sarah Graham sold to Joshua Bennett 79 5/8 acres of BATCHELLORS CHANCE & DARBYS ADDITION.
1827 John Phillips willed to daughter Eleanor Robertson Owens 45 acres.

DARBYS LOTT

Patented in 1762 by William Darby for 100 acres.
Repatented in 1820 by Thomas Darby

DASHIELLS ADDITION

Patented on 7 Apr.1750 by Joseph Dashiell for 25 acres.
1768 Joseph Dashiell willed to grandson John Jones son of Benjamin Jones.
7 Dec.1785 resurveyed to GOOD LUCK by Joseph Dashiell

DASHIELLS AMENDMENT

Patented 1747 by Joseph Dashiell for 321 acres.

DASHIELLS CHANCE

Patented on 5 Dec.1769 Arthur Dashiell for 184 acres a resurvey of 81 acres out of WOODSTOCK and 103 acres of vancant land.
1783 tax - Arthur Dashiell 184 acres - Rewastico 100.

DASHIELLS CONCLUSION

Patented in 1811 by John Dashiell

DASHIELLS FOLLY

Patented on 20 June 1727 by Joseph Dashiell for 108 acres on the south side of the Nanticoke River between Quantico and Wetipquin Creeks.
1783 tax - George Dashiell 108 acres
16 Feb.1802 George Dashiell with wife Elizabeth Dashiell and son Robert Dashiell sold to Ichabod Dashiell 151 1/2 acres of DASHIELLS FOLLY, EASONS CHANCE & SMALL ADDITION.
18 Mar.1805 Ichabod Dashiell with wife Priscilla Dashiell sold to Alexander Stewart 151 1/2 acres, same as above.

DASHIELLS FOLLY

Patented 1805 by John Dashiell for 35 1/2 acres.

DASHIELLS GREEN

Patented 20 June 1782 by John Dashiell for 197 acres, a resurvey of DIXONS GREEN 124 acres sold by Isaac Dixon to John Dashiell.
1783 tax - John Dashiell 75 acres

29 Nov.1798 John Dashiell sold to William Morris 31 acres
25 Oct.1799 William Morris son of Thomas Morris sold to Charles Hammond
23 Dec.1810 William Morris with wife Catherine Morris sold to Charles Hammond, all rights.
1806 DASHIELLS GREEN RENEWED pat. John Dashiell

DASHIELLS LOTT

Patented 10 Oct.1734 George Dashiell for 1740 acres a resurvey out of BENNETTS ADVENTURE.
1739 Col. George Dashiell willed to son Isaac Dashiell and son George Dashiell.
9 May 1748 George Dashiell willed to son Isaac Dashiell 450 acres
12 April 1749 Thomas Marshall guardian of George Dashiell son of Col. George certifies as to condition of DASHIELLS LOTT.
21 Aug 1750 Isaac Dashiell willed to to Louther Dashiell 50 acres out of 450 acres from father George Dashiell.
12 Oct.1752 Isaac Dashiell son of George Dashiell, with wife Henrietta Dashiell sold to Thomas Dashiell son of George Dashiell 400 acres, trade for other lands.
10 Jan 1742 George Dashiell sold to son Clement Dashiell 435 acres
10 Jan 1742 George Dashiell sold to son Louther Dashiell 420 acres
1756 Clement Dashiell willed to son Josiah Dashiell
1765 Louther Dashiell willed to sons Louther Dashiell, William Dashiell and Arthur Dashiell.
1756 Clement Dashiell willed to son Josiah Dashiell
1783 tax - Thomas Dashiell 100 acres, Rewastico 100
1783 tax - Josiah Dashiell 425 acres
1784 Josiah Dashiell willed to wife Henny Dashiell estate, after death to John Jones son of sister Mary Jones, unnamed land.
18 Dec.1789 George Dashiell sold to William McBryde 220 acres.
13 Aug.1791 John Jones father of John Jones devisee of the will of Josiah Dashiell gave to John Jones.
29 May 1791 George Dashiell with wife Rosy Dashiell sold to John Stewart 537 1/2 acres- mortgage.
28 May 1791 William McBryde released mortgage to George Dashiell of 250 acres.
13 Aug.1791 John Jones sold to John Jones his father, all.
6 May 1794 John Holbrook with wife Patience Holbrook sold to Robert Robertson 50 acres.
6 May 1794 Robert Robertson sold 50 acres to John Holbrook.
19 Feb.1800 Dr. Robert Dashiell of Nansemond Co.Va. sold to William Cottman son of Joseph Cottman of Somerset County Md. all rights devised him by Matthias Dashiell.
20 Feb.1800 William Cottman mortgaged to Dr. Robert Dashiell of Va.
11 Dec.1801 Dr. Robert Dashiell with wife Sally Dashiell of Nansemond Co.Va. released mortgage to William Cottman.
20 Oct.1803 Dr. Robert Dashiell with wife Sally Dashiell of Nasamond Co.Va. sold all his lands to William Cottman son of Joseph Cottman.
20 July 1804 William Cottman Jr. with wife Hester Cottman sold to William Cottman Sr. 57 5/8 acres of DASHIELLS LOTT & CHANCE.
26 Feb.1806 Patience Holbrook sold to William Cottman 1/2 acre.
10 Sep.1808 William Malone sold to George Malone 9 acres as William Malone laid off a parcel with pt. GODDARDS FOLLY.

1841 Levin Morris willed to son Warren Jones Morris
1844 Eliza A.F. Denson willed to daughter Annaliza Morris.
1848 George Malone willed real estate to sons Simon Malone and Levi Malone (1850 they are in Trappe District)

DASHIELLS MEADOW

Patented 10 May 1735, a resurvey of PEMBERTON opposite Green Hill Town, for 50 acres by George Dashiell.
1748 George Dashiell willed 50 acres to son Joseph Dashiell.
27 April 1765 Joseph Dashiell sold to John Newman of Som.Co. 50 acres that father George Dashiell bought of William Kibble and John Kibble. Repatented on 9 July 1776 by Capt. Joseph Dashiell of Worc.Co. for 43 acres.
1788 Joseph Dashiell willed to grandson George Dashiell son of George, lands where I live, unnamed.

DASHIELLS MISTAKE

Patented 1765 by Daniel McIntyre for 8 1/2 acres.
1773 Daniel McIntyre willed to wife Elizabeth McIntyre and after death to son William McIntyre
1783 tax - Betty McIntyre 8 1/2 acres- Nanticoke 100.

DASHIELLS PURCHASE

On 17 Feb.1738 Thomas Serman sold part of MEECHES HOPE & YEARS LAND 120 acres, RUNSELL 109 acres and 155 acres vacant land to William Dashiell who repatented for 497 acres.
1745 William Dashiell son of George Dashiell willed to sons James Dashiell and Joseph Dashiell, on the east side of Wetiquin Creek.
1783 tax - William Dashiell Sr. 408 acres.
26 Sep.1806 James Dashiell sold to Doubty Bounds, to settle dispute of boundaries.
26 Apr.1825 Douty Bounds sold 8 1/4 acres to Marcellus Jones.

DASHIELLS REGULATION

Patented 1805 by James Dashiell for 495 acres.
26 Sep.1806 James Dashiell sold to Doubty Bounds, to settle dispute, part.
1868 Daniel J. Dashiell willed to nephew Edgar J. Dashiell 250 acres and to niece Elizabeth White wife of Asa White balance of lands.

DASHIELLS SUCESS

Patented in 1774 by Arthur Dashiell for 224 acres.
6 March 1802 Arthur Dashiell Sr. sold 11 /12 acres to John Byrd.
29 Oct.1803 John Byrd with wife Margaret Byrd sold to John Moore 11 1/2 acres.
1802 Arthur Dashiell willed planation where I live to son Henry Dashiell and balance of lands to son Matthias Dashiell, unnamed.
1804 John Moore willed property to be sold to pay debts. to wife Sarah Moore 1/3rds.

DAUGHTERS DOWRY

see DOUBLE PURCHASE

DAUGHERTYS ADVENTURE

Patented in 1819 by Jesse Dougherty

DAUGHERTYS CONCLUSION

Patented in 1818 by Jesse Dougherty for 246 7/8 acres.

DAVIDS ADDITION

Patented on 18 May 1758 by David Cathell for 50 acres
31 July 1779 Levi Cathell sold to David Cathell 50 acres.

DAVIDS HARDSHIP

Patented on 10 May 1761 by David Cathell for 150 acres
1763 resurveyed by John Cathell for 154 1/2 acres
1764 David Cathell, willed to son John Cathell.
1783 tax - John Cathell 150 acres (CATHELLS HARDSHIP) Wic.100, Worc.Co.
1808 John Cathell willed to eldest son John Cathell with tracts adjacent.

DAVIDS FOLLY

Patented in 1783 by David Cathell

DAVIDS OUTLETT

Patented in 1796 by David Cathell for 237 acres.
1802 David Cathell willed 79 acres to brother John Cathell and balance to be sold
1808 John Cathell willed to son David Cathell tract taken up by David Cathell and willed to me, 80 acres.
18 May 1724 Joshua Cathell sold to Levi Cathell Jr.
23 July 1843 James Cathell sold 29 acres to Jonathan Pollitt.

DAVIDS PRIVILEDGE

Patented 1775 by David Raglin for 30 acres.
20 Mar.1785 David Raglin of Kent Co. Delaware sold to Jacob Morris 30 acres.
15 June 1803 Jacob Morris sold to John Morris son of Joseph Morris, part.
13 Mar.1804 John Morris sold to Jacob Morris son of Joseph Morris, part.

DAVIDS TROUBLE FOR LITTLE

Patented in 1836 by Jonathan Barkley for 412 9/16th acres

DAVIS ADDITION

Patented in 1684 by Samuel Davis for 117 acres.
1756 Samuel Davis willed part to sons Walker Davis and Samuel Davis.
1759 Walker Davis willed to wife Elizabeth Davis and to son James Davis, all lands, unnamed.
1762 resurveyed to SECURITY
18 Oct. 1794 Samuel Davis sold to Edward Hammond, that he swapped with Saul Davis for other land, no acres
28 Oct.1794 Samuel Davis sold to David Cathell part.

DAVIS'S ADVANTAGE

Patented in 1764 by William Turner Davis son of Robert for 189 1/2 acres a resurvey of WILD CAT RIDGE.
2 Nov.1772 William Turner Davis with wife Mary Davis, tailor of Bladen Co. North Carolina sold to Turner Davis, tailor of same
14 Oct.1783 William Turner Davis of North Carolina sold to John Giles of Worcester County Md.
23 Dec.1785 John Giles sold to Hezekiah Davis 27 1/2 acres.

DAVIS CHOICE

Patented in 1732 by John Davis Jr. for 50 acres.
13 Nov.1761 John Davis sold to David Magee 12 acres.
8 July 1762 David Magee resurveyed his part to MAGEES LOTT.
15 Apr.1763 John Davis Sr. sold to Alexander Thomas Russell, near head of the Wicomico River, 38 acres.
2 Sep.1774 Alexander Thomas Russell sold to Price Russell 38 acres.
17 Mar.1777 Price Russell with wife Ann Russell sold to Josiah Russell attorney at law land Alexander Thomas Russell conveyed to him, no name.
1783 tax - Thomas Cox 50 acres, Wic.100, Worc.Co.

DAVIS CHOICE

Patented on 30 Sep.1762 by William Davis for 150 acres.
1767 William Davis willed to daughters Elizabeth Davis, Delitha Davis and Kesiah Davis 150 acres, to share.
1783 tax - James Trader 30 acres- Wic.100 Worc.Co.
1783 tax - William Daley 50 acres.
28 May 1785 William Daley with wife Keziah Daley sold to Boaz Walston 50 acres.
5 Feb.1791 Samuel Taylor with wife Delitha Taylor sold 50 acres to John Parker
16 Apr.1791 Allen Cox and Thomas Cox sold to John Hearn 50 acres
28 June 1800 John Byrd with wife Margaret Byrd sold to John Parker 46 acres.

DAVIS CHOICE

Patented on 8 Oct.1761 by Thomas Davis for 252 acres a resurvey of ISAACS FOLLY.
18 Apr.1759 Thomas Davis gave to John Davis an infant, possessed by dau-in-law Sophia Davis 70 acres.

3 July 1772 Thomas Davis Sr. gave to Thomas Davis Jr. 70 acres.
1775 probably a resurvey by Thomas Davis 650 acres.
1783 tax - Thomas Davis
15 June 1791 Thomas Davis sold part to Benjamin Davis.

DAVIS DISCOVERY

Patented in 1868 by Jesse Davis for 12 acres 5 perches.

DAVIS LOTT

Patented in 1775 by John Davis for 24 3/4 acres
1783 tax - John Davis 25 acres- Wic.100, Worc.Co.
1789 John Davis willed to son Reuben Davis 24 acres.
10 Mar.1798 John Reddish sold to Benjamin Johnson 100 acres.

DAVIS MILL LOTT

Patented on 16 Mar.1757 by Samuel Davis for 66 acres.

DAVIS NECK

Patented on 2 Mar.1722 by Samuel Davis for 150 acres.
Rent Rolls 1666-1723, possessed by Samuel Davis
1756 Samuel Davis willed 150 acres to son James Davis
1783 tax - Samuel Davis 100 acres, Wic.100 Worc.CO.
1787 Samuel Davis willed to daughter Patty Davis.
10 Mar.1798 John Reddish sold to Benjamin Johnson 18 1/2 acres
29 Aug.1794 James Davis with wife Ann Davis sold to Samuel Truitt 18 1/2 acres
8 Jan.1797 Samuel Truitt with wife Nancy Truitt sold to John Reddish 18 1/2 acres
5 Nov.1809 Benjamin Johnson Sr. with wife Phillis Johnson sold to Nathan Jones 18 1/2 acres.

DAVIS OUTLETT

Patented on 22 Feb.1763 by James Davis for 100 acres on a branch of the Wicomico River.
29 Aug.1794 James Davis with wife Ann Davis sold to Samuel Truitt 100 acres.
8 Jan.1797 Samuel Truitt with wife Nancy Truitt sold to John Reddish 100 acres
15 Apr.1805 John Johnson of Benjamin Johnson with wife Nancy Johnson sold to Matthew Jones 15 acres.
5 Nov.1809 Benjamin Johnson Sr. with wife Phillis Johnson sold to Matthew Jones 100 acres.
22 Sep.1806 Abisha Davis sold to Levin Derrickson 50 acres.
1810 Matthew Jones willed to son Purnell Johnson Jones 118 acres.

DAYS ADDITION

Patented 1737 by Day Scott 50 acres.
1753 Day Scott willed to daughter Betty Fortune 50 acres where he lives (no name of land)

DAYS BEGINNING

Patented on 15 May 1688 by Edward Day, for 295 acres.
Rent Rolls 1666-1723, belongs to the heirs of Edward Day, the widow refuses to pay the rent.
April 1708 I Phillip Todd of King & Queen Co.Va. mortgage to John Morse 1/4 pt in Somerset County containing 295 acres.
17 June 1746 Day Scott sold to John Goddard 147 1/2 acres.
1760 John Goddard willed 290 acres, 1/2 to son Francis Lane Goddard on Broad Creek and to son George Goddard other 1/2.
4 July 1775 Francis Lane Goddard sold 294 acres to William Horsey and Isaac Horsey (with all goods and chattels)
1815 Abisha Davis willed to son John B. Davis.

DEANS CHANCE

Patented in 1753 by Charles Dean for 20 acres.
1764 Charles Dean willed land on upper side of Walters Road, unnamed to son James Dean.
1782 Dean Badley willed to daughter Eleanor Parremore my plantation above James Dean, unnamed.
1783 tax - James Dean 10 acres- Rewastico 100
1783 tax - Dean Badley 5 acres
13 Nov.1787 James Dean and Susanna Dean and William Dean of Dorc. Co.Md. sold to Jonathan Waller of Dorc.Co. 15 acres.
4 Jan 1788 Joseph Parremore with wife Eleanor Parremore sold to Jonathan Waller of Dorcester Co.Md., all, no acres mentioned.
16 Oct.1807 William Waller of Washington Co.Ga. sold to Isaac Phillips of Sussex Co.Del. 34 1/2 acres of DEANS CHANCE & ROYAL EXCHANGE.

DEANS DISAPPOINTMENT

Patented in 1793 by Priscilla Waller for 31 3/4 acres.

DEANS FOLLY

Patented in 1800 by Levi Dean for 16 1/2 acres.

DEANS LOTT

Patented in 1753 by Charles Dean for 10 acres.
1764 Charles Dean willed lands, unnamed , to son James Dean
1783 tax - James Dean 10 acres, Rewastico
13 Nov.1787 James Dean and wife Susanna Dean of Dorc.Co.Md. sold to Levi Dean (aka STILLEYS ISLAND)
21 Aug.1795 Levi Dean sold to John Twiford of Dorc. Co.Md. for 5 shillings, 10 acres.

DEANS OUTLETT TO JONES LOT

Patented in 1803 by James Dean for 15 acres.
1805 James Dean willed to negro child Rhoda daughter of Peggy 15 acres bought of Thomas Huffington, no name of land.

DEANS PURCHASE

Patented in 1795 by James Dean for 174 3/4 acres.
26 May 1797 James Dean, merchant sold to George Bennett of Sussex Co.Del. 17 acres on division line between Maryland and Delaware.

DEANS TRAVEL

Patented 1850 by Jesse A.D. Bradley for 3 3/4 acres.

DEANS VENTURE

Resurveyed from ROYAL EXCHANGE patented in 1754 by James Dean 50 acres.
1783 repatented by Charles Dean for 286 acres.
2 May 1799 Charles Dean sold to Levi Dean 189 acres.
1783 tax - Levin Dean, 182 1/2 acres- Rewastico 100
1783 tax - James Dean, 50 acres
25 Jan 1806 Levi Dean with wife Margaret Dean and mother Elizabeth Dean sold to Thomas Badley 189 acres.
24 Jan 1806 Noble Dean of Dorc.Co. Md. sold to Thomas Badley his interest with WOLCOTTS MANOR.
1816 Thomas Badley willed lands to sons John Badley, William Badley and Thomas Badley, unnamed.

DEAR HARBOUR

Patented in 1768 by Stanton Adkins for 50 acres
Resurveyed 8 Oct.1764 Stanton Adkins to 535 acres
24 Aug.1770 I Stanton Adkins lease to father-in-law Joseph Holloway and wife Priscilla Holloway 100 acres.
Repatented in 1782 by Stanton Adkins 815 3/4.
1783 tax- Stephen Adkins 167 1/2 acres
1783 tax- Middleton Adkins 143 acres
1783 tax- Nimrod Adkins 20 acres
1783 tax- William Adkins 39 acres
1783 tax- Hunter Adkins 30 1/2 acres
1783 tax- Joseph Holloway 100 acres
7 Sep.1784 Stanton Adkins sold to Zachariah Parsons 197 acres
5 Sep.1795 Joseph Adkins with wife Sarah Adkins sold to Nimrod Adkins 100 acres DEAR HAROUR & HOG QUARTER.
4 Mar.1797 Nimrod Adkins, Stanton Adkins, Milby Adkins, Ayres Parker, Unice Parker and David Adkins sold to William Adkins. Came Hannah Adkins widow of Stanton Akins, relinquished dower rights.
1790 Stanton Adkins willed to son Nimrod Adkins 100 acres and to son Stanton Adkins 100 acres, unnamed. land.
26 Mar.1804 William Adkins sold to Milby Adkins 7 1/2 acres
26 Mar.1804 Milby Adkins sold to William Adkins 29 3/4 acres.
1835 Nimrod Adkins willed mill lot to be sold by son Elijah Adkins, land unnamed.

DEAR LOTT

Patented on 10 May 1676 by William Elgate for 96 acres.
1725 William Elgate willed residue of land to be divided between daughters Sarah Byrd, Kathryn Driskell, Rebecca Bready and Ann Hall,

no name.
15 Sep.1753 Benjamin Venables, Elgate Hitch, Thomas Byrd, Ann Hall, Rebecca Evans, Moses Driskell, sold to Jonathan Stott 96 acres with SUPPLY, BLACKWATER, WHAT YOU PLEASE.
10 Feb.1762 Jonathan Stott sold to Christopher Piper 96 acres.
5 Aug.1762 Christopher Piper and wife wife Mary Piper sold to Ezekiel James 25 acres.
13 Jan 1767 Christopher Piper sold to Esme Bayley of Worc.Co. all except that part conveyed to Ezekiel James.
1799 Esme Bayley willed plantation, unnamed to son Thomas Bayley. This land not named.

DEAR PURCHASE

Patented in 1759 by Elisha Parker for 50 acres.
13 Sep.1763 Elisha Parker sold to Isaac Phillips 50 acres, in Wicomico Forrest.
1821 William Parsons willed to wife Nancy Parsons 50 acres.

DEAR PASTURE

Patented on 4 July 1728 by Robert Givans for 100 acres
1735 Robert Givans of Stepney Parish willed to son Robert, at Nanticoke River.
6 Aug.1763 Ephraim King apointed to resurvey lands of William Givans orphan son of Robert Givans deceased.
22 Mar.1770 William Givans s/o Robert Givans, sold to John Phillips 100 acres.
24 Oct.1774 John Phillips sold to Thomas Lloyd 25 acres for 5 shillings.
1783 tax - William Lloyd 25 acres
1783 tax - Jacob Rhoads, 75 acres, Rewastico 100.
5 June 1783 John Phillips sold to Jacob Rhoads 75 acres.

DEBTFORD

Patented on 10 March 1679 by William Stevens who assigned to John Winder for 110 acres.
Rent Rolls 1666-1723, possessed by John Winder son of John Winder.
Resurveyed in 1768 by Matthew Cannon for 610 acres
1764 Matthew Cannon and wife Mary Cannon sold to George Dashiell Sr. for 5 shillings 23 1/2 acres.
1768 George Dashiell willed to granddaughter Peggy Nicholson daughter of Joseph Nicholson lands Matthew Cannon deeded me, part of DEBTFORD and WHITTYS INVENTION.
1785 Matthew Cannon willed to son Thomas Cannon.
1783 tax - Matthew Cannon 110 acres.
15 Jan 1801 Thomas Cannon sold to William Mezick 9 acres.
15 June 1802 Mary Cannon sold all interest to Thomas Cannon.
1807 Thomas Cannon willed to son Matthew lands entailed me by my father Matthew Cannon, not named.
1818 William Mezick willed to daughter Martha Washington Handy Mezick.

DEFENSE

Patented in 1794 by Jacob Adams for 70 acres.

DEFIANCE

Patented in 1751 by Thomas Fletcher for 289 acres.

DELIGHT

Patented on 20 Dec.1741 by Richard Crockett for 50 acres.
14 Dec.1743 Richard Crockett of Som.Co.with wife Elizabeth Crockett sold to Adam Muir of Dorc.Co. Md.
1765 Richard Crockett willed to wife Elizabeth Crockett CROCKETTS DELIGHT on Gravely branch.

DELIGHT

Patented in 1725 by Christopher Nutter for 383 acres in Rewastico 100.
6 Mar.1752 George Handy and wife Sarah Handy former relic of Christopher Nutter, sold to John Handy 194 acres.
1756 John Handy willed to wife Ann Handy 1/3rds, and to son Thomas Handy lands where I live adjacent William Nutter, no name.
10 Sep.1759 Ephraim King and wife Ann King conveyed to Samuel King, prop. that became right of Ann Handy by the death of her brother Christopher Nutter that was not heretofore conveyed by Ann to her son Thomas Handy.
1783 William Nutter willed to sons William and Charles Nutter, lands unnamed.
1783 tax - Samuel King 256 acres
1783 tax - William Nutter Sr. 127 1/4 acres.
29 May 1793 William Nutter to Charles Nutter- division of lands DELIGHT aka KINGSTON.
22 Sep.1800 William Bond with wife Priscilla Bond sold 30 aces to John Nelson.
26 Apr.1805 Priscilla Bond sold to Levin Farrington, devised by death of her father, mother and brothers, Ephraim King or Samuel King.
24 Aug.1806 Charles Nutter with wife Louisa Nutter sold part to Henry E. Bayley.
21 Oct.1808 Henry E. Bayley with wife Sarah Bayley sold part to Thomas Mitchell.
1808 Levin Farrington willed lands to daughters Emmy Farrington and Charlotte Farrington, no name.
14 May 1810 Thomas Winder and wife Harriett Winder sold to Henry E. Bayley and Samuel Vincent, willed by Levin Farrington to daughters, no name.
25 Aug.1841 Henry Gale and Susan Gale sold to James Bounds 33 acres
10 Nov.1841 John Austin and wife Jane Austin sold to James Bounds 112 acres lands belonging to Francis D. Nelson and Henry Gale with MONMOUTH & CHELSEA.

DENNIS ADDITION

Patented on 26 Jan.1721 by John Caldwell and assigned to Dennis Driscoll for 100 acres.

Rent Rolls 1666-1723, possessed by Dennis Driscoll
1720 Dennis Driscoll willed to son Dennis 100 acres of ADDITION
17 Mar.1740 Dennis Driskell sold to Moses Gordey 50 acres, part.
7 Nov.1759 Moses Gordy Sr. sold to Matthias Christopher 50 acres.
2 Apr.1761 James Driskell s/o Dennis Driskell sold to Matthias Christopher (confirmation of last deed.)
1783 tax - Matthias Christopher 100 acres, Wic.100 Worc.Co.
19 July 1796 Levin Pollitt, sheriff per judgement against Matthias Christopher sold to Thomas Robertson of Sussex Co. Delaware 100 acres

DENNIS'S CHOICE

Patented on 31 May 1763 by Affradozy Dennis for 18 acres.
6 Mar.1793 Annanias Dennis sold to James Dennis 18 acres.

DENN PARK

Patented 1760 Thomas Lloyd for 36 acres in Rewastico 100.
1783 tax - William Lloyd Jr. 36 acres.

DENN TOWN LOTT

Patented by Thomas Lloyd for 51 acres in Rewastico 100
1768 second patent by Thomas Lloyd for 108 1/2 acres.
1783 tax - William Lloyd 18 1/2 acres.
1810 William Lloyd willed lands to daughter Peggy Lloyd, unnamed.

DENWOODS DEN

Patented on 16 Dec.1681 by Levin Denwood for 300 acres near head of Wicomico River.
Rent Rolls 1666-1723, possessed by Levin Denwood for 150 acres and James Hill for 150 acres.
12 Feb.1729 Thomas Hill sold to Samuel Tull 150 acres that Levin Denwood willed to Thomas Hill, for 5 shillings.
25 Feb.1734 Thomas Denwood and George Denwood sold to Levin Gale 150 acres that Levin Denwood willed to afsd.
7 Sep.1737 Samuel Tull sold to Levin Gale his part.
23 Mar.1753 George Gale sold 300 acres to Joseph Gillis that Levin Gale inherited and willed to be sold by George Gale, John Gale, Matthias Gale and daughter Leah Gale. John and Matthias Gale are now dead and Leah Gale is an infant.
20 Aug.1760 Joseph Gillis sold to Nehemiah Hitch 229 acres.
20 Aug.1760 Joseph Gillis sold to Isaac Vinson 292 1/2 acres.
17 Nov.1762 Nehemiah Hitch sold to Nathan Culver 60 acres (this part resurveyed to PEACE AND QUIETNESS)
1774 Nehemiah Hitch willed to son Thomas Hitch 40 acres and to wife Sarah Hitch 1/2 of manor planation and then to son Elias Hitch, all lands unnamed.
1783 tax - Benjamin Byrd 50 acres
1783 tax - Thomas Hitch Sr. 98 1/2 acres.
1783 tax - Elias Hitch 117 1/2 acres.
1783 tax - Isaac Wilson 220 1/2 acres.
5 June 1786 Isaac Vinson sold 50 acres to Benjamin Byrd.
1792 Benjamin Byrd willed 50 acres to son Thomas Byrd.

1805 Isaac Vincent willed 100 acres to Isaac Vincent of Elijah Vincent.
1821 Thomas Byrd willed to son Benjamin Harvey Byrd.
1827 William Hitch willed to son Marsalas B. Hitch 20 acres and 20 acres unnamed. to son Andrew Elliot Hitch.

DESART

Patented 21 May 1689 by John Caldwell for 250 acres
Rent Rolls 1666-1723, possessed by John Caldwell.
1742 John Caldwell willed to Joshua Caldwell, part.
27 Sep.1744 Robert Caldwell sold to Joseph Ennals of Dorc.Co. several tracts DESERT, CALDWELLS LOTT where in the mill of Robert Caldwell stands, taken up by John Caldwell father of Robert Caldwell.
17 Jan 1755 William Kinney gave to son Isaac Kinney 50 acres, on branch of Broad Creek.
3 Nov.1759 Joshua Caldwell of Worc.Co. sold to William Kinney per his fathers will 120 acres.
17 Mar.1768 William Kinney sold 100 acres to Joshua Kinney.
21 Dec.1771 Elverton Caldwell sold to Isaac Kinney 140 acres
1 May 1776 Sussex Co.Delaware land warrants by Isaac Kinney.

DICKERSONS FANCY

Patented in 1763 by Teague Dickerson for 25 acres in Nanticoke 100.
1764 Teague Dickerson willed land on Broad Creek to grandson Isaac Dickerson son of Levi Dickerson.
1783 tax - John Dougherty 25 acres (married Leah Dickerson)
3 Aug.1799 Isaac Dickerson sold to Solomon Winright 25 acres.
1799 Solomon Winright willed to son Levin Winright plantation, unnamed.

DICKINSONS VENTURE

Patented in 1765 by John Dickenson for 36 acres.

DIKES CHOICE

Patented on 29 Jan.1762 by Daniel Dykes for 100 acres
18 Oct.1765 Daniel Dykes sold 100 acres to Samuel Davis
1774 Samuel Davis willed to son Seymore Davis and daughter Sarah Davis and wife Sarah Davis, lands unnamed.
1783 tax - Col. Joseph Dashiell Wic.100 Worc.Co.
4 Nov.1786 Saul Davis sold to Joseph Dashiell, as Samuel Davis died leaving daughters Mary Davis and Sarah Davis and to son Powell who is since dead without issue.
22 Oct.1790 Zadock Sturgis, sheriff, sold to Thomas Harwood of Annapolis per judgement against Benjamin F.A. C. Dashiell s/o Joseph Dashiell, except dower right of Susanna Dashiell widow of Joseph.
18 Dec.1790 Thomas Harwood of Annapolis with wife Margaret Harwood sold to Purnell Johnson, part.
11 Feb.1791 Purnell Johnson sold part to Thomas Johnson.
14 Sep.1792 Purnell Johnson, Elijah Johnson and William Hearn sold to Benjamin Johnson.

DIKES FIRST ATTEMPT

Patented 1783 by Stephen Dykes for 50 acres
1783 tax - Stephen Dykes 50 acres, Wic.100 Worc.Co.
27 Apr.1797 Peter Gordy, Elisha Parker with wife Eleanor Parker, Samuel Parker with wife Hetty, Benjamin Hearn son of Samuel Hearn, William Hearn of Sussex Co.Delaware with wife Polly Hearn sold rights to William Gordy.

DISCOVERY

Patented on 18 May 1688 by James Weatherly for 160 acres.
Rent Rolls 1666-1723, possessed by James Weatherly
14 Sep.1695 James Weatherly sold to Robert Bowditch with adj. ACWORTHS FOLLY.
1710/15 Robert Bowditch willed to wife Ann Bowditch and then to daughters Joanna Bowditch and Rebecca Clark and heirs, unnamed land.
18 Feb.1751 triparte agreement- Levin Hitch son of Rebecca Hitch formerly Rebecca Clark, and Mary Storey of Dorc.Co. spinster and only surviving daughter of her mother Joanna Storey, formerly Joanna Clarke, sold to Robert Twilley and John Kellum the younger, 160 acres.
9 Dec.1803 Priscilla Kennedy sold 160 acres to John Kellum.

DISCOVERY

Patented on 29 Sep.1764, a resurvey from WOLF TRAP NECK, LOCUST RIDGE and vacant land, by Jesse Dashiell for 406 acres.(aka DASHIELLS DISCOVERY)
17 Aug.1768 Jesse Dashiell sold to Winder Dashiell.
1773 Jesse Dashiell willed to son Benjamin Dashiell (WOLF TRAP NECK.)
1783 tax - John Dashiell 12 acres- Nanticoke 100
1783 tax - James Dashiell 200 acres
1783 tax - Susannah Dashiell 100 acres
1783 tax - Samuel Willin 76 acres
1783 tax - Isaac Hopkins 2 1/2 acres.
1779 Winder Dashiell willed lands to son John Dashiell.
1778 Jesse Dashiell willed to wife Susannah Dashiell and daughters, then to sons James Dashiell, Benjamin Dashiell and Isaac Dashiell.
1785 John Dashiell of Winder Dashiell resurveyed 6 1/2 acres to CONTENTION.
29 June 1787 John Dashiell s/o Winder Dashiell, with wife Nancy Dashiell, and Ann Dashiell mother of John sold to Thomas Smith 164 acres of CONCLUSION & DISCOVERY.
25 Aug.1791 James Dashiell of Jesse Dashiell sold to Isaac Hopkins 13 acres and another deed of same date for 82 acres.
2 May 1810 Matthias Dashiell Hopkins with wife Eleanor Hopkins sold to Jesse Dashiell 45 1/4 acres.

DISCOVERY

Patented in 1772 by Train Acworth for 75 acres in Rewastico 100
1783 tax - Train Acworth 75 acres
1791 Train Acworth willed to wife Priscilla Acworth 1/3rd and to son Beaucham Acworth.

DISCOVERY

Patented on 17 Apr.1760 for 25 acres.
Repatented on 21 Oct.1768 by Elijah Tindell son of Charles Tindell, 50 acres.
1761 Charles Tindell willed to son Charles Tindell 22 acres.

DISCOVERY

Patented in 1749 by John Williams for 15 1/2 acres.

DISCOVERY IN TIME

Patented in 1773 by Henry Lowe.

DISHAROONS ADVENTURE

Patented in 1772 by George Disharoon for 123 1/2 acres.
28 Apr.1785 Gabriel Duvall comissioner to sell confiscated property sold to George Disharoon of Worc.Co. 110 1/2 acres, part in Worc.Co.
11 Apr.1795 Stephen Disharoon of Worc.Co. sold to John Stewart 1 1/2 acres(purchased under confiscated property by George Disharoon father of Stephen Disharoon.)
20 Mar.1802 Joshua Morris of Worc.Co. sold to Eben Disharoon 3/8 acres.
1815 Eben Disharoon willed to son Francis Disharoon 1 acre adj. Kirk Gunby that he got from Joshua Morris, unnamed.

DISHAROONS CHOICE

Patented in 1861 by Amelia J. Disharoon for 43 acres, 2 rods, 37 perches.

DISPUTE

Patented in 1783 by John Robertson for 92 acres in Rewastico 100.
1783 tax- John Robertson Jr. 92 acres.
24 Oct.1794 John Robertson sold to Spencer Walker of Sussex Co. Del. 80 acres.
1799 John Robertson willed to son James Robertson.

DISPUTE

Patented 1816 by Levin Dorman for 2 1/4 acres.

DISPUTE

Patented 1858 by Isaac Kennerly for 19 acres.
(in 1850 he is in Barren Creek District.)

DIXONS CHANCE

Patented on 17 Feb 1762 by Isaac Dixon for 250 acres

DIXONS GOOD LUCK

Patented in 1762 by Isaac Dixon for 250 acres
8 June 1768 Isaac Dixon with wife Frances Dixon sold to Nathaniel Dixon 250 acres.
1 June 1798 Nathaniel Dixon mortgaged to James B. Robins

DIXONS GREEN

Patented on 24 Mar.1772 by Isaac Dixon for 641 acres.
15 May 1772 Isaac Dixon with wife Frances Dixon sold to Nathaniel Dixon 57 acres.
15 May 1772 Isaac Dixon with wife Frances Dixon sold to Samuel Dixon 293 acres.
8 June 1773 Isaac Dixon with wife Frances Todd Dixon sold to Outerbridge Dixon 150 acres.
9 May 1777 Isaac Dixon sold 140 acres to John Dashiell
20 Dec.1779 William Dixon sold to Ambrose Dixon Jr. 293 acres.
20 June 1782 Isaac Dixon sold 124 acres to John Dashiell who resurveyed to DASHIELLS GREEN. 140 acres was a defiency of 16 acres in original tract.
1783 tax - Nathaniel Dixon 57 acres. Wic.100 Worc.Co.
1783 tax - Ambrose Dixon 293 acres
1783 tax - Outerbridge Dixon 150 acres
1783 tax - John Dashiell 140 acres.
9 March 1791 Outerbridge Dixon sold to George Parsons 150 acres
1792 Ambrose Dixon willed to son William Dixon lands unnamed, after death to grandson William Dashiell Dixon
22 Nov.1794 William Morris sold to Eli Showell 10 acres
1 June 1798 Nathaniel Dixon mortgaged to James B. Robins.
17 Jan. 1801 Nathaniel Dixon sold to George Parsons 5 acres
12 Mar.1806 Eli Showell of Kent Co.Delaware with wife Sarah Showell sold to Hezekiah D. Shockley, rights.
1812 Nathaniel Dixon willed all lands to son Nathaniel, not named.
1842 Joshua Carey willed to son Henry M. Carey 80 acres and after death to grandson William Dashiell Dixon.

DIXONS HARD LUCK

Patented on 5 Sep.1752 by Risdon Dixon for 150 acres.

DIXONS LUCK

Patented in 1816 by Huett N. Dixon for 217 1/4 acres.

DOE BETTER

Patented on 20 Aug.1670 by Thomas Gillis 200 acres.
14 March 1676 Thomas Gillis sold to Thomas Humphries 50 acres
15 May 1710 John Gillis s/o Thomas sold to Robert Crouch.
21 Mar.1746 John Crouch with wife Elizabeth Crouch sold 150 acres to Joshua Turpin. Robert Crouch died and left to sons Robert and John. Robert died without issue so John Crouch became heir at law.
1764 resurveyed by Joshua Turpin.

12 Aug.1774 Joshua Turpin, joiner with wife Grace Turpin sold 160 acres to Hiram Reddish, part.
25 Sep.1773 Adam Carlysle of Cumberland Co. Great Britain son of Alexander Carlysle sold 50 acres to Josiah Polk, conveyed by Thomas Humphries to William Carlylse (with Hopewell)
1773 Francis Chattam willed to son John Chattam
1783 tax - Josiah Polk
1783 tax - James Anderson 13 1/2 acres
1783 tax - John Chattam 2 1/2 acres
1783 tax - Hiram Reddish 160 1/2 acres
1784 Josiah Polk willed to brother James Polk
2 May 1785 Thomas Humphries sold to Alexander Carlylse 50 acres
1795 James Polk willed to wife Nancy Polk
10 Apr.1798 John Reddish with wife Rebecca Reddish sold to John Reddish 160 1/2 acres.
3 Nov.1806 Richard Ingersol and Richard Bennett sold to Benjamin Johnson Sr. of Worc.Co. all interest with CASTLE HAVEN, PLAIN DEALING.
24 Sep.1808 John Reddish of Worc.Co. sold 160 1/2 acres to Benjamin Johnson.

DOES HARBOUR

Patented in 1794 by Stephen Townsend for 11 acres.

DOES PARK

Patented on 14 Oct.1765 by Andrew Smith for 50 acres.
2 Dec.1774 Andrew Smith with wife Elizabeth Smith sold to Elijah Hearn 50 acres, in Wicomico Forrest.
1783 tax - Elijah Hearn 50 acres, Wic.100 Worc.Co.
1 Dec.1791 Elijah Hearn sold to George Parker 50 acres
24 Sep.1808 George Parker sold part to Joshua Trader

DOGS DOWN BOTTOM

Patented on 13 Nov.1685 by Phoenix Hall for 200 acres.
Rent Rolls 1666-1723 possessed by Phoenix Hall
1730 William Hill willed to son James Hill
5 Nov.1747 James Hill sold 75 acres to Moses Smith at head of the Wicomico River.
5 May 1758 resurveyed to SMITHS DISCOVERY.

DOGWOOD POINT

Patented on 22 Sep.1763 by William Bassett for 41 acres.
1795 William Bassitt willed to son John Bassett
2 Feb.1799 John Bassett sold to James McLaughlin Duncan that William Basset willed to daughter Alice Bassett, reversion. 45 acres.
1804 John Bassett willed to daughter Sophia Parsons (wife of George Parsons) 41 acres, on north side of Savanah branch.
1848 Henry J. Adkins willed to grandson William H. Adkins son of Ephraim Adkins.

DOGWOOD RIDGE

Patented in 1773 by William Bethards for 50 acres.

1783 tax - William Bethards of William, Acquango 100
1823 William Bethards willed 50 acres to daughter Mary Bethards.

DONOHOES CONCLUSION

Patented 1817 by Joshua Donoho for 340 acres.

DONNIGALL

Patented on 17 Oct.1696 by Andrew Spear for 200 acres
Rent Rolls 1666-1723, possessed by Andrew Spear
20 June 1746 Thomas Spear sold 70 acres to Levin Fletcher. (Henry Spear eldest son of Andrew did not devise so became right of Thomas Spear eldest son of the eldest son of Henry Spear.)
16 Mar.1753 Henry Spear s/o Andrew sold to son Jacob Spear 130 acres at Barren Creek for 5 shillings.
1758 Henry Spear willed to son Henry Spear 200 acres.
10 June 1758 James Polk gave to son Joshua Polk 200 acres of DONNIGALL AND MOANIN.
26 Jan.1770 Jacob Spear and wife Elizabeth Spear and Andrew Spear with wife Betty Spear of Worc.Co. sold to Capt. Charles Dashiell. (Pat.by Andrew Spear grandfather of Andrew and Jacob sons of Henry)
20 Mar.1770 Andrew Spear of Worc.Co. sold 100 acres to Levin Fletcher.
1783 tax - Levin Fletcher (183 a. resurv. to Crooked Chance.)
1783 tax - Charles Dashiell 130 acres.
19 Nov.1791 Levin Fletcher Sr. with wife Betty Fletcher sold to Arthur Dashiell his rights with CROOKED CHANCE and WOOLF PITT HILL.
1835 ADDITION TO DONNIGALL patented by Edward Fowler for 13 7/8 acres.

DORMANS CHANCE

Patented on 5 Sep.1720 by Matthew Dorman on the south side of the Wicomico River, south side of Gordon branch on east fork of the River, for 100 acres.
2 May 1727 Matthew Dorman with wife Frances Dorman sold 100 acres to John Dorman.
Resurveyed 19 March 1755 by John Dorman, 100 acres.
14 Mar.1755 John Dorman gave to son John Dorman 100 acres.
3 Aug.1763 John Dorman sold to George Maglamery 50 acres.
3 Aug.1762 John Dorman sold to Isaac Shockley 50 acres.
11 Feb.1759 Isaac Shockley sold to James Magee 50 acres with LONG ACRE.
4 May 1771 Geoge Maglamery and William Winder sold to Samuel Ingersol 50 acres.
1783 tax - Rueben Magee 100 acres, Wicomico 100.

DORMANS DELIGHT

Patented on 5 Dec.1670 by John Dorman for 300 acres.
12 Mar.1675 John Dorman sold to Thomas Purnell
3 Feb.1678 Thomas Purnell with wife Sarah sold to Christopher Nutter.
Rent Rolls 1666-1723, possessed by Christopher Nutter 150 acres.
Matthew Nutter 150 acres.
14 July 1700 John Nutter of Sussex Co.Del. appointed Robert Jones attorney to convey lands.

3 Oct.1720 Robert Jones attorney of John Nutter sold to Matthew Nutter part. If Matthew has no heirs lands to go to his brother John Huett Nutter.
3 Oct.1720 Robert Jones attorney sold 150 ares to Christopher Nutter.
3 Oct.1720 Robert Jones attorney for John Nutter sold to John Huett Nutter part.
1703 Christopher Nutter willed all land, unnamed, to sons Christopher and Matthew Nutter.
1728 Christopher Nutter willed lands to sons Christopher and William Nutter.
16 Apr.1736 Matthew Nutter of Quantico sold to John Huett Nutter 205 acres of SHILES CHOICE, DORMANS DELIGHT & NUTTERS ADVENTURE
23 Mar.1752 Huett Nutter, mariner, late of Som.Co. but now of London son of Huett deceased who was s/o Matthew Nutter sold to Henry Lowe 400 acres devised Huett by his brother Charles Nutter.
24 Mar.1752 Huett Nutter of London sold to Day Scott, John Shiles and Richard Waters 400 acres occupied now by Robert Handy.
24 Mar.1752 triparte agreement, Huett Nutter with Henry Lowe and Richard Waters for 100 acres.
22 Mar.1755 Huett Nutter sold to Henry Lowe Jr. lands devised to John Nutter brother of Huett by his father John Nutter, unnamed land.
1761 Henry Lowe willed to Huett Nutter.
11 Mar.1774 Henry Lowe with wife Esther Lowe sold to John Waters late of Calvert Co. but now of Somerset, from father Henry Lowe.
24 Mar.1774 Thomas Smith of Sussex Co.Del. sold to John Waters. Thomas Smith heir of John Nutter sold 1/2 of all land in Nutters Neck SHILES CHOICE, NUTTERS ADVENTURE, DORMANS DELIGHT.
1783 tax - William Nutter Sr. 50 acres, Nanticoke 100.
1783 tax - John Waters 250 acres.
1784 John Waters willed to daughter Mary King 200 acres on n/w fork of Nanticoke River, unnamed. and dwelling plantation to wife Elizabeth Waters and then to son Francis Hutchins Waters.
31 Mar.1787 Francis Hutchins Waters sold to John Gale, land that John Waters father of Francis willed, plantation in Quantico Ck. unnamed.
29 Aug.1793 Charles Nutter and William Nutter divided lands.
27 Aug.1806 Henry E. Bayley and wife Sarah Bayley sold to Charles N. Nutter.

DORMANS IMPROVEMENT SECURED

Patented on 18 March 1746 by Thomas Gillis for 40 acres.
18 June 1755 Thomas Gillis sold 40 acres to Nicholas Evans.
1783 tax - John Evans of Nicholas, 40 acres, Nanticoke 100.

DORMANS INLET

Patented in 1842 by Matthias Dorman for 10 acres.
1850 he is in Quantico District.

DOUBLE PURCHASE

Patented in 1740 by William English for 100 acres.

DOUBLE PURCHASE

Patented on 6 July 1762 by Benjamin Christopher and Joseph Christopher

for 50 acres in Wicomico Forrest.
5 Feb.1767 Joseph Christopher with wife Hannah Christopher and Benjamin Christopher with wife Elizabeth Christopher sold to William Parsons 50 acres.
1783 tax - William Parsons, 50 acres, Wic.100 Worc.Co.
1792 William Parsons willed part to son Samuel Parsons and part to son William Parsons.
2 Jan.1809 Samuel Parsons son of William Parsons sold rights to William Parsons of William.

DOUBT NOT REMOVED

6 Sep.1783 Nathaniel Ramsey comissioner to sell confiscated land sold to Rachel Chambers 185 1/2 acres on the south side of the Wicomico River.
1800 Rachel Chambers willed dwelling plantation, unnamed, to daughter Peggy Chambers.

DOUGHTYS LOTT

Patented on 8 Apr.1674 by Stephen Cannon for 150 acres on the south side of Wetipquin Creek.
5 Nov.1678 Stephen Cannon with wife Judith Cannon sold to Peter Douty
Rent Rolls 1666-1723, possessed by William Winright and co-heirs of Stephen Cannon 150 acres, Peter Douty 100 acres.
(Peter Douty married Frances Cannon daughter of Stephen Cannon)
1709 Peter Douty willed 150 acres to Henry Dashiell son of Thomas Dashiell.
1 Jan 1728 Henry Dashiell with wife Alice Dashiell sold 150 acres to Robert Collier.
1756 Robert Collier willed to wife Ann Collier. This land not mentioned in the will.
1783 tax - Betty Handy 26 1/4 acres- Nanticoke 100.

DOUGHTYS MISFORTUNE

Patented in 1744 by Douty Collier for 41 1/2 acres in Nanticoke 100.
1775 Douty Collier willed to daughter Betty Collier.
1774 George Collier willed to son Robert Collier 12 1/2 acres, after death to grandson Ebenezer Collier son of George Collier.
1783 tax - Robert Collier Jr. 12 1/2 acres
1783 tax - Elizabeth Handy 28 1/2 acres
6 Dec.1785 Douty Bounds sold to William Bounds and wife Mary Bounds, 4 1/2 acres.
6 Dec.1785 William Bounds and wife Mary Bounds sold to Douty Bounds 4 1/2 acres.
6 Dec.1785 William Bounds and wife Mary Bounds sold to Solomon Winright 4 1/2 acres.
26 Mar.1784 Solomon Winright with wife Bridget Winright sold to Betty Handy, with tract PARIS
7 June 1795 John Crockett sold 8 acres to Elizabeth Handy.
27 June 1795 Solomon Winright, Levin Winright, Elizabeth Handy, William Bounds and wife Mary Bounds sold to John Crockett PARIS & DOUGHTYS MISFORTUNE which said tract was devised to Ann Collier by the will of Peter Douy, 8a acres.
27 July 1799 George Handy sold to George Collier 7 3/8 acres.

22 Aug.1808 George Collier with wife Martha Collier sold to Matthias Dashiell Hopkins 7 3/8 acres.
5 Nov.1808 Matthias D. Hopkins with wife Eleanor Hopkins sold to James Walter 7 3/8 acres.
1827 James Walter willed to daughter Ann Maria Dorothy Walter, part.

DOVER

Patented in 1780 by William Venables for 50 acres.
5 June 1787 John Venables sold to Saul Davis 50 acres

DOWGATE

Patented 17 July 1679 by John Rixon for 200 acres.
Rent Rolls 1666-1723, possessed by David Shehee who purchased of Rixon's heirs.
1729 David Shehee willed estate to wife Sarah Shehee and her children David Shehee and Margaret Shehee.
1744 John Haywood willed to wife Sarah Haywood.
5 Nov.1748 William Toadvine of Worc Co. and wife Miriam Toadvine (formerly Miriam Watts daughter of John Watts and Ann Watts) and Isaac Tull, carpenter with wife Winifred Tull (formerly Winifred Watts d/o John Watts) sold to Henry Lowe 200 acres, with SARAHS NECK purchaed by John Watts of James Caldwell.
2 Jan 1772 Henry Lowes sold 50 acres to William Kennerly.
15 Oct.1792 The Honorable Alexander Contee Hanson, chancellor of the state of Maryland, sold to Willen McBryde 31 1/2 acres late property of William Kennerly.
23 June 1804 Tubman Lowe, heir of Henry Lowe sold 150 acres to William Anderson.
1 March 1806 William Anderson sold 28 acres to Henry Banks.
10 Sep.1808 William Anderson released mortgage to George Wilson 140 acres.
27 Dec.1809 James Ritchie as trustee to sell land of William McBryde sold part to Samuel Hilman of Worc.Co.

DOWNS CHANCE

Patented on 11 May 1689 by Robert Downs for 62 acres on Quantico Creek.
5 Sep.1719 Robert Downs Jr. s/o Robert sold to Christopher Dashiell 62 acres.
17 Oct.1752 William Owens with wife Betty Owens and John Nicholson with wife Mary Nicholson (wives are coheirs of Christopher Dashiell) sold to Henry Richards 62 acres.
10 Sep.1754 Henry Richards with wife Elizabeth Richards sold to John Jones 62 acres.
27 Mar.1769 James Jones son of John Jones, with wife Prisey Jones sold to Henry Lowe 60 acres.
11 Mar.1774 Henry Lowe s/o Henry, with wife Esther Lowe sold to John Waters late of Calvert Co. but now of Somerset County.
1783 tax - John Waters 60 acres, Rewastico 100.
1784 John Waters willed to wife Elizabeth Waters, dwelling planation and to daughter Mary King, lands, unnamed.

DOWNS CHANCE

Patented on 22 Nov.1760 by Jacob Downs for 50 acres
4 Mar.1752 Robert Downs sold to Phillip Wingate 100 acres on the Nanticoke River.
8 Aug.1766 Jacob Downs sold to John Wingate, all, no acres given.
23 Apr.1777 Sussex Co. Del. land warrants, that was patented by Jacob Downs, now patented by Shadrack Short.
26 Mar.1776 Sussex Co.Del. warrants DOWNS CHANCE INCLUDED 291 acres by John Wingate.
1849 Robert Downs willed to son John Downs (in 1850 he is in the 4th district of Worc.Co. so this could be other lands.)

DRISKILLS FOLLY (aka DUSKYS FOLLY)

Patented 1746 by Jonathan Cathell for 50 acres.
1762 resurvey, (original 50 acres only 48 acres) added 1623 acres.
5 Oct.1762 Jonathan Cathell resurveyed 50 acres to SAFEGUARD
1772 Jonathan Cathell willed to son Thomas Cathell.
1783 tax- David Cathell 50 acres.
1815 Levi Cathell willed to sons Clement Cathell, William Cathell, Haste Cathell, Levi Cathell.

DRISKILLS HAZZARD

Patented on 4 Aug.1764 by Moses Driskell for 388 acres a resurvey of PHILLIPS FOLLY in Wicomico forrest.
11 July 1803 Robert Fergusson of Charles Co. Maryland sold to Benjamin Johnson of Worc.Co. Md. that Moses Driskill sold to Thomas Carbury and sold by Thomas to Robert Fergusson 388 acres.
21 Feb.1807 Benjamin Johnson Sr. sold to John Reddish

DRISKILLS INDUSTRY

Patented on 6 Dec.1765 by William Driskell for 317 acres a resurvey of ADDITION TO EXCHANGE in Wicomico Forrest..
2 Mar.1772 Moses Driskell with wife Elizabeth Driskell sold to Thomas Carberry of Somerset Co.,merchant 388 acres a resurvey.
1783 tax - Stephen Stanford, Wic.100, Worc.Co.
8 Apr.1786 Stephen Stanford with wife Judah Stanford and Robert Stanford with wife Lotty Stanford, Harris Austin with wife Sarah Austin sold to Jesse Fooks 317 acres.
17 Feb.1792 Robert Stanford of Columbia Co. Georgia, attorney of Elizabeth Driskill of same place sold to Jesse Fooks of Worc.Co. Md. rights 1/3rd part.
22 Aug.1797 Jesse Fooks sold to George Fooks 317 acres
5 Apr.1800 George Fooks sold to John Fooks, all.

DRUMANY

Patented in 1732 by George Oliphant for 50 acres.
8 Sep.1764 George Oliphant of Sussex Co. Del. sold to George Culver on the east side of the Nanticoke River.
21 Mar.1770 George Culver sold to John Winright 50 acres.
17 Oct.1772 John Winright sold to Isaac Phillips 50 acres.

DUBLIN

Patented in 1759 by William Strawbridge for 54 acres in Rewastico 100.
14 Oct.1763 William Strawbridge of Worc.Co. sold to Isaac Moore of Som.Co.
1784 Isaac Moore willed to son Newbold Moore, 54 acres.

DUDLEY

Patented on 17 Nov.1675 by Stephen Cannon who assigned to John Peasey for 100 acres, near Oyster Creek.
14 Nov.1683 John Peasey and wife Elizabeth Peasey sold 100 acres to Robert Collier.
Rent Rolls 1666-1723, possessed by James Collier 80 acres, and 20 acres by Robert Collier.
1702 Robert Collier willed to son James Collier 400 acres unnamed and 220 acres to son Robert Collier, unnamed.
15 Aug.1751 Phillip Jones and wife Mary Jones and Priscilla Nicholson and Robert Graham partitioned land that John Nicholson had.(who was named brother of George Betts Collier. Mary Collier widow of James Collier married 2nd. Nehemiah Nicholson) It was resurveyed to COLLIERS GOOD LUCK & DUDLEYS and now called BETSYS GIFT. John Nicholson died intestate and had three daughters Ann Nicholson, Mary Nicholson and Priscilla Nicholson. Ann Nicholson married William Graham and had sons Robert Graham and then died. Mary Nicholson married Phillip Jones, Priscilla married Phillip Covington, except 21 acres left by John Nicholson to Robert Walter.
6 July 1784 Phillip Jones and wife Mary Jones sold their share to Phillip Covington.
1796 resurveyed to BETSYS GIFT 405 1/2 acres.

DUKES FOLLY

Patented in 1748 by William Farlow for 50 acres.

DUMBARTON

Patented in 1800 by William E. Hitch
6 Jan 1800 William Elgate Hitch with wife Polly Hitch sold to Sarah Elligood Aires for 5 shillings. no acres mentioned.
6 Jan.1800 Sarah Ellegood Aires sold to William Elgate Hitch and Littleton Aires.
22 Dec 1808 Littleton Aires and wife Sarah Elligood Aires sold to George Collier 237 acres.

DUNKIRK

Patented in 1735 by Robert Atkins for 50 acres. (part of this land is in Worcester County now)
4 Nov.1761 William Atkins sold to Jacob Christopher 50 acres with MAGDALENES CHOICE.
9 Mar.1765 Jacob Christopher sold to Stephen Horsey 50 acres.
15 Mar.1783 Samuel Horsey with wife Ann Horsey sold 50 acres to Stephen Toadvine.
1783 tax - Stephen Toadvine, 50 acres Wicomico 100.

26 Sep.1801 Stephen Toadvine sold to Elijah Ennis 50 acres and 9 acres of ADDITION TO DUNKIRK. (see Worcester Co. Lands too)

DURHAM

Patented in 1735 by Robert Atkins for 50 acres.
4 Nov.1761 William Atkins sold to Jacob Christopher 50 acres.
9 Mar.1765 Jacob Christopher sold to Stephen Horsey of Som. Co. 50 acres.
7 Feb.1771 Stephen Horsey sold to Samuel Horsey 50 acres.
15 Mar.1783 Samuel Horsey with wife Ann Horsey sold to Stephen Toadvine 50 acres.

DURHAM

Patented in 1794 by James Dean for 121 1/4 acres.
20 Mar.1795 James Dean sold to David Gray 121 1/4 acres
7 June 1799 David Gray sold to Horatio Taylor 19 1/2 acres.

DURHAMS RESOLUTION

Patented in 1758 by Richard Durham for 100 acres.
17 Mar.1763 Richard Durham sold to Joseph Dashiell 100 acres.
5 Dec.1787 John Newman gave to brother in law John Stanton of Baltimore County and Ann Stanton his wife (alias Ann Newman) during their lifetimes 20 acres.
8 March 1794 George Revel son of Samuel Revel sold to John Newman son of John 100 acres.

DUNNS FANCY

Patented in 1748 by Valentine Insley
1850 Valentine Insley is in Tyaskin District

DYKES DISPUTE

Patented in 1784 by Daniel Dykes for 306 acres.
1783 tax- Daniel Dykes 306 acres, Wic.100, Worc.Co.
14 Dec.1786 Daniel Dykes sold to Benjamin Johnson 11 1/2 acres

EAGLES POINT

Patented on 20 Sep.1737 by Patrick Kersey for 40 acres, near Parsonburg.
1733/48 debt books, Patrick Kersey
10 Aug.1744 Patrick Causey sold to Robertson Lingo
7 Mar.1755 Robertson Lingo with wife Ann Lingo sold to John Perdue 40 acres.
1773 ADDITION TO EAGLE POINT, pat. John Perdue 158 acres.
25 Jan 1796 I John Perdue am bound to James Perdue for BEAVER DAM, ADDITION TO EAGLE POINT, END OF STRIFE.
27 Oct.1782 John Perdue gave to son James Perdue 1 1/2 acres
1783 tax- John Perdue 155 acres

23 July 1802 James Perdue willed lands to sons James W. B. Perdue, John K.H. Perdue and Elijah S.W. Perdue, unnamed.
29 June 1805 George Perdue son of John Perdue sold to Kendal H. Perdue part.
12 Aug.1809 John K.H. Perdue sold rights to John S. Parsons.

EAGLE TOWER

Patented 10 Apr.1744 by Thomas Hearn for 100 acres.
17 Nov.1759 Thomas Hearn gave to son Thomas Hearn Jr. 100 acres.
22 Sep.1764 Thomas Hearn sold to Robertson Lingo of Worc.Co. 100 acres.
1772 Robertson Lingo willed to grandsons, John Lingo, Joshua Lingo, William Lingo and Elijah Lingo sons of William, unnamed land.
25 Apr.1795 Elijah Lingo sold to George Waller, millright, of Sussex Co.Del. 25 acres.

EASON

Patented on 20 July 1679 by Thomas Bloyes and assigned to William Wright for 50 acres in Nanticoke 100.
Rent Rolls 1666-1723, possessed by the widow of William Wright.
10 Jan.1709 Bloyce Wright heir of William conveyed to brothers Solomon Wright and William Wright.
7 Dec.1720 Solomon Wright and wife Sarah Wright sold to Capt. Charles Ballard, his part.
1723 Charles Ballard willed to son Charles land in Wicomico, unnamed.
15 Sep.1742 Henry Ballard son of Col. Charles Ballard sold to Isaac Handy 25 acres his moity.
1760 Isaac Handy willed to sons George Handy, Thomas Handy, Henry Handy, all lands, unnamed.

EASOMS CHANCE

Patented 8 Sep.1723 by Benjamin Easum for 34 acres.
Rent Rolls 1666-1723, possessed by Benjamin Easum
1755/61 possessed by Joseph Bounds
16 Mar.1767 John Bounds sold to Jonathan Bounds 34 acres.
9 June 1794 William Stewart sold to Robert Dashiell son of George Dashiell.
16 Feb.1802 George Dashiell with wife Elizabeth Dashiell and son Robert Dashiell sold to Ichabod Dashiell 151 /12 acres of DASHIELLS FOLLY, EASOMS CHANCE & SMALL ADDITION.
1808 William Stewart willed to nephew Alexander Stewart.

EAST CONCLUSION

Patented 1814 by John Nelson for 228 3/4 acres.

EASTWOOD

Patented 2 Oct.1710 by Alexander Adams for 234 acres.
Rent Rolls 1666-1723, possessed by Alexander Adams
2 Nov.1762 Alexander Adams sold to son Samuel Adams 234 acres on the east side of a branch of Broad Creek s/s Nanticoke River.

EBBYS FROLIC

Patented on 27 Nov.1749 by Isaac Cooper for 10 acres.
1783 tax - Mary Williams 10 acres- Rewastico 100.
11 Apr.1800 Isaac Cooper sold 10 acres to John Grumble on road from Vienna Ferry to Barren Creek Mills.
1796 John Grumble willed land to wife Temperance Grumble, no name.

ECCLEFECHAN

Patented 1794 by William Stone for 93 acres.
1805 2nd. patent by William Stone for 258 acres.

EDGES CHANCE

Patented 3 Oct.1759 Nehemiah Edge
28 May 1776 Sussex Co.Del. land warrants, pat. to Joseph Foreman

EDWARDS CHOICE

Patented in 1768 by Edward Ellis for 50 acres.

EDWARDS LOTT

This is 25 acres, part of NOBLE QUARTER- no patent found.
23 Jan 1732 John Evans sold to Edward Willin 25 acres sold to John Evans by Robert Crockett taken out of NOBLE QUARTER & LITTLE MONMOUTH.
6 Apr.1742 Edward Willin and wife Hannah Willin sold 25 acres to William Nelson.
5 Apr.1753 John Evans sold to William Nelson 5 acres.
1762 William Nelson willed to grandson William Atkinson 25 acres bought of Edward Willin.

EGYPT

Patented on 14 oct.1674 by James Jones on south side of Quantico Creek in Nanticoke 100 for 200 acres.
1680 James Jones wlled to Andrew Jones.
3 June 1680 Andrew Jones, heir of James Jones sold to Edward Bennett.
Rent Rolls 1666-1723, possessed by Edward Bennett
1706 Edward Bennett willed to son Edward Bennett and to his daughter Jane Tully wife of Stephen Tully.
7 June 1720 Stephen Tully and wife Jane Tully sold 82 acres to son Stephen Tully Jr.
10 Feb.1747 Edward Bennett and wife Sarah Bennett sold to Daniel Goslin two tracts EGYPT & FAREHAM, 55 acres.
10 Feb.1747 Edward Bennett with wife Sarah Bennett sold 8 acres to Richard Tully.
7 Mar.1749 I Edward Bennett am bound to Isaac Serman for 100 pounds to convey part of tracts EGYPT & FAIRHAM 12 acres.
1 Jan 1761 I Edward Bennett am bound to Richard Phillips for 65 acres of EGYPT & FARHAM.
7 Jan 1768 Daniel Goslin with wife Elizabeth Goslin sold 55 acres of EGYPT & FAIRHAM to John Leatherbury.
17 May 1769 Richard Tully and wife Mary Tully sold 23 acres to John

Nelson.
30 Nov.1770 Richard Tully sold to John Nelson 28 1/2 acres of CHESSEY & EGYPT.
30 Nov.1770 Richard Tully sold to John Leatherbury 32 acres.
17 May 1769 Richard Tully with wife Mary Tully sold to John Nelson 23 acres.
22 Feb.1780 Littleton Bennett sold to Douty Collier son of Robert Collier 65 acres.
1783 tax - James Anderson 12 acres
1783 tax - Douty Collier (with FAIRHAM 62 1/2 acres)
1783 tax - John Leatherbury 32 acres
1783 tax - John Nelson 68 acres
1784 ADDITION TO EGYPT patented to John Leatherbury for 100 acres.
1784 John Nelson willed to son John Nelson tract bought of Richard Tully, unnamed.

ELBA

Patented 1816 by Jonathan Bayley for 71 1/4 acres.

ELGATES LOTT

Patented on 25 April 1680 by William Stevens who assigned to William Elgate for 100 acres.
Rent Rolls 1666-1723, possessed by William Elgate
1725/8 William Elgate willed to daughter Sarah Byrd part and to granddaughter Catherine Hitch daughter of Hannah Hitch.
1 Aug.1737 William Elgate gave to Catherine Byrd wife of Thomas Byrd Jr. 50 acres.
5 Aug.1737 William Elgate gave to daughter Sarah Byrd wife of Thomas 100 acres part of HAKALAH & ELGATES LOTT not given William Byrd nor Catherine Hitch.
1752 Thomas Byrd Sr willed to son Elgate Byrd 50 acres and to son Thomas Byrd 50 acres given to Sarah Byrd by William Elgate.
13 Sep.1760 Catherine Byrd with Josiah Polk and George Hayward divided lands JESHEMON & ELGATES LOTT
3 Apr.1764 Catherine Byrd sold to Levin Ballard 50 acres.
1783 tax - William Johnson 50 acres.
1783 tax - John Smith 25 acres
1783 tax - Reuben Roberts 25 acres.
5 July 1785 Elijah Johnson and wife Margaret Johnson sold to Nathan Adams 100 acres of HAKALAH & ELGATES LOTT, that William Elgate conveyed to Catherine Byrd.
9 Apr.1792 Nathan Adams with wife Betty Adams of Sussex Co.Del. sold to William Ellegood 100 acres of HACHILAH & ELGATES LOTT.
29 Mar.1790 William Ellegood sold to Levin Handy and William Elgate Hitch 1 acre, lease for 22 years.

ELIASES DISCOVERY

No patent found was part of HORSEHEAD 25 acres Elias Venatson.
1746 Elias Venatson willed to sister Bridget Venatson 25 acres.
7 Oct.1760 Elias Venatson resurveyed to ADDITION TO ELIAS DISCOVERY 109 acres.

ELIZABETHS CHOICE

Patented on 23 Mar.1687 Manasses Morris for 200 acres
15 May 1689 Manasses Morris, cooper with wife Elizabeth Morris sold 200 acres to George Bayley.
Rent Rolls 1666-1723, possessed by Manasses Morris in Dor. Co. but now conveyed to John Parsons by George Bayley.
4 Nov.1718 John Parsons of Wicomico sold 200 acres to William Moore.
26 Nov.1746 Ahab Coston with wife Abigail Coston (was Abigail Parsons) sold to John Leatherbury 200 acres that John Parsons who died intestate left only surviving heir Abigail afsd.
18 Aug.1747 John Leatherbury sold to Richard Harris and his son Levin Harris 100 acres now called HARRIS'S LOTT.
1756 John Lamberson willed to William Austin, bought of Ahab Coston
1766 Richard Harris willed to daughter Eunice Harris HARRIS LOTT.
21 Mar.1770 Eunice Harris sold to William Giles 3 acres that descended from her father Richard Harris.
1771 William Giles Jr. willed to Leah Duncan 3 acres.
15 Oct.1775 Jesse Austin of Som.Co. sold to Benjamin Atkinson, 95 1/2 acres willed by his father William Austin.
19 May 1796 Lazarus Huffington and daughters Sarah Huffington and Mary Huffington mortgaged to Benjamin Atkinson.
5 June 1797 Amelia Harris sold to Thomas Skinner that was sold by John Leatherbury to Richard Harris.

ELLINGSWORTHS HOPE

Patented on 9 Apr.1674 by Stephen Cannon who assigned to Richard Ellingsworth for 200 acres on Wetipquin Creek.
6 Oct 1726 Richard Ellingsworth Jr. son of Richard, with wife Elizabeth Ellingsworth sold 100 acres to Roger Nicholson. (other half was sold to Jacob Mezick.)
9 Mar.1731/2 Jacob Mezick sold 50 acres to Nehemiah Mezick
29 Aug.1746 Nehemiah Mezick of Som. Co. and John Mezick of Worc.Co. sold to Elihu Mezick, bricklayer, 50 acres.
1783 tax - Mary Mezick 50 acres
1783 tax - Mary Mezick 39 acres
1783 tax - Henry Nicholson 117 acres
1788 Elihu Mezick willed to wife Margaret Mezick 20 acres and then to sons Elihu Mezick, John Mezick and Daniel Mezick.
4 Nov.1799 Henry Nicholson with wife Elizabeth Nicholson sold to Levin William Mezick their interest.

ELLIOTTS ADDITION

Patented on 21 Nov.1760 by Daniel Elliott for 50 acres.

ELLIS'S ADDITION

Patented in 1765 by Joseph Ellis, a resurvey from QUIET ENTRANCE for 148 1/2 acres.
2 Apr.1771 Joseph Ellis Sr. sold to Stephen Ellis 28 acres with ELLIS'S CHANCE.
6 Nov.1779 Joseph Ellis Sr. sold to Louther Hitch 23 1/4 acres.
1783 tax - Louther Hitch 20 acres.

1783 tax - Joseph Ellis 96 acres
1783 tax - Isaac Dashiell 70 acres
8 Oct.1785 Esther Ellis sold to Stephen Ellis of Sussex Co.Del. 148 1/2 acres formerly belonging to Joseph Ellis Sr. who willed to Esther Ellis to be sold.
16 May 1789 Stephen Ellis of Sussex Co.Del. sold 56 3/4 acres to Louther Hitch of ELLIS ADDITION & ELLIS CHANCE
3 Nov.1791 Louther Hitch sold to Stephen Ellis of Sussex Co.Del. 56 3/4 acres of afsd.
3 Nov.1791 Stephen Ellis of Sussex Co.Del. sold to Louther Hitch 61 1/4 acres of ELLIS CHANCE, ELLIS ADDITION.
23 Sep.1797 Stephen Ellis of Sussex Co.Del. sold to Isaac Dashiell 104 acres of ELLIS CHANCE & ELLIS ADDITION.
23 Sep.1797 Louther Hitch with wife Betsy Hitch sold to Curtis Hitch part.
11 March 1801 Louther Hitch sold to Ezekiel Hitch 23 1/4 acres.
9 Oct.1802 Isaac Dashiell with wife Nancy Dashiell sold to Thomas Humphries 104 acres of ELLIS CHANCE & ELLIS ADDITION.

ELLIS'S CHANCE

Patented in 1760 by Joseph Ellis for 50 acres.
2 Apr.1771 Joseph Ellis Sr. sold 50 acres to Stephen Ellis
16 May 1789 Stephen Ellis of Sussex Co.Del. sold to Louther Hitch part.
3 Nov.1792 Louther Hitch sold to Stephen Ellis 56 3/4 acres of ELLIS CHANCE & ELLIS ADDITION
3 Nov.1792 Stephen Ellis of Sussex Co.Del. sold to Louther Hitch 61 1/4 acres of ELLIS CHANCE & ELLIS ADDITION
3 Nov.1792 Stephen Ellis sold to Isaac Dashiell 104 acres of ELLIS CHANCE & ELLIS ADDITION.
23 Sep.1797 Louther Hitch with wife Betsy Hitch sold to Curtis Hitch 58 3/4 acres of GRAVELY HILL, ELLIS CHANCE & ELLIS ADDITION.
1800 Elijah Ellis patented another 18 1/8 acres.
9 oct.1802 Isaac Dashiell with wife Nancy Dashiell sold to Thomas Humphries 104 acres of ELLIS CHANCE & ELLIS ADDITION.
1830 Elijah Ellis willed lands to daughter Matilda McNeal wife of John McNeal, unnamed.

ELLIS'S FROLIC

Patented in 1762 by Edward Ellis for 50 acres.
23 Dec.1769 Edward Ellis with wife Rachel Ellis sold to John Nelms.
1783 tax - Samuel Howard 50 acres, Rewastico 100.

ELLIS'S MISCHANCE

Patented by Jacob Bell for 7 1/2 acres
11 Fe.1775 Jacob Bell sold to Joshua Hitch 7 1/2 acres with FIRST CHOICE, 3 miles from the Wicomico River.

ELLIS'S VENTURE

Patented in 1802 by Elijah Ellis for 50 acres.
1830 Elijah Ellis willed to daughter Matilda McNeal wife of William

McNeal land on road from Spring Hill Chapel to Salisbury. At her death to her son William McNeal. (land not named.)

ELZEYS CARE
ELZEYS CARE VACATED

Patented 1715 by Levin Denwood for 300 acres.
VACATED patented in 1734 by Levin Denwood.
1757 Levin Denwood willed to brother Spencer Waters, tract on the n/w fork of the Nanticoke River, in Dorcester County, unnamed.

ELYS PRIVILDEDGE

Patented 1794 by Ely Bradley for 11 acres.

END OF CONFUSION

Patented in 1776 by Isaac Rhoads for 54 1/4 acres.

END OF STRIFE

Patented on 20 Dec.1741 by Elenor Dobson on the south side of the Nanticoke River for 40 acres.
4 Sep.1769 Jane Kimmey of Sussex Co.Del. widow, sold to John Clowes 40 acres that her mother Eleanor Dobson willed to her.

END OF STRIFE

Patented in 1750 by James Reed for 272 acres.
18 June 1759 James Reed and wife Mary Reed sold to William Donoho, tailor 40 acres, part added to tract CARTERS LODGE and is called END OF STRIFE that bounds ELLINSWORTHS HOPE.
8 Apr.1763 James Reed and wife Mary Reed sold to John Cave of Acco.Co.Va. 232 acres, at Wetpquin Creek.
26 Feb.1783 Benjamin Cave and Henry Cave sold to Elihu Mezick 75 acres that Elihu and his brother Joseph Mezick bought of Benjamin Cave
26 Feb.1783 Benjamin Cave of Dorc.Co. sold to Jacob Mezick 150 acres.
1783 tax - Elihu Mezick 100 acres, Nanticoke 100
1783 tax - John Douglas 9 acres
1783 tax - Jacob Mezick 132 acres
1788 Jacob Mezick willed to son Covington Mezick
1788 Elihu Mezick willed 75 acres to wife Margaret Mezick and after death to sons Elihu Mezick, John Mezick and Daniel Mezick.
4 July 1799 John Mezick sold to Elihu Mezick 135 acres of END OF STRIFE, LEES SITUATION, GORE and RIVER TRACT within the same tracts.
1828 Covington Mezick willed to son Levin W. Mezick, SPIE being part of STRIFE & COVINGTONS CHANCE.

END OF STRIFE

Patented on 15 May 1762 by John Perdue for 63 acres in Wicomico Forest.
1783 tax - John Perdue Wic. 100 Worc.Co.
12 Nov.1806 George Perdue sold to William Parsons 57 1/2 acres
1845 resurveyed by John Perdue

END OF STRIFE

Patented on 19 Oct.1757 by Joseph Dashiell for 6 1/2 acres in Nanticoke 100.
1783 tax - George Dashiell 6 1/2 acres
1788 Joseph Dashiell willed to grandson Joseph Dashiell son of George Dashiell, all lands.

END OF STRIFE

Patented in 1764 by John Langsdale for 192 1/2 acres
24 Sep.1768 John Langsdale Sr. with wife Eleanor Langsdale sold 45 /34 acres to Arthur Dashiell.
1783 tax - John Langsdale 151 3/4 acres in Rewastico 100
1783 tax - Arthur Dashiell 40 1/2 acres.
29 Apr.1803 Henry Langsdale son of John Langsdale sold to Esther Langsdale widow of John Langsdale.

END OF STRIFE

Patented in 1773 by Benjamin Savage for 200 acres.
1783 tax - Benjamin Savage 200 acres in Wic. 100
13 Jan.1792 Benjamin Savage sold part to Boaz Walston
1794 Benjamin Savage willed lands unnamed to son Zorobable Savage and Benjamin Savage.
2 July 1808 Boaz Walston with wife Bathsheba Walston sold to James Walker Bayley.
1823 John Parker of E. willed to daughter Elizabeth Parsons NO END OF STRIFE purchased of Zerobable and Benjamin Savage.

END OF STRIFE

Patented in 1749 by Daniel McIntyre for 94 acres.
25 Oct.1752 Daniel McIntyre and wife Elizabeth McIntyre sold 9 acres to William Nelson.
21 Oct.1752 Daniel McIntyre and wife Elizabeth McIntyre sold 5 acres to Thomas Willin.
1773 Daniel McIntyre willed to wife ELizabeth McIntyre and after death to son William McIntyre.
1773 will of Thomas Willin, to wife Priscilla Willin use of remainder of land until Samuel Willin is of age except what I have divided with my brother in law Daniel McIntyre.(this land not mentioned by name)
1783 tax - Betty McIntyre 5 acres.
1765 this was resurveyd to FINIS ALL for 106 3/4 acres.

END OF STRIFE

Patented in 1774 by Isaac Rhoads for 40 acres.
1783 tax - Isaac Rhoads 40 acres in Rewastico 100.

END OF STRIFE

Patented in 1774 by George Bayley
12 Aug 1776 Robins Bayley son of George Bayley and heir of Isaiah Bayley sold to Benjamin Bayley

1783 tax - George Bayley Jr. 2 acres- Wico. 100
5 Dec.1795 Boardvine Bayley sold to Obed Bayley 9 acres.

END OF STRIFE

Patented 1850 Henry Dulaney 11 acres
1850 he is in Salisbury District

ENGLISH'S ADVENTURE

Patented 1735 by James English for 47 acres
9 Mar.1774 James English sold to John Williams 47 acres.

ENGLISH'S LOTT

Patented in 1748 by James English for 50 acres.

ENNALS FROLIC

Patented in 1726 by William Ennals for 577 acres.
19 Nov.1729 William Ennals of Dorc.Co., merchant, sold 150 acres to Ezekiel Green on the east side of the Nanticoke River in Somerset County.
11 Mar.1736 Ezekiel Green sold 150 acres to William Cope.

ENTERPRIZE

Patented in 1826 by Charles Leary for 11 1/2 acres.

ESME'S CONCLUSION

Patented in 1801 by Esme Marshall Waller
24 Feb.1810 Esme Marshall Waller sold to Richard Waller 8 3/4 acres
24 Oct.1810 Esme Marshall Waller sold to Eleanor Waller of Sussex Co.Delaware 14 acres.

EPHRAIMS HOOK

Patented in 1803 by Ephraim Wilson for 20 3/4 acres.
21 Oct.1808 Ephraim Wilson of George Wilson with wife Esther Wilson and George Wilson with wife Amelia Wilson sold to Charles Jones 298 acres of RECOVERY, MT. EHPRAIM, WILSONS VENTURE, EPHRAIMS HOOK

EVANS CHANCE

Patented in 1763 by John Evans for 449 1/2 acres

EVANS CONTRIVANCE

Patented in 1812 by Solomon Evans for 7 acres

EVANS HARD LUCK

Patented in 1804 by Solomon Evans

EVANS PURCHASE

Not Patented - 12 Feb.1680 William Stevens sold 300 acres of GETHSEMANE to John Evans, called EVANS PURCHASE.

EVANS PURCHASE

Patented in 1729 by Edward Fowler for 140 acres, was part of tract STANAWAY
1727 William Hangline willed to wife Isabel Hangline. (she married John Twiford) EVANS PURCHASE being part of STANAWAY
29 March 1729 John Twiford and wife Isabella Twiford sold to Edward Fowler.
29 Jan.1742 John Fowler, heir of Edward Fowler sold 140 acres to William Harris.
1783 tax - John Hughes 46 acres
1783 tax - Kezia Harris 92 acres
13 July 1803 Isaac Hopkins with wife Matilda Hopkins sold to Gowan White 16 3/4 acres.
6 Apr.1805 Isaac Hopkins with wife Martha Hopkins sold to Gowan White 16 1/4 acres.
19 Oct.1805 Gowan White sold to Easter (no last name)
21 Aug.1809 Isaac Hopkins with wife Martha Hopkins sold to Matthew Travis (per dividing lines of heirs of John Harris deceased.)
21 Aug 1809 Matthew Travis and wife Priscilla Travis sold to Isaac and Martha Hopkins.
21 Aug.1809 James Ritchie and wife Betsy Ritchie sold all rights to Matthew Travis
1854 William Riall willed to wife Hetty Ann Riall(in 1850 he lived in Tyaskin)

EVANS SECOND CHANCE

Patented in 1773 by John Evans Sr. for 540 1/2 acres.
1789 ADDITION TO patented by John Evans for 8 acres.
14 Dec.1808 Benjamin Dashiell of James with wife Isabella sold to Chaplin Conway 280 1/4 acres of EVANS SECOND CHANCE & MOORFIELDS.
14 Dec.1808 Chaplin Conway with wife Ann Conway sold to Tubman Willin 64 3/4 acres EVANS SECOND CHANCE & SIDNEY
14 Dec.1809 Chaplin Conway with wife Ann Conway sold to Mansfield Street for 5 shillings 90 acres EVANS SECOND CHANCE & SIDNEY.
1836 Stephen Winright willed to son Cannon Winright.

EVANS SLIPE

Patented 1788 by George Aires for 3 /14 acres
5 Nov.1803 George Aires Sr. sold to Robert Willin 3 1/4 acres for 5 shillings.

EVENINGS CHANCE

Patented on 18 Nov.1768 by Joshua Holloway for 50 acres
14 Oct.1768 Resurveyed to WHAT YOU PLEASE.

EVERSHAMP

Patented on 16 March 1673 by Thomas Holbrook and John Holland.
23 Aug.1680 Thomas Holbrook and wife Alice Holbrook, John Holland with wife Ann Holland sold to Thomas Walker.
Rent Rolls 1666-1723, possessed by Thomas Walker but sold to Alexander Adams.
31 Jan 1751 Alexander Adams rector of Stepney Parish gave to son William Adams.
21 Dec.1771 William Adams with wife Leah Adams sold to John Scott.
18 Sep.1776 John Scott rector of Stephney Parish, and wife Elizabeth sold to Isaac Horsey and William Horsey 500 acres.
20 May 1782 Isaac Horsey with wife Mary Horsey of Sussex Co.Del. sold to William Horsey of Som.Co.
1783 tax - William Horsey 350 acres
1783 tax - Cannon Lank 150 acres.
1786 William Horsey willed to son Isaac Horsey plantation bought of Rev. John Scott.
21 Feb.1801 Isaac Horsey sold to Hugh Gemmill 14 3/4 acres
28 Apr.1804 Isaac Horsey s/o William Horsey sold to John Byrd 200 acres
1 Jan 1805 Hugh Gemmill sold to Richard Henry Handy 14 3/4 acres
14 Jan 1805 Richard Henry Handy sold to Hugh Gemmill.

EXCHANGE

Patented on 7 Mar.1754 by William Winder for 50 acres.
2 Mar.1757 William Winder, merchant sold to John Maglamery Jr.
23 Oct.1762 ADDITION TO EXCHANGE pat. John Maglamery 498 acres.
18 Aug.1765 John Maglamery sold to Stephen Scady 9 acres
6 Sep.1765 John Maglamery sold 100 acres to William Driskell of ADDITION TO EXCHANGE.
6 Dec.1765 William Driskell resurveyed ADDITION TO EXCHANGE, to DRISKELLS INDUSTRY 317 acres.
1769 John Maglamery willed to sons Edward Maglamery, Levin Maglamery and Elijah Maglamery.
21 AUg.1769 Sarah Maglamery spinster sold to John Richardson 200 acres of ADDITION TO EXCHANGE that her husband John Maglamery willed to be sold to pay debts.
21 Mar.1783 Edward Maglamery son of John sold to Jesse Fooks 189 acres ADDITION TO EXCHANGE
1783 tax - Jesse Fooks 126 acres (ADDITION TO EXCHANGE)
19 Apr.1788 Sarah Scady, Leah Scady, Major Dorman with wife Sarah Dorman, Selby Dakes with wife Dinah Dakes sold to Jesse Fooks ADDITION TO EXCHANGE 9 acres.
22 Aug.1797 Jesse Fooks sold to George Fooks part. ADDITION.

EXCHANGE

Patented in 1796 by Esme Bayley for 22 1/2 acres
1799 Esme Bayley willed to son Henry Bayley 22 /2 acres.

EXETOR BRIDGE

Patented on 2 Sep.1755 by Thomas Brown for 19 acres at the Nanticoke

River.

EXPENSE

Patented in 1794 by George Smith for 7 7/8 acres
5 Dec.1795 George Smith son of Andrew Smith sold to James Ritchie 2 3/4 acres and 1 3/16th acres
5 Dec.1795 George Smith sold to Nancy Nelms 3 1/4 acres and 1 3/8 acres.
16 Aug.1803 James Ritchie, merchant sold to Robert Dashiell 1 1/4 acres.
26 Nov.1811 John Bounds with wife Nancy Bounds (daughter of Edmund Northern Nelms) sold to Peter Dashiell sold all except one lot of 5 acres.
15 Apr.1813 John Bounds with wife Nancy Bounds sold part to David Howard.

EZEKIELS CONVENIENCY

Patented 7 March 1765 by Henry Graham for 40 1/2 acres.
1783 tax - Ann Huffington 20 acres in Rewastico 100
1783 tax - Ezekiel Graham 20 acres
23 July 1785 Ezekiel Graham sold 16 acres to Charles Weatherly (8 acres) and George Fletcher (8 acres)
26 Nov.1801 Charles Weatherly sold to William Russum, part marsh bought of Ezekiel Graham, no name or acres.

FAIRFIELD

Patented in 1763 by William Bennett for 15 acres.
7 Jan 1768 William Bennett and wife Dorothy Bennett sold to John Leatherbury 15 acres.

FAIRFIELDS

Patented 2 Feb.1682 by Thomas Pemberton a resurvey from KELLUMS FOLLY in a fork of the Wicomico River, for 900 acres
29 Oct.1684 Thomas Pemberton with wife Elizabeth Pemberton sold to Richard Stevens 900 acres at Cowsicks Creek.
1683 Richard Stevens gave to sons John Stevens and Richard Stevens.
1713 Richard Stevens willed 300 acres to daughters Ann Stevens, Abigail Stevens and Hannah Stevens. To daughter Sarah Stevens 300 acres, if no issue to other daughters. Part to sons John Stevens and Isaac Stevens and balance to son Richard Stevens. (note: Sarah Stevens married James Bounds, called COWES SIX plantation.)
3 Aug.1722 Richard Stevens and John Stevens with wife Ann Stevens sold 165 acres to William Kibble.
1727 William Kibble willed to son John Kibble 80 acres, if no issue to son Richard Kibble. To son William Kibble residue of afsd.tract sold by Richard and John Stevens. To wife Ursly Kibble 1/3rds- no name of land.
2 Feb.1736 William Kibble sold to Henry Lowe 1 acre, LOWES HIS PRIZE HOUSE part of KELLUMS FOLLY.
1740 John Richards with wife Ann Richards gave to son John Richards 100 acres bought from Edward Clark.

19 Aug.1743 William Kibble with wife Hannah Kibble sold to Henry Lowe, merchant 15 acres of ADDITION TO LOWES PRIZE HOUSE part of KELLUMS FOLLY, on the east side of the Wicomico River.
1751 Jonathan Bounds lived at COWS SIX plantation, He resurveyed 274 1/2 acres to BOUNDS CHANCE near the town of Allen, Trappe District.
1761 Henry Lowe willed to son Tubman Lowe (now missing) LOWES HIS PRIZE HOUSE or LOWES POINT.

FAIRFIELDS

Patented on 17 Oct.1743 by Sarah Scroggin and Joseph Scroggin for 179 acres at head of the Wicomico River.
22 Feb 1755 Joseph Scroggin with wife Sarah Scroggin sold 37 acres to Nehemiah Hearn.
1760 Nehemiah Hearn willed 37 acres to son Elisha Hearn.
19 May 1766 Elisha Hearn son of Nehemiah Hearn sold to Elijah Hearn 116 acres part of STAINS & FAIRFIELDS.
1768 ADDITION patented John Scroggin for 84 1/2 acres
1772 Joseph Scroggin willed to son John 129 acres and ADDITION TO FAIRFIELDS 84 1/2 acres, except 37 acres given to Elijah Hearn.
12 Apr.1773 John Scroggin sold to Elijah Hearn for 5 shillings 9 acres of FAIRFIELDS and 28 acres of ADDITION.
12 April 1773 Elijah Hearn and wife Sarah Hearn sold 37 acres to John Scroggin.
1783 tax - Elijah Hearn
1783 tax - Robert Scroggin - resurvey to HAZZARD 2 1/2 acres
1783 tax - John Scroggin 170 acres, Rewastico 100
1783 tax - John Scroggin 47 1/2 acres of ADDITION
7 Aug.1790 John Scroggin with wife Eunice Scroggin sold to John Dashiell of Jesse Dashiell 245 acres of FAIRFIELDS & BAD LUCK except for 9 acres of FAIRFIELDS deeded to Elijah Hearn and burying ground.
3 Oct.1794 John Dashiell of Jesse Dashiell sold to Benjmain Jones for 5 shillings 245 acres of FAIRFIELDS & BAD LUCK
9 Mary 1795 Benjamin Jones sold to John Dashiell afsd 245 acres.
1815 Major John Dashiell of Jesse Dashiell willed to wife Nelly Dashiell FAIRFIELD & ADDN. TO FAIRFIELD 400 acres. after death to daughter Eleanor T. Savage (married Joseph Savage of Virginia 1st and 2nd. Capt. William Wailes in 1818)

FAIRHAM

Patented on 30 July 1681 by Edward Bennett for 150 acres on the south side of the head of Quantico Creek.
13 Nov.1693 Edward Bennett with wife Dorothy Bennett gave 50 acres to daughter Mary Tully wife of John Tully.
1706 Edward Bennett willed to son Edward Bennett and his daughter Jane Tully wife of Stephen Tully plantation at Quantico Ck. no name.
7 Aug.1716 Walter Redman and wife Mary Redman (was Mary Tully) gave to son John Tully 50 acres. If no issue to son Joseph Tully (John died without issue)
7 June 1720 Stephen Tully Sr. with wife Jane Tully gave 78 acres to Stephen Tully Jr.
Rent Rolls 1666-1723, possessed by James Tully 50 acres, Stephen Tully 50 acres and Edward Bennett 50 acres.
2 Dec.1728 Joseph Tully sold to John Twiford 100 acres being 50 acres

of FITCHFIELD & 50 acres of FAIRHAM.
14 Aug.1732 Edward Bennett son of Edward, sold to John Twiford 50 acres.
15 Dec.1746 John Twiford gave to William Moore of Quantico 100 acres of FITCHFIELD & FAIRHAM (for support and maintenance during life)
10 Feb.1747 Edward Bennett with wife Sarah Bennett sold to Daniel Goslin 55 acres part of EGYPT & FAIRHAM.
10 Sep.1757 William Moore sold to William Bennett 100 acres of FITCHFIELD & FAIRHAM now called BENNETTS PURCHASE
7 Mar.1749/50 I Edward Bennett am bound to Isaac Serman (mtg.) 12 acres of EGYPT & FAIRHAM. Jan 1761 Edward Bennett am bound to Richard Phillips for 65 acres of EGYPT & FAIRHAM.
7 Jan 1768 Daniel Goslin with wife Elizabeth Goslin sold 55 acres to John Leatherbury of EGYPT & FAIRHAM.
7 Jan 1768 William Bennett with wife Dorothy Bennett sold to John Leatherbury 100 acres of FITCHFIELD & FAIRHAM called BENNETTS PURCHSE
17 May 1769 Richard Tully with wife Mary Tully sold to John Nelson 32 acres of EGYPT & FAIRHAM.
13 Nov.1770 Richard Tully sold 36 acres to John Nelson
30 Nov.1770 Richard Tully sold to John Leatherbury 2 acres.
1783 tax - Douty Collier (with Egypt 62 1/2 acres) Rewastico 100
1783 tax - John Leatherbury 55 acres
1783 tax - James Moore 15 acres
1783 tax - John Nelson 62 acres
1784 John Nelson willed to son John tract bought of Richard Tully, unnamed.

FAIR MEADOW

Patented on 15 Dec.1703 by John McClester for 700 acres near the mouth, on the n/w side of the Wicomico River.
Rent Rolls 1666-1723, possessed by John McClester
18 Apr.1760 William Hickman sold to Jonathan Hickman 350 acres, purchased of John McClester.
8 Jan 1763 William Hickman sold to John Barkley 1/2 of tract bought of John McClester, in Nanticoke.
11 Apr.1776 Charles Barkley of Frederick County sold to Henry Wallace Barkley 175 acres of MEADOW BEGINNING at FAIR MEADOW
1783 tax - Henry Barkley 150 acres
1783 tax - Jonathan Hickman 350 acres
8 June 1788 James Dashiell of Stepney parish sold to Henry Wallace Barkley ST ALBANS, STANAWAY, FAIR MEADOW.
8 June 1788 Henry Wallace Barkley sold to James Dashiell, same as above.

FAIR RIDGE

Patented on 26 June 1676 by John Windsor who assigned to Richard Samuels for 100 acres, near the mouth of the Nanticoke River.
10 Jan.1706 Richard Samuels sold 77 acres to James Dashiell.
Rent Rolls 1666-1723, possessed by Capt. James Dashiell vide account of Richard Samuels.
1708/9 James Dashiell willed to son Joseph Dashiell
29 Aug.1763 Joseph Dashiell resurveyed to MORE LOSS THAN GAIN, a total of 185 acres.

FALSE DISPUTE

Patented in 1772 by Edward Ellis for 22 1/2 acres
31 Dec.1774 Edward Ellis with wife Rachel Ellis sold to George Handy
1782 George Handy willed to daughter Leah Irving
1783 tax - Levin Irving - Rewastico 100
226 Jan 1803 Levin Irving with wife Leah Irving sold 22 1/2 acres to Hugh Gemmill.
1 Jan 1805 Hugh Gemmill with wife Jane Gemmill sold to Richard Henry Handy 22 1/2 acres.
14 Jan.1805 Richard Henry Handy sold to Hugh Gemmill, same.

FANCY

Patented 1740 by James Parremore for 70 acres
4 July 1740 James Parremore willed to son James his manor plantation.
17 Feb.1775 Thomas Parremore son of James Parremore who was the only devisee of James deceased sold to Isaac Coulbourn all rights, no name or acreage. (as James Parremore the younger died leaving Thomas Parremore heir at law)

FANNINGHAM

Patented 22 Nov.1672 by Richard Acworth for 300 acres.
4 Aug.1674 Richard Acworth with wife Ann Acworth sold to Michael Williams 300 acres.
1699 Michael Williams died leaving sons Michael Williams, Nathaniel Williams and Walter Williams.
Rent Rolls 1666-1723, apportains to the orphans of Michael Williams, on the north side of Barren Ck.

FARLOWS CONCLUSION

Patented in 1742 by George Farlow for 525 acres
1850 he is in the 4th district Worc.Co.

FARLOWS DELIGHT

Patented on 21 Apr.1768 by John Farlow for 50 acres.(is in Dennis Election district)
1802 Violetta Fooks wife of Daniel Fooks, willed to daughter Sarah Fooks and Sabrough Fooks 1/3rd and to son Thomas Fooks after the decease of daughters single life.

FARLOWS VENTURE

Patented in 1836 by David Farlow for 227 1/2 acres
1853 ADDITION TO FARLOWS VENTURE patented by Benjamin Farlow and Daniel Farlow for 225 3/4 acres.

FARMERS DELIGHT

Patented 1801 John Maddux for 534 acres and resurvyed by him for 603 acres.

FARRINGTONS ADVENTURE

Patented in 1795 by Levin Farrington for 650 acres
1808 Levin Farrington willed to son Levin Farrington lands in Rewastico Neck, not named.
13 Sep.1808 Levin Farrington mortgaged to the Farmers Bank of Md. 1479 acres with WEATHERLYS PURCHASE, WILSON, SALISBURY PLAIN, TRAINS LOTT & MORRIS LOTT.

FARRINGTONS PURCHASE

Patented in 1766 by William Winder for 261 acres in Rewastico 100 acres a resurvey of PACHINGO RIDGE.
1783 tax - William Winder 261 acres
1792 William Winder willed lands to sons William and Levin Winder (died young) not named.
1808 William Winder willed to son William Henry Winder, all lands, not named.

FATHERS ADVICE

Patented on 17 May 1758 by Joshua Nelms for 50 acres
4 Mar.1765 Joshua Nelms with wife Sarah Nelms sold to Joseph Dashiell son of Col. George Dashiell.
1783 tax - Col. Joseph Dashiell 50 acres.
22 Oct 1790 Zadock Sturgis, sheriff per judgement against Benjamin F.A.C. Dashiell son of Joseph Dashiell, sold to Thomas Harwood of Annapolis 57 acres.
25 July 1796 Thomas Harwood of Annapolis, sold to Joshua Johnson and Isaac Hearn 50 acres.
1797 resurveyed to PARTNERSHIP

FATHERS CARE

Patented 3 July 1683 by Thomas Walker and Susanna Walker children of Thomas Walker for 200 acres
Rent Rolls 1666-1723, possessed by Thomas Walker and Capt. Nicholas Evans who married Susanna Walker.
31 Jan.1751 Alexander Adams gave to son William Adams 200 acres. As Nicholas Evans and Susanna Evans had a son John Evans and Thomas Walker son of Thomas and John Evans and Ann Evans sold to Alexander Adams.
21 Dec.1771 William Adams with wife Leah Adams sold 200 acres to John Scott rector of Stepney Parish.
18 Sep.1776 John Scott with wife Elizabeth Scott sold 200 acres to Isaac Horsey.
20 May 1782 Isaac Horsey with wife Mary Horsey of Sussex Co. Del. sold 200 acres to William Horsey and wife Elinor Horsey.
1783 tax - William Horsey 200 acres
1786 William Horsey willed to son Isaac Horsey plantation and lands bought of Rev. John Scott.
28 Apr.1804 Isaac Horsey sold to John Byrd 200 acres.

FATHERS DELIGHT

Patented on 7 Dec.1678 by John Manlove for 100 acres.

Rent Rolls 1666-1723, possessed by James Weatherly (he married Ann Manlove widow of Richard Acworth)
6 July 1760 Jonathan Manlove with wife Rachel Manlove, grandson of John Manlove sold to John Weatherly 100 acres for 5 shillings.
2 June 1769 John Weatherly sold 100 acres to McKimmea Porter
1783 tax - McKimmea Porter 100 acres.
1790 McKimmea Porter willed to son Levi Porter.
11 June 1810 Levi Porter with wife Hetty Porter sold to Joshua Brattan lands in Rewastico devised by father McKimmea Porter. no name.

FATHERS NEGLECT

Patented in 1734 by John Hitch for 126 acres
1762 John Hitch willed plantation to son Joshua Hitch, unnamed.
1783 tax - Joshua Hitch 100 acres in Rewastico 100
1792 Joshua Hitch made a will. This land not mentioned but he gave lands to son Joshua.
20 Feb.1801 Levin Handy of Rhode Island now of Worc.Co. with wife Eleanor Handy, Joshua Pollitt and wife Sarah Pollitt, Nancy Hitch, Peggy Hitch, William Elgate Hitch with wife Mary Hitch and Molly Hitch sold 400 acres to Hugh Gemmill of HIGH SUFFOLK, FATHERS NEGLECT, WILSONS DISOVERY & HITCHES HARD LUCK (children of Joshua Hitch)
9 Aug.1803 John Wilkins, sheriff, sold to Hugh Gemmill 400 acres per judgement by George W. Handy against Edward Brown and wife Betsy Brown, William E. Hitch and wife Mary Hitch, Joshua Pollitt and wife Sarah Pollitt, Levin Handy and wife Eleanor Handy, William Hitch, Peggy Hitch and Nancy Hitch heirs of Joshua Hitch.
1 Jan.1805 Hugh Gemmill with wife Jane Gemmill sold to Richard Henry Handy the 400 acres of afsd land.
14 Jan 1805 Richard Henry Handy sold to Hugh Gemmill, same.
9 Sep.1806 John Wilkins, sheriff sold to Thomas Rencher 125 acres per judgement against heirs of Joshua Hitch.
1806 Thomas Rencher willed to son Samuel Rencher land purchased at sheriff's sale of heirs of Joshua Hitch.

FATHERS PURCHASE

No patent found for this land. 17 Aug.1715 Richard Crockett and wife Alice Crockett sold to Charles Lowe.
29 Mar.1726 Charles Lowe sold to Thomas Dashiell 100 acres w/s of Shiiles Creek (Charles Lowe son of Hannah Burke now wife of Tobias Burke)
24 Dec.1731 Thomas Dashiell sold 100 acres to son Charles Dashiell
17 June 1743 Charles Dashiell with wife Elizabeth Dashiell traded to Thomas Dashiell for 105 acres of MOUNT ALEXANDER..
9 Jan.1759 Thomas Dashiell son of Thomas gave to son Josiah Dashiell 100 acres.
18 June 1762 Nehemiah Crockett sold to Isaac Atkinson 40 acres of marsh formerly belonging to Thomas Dashiell,unnamed
1 June 1765 Josiah Dashiell son of Thomas Dashiell with wife Mary Dashiell sold 100 acres to Isaac Atkinson.
1783 tax - Elizabeth Atkinson 100 acres.

FATMANS FOLLY

Patented 9 Nov.1718 by John Reed for 50 acres on the south side of the main branch of Broad Creek.
12 Apr.1743 John Reed of Dorc.Co. sold to Dudson Bacon 50 acres.
This land was probably resurveyed to Sussex Co.Delaware.

FAWN HILL

Patented by James Dennis for 38 1/2 acres

FELLOWSHIP

Patented on 16 Sep.1720 by Robert Owens and Samuel Owens in a fork of the Nanticoke River for 200 acres.
Rent Rolls 1666-1723, possessed by Robert Owens and Samuel Owens.
Resurveyed and patented 10 June 1734 Robert Owens 200 acres.
1750 Robert Owens willed to son Samuel Owens
21 Feb.1756 Samuel Owens son of Robert Owens sold to John Laws 200 acres.
7 Sep.1770 John Laws sold to Alexander Laws 200 acres.
1783 tax - Jacob Mezick 50 acres. Nanticoke 100

FIGGS CHANCE

Patented on 15 Sep.1752 by William Figgs for 160 acres a resurvey of ABSALOMS LOTT.
6 Feb.1761 William Figgs sold to Moses Gordy 180 acres on Broad Creek out of the Nanticoke River.
1774 Moses Gordy willed to son Eli Gordy 70 acres and to sons John Gordy and Peter Gordy
25 June 1776 Sussex Co. Delaware land warrants- by John Gordy.

FIGGS PURCHASE

No patent found for this land
31 May 1744 George Maglamery sold to Alexander Adams FIGGS PURCHASE that Thomas Figgs conveyed to John Perdue who conveyed to George Maglammery on the south side of a branch of the Wicomico River.

FINIS

Patented in 1769 by John Evans for 181 1/2 acres.
1783 tax - John Evans of Nicholas, 181 1/2 acres, Nanticoke 100
12 July 1802 Sarah Evans relic of John Evans sold to Thomas Jones and Ichabod Dashiell her dower rights to lands of John Evans, unnamed.
11 Apr.1806 Thomas Jones of Thomas, with wife Ann D. Jones and Ichabod Dashiell with wife Priscilla Dashiell sold to Matthias D. Hopkins 54 acres sold by John Evans to Levi Hopkins

FINIS ALL

Patented in 1765 by Daniel McIntyre for 10 3/4 acres a resurvey of END OF STRIFE
3 Sep.1771 Daniel McIntyre sold to Robert Willin 31 1/4 acre of VAIN

except 1 2/4 acres FINIS
1773 Daniel McIntyre willed to wife Elizabeth McIntyre and after death to son William McIntyre.
1789 ADDITION TO FINIS ALL pat. William McIntyre for 1183 3/4 aces.
18 May 1791 William McIntyre and Charles Willin sold to Samuel Willin 11 /12 acres of ADDITION, in Muddy hole.
18 May 1791 Samuel Willin and Charles Willin sold to Willin McIntyre for 5 shillings ADDITION TO FINIS ALL. no acres given.

FINISH ALL- Alias MIGHT HAD MORE

This is part of NOBLE QUARTER

FINISH

Patented 1752 for 58 acres by John Shiles
1783 tax - John S. Conway 58 acres   Nanticoke 100

FIRM LAND

Patented on 4 July 1764 by Daniel Fooks for 88 acres

FIRST CHOICE

Patented 2 Jan 1676 by William Stevens who assigned to William Manlove near the main branch of Rewastico Creek for 500 acres.
1684 William Manlove deeded to Henry Layton.
1696 Henry Layton willed to to Thomas Johnson s/o Thomas and to Charles Williams residue of FIRST CHOICE.
3 Sep.1716 Thomas Johnson sold to Benjamin Cottman 150 acres.
7 July 1720 John Layton sold for 5 shillings to James Caldwell 1/2 of tract, that descended to John Layton as sole heir of Henry Layton.
1 Apr.1732 Benjamin Cottman sold to Abraham Taylor 100 acres.
25 Sep.1734 James Caldwell traded 10 acres with Ebenezer Cottman for 10 acres of ST GILES.
15 Sep.1756 James Caldwell Sr. gave 100 acres to James Caldwell Jr.
26 Aug.1757 James Caldwell Jr. sold to Henry Dashiell 100 acres.
4 May 1782 Ebenezer Waller sold to Everton Kennerly 10 acres of ST GILES, WEATHERLYS ADVENTURE & FIRST CHOICE (that Ebenezer Cottman bought of James Caldwell. Ebenezer Waller is the son of Richard Waller and Ann Waller (Ann Cottman)
5 July 1782 Ebenezer Moore of Granville N.C. sold to Everton Kennerly his rights.
1783 tax - Everton Kennerly 10 acres- Rewastico 100
1783 tax - Levi Dashiell 100 acres
1783 tax - John Bennett 50 aces
1783 tax - Gillis Howard 150 acres
1783 tax - Levin Irving 36 1/3 acres
1783 tax - Ezekiel Taylor 100 acres.
1784 William Taylor willed to son William Taylor
1786 Levi Dashiell willed 100 acres to son George Dashiell
25 Aug.1786 George Young son of Jonathan Young of Worc.Co. sold to Everton Kennerly all his rights.
28 Feb.1787 Fisher Roberts with wife Elizabeth Roberts sold to Everton Kennerly 150 acres of FIRST CHOICE, ST GILES & GOOD LUCK

28 Feb.1787 John Smith with wife Mary Smith sold to Fisher Roberts 150 acres of ST GILES, FIRST CHOICE, GOOD LUCK
18 Feb.1782 Fisher Roberts and wife Elizabeth Roberts sold to John Smith and wife Mary Smith 150 acres.
15 Jan 1791 Robert Venables and wife Amelia Venables sold 300 acres of FIRST CHOICE & ST. GILES (formerly property of James Caldwell grandfather of Amelia Venables) to Everton Kennerly
15 Jan 1791 Robert Dashiell and Mary Caldwell Dashiell sold 300 acres of FIRST CHOICE & St.GILES (grandaughter of James Caldwell)
15 Oct.1796 William Taylor with wife Sarah Taylor sold 100 acres to James Evans.
10 Dec.1802 James Evans with wife Betty Evans sold to John Hopkins
26 Mar.1803 Henry Dashiell with wife Jane Dashiell sold 100 cres to John Hopkins.
1812 John Hopkins willed to wife Eleanor Hopkins land bought of James Evans and Henry Dashiell.
1836 John Horsey willed to wife Susan Horsey, formerly belonging to Joseph Kennerly.

FIRST CHOICE

Patented in 1761 by George Vinson for 50 acres

FIRST CONCLUSION

Patented in 1770 by Matthias Miles for 92 acres

FIRST PURCHASE

Patented in 1761 by Joseph Jenkins for 110 1/2 acres.
1783 tax - Joseph Jenkins 110 1/2 acres in Wicomico 100
9 Sep.1797 Leah Jenkins and daughters Siner Gray and Levinah Serman sold 25 acres to Joshua Disharoon.

FIRST VENTURE

Patented on 5 Apr.1763 by John Talbot at head of the Wicomico River for 198 acres a resurvey of CLAYS ADVENTURE of 160 acres.

FISHERMANS QUARTER

Patented on 24 Nov 1676 by William Stevens who assigned to Lewis Beard for 150 acres. aka FISHERMANS LOTT
1734 Lewis Beard gave to son Lewis Jr. 130 acres out of FISHERMANS QUARTER & BETTYS ENLARGEMENT
28 Oct.1752 John Beard eldest son of Lewis Beard, with wife Rachel Beard sold to Samuel Fluellin, all that Lewis Beard conveyed to son Lewis, except the graveyard.
1766 Samuel Fluellin willed to son Samuel Fluellin land bought of John Beard, unnamed.
17 May 1771 Samuel Fluellin sold to Ephraim King 130 acres of FISHERMANS QUARTER & BETTYS ENLARGEMENT
1777 Ephraim King willed to Richard Crockett Fluellin and Samuel Fluellin that their father Samuel Fluellin conveyed to me.
1783 tax - Samuel King 130 acres- Nanticoke 100

1783 tax - William Ellingsworth 16 acres
26 July 1784 Samuel King with wife Mary sold to John Stewart
27 May 1792 Samuel Fluellin sold to James Winright his rights
24 Dec.1793 Jarvis Beard sold to James Mezick 130 acres of FISHERMANS QUAARTER & BETTYS ENLARGEMENT
3 Aug.1799 Samuel Fluellin sold to Covington Cordrey 100 acres of TURNSTILE aka FISHERMANS QUARTER, BETTYS ENLARGEMENT & CALLOWAYS ADDITION.

FISHING LOT

Patented 1844 by Hambleton E. Bennett for 2 1/2 acres

FITCHFIELD

Patented in 1688 by Edward Bennett for 150 acres
13 Nov.1693 Edward Bennett gave to daughter Mary Tully wife of John Tully 150 acres. Mary Tully afterwards married Walter Redman.
7 Aug.1716 Walter Redman and wife Mary Redman gave to her son John Tully 50 acres, if no issue to son Joseph Tully.
2 Dec.1728 Joseph Tully sold 50 acres to John Twiford.
14 Aug.1732 Edward Bennett son of Edward sold to John Twiford 50 acres.
21 Aug.1744 Edward Bennett s/o Edward who was the son of Edward Bennett sold 100 acres to his brother George Bennett
15 Dec.1746 John Twiford sold to William Moore of Quantico 50 acres.
27 Feb.1746 George Bennett and wife Jean Bennett sold to William Moore 100 acres on the south side of Quantico Branch.
10 Sep.1757 William Moore sold to William Bennett 100 acres of FITCHFIELD & FAIRHAM now called BENNETTS PURCHASE.
7 Jan 1768 William Bennett and wife Dorothy Bennett sold 100 acres to John Leatherbury of FITCHFIELD & FAIRHAM
29 Oct.1803 John Moore with wife Margaret Moore sold to John Byrd 287 2/3 acres of WOOD YARD, FITCHFIELD & TURKEY COCK HILL

FITCHWATERS STUDY

Patented in 1770 by Ambrose Fitchwater
Resurveyed in 1783 by Benjamin Henderson for 350 acres, Wicomico 100.
27 Mar 1787 Benjamin Henderson with wife Elizabeth Henderson sold 344 3/4 acres to Levin Miles.
5 Mar.1796 Levin Miles with wife Elizabeth Miles sold to Isaac Henderson 344 3/4 acres
21 Feb.1797 Isaac Henderson sold to Joshua Knight for 5 shillings 34 acres and 1/4 acre and 7 acres of same.
21 Feb.1797 Isaac Henderson sold 20 1/2 acres to Obed Bayley for 5 shillings.
8 oct.1799 Talman Dorsey and wife Betty Dorsey sold part to James Bennett.
10 Dec.1799 Stephen Roach and wife Mary Roach sold all rights to James Bennett
13 Dec.1799 Jenkins Henderson, Benjamin Henderson, John Henderson, Lemuel Henderson, Isaac Henderson and Taby Henderson of Worc.Co. sold all rights to James Bennett.
22 Oct.1801 James Knight with wife Eliza Knight, Peter Manlove and

wife Sarah Manlove, John Reddish with wife Rhoda Reddish sold to William Brereton, part Isaac Henderson sold to Joshua Knight.
1 Dec.1801 Elzey Davis with wife Mary Davis (late Mary Knight) sold to William Brereton their rights.
1 June 1804 William Brereton with wife Nancy Brereton sold to William Cottman, lands conveyed him by James Knight, Peter Malone and wife Sarah Malone, John Reddish and Elzey Davis with wife Mary Davis. no name of land.
1805 William Cottman willed property to be sold to pay debts, unnamed.

FLANDERS

Patented in 1754 by Ebenezer Hearn for 66 acres
27 May 1765 Ebenezer Hearn sold 66 acres to John Martin at Wicomico River
10 Sep.1769 John Martin sold 66 acres to William Cottman Waller.

FLAT GLADE

Patented in 1763 by Joseph Venables for 100 acres in Rewastico 100.
1783 tax - Joseph Venables 100 acres
1788 Joseph Venables willed to granson Benjamin Venables son of Benjamin and Betsy Venables.
12 Dec. 1788 Joseph Venables sold 15 3/4 acres to William Phillips.
1827 William Phillips willed to son Peregrine Phillips the Venables plantation, unnamed.

FLAT RIDGE

Patented on 8 May 1762 by William Smith for 9 acres

FLETCHERS CHANCE

see CROOKED CHANCE

FLUELLINS NEGLECT

Patented in 1767 by Isaac Handy for 185 1/2 acres in Nanticoke 100
1772 Isaac Handy willed to wife Betty Handy dwelling plantation.
1783 tax - Elizabeth Handy 185 1/2 acres
31 Aug.1799 George Handy grandson of Isaac Handy sold to Chaplin Conway 240 acres of HANDYS DISCOVERY, HANDYS CHANCE & FLUEULLINS NEGLECT.
29 Mar.1803 Chaplin Conway with wife Ann Conway sold for 5 shillings to William Robertson 29 1/2 acres of FLUELLINS NEGLECT, HANDYS CHANCE & PASTURAGE.
14 Dec.1808 Chaplin Conway with wife Ann Conway sold 50 acres to James Harris
1 Feb.1810 Chaplin Conway with wife Ann Conway sold to Samuel Robertson 46 3/4 acres
19 May 1809 Chaplin Conway with wife Ann Conway sold 32 1/2 acres to William Robertson.

FLUELLINS PLEASURE

Patented in 1762 by James Winright for 30 acres
1783 tax - James Winright, Nanticoke 100, 30 acres
1794 James Winright willed to wife Eleanor Winright, in Muddy Hole, and then to grandson Levi Selby son of Henry Selby and Rebecca Selby.

FLUELLINS PURCHASE

Patented on 23 Oct.1696 by Samuel Fluellin for 50 acres 4 miles from the south side of the Nanticoke River.
Rent Rolls 1666-1723, possessed by the widow Fluellin
1783 tax - Charles Fullerton 50 acres
13 July 1789 Samuel Fluellin sold to George Robertson 50 acres in Muddy Hole.
26 Mar.1793 Gillis Polk, surviving trustee of Ephraim King and Samuel Fluellin sold to Isaac Atkinson son of Isaac, CLEAR OF CANNON SHOTT, FLUELLINS SETLEMENT, ADDN. TO COW RIDGE,TICKNELL,CANNONS LOTT, SECURITY, etc.
1827 Isaac Atkinson willed lands unnamed to wife Priscilla Atkinson, and sons George Atkinson and Isaac Atkinson Jr.

FLUELLINS SETTLEMENT

Patented 1751 by Samuel Fluellin, a resurvey of CHANCE with vacancy for 137 acres.
19 Mar.1770 Richard Crockett Fluellin son of Samuel sold to Ephraim King 137 acres (This land Samuel Fluellin devised to son John Fluellin who died without issue)
1777 Ephraim King willed to Richard Crockett Fluellin and Samuel Fluellin lands their father Samuel bought and was conveyed by Samuel Fluellin son of Samuel Fluellin to me, unnamed.
1783 tax - Charles Fullerton 137 acres.
26 Mar.1793 Gillis Polk surviving trustee of Ephraim King and Samuel Fluellin sold to Isaac Atkinson son of Isaac.
1794 resurveyed by ISAAC ATKINSON for 578 1/2 acres.
1827 Isaac Atkinson willed lands to wife Priscilla Atkinson and to sons George Atkinson and Isaac Atkinson Jr, unnamed.

FLINTS SAFE GUARD

Patented on 19 May 1766 by John Flint for 113 acres a resurvey of HUGGS PURCHASE.
1771 Thomas Flint willed to son Thomas, where father John Flint lived.
6 Dec.1782 John Flint and Thomas Flint sold to Benjamin Nutter 113 acres.

FLORIDA

Patented 1822 by Samuel Lecompte 62 1/2 acres

FLOWERFIELD

Patented 8 Oct.1710 Robert Givans for 165 acres on the south side of Rewastico Branch.

Rent Rolls 1666-1723, possessed by Robert Givans
13 June 1721 Robert Givans with wife Mary Givans sold to Patrick Donelson 165 acres.
9 Apr.1744 George McKean of Brunswick Co. Va. sold to Thomas Roberts 107 acres of PHARSALIA & FLOWERIFLED that Patrick Donelson willed to grandsons Patrick McKean and George McKean.
5 May1744 Patrick McKean sold to Thomas Roberts, same as above.
1783 tax- Fisher Roberts (s/o Thomas Roberts) 165 acres
1795/6 Thomas Roberts wiled to son William Roberts
26 Oct.1803 William Roberts with wife Sarah Roberts sold to Joshua Roberts and Levin Taylor FLOWERFIELD & part of PHARSALIA purchased by Thomas Roberts.

FLOWERFIELD

Patented 1756 by Henry Lowe for 576 acres
ADDITION TO FLOWERFIELD pat. 1773 by Henry Lowe for 450 acres.
23 Nov.1779 Henry Lowe sold to Joseph Morris 450 acres of ADDITION
1783 tax - Joshua Hitch 222 acres
1783 tax - Willen McIntyre 52 acres
11 Nov.1784 Joseph Morris Sr. with wife Elizabeth Morris sold to Esme Bayley 229 acres.
9 Sep. 1799 Jacob Morris and Joseph Morris, John Morris, Elizabeth Adams sold 221 acres to John Hitch devisee of Joshua Hitch.
1799 Esme Bayley willed ADDITON TO FLOWERFIELD to wife Sinah Bayley and plantation to son Henry Bayley after wife's death.
8 Mar.1800 Robert Morris and Polly Ray sold to John Hitch 221 acres per bond of conveyance of Joseph Morris to Joshua Hitch.
22 Dec.1801 Henry E. Bayley sold to Thomas Bayley 229 acres of ADDITION .
6 May 1800 John Hitch with wife Jane Hitch sold to Levin Handy of Worc.Co. 221 acres.

FOES CONFUSION

Patented 1774 by Thomas Lloyd for 60 acres

FOLLY

Patented in 1735 by Richard Willis for 50 acres.

FOLLY

Patented in 1766 by Richard Samuels for 50 acres

FOLLY

Patented in 1774 by Elijah Cannon for 75 acres.
21 Jan.1775 Elijah Cannon sold 75 acres to Wingate Cannon on east side of the Nanticoke River. As Joseph Eckley and wife Susanna Eckley daughter of John Records appointed Ebenezer Cannon or James Cannon to make over to Wingate Cannon 75 acres.
7 Mar.1776 Sussex County Delaware land warrents, patented by Wingate Cannon

FOLLY

Patented in 1762 by Isaac Taylor for 25 acres
1783 tax - William Taylor 25 acres, Rewastico 100

FOOKS BEGINNING

Patented in 1834 by James M. Fooks and Benjamin H. Byrd for 50 acres.

FOOKS CHOICE

Patnented in 1790 by Ezekiel Ruark for 30 acres at head of Wicomico River
14 Mar.1795 Ezekiel Ruark sold to Henry Toadvine 30 acres

FOOKS COST

Patented on 25 Nov.1765 by William Fooks for 400 acres a resurvey from LONG ACRE.
1764 David Cathell willed to son David 100 acres of a resurvey with William Fooks, FOOKS COST.
5 Aug.1767 William Fooks sold to Levi Cathell 100 acres
5 Aug.1767 William Fooks sold to David Cathell 100 acres
5 Aug.1767 William Fooks sold to James Fooks 21 acres.
1774 William Fooks willed to wife Mary Fooks and then to son Benjamin Fooks and to son Jesse Fooks 50 acres.
21 June 1779 Jesse Fooks sold to Jonathan Riggin 49 acres.
1783 tax - Thomas Fooks 21 acres
1783 tax - Levi Cathell 100 acres
1783 tax - David Cathell 100 acres.
25 Jan.1803 Levi Cathell with wife Rebecca Cathell sold 99 acres to William Brown.
25 May 1805 Joseph Fooks sold to Thomas Fooks.
11 Apr.1809 Benjamin Fooks with wife Hannah Fooks sold to Outten Toadvine, part.

FOOKS DISAPPOINTMENT

Patented on 3 Aug.1784 by William Pollitt for 30 acres.
3 Mar.1790 William Pollitt sold to Samuel Pollitt 30 acres.

FOOKS HARD LUCK

Patented in 1797 by Thomas Fooks for 115 1/2 acres
5 Apr.1800 Thomas Fooks sold to James Fooks and Benjamin Fooks, all.
3 Nov.1801 James Fooks sold to Benjamin Fooks his half.
29 Jan.1803 Benjamin Fooks with wife Hannah Fooks sold to Charles Fooks 115 1/2 acres.

FOOKS LOTT

Patented in 1813 for 270 1/2 acres by William Fooks in Wicomico 100, Worc.Co.
1833 William Fooks willed part to wife Ann Fooks and to son William Fooks.

FOOKS RIGHT

Patented in 1794 by William Fooks for 314 acres.
5 May 1801 William Fooks with wife Nancy Fooks sold to Todd Livingston 41 1/4 acres.

FOOT HOLD

Patented in 1800 by Jonathan Waller.
1828 William Phillips willed to son Peregrine Phillips.

FORCE PUTT

Patented 9 Oct. 1700 by Peter Douty for 50 acres on the west side of the Wicomico River, east side of Broad Creek
Rent Rolls 1666-1723, possessed by Peter Douty
1709 Peter Douty willed to Peter son of John Furbush 50 acres.
16 Mar.1729 Peter Furbush sold to John Larramore 50 acres.
9 Mar.1747 Levin Larramore and mother Mary Larramore sold to Teague Dickerson 50 acres.
22 Aug.1764 John Furbush sold to John Dougherty and Teague Dickerson 50 acres
1765 Teague Dickerson willed land on Broad Creek to son Levi Dickerson.
1795 John Dougherty willed lands to wife unnamed and after her death to son Robert Dougherty (he married Leah Dickerson daughter of Teague Dickerson)

FORK

Patented in 1762 by Duncan Baine. He patented ADDITION TO FORK in 1768 for 50 acres, also.
11 Dec.1787 Stephen Baine sold to John Hitch 30 acres of FORK & ADDN.
11 Dec.1787 Stephen Baine sold to Jacob Morris 32 acres of FORK, ADDN. TO FORK, & A THIRD POINT OF THE FORK.
7 Sep.1793 Stephen Baine with wife Ann Baine sold 22 1/2 acres to Joshua Morris of Worc.Co. FORK & POINT OF THE FORK
3 May 1794 Stephen Baine sold to Jacob Morris 16 3/4 acres of FORK & POINT OF THE FORK
3 May 1794 Stephen Baine with wife Ann Baine sold to John Morris son of Joseph part of FORK & POINT OF THE FORK.
13 Mar.1804 John Morris sold to Jacob Morris son of Joseph Morris part FORK & POINT OF THE FORK.
15 Mar.1806 William Pollitt sold to Jacob Morris part called Middle Neck 7 3/4 acres.
1825 John Morris of Jacob Morris willed to nephew William P. Morris.

FORK (of the) BRANCH

Patented on 6 Mar.1766 by Thomas Humphries for 9 acres.
Thomas Humphries gave to son Joseph. Joshua Humphries son of Joseph inherited.
1783 tax - Phillis Humphries 9 acres in Rewastico 100
1783 tax - Joseph Humphries 6 acres
1804 Joseph Humphries willed, to be sold.

26 Aug.1806 Thomas Humphries sold to Joshua Humphries 1 acre agreeable to the will of Joseph Humphries son of Thomas Humphries, no name.
1842 Josephus Humphries, Charles W. Humphries, Hugh Jackson, Sarah McB. Jackson, Archellus Humphries, Margaret W. Humphries sold 9 acres, of estate of Joshua Humphries, to Purnell Toadvine and Josiah Ellinsworth and John Slemons.

FORKED MULBERRY TREE

Patented in 1760 by Thomas Huffington for 20 acres
1783 tax - Thomas Huffington 20 acres, Rewastico 100
9 Mar.1786 Thomas Huffington with wife Mary Huffington and Richard Huffington sold to James Dean, 20 acres.
1805 James Dean willed 15 acres bought of Thomas Huffington to negro child Rhoda daughter of Peggy- no name.

FORKED NECK

Patented 20 Oct.1683 by William Stevens who assigned to Francis Jenkins.
1708 Francis Jenkins willed 200 acres to brother Robert King.
16 Jan 1719 Robert King and wife Priscilla King sold to Robert Hopkins 300 acres.
15 Aug.1730 Robert Hopkins and wife Jane Hopkins sold to Peter Samuels 300 acres.
5 July 1742 Peter Samuels Sr. sold to John Kilby 300 acres, north side of Deep Creek.
5 Feb.1746 John Kilby sold 300 acres to Charles Banister.
19 Aug.1771 Charles Bannister sold to the propietors of the DEEP CREEK FURNACE, Edward Vaughan and Company 300 acres.

FORKED NECK

Patented on 15 Apr.1695 by John Jenner about 2 miles from Tundotank.
20 Oct.1694 John Jenner willed to daughter Deborah Mechan, Dennis Driskell & James Driskell, at Quapongo Indian Town, no name.
Rent Rolls 1666-1723, claimed by the heirs of John Jenner under the guardianship of her brother James Train.
12 May 1725 Deborah Mechan sold to Dennis Driskell 400 acres.
6 Dec.1756 James Driskell sold to William Fooks 100 acres
6 Fec.1756 James Driskell sold to John Talbot 100 acres.
1756 James Driskell son of Dennis Driskell sold to Mary Fooks 200 acres, part not before sold to William Fooks or John Talbot.
8 Aug.1761 Mary Fooks sold 11 acres FORT NECK to George Handy and David Cathell.
16 Apr.1770 Mary Fooks sold to Thomas Fooks 139 acres.
16 Apr.1770 Mary Fooks sold to James Fooks 50 acres.
11 Apr.1772 George Handy Sr. sold to John Cathell 11 acres that George Handy and David Cathell bought of Mary Fooks.
1774 William Fooks willed to wife Mary Fooks 100 acres, and then to son Benjamin Fooks.
1783 tax - John Broughton 100 acres, Wic.100 Worc.Co.
1783 tax - Thomas Fooks 50 acres
1783 tax - Thomas Fooks 200 acres.

24 May 1786 John Venables sold to Phillip Scroggin 100 acres to pay debts, late property of George Talbot.
13 June 1791 William McBryde empowered gy John Scroggin and Robert Scroggin sold to William Toadvine and Stephen Toadvine
13 June 1791 George Talbott sold 100 acres to William and Stephen Toadvine.
28 Dec.1793 Stephen Toadvine and William Toadvine with wife Priscilla Toadvine, sold to Thomas Fooks 100 acres
1 Mar.1794 Benjamin Fooks to Thomas Fooks,division of lands.
25 Mar.1797 Joseph Fooks sold to Thomas Fooks, division of lands.
11 Apr.1801 Joseph Fooks with wife sold to John Cathell 16 acres
10 Dec.1803 Benjamin Fooks of William Fooks, with wife Henny Fooks sold to Sampson Davis 5 acres, 2 rods.
25 May 1805 Joseph Fooks with wife Anne Fooks sold to Thomas Fooks, part.
11 Apr.1809 Benjamin Fooks with wife Hannah Fooks sold to Outten Toadvine.
1818 Charles Fooks willed to daughter Sally Fooks

FORKED NECK

Patented 20 Aug.1675 by George Betts for 250 acres
18 Nov.1686 George Betts with wife Bridget Betts sold to Barnet Ramsey and Alexander Johnson both of Acco.Co.Va. now called SECOND PURCHASE.

FORKED NECK

75 acres, part FIRST CHOICE

FOR LITTLE OR NOTHING

Patented in 1803 by William Donoho for 21 1/4 acres.
1785 William Donoho willed to daughter Rebecca Powell and her children NOTHING BE IT MORE OR LESS.

FORREST GROVE

Patented in 1761 by Alexander Mitchell for 100 acres in Wicomico Forest.
8 Mar.1765 Alexander Mitchell sold to Moses Gordy 100 acres
17 Apr.1776 Sussex Co. Delaware land warrants, patented by Moses Gordy.

FORREST GROVE

Patented on 4 Sep.1749 by James McDaniel for 52 acres.
21 Mar.1752 James McDaniel, bricklayer, with wife Margaret McDaniel sold to Peter Parsons, planter 52 acres.
30 Nov.1759 Peter Parsons with wife Martha Parsons sold to Charles Parker Jr. 52 acres.
3 Nov.1762 Charles Parker with wife Ann Parker sold to Thomas Biffen Bayley 52 acres.
17 Dec.1774 Thomas Biffin Bayley with wife Tabitha Bayley sold to Joshua Holloway 12 acres.
1783 tax - William Parsons 25 acres
2 Feb.1797 Nimrod Adkins with wife Betsy Adkins, John Melson with wife

Hannah Melson, William Brewington with wife Sarah Brewington, Milby Adkins with wife Mary Adkins sold to Elizabeth Trader 42 1/2 acres of FORREST GROVE & JAMES PURCHASE that William Parsons willed to daughters.
2 Feb.1797 Same as above, sold to James Perdue except part sold Elizabeth Trader.
1823 John Parker of E. willed to son Elisha Parker 50 acres and mills bought of Peter Parsons.
1843 James Rounds willed to daughter Elizabeth Parsons, then to her son John J. Parsons.

FORREST GROVE

Patented in 1762 by James Perdue for 75 acres about 6 miles back from Salisbury Town on head of Wicomico River.
11 Oct.1769 James Perdue Sr. with wife Susanna Perdue sold to John Taylor son of Thomas Taylor 50 acres.
11 May 1771 James Perdue Sr. with wife Susanna Perdue sold 25 acres to William Parsons.
1783 tax - James Perdue of John Perdue, 50 acres
24 Oct.1795 James Perdue sold to Eli Perdue 50 acres.

FORREST GROVE

Patented on 4 June 1773 by Joshua Holloway for 417 1/2 acres
1786 FORREST GROVE ENLARGED, Joshua Holloway 458 1/2 acres
27 June 1774 Joshua Holloway with wife Mary Holloway sold to Elihu Bridell 98 acres, near the nead of Nasango Creek.

FORREST GROVE

Patented in 1783 by Jacob Parker in Wicomico 100, Worc.Co.
1787 Elisha Parker son of Jacob, willed to daughter Abigail Turner wife of Henry Turner 39 acres.
6 Oct.1787 Jacob Parker with wife Mary Parker sold to Elisha Parker 187 acres.
6 Oct.1787 Jacob Parker with wife Mary Parker sold to Elisha Parker 276 acres.
24 Feb.1810 John Parker and Elisha Parker both of Elisha, sold to Billy Parker son of John Parker, 172 acres.

FORTUNE

Patented on 19 Oct.1677 by William Stevens and assigned to Daniel Haste for 100 acres
1701 Daniel Haste willed Benjamin Wailes 100 acres
Rent Rolls 1666-1723, possessed by Benjamin Wailes (he married Elizabeth Haste)
1726/9 Benjamin Wailes willed to son George Wailes 100 acres
1736/7 Joseph Wailes willed to sons Daniel Wailes and Haste Wailes dwelling plantation, unnamed.
22 Mar.1758 Haste Wailes quitclaimed to brother Daniel Wailes TOSITER, FORTUNE, MIGHT HAVE HAD MORE & JOSEPHS LOTT

FORTUNE

Patented in 1744 by David Polk, a resurvey of LITTLE BELEAN for 305 acres
27 Feb.1750 David Polk sold 60 acres to William Davis
1752 William Davis willed to son-in-law Joseph Allen and daugter Betty Allen 60 acres.
1766 Joseph Allen willed to son William Davis Allen, lands unnamed.
14 Sep.1773 William Davis Allen, mtg. to Alexander Spicer, William French, John Bowman, Charles Crookshank, John Crawford and George Crawford of Great Britain, that was conveyed to grandfather William Davis by David Polk, with SLIGO.
1778 David Polk willed to son Josiah Polk.
1783 tax - William Allen 60 acres
1783 tax - Josiah Polk 230 acres
2 June 1785 William Davis Allen mortgaged Archibald Patison of Dorc.Co. 60 acres.
24 Mar.1786 William Davis Allen sold 60 acres to Planner Williams
13 Jan.1786 Archibald Patison of Dor. Co. released mortgage to Planner Williams
1788 Planner Williams willed estate to daughter Amelia Gale
2 Nov.1797 John Gale and wife Amelia Gale sold to William Polk all lands of Planner Williams.
1812 William Polk willed to son William Winder Polk land bought of John Gale and Amelia Gale, unnamed.

FORTUNE

Patented in 1748 by John Horseman and E. L. Horseman for 15 3/4 acres
1850 they are in Tyaskin District.

FORTUNE

Patented in 1748 by Robert Collier for 40 acres

FOUNTAINS CHOICE

Patented in 1762 by Stephen Fountain for 413 acres.
22 Jan.1774 Stephen Fountain with wife Judah Fountain sold to Benjamin Shockley 259 acres.
15 Mar.1783 Benjamin Shockley gave to Benjamin Shockley son of Sampson Shockley 83 acres.
12 Oct.1787 William Stevens with wife Agnes Stevens and Stephen Fountain with wife Judah Fountain sold to Levin Watson 100 acres.
1791 Benjamin Shockley willed to son John Shockley 83 acres and to son Elijah Shockley.
27 Nov.1792 William Stevens and Judah Fountain widow of Stephen and Levin Watson sold to Levin Watson 70 acres.
27 Dec.1792 William Stevens and William Morris sold to William Watson 30 acres.
14 Sep.1792 Belitha Nicholson sold rights to William Morris
19 Mar.1799 Eli Shockley with wife Zilpah Shockley sold to Jethro Morris
26 Mar.1799 Benjamin Johnson sold to John Shockley of Benjamin Shockley 82 acres.
25 Oct.1799 William Morris son of Thomas Morris sold rights to Charles

Hammond.
1 Aug.1800 Levin Watson with wife Joyce Watson and William Watson sold to Joshua Morris son of William Morris.
23 Dec.1801 William Morris with wife Catherine Morris sold to Charles Hammond all.
7 June 1802 Joshua Morris sold to Benjamin Briddell 105 acres.
2 Apr.1803 John Culver with wife Ibby Culver sold to William Dixon
24July 1803 Nathan Culver of Hancock Co. Georgia appointed brother John Culver of Salisbury trustee to sell the real estate of Richard Powders in right of wife Nancy Culver formerly Nancy Powders.
11 Feb.1804 William Dixon of Nathaniel Dixon, with wife Leah Dixon and Pierce Powell sold to Jethro Morris all from Richard Powders.
7 Apr.1807 Benjamin Shockley with wife Sarah Shockley sold to James Noble 83 acres.

FOUNTAINS FROLICK

Patented in 1771 by Edward Serman for 122 acres
1783 tax - Edward Serman 96 1/2 acres, Wic.100
22 APr.1785 Edward Serman sold to Capt. Benjamin Nutter 28 acres
21 Mary 1783 Clement Holliday and Nathaniel Ramsey comissioners to sell confistated property sold 122 acres to Edward Serman
28 May 1787 Edward Serman sold 24 1/2 acres to Peter Cahoon
13 July 1805 Betsy Cahoon sold to William Williams 24 1/2 acres
22 Nov.1806 Heirs of Richard Powders sold to Thomas Wimbrow. Signed Ebe Culver and Perch Powell.
24 Feb.1810 Betsy Cahoon widow of Peter Cahoon and Sally Cahoon her daughter sold to William Williams 24 acres.

FOUNTAINS LOTT

Patented in 1739 by Nicholas Fountain for 100 acres
16 Apr.1770 Nicholas Fountain with wife Tabitha Fountain sold to Hezekiah Carey 75 acres
9 July 1772 Nicholas Fountain sold to Boaz Wright 25 acres
19 May 1786 Hezekiah Carey sold to William Morris son of Thomas Morris 75 acres.
30 Oct.1789 Boaz Wright of Sussex Co.Delaware sold to Outerbridge Dixon of Worc.Co. 25 acres.
9 Mar.1791 Outerbridge Dixon sold to George Parsons 25 acres.

FOWLERS CHANCE

No patent found
8 Mary 1758 Arthur Fowler Sr. sold to Jonathan Fowler 124 acres, part on the south east side of the Nanticoke River
1772 Arthur Fowler willed to son Jonathan Fowler 124 acre, part and to sons Arthur Fowler and Jesse Fowler, residue of lands.

FOWLERS LOTT

Patented in 1756 by Isaac Fowler for 10 acres

FOX DEN

Patented in 1807 by Joshua Holloway for 24 acres

FOX STALL

Patented on 4 Oct.1682 John Evans for 50 acres.
Rent Rolls 1666-1723, possessed by Capt. Nicholas Evans (son of John)
1768 Thomas Records willed to wife Sarah Records and children
1783 tax - John Evans of Nicholas 50 acres
1783 tax - Archelus Records 28 acres- Rewastico 100(possibly another tract by this name or FOX HALL.)
9 Apr.1798 Archelus Records sold to Thomas Reddish 15 1/2 acres.
8 Sep.1810 Thomas Reddish wife wife Nancy Reddish and Isabella Morris sold to Caleb Kennerly 158 acres of PARTNERS CHOICE, GODDARDS ADDITION, FOX HALL.

FOX HARBOUR

Patented in 1811 by William J. Coulbourn 37 acres

FOX HARBOUR

Patented in 1798 by William Gordy for 120 1/4 acres
9 Nov.1809 William Gordy with wife Eliza Gordy sold to Betty Gordy part.

FOX HILL

Patented in 1775 by Thomas Pollitt for 46 acres

FOX HILL

Patented in 1796 by Elihu Jackson for 70 1/2 acres
5 Nov.1796 Elihu Jackson with wife Betty Jackson sold to George Parker 189 1/2 acres of COLLINS ADVENTURE & FOX HILL.
29 Apr.1797 George Parker sold to John Byrd, same as above.
13 July 1799 John Byrd sold to Elihu Jackson 189 1/2 acres,as above.
1836 Elihu Jackson willed lands, no named to sons Noah Jackson and John Jackson.

FOX ISLAND

Patented on 16 Aug.1753 by Jonathan Jenkins for 67 acres (his wife was Esther Hilman.)
1783 tax - Samuel Sockwell 67 acres.
25 Nov.1791 Samuel Sockwell with wife Esther Sockwell sold to Cyrus Sharp.

FOYS DISCOVERY

Patented in 1747 by Adam Foy for 50 acres
8 June 1753 Adam Foy, woodsman sold to Thomas Duncan 50 acres.
1 April 1756 Thomas Duncan sold to Charles Duncan 50 acres.
1783 tax - Charles Duncan 100 acres, Acquanto 00
                                                N
9 Apr.1805 Josiah Duncan with wife Martha Duncan sold to Richard Sampson and Seth Whaley rights. Came Kesiah Duncan mother of Josiah, released her dower rights.

FREE PURCHASE

100 acres PART OF DOUBLE PURCHASE

FEEEMANS ADVENTURE

Patented in 1764 by Henry Alexander for 80 acres.

FREENEYS HARD FATE

Patented in 1799 by Joshua Freeney
1822 Joshua Freeney willed lands in Somerset County to son John Freeney, unnamed.
1850 John Freeney in Salisbury district.

FRIENDS ADVENTURE

Patented in 1775 by Charles Vaughan for 461 1/2 acres
11 Mar.1782 Charles Vaughan sold to Zorobable King, Jesse Walston and Solomon Long 200 acres, to sell real estate of William Gray, with SCOTTS CHANCE.
11 Dec.1792 John Denwood, sheriff on behalf of Gustavous Scott against Charles Vaughn, sold to Charles Badley, SCOTTS CHANCE, FRIENDS ADVENTURE, no acres given.
26 May 1797 Levin Gray sold to Ephraim Badley
16 Jan 1802 David Gray sold to Charles Badley, part.
15 Sep.1804 Polly Badley widow of Ephraim Badley sold to Severn Badley 75 acres.
1843 Polly Cooper willed to son Severn B. Cooper (also names brother Severn Badley)
1850 Severn Badley in Barren Creek.

FRIENDS ADVICE

Patented in 1808 by Sandy Robertson for 7 1/4 acres
1814 Sandy Robertson willed to son William S. Robertson, plantation.

FRIENDS ASSISTANCE

Patented on 15 Nov.1685 by William Elgate.
Rent Rolls 1666-1723, possessed by Thomas Ralph. William Elgate having
1764 Robert Jenkins Henry willed to daughter Elizabeth Henry 300 acres.
1783 tax - Richard Haynie 300 acres- Rewastico 100
12 Aug.1794 Tract for Sale- FRIENDS ASSISTANCE around 280 acres, Isaac Henry and John Henry.
28 Aug.1793 Andrew Raglate of Aberdeen, North Britain, had 280 acres in Som. Co. He died intestate leaving Anna Rigg his only daughter. Appoints attorneys to sell, now in possession of Isaac Henry.
18 June 1796 Anna Riggs of Aberdeen North Britain sold to Jane Ker 358 3/4 acres.
17 Jan.1797 Jane Ker sold 268 3/4 acres to Hugh Gemmill, except part taken out of MAIDENHEAD.

FRIENDS CHOICE

Patented on 6 Feb.1672 by William Layton for 300 acres.
Rent Rolls 1666-1723, possessed by Thomas Ralph who purchased from William Layton 300 acres.
14 Nov.1721 Thomas Ralph sold to Affradozi Johnson 300 acres.
8 Dec.1742 Affradozi Johnson sold 125 acres to Purnell Johnson.
21 Aug.1746 Purnell Johnson sold to Isaac Handy, merchant 10 acres.(adjacent PEMBERTON plantation)
1750 Samuel Johnson willed to son Benjamin Johnson, willed me by my father.
26 Mar.1768 Benjamin Johnson sold 87 1/2 acres (lower part) to Affradozi Johnson.
15 May 1769 Thomas Johnson of Worc.Co. sold to Purnell Johnson of Somerset Co. 87 1/2 acres.
1743 Affradozi Johnson willed to son Thomas Johnson 87 acres at Rockawalkin and 125 acres to son Purnell Johnson and 87 acres to son Samuel Johnson.
1777 Affradozi Johnson willed to brother William Johnson 87 1/2 acres
1778 Purnell Johnson willed to sons Elijah Johnson and William Johnson
1783 tax - William Johnson 106 acres, Wicomico 100
1783 tax - William Johnson 124 acres
1783 tax - Henry Handy 10 acres
22 June 1785 William Johnson willed to brother Thomas Johnson, if he returns to the county, if not to brother Purnell Johnson.
14 Jan.1786 Elijah Johnson sold to Henry Handy and William Handy (Elijah Johnson brother of William Johnson, no deceased) two tracts with PEMBERTON, no acres.
10 Mar.1787 Thomas Johnson sold to William Handy and Henry Handy, to adjust lands of PEMBERTON & FRIENDS CHOICE, to determine lines of a parcel deeded Purnell Johnson to Isaac Handy for 10 acres called MULBERRRY LANDING.
9 Feb.1793 Purnell Johnson of Worc.Co. and William Hearn of Som. CO. sold to Elijah Johnson and William Purnell Johnson son of Elijah Johnson, FRIENDS CHOICE, SPENCES CHOICE.(Purnell Johnson and William Johnson representatives of Sarah Hearn late Sarah Johnson sister of Purnell and Elijah became equally entitled.) after death of Elijah Johnson to go to William Purnell Johnson and heirs.
April Court 1807, Thomas Handy petitioned the court to sell the real estate of Henry Handy, his brother, 10 acres.
1817 Purnell Johnson willed to Purnell Johnson conveyed by William Purnell Johnson to his mother Annie Dashiell (wife of Purnell Johnson and Thomas Dashiell.)

FRIENDS DISCOVERY

Patented on 18 May 1688 by James Weatherly for 300 acres
Rent Rolls 1666-1723, possessed by Henry Acworth (he married Sarah Weatherly daughter of James Weatherly)
1715 Henry Acworth willed to sons Henry Acworth, John Acworth and Samuel Acworth.
1783 tax - Henry Acworth 300 acres , Nanticoke 100
26 Jan 1782 Henry Acworth with wife Elizabeth Acworth sold 46 acres to James Phillips.
1784 James Phillips willed land unnamed to son Henry Phillips.

FRIENDS DISCOVERY

Patented on 4 June 1695 by Roger Burkum upon the Quantico for 30 acres.
1695 Roger Burkum sold to Roger West
13 Apr. 1732 James West and wife Mary West sold to John Anderson 30 acres
1783 tax - John Anderson 30 acres.

FRIENDS DENIAL

Patented 23 June 1727 by Alexander Adams for 50 acres
1 Oct.1752 Alexander Adams sold to George Adams 50 acres, in Deep Creek on the south side of the Nanticoke River.

FRIENDS DENIAL
FRIENDS DENIAL ENLARGED

Patented 18 Apr.1680 by Thomas Walker who assigned to Thomas Cox for 300 acres.
3 Oct.1684 Thomas Cox with wife Rebecca Cox sold to Phoenix Hall
5 Oct.1687 Phoenix Hall with wife Elizabeth sold 300 acres to Matthew Wallace.
Rent Rolls 1666-1723, belongs to Matthew Wallace who is now in Cecil County or thereabouts, two miles from the fork of the Wicomico River.
28 Sep.1723 Thomas Hugg and wife Joanna Hugg sold to John Caldwell that was conveyed to John Polk late husband of Joanna Hugg.
7 June 1723 William Polk of Dorc Co.Md. and wife Priscilla Polk sold to John Caldwell, that Matthew Wallace conveyed to John Polk, who gave to son William Polk.
1731 John Caldwell gave 300 acres to son Joshua Caldwell.9 June 1740 John Caldwell and Joshua Caldwell with wife Elizabeth Caldwell sold 100 acres to John Flint.
19 Nov.1747 Joshua Caldwell sold 150 acres to George Parsons.
7 Mar.1759 John Flint sold to Thomas Flint 150 acres.
3 Mar.1763 George Parsons gave to son George Parsons 150 acres.
1771 Thomas Flint willed to son John Flint, plantation, unnamed.
6 Dec.1782 John Flint and Thomas Flint sold to Benjamin Nutter part of FRIENDS DENIAL called FLINTS SAFEGUARD, 113 acres.
1795 FRIENDS DENIAL ENLARGED patented by John Flint for 226 acres.
1783 tax - George Parsons 150 acres, Wicomico 100, Worc.Co.
1783 tax - John Flint 150 acres
1808 George Parsons willed to son George Parsons.

FRIENDS ENDEAVOUR

Patented on 3 Oct.1689 by William Joseph for 2700 acres
4 Sep.1763 William Joseph Sr. of St. Marys Co. Md. sold to George Adams and Richard Crockett and William Turner of Worc.Co. patented William Joseph grandfather to William afsd on the south side of the Nanticoke River.

FRIENDS FOLLY

Patented in 1772 by William Paca of Annapolis for 975 acres.

5 Jun.1773 William Paca with wife Mary of Annapolis, attorney, sold to Christopher Cardiff of Dorc.Co. 643 3/4 acres that was resurveyed and found short, except part sold to James Hust but not deeded 104 acres.
20 Oct.1777 Christopher Cardiff with wife Margaret of Dorc.. Co.Md. sold 500 acres to John Phillips of Som. Co. (on the north side of Barren Creek.)
1783 tax - John Phillips 230 acres- Rewastico 100
1783 tax - Levin Smith 50 acres
1783 tax - Charles Weatherly 174 acres
1783 tax - Stephen Wright 150 acres
1808 Levin Smith willed lands to wife Mary Smith, unnamed. after death to Adam Moore
1810 William Russum willed to son William Russum

FRIENDS GOODWILL

Patented on 8 Apr.1703 by John Disharoon and Lewis Disharoon on the south east branch of Wicomico River between the fork and Long Bridge for 200 acres..
Rent Rolls 1666-1723, possessed by same
8 July 1738 John Disharoon with wife Margaret Disharoon, Lewis Disharoon and wife Jean Disharoon sold to William Hayman 200 acres.
1746 William Hayman willed to son Henry Hayman 50 acres, to son William 100 acres and to son Nicholas Hayman 50 acres, unnamed land.
18 June 1756 Henry Hayman sold to Eleanor Toadvine (daughter of William Hayman) 50 acres.
13 Mar.1761 Nicholas Hayman sold to William Venables 50 acres
13 Mar.1761 William Hayman son of William, sold to William Venables 25 acres.
18 Aug.1763 Charles Cottingham with wife Eleanor Cottingham (was Eleanor Toadvine)sold to William Winder 50 acres
8 June 1764 William Hayman sold to William Harrison 75 acres.
2 June 1767 Solomon Harrison sold to Elizabeth Harrison 75 acres.
1783 tax - Jonathan Shockley, Wic. 100 75 acres
1783 tax - John Sturgis
10 Sep.1786 Elizabeth Shockley sold part to Joshua Sturgis
13 July 1791 Esme Bayley, Gillis Polk, William McBryde to sell the real estate of John Mitchell late of Sussex Co.Del. for debts sold to William Winder 75 acres.
11 Apr.1792 Elizabeth Shockley sold all rights to William Winder Jr.

FRIENDSHIP

Patented 27 Nov.1685 Thomas Jones for 500 acres
Rent Rolls 1666-1723, possessed by Robert Catherwood for orphans (the widow Martha Jones married 2nd Robert Catherwood)

FRIENDSHIP

Patented in 1707 by Joseph Gray for 100 acres

FRIENDSHIP

Patented in 1759 by David Cordrey for 100 acres
1774 David Cordrey willed all lands to be sold, unnamed.

19 Apr.1777 Thomas Cordrey exec. of David sold to Joseph Melson 79 acres on the north side of Barren Creek.
1783 tax - Joseph Melson 79 1/2 acres
1787 Joseph Melson willed to son Joseph Melson, if no issue to daughters Sary Melson and Mary Melson (his was was Eunice Melson)
1849 Joseph Weatherly willed 100 acres to son Marcellus Weatherly.

FRIENDSHIP

Patented in 1771 by John Phillips for 50 acres
5 Dec.1772 John Phillips with wife Rhoda Phillips sold to John Sterling 1/2 part of undivided right of inheritance, 50 acres on south side of Barren Creek.
1777 John Sterling willed to wife Mary Sterling, estate, then to sons Travis Sterling, John Sterling and Aaron Sterling
1783 tax - Aaron Sterling 25 acres, Rewastico 100
1783 tax - William Gillis 25 acres

FRIENDSHIP

Patented in 1776 by Isaac Horsey and William Horsey for 50 acres.
1786 William Horsey willed to son William Horsey part of BEAVER DAM called FRIENDSHIP
20 May 1782 Isaac Horsey with wife Mary Horsey of Sussex Co.Del. sold to William Horsey with wife Eleanor Horsey of Somerset County his part of 50 acres.
1783 tax - William Horsey- Rewastico 100.

FRIENDSHIP

Patented in 1811 by Henry Banks

FRIZELLS ENJOYMENT

Patented on 12 Nov.1685 by John Frizzell for 150 acres
Rent Rolls 1666-1723, possessed by John Frizzell
12 Jan 1722 James Jones and wife Sarah Jones and Andrew Bashaw with wife Mary Bashaw divided the lands of John Frizzell father of Sarah and Mary, two miles from head of Wicomico River 150 acres.
2 Mar.1725 Andrew Bashaw with wife Mary Bashaw sold to John Disharoon 150 acres.
1754 John Disharoon willed to son William Disharoon
1783 tax - Mary Disharoon 150 acres, Wicomico 100
1831/2 James Disharoon willed to grandson William Disharoon son of James Disharoon.

FRUITLAND TOWN

Originally part of Wicomico Manor. During the revolution was knows as Disheroons Cross Roads and later called FORKTOWN, on road from Salisbury to Princess Anne Md, in Trappe District.

FRUITFUL PLAIN

Patented on 24 Apr.1684 by George Layfield four miles from the north

east br. of the Nanticoke River in Smiths Neck, for 540 acres.
1733 Thomas Layfield willed to son Thomas Layfield 540 acres
17 May 1743 Thomas Layfield mortgaged to Francis Newbold.

GABRIELS SECOND PURCHASE

Patented on 15 May 1760 by Gabriel Powell for 100 acres

GALES DISCOVERY

No patent found.
13 Jan.1804 James Nelson with wife Esther Nelson sold to Augustus Cannon 6 1/2 acres with MONMOUTH & HARRIS LOTT
9 Nov.1804 John Nelson sold part to Augustus Cannon
8 Aug.1809 Daniel Ballard, sheriff sold to Alexander Stewart, per judgement against Augustus Cannon, 156 3/4 acres MONMOUTH, ADDITION TO GALES DISCOVERY, HARRIS LOTT.
9 Oct.1810 Daniel Wailes sold his part of the real estate of Alexander Stewart, to John Stewart, no name.

GALES PURCHASE

Patented in 1737 by John Gale for 713 acres (was part of ADDITION)
10 oct.1738 John Gale of Stepney Parish with Milcah Gale his wife sold 17 acres to Thomas Ralph
1743 Thomas Ralph willed to daughter Susanna Serman 17 acres
1783 tax - Elizabeth Gale 696 acres, Nanticoke 100
1783 tax - Charles Serman 17 acres
4 Mar.1797 Charles Serman sold 17 acres to Charles Rider
1801 Charles Rider willed to son Thomas Rider
8 Apr.1806 Thomas Rider with wife Priscilla Rider of Sussex Co.Del. sold to John Rider, 17 acres.

GALES SUPPLY

Patented in 1726 by Levin Gale for 384 acres
1742 Levin Gale willed to brother Matthias Gale, near Whitehaven town, land unnamed.
9 Aug.1800 Jesse Fooks sold to Charles Fooks with STAND FAST
8 Apr.1806 George Gale, Littleton Gale with Anne Maria Gale who released her dower rights sold 1/2 to Thomas Layfield.
13 June 1806 Jonathan Noble sold to Edward Morris 87 3/4 acres
13 June 1806 Edward Morris sold same to Jonathan Noble.

GALES UNION

Patented in 1787 by John Gale for 1450 acres.
21 Jan 1794 John Gale traded 19 1/2 acres with William Bounds for same of LOCKLAMON
4 Mar.1794 John Gale traded with Edward Austin 33 2/3rds acres for BETTS PRIVILDEDGE
5 June 1798 Edward Austin with wife Mary Austin sold 33 2/3rds acres to John Gale
27 Feb.1807 John Gale sold to John Taylor 1 1/2 acres.

GARDEN SPOT

Patented on 7 Oct.1761 by Smith Brewington for 100 acres In Wicomico forest
29 May 1763 ADDITION TO GARDEN SPOT patented for 278 acres by Smith Brewington
1783 tax - Smith Brewington 280 acres of ADDITION
1823 SECOND ADDITION patented by Smith Brewington for 359 3/4 acres.

GEDDES OUTLETT

Patented in 1763 by Robert Geddes

GENTLEMENTS MISTAKE

Patented in 1794 by Henry Banks for 35 acres
3 Jan.1795 Henry Banks sold to William Beard 35 acres
1800 William Beard willed to children lands unnamed, James Beard, Thomas Beard, Eliab Beard and Molly Beard.
6 June 1808 Eliab Beard sold to William Bounds of Richard Bounds 16 acres of LATENS DISCOVERY & GENTLEMENTS MISTAKE on south side of Wic. River on road from Upper Ferry to Salisbury
1828 Smith Sims willed to daughter Polly Murray where Thomas Murray now lives purchased of George Marshall.

GEORGES ADDTION

Patented in 1851 by William Laws for 236 acres
1850 he is in the Coulbourns, 6th district of Worc.Co.

GEORGES CHANCE

Patented on 2 Sep.1730 by George Oliphant for 50 acres
31 Mar.1733 George Oliphant with wife Margaret Oliphant of Step. Parish sold to John McDowell.
8 Feb.1759 John McDowell sold 50 acres to David Greer.

GEORGE GALES GENEROSITY

Patented in 1788 by Henry Gale for 291 1/2 acres
17 Aug.1804 Henry Gale sold to John Gale, agreement to divide land of Capt. Henry Gale.
26 Apr.1805 Henry Gale sold 1 acres to James McCree
5 Dec.1806 Henry Gale sold 1 acres to James McCree
27 Feb.1807 Henry Gale sold 2 acres to John Gale, at Quantico Creek.

GEORGES LOT

Patented on 1 Dec.1762 by George Smith son of Andrew Smith for 247 acres a resurvey of CHOICE
4 Apr.1768 George Smith with wife Deborah Smith sold to Marcellus Hobbs 211 acres
14 Jan.1789 George Smith sold to Edmond Northern Nelms 24 acres.
25 Nov.1795 Warren County Georgia- Milbourn Magee with wife Nelly Magee ordained Davis Magee of Hancock Co.Georgia to sell to Archibald

Smith, HOBBS ADVENTURE, GEORGES LOTT, devised Nelly Magee and Betsy Hobbs by father Marcellus Hobbs.
5 Dec.1797 Davis Magee late of Georgia sold to Archibald Smith 134 acres.
8 Dec.1798 Matthias Hobbs son of Marcellus Hobbs sold to Samuel Turner Parker, rights.
1802 Archibald Smith of Lawrence Co. South Carolina by son Joshua Smith sold to Samuel Turner Parker 125 1/4 acres of GEORGES LOTT & HOBBS ADVENTURE
3 June.1806 George Smith son of Andrew Smith sold to Samuel Turner Parker 211 acres.
4 Mar.1808 John Bounds of Dorc.Co. with wife Nancy Bounds heir of Edmond Northern Nelms, sold to Ebenezer Lowe, part.

GEORGES LOT

Patented in 1803 by William Pollitt for 51 acres
3 Nov.1807 William Pollitt of Worc.Co. sold 42 acres to John Austin.

GEORGES MEADOW

Patented 9 Nov.1763 by George Dashiell for 40 acres
1768 George Dashiell willed to granddaughter Peggy Nicholson daughter of Joseph Nicholson, or if Nancy McMurray and Rebecca McMurray will pay expenses, then to them.
1783 tax - Arthur Denwood 20 acres- Nantticoke 100
1783 tax - Price Russell 20 acres (he married Ann McMurray)

GEORGES PLEASURE

Patented in 1749 by Day Scott for 50 acres
12 Oct.1754 Day Scott sold 50 acres to Betty Game, spinster
5 Dec.1772 Betty Game of Worc.Co. sold to George Collier Hopkins 50 acres.
1783 tax -. George Collier Hopkins 50 acres, Nanticoke 100.

GEORGES PLEASURE

Patented in 1763 by George Collier for 24 1/4 acres
1774 George Collier willed to son George 24 1/4 acres
22 Aug.1808 George Collier with wife Martha Collier sold to Matthias Dashiell Hopkins 24 14 acres
5 Nov.1808 Matthias D. Hopkins with wife Eleanor Hopkins sold 24 acres to James Walter
1783 tax - James Walter 24 1/4 acres- Nanticoke 100
1844 Jacob Dashiell colored man, willed to sons George Dashiell, James Dashiell, Rufus Dashiell, John Dashiell and Etamus Dashiell 2 1/2 acres purchased of George Hopkins of Matt Hopkins.

GEORGES PRIVILEDGE

Patented in 1746 by Day Scott for 50 acres
7 Dec.1750 Capt. Day Scott sold 50 acres to Daniel Wailes.
1774 George Collier willed to son John Collier GEORGE COLIERS PRIVILDEGE 13 1/2 acres, after his death to grandson George Collier

1783 tax - Ann Collier 13 1/2 acres
22 Aug.1808 George Collier with with Martha Collier sold to Matthias
Dashiell Hopkins 15 3/4 acres GEORGE COLLIERS PRIVILDEGE.
5 NOv.1808 Matthias Dashiell Hopkins with wife Eleanor Hopkins sold to
James Walter 15 3/4 acres.
1827 James Walter willed to son Littleton Robertson Walter 15 3/4
acres of GEORGE COLLIERS PRIVILEDGE

GEORGES PURCHASE

Patented on 30 Jan.1721 by George Benston for 100 acres
Rent Rolls 1666-1723, possessed by George Benston
23 Mar.1726 George Benston with wife Rebecca Benston sold 100 acres to
James Cathell
1772 Jonathan Cathell willed to father James Cathell for life
1772 James Cathell willed to grandson Josiah Cathell
27 Mar.1780 Josiah Cathell sold to Levi Cathell 100 acres
1 Apr.1782 Levi Cathell with wife Rebecca Cathell sold to Jonathan
Riggin 91 1/4 acres.
29 Aug.1782 Jonathan Riggin sold to Henry Toadvine 100 acres 4 miles
from head of Wicomico River, no name.
6 Apr.1808 John Cathell sold to Levi Cathell and David Cathell 102 1/2
acres of SAFEGUARD & GEORGES PURCHASE.
2 Jan.1810 Levi Cathell son of David, sold 100 acres to David Cathell
16 Jan.1812 David Cathell sold to Nancy Jones 100 acres.
17 Jun.1815 John Cathell and Nancy S. Cathell sold to Matty Cathell

GEORGES PURCHASE

Patented in 1834 by James Derrickson, John C. Derrickson, Isaac
Covington and Elisha L. Purnell for 46 acres.

GEORGES STRUGGLE

Patented in 1833 by George H. Parsons for 165 1/2 acres
1850 he is in 4th district Worc.Co.Md.

GETHSEMANE

Patented on 3 Oct.1674 by William Stevens for 900 acres in Quantico
Creek.
Jan 1676 William Stevens with wife Elizabeth Stevens sold 600 acres to
Edward Lumm
9 May 1678 Edward Lumm sold to William Hatheley 300 acres called LUMMS
PURCHASE out of GETHESEMANE and now called HATHELEYS PURCHASE or
CHOICE.
12 Feb.1680 William Stevens with wife Elizabeth Stevens sold 300 acres
to John Evans called EVANS PURCHASE.
13 July 1683 John Evans with wife Mary Evans sold to John Hamblin,
EVANS PURCHASE 300 acres.
1687/88 William Hatheley willed to daughters Judith Hatheley and
Catherine Hatheley 300 acres of HATHELEYS CHOICE.
Rent Rolls 1666-1723, possessed by Samuel Worthington 300 acres, John
Hamblin 300 acres, John Kemp 300 acres.
15 Oct.1709 Samuel Worthington sold 300 acres to Thomas Dashiell now

called BATCHELLORS CHOICE
5 Dec 1735 Thomas Dashiell exchanged with John Jones son of Robert Jones for lands on the south side of Money Creek devised by Robert Jones father of said John Jones.
10 Sep.1759 Ephraim King with wife Ann King conveyed to Samuel King three tracts DELIGHT, GETHESAME & ROSS all property that became right of Ann King by the death of her brother Christopher Nutter.
1783 tax - Samuel King 300 acres- Rewastico 100.
9 Nov.1797 George Gale, Littleton Gale of Cecil Co., Levin Gale, Samuel Wilson with wife Leah Wilson sold to Edward Austin 1100 acres called MEMUNQUAK in Nutters Neck, that Samuel King was seized of (bond provided against claims by Charles Rogers with wife Amelia Rogers against children of Levin Handy or wife.)
8 Nov.1798 William B. Bond with wife Priscilla Bond sold to George Gale, Levin Gale, Littleton Gale and Samuel Wilson with wife Leah Wilson prop of Samuel King deceased.,no name or acrege.
8 Nov.1797 George Gale, Littleton Gale of Cecil Co., Levin Gale, Samuel Wilson with wife Leah Wilson sold to Thomas Garrettson of Som.Co. devised by Ephraim King to Levin Gale, all with LONG DELAY
6 Jan.1798 George Robertson with wife Mary Robertson sold to Levin Gale
26 Apr.1805 Priscilla Bond sold to Levin Farrington GETHSEMANE, DEIGHT, ROSS devised her by deaths of father, mother and brothers and Ephraim King and Samuel King.

GILES FOLLY

Patented in 1764 by William Giles for 271 3/4 acres a resurvey from PARREMORES FIRST CHOICE & SALLOP
1772 William Giles willed to Leah Duncan and balance of plantation to son Isaac Giles, unnamed.
11 Sep 1775 Isaac Giles with wife Elizabeth Giles sold 271 3/4 acres to Ralph Moore
29 May 1778 Leah Duncan sold 50 acres to Ralph Moore
1783 tax -. Ralph Moore 271 3/4 acres, Nanticoke 100
20 Mar.1784 Isaac Giles son of Jacob Giles sold all rights to John Leatherbury
18 May 1784 Isaac Giles Jr. sold to John Leatherbury, on south side of Quantico Creek, now possessed by Ralph Moore, his interest.
6 Mar.1786 Ralph Moore and wife Mary Moore sold to Mary Bonnewel wife of Michael Hall Bonnewell of Dorc.Co. 50 acres of PARREMORES FIRST CHOICE, SALLOP AND GILES FOLLY.
6 Mar.1786 Ralph Moore with wife Mary Moore sold to Sarah Moore wife of Levin Moore 50 acres.
18 May 1791 Ralph Moore leased for seven years to James Anderson 600 acres of PARREMOURS FIRST CHOICE, GILES FOLLY, SALOP
9 Nov.1791 Ralph Moore with wife Mary Moore and James Moore sold to James Anderson, part.
9 Mar.1793 Michael Hall Bonnewell with wife Mary Bonnewell of Kent Co.Del. sold to James Anderson of Som. Co. that Mary Bonnewell at death of her parents Ralph Moore and Mary Moore was seized, 50 acres.
25 Aug.1794 Ralph Moore and James Anderson sold 1 acre to the Methodist Society in Quantico for a chapel.
1804 James Anderson willed to son James, land purchased of Michael

Hall Bonnewell.
10 Apr.1809 Richard K. Moore with wife Priscilla Moore sold to John Rider 196 acres.

GILES LOT

Patented on 11 June 1696 by William Giles Jr for 450 acres.
Rent Rolls 1666-1723, possessed by William Giles Jr.
1749 William Giles willed to son Thomas Giles.
12 Jan 1755 Thomas Giles sold 50 acres to Jacob Giles for 10 shillings
1769 Thomas Giles, planter willed to son Jacob Giles 125 acres, on road from Wicomico Ferry to Broad Creek. To son Thomas his dwelling plantation on the south side of afsd tract and plantations to sons Isaac Giles and William Giles where they live.
1 Sep.1770 Thomas Giles s/o Thomas with wife Mary Giles sold to John Wailes 120 acres.
15 Nov.1774 William Giles s/o Thomas, with wife Mary Giles sold to George Twilley 50 acres
1783 tax - Isaac Giles 250 acres- Nanticoke 100
1783 tax - Eunice Giles 175 acres
1783 tax - John Wailes 120 acres
9 Aug.1784 Isaac Giles son of Thomas sold to Levin Wailes, his interest.
22 Mar.1787 Isaac Giles Jr. sold 20 acrees to Benjamin Wailes.
13 Aug.1787 Isaac Giles s/o Thomas with wife Elizabeth Giles sold to Levin Wailes 175 acres
10 Oct.1789 Isaac Giles s/o Thomas sold to Benjamin Wailes 20 acres
10 Oct.1689 Isaac Giles sold his rights to William Giles for 5 shillings.
10 Oct.1789 Isaac Giles son of William Giles deceased sold 10 acres to Denwood Turpin.
10 Oct.1789 Denwood Turpin sold 20 acres to George Twilley
16 May 1794 William Giles Jr. and Isaac Giles sold 70 acres to Benjamin Wailes.
16 May 1794 Isaac Giles sold part to William Giles Jr.
17 Sep.1794 George Twilley son of John Twilley sold to Benjamin Venables 10 acres.
1796 Benjamin Venables willed to wife Elizabeth Venables 1/3 of lands unnamed and to sons John Venables, Charles Venables & Robert Venables
2 Apr.1803 Benjamin Wailes sold to William Horsey 234 acres.
4 Dec.1804 William Horsey of Delaware sold to Richardson Donoho 189 1/2 acres.
7 Oct.1805 Benjamin McClennan (married Ann Venables in 1804) sold to William Andrews, his wifes dower interest.
21 Apr.1807 James B. Robins sold to Arthur Dashiell part that Isaac Giles had from his father Thomas Giles 175 acres that he conveyed to Levin Wailes; for debts.
22 April 1807 Arthur Dashiell sold to James B. Robins of Worc.Co.

GILES VENTURE

Patented in 1764 by William Giles
1772 William Giles willed to Esther Duncan 50 acres on road from Quantico Mill to Rewastico Mill
22 Apr.1785 Isaac Giles son of Jacob Giles, and Isaac Giles Sr. and

Samuel King sold to John Hopkins 50 acres
1812 John Hopkins willed to son William Hopkins plantation on road from Quantico Mills to Rewastico Mills, unnamed.

GILLIS ADDITION

Patented on 21 Nov.1685 by John Gillis for 100 acres
1720 John Gillis willed to sons Thomas Gillis and Ezekiel Gillis
18 Nov.1766 James Collins sold 100 acres to James Houston.
1771 Patented GILLIS ADDITION by Joseph Gillis 18 acres
1783 tax - Joseph Gillis 18 acres
1783 tax - William Stone 100 acres
15 May 1784 James Houston sold 100 acres to William Stone
24 Oct.1802 George Gillis sold to James H. West 18 acres.
12 Apr.1802 James H. West sold to Arthur Dashiell 18 acres.
1802 Arthur Dashiell willed to son Levin Dashiell
30 July 1803 George H. Dashiell of Acco.Co.Va. sold his part from father Levin Dashiell, to Martha Holt.

GILLIS ADVENTURE

Patented 16 Dec.1682 by William Merrill and assigned to John Gillis for 100 acres.
1720 John Gillis willed 100 acres to sons Thomas Gillis and Ezekiel Gillis.
25 Feb.1775 James Holder and wife Esther Holder, Margaret Duncan spinster sold 50 acres to John Hopkins.
1755 Joseph Allen willed lands unnamed to son William Davis Allen
1783 tax - William Davis Allen 100 acres
1783 tax - Thomas Gillis 5 acres
1783 tax - John Hopkins 150 acres
(there must have been more that one patent by this name.)
15 Mar.1797 Ninian Pinkney sold for Joseph Gillis of the Island of Madeira to William Stone.
1838 William Murray Stone s/o William, willed to son John Witmer Stone land purchased from Ninian Pinkney by my father.

GILLIS'S CARE

Patented in 1746 by Thomas Gillis for 22 acres
18 June 1755 Thomas Gillis sold to Nicholas Evans 22 acres
1783 tax - John Evans of Nicholas 22 acres, Nanticoke 100

GILLIS'S MEADOW

Patented in 1762 by Thomas Gillis 4 miles from head of the Wicomico in the forrest
4 May 1669 Thomas Gillis sold to Jonathan Riggin 100 acres.
4 May 1779 Thomas Gillis gave to son Joseph Gillis 50 acres.
1783 tax - John Jenner 50 acres, Wic.100.

GILLIS SWAMP

Patented in 1796 by Thomas Gillis for 4 1/4 acres

GILLIS'S VENTURE

Patented in 1763 by Thomas Gillis for 5 acres

GIVANS ADVENTURE

Patented in 1762 by Samson Burbage for 30 acres
1850 he is in the 6th district Coulbourns, Worc.Co.Md.

GIVANS CARE

Patented in 1749 by Hiram Givans for 57 acres

GIVANS DISCOVERY

Patented in 1765 by Day Givans for 50 acres
7 Mar.1754 Day Givans sold to Elizabeth Hall 40 acres.
1765 Day Givans sold to Joseph Collins 70 acres of GIVANS HIS DISCOVERY
1767 Joseph Collins willed to daughter Margaret Collins
1783 tax - James Phillips- Rewastico 100, 50 acres
15 Feb.1786 Negro Bridget sold to James Lloyd 50 acres pat. Day Givans and devised her by will, on the north side of Rewastico Creek.

GIVENS LAST CHANCE

Patented on 19 June 1698 by Robert Givans on the north side of Deep Creek.
4 July 1728 repatented by Robert Givans for 200 acres.
21 Sep.1730 Robert Givans sold to David Smith 200 acres for 5 shillings.

GIVANS LIBERTY

Patented in 1772 by Solomon Givans
14 Apr.1774 Solomon Givans sold to James Tull 229 1/2 acres
23 Dec.1774 James Tull sold to Spencer Haris 224 acres
26 Mar.1784 Spencer Harris sold 224 acres to William McBryde
1783 tax - Spencer Harris 129 acres, Wic.100 Worc.Co.
1783 tax - Solomon Givans 79 acres
12 May 1788 Solomon Givans sold rights to Jethro Morris son of Thomas Morris.
25 Apr.1791 William McBryde with wife Sarah McBryde sold to Joshua Dorman 75 acres.
1795 Elias Burbage willed to son Thomas Burbage 115 acres
1795 Spencer Harris willed lands unnamed, to wife Sinah Harris
16 Sep.1801 Thomas Burbage son of Elias Burbage sold to Jethro Morris CORN HILL & GIVANS LIBERTY 115 acres
18 Feb.1809 James Ritchie trustee to sell real estate of William McBryde sold to William Johnson Coulbourn.

GIVANS LOTT

Patented on 1 Mar.1688 by Robert Givans for 150 acres near Tuseky Branch
1783 tax - Robert Givans

15 Dec.1740 Robert Givans son of Robert of Rewastico Creek sold 150 acres to John Records Jr.of Tuseky Branch.
17 Mar.1749 Jarrad Wyley of Worc.Co. sold 100 acres to Joseph Ennals of Dorc.Co., bought of Robert Givans.

GIVANS SECURITY

Patented in 1749 by James Givans for 300 acres.
8 Apr.1753 David Kirkpatrick and wife Jane Kirkpatrick (late widow of Robert Givans deceased) sold to Joshua Whittington of Dorc.Co. 200 acres.
(Joshua Whittington married Elizabeth Nairn. She married 2nd. Huett Nutter by 1767 and had son William Whittington)
1783 tax - Huett Nutter 100 acres (escheat of White Marsh) Rewastico
1783 tax - William Whittington 200 acres
19 Dec.1817 Matthias Whittington sold to William Bounds 56 acres of GIVANS SECURITY & BOWER HILL.
28 July 1825 Matthias Whittington sold to John Bounds 12 acres.
26 Feb.1825 William Bounds son of James Bounds sold to John Bounds 265 3/4 acres of BOWER HILL & GIVANS SECURITY.

GLADE SIDE

Patented in 1755 by John Gupton for 50 acres
19 Sep.1763 John Gupton sold to Thomas Humphries Jr. 50 acres
25 Sep.1797 Thomas Humphries Jr. sold 50 acres to George Wilson
5 Sep.1809 George Wilson Sr. sold 50 acres to Caleb Kennerly

GLADSTEANS ADVENTURE

Patented on 15 June 1682 by John Gladstean for 150 acres
Rent Rolls 1666-1723, possessed by John Gladstean
Repatented in 1689 by Peter Elzey for 150 acres
6 Dec.1723 Francis Elzey, Levin Rigby with wife Elizabeth Rigby sold to Thomas Marvel.
18 Mar.1752 Robert Marvel son of Thomas Marvel sold to Thomas Cooper and Samuel Cooper 150 acres.
20 Mar.1753 I Thomas Marvel give to son David Marvel 100 acres in the middle of a tract. To son Thomas Marvel 100 acres at back of the tract. Son Phillip Marvel to Job Gasteneau. To son Robert Marvel dwelling plantation 150 acres, unnamed.
16 Mar.1756 David Marvel son of Thomas Marvel sold to Joseph Rolle 100 acres part of HARDSHIP & GLADSTEANS ADVENTURE.
12 Aug.1758 Thomas Marvell sold to Abraham Taylor 100 acres part of GLADSTEANS ADVENTURE & HARDSHIP.
17 Feb.1765 Thomas Cooper and Samuel Cooper sold to John Badley 75 acres of GLADSTEANS ADVENTURE & HARDSHIP
23 May 1774 Samuel Cooper sold to Charles Badley 75 acres of HARDSHIP & GLADSTEANS ADVENTURE.
1783 tax - Robert Brown 64 acres- Rewastico 100
1783 tax - Dean Badley (resurvey to hardship)11 acres
1783 tax - Joseph Rolle
1783 tax - Abraham Taylor
1783 tax - Dean Badley 64 acres
1791 Abraham Taylor willed part to son William Taylor

1799 Ephraim Badley willed to daughter Adah Badley
3 June 1803 Abraham Taylor with wife Molly Taylor sold to Horatio Taylor 100 acres of GLADSTEANS ADVENTURE & HARDSHIP
17 May 1810 Louther Taylor of Kent Co.Del.attorney for Bartholomew Taylor and Abraham Taylor of Bracken Co. Ky sold to Horatio Taylor of Som. Co.Md.
1843 Polly Cooper w/o Samuel Cooper willed to sons Martin Cooper and Severn Cooper.

GLADSTEANS CHOICE

Patented 2 Nov.1682 by John Gladstean for 150 acres and assigned to Peter Elzey
1715 Peter Elzey willed to daughters Francis Elzey and Elizabeth Elzey 150 acres on Nanticoke River, unnamed.
Rent Rolls 1666-1723, possessed by Richard Austin
1783 tax - Joseph Rolle (with GLADSTEANS ADVENTURE 100 acres)
1783 tax - Abraham Taylor (with GLADSTEANS ADVENTURE 100 acres)

GLADSTEANS INDUSTRY

Patented on 18 June 1689 by John Panter for 170 acres 2 miles from Broad Creek, Nanticoke 100
Rent Rolls 1666-1723, possessed by John Panter
20 Nov.1729 James Rowley of Dorc.Co. sold to Charles Dean of Dorc.Co. 170 acres.

GLASCOE

Patented on 30 May 1706 by Thomas Gordon for 300 acres, at side of Broad Creek.
Rent Rolls 1666-1723, possessed by Thomas Gordon
8 Mar.1734 John Smith son of Charleton Smith with wife Elizabeth Smith sold to John Collins 150 acres that Thomas Gordon sold to Charleton Smith.
29 Oct.1753 John Collins sold 100 acres to John Stilley.
12 Aug.1758 John Stilley sold 100 acres to Solomon Collins.
22 Aug.1769 John Collins sold 50 acres to William Figgs
23 Oct.1772 John Smith sold 150 acres to Fountain Stilley for 5 shillings.
16 Sep.1774 Fountain Stilley with wife Margaret Stilley sold 150 acres to Stephen Davenport of Kent Co.
(probably to Sussex Co.Delaware)

GLASCOW GREEN

Patented on 16 Nov.1772 by William Adams
19 Nov.1773 William Adams sold to John Scott for 25 1/4 acres.
18 Sep.1776 John Scott rector of Step.Parish, with wife Elizabeth Scott sold to Isaac Horsey.
20 Mary 1782 Isaac Horsey with wife Mary Horsey of Sussex Co.Del. sold 25 1/4 acres to William Horsey and wife Elinor Horsey of Som.Co.Md.
25 Dec.1784 William Adams sold to William Horsey 25 1/4 acres for 5 shillings.
1786 William Horsey wiled plantation unnamed to son Isaac Horsey
28 April 1804 Isaac Horsey sold to John Byrd 25 1/4 acres.
1858 ADDITION TO GLASCOW GREEN, patented by John Parsons.

GLOSTER

Patented on 28 July 1768 by William Whittington for 68 acres
23 Oct. 1794 William Whittington docked and entailed 68 acres.

GLOUCESTER

Patented on 8 Nov.1672 by John Keen and John Okey for 150 acres
13 Apr.1680 John Keen with wife Mary sold to John Richards 150 acres
1 Aug.1678 John Okey with wife Mary Okey sold 150 acres to John Richards and wife Elizabeth Richards.
20 Nov.1690 John Richards, joiner with wife Elizabeth Richards sold to Thomas Dullahide, planter.
27 July 1716 George Bayley gave to son George Bayley 150 acres.
19 Feb.1744 John Richards sold 60 acres to George Bayley
5 Feb.1747 Phillip Richards of Dorc.Co. sold to Elias Bayley, part.
1 Jan 1771 Newton Bayley (widow of George Bayley) and Isaiah Bayley sold to Jacob Meek 1 acre
9 May 1771 Jacob Meek with wife Sarah Meek sold 1 acre to Newton Bayley.
12 Aug.1776 Robins Bayley heir of George Bayley and Isaiah Bayley deceased, released his rights to Benjamin Bayley where his father George Bayley lived, in consideration of money to be paid to Robins Bayley after death of mother Newton Bayley.
16 Sep.1782 Deposition- came Littleton Bayley age 22 years-witnessed that George Bayley ahd GLOUSTER and was burried on same and had son George Bayley, now possessed.

GODDARDS ADDITION

Patented in 1815 by Thomas Goddard, John Goddard and George Goddard
8 Sep.1810 Thomas Reddish with wife Nancy Reddish and Isabella Morris sold to Caleb Kennerly 158 acres of PARTNERS CHOICE, GODDARDS ADDN. & FOX HALL
1847 Caleb.Kennerly willed to wife Juliann Kennerly, 1/3rds, no land mentioned. (she is in Quantico in 1850)

GODDARDS FOLLY

Patented on 10 Oct.1677 by John White for 600 acres, who assigned to Richard Stevens.
Rent Rolls 1666-1723, possessed by Richard Stevens 600 acres
13 Mar 1685 Richard Stevens with wife Abigail Stevens sold 200 acres to Peter Parsons.
1713 Richard Stevens willed to son Richard and wife Abigail Stevens and then to son Isaac Stevens.
12 May 1737 John Parsons son of John, with wife Mary Parsons sold to Robert Malone 100 acres.
17 Nov.1743 John Parsons of Worc.Co. sold to Ann Deverix and her son John Deverix part formerly sold Peter Parsons grandfather of John afsd.
6 Nov.1764 John Deverix sold to Joseph Morris 90 acres for 5 shillings.
15 Mar.1768 John Malone sold 100 acres to Robert Malone.
1783 tax - Robert Malone 100 acres

1783 tax - Joseph Morris 90 acres
1786 Joseph Morris willed 90 acres to John Malone Morris.
23 July 1793 Stephen Malone with wife Elizabeth Malone sold to John Morris 20 acres.
7 Mar.1795 Stephen Malone son of Robert Malone sold 9 acres to William Malone.
12 May 1795 Stephen Malone sold to William Bounds 106 3/4 acres per deed from John Parsons to Robert Malone adj. TURKEY RIDGE, no name.
5 Oct.1797 Stephen Malone sold to John Morris 10 acres.
10 Sep.1808 William Malone sold part to George Malone.
1810 John Morris son of Joseph Morris, willed to sons Joseph Morris and John H. Morris 120 acres.

GOLDEN GROVE

Patented in 1771 by John Robinson for 9 acres

GOLDEN QUARTER

Patented in 1695 by William Wallace for 100 acres
Rent Rolls 1666-1723, possessed by John Hall
2 Nov.1738 Moses Duskey sold to Samuel Davis 100 acres that William Wallace sold to John Hall who conveyed to Moses Duskey
1756 Samuel Davis willed to son Walker Davis 100a cres
1783 tax - Samuel Davis 100 acres, Wicomico 100
19 July 1788 Samuel Davis sold to John Johnson 32 3/4 acres
11 Oct.1794 Samuel Davis sold to Thomas Fooks 52 acres
17 Oct.1807 Thomas Fooks sold to James Fooks of Thomas 52 acres
1826 Benjamin Johnson willed to grandaughter Phillis Nutter
1872 Phillis Dykes Nutter willed to be sold land on road from Salisbury to Snow Hill.

GOLDEN QUARTER

Patented on 27 Dec.1715 by Thomas Jones at Little Creek
Rent Rolls 1666-1723, possessed by Thomas Jones.
Repatented in 1730 by John Moore for 50 acres
7 Oct.1755 John Moore of Dorc.Co. sold to Joshua Calloway 50 acres on the north side of Little Creek, at Nanticoke River
22 June 1758 John Calloway son of John sold to William Winder 50 acres.
22 June 1758 Thomas Savage sold to William Winder.
16 Aug.1763 William Winder sold to Levin Calloway 50 acres.

GOLDEN VALLEY ADDITION

Patented 1767 by Joshua Mitchell for 426 acres
Patented 1767 SECOND ADDITION 1135 1/4 acres Joshua Mitchell
26 May 1787 Col. Joshua Mitchell sold to John Pope Mitchell 1000 acres of GOLDEN VALLEY SECOND ADDITION & AYDELOTTES BEAVER DAMS

GOLDS DELIGHT

Patented 8 Sep.1695 by Edward Gold for 450 acres, near Spring Hill
Rent Rolls 1666-1723, possessed by Edward Gold

18 Oct.1716 Edward Gold sold 50 acres to John Matthews
12 July 1721 Edward Gold sold 400 acres to Benjamin Wailes
2 Feb.1725 John Matthews and wife Sarah Matthews sold to Mary Hampton, gentlewoman 50 acres.
1737 Joseph Wailes willed to wife Helena Wailes and to sons John Wailes and George Wailes.
1744 Mary Hampton willed to son John Henry bought of John Matthews 50 acres.
1783 tax - John Wailes, 200 acres Rewastico 100
1783 tax - George Wailes 200 acres
1788 George Wailes willed to son John Irving Wailes manor plantation where I live and to grandson William Wailes son of Levin Wailes and Mary Wailes, when of age GOLDS DELIGHT from son John Wailes.
7 Sep 1794 George Twilley soon of John Twilley sold to Benjamin Venables 50 acres where mother Eleanor McAllen now lives with GILES LOTT & WESTERN FIELDS.
1797 John Wailes willed to son Benjamin Wailes 20 acres and then to grandson John Wailes son of Benjamin Wailes.
1799 Joseph McClellan sold to friend Horatio Stayton, where Jesse Vinson lives.
4 Dec.1804 William Horsey of Delaware sold 21 3/4 acres to Richardson Donoho.
5 Jan 1805 William Horsey of Dover Del. sold to John Wailes 261 1/4 acres of GOLDS DELIGHT & WAILES RETREAT.

GOOD HOPE

Patented in 1745 to Daniel Melson for 100 acres
12 Mar.1654 Daniel Melson patented ADDITION TO GOOD HOPE 45 acres.
1783 tax - Daniel Melson 87 acres Wic.100
1783 tax - Daniel Melson ADDITION TO GOOD HOPE 45 acres
1785 Daniel Melson willed land to grandson Daniel Melson, unnamed.
10 Oct.1796 Daniel Melson Jr. sold to Daniel Melson his father 100 acres GOOD HOPE, 45 acres of ADDITION TO GOOD HOPE
29 May 1798 Daniel Melson of Sussex Co.Delaware sold to John Hearn 100 acres.

GOOD HOPE

Patented 2 Oct.1713 Morris Morris for 100 acres on the south side of Broad Creek
Rent Rolls 1666-1723, possessed by Morris Morris
1716 Morris willed to Robert Givans 100 acres on Broad Creek, unnamed
5 June 1733 Robert Givans sold 100 acres to Isaiah Quartermus.

GOOD INCREASE

Patented in 1760 for 50 acres by George Vance
27 Sep.1763 Patented 116 acres by George Vance, resurvey
1774 Patented 181 1/4 acres by George Vance
20 Jan 1764 George Vance sold to Edward Northern Nelms condemmed land 20 acres

GOOD INCREASE

Patented in 1784 by Jarvis Jenkins for 5 1/2 acres

1783 tax - Kibble Jenkins 5 1/2 acres, Wic.100

GOOD INTENTION

Patented in 1769 by John Disharoon for 177 acres
Repantented in 1783 by Newton Disharoon 177 acres
13 Mar.1787 Newton Disharoon with wife Mary Disharoon sold 14 3/4 acres to George Disharoon of Worc.Co.
9 July 1788 Newton Disharoon sold to George Disharoon, out of two patents 20 1/4 acres and 14 3/4 acres
9 Sep.1796 Stephen Disharoon son of George Disharoon sold 19 1/2 acres to Joshua Morris
19 Mar.1796 Stephen Disharoon son of George Disharoon sold 14 acres to Cyrus Sharp
1799 Newton Disharoon willed to sons William Disharoon and John Disharoon.
1802 Cyrus Sharp willed lands unnamed to brothers William Sharp and Daniel Sharp.
31 May 1810 Daniel Sharp with wife Rebecca Sharp sold to James Bennett, now called WHITE PLAINS
1815 resurveyed to WHITE PLAINS

GOOD LUCK

Patented on 15 Nov.1685 Alexander Thomas for 100 acres on Quantico Creek.
May 1720 James Boucher with wife Frances Boucher sold to Thomas Ralph of Quantico 48 acres that Alexander Thomas willed to Gamer Waller and to daughters Elizabeth Thomas and Frances Thomas. Elizabeth married James Russell and Frances married Thomas Boucher.
1732 William Ralph repatented as GOOD LUCK AT LAST
8 Sep.1733 William Ralph and wife Sarah Ralph sold 50 acres to Thomas Parremore
6 Jan 1745/6 James Russell, cooper, son of James sold to Alexander Thomas Russell 62 1/2 acres of TULLOCK GRANGE & pt. of ALEXANDERS GOOD LUCK.
10 Nov.1770 Thomas Ralph son of William Ralph sold to William Ralph part.
1769 William Ralph willed to Joseph Parremore 25 acres, he to pay for said land, and parts to sons Mitchell Ralph and George Ralph.
2 Jan 1775 Thomas Parremore and William Ralph sold 73 1/2 acres to Joseph Parremore
6 Apr.1776 Sussex Co.Delaware, land warrents patented by Thomas Ralph

GOOD LUCK

Patented on 28 Aug.1717 by John Caldwell who assigned to James Caldwell for 63 acres
Rent Rolls 1666-1723, possessed by James Caldwell
18 Aug.1741 John Lewis of Accoc.Co. sold to George Dashiell, where Elizabeth Lewis mother of John owned devised to said John Lewis, proceeds to be paid to her grandson Josiah Lewis, also known as TO HAVE & TO HOLD 45 acres.
10 Jan 1742 George Dashiell gave to son Clement Dashiell 15 acres bought of John Lewis and to son Louther Dashiell 30 acres.

2 June 1745 William Dashiell sold 32 acres to Robert Kirby of Northampton Co.Va. with PHARSALIA
20 Aug.1755 Robert Kirby sold to Isaac Dashiell 32 acres.
10 June 1756 Clement Dashiell willed to son Josiah Dashiell 450 acrs of DASHIELLS LOTT & CHANCE given me by father George Dashiell.
23 Mar.1758 Isaac Dashiell with wife Henrietta Dashiell sold to Mitchell Jones 32 acres.
28 Mar.1758 Isaac Dashiell sold to Mitchell Jones land bought of Robert Kirby.
1769 Mitchell Dashiell willed to son George Dashiell
1783 tax - George Dashiell 3 1/2 acres- Rewastico
1783 tax - Esther Jones 32 acres
1783 tax - William Johnson 32 acres
3 Mar.1795 George Dashiell son of Mitchell Dashiell sold to Robert Dashiell his part.
12 Feb.1798 Benjamin Jones son of Mitchell Jones sold to George Robertson 300 acres of PHARSALIA, GOOD LUCK HENRYS CONCLUSION
12 Jan 1799 Esther Jones widow of Mitchell Jones sold her interest to Shiles Crockett
9 Mar.1799 Robert Dashiell Sr. with wife Isabella Dashiell sold to Arthur Dashiell Jr.

GOOD LUCK

Patented in 1730 by John Records for 40 acres
24 Aug.1759 Ann Records widow of John Records sold to Thomas Records
Repatented in 1764 by Thomas Records for 207 1/2 acres
1768 Thomas Records willed to son Lame Records
28 Feb.1787 Fisher Roberts with wife Elizabeth Roberts sold 150 acres of FIRST CHOICE, ST GILES, GOOD LUCK to Everton Kennerly on Rewastico Creek.
1783 tax - Archelus Records 77 acres
18 Feb.1787 John Smith with wife Mary Smith sold to Fisher Roberts 150 acres of St.GILES,FIRST CHOICE,GOOD LUCK
1810 Lame Records son of Thomas Records willed to three daughters Betty Records, Polly Records and Phillis Records.

GOOD LUCK

Patented on 16 Sep.1731 by Patrick Caldwell for 100 acres.
5 Nov.1740 Patrick Caldwell with wife Mary Caldwell sold to John Polk 100 acres.
1776 Sussex Co.Del. resurvey William Polk son of John Polk

GOOD LUCK

Patented on 20 Aug.1762 by William Roach for 25 acres
1765 William Roach willed to son James Roach
1783 tax - James Roach 25 acres, Wic.100

GOOD LUCK

Patented in 1769 by Constant Disharoon for 50 acres
1783 tax - Constant Disharoon 50 acres, Wic.100
1795 Constant Disharoon willed to daughter Milla Stanford

1 Sep.1810 Amelia Stanford daughter of Constant Disharoon sold to John Disharoon 44 acres.
1849 John Disharoon willed to son James Disharoon

GOOD LUCK

Patented in 1774 to Henry Toadvine for 103 acres
1782 Henry Toadvine willed 50 acres to wife Mary Toadvine and part to son William Toadvine.
1783 tax - William Toadvine 103 acres
1804 William Toadvine willed to sons William Toadvine and Henry Toadvine.

GOOD LUCK

Patented in 1776 by Joshua Cathell for 91 3/4 acres
1808 John Cathell willed to son George Cathell 472 acres with HUNGER & THIRST. (George Cathell died and it descended to brother John Cathell Jr.who died and descended to James Martin Cathell.)
27 Oct.1821 Levi Cathell sold to James Toadvine part (Levi as trustee to sell real estate of John Cathell Jr.)
1822 James Toadvine willed to daughters Catherine Toadvine, Mary Ann Toadvine and Harriett Toadvine land bought of the estate of John Cathell.

GOOD LUCK

Patented in 1783 by William Willis for 50 acres
1783 tax - William Willis
Patented in 1786 ADDITION TO GOOD LUCK 138 acres, William Willis
9 Apr.1790 Zadock Sturgis, sheriff sold to Nathan Culver, per judgement against William Willis.

GOOD LUCK

Patented on 7 Dec.1785 by Joseph Dashiell a resurvey of DASHIELLS ADDITION, LAST CHOICE 7 vacant lands, for 57 1/4 acres
1788 Joseph Dashiell willed to grandson Joseph Dashiell son of Benjamin Dashiell.

GOOD LUCK

Patented in 1815 by Elisha Parker

GOOD LUCK

Patented in 1816 by John Twilley for 40 acres

GOOD LUCK

Patented in 1853 by John Windsor and George Bounds for 6 7/8 acres
1850 they are in Barren Creek district.

GOOD NEIGHBOURHOOD

Patented on 4 Nov.1686 by Thomas Farnel for 200 acres on the south side of the Nanticoke River
Thomas Farnel with wife ELizabeth Farnel sold to Patrick Quartermus who sold to Thomas Johnson.
12 Oct.1723 Thomas Johnson with wife Elizabeth Johnson sold to Richard Kellum 200 acres.
4 Dec.1729 Richard Kellum of Sussex Co.Del,weaver with wife Jane Kellum sold to John Phillips, schoolmaster, 200 acres now called CAMBRIDGE.
1762 John Phillips willed to son John, lands unnamed.
Absalom Phillips sold to Obed Outten, a little below Deep Creek and it was surveyed in Sussex Co. Delaware 30 Mar. 1776 and patented to Solomon Turpin.

GOOD NEIGHBOURHOOD

Patented in 1749 by Ephraim King for 194 acres.

GOOD NEIGHBORHOOD

Patented on 31 May 1756 by James Staton for 10 acres at the head of the Nanticoke River.
1 Mar.1758 James Staton with wife Grace Staton sold to John Laws 10 acres
7 Sep.1770 John Laws with wife Anne Laws sold to Robert Mitchell, merchant 10 acres

GOOD SUCESS

Patented on 28 Nov.1685 by Alexander Thomas for 100 acres
1695 Alexander Thomas willed plantation to daughters Eliza Thomas and Frances Thomas.
Rent Rolls 1666-1723, possessed by James Russell 50 acres and John Bouger 50 acres, who married the coheirs of Alexander Thomas.
1783 tax - Charles Serman 48 acres, Nanticoke 100
4 Mar.1797 Charles Serman sold 48 acres to Charles Rider with RALPHS VENTURE & GALES PURCHASE
1801 Charles Rider willed to son Thomas Rider
8 Spr.1806 Thomas Rider with wife Priscilla Rider of Sussex Co.Del. sold 48 acres to John Rider.

GOOD WILL

see CHANCE pat.1688

GORDONS DELIGHT

Patented 14 May 1689 by Thomas Gordon at head of Tuskey Branch issuing out of Broad Creek for 100 acres.
Rent Rolls 1666-1723, possessed by Thomas Gordon
11 Jan.1713 Thomas Gordon sold 100 acres to Robert Dashiell.
1718 Robert Dashiell willed 100 acres to son Matthias Dashiell
1744 Matthias Dashiell willed 100 acres to Capell King
6 Jan 1745 Capell King with wife Sarah King sold to John Moore 100

acres.
5 Nov.1769 John Moore sold to George Lane Moore 100 acres.
25 Mar.1771 George Lane Moore with wife Mary Moore sold 100 acres to James Layton of Dorc. Co. with SHILES RIDGE.

GORDONS GAIN OVER

Patented in 1783 by Gideon Badley for 13 1/2 acres
13 Nov.1787 Gideon Badley of Sussex Co.Del. sold 13 1/2 acres to James Robertson with one half of saw mill.

GORDONS LOTT

Patented 9 June 1689 by Thomas Gordon for 200 acres, 2 1/2 miles above the Wading place over Deep Creek.
Rent Rolls 1666-1723, possessed by William Broadwater in Acco.Co.Va.
1725/6 William Broadwater of Acco.Co Va. willed to son Caleb 200 acres
8 June 1742 John Bevans Sr. sold to John Lord, that Caleb Broadwater of Va. sold to him.
13 Aug.1767 John Lord sold to Jonathan Vaughan, William Douglas, ironmaster, David Murtre, Persisor Frazier, Christopher Marshall, William Wishart and Jemimah Edwards of Philadelphia,merchants, 175 acres.
1786 John Lord willed dwelling plantation to son William Lord, unnamed.
1788 William Lord willed to daughter Betsy Acworth daughter of Mary Acworth dwelling plantation, no name.

GORDONS LUCK

Patented in 1837 by Samuel Gordon for 328 3/4 acres

GORDYS ADVENTURE

Patented in 1775 by Peter Gordy Jr. for 25 acres
1772 Peter Gordy willed to son Peter Gordy 25 acres, unnamed.
1783 tax- Peter Gordy, Wic.100 Worc.Co.
10 June 1805 William Gordy sold to Joshua Freeney 25 acres.

GORDYS CHANCE

Patented in 1735 by Peter Gordy for 100 acres
1772 Peter Gordy willed to son Peter 100 acres, in Somerset Co. and Worc.Co.
ADDITION TO GORDYS CHANCE Patented in 1773 by Peter Gordy 25 acres
1783 tax - Peter Gordy 125 acres Wic.100 Worc.Co.
27 Apr.1797 Peter Gordy, Elisha Parker with wife Eleanor Parker, Samuel Parker with wife Hetty Parker, Benjamin Hearn son of Samuel Hearn of Sussex Co.Del. with wife Polly Hearn sold rights to William Gordy, 125 acres.
9 Nov.1809 William Gordy with wife Eliza Gordy sold to Betty Gordy.

GORDYS DELIGHT

Patented on 17 July 1760 by Moses Gordy for 75 acres

18 Apr.1776 Sussex Co.Del.land warrants orig. pat. Moses Gordy
1787 George Smith willed to son Seth Smith. Will probated Sussex Co.Delaware.
14 Apr.1789 Isaac Cooper of Sussex Co.Del. executor of George Smith sold to George Smith son of Andrew Smith of Worc.Co. lands left by will of George Smith, no name, or acreage.

GORDYS DISAPPOINTMENT

Patented on 1 Dec.1751 by Jacob Phillips 50 acres
23 Aug.1762 resurveyed by Jacob Phillips 100 acres
1783 tax - Jacob Phillips 100 acres
30 May 1785 Jacob Phillips sold 100 acres to Benjamin Hearn
23 Apr.1796 Benjamin Hearn sold to Hezekiah Maddux
1805 Hezekiah Maddux willed to son Wilson Maddux

(The) GORE

Patented in 1788 by Elihu Mezick for 12 acres
1788 Elihu Mezick willed to wife Margaret Mezick 12 acres, and then to sons Elihu Mezick, John Mezick and Daniel Mezick.
4 July 1799 John Mezick sold to Elihu Mezick 135 acres of END OF STRIFE, LEES SITUATION, GORE & River Tract adjoining.

GOSHEN

Patented on 20 Oct.1721 by Samuel Owens and Robert Owens for 100 acres on the east side of the main branch of the Naticoke River
Rent Rolls 1666-1723, possessed by same.
1727 ADDITON TO GOSHEN James Owens 184 acres.
1760 James Owens willed to son Samuel Owens 100 acres and part of ADDITION TO GOSHEN to son James Owens (wife Kesia Owens)
10 Jan 1775 Samuel Owens, joiner sold to Alexander Laws 100 acres
20 Feb.1775 William Owens, yoeman sold to Boaz Manlove Esq. of Sussex Co.Delaware GOSHENS ADDITION sold 45 acres.
20 Feb.1775 William Owens son of James Owens sold to Alexander Laws 45 acres ADDITION TO GOSHEN.

GOSHEN

Patented on 20 April 1762 by David Smith for 100 acres in Wicomico forest.
7 Sep.1776 Isaiah Smith son of David, with wife Jannet Smith sold to Henry Trader 100 acres
1783 tax - Elijah Smith 46 acres, Wic.100, Worc.Co.

GOSHEN

Patented in 1790 by Barkley Townsend for 60 acres
14 Sep.1793 Barkley Townsend of Sussex Co.Delaware sold to Elisha Parker of Worcester COunty, 28 1/2 acres
14Sep.1793 Barkley Townsend of Sussex Co.Del. sold to Spencer Davis Sr. of Maryland 31 1/2 acres.

GOSLEES CHANCE

Patented in 1774 by Joseph Goslee
1 Jan 1776 John Goslee gave to son Matthew Goslee CHANCE and part of GOSLEES LOT 50 acres.
1783 tax - Joseph Goslee 25 1/4 acres
13 Jan 1806 William Malone with wife Frances Malone sold to John Dorman and wife Nancy Dorman for 5 shillings 82 acres formerly belonging to Samuel Goslee, GOSLEES CHANCE, pt. LITTLE BALEAN
13 Jan.1806 John Dorman with wife Nancy Dorman sold to William Malone and wife Frances Malone, same- division of lands.
20 Aug.1808 William Malone sold his interest to Robert Malone
1848 George Malone willed real estate to sons Simon Malone and Peter Malone, unnamed.(They are in Trappe District in 1850.)

GOSLEES CONTENT

see HOGSDOWN

GOSLEES LOTT

Patented on 28 Nov.1688 by John Goslee for 100 acres
Rent Rolls 1666-1723, possessed by John Goslee
1721 will of John Goslee, no land in will, sons Richard Goslee, John Goslee, Matthew Goslee, Thomas Goslee and James Goslee.
1762 Richard Goslee willed LOTT to daughter Sarah Goslee
5 Apr.1768 John Goslee with wife Hannah Goslee sold 34 acres to Joseph Goslee.
1765 another patent by John Goslee
1 Jan 1776 John Goslee gave to son Matthew Goslee 50 acres with CHANCE
1783 tax - John Goslee 150 acres
1783 tax - Joseph Goslee 35 acres
1795 John Goslee willed to son Josiah Goslee 8 acres in northwest corner of GOSLEES LOTT, to wife Hannah Goslee land and to son George Goslee 50 acres, unnamed and to sons James Goslee and Thomas Goslee 100 acres unnamed land.
22 Oct.1805 Josiah Goslee with wife Leah Goslee sold to Isaac Harris 58 acres
1 Mar.1806 Thomas Goslee sold 50 acres to Isaac Harris.
1836 Patented John Goslee 5 3/4 acres of GOSLEES LOTT

GRAHAMS NEGLECT

Patented in 1832 by Levin Bennett for 116 acres
(1850 he is in Barren Creek District)

GRANDFATHERS CARE

Patented in 1775 for Esther Dashiell daughter of Robert Dashiell for 548 1/2 acres, a resurvey of IMPROVEMENT & RECOVERY
31 Mar.1764 Henry Lowe and wife Esther Lowe, mortgaged to George Day Scott and William Hayward.
1783 tax - Henry Lowe Jr. (he married Esther Dashiell)
17 June 1800 Tubman Lowe son of Henry Lowe sold to Frederick Augustus Dashiell 600 acres RECOVERY,IMPROVEMENT, GRANDFATHERS CARE, LOWES MEADOW & VENTURE PRIVILEDGE
1817 Benjamin Frederick A. Dashiell willed real estate to daughter

Elizabeth Leah Dennis, no named. Son-in-law John Upshur Dennis.

GRANVILLE

Patented in 1808 by Samuel Robertson for 100 acres

GRAVELLY BRANCH

Patented in 1740 by John Sharp for 100 acres

GRAVELLY HILL

Patented on 10 Dec.1721 by John Cotton for 50 acres
Rent Rolls 1666-1723, possessed by John Cotton
31 Dec.1728 John Cotton of Kent Co. Delaware, with wife Agnes Cotton sold to John Gray Jr. 50 acres
20 Nov.1750 Allen Gray sold to Ezekiel Hitch 50 acres that John Gray willed to Allen Gray.
22 Apr.1784 Ezekiel Hitch sold to Louther Hitch 50 acres
23 Sep.1797 Louther Hitch with wife Betsy Hitch sold to Curtis Hitch 58 3/4 acres of GRAVELY HILL, ELLIS CHANCE, ELLIS ADDITION.
11 March 1791 Louther Hitch sold 50 acres to Ezekiel Hitch.

GRAVENORS FIRST CHOICE

Patented in 1850 by Benjamin Gravener for 4 acres in Barren Creek.

GRAHAMS LOTT

Patented in 1802 by Benjamin Graham for 15 acres.

GRAYS LOTT

Patented in 1804 by David Gray for 84 1/2 acres.

GREAT CRY AND LITTLE WOOL

Patented in 1801 by Thomas Culver for 28 7/8 acres
29 Sep.1801 Thomas Culver sold to Thomas Humphries 28 7/8 acres adjacent COVINGTONS CHOICE & ELLIS ADDITION

GREAT NECK

Patented on 4 Sep.1695 by William Wallace for 100 acres
Rent Rolls 1666-1723, possessed by William Hayman
11 Mar.1711 John Smith, Thomas Layton, William Hayman and Thomas Byrd mortgaged to Charles Phillips.
8 Mar.1721 Henry Phillips son of Charles Phillips assigned to John Shockley
6 Oct.1729 William Wallace son of William sold to John Shockley 100 acres.
5 Mar.1745/6 John Shockley sold to son Richard Shockley 50 acres
7 Nov.1750 John Shockley with wife Sarah Shockley sold to George Austin of Somerset Co., joiner.
23 Nov.1752 George Austin with wife Priscilla Austin sold 50 acres to

Risdon Dixon.
3 Nov.1763 Richard Shockley sold 50 acres to George Toadvine
5 Aug.1772 John Toadvine sold to John Cathell tract conveyed by
Richard Shockley to George Toadvine 12 1/2 acres, no name.
4 Nov.1792 Sarah Toadvine sold to John Cathell 57 acres.

GREAT OAK ISLAND

see LARGEE

GREEN BANK

Patented in 1797 by William Bowland for 8 3/4 acres

GREEN BRIAR

Patented in 1785 by John Brown for 174 acres
Another patent by John Brown in 1786 for 83 acres
1783 tax - John Brown 77 1/4 acres
1783 tax - James Roach 96 1/3 acres
16 Aug.1785 John Brown gave to Anna Roach, Matty Roach, Mary Bozman Roach, Nelly Roach and Betty Roach 96 3/4 acres (children of James Roach deceased that John Brown gave to James Roach.)
22 Aug.1786 John Brown sold 9 acres to Joshua Stanford
3 Nov.1802 Joshua Stanford sold to John Cathell 131 1/2 acres of LITTLE NECK, ADDN. TO LITTLE NECK,STANFORDS FINDING, GREEN BRIAR
1808 John Cathell willed to son George Cathell
1871 Salisbury Advertiser, trustees sale of GREEN BRIAR & WILL HAVE MORE 100 acres which James Stevens purchased of R.K. Truitt.

GREEN HAMMOCK

Patented in 1772 by Henry Lowe for 134 3/4 acres
1783 tax - Henry Lowe Wic.100

GREEN HILL

Patented on 22 Apr.1680 by William Stevens who assigned to Thomas Humphries for 50 acres
18 Aug.1740 Thomas Humphries sold to brother Joshua Humphries 25 acres
1783 tax - Phillis Humphries 8 1/2 acres   Rewastico 100
1783 tax - Joseph Humphries 16 acres
1783 tax - Joshua Humphries 25 acres
21 Aug.1789 Joseph Humphries sold 1 1/8 acres to Charles Winright that his father devised to him.
2 Jan 1796 Charles Winright with wife Jane Winright sold to Joseph Humphries 1 3/8 acres.
8 May 1800 Joseph Humphries sold 2 acres to John Hitch, Littleton Aires and Sally E. Aires
8 May 1800 John Hitch, Sarah Hitch, Littleton Aires with wife Sally E. Aires sold to Mary Moore 2 acres.
13 Dec.1806 Jesee Byrd and Thomas Byrd Jr. with wife Sarah Byrd sold 1/2 acres lott to John C. Hatton
1804 Joseph Humphries willed to David V. Jenkins lot where James Nicholson lives and to Joseph Humphries son of Jacob Humphries, no name.
6 May 1808 David Vance Jenkins with wife Rebecca Jenkins sold to

Samuel Gover 1 3/8 acres
6 Jan 1810 Joseph Humphries with wife Dorothy Humphries sold to Joseph Moore 3/4 acre and 1/8 acres
1 June 1810 John Cheney Hatton with wife Esther Hatton sold to James Handy 1/2 acre
1811 Joshua Humphries sold 1 acre to Aaron Mezick.
22 Sep.1835 Archelus R. Humphries with wife Margaret W. Humphries, Charles W. Humphries and wife Amelia Humphries, Sarah McBryde Humphries sold to Josephus Humphries part of GREEN HILL & KEENS LOTT 195 acres that came them at death of father Joshua Humphries.

GREEN HILL

Patented on 23 Nov.1728 by Jacob Ingram for 50 acres
7 Aug.1738 Jacob Ingram with wife Charity Ingram of Sussex Co.Del. sold to Robert Hall 50 acres.
7 Aug.1748 Spence Hall of Kent Co. Del. tailor and Thomas Hall of Kent Co.,shoemaker and Moses Hall of Kent Co. yoeman, sold 50 acres to Daniel Boyce, at Deep Creek.
1755 Daniel Boyce willed to son Joseph Boyce part of GREEN HILL & TRYAL.

GREEN HILL TOWN

19 Apr.1730 Day Scott sold to George McClester 3/4 acre, lot #18
19 Apr.1731 Neal McClester sold lot #16 to Vestry of Stepney Parish
20 Aug.1737 Robert Jones sold lot #10 to Neal McClester
2 Aug.1737 Neal McClester sold to Day Scott lot #4
1753 Day Scott willed to son George Day Scott plantation I live GREEN HILL being part of SUNKEN GROUND.
1751 Neal McClester willed to nephew Samuel McClester son of John McClester lot #10
1796 George Day Scott willed lands to Ware Cheney, unnamed.

GREEN LAND

Patented by Col. William Stevens for 2500 acres who assigned to William Green.
Rent Rolls 1666-1723, possessed by William Green an inhabitant of Dorcester County.
3 Jan 1759 Ann Pincher, an indian, and Thomas Wingate sold for 99 years 100 acres WADING PLACE on Broad Breek.
11 Sep.1764 Jonathan Young sold to George Adams 500 acres on the south side of Nanticoke River s/s of Deep Creek below WADING PLACE.
17 Nov.1768 William Allen, Levin Gale, Henry Steele trustees for Nanticoke Indians, compensation of lands to John Mitchell merchant. To lay out 3000 acres for use of Nanticoke Indians adjacent Broad Creek originally patented for 500 acres 8 June 1712. Sold 2236 acres part of 2500 acres laid out for the Indians.
17 Nov.1768 Same as above, sold to Barkley Townsend son of William Barkley Townsend 514 acres.
10 Dec.1768 John Mitchell sold to Josiah Polk and Joseph Dashiell, at Wading Place on Broad Creek.

GREEN LAND

Patented on 18 Mar.1724 by Matthew Rain for 200 acres
1726 Matthew Rain Sr. with wife Arcada Rain, willed 100 acres to son Matthew after his mothers death and 100 acres to son John Rain.
6 Apr.1770 Matthew Rain and wife Peggy Rain sold to William Fassitt
1783 tax - John Rain 100 acres, Acquanto 100
8 Jan.1782 John Rain sold to Caleb Rain, BEE HILL and part of GREENLAND, no acreage mentioned.
9 Sep.1799 John Rain sold with wife Nanny Rain sold to Joseph Timmons 17 1/2 acres
9 Sep.1799 Joseph Timmons with wife Esther Timmons sold to Benjamin Timmons.
9 Apr.1803 Caleb Rain sold to John Brittingham part.
15 Jan.1803 Caleb Rain sold to John Brittingham, purchased from brother John Rain 7 acres of BEE HILL & GREEN LAND.
15 Jan.1803 Caleb Rain with wife Elizabeth Rain sold to John Bassett 17 acres.

GREENS LOSS

Patented in 1769 by David Cope for 150 acres
1767 David Cope willed to brother John Cope 75 acres and to daughter Phoebe Cope dwelling plantation unnamed and lands to mother Margaret Cope, unnamed.
1781 John Henry sold to Robert Henry 75 acres purchased of John Cope from his brother David Cope.
1783 tax - John Henry 75 acres, Rewastico 100
1783 tax - Drummond Simpson 75 acres

GREEN MEADOW

Patented in 1764 by John Calloway for 235 acres
26 Apr.1764 John Calloway son of Peter Calloway sold 96 acres to Thomas Moore
26 Apr.1764 John Calloway sold 139 acres to William Hitch
25 Sep.1765 William Hitch sold 140 acres to Josiah Dashiell
4 Mar.1769 Josiah Dashiell sold 140 acres to Ralph Lowe
21 May 1776 land warrents Sussex Co.Delaware - Ralph Lowe

GREEN MEADOW

Patented on 1 March 1689 by James Givans for 150 acres
1723 James Givans of Rewastico willed to daughters Martha Givans and Jane Givans swamp and 200 acres, unnamed.
1748 John Reed willed plantation to son Jacob Reed and wife Martha Reed, unnamed.
4 Nov.1768 John Davis with wife Martha Davis sold to Thomas Moore 150 acres that was possessed by John Reed former husband of Martha Davis
1783 tax - John Cooksey 40 acres Wic.100
11 Oct.1800 Jesse Fooks sold part to Rachel Fooks.

GREENS DISCOVERY

Patented in 1797 by Samuel Green for 9 3/4 acres

4 Sep.1807 Henry Wilson with wife Catherine Wilson sold to Eleanor Handy 132 1/2 acres of LYONS DEN, WARRINGTON, GREENS DISCOVERY.

GREENS RECANTATION

Patented on 28 July 1679 by William Stevens who assigned to William Green for 200 acres on northside of the main branch of the Quantico river.
3 Oct.1685 William Green with wife Elizabeth Green sold to Robert Burkum 200 acres.
Rent Rolls 1666-1723, possessed by Lucy Burkum 200 acres
28 Feb.1709 John Burkum gave 100 acres to son Roger Burkum
Roger Burkum died and eldest son John Possessed. John Burkum with wife Elizabeth Burkum sold 100 acres to Adam Hitch. Adam Hitch with wife Hannah Hitch sold to Thomas Phillips. Thomas Phillips and wife Mary Phillips conveyed to William Serman who assigned bond to William Young. William Young assiged to James West.
25 Mar.1725 Mary Phillips relic of Thomas Phillips and son Roger Phillips sold 100 acres to James West.
1749 James West willed to wife Abigail West plantation, 200 acres of GREENS RECANTATION to be sold, at the mouth of Broad Creek.
31 Jan 1753 Thomas Phillips sold 20 acres to John Anderson
31 Jan.1753 James West sold too acres to Richard Green
31 Jan.1753 James West sold 100 acres to Thomas Phillips.
10 Oct.1765 Thomas Phillips sold 80 acres to John Anderson
1768 Richard Green willed 90 acres to son Ezekiel Green
23 June 1785 James West son of James sold to John Anderson his moity
22 Oct.1789 John Anderson sold 62 acres to Thomas Caton with BACON QUARTER.
10 Apr.1790 John Anderson sold 13 acres to Thomas Skinner
26 May 1791 John Anderson sold 200 acres to Lambert Hyland.
10 May 1805 Ezekiel Green sold all his interest from father to Thomas Anderson
1829 John Horsey willed to wife Susan Horsey.

GREENS LUCK

Patented in 1763 by Richard Green for 315 acres, a resurvey from MARYS CHOICE
1768 Richard Green willed to son Samuel Green and to son John Green a small lot on south side of MARYS CHOICE obtained in a resurvey with Lazarus Huffington, and to son Isaac Green and son John Green 33 /12 acres.
21 Mar.1770 Isaac Green sold 7 acres to William Giles.
1772 William Giles sold 7 acres to Leah Duncan
11 Apr.1772 Samuel Green with wife Sophia Green sold 204 1/4 acres to Benjamin Atkinson.
11 Apr.1772 Isaac Green sold to Benjamin Atkinson 12 acres
6 Mar.1773 Isaac Green sold 14 acres to John Anderson
6 Mar.1773 Isaac Green sold 55 acres to Charles Leatherbury at Quantico Creek.
15 Apr.1773 Charles Leatherbury sold 55 acres to George Ballard for 5 shillings
1783 tax - Richard Acworth 230 1/2 acres, Rewastico 100
1783 tax - Benjamin Atkinson 88 acres

1783 tax - John Anderson 88 acres
1783 tax - John Hobbs 2 1/2 acres
26 May 1791 John Anderson sold 50 acres to Lambert Hyland.

GREENWICH

Patented on 4 Mar.1679 by William Stevens who assigned to Daniel Haste for 50 acres
1701 Daniel Haste willed to daughter Sarah Haste 50 acres
Rent Rolls 1666-1723, possessed by Robert Dashiell who married Sarah Haste, 50 acres.
1717 Robert Dashiell willed to son Haste Dashiell 50 acres
1749 William Dashiell (brother of Haste Dashiell) willed to son Robert Dashiell
1783 tax - Robert Dashiell 50 acres- Nanticoke 100
1789 Robert Dashiell son of William Dashiell, willed real estate unnamed to step-daughters Esther Lucas, Martha Lucas, Jane Lucas and Margaret Lucas .
13 Mar.1810 John H. Anderson with wife Maria Anderson sold to Thomas Walter lands Robert Dashiell father of Margaret Bloodsworth had that descended to four daughters Jane Lucas, Matilda Lucas, Margaret Lucas and Esther Lucas. Esther died intestate, no issue, Margaret Dashiell married John Bloodsworth who deeded to John H. Anderson, no name of land.
1815 Repatented by Thomas Walter for 338 acres.

GROG

Patented in 1766 by Henry Lowe
1783 tax - Henry Lowe 49 1/2 acres, Wic.100

GROGG HILL

Patented in 1772 by Peter Waters for 310 acres.
10 May 1777 Peter Waters sold 310 acres to John Denwood
20 Aug.1772 John Denwood sold to Peter Hack Waters son of Littleton Waters.
24 Oct.1796 Littleton Waters, mariner appoint brother Edward Waters to sell ENVY & GROG HILL
16 Oct.1797 Edward Waters sold to Solomon Winright and John Jones of Benjamin Jones 310 acres.
16 Oct.1797 Littleton Waters, mariner and Edward Waters sold to Solomon Winright and John Jones of Benjamin Jones one moity.
3 Aug.1799 John Jones sold to Richard Dunn 9 3/4 acres
1799 Solomon Winright willed plantation to son Levin Winright.

GROVE

1785 121 acres AKA ADDITION TO TIMBER LOTT

GRUMBLES FARWELL TO SOMERSET

Patented in 1800 to John Grumble
1799 John Grumble willed lands to son John Grumble and to wife Temperance Grumble.

GUM BRANCH

Patented in 1802 by Joshua Holloway for 8 acres

GUM SWAMP

Patented in 1771 by Samuel Williams for 72 acres from Wicomico Manor
16 May 1783 Clement Holliday and Nathaniel Ramsey comissioners to sell confiscated property sold to Samuel Williams 72 1/2 acres.
5 May 1798 Samuel Richardson sold to Jesse Bratten 60 acres of GUN SWAMP & PARTNERSHIP

GUNBYS LAST ADDITION

Patented in 1760 by James Gunby for 9 1/4 acres

HACHILAH

Patented on 1674 by William Elgate for 150 acres
Rent Rolls 1666-1723, possessed by William Elgate
1725 William Elgate willed to daughter Sarah Byrd wife of Thomas Byrd 100 acres out of HACHILAH & ELGATES LOTT not alienated to William Byrd nor given to Catherine Hitch daughter of Hannah Hitch.
12 June 1736 William Elgate s/o William with wife Sarah Elgate sold 100 acres to William Byrd patented to William Elgate who died intestate.
1752 Thomas Byrd Sr. willed to son Thomas 50 acres given Sarah Byrd.
1770 ADDITION TO HACHILAH 114 1/2 acres Jesse Byrd
1783 tax - Jesse Byrd 117 acres, a resurvey, Nanticoke 100
1783 tax - Elijah Johnson 50 acres
5 July 1785 Elijah Johnson with wife Margaret Johnson sold to Nathan Adams 100 acres HACHILAH & ELGATES LOTT that William Elgate conveyed to Sarah Byrd.
9 Apr.1792 Nathan Adams with wife Betty Adams of Sussex Co. Del. sold 100 acres to William Ellegood of HACHILAH & ELGATES LOTT

HAILS DISAPPOINTMENT

Patented in 1769 by Jarvis Jenkins for 29 1/4 acres

HAINES GROVE

Patented in 1730 by Francis Haines for 50 acres
11 Mar.1757 Francis Haines with wife Martha Haines gave to son David Haines 50 acres.

HALLS ADVENTURE

Patented in 1743 by Ann Hall for 168 acres a resurvey from MUNSLEY & AVERS POLICY
3 Oct.1751 Ann Hall and Thomas Hall sold to Robert Banks 168 acres.
1759 Robert Banks willed to son Isaiah Banks
1776 Isaiah Banks willed 170 acres to brother Henry Banks
1783 tax - Priscilla Banks 168 acres, Rewastico 100

22 Apr.1784 Henry Banks sold 168 acres to William McBryde with ADAMS DISCOVERY, KINGS NEGLECT.
1821 Thomas Byrd willed to daughter Sarah Ann Byrd.

HALLS CHOICE

Patented 29 Sep.1749 by John Hall at head of Deep Creek out of the Nanticoke River, for 50 acres.
24 Mar.1773 Robert Marvel sold to Thomas Hall son of John 50 acres.

HAMBLINGS INDUSTRY

Patented on 4 June 1763 by Maddux Hamblin for 80 acres
14 Apr.1791 Maddux Hamblin sold to Zedekiah Lamberson 80 acres.

HAMMONDS CHOICE

see SIMPLETON

HANCOCKS TROUBLE

Patented in 1869 by John Hancock for 5 1/4 acres

HANDYS BEGINNING

Patented on 13 July 1724 for 100 acres by Thomas Cox and sold to Ebenezer Handy out of ALDERBURY & WILTON
1735 Ebenezer Handy willed to son Robert Handy
1765 Robert Handy willed to son Ebenezer 500 acres that father Ebenezer Handy bought of Thomas Cox
1783 tax - Elisha Parker 50 acres Wic.100, Worc.Co.
1783 tax - Ebenezer Handy (ALDERBURY & WILTON)

HANDYS CARE

Patented in 1753 by John Handy and wife Ann Handy for 235 acres
1756 John Handy willed to wife Ann Handy and to son Thomas Handy land I live adjacent William Nutter and to son Levin Handy lands on the Wicomico River, unnamed.
1783 tax - William Nutter Sr. 37 acres Rewastico 100
1783 tax - Isaac Handy 41 acres
22 Sep.1810 William Handy and Edward G. Handy sold to Josiah Bayley of Dorc.Co. lands at Salisbury at Handys Mill Pond 43 5/8 acres, unnamed.
26 Sep.1810 William Handy and Edward G. Handy of Washington DC sold to Spencer Todd lands of Isaac Handy 40 acres of NEWHAVEN, CORKLAND, SMALL LOTT & HANDYS CARE.
26 Sep.1810 William Handy and Edward G. Handy sold to Thomas Byrd 312 acres of NEW HAVEN, CORKLAND, & HANDYS CARE.

HANDYS CHANCE

Patented in 1763 by Isaac Handy for 54 acres
1772 Isaac Handy willed dwelling plantation to wife Betty Handy
1783 tax - Elizabeth Handy 54 acres Nanticoke 100
31 Aug.1799 George Handy grandson of Isaac Handy sold to Chaplin Conway 240 acres of HANDYS DISCOVERY, HANDYS CHANCE, FLUELLINGS NEGLECT.

29 Mar.1803 Chaplin Conway with wife Ann Conway sold to William Robertson for 5 shillngs 29 1/2 acres of above land.
1846 William Robertson willed to son William Robertson
(1850 he is in Tyaskin)

HANDYS CHANCE

Patented in 1769 by George Handy for 4 1/2 acres

HANDYS DISCOVERY

Patented in 1744 by Isaac Handy for 303 acres
22 Aug.1769 Col. Isaac Handy sold to Isaac Atkinson 33 acres for 5 shillings.
1772 Isaac Handy willed dwelling plantation to wife Betty Handy
1783 tax - Elizabeth Handy 270 acres Nanticoke 100
31 Aug.1799 George Handy grandson of Isaac Handy sold to Chaplin Conway 240 acres of HANDYS DISCOVERY, HANDYS CHANCE, FLUELLINGS NEGLECT.
29 Mar.1803 Chaplin Conway with wife Ann Conway sold to William Robertson 29 1/2 acres of above land for 5 shillings.
1813 resurveyed by William Handy for 240 acres
1846 William Robertson willed to son William Robertson
(1850 he is in Tyaskin)

HANDYS FROLICK

Patented on 4 April 1755 by Benjamin Handy for 5 acres.
1764 Benjamin Handy died intestate, he had a son John Handy
1772 John Handy willed to son Haste Handy
1783 tax - Joseph Dashiell for Haste Handy 5 acres, Wic. 100 Worc.Co.
13 June 1792 Haste Handy sold to Gabriel Slocomb 5 acres.

HANDYS MEADOW

Patented in 1768 by George Handy for 48 acres
20 June 1772 division of lands between George Handy and Henry Handy that George Handy gave to brother Henry Handy
5 Jan.1782 George Handy sold to Henry Handy
1785 resurveyed to HANDYS NECK

HANDYS NECK

Patented in 1786 by William Handy for 793 1/2 acres
1782 George Handy willed to son William Handy, lands in a resurvey to be arbritrated and to wife Betty Handy manor plantation
5 Jan 1782 George Handy settled dispute with Henry Handy
1783 tax - Betty Handy 793 acres- Rewastico 100 a resurvey of PEMBERTON, SURVEYORS MISTAKE, HANDYS MEADOW, WHITTINGTON NEGLECT, HANDYS PASTURE.
1858 ADDITION TO HANDYS NECK 24 1/2 acres by Allison C. Parsons.

HANDYS OUTLETT

Patented on 2 Oct.1763 by Benjamin Handy for 50 acres

1764 Benjamin Handy died intestate. he had a son John Handy
1772 John Handy willed to son Haste Handy
1783 tax - Joseph Dashiell for Haste Handy 50 acres,Wic.100 Worc.Co.
14 June 1792 Haste Handy sold to Gabriel Slocomb 50 acres.
13 May 1800 Gabriel Slocomb with wife Catherine Slocomb of Dorc.Co. sold to Marcellus Slocomb of same 50 acres.
17 Nov.1807 Sarah Slocomb widow of Marcellus of Dorc.Co., Barzilla Slocomb guardian of John Slocomb, Barzilla Slocomb, Marcellus Slocomb, Nelly Slocomb and Gabriel Slocomb sold to William Bassett of Worcester County.
1832 William Bassett willed to daughters Mary Brittingham, Sarah Brittingham, Rachel Adkins and Betsy Davis.

HANDYS PASTURE

Patented on 6 Sep.1735 by Thomas Dashiell who sold 300 acres to Isaac Handy, part of SHIELLS FOLLY now called HANDYS PASTURE.
1760 Isaac Handy willed lands on Wicomico River to all sons Henry Handy, William Handy and George Handy, unnamed.
1773 Daniel McIntyre willed to wife Elizabeth McIntyre, after her death to son Willin McIntyre.
1783 tax - Betty McIntyre 2 1/2 acres, Nanticoke 100

HANDYS PURCHASE

Patented in 1764 by Thomas Handy for 209 1/4 acres
1783 tax - James Bennett 200 acres Rewastico 100

HANDYS SECURITY

Patented in 1736 by Ebenezer Handy for 350 acres
1735 Ebenezer Handy willed 350 acres to son Benjamin Handy
1768 Patented by George Handy for 2 acres HANDYS SECURITY
1772 John Handy willed 350 acres to son Haste Handy
1783 tax - Joseph Dashiell for Haste Handy 350 acres, Wic.100 Worc.Co.
13 May 1800 Gabriel Slocomb of Dorc.Co. sold to Marcellus Slocomb 8 acres.
14 June 1792 Haste Handy sold to Gabriel Slocomb 350 acres.
1794 ADDITION TO HANDYS SECURITY 319 1/2 acres Gabriel Slocomb
17 Nov.1807 Sarah Slocomb widow of Marcellus Slocomb and Barzilla Slocomb sold to William Bassett of Worcester County Md.
1832 William Bassett willed to daughter Mary Brittingham, Sally Brittingham, Rachel Adkins and Betsy Davis

HAPHAZZARD
see WILSONS DISCOVERY

HAP AT A VENTURE

Patented in 1769 by James Winright for 25 acres
16 Aug.1769 James Winright with wife Eleanor Winright sold to Solomon Winright 25 acres with CANNON SHOTT
1783 tax - Solomon Winright 25 acres, Nanticoke 100
1799 Solomon Winright willed to son Levin Winright

HAPPY ENTRANCE

Patented on 1 April 1767 by Oliver Griffin for 40 acres
1783 tax - John Griffin 40 acres, Acquango 100 Worc.Co.
1784 HAPPY ENTRANCE ENLARGED pat. Oliver Griffin
15 July 1785 Oliver Griffin sold to JohnGriffin 169 acres of HAPPY ENTRANCE ENLARGED.

HARDEKNIGHTS DELIGHT

Patented in 1758 by James Hardeknight for 25 acres
28 July 1769 Mary Hardeknight, Moses Culver and Susanna Hardeknight sold 25 acres to Samuel Jackson Bayley.

HARD BARGAIN

Patented in 1785 by Thomas Russell for 25 acres

HARD BARGAIN

Patented in 1799 by William Gordy for 50 acres
5 Apr.1800 William Gordy sold to Joshua Freeney 19 1/2 acres.

HARD FORTUNE

Patented in 1767 by John Graham for 30 acres
1767 John Graham willed to brother Phillip Graham (under 21) lands unnamed.
1783 tax - James Beard 30 acres, Rewastico 100
1787 Phillip Graham willed to sons John Graham and William Graham all lands in Wicomico that James Beard rents, unnamed.
11 Feb.1806 Henry Boston and wife Nancy Boston (late Nancy Graham) sold to John Graham, land Phillip Graham devised to sons John and William Graham.
15 Mar.1806 Francis Collier with wife Betsy Collier (lately Betsy Graham) sold to John Graham
13 Oct.1807 Ralph Milbourn with wife Sarah Milbourn (lately Sarah Graham) sold rights for 10 shillings to John Graham.

HARD FORTUNE

Patented in 1769 by Benjamin Gillis for 141 acres
14 Mar.1772 Benjamin Gillis with wife Esther Gillis sold to John Nelson 15 acres with STEPHENSON (STEVENSON)
1784 John Nelson willed to son John Nelson lands I live bought of Benjamin Gillis
1783 tax - John Nelson 100 acres (STEVENSON)

HARD FORTUNE

Patented in 1765 by Isaac Cooper a resurvey from QUAIKENSON NECK for 330 1/2 acres.
4 Feb.1767 Isaac Cooper sold 50 acres to Abraham Smith
18 Feb.1768 Isaac Cooper sold 74 acres to John Huffington, at Barren creek mill.
1782/4 Levin Huffington willed to son Isaac Huffington land unnamed.

1783 tax - John Cooper 224 acres- Rewastico 100
1783 tax - Joshua Huffington 37 1/2 acres
1783 tax - Abraham Smith 50 acres
1783 tax - Jonathan Huffington 37 1/2 acres
1785 ADDITION TO HARD FORTUNE 172 acres patented by Angelo Huffington
1791 John Cooper willed lands to son Isaac Cooper
1802 Jonathan Huffington willed to wife Sarah Huffington land on road from Vienna Causeway to Barren Creek mills, no name.
13 Nov.1807 Isaac Cooper sold to John Elliott HARD FORTUNE PUZZLE & PARTNERS CHOICE
13 Nov.1807 James Huffington and John Huffington sold to Charles Venables.
2 Dec 1847 George W. Bounds and wife Rachel Bounds sold to Luther Kennedy 1 acres and 5 perches of HARD FORTUNE or WHITE HALL on rd from Vienna to Bacon Quarter.

HARD FORTUNE

Patented in 1798 by John Hopkins for 64 1/2 acres
1812 John Hopkins willed to son William Hopkins, dwelling plantation, unnamed on road from Quantico mills to Rewastico mills.

HARD LUCK

Patented in 1812 by John Parker for 2 3/4 acres

HARD LUCK

19 Aug.1762 Priscilla Toadvine who married Isaac Banks assigned Henry Toadvine the warrant for HARD LUCK 76 acres.
Patented in 1769 by Henry Toadvine for 76 acres
11 Jan.1772 Henry Toadvine with wife Mary Toadvine sold part to Charles Roach 32 acres.
23 Aug.1776 Charles Roach sold to William McBryde part.
19 Nov.1779 Charles Roach sold to Stephen Roach 32 acres.
1782 Henry Toadvine willed to son Henry 44 acres
1783 tax - Stephen Toadvine 30 acres
1783 tax - Henry Toadvine 44 acres
1783 tax - William Toadvine 6 acres
28 Dec.1793 Stephen Toadvine with wife Mary Toadvine sold to Henry Toadvine 1 acre for a saw mill.
13 May 1795 Stephen Toadvine sold to John Ingersol 46 acres.
26 Aug.1803 John Ingersol sold to Outten Toadvine 46 acres.

HARDSHIP

Patented on 13 May 1689 by John Anderson for 200 acres
Rent Rolls 1666-1723, possessed by Phillip Fleming who married the relic of William Phillips who had the right
14 July 1725 William Phillips and wife Elizabeth Phillips sold to Thomas Marvell.
16 Mar.1746 David Marvell son of Thomas sold to Joseph Rowle 100 acres part of GLADSTONES ADVENTURE & HARDSHIP
18 May 1752 Robert Marvell sold to Samuel Cooper and Thomas Cooper 150 acres of GLADSTEANS ADVENTURE & HARDSHIP.

20 Mar.1753 Thomas Marvell gave to son David Marvell 100 acres in the middle of tract, to son Thomas Marvell 100 acres in back of the tract and 150 acres to son Robert Marvell dwelling plantation, all unnamed.
12 Aug.1758 Thomas Marvell sold to Abraham Taylor 100 acres of HARDSHIP & GLADSTONES ADVENTURE
17 Feb.1765 Thomas Cooper and Samuel Cooper sold to John Badley 75 acres of GLADSTEANS ADVENTURE & HARDSHIP
23 May 1774 Samuel Cooper sold to Charles Badley 75 acres of HARDSHIP & GLADSTEANS ADVENTURE
1776 John Badley willed to son Dean 1/2 of upper plantation, no mamed.
1782 Dean Badley willed to son Charles Badley, part of OLD PLACE, unnamed.
1783 tax - Dean Badley 11 acres
1783 tax - Charles Badley 75 acres
1803 ADDITION TO HARDSHIP patented by Charles Badley for 109 acres
3 June 1803 Abraham Taylor with wife Molly Taylor sold to Horatio Taylor 100 acres of HARDSHIP & GLADSTEANS ADVENTURE
17 May 1810 Louther Taylor of Kent Co. Del. attorney to sell the real estate of Bartholomew Taylor and Abraham Taylor of Barren Co. Ky sold to Horatio Taylor of Somerset Co.
1843 Polly Cooper w/o Samuel Cooper willed to children Brittana Vincent wife of Ephraim Vincent, Levin Cooper, Mary Badley wife of Gideon Badley 75 acres on Nanticoke River and to sons Martin Cooper and Severn B. Cooper.

HARDSHIP

Patented in 1764 by Job Truitt for 356 acres, a resurvey of COW HOUSE RIDGE.
1783 tax - Job Truitt 356 acres, Acquango 100
1793 Daniel Fooks willed to son Billy Fooks HARDSHIP and tract unnamed to son Jonathan Fooks and to son Benjamin Fooks ADDITION TO HARDSHIP
17 Apr.1797 Billy Fooks sold to Benjamin Shockley 134 acres
5 Dec.1795 George and Boaz Walston sold to William Parsons 50 acres
7 Sep.1799 Charles Shockley sold his 1/6th interest from Benjamin Shockley to Betsy Schockley.
16 Jan.1806 Arcada Truitt and George Truitt of Job Truitt sold to John Parsons 115 acres of COW HOUSE RIDGE & HARDSHIP
23 Jan. 1808 Benjamin Shockley of Benjamin, sold to Billy Fooks, ADDITION TO HARDSHIP, part.
8 Sep.1809 Daniel Fooks, Jonathan Fooks, James Fooks and Thomas Fooks sold to Billy Fooks 75 acres HARDSHIP and ADDITION TO HARDSHIP
8 Dec.1809 Same as above, division of lands.
1830 Jonathan Fooks willed to daughter Henrietta Byrd 21 acres of ADDITON TO HARDSHIP and to son James Minos Fooks 25 acres of HARDSHIP

HARDSHIP

Patented in 1784 by William Dennis for 75 acres.
8 Oct.1785 William Dennis sold to Daniel Fooks 75 acres.
15 Sep.1809 William Dennis and Betty Dennis sold to Henry Dennis 50 acres.

HARDSHIP

Patented in 1788 by Abraham Cooper for 450 3/4 acres
21 May 1791 Abraham Cooper with wife Mary Cooper of Sussex Co.Del.

sold to Benjamin Venables of Som.Co. 125 1/2 acres of HARSHIP & BEDFORD.
27 Aug.1791 Abraham Cooper of Sussex Co.Del. sold 134 acres to James McDaniel of Som. Co.
13 Oct.1804 James McDaniel sold 134 acres to Joseph Howard of Sussex Co.Delaware
21 Nov.1807 Benjamin Venables sold to Joseph Venables 125 1/2 acres of HARDSHIP & BEDFORD.

HARDSHIP

Patented in 1789 by Abraham Taylor for 130 3/4 acres
1791 Abraham Taylor willed to son William Taylor, part and to son in law Isaac Kenny part.
16 Jan.1802 Isaac Kenney sold 77 acres to David Gray.

HARDSHIP

Patented in 1789 by Clement Hearn for 79 acres
1806 John Hearn willed to son Solomon Hearn, near Salisbury.

HARDSHIP

Patented in 1823 by William Laws for 28 1/2 acres

HARD TO COME AT

Patented in 1790 by John Scroggin for 135 1/2 acres
13 June 1789 John Scroggin with wife Eunice Scroggin sold to Eli Vinson 30 acres of HARD TO COME AT & ADDITION TO ANYTHING
8 Oct.1790 John Scroggin with wife Eunice Scroggin sold to Joseph Scroggin 135 1/2 acres
10 April 1792 Eli Vinson with wife Ann Vinson sold 55 acres to James Selby with ADDITION TO ANYTHING total 85 1/4 acres
19 Jan 1793 Joseph Scroggin with wife Betsy Scroggin sold to Eli Vinson 28 acres of HARD TO COME AT & ADDN. TO ANYTHING.
20 July 1794 Eli Vinson sold to James Selby son of Ezekiel Selby of Worc.Co. 80 acres of HARD TO COME AT & ADDN. TO ANYTHING
3 Dec.1794 Phillip Scroggin with wife Polly Scroggin sold to John Dashiell 224 1/2 acres of STAINS, ANYTHING & HARD TO COME AT.
17 Sep.1804 James Selby with wife Mary Selby of Worc.Co. sold to Eli Vinson, no acreage mentioned.
16 Oct.1804 Benjamin Waller son of Richard Waller with wife Mary Whittington Waller sold part to John Dashiell.
16 Oct.1804 Eli Vinson with wife Ann Vinson sold to Benjamin Waller with ANYTHING, to settle division of lines.

HARD TO COME

Patented in 1815 by William Hearn for 13 acres

HARD VENTURE

Patented on 4 Feb.1763 by Outten Truitt for 52 acres
14 Feb.1805 Nancy Martin daughter of Wm. Whittington and William

Whittington s/o William sold to Thomas Dennis 52 acres.
1816 ADDITION TO HARD VENTURE, patented Thomas Dennis 167 1/2 acres

HARDYS ADDITION
see WEATHERLYS RESERVE

HARRIS LOTT
see ELIZABETHS CHOICE 100 acres.

HARRIS SMALL LOTT

Patented in 1768 by Solomon Harris for 52 1/2 acres who sold to John Nelson.
1783 tax - John Nelson 52 1/2 acres in Rewastico 100
1784 John Nelson willed to sons James Nelson and John Nelson
21 Sep.1803 William Harris sold to John Nelson 42 acres.
13 Jan.1804 James Nelson with wife Esther Nelson sold to Augustus Cannon 43 1/2 acres
20 Jan 1804 John Nelson sold 7 acres to John Hopkins
9 Nov.1804 John Nelson sold to Augustus Cannon, no acreage given.
8 Aug.1809 Daniel Ballard, sheriff sold to Alexander Stewart, per judgement against Augustus Cannon, MONMOUTH, HARRIS LOTT, GALES DISCOVERY total 156 3/4 acres.
9 Oct.1810 Daniel Wailes sold to John Stewart his part of the distribution of the real estate of Alexander Stewart, unnamed.

HARTFORD

Patented on 29 Nov.1672 by Charles Hutchins for 200 acres in Nanticoke 100 who assigned to Richard Samuels.
Rent Rolls 1666-1723, possessed by Richard Samuels 200 acres
1709 Richard Samuels gave to son Peter Samuels 200 acres
15 Aug.1730 Peter Samuels with wife Hannah Samuels sold 200 acres to Robert Hopkins.
6 Jan 1737 Stephen Hopkins son of Robert Hopkins, with wife Elizabeth Hopkins sold 200 acres to Thomas Jones and wife Susannah Jones.
22 Aug.1740 Thomas Jones with wife Susannah Jones sold 200 acres to Benjamin Townsend and wife Mary Townsend.
10 May 1745 Benjamin Townsend with wife Mary Townsend sold 100 acres to Daniel Walter and Jonathan Hickman.
8 Jan.1763 Jonathan Hickman with wife Jean Hickman sold to John Barkley 100 acres.
4 Feb.1767 John Barkley sold 50 acres to Samuel Townsend.
1774 John Barkley willed to son Charles Barkley
11 Apr.1776 Charles Barkley sold to John Barkley 70 acres.
29 Aug.1808 Mary Dean sold to Polly Smith and Peggy Hughes wife of Josiah Hughes, sold by Benjamin Townsend to Daniel Walter father of Mary Dean.
1839 John Turner willed to son John Turner, formerly property of John Insley purchased of William Willin.

HATHELEYS CHOICE
see GETHESEME

HAVANNAH

Patented in 1786 by Thomas Huffington for 20 acres

1783 tax - Thomas Huffington 20 acres in Rewastico 100.

HAVANNAH

Patented in 1764 by William Adams for 879 1/2 acres
2 Mar.1767 William Adams sold 100 acres to Christopher Glass
10 Oct.1768 Christopher Glass with wife Alice Glass sold 14 1/2 acres to Francis Disharoon.
1783 tax - Francis Disharoon 100 acres
1783 tax - James Bennett 200 acres
1783 tax - Robert Dashiell 289 1/2 acres.
20 Feb 1790 Frederick Hill mortgaged to Robert Dashiell 14 acres, 25 acres adjacent and 25 acres.
21 Jan.1797 John Whittingham Adams, John Timmons and wife Christina Timmons of Sussex Co.Del. sold to William Cottman claim on plantation of William Adams, no name or acreage.
23 July 1799 John Dashiell with wife Mary Dashiell sold to William Cottman, land in Duck cove William Adams died possessed, no name or acreage.
17 Feb.1800 Charles Nutter and wife Louisa Nutter sold to William Cottman rights to estate of William Adams in Duck Cove.
8 Oct.1805 Levin Farrington, William Cottman, Lazarus Cottman execs. of William Cottman sold to Andrew Adams land willed to be sold purchased from William Adams, no name or acreage.

HAYFIELD

Patented in 1773 by Henry Steele for 35 acres

HAYMANS HARDSHIP

Patented on 11 July 1762 by William Hayman for 54 acres.
8 June 1764 William Hayman sold to William Harrison with FRIENDS GOOD WILL
1765 William Harrison willed to son Joseph Harrison
2 June 1767 Solomon Harrison sold to Elizabeth Harrison 54 acres
19 Apr.1769 Elizabeth Harrison widow, gave to daughters Sarah Robinson Armatrader and Patience Harrison 52 acres.
1783 tax - Joseph Riggs 52 acres Wic.100 Worc.Co.
9 Apr.1790 Joseph Riggs and wife Sarah Riggs and Elizabeth Shockley mother of Sarah sold 54 acres to John Biglands.
9 Sep.1798 John Biglands sold to Isaac Henry 54 acres

HAYMANS LUCK

Patented in 1833 by William B. Hayman for 10 acres

HAYMANS OUTLETT

Patented on 26 Sep.1763 by James Hayman for 50 acres
1783 tax - Margaret Hayman 50 acres, Wic.100 Worc.Co.
1783 tax - Rachel Hayman 15 acres
1819 Joshua Hayman willed to daughter Priscilla Morris HAYMANS ADDITION 15 acres.

HAY MARKET

Patented in 1769 by William Whaland for 50 acres

HAZEL RIDGE

Patented in 1791 by Thomas White for 148 1/2 acres
7 Apr.1794 Thomas White sold to Peter Parsons 52 acres
7 Apr.1797 Thomas White sold to Henry Corkill 26 acres

HAZZARD

Patented on 20 May 1705 by Richard Samuels for 100 acres
10 Jan.1705 Richard Samuels sold to James Dashiell 100cres
1708/9 James Dashiell willed to son Joseph Dashiell
20 Aug.1763 resurveyed by Joseph Dashiell to MORE LOSS THAN GAIN

HAZZARD

Patented in 1786 by Smith Lingo for 13 1/2 acres
1783 tax - Nathaniel Whaley 13 acres Wic.100 Worc.Co.
4 Sep.1787 Smith Lingo son of Robertson Lingo sold to James Perdue 13 1/2 acres.

HAZZARD

Patented in 1756 by William Adams for 29 acres

HAZZARD

Patented in 1783 by Joseph Scroggin for 105 acres
1772 Joseph Scroggin willed 105 acres to son Robert Scroggin
1783 ADDITION TO HAZZARD, pat. Robert Scroggin for 131 1/4 acres
1783 tax - Joseph Scroggin 33 1/2 acres Rewastico 100
1783 tax - Robert Scroggin
16 May 1785 Robert Scroggin and Nathan Culver sold to Joshua Hastings of Sussex Co.Del. HAZZARD & ADDN. TO COLLINS ADVENTURE 81 acres.
5 June 1790 Robert Scroggin son of Joseph Scroggin sold to brother Joseph Scroggin 33 1/2 acres
3 Aug.1790 Robert Scroggin sold to Elijah Moore for 5 shillings 25 acres of HAZZARD and 4 1/2 acres of ADDITION TO HAZZARD.
19 Jan.1793 Joseph Scroggin with wife Elizabeth Scroggin sold 33 1/2 acres to John Dashiell.
3 Oct.1794 John Dashiell of Jesse Dashiell sold 33 /12 acres to Benjamin Jones.
28 Oct.1794 Elijah Moore with wife Betsy Moore sold to George Parker 186 acres of ADDN. TO COLLINS ADVENUTE, HAZZARD & ADDN. TO HAZZARD.
9 May 1795 Benjamin Jones sold 33 1/2 acres to John Dashiell of Jesse Dashiell
14 Dec. 1799 Daniel Hastings of Sussex Co.Del. son of Joshua Hastings sold to Hezekiah Hastings of Somerset all rights.
3 Sep.1808 George Parker with wife Sarah Parker sold 179 acres to John Rider of ADDITION & ADDITION TO HAZZARD.
18 Feb.1809 John Rider with wife Nelly Rider sold to John Freeney 179 acres of afsd.

1839 Hezekiah Hastings willed plantation unnamed to wife Agnes
Hastings and son William Hastings.

HAZZARD

Patented in 1742 by Charles Thompson for 75 acres

HEARNS ADDITION

Patented in 1773 by Daniel Melson for 70 1/2 acres
1783 tax - Daniel Melson 70 acres, Wic.100 Worc.Co.
29 May 1798 Daniel Melson of Sussex Co.Delaware sold to John Hearn 59 1/4 acres.

HEARNS DISCOVERY

Patented in 1893 by Benjamin G. Hearn for 13 acres 34 perches
Resurveyed in 1804 by Joshua Dryden 13 acres 34 perches

HEARNS LIBERTY

Patented on 10 Dec.1757 by Benjamin Hearn for 34 acres
13 Nov.1771 Benjamin Hearn sold to Isaiah Calloway 34 acres

HEARNS VENTURE

Patented in 1760 by Thomas Hearn for 100 acres
1762 Thomas Hearn willed to son John Hearn, daughters Elizabeth Moore wife of Isaac Moore, Jemima Hearn, Sarah Hearn and Ann Hearn.
9 Sep.1774 Ann Hearn sold to Samuel Haynie for 5 shillings 33 1/2 acres.
18 June 1768 Joseph Hitch with wife Jemima Hitch sold 33 /12 acres to Samuel Haynie
14 Mar.1772 Francis Disharoon with wife Sarah Disharoon sold to Samuel Haynie for 5 shillings, with part of ST KITTS.

HEATHS GIFT

Patented in 1788 by William Heath

HEATHS VENTURE

Patented on 4 Oct.1761 for 50 acres by Smith Heath
15 Oct 1768 resurveyed 186 acres by Smith Heath
1783 tax - Smith Heath 95 acres, Wic.100 Worc.Co
27 Oct.1786 Smith Heath sold to James Perdue 186 acres.
1842 John Perdue and George L. Perdue patented ADDITION TO HEATHS VENTURE for 210 1/2 acres.

HELP

Patented in 1771 by Richard Waller for 13 1/4 acres
6 Oct.1804 Benjamin Waller with wife Polly Waller sold 13 1/4 acres to Eli Vinson

HENDERSONS CHOICE

Patented in 1760 by Daniel Henderson for 65 acres
18 Feb.1768 Daniel Henderson sold 33 acres to Joseph Alpha
18 Feb.1768 Daniel Henderson and Daniel Rhoads sold 32 acres to John Phillips
5 June 1783 John Phillips sold 32 acres to Jacob Rhoads
1783 tax - Joseph Alpha 33 acres Nanticoke 100
1783 tax - Jacob Rhoads 32 acres Rewastico 100
1787 Jacob Rhoads willed lands to sons Nathan Rhoads and Charles Rhoads, this land not named.
1789 Joseph Alpha willed lands to wife Mary Alpha.

HENRYS

see WESTERN FIELDS

HENRYS CHANCE

Patented on 5 Nov.1764 by Henry Toadvine for 285 acres, a resurvey of CHANCE.
1782 Henry Toadvine willed to wife Mary Toadvine, sons Henry Toadvine, James Toadvine and Isaac Toadvine, this land not mentioned.
1783 Second Patent by Henry Toadvine Jr. for 33 acres.
1783 tax - Mary Toadvine 107 acres Worc.Co. Wic.100

HENRYS CONLUSION

Patented in 1786 by Isaac Henry for 463 3/4 acres
15 Jan.1795 Isaac Henry with wife Dorothy Henry sold to Benjamin Jones 56 1/4 acres of HENRYS CONCLUSION & PHARSALIA
26 Oct.1798 Isaac Henry sold 16 3/4 acres to Arthur Dashiell
12 Feb.1798 Benjamin Jones son of Mitchell Jones sold to George Robertson 300 acres of PHARSALIA, GOOD LUCK & HENRYS CONCLUSION
6 Feb.1801 Isaac Henry with wife Dolly Henry sold to Horatio Stayton 390 perches.
1802 Arthur Dashiell willed balance of lands to son Matthias Dashiell, unnamed.

HENRYS ENDEAVOR

Patented in 1763 by Henry Dorman for 50 acres
23 Jan.1770 Henry Dorman wife wife Sarah Dorman sold 50 acres to Stephen Redden with WHAT YOU PLEASE.
12 Jan 1779 Stephen Redden with wife Mary Redden sold 50 acres to Joseph Morris on branch of the Wicomico Creek.
19 Mar.1782 Joseph Morris Jr. sold 50 acres to George Dashiell son of George Dashiell.
19 Mar.1788 George Dashiell sold 50 acres to Mills Bayley
21 Aug.1805 George Bayley sold to Negro Jesse Purnell 28 acres.

HENRYS HARDSHIP

Patented in 1775 by Henry Toadvine for 41 acres
6 Apr.1779 Henry Toadvine sold to George Bayley 31 acres
12 Nov.1779 George Bayley with wife Fanny Bayley sold to Arnold Toadvine 31 acres

1783 tax Arnold Toadvine 41 acres Wic.100 Worc.Co.
20 Apr.1787 Arnold Toadvine sold to Nathan Culver 32 acres.
5 Nov.1789 Nathan Culver sold 31 acres to Benjamin Shockley.
1791 Benjamin Shockley willed to son John Shockley
26 Mar.1799 Benjamin Johnson sold to John Shockley of Benjamin 32 acres.

HENRYS LOT

Patented in 1765 by Henry Parsons for 21 acres 3 perches 15 rods

HENRYS MEADOW

Patented in 1775 by Hugh Henry for 12 acres a resurvey from WOODFIELDS
22 May 1784 Charles Davis quitclaimed to Isaac Henry WOODFIELD on the south side of Rewastico branch near Spring Hill Church. HENRYS MEADOW taken up by Hugh Henry father of Isaac Henry that Charles Davis purchased and agreed to quitclaim to him.

HICKMANS PROFIT

Patented in 1775 by Jonathan Hickman for 2 1/2 acres
1783 tax - Jonathan Hickman 2 1/2 acres- Nanticoke 100

HICKORY LEVEL

Patented on 5 Sep.1718 by William Twiford for 40 acres
Rent Rolls 1666-1723, possessed by William Twiford
14 Aug.1727 William Twiford sold 40 acres to John Huffington.

HICKORY NECK

Patented in 1758 by Jacob Heath for 50 acres
1775 Jacob Heath willed to wife Mary Heath 1/2 and after death to son Jacob Heath and to the rest of my children, land unnamed.
1783 tax - James Heath 50 acres Acquango 100, Worc.Co.
7 Oct.1786 Jacob Heath sold to James Heath 50 acres.

HICKORY RIDGE

Patented on 22 Sep.1676 by William Stevens for 50 acres.
20 Sep.1701 William Stevens assigned to John Shiles.
Rent Rolls 1666-1723, possessed by John Shiles near the mouth of the Wicomico River
1714 John Shiles willed plantation to son John Shiles, unnamed.
15 April 1745 John Shiles sold to Thomas Willin 210 acres of HOGG QUARTER, SAFETY, SHILES MEADOW, IGNOBLE QUARTER & WHITTY CONTRIVANCE six parcels including 50 acres of tract alienated to John Shiles by William Whittington.
1749 resurveyd by Thomas Willin 99 acres.
25 Oct 1752 Thomas Willin and wife Major Willin sold 23 acres to Thomas Willin Jr. 99 acres.
1773 Thomas Willin Jr. willed lands unnamed to son Samuel Willin
1783 tax - Samuel Willin 76 acres in Nanticoke 100
1812 Samuel Willin willed lands to son James Willin.

HIGH SUFFOLK

Patented on 10 Oct.1677 by Thomas Walker with wife Sarah Walker and Nicholas Evans and wife Rachel Evans for 1450 acres.
Rent Rolls 1666-1723, possessed by Adam Hitch who purchased from Thomas Walker and Nicholas Evans.
8 Feb.1721 Adam Hitch with wife Anne Hitch sold 30 acres to John Cordrey.
1 July 1721 Adam Hitch with wife Ann Hitch sold 83 acres to Francis Langeake.
1728 Thomas Walker Jr. son of Thomas sold to Adam Hitch 100 acres
6 May 1728 Adam Hitch with wife Mary Hitch gave to son Samuel Hitch part of HIGH SUFFOLK & COME BY CHANCE 212 acres, and to son John Hitch 94 acres of SUFFOLK and to son Solomon Hitch 310 acres and to son William Hitch 405 acres.
1730 William Hitch willed to sons William Hitch, Thomas Hitch, Nehemiah Hitch and John Hitch 405 acres.
1730 Adam Hitch willed to son Elgate Hitch, wife Mary Hitch and part to grandson John Price 90 acres where he lives.
23 Jan.1746 Elgate Hitch sold 100 acres to John Crouch
31 Jan 1746/7 Morgan Cordrey and John Cordrey sold to Dennis Dulaney, tailor, 30 acres.
22 Mar.1754 Nehemiah Hitch, William Hitch and John Hitch brothers sold to John Hitch, 100 acres that Adam Hitch gave to son William Hitch.
20 Feb.1757 William Hitch, John Hitch sold 100 acres to Solomon Hitch
7 Mar.1757 William Hitch with wife Mercy Hitch and John Hitch sold 200 acres to George Wilson.
26 Feb.1757 Solomon Hitch, William Hitch Jr.sons of Solomon Hitch with William Hitch Jr. son of William sold 310 acres to William Murray.
2 Mar.1763 George Wilson and wife Birdy Wilson sold 200 acres to Joshua Hitch
20 Jan.1751/2 We Mary Price and Adam Price give bond of mortgage to William Adams for 80 acres.
1767 Robert Hitch with wife Eva Hitch gave 200 acres to son Isaac Hitch.
7 Sep 1769 triparte agreement Francis Lank to Josiah Polk and Robert Hitch 250 acres that Francis Langeake devised to grandson Francis Lank son of George Lank with COME BY CHANCE & HIGH SUFFOLK.
5 Sep.1769 William Lank sold to Isaac Coulbourn and Joshua Hitch all 150 acres that Francis Lank willed to grandson William Langeake son of Stephen Langeake.
25 July 1772 Francis Lank sold to Esme Bayley land devised by Francis Lank to Francis Lank the eldest, unnamed.
17 July 1770 Robert Hitch sold to Esme Bayley 250 acres of COME BY CHANCE, HIGH SUFFOLK.
31 Aug.1774 Betty Handy sold to William McBryde and wife Sarah McBryde (division of lands that Capt. William Murray father of Betty Handy and Sarah McBryde left NEATHERDALE, VULCANS VINEYARD & HIGH SUFFOLK, Betty Handy to have 310 acres in Rokiawalkin and balance to Sarah McBryde.
21 Jan 1775 Isaac Hitch sold to William Handy 212 acres of COME BY CHANCE & HIGH SUFFOLK.
21 Jan.1775 Eve Nichols widow of Richard Nichols had before marriage to Nichols as widow of Robert Hitch deceased who was the son of Samuel Hitch, sold all rights to William Handy.
19 Jan 1778 Spencer Hitch of Sussex Co.Del. sold 10 1/2 acres to

William Handy of Somerset Co. purchased of Isaac Hitch.
1783 tax - Esme Bayley 150 acres, Rewastico 100
1783 tax - William Handy Sr. 220 acres
1783 tax - Sarah Hitch 100 acres
1783 tax - Thomas Hitch Jr. 224 acres
1783 tax - William Stone 210 acres
1783 tax - John Smith 100 acres.
25 Nov.1783 Esme Bayley with wife Sinah Bayley sold to Sarah Ellegood Hitch daughter of Robert Hitch for 5 shillings, 100 acres.
16 Jan.1784 William McBryde with wife Sarah McBryde sold to William Stone and wife Betty Stone 110 acres that fell to Betty and Sarah daughters of William Murray, division of land.
15 May 1793 William Elgate Hitch son of Joshua Hitch sold 150 acres to William Adams.
17 Oct.1796 William Stone with wife Betty Stone gave 300 acres to Henry Stone their second son.
21 Apr.1798 Esme Bayley sold to William Elgate Hitch 150 acres of COME BY CHANCE & HIGH SUFFOLK.
20 Feb.1801 Levin Handy of Rhode Island, now of Worc.Co. with wife Eleanor Handy, Joshua Pollitt and wife Sarah Pollitt, Nancy Hitch, Peggy Hitch, William Elgate Hitch with wife Mary Hitch, & Molly Hitch sold to Hugh Gemmill 400 acres of HIGH SUFFOLK, FATHERS NEGLECT, WILSONS DISOVERY, etc.
9 Aug.1803 John Wilkins, sheriff sold to Hugh Gemmill 497 1/2 acres per judgement against the heirs of Joshua Hitch.
1 Jan 1805 Hugh Gemmill sold part to Richard Henry Handy.
14 Jan.1805 Richard Henry Handy sold same to Hugh Gemmill.
9 Sep.1806 John Wilkins Esq, sheriff sold to Thomas Rencher 497 1/2 acres per judgement against Edward Brown with wife Betsy Brown, William E. Hitch and wife Mary Hitch, Joshua Pollitt and wife Sarah Pollitt, Levin Handy with wife Eleanor Handy, John Hitch, William Hitch, Peggy Hitch and Nancy Hitch heirs of Joshua Hitch.
1806 Thomas Rencher willed to son Samuel Rencher QUARTER LANDS purchased at sheriff's sale from the heirs of Joshua Hitch
18 Nov.1808 John Byrd with wife Margaret Byrd formerly Margaret Handy widow of William Handy sold to son William Smith Handy her dower rights.
18 Nov.1808 William Smith Handy with wife Phoebe Handy mortgaged to Thomas Hooper of Worc.Co. 425 acres.
5 Aug.1810 Thomas Hitch sold 150 acres to Thomas Rencher
28 Feb.1810 Henry Dulaney sold 30 acres to William Hearn
5 May 1810 Thomas Hitch sold 35 acres to William Stone.
1838 William Murray Stone willed to son William Murray Stone tract purchased of Thomas Hitch, unnamed.
1743 Mary Hitch willed 150 acres to daughter Sally Hitch.

HILMANS FIRST PURCHASE

Patented in 1762 by John Hilman
1783 tax - John Hilman 34 1/2 acres HILMANS FIRST CHOICE
13 May 1775 Joshua Hilman sold 44 1/4 acres to Levin Dashiell.

HILLS VENTURE

Patented in 1800 by James Hill for 12 acres

HILLSBOROUGH

Patented in 1793 by Frederick Hill
10 Jan 1798 Frederick Hill sold 28 1/2 acres to Robert Dashiell adjacent MT.SINAI

HITCHES CHANCE

Patented in 1782 by Thomas Hitch for 22 1/2 acres

HITCHES CHOICE

Patented in 1761 by Joshua Hitch for 30 acres
1783 tax - Joshua Hitch 30 acres Rewastico 1001793 Joshua Hitch willed dwelling plantation to son Joshua Hitch
9 Aug.1803 John Wilkins, sheriff sold to Hugh Gemmill 28 1/2 acres per judgement against heirs of Joshua Hitch
9 Sep.1806 John Wilkins, sheriff sold to Thomas Rencher 28 1/2 acres.
1806 Thomas Rencher willed to son Samuel Rencher QUARTER LANDS bought at sheriffs sale, property of Joshua Hitch.

HITCHES CHOICE

Patented in 1757 by Ezekiel Hitch for 50 acres
1783 tax - Ezekiel Hitch 50 acres, Rewastico 100

HITCHES DISCOVERY

Patented in 1767 by Joshua Hitch for 15 1/4 acres
1792 Joshua Hitch willed plantation to son Joshua Hitch.

HITCHES HARD LUCK

Patented in 1801 by William Hitch, John Hitch, Laban Hitch, Nancy Hitch, Betty Hitch and William Hitch for 1256 acres (children of Joshua Hitch Sr.)a resurvey of MADDOX LUCK & WILSONS DISCOVERY
6 May 1800 John Hitch, Edward Brown with wife Betsy Brown, Levin Handy and wife Nelly Handy, Joshua Pollitt with wife Sally Pollitt and William Elgate Hitch with wife Polly Hitch, Nancy Hitch and Peggy Hitch sold 300 acres to Thomas Rencher Sr.
2 Jan.1801 Edward Brown with wife Elizabeth Brown and John Hitch of Baltimore with wife Jane Hitch sold to William E. Hitch.
20 Feb.1801 Levin Handy with wife Eleanor Handy, Joshua Pollitt with wife Sarah Pollitt, Nancy Hitch, Peggy Hitch and William Elgate Hitch with wife Mary Hitch & Molly Hitch sold 400 acres to Hugh Gemmill of this and HIGH SUFFOLK, WILSONS DISCOVERY, FATHERS NEGLECT.
26 Jan.1802 Hugh Gemmill with wife Ann Gemmill sold 29 1/8 acre to Levin Irving.
9 Aug.1803 John Wilkins, sheriff sold to Hugh Gemmill per judgement.
1 Jan.1805 Hugh Gemmill sold to Richard Henry Handy
14 Jan.1805 Richard Henry Handy sold to Hugh Gemmill
9 Sep.1806 John Wilkins, sheriff sold to Thomas Rencher 100 1/2 acres.
1806 Thomas Rencher willed to son Samuel Rencher lands purchaed at sheriff's sale QUARTER LANDS of Joshua Hitch.

HOBBS ADVENTURE

Patented on 29 Dec.1769 by Marcellus Hobbs for 63 acres
1778 Marcellus Hobbs willed to son Matthias Hobbs dwelling plantation on road from Salisbury to Cypress Swamp(unnamed) and to son Levin Hobbs part of the same and to daughters Betsy Hobbs and Nelly Hobbs.
1783 tax - Matthias Hobbs 63 acres, Wic.100.Worc.Co.
25 Nov.1795 at Warren Co. Georgia, Milbourn Magee with wife Nelly Magee ordain Davis Magee of Hancock Co. Ga. attorney to sell to Archibald Smith, devised to Nelly and Betsy Hobbs.
8 Dec.1798 Matthias Hobbs son of Marcellus Hobbs sold to Samuel Turner Parker, rights.
5 Dec.1797 Davis Magee of Georgia, sold to Archibald Smith 13 1/2 acres.
16 Mar.1799 Samuel T. Parker with wife Hetty Parker sold to William Dayley 2 acres.
27 pr.1802 Archibald Smith of Lawrence Co. South Carolina appoint son Joshua Smith attorney. 17 Apr.1802 Joshua Smith sold to Samuel Turner Parker 125 1/4 acres of GEORGES LOTT & HOBBS ADVENTURE.

HOBBESSES MISCHANCE

Patented in 1773 by George Vance for 79 acres.
1777 George Vance willed to wife Margaret Vance and to daughter Sally Vance, land unnamed.
1783 tax - Matthias Vinson 79 acres, Wic.100, Worc.Co.

HOBSONS CHOICE

Patented on 7 May 1758 by Nathaniel Willis for 50 acres.
1761 Nathaniel Willis willed 50 acres to son Nathaniel.
8 Aug.1761 John Willis with wife Elizabeth Willis sold to Nathaniel Willis for 5 shillings hear head of Wicomico River.
1783 tax- Matthias Austin 50 acres, Wic.100. Worc.Co.
1788 Matthias Austin willed lands unnamed to son John Austin.

HOG DEN

Patented in 1784 by William Brittingham for 24 acres
1783 tax - William Brittingham 24 acres, Nanticoke 100

HOGGS DOWN

Patented on 10 July 1679 by George Southern for 450 acres.
15 July 1680 Edward Southern now of Horekill with wife Mary Southern sold to James Jarrett and Richard Jarrett.
1704 Richard Jarrett willed to brother Graves Jarrett 225 acres, if no issue to cousin Joyles Bashaw.
Rent Rolls 1666-1723, possessed by Graves Jarrett who with his brother Richard purchased of George Southern and by death of Richard Jarrett it fell to Graves Jarrett.
1722 Graves Jarrett willed to wife Mary Jarrett plantation and then to Graves Boardman son of Francis Boardman.
1728/30 Thomas Bashaw willed to eldest sons Jarrett Bashaw and William Bashaw 100 acres bought of Giles Bashaw and to son Thomas Bashaw 100

acres of dwelling plantation, unnamed and to youngest son William Bashaw 70 acres adjacent plantation bought of Graves Jarrett.
14 Sep.1734 Joyles Bashaw sold 50 acres to Thomas Goslee of Stepney Parish.
1738 Giles Bashaw willed to Jarrett Bashaw, if no issue to his sisters Ann Bashaw and Eleanor Bashaw. To Graves Boardman 40 acres.
24 May 1745 Graves Boardman with wife Susannah Boardman sold 50 acres to David Polk.
13 Jan.1747 Graves Boardman sold 50 acres to Thomas Goslee now called GOSLEES CONTENT.
1748 Thomas Goslee willed to son Samuel Goslee (minor)plantation bought of Graves Boardman.
11 May 1761 George Robertson with wife Eleanor Robertson sold to Ezekiel Humphries 70 acres given Eleanor by her brother William Bashaw in his will.
11 May 1761 Ezekiel Humphries sold 70 acres to Jacob Thorns that Graves Jarrett alienated to Thomas Bashaw who gave to son William Bashaw.
13 Dec.1767 Samuel Goslee sold 100 acres to Josiah Polk.
11 Sep.1771 Thomas Bashaw of Norfolk Va. son of Jarrett Bashaw who was the son of Thomas Bashaw of Somerset County sold 50 acres to Josiah Polk.
1778 David Polk willed to son Josiah Polk.
1783 tax - Joshua Humphries 170 acres Wic.100
1783 tax - Josiah Polk 100 acres.
1784 Josiah Polk willed to brother William Polk lands purchased to Samuel Boardman Goslee.
1784 Josiah Polk sold to brother James Polk part.
18 Mar.1786 William Humphries sold to Joshua Humphries for 5 shillings the rights of his mother Ann Humphries daughter and coheir of Jacob Cordrey, no acres mentioned.
10 Sep.1793 Stephen Thorns and Joshua Humphries with wife Sarah Humphries sold 57 3/.4 acres to William Polk, attorney.
20 Feb.1796 Louther King of Sussex Co.Del. sold to Esme Bayley and William Polk his interest.
1795 James Polk willed part to wife Nancy Polk.
1799 Esme Bayley willed to wife Sinah Bayley, that Louther King sold him.
1802 Sinah Bayley willed to daughter Patience Done.
2 Feb.1805 Sarah Humphries and Elijah Humphries sold 122 acres to Kirk Gunby.
26 Feb.1805 Elijah Humphries son of Joshua Humphries and Esther Neal sold to Kirk Gunby all rights to their part of 450 acres that Joshua Humphries bought of William Humphries. Sarah Humphries signed off her dower rights.
18 May 1805 Kirk Gunby and wife Mary Gunby sold to William Mitchell
25 Mar.1807 John Done and wife Patience Done sold to Josiah Bayley of Dorc.Co. and Thomas Bayley of Somerset Co.(agreement) for 5 shillings 1/3rd part that James Polk willed to wife Nancy Polk and after her death to brother William Polk and sister Sinah Bayley and children of his brother Gillis Polk. Sinah Bayley willed her part to daughter Patience Done.(children of John Done and Patience Done were Elizabeth Bayley Done, Juliet Henrietta Done and Leah Bayley Done) no name of land mentioned.
1832 William Bassett, wife Elizabeth Bassett, willed 211 acres to

daughter Betsy Bassett and Benjamin Bassett children of John Bassett.

HOGGSDOWN

Patented on 10 July 1682 by Richard Stevens for 150 acres.
Rent Rolls 1666-1723, possessed by Madam Mary King 150 acres.

HOGG HILL

Patented on 3 Apr.1763 by Charles Duncan for 50 acres
1783 tax - Charles Duncan 50 acres, Acquango 100 Worc.Co.

HOG ISLAND

Patented in 1734 by John Carter for 50 acres.
3 July 1750 Isaac Carter son of John Carter Jr., with wife Sarah Carter sold 50 acres to William Owens on the northmost branch of Barren Creek.
4 June 1757 William Owens sold 50 acres to John Williams
1830 James Larramore willed to granddaughter Leah Selby.

HOG ISLAND

Patented in 1785 by John Robertson for 35 1/4 acres
14 May 1794 John Robertson sold 25 1/4 acres to James Dean.

HOG ISLAND

Patented in 1795 by Henry Corkwell in Wicomico Forest for 32 acres.
10 Oct.1803 Henry Corkwell sold to David Smith Walston 32 acres
31 Mar.1804 David Smith Walston sold to Samuel Turner Parker 32 acres.

HOG NECK

Patented on 1 Oct.1683 by Francis Jenkins for 300 acres
Rent Rolls 1666-1723, possessed by John Crouch who purchased from Francis Jenkins but not conveyed.
1708 Francis Jenkins willed 300 acres to John Crouch. He to pay for as per agreement.
1720/24 John Crouch willed to wife Ann Crouch 200 acres (he had children John Crouch, Isaac Crouch and Ann Crouch.)
4 June 1726 John Crouch sold 5 acres to Andrew Scott.
20 Sep.1729 John Crouch sold 95 acres to George Sharp of the Island of Nevis, upper part.
1 June 1730 Andrew Scott sold 5 acres to George Sharp.
22 Feb.1754 Isaac Crouch sold 100 acres to Jarvis Jenkins.
21 Feb.1760 George Sharp bricklayer, son of George Sharp, with wife Hannah Sharp sold to Jarvis Jenkins 95 acres.
10 Oct.1761 John Crouch son of Isaac Crouch deceased sold 100 acres to Jarvis Jenkins Jr., his interest (a confirmation of conveyance by Isaac Crouch to Jarvis Jenkins.)
13 Sep.1766 John Crouch sold 100 acres to David Jenkins.
1773 David Jenkins willed 100 acres to son David Jenkins and to son Littleton Jenkins 100 acres, land unnamed.
1783 tax - David Jenkins 100 acres.

1783 tax - Kibble Jenkins 250 acres.
1794 resurveyed to MT SINAI
19 Feb.1800 Kibble Jenkins sold to James Bennett, Mt.SINAI a resurvey of HOG NECK, no acres mentioned.
1820 Kibble Jenkins willed to George Willis son of Lotta Willis 100 acres and 70 acres of Mt. Sinai.

HOGG PALACE

Patented on 27 July 1715 by Thomas Jones on the east side of Broad Creek off the Nanticoke River for 100 acres.
Rent Rolls 1666-1723, possessed by Thomas Jones.
Resurveyed and patented by Thomas Waller on 15 Nov.1736
Jan.1756 Thomas Waller gave to William Waller 1/2 part, 50 acres.
26 Oct.1757 Thomas Waller mortgaged to Outerbridge Horsey, HOGG PALACE, LOGSGATE HILL & SHARPES CHANCE.
1785 Outerbridge Horsey willed to son Lazarus Horsey.

HOG PEN

Patented in 1789 by Thomas Stanford for 8 acres
1791 Thomas Stanford willed to son John Stanford (STANFORDS HOG PEN)

HOG PEN RIDGE

Patented in 1762 by Purnell Johnson for 63 acres
1778 Purnell Johnson willed to son Purnell Johnson
1783 tax - Purnell Johnson Wic.100 Worc.Co.
1817 Purnell Johnson willed lands unnamed to William Hearn of Elijah Hearn (nephew) and nephew William Purnell Johnson.

HOG QUARTER

Patented on 21 Nov.1672 by Richard Acworth for 200 acres on the south side of Barren Creek..
Rent Rolls 1666-1723, possessed by Richard Acworth
1727 Richard Acworth willed to sons Charles Acworth and Thomas Acworth.
1 March 1755 Thomas Acworth and Charles Acworth sold to Richard Acworth, blacksmith 100 acres of HOGG QUARTER & ACWORTHS DELIGHT.
1759 Richard Acworth willed to sons James Acworth and Richard Acworth.
23 Nov.1759 Charles Acworth son of Thomas Acworth gave to brother James Acworth 450 acres of ACWORTHS DELIGHT, ACWORTHS CHOICE, HOGG QUARTER, RIDGES & part of MARISH POINT.
20 June 1769 James Acworth sold 30 acres to brother Richard Acworth.
20 June 1769 James Acworth sold to William Acworth 40 acres.
4 July 1769 James Acworth and wife Mary Acworth and William Acworth sold 130 acres to Beauchamp Hull.
1783 tax - Train Acworth 40 acres, Nanticoke 100
1783 tax - Beauchamp Hull 130 acres
1783 tax - Richard Acworth 30 acres.
3 Dec.1795 Richard Acworth mortgaged to Robert Venables ACWORTHS DELIGHT & HOGG QUARTER, part of warrant of resurvey.

HOG QUARTER

Patented on 24 Nov.1674 by Thomas Shiles for 50 acres.
1674/5 Thomas Shiles willed to son John 100 acres, two patents not named.
Rent Rolls 1666-1723, possessed by John Shiles son of Thomas Shiles.
1714 John Shiles willed to son John plantation, unnamed.
15 Apr.1745 John Shiles sold to Thomas Willin 50 acres.
13 June 1764 Thomas Willin with wife Elizabeth Willin sold to son Robert Willin with balance of SAFETY that part not already taken up by his brother Thomas Willin.
30 June 1764 Thomas Willin Sr. with wife Elizabeth Willin gave part to son Thomas Willin Jr.
1773 Thomas Willin Jr. willed to son George Willin 2 acres and to son Levin Willin balance of HOG YARD.
1783 tax - Robert Willin 9 1/2 acres, Nanticoke 100
1783 tax - Levin Willin 21 acres and 25 acres
1783 tax - George Willin 2 acres
20 June 1786 Charles Willin with wife Eleanor Willin, Robert Willin and Ann Willin sold to George Aires 31 acres, for 5 shillings.
27 Feb.1787 Charles Willin sold to George Willin 11 1/2 acres of HOGG QUARTER & WILLENS MISTAKE.

HOG QUARTER

Patented on 10 July 1677 by William Stevens for 700 acres who assigned to William Green to the northward of Wetipquin Creek.
3 Mar.1705 William Green sold to William White.
Rent Rolls 1666-1723, possessed by John White
20 Oct.1721 Charles White son of William gave 350 acres to brother William White.
1 Aug.1727 Charles White with wife Catherine White sold 350 acres to John Reed Sr. of Wetipquin.
15 Nov.1728 William White of Dorc.Co.Md. and Charles White sold upper 1/2 to Isaiah Quartermus.
20 Dec.1731 Isaiah Quartermus sold 200 acres to John Reed Sr., upper part.
1731 John Reed sold 175 acres to James Quartermus.
17 Apr.1740 John Reed Sr. gave part to son John Reed Jr.
1745 John Reed willed to son Hezekiah Reed dwelling plantation and balance of land bought of Charles White that I did not give to son John Reed.
1748 John Reed willed to son Jacob Reed dwelling plantation unnamed. His wife was Martha Reed.
20 June 1753 Patrick Quartermus with wife Sarah Quartermus sold 75 acres to John Barkley.
2 Mar.1764 Hezekiah Reed with wife Judah Reed sold to David Dorman 100 acres.
22 July 1764 Jacob Reed son of John Reed who was the son of John Reed, with wife Martha Reed sold to Ephraim King part.
4 Feb.1767 John Quartermus son of Patrick Quartermus of James Quartermus sold 75 acres to John Barkley.
4 Feb.1767 John Quartermus sold 100 acres to John Phillips for 5 shillings.
4 June 1771 John Phillips sold 100 acres to Ephraim King.

1783 tax - Hezekiah Reed 30 acres- Nanticoke 100
1783 tax - Samuel King 450 acres.
1783 tax - William Porter 100 acres.
26 July 1784 Samuel King with wife Mary King sold to John Stewart 997 3/4 acres of FISHERMANS QUARTER, HOG QUARTER, KINGS MISFORTUNE, MT. EPHRAIM.
19 Apr.1798 James Reed with wife Betty Reed sold 35 acres to David Dutton
1798 David Dutton willed to be sold.
1 Dec.1804 Belitha Wright and wife Mary Ann Wright (Mary Ann Dutton) sold to Stephen Wright that David Dutton purchased of James Reed.
11 Feb.1806 Alexander Stewart sold to Isaac Harris 75 3/4 acres and 17 1/2 acres.
7 Apr.1810 Stephen Wright, shipright, sold to Delaney Wright 101 acres of WESTON, HOG QUARTER, CHANCE.
1823 William Donoho willed to son Alexander Donoho and to son William R. Donoho.

HOG QUARTER

Patented in 1746 by John Jenkins for 319 acres.

HOG QUARTER

Patented on 8 March 1761 by Joseph Christopher for 30 acres in Wicomico forest.
5 Feb.1767 Joseph Christopher with wife Hannah Christopher sold to Benjamin Christopher 30 acres.
7 Mar.1768 Benjamin Christopher with wife Elizabeth Christopher sold to William Parsons 30 acres.
11 May 1771 William Parsons with wife Hannah Parsons sold to James Perdue Sr.
8 June 1772 James Perdue Sr. sold to John Nelms 30 acres.
1783 tax - John Nelms 30 acres, Wic.100 Worc.Co.
1784 John Nelms willed lands to wife Nancy Nelms until children come of age.

HOG QUARTER

Patented on 20 March 1761 by William Jones son of John Jones for 21 acres.
5 Aug.1774 William Jones son of John Jones sold to Phillip Davis 21 acres.

HOG QUARTER

Patented in 1769 by Walter Taylor for 13 acres
1783 tax - Walter Taylor 13 acres
1815 ADDITION TO HOG QUARTER 36 acres patented by Matthias C. Taylor

HOG QUARTER

Patented on 22 Dec 1766 by John Davis for 50 acres.
Resurveyed on 25 Sep.1767 by John Davis HOG QUARTER ENLARGED for 188 acres.
1773 ADDITION TO HOG QUARTER patented by Samuel Davis for 264 acres

1783 tax - John Davis 50 acres, Acquango 100.
3 May 1783 John Davis son of John sold to James Dale son of John Dale 138 acres.
5 Ma.1796 John Davis son of John sold to James Truitt 50 acres
5 May 1796 Jacob Dale heir of James Dale sold to William McGregor 138 acres.
5 July 1796 Joshua Dale of Davidson Co. Tenn. eldest son of James Dale sold rights to William McGregor.
11 Oct.1800 Jesse Fooks sold to Rachel Fooks ADDITION TO HOG QUARTER 161 acres.
12 Aug.1803 Joshua Prideaux commissioner sold to William Mc Gregor (married Mary Dale daughter of James Dale)
1829 William Fooks willed to daughter Delila Fooks 100 acres and balance to daughter Mary Fooks, ADDITION TO HOG QUARTER.

HOG QUARTER

Patented 15 Nov.1757 by Thomas Carey for 20 acres
1783 tax - Hezekiah Carey s/o Thomas 20 acres, Wic.100, Worc.Co.
19 Aug.1786 Hezekiah Carey sold to William Morris 20 acres.

HOG RANGE

Patented in 1796 by William Pollitt for 34 3/4 acres

HOG RIDGE

Patented in 1761 by Joseph Goslee

HOGS ROAD

Patented in 1759 by John Caldwell for 67 acres
4 Feb.1775 Nehemiah Staton with wife Sarah Staton sold to William Laws 67 acres.

HOGG YARD

Patented on 20 Dec.1755 by Isaac Mitchell for 170 acres
1773 Isaac Mitchell willed 170 acres to son Josiah Mitchell in Worcester County.
9 June 1785 Isaac Mitchell of Pocomoke sold to brother Josiah Mitchell all his rights patented by their father Isaac Mitchell.

HOGG YARD

Patented in 1758 by William Nelson for 25 acres.
17 May 1762 William Nelson and wife Ann Nelson sold to Isaac Handy for 5 shillings a parcel of land between them, no name or acreage.

HOGG YARD

Patented in 1763 by Isaac Atkinson for 132 1/2 acres
18 Mar.1772 Isaac Atkinson with wife Elizabeth Atkinson sold 21 3/4 acres to Levin Willin son of Thomas Willin, adjacent NOBLE QUARTER.
18 ar.1772 Isaac Atkinson with wife Elizabeth Atkinson sold 21 3/4 acres to George Willin Sr. son of Thomas Willin

1773 Thomas Willin Jr. willed to son George 2 acres an to son Levin Willin balance of afsd.
1783 tax - George Willin 22 3/4 acres- Nanticoke 100
1783 tax - Levin Willin 21 acres
1783 tax - Elizabeth Atkinson 20 acres.
27 Feb.1787 George Willin sold 9 acres to Robert Willin for 5 shillings.
1797 Levin Willin willed lands unnamed to wife Nancy Willin, afte death to sons Alexander Willin and Chaplin Willin.

HOLD FAST

Patented 1 Oct.1688 by Richard Hull in Virginia, near Tonytank Town
Rent Rolls 1666-1723, belongs to Richard Hull of Northumberland Co. Virginia.
30 Sep.1769 Richard Hull of St. Stephen's Parish in Northumberland Co. Va. sold 400 acres to Thomas Pollitt
1783 tax - William Pollitt 400 acres Wic.100 Worc.Co.
1788 William Pollitt willed part to sons William Pollitt and Samuel Pollitt.

HOLDERS CHANCE

Patented on 25 Oct.1714 by John Holder on road to Cypress Bridge.
Rent Rolls 1666-1723, possessed by John Holder
1716/21 John Holder willed lands unnamed to son Joseph Holder.
15 Mar.1736 Ebenezer Handy mortgaged to John Trehearn 65 acres with COXES FORK.
19 Aug.1767 John Handy of Worc.Co. sold to John Leonard of Som.. Co. 65 acres
1763 Joseph Leonard willed 65 acres to son John Leonard.
1783 tax - John Leonard Wic.100 65 acres.
21 Apr.1787 I James Hill sell to James Fletcher estate of John Leonard, no name or acreage. James Hill married Leah Leonard who had administration of her husbands estate.

HOLDERS FOLLY

Patented in 1734 by Lewis Disharoon for 100 acres
1745 Lewis Disharoon willed to son Levin Disharoon 100 acres
1746 Levin Disharoon willed to son Levin Disharoon
8 June 1766 Levin Disharoon sold to George Smith 100 acres in the fork of the Wicomico River.
1773 SMITHS ADDITION TO HOLDERS FOLLY patented George Smith for 155 acres
1783 tax - James Townsend Wic.100 Worc.Co. 129 acres.
6 Oct.1787 George Smith son of Andrew Smith sold to Nancy Nelms 129 acres.
1 June 1805 George Smith, Isaac Vinson with wife Leah Vinson, Seth Smith, Hetty Wooten of Sussex Co.Delaware sold to Elisha Parker 3/4 acre of SMITHS ADDN. TO HOLDERS FOLLY.

HOLLISES ADDITION

Patented in 1818 by William Hollis for 21 1/2 acres

HOLLOWAYS GOOD LUCK

Patented in 1807 by John Holloway for 34 1/2 acres

HOLLOWAYS PURCHASE

Patented in 1854 by Elijah Holloway for 191 acres

HOLLY GROVE

Patented on 4 July 1764 by Benjamin Perdue for 13 1/2 acres
4 June 1770 Benjamin Perdue sold to James Perdue son of John Perdue 13 1/2 acres with BENJAMINS CHOICE 22 acres.
1783 tax - James Perdue of John, 13 1/2 acres, Wic.100 Worc.Co.

HONEST PURCHASE

Patented in 1777 by William Mills for 99 acres in Rewastico 100.
1783 tax - William Mills 100 acres a resurvey of POOR CHOICE
1823 William Mills willed to son Selby Mills.

HOPEWELL

Patented on 1 July 1669 by John Marvel for 300 acres
20 Sep.1679 John Marvel and wife Hannah Marvel sold 300 acres to William Keen.
2 May 1684 William Keen with wife Mary Keen of Rockawalkin sold 300 acres to Thomas Humphries.
Rent Rolls 1666-1723, possessed by Alexander Carlylse who purchased ot Thomas Humphries.
25 Sep.1773 Adam Carlylse of Cumberland Co. Gr. Britain son of Alexander Carlylse sold 300 acres to Josiah Polk.
1783 tax - Josiah Polk 300 acres
1784 Josiah Polk willed to brother James Polk
1795 James Polk willed to wife Nancy Polk.

HOPEWELL

Patented in 1741 by William Bowman for 100 acres.

HOPKINS ADDITION

Patented in 1758 by Isaac Hopkins for 20 acres
1783 tax - Isaac Hopkins 20 acres, Nanticoke 100
1836 Stephen Winright wiled to daughter Betsy Shores 79 acres bought of Matthias D. Hopkins.

HOPKINS CHOCE

Patented in 1754 by David Hopkins for 20 acres
1783 tax - Stephen Hopkins 25 acres, Nanticoke 100

HOPKINS CONCLUSION

Patented in 1770 by Isaac Hopkins for 80 acres

1783 tax - Isaac Hopkins 80 acres, Nanticoke 100

HOPKINS LAST CONCLUSION

Patented in 1786 by Isaac Hopkins a resurvey of HOPKINS CONCLUSION for 100 acres
1788 Isaac Hopkins willed to daughter Mary Smith 40 acres, after her death to grandson Isaac Smith. To son Levi Hopkins balance of estate, unnamed.
10 Aug.1809 Josiah Hughes and wife Peggy Hopkins Hughes (he married Peggy Smith 12 Oct.1805) sold to Polly Smith land formerly property of Thomas Smith father of Peggy Hughes and formerly of Isaac Hopkins who willed to daughter Mary Smith wife of Thomas Smith at Wetpiquin Creek, no name or acres.

HOPKINS LOTT

Patented in 1761 by Robert Hopkins for 267 1/4 acres.
20 Aug.1762 Robert Hopkins sold to Obediah Disharoon 43 acres, adjacent where Constant Disharoon lives.
14 Sep.1762 Robert Hopkins sold 50 acres to Walter Taylor
28 Sep.1762 Robert Hopkins sold 150 acres to Samuel Adams.
14 Sep.1762 Robert Hopkins sold 21 1/2 acres to Constant Disharoon
31 Dec.1771 Samuel Adams with wife Rebecca Adams sold to William Smith 168 1/2 acres.
1783 tax - Constant Disharoon Wic.100 Worc.Co.
1783 tax - Joshua Disharoon 168 1/2 acres.
14 Dec.1805 Walter Taylor of Kent Co. Delaware sold to David Prior of Somerset County 50 acres now called part of BACK SWAMP.

HORN RIDGE

Patented in 1760 by Jon. Jenkins for 33 acres.

HORSE HEAD

Patented on 16 Nov.1730 by Isaac Ingram for 100 acres.
11 Aug.1744 Jacob Ingram with wife Agnes Ingram sold to Elias Venatson 100 acres, at head of Dove Creek.
1746 Elias Venatson willed to to son Charles Venatson 100 acres of HORSEHEAD.
26 Jan 1764 Charles Venatson of Frederick Co. Md. sold to John Conway of Worc.Co. 100 acres.

HORSE ISLAND

Patented in 1753 by Benjamin Venables for 16 1/2 acres
1783 tax - Joseph Venables son of Benjamin 16 1/2 acres, Rewastcio 100

HORSEYS BAILYWICK

Patented on 16 March 1664 by Stephen Horsey for 500 acres
7 Aug.1667 Stephen Horsey sold to Edward Southern 500 acres.
9 June 1674 Edward Southern with wife Mary Southern sold 200 acres to Phillip Ascue now caled PHILLIPS TOGETHER

1 Apr.1684 Phillip Ascue with wife Grace Ascue sold 100 acres to Thomas Benston.
10 Aug.1675 Edward Southern of Wicomico with wife Mary Southern sold 300 acres to Robert Ridgley.
8 Sep.1677 Phillip Ascue with wife Lydia Ascue sold to Roger Phillips now called BETTER THAN IT PROMISES.
11 Aug.1675 Edward Southern with wife Mary Southern sold 250 acres to John Dorman.
4 Mar.1676 John Dorman sold 250 acres to Thomas Hobbs.
11 Jan 1678 Thomas Hobbs with wife Elizabeth Hobbs sold to William Layton 250 acres.
4 Dec.1695 Richard Phillips sold to Phillip Ascue 50 acres called HOGSDOWN.
Rent Rolls 1666-1723, possessed by Richard Phillips 100 acres, Phillip Ascue 150 acres, Robert Ridgley 250 acres (this included offer of 200 acres made by special warrant for Ridgley called BOLEAN.
1708 Phillip Ascue with wife Grace Ascue sold to Thomas Brown ADDITION.
14 Apr.1721 Thomas Benson sold to Edward Hertz late of the island of Bermuda 100 acres with 50 acres of ADDITION.
26 Apr.1730 Thomas Phillips sold to Roger Kellett 107 acres nd 12 1/2 acre of PHILLIPS ADDITION adj. land left Sarah Phillips by will adjacent land Roger Kellett bought of Richard Phillips, unnamed.
1 Feb.1739 Richard Phillips son of Richard sold to Roger Kellett and wife Eunice Kellett his wife's part of HORSEYS BALIWICK, LITTLE BOLEAN, PHILLIPS ADDITION total 132 1/2 acres 12 1/2 acres being PHILLIPS ADDITION.
26 Apr.1730 Thomas Phillips sold to Roger Kellett with wife Eunice Kellett part.
11 Feb.1739 Richard Phillips sold to Henry Lowe 80 acres with LITTLE BELEAN nor called LOWES ENLARGED
1743 part resurveyed to LOWES ENLARGED..
1 Nov.1751 Robert Ridgley of Baltimore Co.Md. sold to Eunice Kellett 40 acres.
1752 200 acres resurveyed to NORTHS SITUATION
20 May 1754 Robert Ridgley of Baltimore Co.Md. sold to Thomas Gillis, balance.
1783 tax - Samuel Covington
4 Dec.1800 John Webb sold to John Dashiell Sr. 308 acres of PHILLIPS ADDN. HORSEYS BALIWICK, LITTLE BOLEAN AND LOWES ENLARGED.
17 Dec.1801 John Dashiell and wife Elizabeth Dashiell sold to John Webb.

HOT HILL

Patented in 1761 by Nehemiah Hitch for 30 acres
1774 Nehemiah Hitch willed to wife Sarah Hitch all lands unnamed and then to son Elias Hitch.
1783 tax - Elias Hitch 30 acres, Rewastico 100.

HOUGHS CHANCE

Patented on 25 Jan.1762 Edward Hough for 12 acres.

HOUNDS DITCH

Patented on 23 Nov.1685 by John Webb for 500 acres
19 June 1705 John Webb with wife Callebra Webb sold 500 acres to William Bozman on the west side of Broad Creek.
Rent Rolls 1666-1723, possessed by John Bozman
14 July 1722 William Bozman Sr. with wife Sarah Bozman sold to Edward Wooten
12 Nov.1728 Edward Wooten with wife Sarah Wooten sold to Jane Hugg 121 acres that he sold to Thomas Hugg deceased who died before conveyance. Thomas Hugg willed on death to wife Joanna Hugg and after death to daughter Jane Hugg. 16 Feb.1727.
13 Mar.1731 Edward Wooten and wife Sarah Wooten sold to Henry Benston 83 acres at corner of Joannna Hugg alias Joan Cooper.
1761 Henry Benston willed to son James Benston
31 Oct.1763 Edward Wooten sold to John Wooten 200 acres.
3 Nov.1763 John Wooten sold to Benjamin Wooten 150 acres.
26 Jan.1771 James Cooper with wife Jane Cooper sold to Elijah Cooper for 5 shillings, 21 acres.

HOUNDS RIDGE

Patented on 12 Sep.1760 Jonathan Jenkins for 33 acres.
5 Nov.1791 Samuel Sockwell with wife Esther Sockwell sold to Cyrus Sharp.
1802 Cyrus Sharp willed lands unnamed to brothers William Sharp and Daniel Sharp.
31 May 1810 Daniel Sharp with wife Rebecca Sharp sold to James Bennett with SHAVE THE BALD FRIAR, ADDITION, & GOOD INTENT 364 3/4 acres now called WHITE PLAINS
1815 resurveyed to WHITE PLAINS

HOUSTONS ADVENTURE

Patented on 16 April 1767 by Dr. James Houston for 161 acres a survey of COVINGTONS CHOICE a patent that was voided.
1783 tax - Dr. James Houston 161 acres Wic.100, Worc.Co.
1786 William Horsey willed to son George Wailes Horsey 121 acres granted Dr. James Houston. Wife Nelly Horsey.

HOWARDS DISCOVERY

Patented in 1762 by David Howard for 57 acres
2 Apr.1767 David Howard with wife Eleanor Howard sold to Robert Banks 57 acres.
1768 Robert Banks willed to son Henry Banks.
1783 tax - Henry Banks 57 acres.
15 Aug.1783 James Houston sold to Henry Banks 161 acres.
4 Feb.1797 Henry Banks with wife Mary Banks sold to Benjamin Johnson and John Johnson 28 acres.

HUCKSTERS CHOICE

Patented in 1810 by Billy Fooks and others 24 acres
1830 Jonathan Fooks willed to daughter Henrietta Byrd 8 acres.

HUFFINGTONS DISAPPOINTMENT

Patented in 1785 by John Robertson for 62 3/4 acres
1800 John Robertson willed 60 acres to son Solomon Robertson.

HUFFINGTON HILL

Patented in 1804 by James Dean for 15 acres
1805 James Dean willed 15 acres to negro child Rhoda daughter of Peggy bought of Thomas Huffington, unnamed.

HUFFINGTONS LOTT

Patented in 1753 Thomas Huffington for 20 acres
1762 Thomas Huffington willed to daughter Sarah Day.

HUFFINGTONS SWAMP

Patented in 1803 by Thomas Huffington for 28 1/2 acres

HUFFINGTONS VENTURE

Patented in 1762 by Lazarus Huffington for 50 acres
9 May 1778 Lazarus Huffington sold to Benjamin Nelson 50 acres
1783 tax - Benjamin Nelson 100 acres
1783 tax - John Nelson 60 acrees
1784 John Nelson willed to son John Nelson part bought of Henry Gale, unnamed.
5 Nov.1791 John Leatherbury sheriff sold to Arthur Dashiell per judgement by Benjamin Skinner against Benjamin Nelson. 50 acres
5 Nov.1791 Arthur Dashiell sold to John Nelson part bought of John Leatherbury.
28 Dec.1793 John Leatherbury Esq. sheriff sold to John Nelson, highest bidder 50 acres, as Benjamin Nelson a prisioner in jail, sold for debts.

HUGGS PURCHASE

Patented in 1714 by Thomas Hugg for 100 acres
17 June 1720 Thomas Hugg, cooper with wife Joanna Hugg sold 100 acres to John Perdue, planter.
1 July 1729 John Perdue with wife Mary Perdue sold to George Maglamery weaver, 100 acres.
Aug.1760 Alexander Adams rector of Stepney Parish sold to John Flint 100 acres.
1771 Thomas Flint willed to son Thomas Flint where Father John Flint lived with FLINTS SAFEGUARD.
23 Feb.1763 John Flint resurveyed to FLINTS SAFEGUARD.

HUGHES ADDITION

Patented in 1812 by Jesse Hughes for 282 1/2 acres

HULLS FOLLY

Patented in 1818 by Brittingham Hull for 15 acres.

HUMPRHIES CHANCE

Patented in 1761 by Thomas Humphries Jr. for 100 acres
12 Dec.1767 Thomas Humphries Jr. sold to James Nicholson 100 acres.
2 July 1768 James Nicholson sold to Thomas McClemmy
1783 tax - Benjamin McClellan 100 acres
1799 Joseph McClellan willed to friend Horatio Stayton 100 acres.
4 Jan 1800 Horatio Stayton sold to Spencer Hearn 100 acres.

HUMPHREYS HOOK

Patented in 1817 by Thomas Humphries 22 acres.

HUNGARY QUARTER

Patented on 20 Nov.1694 by John Frizzell on the east side of a branch of the Wicomico River for 200 acres.
7 Nov.1752 Graves Bashaw with wife Mary Bashaw sold to Jonathan Sturgis 200 acres.
8 Nov.1753 Jonathan Sturgis withe wife Esther Sturgis sold 112 acres to John Sturgis of Accomack Co.Va.
10 June 1768 John Sturgis sold to Alexander Thomas Russell 112 acres.
2 Sep.1774 Alexander Thomas Russell sold to Price Russell 112 acres.
Resurveyed 1773 for 272 1/2 acres by Alexander Thomas Russell
9 June 1778 Josiah Russell of Frederick County and Price Russell with wife Anne Russell of Somerset Co. sold to William Hopewell
19 June 1782 William Hopewell with wife Nancy Hopewell sold to John Davis 16 acres, 1/2 mile from Salisbury.
1783 tax - John Davis 16 acres. Wic.100 Worc.Co.
1783 tax - Joshua Sturgis Jr. 70 acres.
1789 John Davis willed 8 acres to son Reuben Davis and to son Stephen Davis 8 acres.

HUNGARY QUARTER

Patented on 25 Oct.1789 by William Winder for 50 acres
22 Oct.1790 William Winder gave to daughter Leah Morris part with SAW MILL LOTT 100 acres, except mill belonging to George Dashiell.
20 Aug.1791 William Winder Sr. gave to daughter Leah Morris 50 acres.
4 Dec.1795 Leah Morris and Col. William Morris executors of James Round Morris sold to Reuben Davis 16 acres
22 Nov.1793 James Round Morris with wife Leah Morris sold to Joshua Pollitt pt.
1795 James Round Morris, wife Leah Morris, willed to children William Winder Morris and John Boucher Morris
5 Aug.1798 Leah Morris, William Morris, Levin Winder executors of James Round Morris sold to Reuben Davis who resurveyed to MORRIS DISCOVERY
4 June 1805 James Fooks of Jesse Fooks with wife Sabrey Fooks sold to Joshua Pollitt 7 1/2 acres, at Wicomico River.

HUNGER AND THIRST

Patented in 1800 by Nancy Austin, Prissey Austin and Polly Nairn in for 107 acres daughters of Elijah Austin, in Wicomico Manor.
16 Jan.1801 Robert Nairn with wife Polly Nairn sold to William Pollitt

1/3rd part.
8 July 1809 William Pollitt with wife Sally Pollitt sold to James
Toadvine, part.
1808 John Cathell willed to son George Cathell 472 acres of HUNGER &
THIRST, GOOD LUCK & SUMMER FIELDS.
1816 Wiliam Pollitt willed to nephew James Morris lands bought of
Robert Nairn.
27 Oct.1821 Levi Cathell Jr, trustee to sell real estate of John
Cathell Jr. sold to James Toadvine, part.

HURRY

Patented in 1741 Robert Ingram for 50 acres
1783 tax - Elihu Mezick 50 acres, Nanticoke 100

HYPOCRITES DECEIVED

Patented in 1776 by John Gordy for 652 acres
25 Oct.1776 John Gordy with wife Hannah Gordy sold to Henry Trader 149
acres.
9 June 1789 John Gordy of Sussex Co.Del. with wife Hannah Gordy gave
to Nathan Gordy 227 acres.
20 June 1789 John Gordy with wife Hannah Gordy of Sussex Co.Del. sold
to William Layfield 143 acres.
1783 tax - William Oliphant 100 acres- Wic.100 Worc.Co.
1783 tax - Ignatius Anderson 150 acres
1783 tax - John Gordy 150 acres
1783 tax - James Perdue 50 acres

ICHABOD

Patented in 1773 by William Adams
1788 Josiah Adams willed to sister Louisa Adams, all estate, unnamed.
4 Nov.1809 Charles Nutter with wife Louisa Nutter sold to Andrew Adams
10 1/4 acres as Josiah Adams bequeathed to sister Louisa Adams afsd.

IGNOBLE QUARTER

Patented on 14 Sep.1668 by Thomas Shiles for 300 acres
24 Dec.1698 Thomas Shiles sold 32 acres to Thomas Dashiell
Rent Rolls 1666-1723, possessed by Thomas Shiles
Rent Rolls 1666-1723, possessed by Thomas Dashiell 32 acres
1674 Thomas Shiles willed 300 acres to son Thomas Shiles.
24 Dec.1731 Thomas Dashiell deeded to son Charles Dashiell 32 acres.
17 June 1743 Charles Dashiell sold to Stephen Winright 32 acres
1744 Mary Hampton willed to Thomas Fletcher
15 Apr.1745 John Shiles sold to Thomas Willin 36 acres.
22 Feb.1755 Thomas Willin gave to son John Willin 50 acres.
20 June 1755 Thomas Fletcher s/o Thomas sold to Henry Waggaman 300
acres.
20 Jan 1756 Henry Waggaman sold to Thomas Fletcher 300 acres
ADDITION pat. 1759 by John Robertson 13 1/2 acres.
1763 Stephen Winright willed to son Cannon Winright 32 acres.
17 May 1761 Nehemiah Crockett with wife Alice Crockett sold to Jacob

Mezick with wife Elizabeth Mezick, land sold to John Willin son of Thomas Willin, as John Nelson died intestate and his daughters Elizabeth Mezick and Alice Crockett inherited.
1763 Stephen Winright willed to son Cannon Winright 30 acres bought of Charles Dashiell.
22 Aug.1771 Evans Winright and Cannon Winright sold 32 acres to Thomas Rencher Jr.
17 Sep.1779 Mary Winright widow of Stephen Winright sold to Cannon Winright 100 acres, unnamed.
1783 tax - Thomas Rencher 32 acres.
1783 tax - George Robertson 182 acres
1783 tax - Cannon Winright 100 acres, Nanticoke 100
1783 tax - Evans Winright 100 acres.
16 Dec.1788 John Willin with wife Betty Willin sold to Willin McIntyre 12 3/4 acres for 5 shillings
16 Dec.1788 Samuel Willin with wife Mary Willin sold to Willin McIntyre 8 acres.
(also see NOBLE QUARTER.)

ILL NEIGHBORHOOD

Patented in 1756 by John Huffington for 913 acres a resurvey of BARREN QUARTER, WHAT YOU PLEASE & MORRIS GROUND.
1783 tax - Joseph Hust 50 acres   Rewastico 100
1783 tax - Richard Haynie 450 acres
1783 tax - James Hust 100 acres
1783 tax - John Phillips 118 acres
1783 tax - Charles Weatherly
26 Nov.1801 Jonathan Huffington sold to William Russum 100 acres.
1821 William Russum willed to sons William P. Russum and Robert C. Russum.
Became part of MARDELLA SPRINGS TOWN.

ILL WILL

Patented in 1765 by John Goddard for 32 1/4 acres
1783 tax - William Goddard 32 1/4 acres, Rewastico 100
1802 William Goddard willed lands, unnamed to sons John Goddard and George Goddard.

IMPROVEMENT

Patented in 1725 by George Dashiell for 40 acres on the south side of Quantico Creek.
1733 George Dashiell willed to son Robert Dashiell
12 Apr.1749 Court appoints Mrs. Jane Handy as guardian of Esther Dashiell daughter of Robert Dashiell. Certified inventory includes lands in Quantico Creek, RECOVERY & IMPROVMENT.
1755 Esther Dashiell daughter of Robert Dashiell resurveyed to 548 1/2 acres a combination of lands IMPROVEMENT, and RECOVERY to GRANDFATHERS CARE.

INCLOSED

Patented on 22 Oct.1722 by Edward Wooten for 100 acres on the west

side of Cypress Branch.
Rent Rolls 1666-1723, possessed by Edward Wooten
31 Oct.1762 Edward Wooten sold to John Wooten 100 acres.
3 Nov.1763 John Wooten sold 100 acres to Benjamin Wooten
2 May 1776 resurveyed to Sussex Co.Delaware

INCLOSED

Patented on 4 July 1728 by Robert Givans for 437 acres
1735 Robert Givans of Stepney Parish willed to son Thomas Givans 100 acres and to son George Givans 100 acres adjacent to son Day Givans.
8 Nov.1744 George Givans sold 40 acres to Jarrad Wyley.
24 July 1747 Robert Givans gave bond to George Givans to make over two tracts that fell him by death of brother Thomas Givans 281 acres with CYPRESS SWAMP left Thomas by father Robert Givans.
17 Mar.1749 Jarrad Wyley of Worc.Co. sold to Joseph Ennals of Dorc.Co. on the south side of Broad Creek.
29 July 1755 Day Givans son of Robert Givans sold to Joseph Marshall 437 acres.

INDEPENDENCY

Patented by Jesse Hughes for 480 acres

INDIAN CABBIN BRANCH

Patented in 1728 by Jon. Vaughan for 12 acres

INDIAN LOTT

28 Apr.1785 Gabriel Duvall comissioner to sell confiscated British property sold to Richard Mills, in Wicomico Manor 121 1/4 acres
25 May 1790 Richard Mills sold to Jesse Fooks INDIAN LOTT, part of WICOMICO MANOR 121 1/4 acres.
Patented in 1793 by Jesse Fooks for 121 1/4 acres

INDUSTRY

Patented in 1749 by Charles Tindell for 100 acres.
1763 Charles Tindell willed 100 acres to son Charles Tindell.

INGRAMS LOTT

Patented on 6 Apr.1722 by Jacob Ingram for 50 acres on the north side of Deep Creek Branch.
Rent Rolls 1666-1723, possessed by Jacob Ingram
25 Aug.1740 Jacob Ingram sold 50 acres to John Lord patented Jacob son of Isaac Ingram.
13 Apr.1763 Jacob Ingram with wife Ann Ingram sold to John Spicer 50 acres.
6 Apr.1768 William Spicer sold to Jonathan Vaughan and Company of Deep Creek Furnace 50 acres.

INHERITANCE AND ADDITON

Patented in 1748 by Jarman Bethards for 47 acres (at Pittsville)

5 Mar.1762 Jarman Bethards ADDITION TO INHERITANCE 567 1/2 acres
9 Mar.1770 Jarman Bethards sold to John Parsons 80 acres of ADDITION TO INHERITANCE
8 Sep.1773 Jarman Bethards sold to John Parsons 80 acres
1780 Jarman Bethards willed to son William Jarman Bethards and 50 acres to son Samuel Bethards.
1782 ADDITION TO INHERITANCE resurveyed by Jarman Bethards 567 1/2 acres.
26 Feb.1798 Martha Bethards and Elizabeth Bethards of Kent Co.Delaware sold to Zachariah Parsons of Worc.Co.Md. 230 1/2 acres of ADDITION
26 Feb.1798 Martha Bethards and Elizabeth Bethards of Kent Co.Del. sold to William Campbell 138 1/2 acres ADDITION
22 June 1804 Henry S. Bethards son of Samuel Bethards sold to William Parker three parts, no acres given.
18 July 1807 William Parker sold to Zephaniah Parsons 314 acres of ADDITION TO INHERITANCE & TARR KILL RIDGE.
1814 Zephaniah parsons willed to son William Parsons and part to son John Parsons
12 Jan.1822 John Parsons of Peter Parsons sold to John Selby Parsons 91 1/2 acres of ADDITION
1 Mar.1834 John Selby Parsons sold to James Fooks part
31 Jan.1835 Simon Peter Parsons and wife Ann Parsons sold to John Selby Parsons 138 1/2 acres of RICH POINT, ADDN. TO INHERITANCE.
4 June 1842 Catherine Parsons, John Selby Parsons and Betsy Parsons sold to John Albert Parsons 70 1/2 acres.

INLETT

Patented in 1793 by Whittington White for 41 1/2 acres

INSLEYS LOTT

Patented in 1830 by John Insley for 1 1/2 acres
1850 he is in Tyaskin District

INSLEYS TRIAL

Patented in 1848 by John Insley for 59 acres

INSLEYS TROUBLE

Patented in 1830 by John Insley for 3 3/8 acres

INVERNESS

Patented in 1793 by Levin Taylor for 132 1/2 acres
1854 ADDITION TO INVERNESS, patented by William Taylor for 112 acres.

INVITATION

Patented in 1801 by George Collins for 348 1/4 acres

IRELAND EYE

Patented on 1 Oct.1688 by Lawrence Young for 300 acres above Plumb

Creek
5 May 1698 Lawrence Young and wife Ann Young (Ann Bounds) sold to James Rawley, planter.
Rent Rolls 1666-1723, possessed by James Rawley
18 May 1713 William Rawley son of James sold to John Shores.
29 Jan 1724 John Shores and wife Alice Shores sold to John Nicholson, bricklayer.
8 Nov.1729 John Nicholson sold 300 acres to John Robertson
1748/53 John Robertson willed to son James 150 acres and to son Jacob Robertson 150 acres, dwelling plantation.
1748/523 John Robertson willed to son James Robertson 150 acres and to son Jacob Robertson 150 acres, dwelling plantation.
1783 tax - John Robertson 150 acres, Nanticoke 100
1783 tax - Thomas Connerly 150 acres.

IRON HILL

Patented on 29 Mar.1732 by James Makemorie for 180 acres.
22 Feb.1734 James Makemorie with wife Ann Makemorie sold to William Calloway.
1758 William Calloway willed to son Moses Calloway 50 acres and balance to son Matthew Calloway.
1758 Moses Calloway willed to son Moses part and to son Clammond Calloway
3 Feb.1758 Moses Calloway and wife Ann Calloway sold 50 acres to Matthew Calloway, at head of a branch of the Nanticoke River.
27 May 1776 resurveyed to Sussex Co.Delaware by Matthew Calloway

IRON MINE

Patented in 1816 by Thomas R. Handy for 157 acres, 2 perches and 23 rods.

IRON ORE

Patented in 1764 by Joseph Venables for 10 acres
1788 Joseph Venables willed to Joshua Bratten son of James Bratten and Mary Bratten.

ISAACS BEGINNING

This is part of PHARSALIA

ISAACS CHOICE

Patented in 1782 by Isaac Serman for 234 3/4 acres.
1783 tax - George Serman 39 1/2 acres Wic. 100
1783 tax - Grace Serman 45 1/2 acres
11 Apr.1795 George Serman with wife Rebecca Serman sold to Cornelius Vanderwolf 7 3/4 acres
1797 George Serman willed land unnamed to sons Isaac Serman and George Serman.

ISAACS FOLLY

Patented on 8 Nov.1737 by Andrew Collins for 80 acres.
1728/9 Andrew Collins willed to son William Collins a half and other

half to Thomas Davis.
4 Nov.1747 William Collins Jr. with wife Tabitha Collins sold their
rights to Thomas Davis
1764 resurveyed to DAVIS CHOICE.

ISLAND OF MARSH

Patented to Thomas Dashiell for 17 1/2 acres
1771 Thomas Dashiell willed to son William Dashiell
1783 tax - Thomas Dashiell 17 1/2 acres
20 July 1804 Patience Holbrook widow of John Holbrook sold to William
Cottman Jr. 17 1/2 acres.

ISLAND OF MARSH

Patented on 9 Feb.1682 by William Brereton for 50 acres.
Rent Rolls 1666-1723, possessed by William Brereton son of William.
2nd listing Rent Rolls 1666-1723, possessed by John Frizzell

JACKSONS BEGINNING

Patented in 1801 by Joseph Jackson for 19 1/2 acres
Mar.1805 Joseph Jackson willed entire estate to wife Elizabeth
Jackson, after death to Thomas Nicholson son of Jonathan Nicholson
20 Feb.1805 Thomas Lankford, shoemaker sold to Joshua Nicholson 50
acres of JACKSONS BEGINNNG AND ADDITION TO CUBYS CHANCE.

JACKSONS DELIGHT

Patented in 1811 by Elihu Jackson for 253 3/4 acres
1833 Elihu Jackson willed lands to grandson Isaac B. Jackson
1850 Isaac B. Jackson in Salisbury district.

JACKSONS LOTT

Patented in 1748 by Samuel Jackson for 50 acres
1753 Samuel Jackson willed to grandson Samuel Jackson Bayley, if no
heirs to grandson Benjamin Bayley.

JACKSONS PARADISE

This is part of BEWDLY

JACKSONS PURCHASE

Patented in 1755 by James Jackson for 50 acres

JAMES ADDITION

Patented in 1754 by James Cathell for 50 acres.
1772 James Cathell of Worc.Co. willed to son James, 50 acres
13 Mar.1796 Levin Pollitt sold to John Cathell part bought at
sheriff's sale and taken from James Cathell son of James.
1 Jan.1793 Betty Christopher sold to David Cathell 50 acres
29 May 1824 Joshua Cathell son of David Cathell sold to Joseph
Townsend.

11 Mar.1796 Levin Pollitt, sheriff sold to John Cathell per judgement against James Cathell heir of James 50 acres CATHELLS CHANCE & JAMES ADDITION.

JAMES CHOICE

Patented on 23 Sep.1756 by Levin James for 71 acres
1783 tax - Comfort James 24 acres, Worc.Co. Wic. 100
25 Dec.1805 Joshua Owens with wife Violetta Owens sold 71 acres to John Lamberson at branch of Wicomico River.
7 Oct.1806 John Lamberson with wife Mary Lamberson sold to Joshua Owens and wife Violetta Owens, rights

JAMES CHOICE

Patented on 18 Aug.1768 by James Lewis for 50 acres
9 Nov.1771 James Lewis sold 50 acres to Joseph Timmons.
1783 tax - James Perdue 50 acres, Wic.100 Worc.Co.
20 Aug.1787 Joseph Timmons with wife Mary Timmons sold to Joseph Brittingham 50 acres.
14 Feb.1806 Joseph Brittingham with wife Mary Brittingham sold to James Parsons 50 acres.

JAMES CHOICE

Patented on 24 May 1688 by Richard Chambers for 150 acres in the woods near a branch of the Wicomico River
Rent Rolls 1666-1723, possessed by Richard Chambers
1726/8 Richard Chambers willed to daughter Sarah Chambers.
16 Apr.1768 Richard Tull son of George Tull and wife Sarah Tull of Dorc.Co. sold to John Brown 75 acres.
17 Apr.1768 Richard Tull and wife Sarah Tull of Dorc.Co. sold to Jonathan Stanford of Somerset Co. 75 acres.
7 Ma.1786 Jonathan Stanford sold to David Brown 75 acres
10 Oct.1795 James Perdue with wife Sarah Perdue sold to Jonathan Parsons 50 acres
21 May 1803 David Brown sold 75 acres to son Thomas Brown

JAMES CHOICE

Patented in 1851 by Levin P. White (Salisbury district)

JAMES DEBATE

Patented in 1764 by Ezekiel James a resurvey from BARBERS ADDITION, for 231 acres
1770 Ezekiel James willed to daughter Unice James.
1783 tax - George James 231 acres, Nanticoke 100
2 Dec.1809 Francis James sold to John Chattam Jr. as Dr. Ezekiel James died and willed to daughter Unice James dwelling plantation. Francis James is issue of Eunice James.
2 Dec.1809 John Chattam sold to Francis James.

JAMES ESCAPE

Patented in 1817 by James Toadvine for 129 acres

JAMES FORTUNE

Patented in 1774 by Nathan Culver, a resurvey of SAW MILL SUPPLY for 96 acres
24 Jan 1782 Nathan Culver sold to Thomas Humphries 18 acres.
15 June 1799 William Hitch and John Hitch sons of Joshua Hitch sold to Thomas Humphries 11 1/4 acres
1783 tax - Levin Huffington 15 acres, Rewastico 100.

JAMES LOTT

Patented in 1753 by Jacob Mezick for 34 acres
1751 Jacob Mezick willed to grandson James Mezick son of Elihu Mezick 17 acres and to son Jacob Mezick, balance
1783 tax - Jacob Mezick 17 acres
22 Apr.1785 James Mezick and wife Elizabeth Mezick of Dorc.Co. Md. sold to Solomon Kimmey of Somerset County 1/2 acre
22 July 1786 Solomon Kimmey sold 34 acres to Elihu Mezick Sr. on the north side of Wetpiquin Creek.

JAMES NEGLECT

Patented in 1786 by Matthias Hobbs for 124 acres
1 Apr.1794 Burke Co. Georgia, Elizabeth Hobbs sold to Milby Magee of same 75 acres that Matthias Hobbs willed to Elizabeth Hobbs.
1798 Matthias Hobbs willed lands to son Benjamin Hobbs, unnamed.
8 Dec.1798 Matthias Hobbs son of Marcellus Hobbs sold to Samuel Turner Parker for 5 shillings rights devised by father.

JAMES POINT

Patented in 1815 by James Bennett a part resurvey out of Mt. Sinai, for 5 7/8 acres.

JAMES PURCHASE

Patented on 7 May 1758 by James Perdue for 25 acres
11 May 1771 James Perdue Sr. with wife Hannah Perdue sold to William Parsons 25 acres in Wiomico forrest.
1783 tax - William Parsons 25 acres, Wic.100, Worc.Co.
2 feb.1797 Nimrod Adkins with wife Betty Adkins, John Melson with wife Hannah Melson, William Brewington with wife Sarah Brewington, Milby Adkins with wife Mary Adkins sold to James Perdue land willed by William Parsons.
2 Feb. 1797 same as above, to Elizabeth Trader, 42 1/2 acres.
1808 John Cathell of Worc.Co. willed to son David Cathell.

JEASMANS CHANCE

Patented in 1811 by George Jeasman for 30 acres

JENKINS MISTAKE

Patented in 1792 by Elias Bayley for 47 acres
2 Oct.1793 Elias Bayley sold to James Bennett 47 acres

JENNERS GOOD LUCK

Patented in 1761 by John Jenner for 50 acres
24 June 1763 John Jenner sold to Ephraim Stevens (to put up as bond for bail money)
7 Apr.1778 Josiah Polk executor sold to Ephraim Stevens 50 acres that John Jenner sold to John Caldwell who willed to be sold by executor Josiah Polk.
1783 tax- Ephraim Stevens 50 acres
1785 Ephraim Stevens of Worc.Co. sold 50 acres to son William Augustus Dashiell Stevens.
12 May 1801 John O. Twiford with wife Ann Twiford of Acco.Co.Va. sold to George Kibble of Som. Co. 55 acres.

JERICHO

Patented in 1759 by William Hastings for 42 acres

JESHIMON

Patented 28 Sep.1674 William Stevens assigned to Isaac Foxcroft, 300 acres in Nanticoke 100.
Rent Rolls 1666-1723, possessed by widow Waters (of Sampson Waters) in Boston, New England. The manager Capt. James Dashiell who married Mary Waters daughter of Sampson Waters and Rebecca Foxcroft daughter of Isaac Foxcroft.
1708/10 Francis Jenkins willed 300 acres to wife Mary Jenkins.
2 Mar.1717 Obediah Wakefield and John Wakefield of Boston in Suffolk Co.Mass. sold to Peter Bowden son of John Bowden late of Northampton Co. Va. 875 acres, 1/2 of JESHIMON 300 acres patented by Isaac Foxcroft, with BENTLY, BATCHELORS ADVENTURE, COVENT GARDEN & SUPPLY.
23 Aug.1739 Peter Bowden with wife Susanna Bowden of Northampton Co. Va. sold to Capell King 1/2 of 1750 acres, unnamed.

JESHIMON

Patented on 17 May 1688 by William Elgate for 150 acres
Rent Rolls 1666-1723, possessed by William Elgate.
1725/8 William Elgate willed to grandaughter Catherine Hitch daughter of Hannah Hitch.
1 Aug.1737 William Elgate gave to Catherine Byrd wife of Thomas Byrd Jr. daughter of Hannah Hitch 150 acres.
13 Sep.1750 Catherine Byrd sold to Josiah Polk and George Hayward (for division of lands.)300 acres ELGATES LOTT & JESHIMON
3 Apr.1764 Catherine Byrd sold to Levin Ballard 150 acres for 5 shillings with ELGATES LOTT.

JINNY DANG THE WEAVER

Patented in 1793 by Joshua Jones for 165 3/4 acres
22 Jan.1794 Joshua Jones mortgaged to John Hackett of Baltimore Town between 80 and 89 acres conveyed by Smullen Layfield to Joshua Jones who later patented by this name.
13 Sep.1797 Joshua Jones with wife Dorcas Jones sold to John Cottman Stewart and wife Ann Stewart on the east side of the Wicomico River at

Tony Tank Creek, partition of land.
30 Sep.1797 John Cottman Stewart and wife Ann Stewart sold 82 1/2 acres to William Pollitt
13 Sep.1797 William Pollitt sold 82 1/2 acres to John Cottman Stewart.
22 July 1809 Dorcas Jones widow of Joshua Jones sold to Peter Dashiell 9 3/4 acres.

JOES RIDGE

Patented in 1747 by William Haynie for 10 acres

JOHNS ADVENTURE

Patented in 1792 by John Hitch for 22 1/2 acres
1828 John Hitch willed to wife Amelia Hitch lands unnamed.

JOHNS CHANCE

Patented in 1815 by Josiah Bayley for 9 1/2 acres

JOHNS DEFENSE

Patented in 1819 by Ann Johnson for 172 acres

JOHNS FOREST

Patented on 22 July 1748 by John Brown for 60 acres.
22 Oct.1766 John Brown willed to brother James Brown
4 Sep.1769 James Brown son of James of Dorc.Co. Md. sold to Andrew Collins on road from Broad Creek. 50 acres.

JOHNS MISFORTUNE

Patented in 1775 by John Moore for 13 acres

JOHNSONS ADDITION

Patented in 1811 by Littleton Johnson for 3 1/4 acres
1816 Littleton Johnson willed lands to son William Johnson then to his daughter Esther Johnson.

JOHNSONS DELIGHT

Patented on 7 Aug.1732 by Thomas Johnson for 50 acres
4 Feb.1741 Thomas Johnson of Sussex Co.Del. sold to William Winright 50 acres on east side of the Nanticoke River in Beard Neck.

JOHNSONS DISPUTE

Patented in 1816 by Shepherd Johnson for 175 3/4 acres

JOHNSONS LOTT & JOHNSONS ADDITION

Patented on 20 Oct.1665 by George Johnson for 300 acres
20 Jan 1668 George Johnson sold 300 acres to Daniel Haste.

1701 Daniel Haste willed to daughter Sarah Haste
Rent Rolls 1666-1723, possessed by Robert Dashiell who married the coheir of Daniel Haste who had the right.
6 Feb.1718 Sarah Dashiell widow of Robert Dashiell gave to son Haste Dashiell
1718 Robert Dashiell gave to son Haste Dashiell 300 acres my now dwelling planatation.
1729 Haste Dashiell willed to brother James Dashiell
27 Feb.1735 Capell King gentleman, sold to Matthias Dashiell. He had the right by intermarring with the widow Sarah Dashiell of Robert Dashiell the elder, formerly land of Daniel Haste laying on the east side of a small Creek called Jones Creek, for 5 shillings.
18 March 1749 resurvey to JOHNSONS ADDITION 274 acres by Matthias Dashiell, found that 23 acres was missing.
1752 William Dashiell son of Robert Dashiell willed to eldest son Robert 174 acres, dwelling plantation, JOHNSONS ADDITION
1783 tax - Robert Dashiell 274 acres in Nanticoke 100

JOHNSONS VENTURE

Patented in 1803 by Jesse Johnson for 14 3/4 acres. He repatented in 1807 for 10 acres.

JONATHANS LOTT

Patented in 1738 by Manuel Manlove for 100 acres

JONATHANS PROSPECT

Patented in 1761 by Jonathan Cope for 75 acres
29 Feb.1768 Jonathan Cope sold 75 acres to Levin Huffington
1782 Levin Huffington willed to daughter Matildah Huffington 75 acres
1783 tax - Joseph Dunn 75 acres
28 Sep.1803 Charles Esham with wife Martha Esham sold to Isaac Kennerly 75 acres.

JONES CHANCE

Patented in 1744 by John Jones for 331 acres
21 Aug.1766 Robert Jones sold 231 acres to Ephraim King on the south side of Quantico Creek.
27 Mar.1769 James Jones and wife Prisey Jones sold to Henry Lowe 100 acres devised by father John Jones.
11 Mar.1774 Henry Lowe and wife Esther Lowe sold to John Waters late of Calvert Co. but now Somerset Co. with DOWNS CHANCE & TUBMANS LOTT, QUANTICO, DORMANS DELIGHT, etc.
31 Mar.1787 Francis Hutchins Waters sold to John Gale plantation from his father John Waters, unnamed land in Quantico Creek.

JONES CHOICE

Patented in 1749 by Isaac Jones for 50 acres
21 Feb.1757 Isaac Jones sold to Alexander Records 50 acres
5 Jan.1775 Alexander Records sold 50 acres to Joshua Hitch at Darren Creek

1792 Joshua Hitch willed planatation to son Joshua Hitch.

JONES DEFEAT

Patented in 1762 by Benjamin Riggin for 10 acres 1 perch, 22 rods.

JONES DELIGHT

Patented in 1735 for James Jones for 50 acres
29 Feb.1752 Isaac Jones sold to Joshua Jones for 5 shillings
6 Oct 1764 Isaac Jones and wife Jane Jones of Worc.Co. sold to James Jones of Somerset Co. 50 acres that James Jones father of Isaac Jones devised to son Joshua Jones who died without issue.
3 Oct.1765 James Jones sold 50 acres to Samuel Jackson Bayley.

JONES DELIGHT

Patented in 1739 by William Jones for 65 acres
4 Nov.1756 William Jones of North Carolina sold to Jonathan Cathell 65 acres.
1772 Jonathan Cathell willed to son Laban Cathell.
6 Mar.1782 Daniel Cathell sold 65 acres to John Taylor on Gladys Branch of the Wicomico River.
1783 tax - John Taylor 65 acres Wic.100 Worc.Co.
1790 John Taylor, wife Mary Taylor, willed to son Thomas Taylor.
13 Sep.1794 James Taylor with wife Mary Taylor sold to Sarah Orman 65 acres.
5 Jan.1805 Eben Disharoon, Aaron Mezick with wife Ann Mezick, Patty Disharoon, Matthew Jones with wife Frankey Jones, Molly Disharoon sold to James Fooks son of Thomas Fooks 65 acres
10 Jan.1807 James Fooks with wife Leah Fooks sold to Benjamin Johnson Jr. 18 acres.
17 Oct.1807 Sarah Disharoon of Francis Disharoon sold to James Fooks her part.

JONES DELIGHT

Patented in 1747 by Samuel B.D. Jones for 629 acres.

JONES DISCOVERY

Patented in 1794 by William Jones for 3 3/4 acres

JONES GOOD LUCK

No patent found under this name.
23 Mar.1772 John Jones sold 55 acres of JONES GOOD LUCK to John Caldwell
7 Nov.1825 John Rider sold 55 acres to William Bounds of Richard Bounds, on the south side of Wicomico River near Upper Ferry that he John Rider purchased of Joseph Moore. Came Eleanor Rider widow of John to verify.
1832 William Richard Bounds willed to son James Bounds and Richard Bounds, bought of the heirs of James Collins.
25 Aug.1734 James H. Bounds with wife Hester Bounds sold to John Dorman 1/2 of 55 acres that father William Bounds willed to him and

brother Richard Bounds.
6 July 1742 Richard Bounds sold 27 1/2 acres to William Bounds.

JONES HOLE

Patented on 8 Sep.1663 by James Jones for 250 acres.
1675 James Jones with wife Sarah Jones sold 75 perches to Capt. Paul Marsh.
1662/4 James Jones gave to Andrew Jones (cousin or Nephew)
1684 Andrew Jones died, widow Elizabeth Winder Jones married 2nd. Thomas Brereton.
1723 Nicholas Evans gave part to daughter Rachel Collier, one mile above town of Whitehaven. (she married George Betts Collier)
19 April 1736 John Huett Nutter eldest son and heir of Ann Leckie who was Ann Huett and later Ann Nutter daughter of Rev. John Huett sold to Levin Gale.
1737 resurveyed to AKAM 2162 acres.
9 Apr.1742 Daniel Cordrey and wife Rachel Cordrey sold 200 acres to Levin Gale all interest in tract belonging to Levin Gale, AKAM, part of JONES HOLE & SUNKEN GROUND.
1770 Rachel Cordrey widow of David Cordrey willed to son Nicholas Evans Collier tract mortgaged to Col. Levin Gale.
19 Oct.1779 Moses Parks with wife Elizabeth Parks who was the daughter of Howell Jones son of Howell Jones the elder who was the son of James Jones sold to Salathiel Griffith, conveyed by Nicholas Evans to James Jones.
19 Oct.1779 Salathiel Griffith sold to Moses Parks and wife Elizabeth Parks.
1796 George Day Scott willed lands unnamed to nephew Dr. Ware Cheney.
7 April 1802 Ware Cheney sold to Francis Ware Hayes all interest willed by George Day Scott with SUNKEN GROUND.
7 Apr.1802 Francis Ware Hayes sold same to Ware Cheney.

JONES LOTT

Patented in 1803 by John Jones for 10 acres
11 Apr.1804 John Jones with wife Elizabeth Jones sold to John Walker of Sussex Co.Del. 10 acres on the south side of the Nanticoke River.

JONES' NECK

Patented on 10 May 1728 by Ebenezer Jones 96 acres on branch of Broad Creek out of the Nanticoke River.
16 Sep.1769 Thomas Jones sold to Henry Blair Johnson 96 acres.

JONES VENTURE

Patented in 1734 by James Jones for 50 acres
231 Feb.1757 Isaac Jones sold 50 acres to Alexander Records
5 Jan 1775 Alexander Records sold 50 acres to Joshua Hitch at Barren Creek.

JOSEPHS LOTT

Patented on 19 Apr.1706 by Benjamin Wailes for 70 acres, two miles from the Wicomico River on west side of Jones Creek at corner of tract

DORCHESTER.
1726 Benjamin Wailes willed to son Joseph Wailes.
12 May 1750 Daniel Wailes sold to Robert Collier Jr. 12 acres.
22 Mar.1758 Haste Wailes quitclaimed to brother Daniel Wailes,devised him by the will of Joseph Wailes.
1783 tax - Robert Collier Jr. 12 acres. Nanticoke 100

JOSEPHS LOTT

Patented in 1734 by Joseph Tilghman for 67 acres
23 Mar.1742 Joseph Tilghman sold to Mary Toadvine
28 May 1763 William Toadvine sold to Charles Cottingham 67 acres
21 July 1774 John Toadvine with wife Anne Toadvine sold to Hezekiah Carey 67 acres.
1 Oct.1777 Hezekiah Carey sold to James Houston 57 acres.
15 Mar.1783 Dr. James Houston sold 67 acres to Matthew Oliphant.
9 Apr.1792 Matthew Oliphant with wife Ann Oliphant sold to Elijah Shockley.
27 Sep.1796 ELijah Shockley sold to John Dashiell part.

JOSEPHS PRIVILEDGE

Patented in 1763 by Daniel Wailes for 195 acres.
1783 tax - Joseph Wailes 195 acres, Nanticoke 100
23 Jan 1808 Daniel Wailes sold to Henry Crawford.
1808 William Winder willed to daughters and children, that I have a contracted with Henry Crawford. (his children were William Henry Winder, Arietta Laird, Charlotte Henry Winder, Rider Henry Winder.)
8 Aug.1809 Capt. Henry R. Graham of the Army of the US and wife Charlotte A.H. Graham (lately Winder) sold to Rev. James Laird. 1/2 mills lately property of William Winder, sold 1/2.
6 June 1809 Henry Crawford with wife Esther Crawford sold to Dorothy Arietta Laird and Charlotte Augusta Henry Winder 52 acres with JOSEPHS PRIVILDEGE purchased of Daniel Wailes.

JOSHUAS CHOICE

Patented in 1786 by Joshua Morris for 150 acres
1783 tax - Joshua Morris 90 acres Wic.100
25 Apr.1791 Joshua Morris sold 36 3/4 acres to Jacob Morris.
15 June 1803 Jacob Morris sold to John Morris son of Joseph Morris, part.
13 Mar.1804 John Morris sold to Jacob Morris son of Joseph Morris, part.
1825 John Morris of Jacob willed to nephew William P. Morris of James Morris, being part of two tracts FORK & POINT OF THE FORK.

JUSTICE TO BE DONE

Patented in 1785 by John Evans for 5 acres

KEENS LOTT

Patented on 19 Sep.1672 by William Keen for 300 acres
8 May 1675 William Keen with wife Mary Keen sold to Thomas Humphries.

Rent Rolls 1666-1723, possessed by Thomas Humphries.
18 Aug.1740 Thomas Humphries sold for 5 shillings to Joshua Humphries
125 acres with GREEN HILL.
18 Aug.1747 Thomas Humphries Jr. conveyed to Joshua Humphries 300 acres
1783 tax - Joshua Humphries - Rewastico 100
1783 tax - Joseph Humphries 100 acres
1783 tax - Phillis Humphries 50 acres
1788 ADDITION TO KEENS LOTT pat. Elijah Humphries for 156 3/4 acres.
1804 Joseph Humphries willed THE LOTT to be sold for debts.
22 Sep 1835 Archelus Humphries and wife Margaret W. Humphries, Charles Humphries with wife Amelia A. Humphries, Sarah McBryde Humphries sold to Josephus Humphries 195 acres of KEENS LOTT & GREEN HILL.

KEEP OUT

Patented in 1805 by William White for 28 acres

KELLUMS DISCOVERY

Patented in 1755 by Edward Kellum for 132 acres
1757 Edward Kellum willed to grandson Edward son of John Kellum
5 Dec.1772 Edward Kellum sold to John Sterling son of Aaron 132 acres with KELLUMS LOTT
1783 tax - Aaron Sterling 132 acres, Rewastico 100

KELLUMS FOLLY

Patented on 6 June 1665 by John Ingram for 550 acres.
Rent Rolls 1666-1723, possessed by John Ingram
8 Feb.1682 resurveyed for Thomas Pemberton for 900 acres
1683 Thomas Pemberton sold to Richard Stevens 900 acres. Richard Stevens resurveyed to FAIRFIELDS.

KELLUMS LOTT

Patented in 1765 by John Kellum for 554 acres in Rewastico 100 a resurvey of Weatherlys Discovery.
8 June 1771 John Kellum sold 54 acres to James Phillips.
8 June 1771 John Kellum sold 206 acres to John Collins.
26 Dec.1773 John Collins of Worc.Co. with wife Sarah Collins sold 125 acres to Matthew Dorman.
26 Dec.1772 John Collins with wife Sarah Collins sold 36 acres to Phillip Harris
5 Dec.1772 Edward Kellum sold 35 acres to John Sterling son of Aaron Sterling.
14 Apr.1775 John Collins sold 8 acres to Sarah Johnson
8 Mar.1781 Sarah Johnson of Dorc.Co. sold 8 acres to James Philips, with MAIDENS CHOICE on the south side of Barren Creek.
9 Feb.1782 Edward Kellum sold 29 acres to William Lloyd Sr.
1783 tax - John Lankford 36 acres
1783 tax - Henry Acworth 56 acres
1783 tax - John Hardy 45 acres
1783 tax - Edward Kellum 230 acres
1783 tax - William Lloyd Sr. 22 acres

1783 tax - James Phillips 38 acres
14 April 1792 Phillip Lankford sold 42 acres to James Parremore
3 Dec.1803 Priscilla Kennedy sold her interest in 554 acres to John Kellum
1810 William Lloyd willed lands to daughter Peggy Lloyd.
1853 Rachel Phillips willed to daughters Ann Mills, Jane Lloyd (w/o John Lloyd), Patty Mills and her son William Washington Mills LARGEE & KELLUMS LOTT a total of 180 1/2 acres.

KEMMEYS DESIRE

Patented on 25 June 1697 by Henry Kimmey for 50 acres
5 Nov.1734 Henry Kimmey sold to Spear Langsdale
6 Nov.1766 John Langsdale sold to William Swain, on the east side of the Nanticoke River, 50 acres.

KENNERLYS BEGINNING

Patented in 1818 by Isaac Kennerly for 22 3/4 acres

KENNERLYS CHOICE

This is part of DOWGATE

KENNERLYS FIRST CHOICE

Patented in 1853 by Isaac Kennerly for 18 acres

KENNERLYS FOLLY

Patented in 1851 by Luther Kennerly for 22 3/4 acres
1850 he is in Barren Creek District.

KINNEYS CHANCE

Patented in 1746 by William Kinney for 50 acres
1760 William Kinney planter willed to son William Kinney
2 May 1776 land warrants Sussex Do.Delaware patented John Ready.

KINNEYS SETTLEMENT

Patented by Samuel Kinney for 100 acres
4 Mar.1745 Samuel Kinney sold to Phillip Windsor for 5 shillings 100 acres, on south side of the Nanticoke River.
18 Apr.1776 Sussex Co.Del.land warrants resurveyed by Jesse Windsor to BALL PLAY 319 acres.

KICKOTAN CHOICE

Patented on 2 April 1666 by John Winder for 300 acres
Rent Rolls 1666-1723, possessed by John Winder son of John
1698 John Winder willed to son John Winder 300 acres
13 Nov.1798 Mary Cannon sold to Augustus Cannon 136 acres of KICKOTAN CHOICE & CANNONS ADDITION.
12 Apr.1799 Augustus Cannon with wife Cloe Cannon sold all rights to William Polk.
7 Nov.1799 Thomas Cannon sold to William Polk.

7 Nov.1799 Mary Cannon sold her interest to William Polk
18 June 1802 Mary Cannon sold all interest to Thomas Cannon in
DEBTFORD, DANIELS ADVENTURE & KICKOTANS CHOICE
11 Feb.1806 William Polk sold to Josiah Polk land purchased of
Augustus Cannon and Mary Cannon.
7 Apr.1810 Josiah Polk Jr with wife Rebecca Polk sold to Levin D.
Jones with CANNONS ADDITION.

KIBBLES DESTINY

Patented in 1817 by George Kibble for 243 acres
20 May 1828 Farm advertised for sale by Joshua Moore 300 acres KIBBLES
DESTINY at mouth of Wicomico Creek.
1841 Levin Morris willed to daughter Ann Eliza Morris
(note; Bridget Cottman daughter of George Kibble married 2nd. John H.
Morris in 1820)

KINGS CHOICE

Patented in 1750 by Ephraim King for 50 acres

KINGS LUCK

Patented on 9 Sep.1726 by John Caldwell for 50 acres.
10 Nov.1726 John Caldwell assigned to Phillip King.
31 Mar.1733 Phillip King and now wife Meriam King sold 50 acres to
William Oliphant.
3 June 1756 John Magee and wife Margaret Magee sold 50 acres to James
English. As William Oliphant died intestate and afsd Margaret Magee
became seized.
1784 John Nelson willed to son in law Thomas English tract bought of
him, KINGS LUCK.
7 June 1776 Sussex Co.Del.land warrants, patented James English Sr.

KINGS MISFORTUNE

Patented in 1750 by Ephraim King for 1704 acres.
1783 tax - Samuel King 804 acres Nanticoke 100.
26 July 1784 Samuel King with wife Mary King sold to John Stewart 997
3/4 acres of IRISHMANS QUARTER, HOG QUARTER, KINGS MISFORTUNE, MT.
EPHRAIM.
1787 Samuel King willed to Lucretia Jones land devised by my father
Ephraim King to her mother Elizabeth King, unnamed.
27 June 1810 Miss Lucretia Jones sold to Capt.Alexander Stewart 1704
acres.
1823 William Donoho willed to Asa Phillips part bought of the heirs of
Alexander Stewart and part to eldest son Alexander Donoho.
1839 John Turner willed to grandson John, in Wetqpuin Neck.

KINGS NEGLECT

Patented in 1762 by Isaiah Banks for 2 acres.
1776 Isaiah Banks willed to brother Henry Banks.
22 Apr.1784 Henry Banks sold to William McBryde with HALLS ADVENTURE,
ADAMS DISCOVERY.

21 Jan.1809 James Ritchie sold to Sarah McBryde 154 1/2 acres of KINGS NEGLECT & NEWBERRY.
1849 ADDITION pat. for 18 1/2 acres Francis M. Slemons.

KINGSTON

Patented on 1 Oct.1681 by Thomas Chapell for 100 acres between Quantico and Nanticoke Rivers.
Rent Rolls 1666-1723, Thomas Chapell has an heir in Acco.Co.Va. no rent ever paid.
1 June 1782 John Melton of Dorc.Co.Md. sold to William Nutter of Somerset County as John was the son of Ann Melton who married Richard Melton. She was the daughter of Thomas Chapell.
1783 tax- William Nutter Sr. 100 acres Rewastico 100.
1783 William Nutter willed to son William 1/2 and to son Charles Nutter 1/2.
29 May 1793 William Nutter sold to Charles Nutter DELIGHT aka KINGSTON, division of lands.

KINKINS FOLLY

Patented in 1748 by Samuel Collins
23 Oct.1772 John Stilley sold 49 acres to Ann Moore for 5 shillings.
26 Mar.1776 resurveyed to Sussex Co.Delaware by John Lecompte.

KINIKINS RISK

Patented in 1748 by James Kinikin and William Kinikin for 47 5/8 acres
1850 James Kinikin in Barren Creek district.

KINNEYENGTON

Patented in 1803 by Abraham Taylor for 280 1/4 acres.
2 Apr.1803 Abraham Taylor with wife Molly Taylor sold to Horatio Taylor with TAYLORS ADDITION & TOWER HILL.
3 June 1803 Abraham Taylor and wife Molly Taylor sold to Ebenezer Taylor, same as above.
17 May 1810 Louther Taylor of Kent Co.Del. sold to Horatio Taylor- as Bartholomew Taylor and Abraham Taylor of Bracken Co.Kentucky appointed Louther Taylor to sell the land.

KIRK

Patented in 1858 by Isaac Kennerly for 15 3/4 acres.

KIRKMINSTER

Patented on 29 May 1689 by Matthew Wallace for 200 acres back from the south side of Wicomico River.
Rent Rolls 1666-1723, Matthew Wallace deserted the county and lives in the woods at the head of Delaware Bay. Land not possessed.
7 June 1723 William Polk of Dorc.Co.Md. and wife Priscilla Polk sold to John Caldwell, that Matthew Wallace conveyed to John Polk who gave to son William Polk.
28 Sep.1723 Thomas Hugg and wife Joanna Hugg sold to John Caldwell 200

acres that Matthew Wallace conveyed to John Ralph late husband of Joanna Hugg.
1731 John Caldwell gave to son Joshua Caldwell 200 acres.
11 Sep.1762 William Caldwell with wife Sarah Caldwell sold to Edward Northern Nelms 100 acres.
4 June 1766 William Caldwell sold 100 acres to Edward Northern Nelms.
1783 tax - Edmund Northern Nelms 225 acres- Wicomico 100.

KNAVERY DISOVERED

Patented in 1790 by Barkley Townsend for 46 acres.
13 July 1796 Barkley Townsend of Sussex Co.Delaware sold to Seth Smith and Isaac Vincent Jr. of Worcester Co.Md. 46 acres.

KNIGHTS DISCOVERY

Patented in 1758 by Jonathan Knight for 50 acres
1783 tax - Jonathan Knight 50 acres, Wic. 100
1749 Willin Wright willed to son Isaac K. Wright.

LAND DOWN

Patented on 1 May 1688 by Angelo Richardson for 300 acres on the south side of the Wicomico River
Rent Rolls 1666-1723, possessed by John Davis
1 Feb.1741 Daniel Davis and wife Elizabeth Davis sold to Thomas Davis 150 acres on east fork of the Wicomico River.
8 Oct.1772 Elijah Davis sold to John Davis 150 acres
1783 tax - John Davis 300 acres, Wicomico 100
1789 John Davis willed to son Rencher Davis 140 acres and to son Stephen Davis 160 acres.
17 Nov.1798 Reuben Davis with wife Sarah Davis with Stephen Davis sold to Jordan Parsons 8 acres of LAND DOWN, MORRIS DISCOVERY

LAND OF PROMISE

Patented in 1758 by Arthur Lewis on the south side of the Nanticoke River.
5 Aug.1751 Arthur Lewis sold to Thomas Truitt 100 acres.
1763 Thomas Truitt willed to son Riley Truitt, PROMISE and to son James Truitt
1783 tax - Arthur Lewis 50 acres, Acquango 100
9 Aug.1790 Thomas Lewis sold to Zadock Lewis 19 1/4 acres
2 Mar.1805 Zadock Lewis sold to John Parsons 50 1/4 acres of LAND OF PROMISE, CHOICE, GOOD LUCK
1811 James Lewis willed to son Jesse Lewis 30 3/4 acres.

LANDONS LIBERTY

Patented in 1774 by Arthur Landon for 51 acres.

LANGSDALES DISCOVERY

Patented in 1849 by Robert Langsdale for 32 7/8 acres

1850 he is in Barren Creek District

LANGSDALES SLIPE

Patented in 1809 by Huett Langsdale for 5 1/4 acres.

LANGSDALES VICTORY

Patented in 1818 by Huett Langsdale for 269 acres.
19 Apr.1803 John Wilkins,sheriff sold to Henry Langsdale goods of William Langsdale 2/9ths part.
22 Apr.1803 Henry Langsdale son of John Langsdale sold to Esther Langsdale widow of John Langsdale 60 acres of WOODSTOCK AND END OF STRIFE, repatented to LANGSDALES VICTORY, as John Langsdale died intestate and left issue, William Langsdale, John Langsdale, Henry Langsdale, Eleanor Langsdale, Elizabeth Langsdale, Joshua Langsdale, Whittington Langsdale, James Langsdale, Huett Langsdale and Robert Langsdale. Part was sold to the highest bidder Henry Langsdale. 2/9ths part
17 May 1803 John Wilkins,sheriff sold to Esther Langsdale per suit against William Langsdale, 1/9th part.
1806 Esther Langsdale willed to son James Langsdale 1/2 if he returns and 1/2 to son Huett Langsdale.
13 July 1808 Joshua W. Langsdale son of John sold to Huett Langsdale his 1/9th part 30 acres.
11 July 1808 Elizabeth Langsdale sold to Huett Langsdale 1/9th part.
6 July 1808 Arthur Dashiell sold to Huett Langsdale 1/9th part purchased of Richard Goslee and wife Eleanor Goslee, 30 acres.

LANKFORDS DELIGHT

Patented on 29 Sep.1764 by Thomas Lankford for 42 1/4 acres.
25 Aug.1776 Benjamin Lankford and mother Mary Lankford sold 42 1/4 acres to George Wilson
1783 tax - George Wilson 42 1/4 acres, Rewastico 100
1793 ADDITION TO LANDKORDS DELIGHT patented by George Wilson.

LANKFORDS DISCOVERY

Patented in 1827 by Hiram Lankford for 36 1/2 acres.

LANKFORDS HARD BARGAIN

Patented in 1800 by Ephraim Lankford for 15 acres

LANKFORDS LOTT

Patented in 1798 by John Lankford for 2 1/2 acres

LANKFORDS LUCK

Patented in 1805 by John Lankford for 6 acres

LARGEY ~~George~~ James

Patented on 2 Oct.1706 by ~~George~~ Givans for 600 acres at head of Beaver Dam Creek.
1723 James Givans willed to daughter Margaret Givans part and to other children, unnamed and to son George Givans.
15 Nov.1742 George Givans sold to John Gale land from father James Givans 200 acres part of LARGEY & AKALOW
18 Jan 1741 William Givans s/o James Givans sold 200 acres to William Giles Jr. bequeathed by father.
16 Mar.1753 William Giles sold 100 acres to Solomon Harris.
15 Sep.1756 James Caldwell Sr. gave to James Caldwell Jr. 100 acres that James Givans willed to daughter Margaret Givans, his mother.
1771 John Kellum willed to son Edward Kellum
1772 William Giles willed to Solomon Harris 58 acres and to daughter Leah Duncan LARGEE
14 Apr.1774 Edward Kellum and wife Priscilla Kellum sold to Thomas Bedsworth and Thomas Russell Jr. AKALOW & LARGEE that Margaret Givans conveyed to John Kellum.
20 Feb.1779 John Gale sold 220a. of LARGEY & AKALOW to George Gale.
1783 tax - Abihu Harris 38 1/3 acres- Nanticoke 100
1783 tax - William Harris 62 1/2 acres
1783 tax - John Nelson 72 1/4 acres
1783 tax - Thomas Russell 87 1/2 acres
1783 tax - Cornelius Ready 72 1/2 acres
1783 tax - Thomas Bedsworth 87 1/4 acres
1783 tax - James Nelson 72 1/4 acres
17 June 1783 George Gale son of George sold to James Phillips part of LARGEE & AKALOW 148 1/2 acres.
17 June 1783 George Gale sold to Cornelius Ready 148 1/2 acres of LARGEE & AKALOW
1783 Rachel Phillips willed to daughters Ann Mills, Jane Lloyd, Patty Mills and her son William Washington Mills 180 1/2 acres of LARGEY & KELLUMS LOTT.
1783 Cornelius Ready sold to Isaac Giles 148 1/2 acres of LARGEY & AKALOW.
1791 Isaac Giles willed lands to be sold, unnamed.
13 June 1791 Henry Acworth executor of Isaac Giles sold 148 1/2 acres of LARGEY & AKALOW to William Bedsworth.
1802 Arthur Dashiell willed to son Asa Dashiell.
1 Mar.1805 Levi Russell sold to Charles Rhoads AGALOW, LARGEY, & RUSSELLS HARD BARGAIN, no acreage mentioned.

LAST ADDITION TO FREE PURCHASE

This is part of 1679 DOUBLE PURCHASE

LAST ATTEMPT

Patented in 1833 by Thomas English for 10 3/8 acres
1850 he is in Barren Creek District.

LAST CHOICE

Patented in 1746 by Day Scott for 450 acres

13 Jan 1747 Capt. Day Scott sold 100 acres to Edward Corby now called CORBY.
1748 David Corby willed to wife Sarah Ann Corby 100 acres of CORBY and after death to youngest brother Matthew Corby.
9 Feb.1752 Day Scott sold to Joseph Ennals of Dorc.Co. 350 acres
24 Nov.1755 Joseph Ennals sold 350 acres to Day Scott.
22 Jan.1755 Covington Mezick and wife Sarah Ann sold to Nicholas Evans Collier 100 acres of tract CORBY taken out of LAST CHOICE.
1753 Day Scott willed 50 acres to George Dashiell, balance to be sold to pay debts.
13 Dec.1755 Day Scott sold to Thomas Williams 350 acres with part of SUNKEN GROUND.
1768 Thomas Williams willed to grandson David Williams land bought of Day Scott on Wicomico River, unnamed.
21 Nov.1770 David Williams sold 13 acres to Joseph Dashiell
22 Nov.1770 David Williams sold to Joshua Evans alias Moore, that Thomas Williams left to grandson David, 65 1/4 acres.
1774 George Collier Sr. willed 50 acres to son John Collier
17 Aug.1774 David Williams quitclaimed part to Phillip Graham(exchange for CAUDREYS BEGINNING.
29 Nov.1774 David Williams sold 65 1/4 acres to Joshua Evans at Wetpquin.
1783 tax - Ann Collier 50 acres, Nanticoke 100
1783 tax - Nicholas E. Collier 23 acres
1783 tax - John Holbrook 271 3/4 acres
2 May 1791 Thomas Williams of David Williams sold to William Davis devised by will of David Williams to son Thomas, with SUNKEN GROUND, no acreage mentioned
2 May 1791 William Davis sold same to Thomas Williams of David Williams.
7 Jan.1800 Thomas Williams, John Gale and Amelia Gale sold 540 1/2 acres of SUNKEN GROUND & LAST CHOICE to James Nelson.

LAST CHOICE

Patented in 1757 by Douty Collier for 70 acres
1775 Douty Collier willed to daughter Mary Bounds
1783 tax - William Bounds 70 acres, Nanticoke 100
7 Jan. 1795 William Bounds and wife Mary Bounds sold to Douty Bounds son of William Bounds afsd 70 acres.

LAST CHOICE

Patented on 21 July 1759 by William Polk for 200 acres
21 Feb.1769 William Polk and wife Mary Polk sold 200 acres to John Weatherly.
3 June 1769 John Weatherly sold 62 acres to McKimmea Porter.
31 Jan.1770 John Weatherly sold his rights to Richard Waller, with saw mill adjacent.
23 Nov.1779 Charles Weatherly and James Weatherly, John Weatherly and Jesse Weatherly sold to William Winder with PARTNERSHIP, ACWORTHS CHOICE & PREVENTION.
1783 tax - McKimmea Porter 62 acres, Rewastico 100
1783 tax - William Winder 86 acres
1790 McKimmea Porter willed to son Levi Porter.

LAST CHOICE

Patented on 17 Oct.1759 by John Hitch for 25 acres
8 Apr.1765 George Hitch son of John, in the townshiip of Dartmouth in Mass. sold 25 acres to Joseph Hitch of Somerset Co.
15 June 1799 William Hitch, John Hitch with wife Jean Hitch sons of Joshua Hitch sold 25 acres to Thomas Humphries Jr.

LAST CHOICE

Patented on 4 May 1761 by William Spicer for 18 acres on the Nanticoke River.
9 Nov.1764 William Spicer sold to John Johnson with SECOND CHOICE

LAST CHOICE

Patented on 15 May 1762 by Elisha Parker for 54 acres

LAST CHOICE

Patented in 1763 by George Collier Hopkins for 48 1/2 acres
1783 tax - George Collier Hopkins, Nanticoke 100

LAST CHOICE

Patented in 1768 by George Vinson for 331 1/4 acres
24 Feb.1770 George Vinson sold to Jacob Bell CHARLESTON, SECURITY & LAST CHOICE, 50 acres and 91 acres.
17 Apr.1770 Jacob Bell sold 66 acres to John Nelms at Wicomico River
14 Mar.1772 George Vinson sold 80 1/2 acres to Joshua Hitch
11 Feb.1775 Joshua Hitch sold to Jacob Bell 16 acres in Rockawalkin 3 miles south west of Salisbury Town
2 Aug.1777 Jacob Bell with wife Judah Bell sold to George Handy tract unnamed on road from Spring Hill Church to Salisbury 145 3/4 acres.
1783 tax - George Vinson 100 3/4 acres, Rewastico 100
1783 tax - Joshua Hitch 80 acres.
3 Nov.1792 Curtis Martin Thomason sold to John Maddux 20 acres
12 Jan.1793 Curtis Martin Thomason devisee of the will of George Vinson, sold to Benjamin Hearn 88 1/8 acres
1802 Benjamin Hearn willed to wife Sarah Hearn lands where George Vincent formerly lived, unnamed.
9 Aug.1803 John Wilkins, sheriff sold 67 acres to Hugh Gemmill, per judgement against the heirs of Joshua Hitch.
9 Sep.1806 John Wilkins, sheriff sold 67 acres to Thomas Rencher per judgement.
1806 Thomas Rencher willed to son Samuel Rencher lands purchased at sheriff's sale formerly belonging to heirs of Joshua Hitch called QUARTER LANDS.

LAST CHOICE

Patented in 1769 by John Richardson for 124 acres
19 Feb.1774 John Richardson with wife Mary Richardson of Worc.Co. sold 124 acres to Joshua Hilman
21 Aug.1783 Joshua Hilman sold 100 acres to William Hilman of BRITTAIN

& LAST CHOICE.
17 Mar.1801 James T. Hilman sold to Samuel Hilman part of lands of Joshua Hilman, no name.
11 Oct1806 Winder T. Hilman of Worc.Co sold to Samuel Hilman 17 acres from will of Joshua Hilman, no name.

LAST CHOICE

Patented on 5 Aug.1769 Benjamin Dashiell for 8 3/4 acres
8 Apr.1784 James Dashiell sold to Joshua Evans Moore 8 3/4 acres at Tipiquin Creek (CHOICE)

LAST CHOICE

Patented on 29 Sep.1769 by Arthur Dashiell for 64 3/4 acres
1783 tax - Arthur Dashiell 64 3/4 acres
22 Jan 1791 Arthur Dashiell sold 4 1/2 acres to George Twilley.

LAST CHOICE

Patented in 1797 by William Coulbourn for 8 1/4 acres

LAST CHOICE

Patented in 1795 by Revel Hayman for 6 acres
1796 Revel Hayman willed to wife Sarah Hayman lands and mills in Somerset Co. and Worc. Co. and after death to son William Brown Hayman, unnamed lands.

LAST CHOICE

Patented in 1801 by Thomas Tull for 7 1/4 acres

LAST CONCLUSION

Patented on 5 Sep.1779 by Lazarus Huffington for 182 3/4 acres a resurvey from COMMONS.
20 Sep.1779 Lazarus Huffington sold to John Atkinson son of Benjamin Atkinson.
1783 tax - Richard Acworth 182 3/4 acres- Rewastico 100.

LAST DISCOVERY

Patented in 1763 by Nathan Culver for 23 acres.
25 Feb.1764 Nathan Culver sold to William Stephens 22 1/2 acres with MADDOX FANCY & CONFUSION.
16 Dec.1769 William Stephens sold to Henry Trader 22 1/2 acres
5 Apr.1771 Henry Armatrader with wife Agnes Armatrader sold 22 1/2 acres to William McClemmy
17 Aug 1774 William McClemmy mortgaged to Zorobable King and Solomon Long lands purchased of Henry Trader.
1783 tax - William McClemmy 22 1/2 acres- Rewastico 100
7 Apr.1792 John Leatherbury, sheriff sold to Joshua Hitch 8 1/2 acres, lands of William McClemmy
7 Apr.1792 Joshua Hitch Jr. sold to Levin Irving 8 1/2 acres

9 Feb.1793 Levin Irving sold 8 1/2 acres to John Maddux.

LAST OF ALL

Patented in 1791 by Josiah W. Heath for 8 3/4 acres.

LAST PICKING

Patented in 1791 by Josiah W. Heath for 9 1/4 acres

LAST SHIP

Patented in 1775 by Elijah Matthews for 4 acres

LATE AT NIGHT

Patented in 1734 by James Nicholson for 50 acres
15 Aug.1775 Roger Nicholson sold 50 acres to Arthur Dashiell
1783 tax - Arthur Dashiell 50 acres, Rewastico 100

LATE AT NOON

Patented in 1760 by George Phillips for 50 acres
17 Apr.1767 George Phillips with wife Elizabeth Phillips sold to Arthur Dashiell 50 acres, at Barren Creek adj. WOODSTOCK
1783 tax - Arthur Dashiell 50 acres, Rewastico 100
1803 Arthur Dashiell willed to son Henry Dashiell.

LATE DISCOVERY

Patented on 7 Nov.1686 by Robert Collier for 50 acres.
Rent Rolls 1666-1723, possessed by Robert son of Robert Collier
1 Jan.1728 Robert Collier sold to Richard Dunn part of SHADWELL with LATE DISCOVERY and other lands adjacent.
1783 tax - Richard Dunn 50 acres- Nanticoke 100
6 July 1785 William Dunn son of Nicholas Dunn sold to Richard Dunn son of Thomas, that Robert Collier sold to Richard Dunn grandfather of afsd. William Dunn.

LAUGH ABOUT

Patented on 25 Apr.1761 by Andrew Smith for 50 acres in Wicomico Forest
3 Dec.1774 Andrew Smith with wife Elizabeth Smith sold to Elijah Hearn Jr. 50 acres.
1 Dec.1791 Elijah Hearn sold to George Parker 50 acres.

LAWS ADDTION

Patented on 2 Sep.1761 by Elijah Laws for 50 acres
1 Aug.1775 Elijah Laws sold to William Laws Jr. for 5 shillings, 50 acres.

LAWS MISTAKE

Patented in 1790 by Littleton Timmons for 7 1/2 acres

LAWSONS REST

Patented on 26 Jan.1748 by Richard Lawson for 50 acres
17 Aug.1768 Joshua Tennis with wife Sarah Tennis, William Price and wife Molly Price of Dorc.Co. and Leah Lawson sold to James Moore of Dorc.Co. Md. 50 acres that Richard Lawson willed to daughters Sarah Lawson, Molly Lawson and Leah Lawson.
4 Aug.1773 James Moore sold to William Douglas, Joseph Pennell, William Wishart, Benjamin Marshall, Christopher Marshall Jr. and Charles Marshall on the east side of the Nanticoke River.

LAYFIELDS CHANCE

Patented in 1773 by William Layfield for 50 acres
1783 tax - William Layfield 50 acres Wic.100 Worc.Co.

LAYFIELDS CHANCE

Patented on 13 May 1785 by Solomon Layfield for 50 acres
also Patented in 1795 by Solomon Layfield for 18 1/2 acres
15 Nov.1788 Solomon Layfield sold to Louther Carmean 50 acres.

LAYFIELDS CHOICE

Patented in 1753 by Robert Layfield for 75 acres

LAYFIELDS INDUSTRY

Patented in 1793 by William Layfield for 497 acres

LAYFIELDS PRIVILDEGE

Patented in 1772 by George Sockwell for 33 1/4 acres

LAYTONS DISCOVERY

Patented on 22 Mar.1695 by William Layton for 300 acres
Rent Rolls 1666-1723, possessed by William Layton Jr.
29 Aug.1723 William Layton Jr. s/o William of Sussex Co.Del. sold to John Leatherbury 300 acres.
23 Feb.1725 John Leatherbury and wife Sarah Leatherbury sold to Jacob Morris part.
22 Mar.1758 Charles Leatherbury son of John Leatherbury sold to Thomas Beard 100 acres
1783 tax - Thomas Beard 100 acres - Wicomico 100
1790 ADDITION TO LAYTONS DISCOVERY 5 acres pat. Thomas Beard.
26 June 1797 William Beard and wife Sarah Beard sold 1/2 acre to William Anderson.
24 Jan.1807 Joseph Morris Sr. of Sussex Co.Del. sold to Robert H. Morris of Somerset Co. 105 acres
24 Jan.1807 Joseph Morris of Sussex Co.Del. sold to Martin Bowles 14 1/2 acres
27 Aug.1808 Robert Morris sold part to Peter Dashiell, no acreage.
1814 James Beard willed plantation to brother Eliab Beard
6 June 1818 Eliab Beard sold to William Bounds of Richard Bounds part

16 acres 68 perches of LATONS DISCOVERY & GENTLEMENS MISTAKE.
1812 Robert Morris willed 105 1/2 acres to son John Morris.
1830 John Chattam willed to grandsons John and James Chattam sons of daughter Priscilla Chattam tract bought of Eliab Beard.
23 Aug.1826 William Collins of Jefferson Co.Ky sold to William Bounds 48 1/4 acres.
1832 William Bounds of Richard Bounds willed to sons John M.Bounds and George Washington Bounds 41 acres and to son Jones Bounds 48 acres bought of the heirs of Robert Morris.

LAZY HILL

Patented on 15 March 1723/4
28 Mar.1748 Josiah Wroughton of Sussex Co.Del. sold to Levin Huffington 85 acres.
1783 tax - Levin Huffington
1782 Levin Huffington willed to son Angelo Huffington 85 1/2 acres.

LEATHERBURYS FANCY

Patented in 1749 by John Leatherbury for 8 acres.
1753 John Leatherbury willed lands in Quantico to son Thomas Leatherbury, unnamed (he also had a son Charles Leatherbury.
3 May 1774 Thomas Leatherbury sold 2 acres to Thomas Rider on the south side of Quantico Creek.
1783 tax - Charles Leatherbury 8 acres, Nanticoke 100
12 Feb.1790 Thomas Moore with wife Mary Moore of Sussex Co.Del. sold to Charles Rider and Edward Austin of Som. Co. WARWICK, MIDFIELD, LEATHERBURYS FANCY, formerly belonging to John Rider.
2 Feb.1791 Charles Serman with wife Sarah Serman sold rights to Edward Austin and Charles Rider.

LEBANON

Patented in 1774 by John Cottingham for 383 acres

LEBANON

Patented in 1786 by Joseph Venables for 381 acres
1788 Joseph Venables willed to grandson Samuel Venables and part to Joshua Venables son of James Venables and Mary Venables.
9 Nov.1799 William Russum, executor sold to Joshua Bennett Jr. of Sussex Co.Del. that Joseph Venables devised to be sold if Samuel Venables his grandson died with issue, 322 acres of ALGATE & LEBANON.
1831 Eli Bennett willed to brothers Turpin Bennett and Levin Bennett
1833 Turpin Bennett willed to brothers Eli Bennett and Levin Bennett of Joshua Bennett.

LECKIES ADVENTURE

see DANIELS ADVENTURE

LEES SITUATION

Patented in 1763 by Elihu Mezick for 27 acres
1783 tax - Elihu Mezick - Nanticoke 100
1788 Elihu Mezick willed to wife Margaret Mezick and after death to

sons Elihu Mezick, John Mezick and Daniel Mezick.
4 July 1799 John Mezick sold to Elihu Mezick.

LEONARDS ADVENTURE

Patented in 1791 by Joseph Leonard for 140 acres

LEONARDS LAST CONCLUSION

Patented in 1814 by Joseph Leonard for 92 1/4 acres

LESS

Patented in 1822 by John Williams for 17 3/4 acres

LET ME BE

Patented in 1817 by William Donoho for 62 1/2 acres

LEVEL GROUND

Patented in 1754 by Dudson Bacon for 21 1/2 acres
17 Apr.1776 resurvey to Sussex Co. Del.by Dudson Bacon

LEVEL LAND

see MEECHES HOPE

LEVINS CHANCE

Patented in 1734 by Levin Disharoon for 50 acres
23 Aug.1742 Levin Disharoon mortgaged 50 acres to Joseph Leonard at head of Wicomico River.
23 Feb.1762 Levin Disharoon the younger of Worc.Co. sold 50 acres to Joseph Leonard.
1767 Joseph Leonard willed 50 acres to son Joseph
1783 tax - Joseph Leonard 50 acres.

LEVINS CHANCE

Patented on 20 Aug. 1762 by Levin Carey for 50 acres
1783 tax - Levin Carey 50 acres, Wic.100, Worc.Co.
1791 Levin Carey willed lands to wife Lidy Carey, unnamed. (also had son Thomas Carey.)
24 Oct.1795 Samuel Carey sold to Samuel Pollitt.

LEVINS FOLLY

Patented in 1754 by Levin Calloway for 33 acres
Resurveyed 11 Apr.1776 to Sussex Co.Del. warrents by Levin Calloway

LEVINS GRIEF

Patented in 1752 by Matthew Kemp for 12 acres

LEWIS CHANCE

Patented in 1729 by **Lewis Beard** for 15 acres

LEWIS LOTT

Patented in 1831 by **William Taylor** for 15 3/8 acres

LIBERTY

Patented in 1763 by **Thomas Price** for 10 acres

LIBERTY

Patented in 1774 by **Belitha Phippen** for 25 acres

LIFFORD

Patented in 1679 by **John Evans** for 100 acres
1740 Alexander Leckie willed to son-in-law Nicholas Evans 100 acres LIFFORDS at death of wife. (He married Ann Evans widow of John Evans)

LIGHTWOOD RIDGE

No patent found.
1769 John Hearn willed 50 acres to sons Isaac Hearn, John Hearn, Peter Gordy, to share.
1783 tax - John Hearn 34 acres- Wic.100, Worc.Co.
1806 John Hearn willed to son John Hearn.

LINANKES ON NECK

see QUIAKENSON NECK

LINCHOYLE

Patented on 10 Mar.1679 by **William Stevens** who assigned to John Winder
Rent Rolls 1666-1723, possessed by John Winder son of John 40 acres.

LIME HOUSE

1in 1680 by **William Stevens** for 40 acres.
1 Sep.1768 Matthew Cannon with wife Mary Cannon sold 40 acres to Thomas Irving for 5 shillings.
Repatented in 1768 by Thomas Irving for 25 1/8 acres
1783 tax- Thomas Irving 25 1/2 acres
1784 Thomas Irving willed to son Joseph Irving 25 1/2 acres.
14 Sep.1789 Joseph Irving sold to Levin Irving with DANIELS ADVENTURE, WARWICK & MIDFIELD.
19 Jan.1799 Levin Irving son of Thomas Irving, with wife Leah Irving sold to William Mezick.
1818 William Mezick willed to daughter Martha Washington Handy Mezick.

LINGOES OUTLETT

Patented on 19 May 1763 by **Robertson Lingo** for 50 acres in Wicomico Forest.

1772 Robertson Lingo willed to son Smith Lingo.
ADDITION patented by Robertson Lingo for 123 acres.
1783 tax - Nathaniel Whaley 50 acres, Wic.100, Worc.Co.
4 Sep.1789 Smith Lingo of Sussex Co.Del. sold to James Perdue 50 acres.
SECOND ADDITION patented in 1851 by Elijah Holloway

LINGOES PRIVILEDGE

Patented on 1 May 1764 by Robertson Lingo for 50 acres in Wicomico Forrest.
1783 tax - Smith Heath 11 acres, Wic.100, Worc.Co.
26 Feb.1774 John Lingo sold to Smith Heath 11 acres.
10 Dec. 1774 John Lingo sold to James Perdue, balance.

LINGOES SECURITY

Patented on 18 May 1753 by Robinson Lingo for 100 acres
10 Dec.1774 John Lingo sold to James Perdue 100 acres, in Wicomico Forrest.

LITTLE

Patented in 1759 by William Donoho for 4 1/2 acres
1783 tax - William Donoho - Nanticoke 100
1785 William Donoho willed to daughter Rebecca Powell and her children, NOTHING BE IT MORE OR LESS.

LITTLE BELEAN

Patented on 31 Jan 1677 for 1200 acres by Robert Ridgley
1680 Robert Ridgley St.Ingoes, St. Marys Co.Md. willed to wife Martha Ridgley 1200 acres in Somerset County.
1701 Robert Ridgley willed lands to be sold, unnamed.
Rent Rolls 1666-1723, possessed by John Davis 525 acres, Richard Phillips 200 acres, John Pearce 400 acres, Richard Grudman? 75 acres.
15 April 1688 Anthony Underwood with wife Martha Underwood (Martha Ridgley) sold 100 acres to Simon Perkins.
24 Oct.1692 Simon Perkins and wife Marian Perkins sold 100 acres to John Winder.
24 Mar.1697 John Winder sold to Ephraim Wilson 500 acres called SLIGO
20 Jan.1704 Ephraim Wilson with wife Elizabeth Wilson sold to William Davis 500 acres SLIGO
1716 John Winder willed to John Watts and heirs 75 acres.
28 Feb.1721 William Serman and wife Sarah Serman sold to Roger Phillips 100 acre of 200 acres purchased by Roger Phillips of Simon Perkins and wife Marian Perkins.
18 Nov.1729 Benjamin Tull and wife Mary Tull sold to Samuel Boardman son of Francis Boardman 80 acres that William Davis willed to widow Sarah Davis who conveyed to Benjamin Tull called SLIGO.
29 June 1733 William Davis son of William with wife Bridget Davis sold 100 acres to Richard Goslee.
13 Aug.1735 William Davis with wife Bridget Davis sold to Matthew Goslee 50 acres.
11 Feb.1739 Richard Goslee and wife Tabitha Goslee sold to Henry Lowe 100 acres now called SALEM.

1 Feb.1739 Richard Phillips son of Richard sold to Roger Kellett and wife Eunice Kellett 132 1/2 acres that Roger Phillips left to son Richard who since died intestate, part of three tracts HORSEYS BALIWICK, LITTLE BELEAN and 12 1/2 acres of PHILLIPS ADDN. except 80 acres sold to David Hurt.
11 Feb 1739 Richard Phillips sold to Henry Lowe 80 acres out of HORSEYS BALIWICK & LITTLE BELEAN now called LOWES.
29 June1741 John Bluett and wife Miarian Bluett one of the daughters of John Watts, Winifred Watts daughter of John and Thomas Collier and wife Ann Collier sold 75 acres to David Polk.
26 Apr.1746 Thomas Phillips sold to Roger Kellett and wife Eunice Kellett 107 acres and 12 1/2 acres of marsh adjacent land left Sarah Phillips by Roger Phillips, bought of Richard Phillips.
27 Jan.1746 Graves Boardman sold to John Williams 80 acres conveyed by Benjamin Tull to Samuel Boardman who died intestate SLIGO
1752 William Davis willed to son-in-law Joseph Allen and daughter Betty Allen dwelling plantation adjacent FORTUNE and 60 acres to wife Bridget Davis lands, after death to grandson William Davis Allen.
25 Mar.1762 Purkins Venables sold to James Racey 163 acres of LITTLE BELEAN.
14 Sep.1773 William Davis Allen sold to Alexander Spicer, William French, John Bowman, Charles Crookshank, John Crawford and George Crawford of Great Britian 500 acres SLIGO being part of LITTLE BELEAN (prob. mortgage)
1783 tax - William Allen 471 1/2 acres
1783 tax - Salathiel Griffith 150 acres
1783 tax - John Shiles 163 acres
1783 tax - John Dashiell 100 acres
1783 tax - William Allen 171 1/2 acres
2 June 1785 William Davis Allen sold to Archibald Patison of Dorc.Co. 560 acres with tract FORTUNE.
24 Mar.1786 William Davis Allen sold to Planner Williams lands conveyed by Ephraim Wilson to William Davis his grandfather.
13 Jan.1786 Archibald Patison of Dorc.Co. released mortgage to Planner Williams of SLIGO, LITTLE BELEAN, FORTUNE.
1786 Joseph Morris willed to son John Malone Morris or son Robert Morris 103 acres.
2 Nov.1797 John Gale with wife Amelia Gale sold to William Polk deed of mortgage conveyed by Archibald Patison to Planner Williams.
7 Dec.1800 John Webb mortgaged to John Dashiell part.
17 Dec.1801 John Dashiell with wife Elizabeth Dashiell released mortgage to John Webb.
21 May 1800 Tubman Lowe sold to John Dashiell 100 acres that William Davis and Bridget Davis conveyed to Richard Goslee who sold to Henry Lowe grandfather of Tubman Lowe.
15 Nov.1803 John Dashiell sold to John Morris 66 1/2 acres purchased of Josiah Polk, adjacent SLIGO.
25 June 1805 John Dashiell sold 33 1/2 acres to George Kibble SLIGO
13 Jan.1806 division of lands between William Malone and wife Frances Malone and John Dorman and wife Nancy Dorman 82 acres belonging to Samuel Goslee GOSLEES CHANCE & LITTLE BELEAN.
1812 William Polk willed to son William Winder Polk land bought of John Gale and Amelia Gale.
1818 John M. Morris willed to son Joseph Morris part and to son John H. Morris 56 1/2 acres.

LITTLE BIT

Patented in 1763 by William Bennett for 14 acres
7 Jan 1768 William Bennett and wife Dorothy Bennett sold 14 acres to John Leatherbury
1783 tax - John Leatherbury 14 acres, Rewastico 100

LITTLE BIT

Patented in 1796 by John Robertson for 3 acres
1799 John Robertson willed to friend Thomas Connerly 2 acres on the south side of the Nanticoke River, no name.

LITTLE BIT

Patented in 1763 by Dennis Dulaney for 4 1/4 acres
Patented again in 1803 by Henry Dulaney for 5 acres.

LITTLE CONVENIENCY

Patented in 1807 by Jesse Johnson for 2 1/4 acres

LITTLE EDEN

1794 ADDITION TO LITTLE EDEN patented by Stephen Disharoon for 212 1/2 acres
1795 Stephen Disharoon willed to wife Sarah Disharoon lands unnamed.
19 Mar.1796 Stephen Disharoon son of George Disharoon sold 87 acres to Cyrus Sharp.
19 Mar.1796 Stephen Disharoon sold 133 acres to James Bennett.
LITTLE EDEN Patented in 1805 by James Bennett a resurvey from SHAVE THE BALD FRIAR & ADDITION TO LITTLE EDEN for 848 3/4 acres.
1849 John Disharoon willed to daughter Betsy Fooks 43 acres and part to daughter Mariah Fooks.

LITTLE HELP

Patented in 1814 by Elisha Parker for 6 acres
1812 James Bennett willed 6 acres to be sold.

LITTLE HOPE

Patented in 1770 by Nehemiah Crockett for 27 acres
10 Jan.1787 John Crockett sold 27 1/2 acres to Joshua Donoho.

LITTLE IS BETTER THAN NONE

Patented in 1817 by McMurray Johnson for 15 acres

LITTLE IS BETTER THAN NONE

Patented in 1817 by Benjamin Weatherly for 1 3/4 acres

LITTLE MONMOUTH

Patented on 27 Aug.1679 by Thomas Brereton for 100 acres on the south

side of Quantico Ck. in a swamp.
Rent Rolls 1666-1723 possessed by John Evans who repatented.
1686 John Evans willed to son John Evans
1732 John Evans sold to Edward Willin part called EDWARDS LOTT 25 acres
6 May 1734 Robert Crockett gave 100 acres to Robert Crockett part of LITTLE MONMOUTH alienated by John Evans.
20 Aug.1739 John Evans gave to daughter Mary Winright wife of Stephen Winright 50 acres.
14 April 1798 Isaac Atkinson sold to Sarah Robertson 100 acres of NOBLE QUARTER & LITTLE MONMOUTH
3 Nov.1801 Sarah Robertson sold same to Samuel Robertson.

LITTLE NELSEY

Patented on 13 Sep.1678 by William Stevens who assigned to William Keen for 300 acres.
8 Feb.1685 William Keen with wife Ann Keen sold to Pascoe Bartlett
Rent Rolls 1666-1723 possessed by Pascoe Bartlett 100 acres and Thomas Lucas both marrying the daughters of William Keen.
14 Oct.1755 Newell Bell sold to Benjamin Venables 200 acres of KEEN called LITTLE NELSEY deeded by William Keen to John Bell.
4 Oct.1758 Benjamin Venables and wife Ann Venables sold to Thomas Fletcher 200 acres.
March 1760 deposition- Benjamin Venables says that in conversation between Samuel Caldwell late of St. Marys County, deceased, and William Venables where they exchanged LITTLE NELSEY 200 acres and BELLS FIRST CHOICE. Samuel Caldwell gave William Venables MILLS SECURITY 25 acres with all mills per will of father John Venables. This deponant at the same time had a bond from one Bell for conveyance of both LITTLE NELSEY and BELLS FIRST CHOICE to Joseph Venables father of afsd. Benjamin Venables and William Venables who claimed the said land as heir at law to said Joseph. This deponent says he conveyed the same to Thomas Fletcher to whom Samuel Caldwell had sold same.
4 May 1765 Pascoe Bartlett and wife Sarah Bartlett sold to Thomas Stanford 100 acres, from Pascoe Bartlett and wife Hannah Bartlett.
17 June 1777 William Stanford and wife Patience Stanford sold to Thomas Stanford 100 acres.
1783 tax- Thomas Stanford 100 acres   Rewastico 100
1783 tax - Margaret Stevens 100 acres
1783 tax - Elizabeth Fletcher 200 acres
1791 Thomas Stanford willed 100 acres to son John Stanford.

LITTLE NECK

20 April 1738 Robert Givans eldest son of Robert sold 50 acres to Thomas Shiles in a mouth between Broad Creek and Deep Creek, south side of Nanticoke River.
1766 William Marine willed 50 acres to son William.

LITTLE NECK

Patented in 1762 by David Stanford for 71 acres
Repatented in 1774 by David Stanford for 220 3/4 acres.
17 Apr.1775 David Stanford with wife Sarah Stanford sold for 5

shillings to Joshua Stanford 100 acres.
29 Nov.1785 David Stanford traded for ADDITION TO LITTLE NECK with Joshua Stanford
1787 ADDITION TO LITTLE NECK patented by Joshua Stanford.
21 Mar.1789 Joshua Stanford sold to David Stanford 75 1/4 acres of LITTLENECK & ADDITION TO LITTLE NECK.
3 Nov.1802 Joshua Stanford sold to John Cathell 131 1/4 acres of LITTLE NECK, ADDN. TO LITTLENECK, STANFORDS FINDING & GREEN BRIAR.

LITTLEWORTH

Patented in 1728 by George Dashiell for 50 acres.
21 Oct.1766 George Dashiell sold 50 acres to John North
1783 tax- John North 50 acres.Nanticoke 100
20 July 1784 John North sold 39 acres to Joseph Austin of BEWDLY & LITTLEWORTH.
1783 John North willed to John Grant and to daughter Elizabeth Grant.
15 Nov.1792 Joseph Austin sold 39 acres to George Austin of BEWDLY & LITTLEWORTH.
15 Nov.1796 Edward North sold part to Levin Horner, no acres given.
16 Feb.1799 Edward North and Levin Thomas sold to Ebenezer Collier their interest in BEWDLY & LITTLEWORTH
19 June 1799 Ebenezer Collier sold 21 1/2 acres to Richard Dunn of BEWDLY & LITTLEWORTH.

LITTLEWORTH

Patented in 1761 by John Perkins for 102 acres

LITTLEWORTH

Patented in 1725 by Richard Huffington for 50 acres.

LITTLEWORTH

Patented on 9 May 1767 by Levin Gunby for 150 acres, a resurvey of MURCKLE ISLAND
8 June 1772 Levin Gunby with wife Sabra Gunby sold to William Fooks 50 acres
1774 William Fooks willed 150 acres to son Daniel Fooks
1829 William Fooks willed to son Daniel Fooks.

LIVERPOOL

Patented on 27 Nov.1685 by Thomas Holston for 500 acres
4 May 1762 John Osborn grandson and heir to Thomas Holston sold to Andrew Spear. As Thomas Holston died intestate and land fell to his daughter Jane Holston who married John Osborne.
29 Mar.1770 Andrew Spear sold to George Farrington 500 acres on the north east branch of the Nanticoke River with 1/2 of saw mill.

LOCK HARBOUR

Patented in 1771 by James Houston for 497 3/4 acres
9 Apr.1798 Purnell Johnson sold to William Adkins 200 acres of

ADDITION TO LOCK HARBOUR.
1823 John Parker of E. willed to daughter Elizabeth Parsons and daughter Sarah Parsons and son Elisha P. Parker
1850 Elisha Parker in 8th district, Nutters, Worc.Co.

LOCKLAMON

Patented 19 Dec.1789 by William Bounds for 403 acres in Tyaskin
21 Jan 1794 William Bounds traded John Gale 19 1/2 acres for same of GALES UNION.
1805 William Bounds willed to son Douty Bounds.
26 Sep.1806 Douty Bounds son of William Bounds sold to James Dashiell, arbitration of bounds of CHANCE & LOCHLAMON at head of Wetpquin Creek to Green Hill, with YEARSLAND.
26 Sep.1806 Douty Bounds sold to Charles Leatherbury part.
26 Sep.1806 Charles Leatherbury sold to Douty Bounds, same.
26 Sep.1806 James Dashiell sold to Douty Bounds, to resolve dispute over land boundaries.
26 Apr.1825 Douty Bounds sold to Marcellas Jones 394 3/4 acres.
1845 ADDITION TO LOCKLAMON patented by Marcellas Jones for 650 4/8 acres.

LOCUST RIDGE

Patented in 1753 by Littleton Dennis for 122 1/2 acres.
16 Jan.1753 Littleton Dennis sold to Jesse Dashiell
29 Sep.1764 Jesse Dashiell resurveyed to DISCOVERY.

LOCUST RIDGE

Patented in 1807 by Abraham Taylor for 93 acres.

LOGSGATE HILL

Patented on 17 Nov 1719 by John Quigley for 100 acres on the south side of Broad Creek at Tarkill Branch
Rent Rolls 1666-1723 possessed by John Quigley
13 Sep.1729 David Robinson with wife Mary Robinson sold to Charles Dashiell, Mary Robinson was the relic of John Quigley who had the rights.
21 Feb.1735 Charles Dashiell sold to John Gibbons, blacksmith.
7 Aug.1753 John Gibbons with wife Mary Gibbons of Worc.Co.,blacksmith sold to Thomas Waller Jr. 100 acres.
17 Mar 1757. Thomas Waller Jr. mtg. to Thomas Moore with SHARPES CHANCE
26 Oct.1757 Thomas Waller mortgaged to Outerbridge Horsey HOGG PALACE, LOGSGATE HILL, SHARPES CHANCE.
16 Aug.1758 Thomas Moore sold to Outerbridge Horsey mortgage he had from Thomas Waller.
1785 Outerbridge Horsey willed to son Lazarus Horsey with ROUND SAVANAH & SHARPES CHANCE.

LONDON

Patented in 1748 by John Cox for 50 acres.
26 Nov.1762 John Cox with wife Ann Cox sold 50 acres to John Hearn.
1769 John Hearn willed 50 acres to sons John Hearn, Isaac Hearn and

Peter Gordy.
4 Nov.1799 John Hearn and Elijah Smith of Sussex Co.Delaware sold to Hezekiah Maddux 50 acres of LONDON & CANNAAN.

LONDON

Patented in 1759 by David Wilson for 35 acres
17 Nov.1767 David Wilson sold to Henry Trader 35 acres
19 May 1769 Henry Armatrader and wife Agnes Armatrader sold to George Smith son of Andrew Smith of Worc.Co. 35 acres
11 Mar.1771 George Smith sold 35 acres to John Elzey
17 Aug.1773 John Elzey sold 35 acres to John Nelms
1783 tax- Elijah Smith 15 acres, Wicomico 100

LONE TREE ISLAND

Patented in 1730 by James Train for 374 acres
1783 tax- John Collins 374 acres- Rewastico 100

LONG ACRE

Patented on 23 Oct.1673 by James Jones for 200 acres.
10 Aug.1674 James Jones sold to David Williamson. (the whole family was murdered by Indians. He married Jane Covington daughter of Nehemiah Covington.)
Repatented on 1679 by John Covington
1679 John Covington and wife Mary Covington sold to Thomas Walker 200 acres.
Rent Rolls 1666-1723 possessed by John Caudrey 200 acres.
1721/2 John Caudrey willed to son Abraham Caudrey 200 acres
1 July 1741 Abraham Caudrey sold to Robert Graham.
1755 Robert Graham willed to son John Graham, when he is of age lands and to daughter Mary Graham and son Phillip Graham lands unnamed.
1767 John Graham willed to brother Phillip Graham all lands.
1783 tax- James Beard 200 acres.
1787 Phillip Graham willed to sons John Graham and William Graham all lands that James Beard rents.
11 Oct.1806 Henry Boston with wife Nancy Boston (lately Nancy Graham) sold to John Graham all interest that Phillip Graham devised to sons John Graham and William Graham.
14 Mar.1806 Francis Collier with wife Betsy Collier (lately Betsy Graham) sold to John Graham.
13 Oct.1807 Ralph Milbourn and wife Sarah Milbourn (lately Sarah Graham sold to John Graham for 10 shillings all rights to LONG ACRE, CAUDRYS BEGINNING, HARD FORTUNE, ADDITION TO CHANCE.
19 Sep.1809 Henry Boston with wife Nancy Boston sold to John Graham 2/5ths of 1/5th of 30 acres.
1804 resurveyed to SALLY

LONG ACRE

Patented on 31 July 173 to John Roach for 548 acres
Rent Rolls 16666-1723 possessed by John Roach
1726/7 John Roach gave to son Isaac Roach 250 acres and to son-in-law Benjamin Fooks and Sarah Fooks his wife 120 acres.

13 Oct.1721 John Roach with wife Alice Roach sold to John Shockley 176 acres.
1737 Benjamin Fooks resurveyed 100 acres and patented.
4 June 1766 Isaac Roach sold to Samuel Ingersol 19 acres.
29 Jan.1768 Isaac Roach sold to John Cathell 25 acres
11 Feb.1769 Isaac Shockley sold to James Davis 16 acres
4 Aug.1769 Isaac Roach sold to Samuel Ingersol 50 acres.
19 Jan.1770 Isaac Roach sold to Thomas Cannon and wife Sarah Cannon for 5 shillings, balance, for his maintenance.
4 June 1770 Thomas Cannon and Isaac Roach sold 30 acres to Samuel Ingersol on a branch of Tony Tank Creek.
29 Jan.1773 Thomas Cannon with wife Sarah Cannon sold 23 acres to Samuel Ingersol.
6 Apr.1775 Thomas Cannon with wife Sarah Cannon sold to Jesse Fooks 1 acre.
16 Aug.1777 Samuel Ingersol, shipcarpenter with wife Catherine Ingersol sold to Jesse Fooks part LONG ACRES & LONG CHANCE 120 acres.
1783 tax- William Toadvine 50 acres, Wicomico 100
1783 tax- Thomas Fooks 121 acres
1783 tax- John Cathell 80 acres
1783 tax- Mary Toadvine 6 acres
1783 tax- Samuel Ingersol 100 acres
1782 Henry Toadvine willed to son Purnell Toadvine.
7 Oct.1783 Jesse Fooks wife wife Leah Fooks sold 80 1/2 acres to John Cathell.
21 Nov.1783 Jesse Fooks sold 1 acre to William Toadvine
21 Nov.1783 Jesse Fooks with wife Leah Fooks sold to Samuel Ingersol 7 acres of LONG ACRE, 100 acres LONG CHANCE
17 Mar.1790 John Roberts and Rachel Roberts sold to William James of Worc.Co. property of Samuel Ingersol.
4 Apr.1790 John Roberts with wife Rachel Roberts sold to William James property of Samuel Ingersol, no name.
24 Apr.1790 Mary Ingersol sold to William James lands held by her father Samuel Ingersol. no name or acreage.
27 July 1792 William James sold to John Roberts part.
13 May 1795 John Ingersol sold to Stephen Toadvine from father Samuel who died intestate.
29 Mar.1796 Whittington White with wife Tabitha White child of Samuel Ingersol sold to Stephen Toadvine
31 Mar.1800 Underwood Roberts sold to Samuel Serman and Betty Serman part. of LONG ACRE & LONG CHANCE, had by Samuel Ingersol.
25 May 1805 Joseph Fooks with wife Anne Fooks sold to Thomas Fooks 50 acres.

LONG ACRE

Patented in 1737 by Benjamin Fooks a resurvey from LONG ACRE for 100 acres
1752 Benjamin Fooks willed to son William Fooks 100 acres and to son James Fooks 120 acres.
7 July 1764 William Fooks resurveyed pt. to FOOKS COST.
1774 William Fooks willed to wife Mary Fooks 50 acres and to son Jesse Fooks and to son Joseph Fooks son of James Fooks rights to LONG ACRE taken up by John Roach.
1783 tax- Mary Fooks 100 acres.
11 Apr.1809 Benjamin Fooks sold to Outten Toadvine

LONG ACRE

Patented on 17 May 1737 by William Waples and Paul Waples for 300 acres.
12 Oct 1739 William Waples of Sussex Co.Del. and wife Margaret Waples and Paul Waples and wife Elizabeth Waples sold lower part to John Collins.
13 Oct.1739 William Waples and wife Margaret Waples and Paul Waples and Elizabeth Waples sold to James O'Neal 100 acres, middle part.
13 Oct.1739 They all sold to Phillip Wingate 100 acres, upper part.
1748 James O'Neal willed to son Thomas O'Neal 200 acres
7 Aug.1750 John Collins sold 100 acres to Joseph Collins, in Parsons Neck on the south side of the Nanticoke River.

LONG CHANCE

Patented on 19 Sep.1766 by Samuel Ingersol for 36 acres
Resurveyed 28 Oct.1767 by Samuel Ingersol for 65 acres.
29 Jan.1773 Samuel Ingersol sold to Henry Toadvine 8 acres.
16 Aug.1777 Samuel Ingersol sold to Jesse Fooks 120 acres of LONG CHANCE & LONG ACRE.
21 Nov.1783 Jesse Fooks with wife Leah Fooks sold to Samue Ingersol
1783 tax- Samuel Ingersol Wicomico 100.
17 Mar.1790 John Roberts and wife Rachel Roberts sold to William James of Worc.Co. property of Samuel Ingersol.
24 Apr.1790 Mary Ingersol daughter of Samuel sold to William James her rights.
17 Mar.1790 Tabitha Roberts gave to Richard Ingersol his rights to his fathers lands in Somerset & Worcester Counties, no name.
27 July 1792 William James sold to John Roberts part on Tony Tank Creek.
23 June 1795 Richard Ingersol and wife Rebecca Ingersol sold 30 acres to William Roberts.
13 May 1795 John Ingersol s/o Samuel sold to Stephen Toadvine
29 Mar.1796 Whittington White and Tabitha White child of Samuel Ingersol sold to Stephen Toadvine
30 Dec.1798 Catherine White d/o Samuel Ingersol and wife of Peter White sold to Stephen Toadvine
13 May 1800 John Ingersol of Worc.Co. sold to Richard Ingersol of Somerset Co. all lands of Samuel Ingersol, unnamed.
31 May 1800 Underwood Roberts sold to Isaac Serman and Betty Serman had of Samuel Ingersol.

LONG DELAY

Patented in 1766 by Ephraim King for 17 1/2 acres
1777 Ephraim King willed to son Samuel King on the south side of Quantico, if no issue to Levin Gale.
1783 tax- Samuel King 17 1/2 acres, Rewastico 100
8 Nov.1797 George Gale and Littleton Gale of Cecil Co. and Levin Gale and Samuel Wilson with wife Leah Wilson sold to Thomas Garrettson of Som.Co. devised by Ephraim King to Levin Gale.
6 Jan.1798 George Robertson and wife Mary Robertson sold to Levin Gale
13 June 1810 John A. Garrettson sold to Francis Brady 1/6th part of 1/6th of lands inherited.

LONG DELAY

Patented in 1746 by John Robertson for 100 acres on Plumb Creek.
1748 John Robertson willed to son John 100 acres 1783 tax- John Robertson Sr. 100 acres.
1800 John Robertson willed to wife Phillis Robertson.
1828 Asher Burroughs willed to son Joshua Burroughs.
1830 Jonathan Fooks of David Fooks willed to daughter Henrietta Byrd, bought of Asher Burroughs.

LONG EXPECTED

see GETHESEME

LONG HILL

Patented on 23 July 1668 by Samuel Jackson for 300 acres.
12 Aug.1668 Samuel Jackson sold to James Dashiell 300 acres
1697 James Dashiell willed to son Robert Dashiell.
Rent Rolls 1700 possessed by Ann Dashiell widow of James.
Rent Rolls 1705 had by Capt. James Dashiell trustee for Robert Dashiell.
1718 Robert Dashiell willed to son Robert 150 acres and to James Dashiell 150 acres.
19 Dec.1743 Capell King with wife Sarah King gave to her son Matthias Dashiell. He not to claim interest in the land where his brother William Dashiell lives. 150 acres upper half.
1744 Matthias Dashiell son of Robert willed 150 acres to John Stewart son of sister Rebecca Stewart (she married Alexander Stewart)
1749 William Dashiell son of Robert Dashiell willed to son Haste Dashiell on Tipqueen Creek.
1783 tax- William Francis Dashiell 150 acres, Nanticoke 100
1783 tax- John Stewart
22 July 1786 Robert Dashiell with wife Jane Dashiell sold to William Francis Dashiell 158 1/2 acres.
6 Aug.1884 Cadmus Dashiell sold to Thomas Hambury 271 acres of LONG HILL & MOUNT EPHRAIM.
This became part of the town of Wetpiquin.

LONG RANGE

Patented in 1771 by Joshua Davis for 165 acres

LONG RIDGE

Patented in 1760 by William Maddux for 44 1/4 acres
24 Feb.1810 Samuel Rencher sold 30 acres to John Maddux Jr.

LONG SWAMP

1762 William Owens willed to son William Owens with OWENS SECURITY
7 Mar.1776 resurveyed to Sussex Co.Delaware by William Owens.

LONG SLIPE

Patented in 1785 by Solomon Winright for 8 acres.

LONG WAIT FOR

Patented in 1775 by William Layfield for 100 acres
1783 tax- William Layfield 100 acres, Wic. 100, Worc.Co.

LOOK OUT

Patented in 1833 by Joseph S. Barnard for 300 acres.

LOTT

Patented in 1681 by Robert Ridgley for 200 acres
Patented 2nd. 200 acres by Robert Ridgley 1736
1701 Robert Ridgley of St. Mary's County willed land in Somerset County to be sold.
1745 George Handy willed to son Levin Handy 200 acres.
19 Dec.1755 Samuel Handy sold to John Handy 200 acres with part of BELEAN
1783 tax- Levin Handy 200 acres, Rewastico 100
17 Feb.1810 Thomas J. Winder with wife Harriett Winder (daughter of Levin Handy) sold to William Hopkins.

LOTT

Patented on 9 July 1737 by William Gray for 100 acres.
6 July 1739 William Gray sold 100 acres to George Dashiell
1749 George Dashiell willed to son Joseph Dashiell at head of Deep Creek out of the Nanticoke River.
30 Nov.1759 Joseph Dashiell sold to Joshua Caldwell and William Boyce 100 acres, all except burying ground.
23 Feb.1760 William Boyce resurveyed to LOTTS SUPPLY

LOTT

Patented in 1741 by Thomas Methven for 50 acres

LOTT

Patented in 1762 by John Carmichael for 2 acres

LOTT

Patented in 1777 by Elizabeth Maddux for 15 1/4 acres.

LOTT

Patented in 1813 by Henry Graham and John Graham for 8 acres.

LOTTS SUPPLY

Patented on 23 Feb.1760 by William Boyce and Joshua Caldwell for 189 acres a resurvey from LOTT
26 July 1763 William Boyce sold to Joshua Caldwell, millright LOTT that Joseph Dashiell sold to Joshua Caldwell and William Boyce.

LOW MEADOW

Patented on 22 June 1765 by Elizabeth Handy for 13 acres.
14 JUne 1792 Haste Handy sold to Gabriel Slocomb 13 acres.

LOWES CONCLSION

Patented in 1844 by Ralph Lowe in Barren Creek.

LOWES ENLARGED

Patented in 1743 by Henry Lowe for 194 acres, part of LITTLE BELEAN & HORSEYS BALIWICK
1761 Henry Lowe willed to Robert Kellett
1783 tax - Samuel Covington 31 acres
1783 tax - Henry Fitzgerald 103 3/4 acres
21 July 1796 Tubman Lowe sold to John Morris 103 acres from grandfather Henry Lowe.
1792 John Morris patented MORRIS ADDITION TO LOWES ENLARGED 132 1/4 acres
7 Dec.1800 John Webb mortgaged to John Dashiell Sr.
17 Dec.1801 John Dashiell and wife Elizabeth Dashiell released mortgage to John Webb
4 Oct.1805 John Webb and wife Hetty Webb sold to John Dashiell Jr. PHILLIPS ADDN. HORSEYS BALIWICK, LITTLE BELEAN and part of LOWES ENLARGED 308 acres.
1810 John Morris willed to sons Joseph Morris and John H. Morris 132 acres of MORRIS ADDITION TO LOWES ENLARGED.

LOWES HIS PRIZE HOUSE

see FAIRFIELDS

LOWES MEADOW

Patented in 1760 by Henry Lowe for 17 1/2 acres
17 June 1800 Tubman Lowe son of Henry sold to Frederick A. C. Dashiell.

LUCK

Patented in 1769 by Alexander Thomas Russell for 5 acres.
1 May 1773 Alexander Thomas Russell sold to son Price Russell all his land, no name.
1783 tax- Price Russell 5 acres, Nanticoke 100

LUCK BY CHANCE

Patented in 1804 by William Anderson for 22 3/4 acres

LUCK BY CHANCE

Patented in 1805 by Joshua Nicholson for 15 3/4 acres

LUCK BY CHANCE

Patented on 13 Apr.1771 by James Hust for 60 acres.
17 Apr.1775 James Hust with wife Mary Hust sold 60 acres to Richard

Williams, on north side of the main road from Barren Creek Mills to Vienna Ferry.
1783 tax - Mary Williams 60 acres, Rewastico 100
28 Mar.1800 William Giles and wife Ganer Giles sold to John Grumble of Sussex Co.Del. 60 acres deeded to Richard Williams.
26 Nov.1801 William Russum sold to William Wilson 60 acres of WILLIAMS LOTT adj. ACWORTHS DELIGHT & LUCK BY CHANCE.

LUCK BY CHANCE

Patented in 1774 by Train Acworth for 100 acres
1783 tax - Train Acworth 100 acres
1791 Train Acworth willed to son Train.

LUKES CHANCE

Patented in 1767 by Luke Mezick for 2 acres

LUMMS PURCHASE

see GETHESEME & LONG EXPECTED.

LYONS DEN

Patented on 26 June 1676 by John Lyon for 200 acres
2 June 1679 John Lyon with wife Margery Lyon sold to John Smith, Edward Williams and August Morrow 200 acres.
Rent Rolls 1666-1723 possessed by the widow Marrett relict of John Marrett.

LYONS DEN

Patented in 1763 by James Russell for 55 1/4 acres
14 Sep.1795 Jesse Russell sold to John Carmichael 55 1/4 acres
7 Apr.1801 Levin Carmichael sold to Henry Walston 55 1/4 acres.
11 April 1803 Levin Carmichael with wife Elizabeth Carmichael sold to Henry Wilson 55 1/4 acres.
4 Sep.1807 Henry Wilson with wife Catherine Wilson sold to Eleanor Handy 132 1/2 acres of LYONS DEN, WARRINGTON, GREENS DISCOVERY.

LYONS FOLLY

Patented on 26 Nov.1678 by John Lyon for 150 acres.
Rent Rolls 1666-1723 possessed by John Cheeseman. As John Lyon conveyed to Robert Bowdith who sold to William Merrill of Dorc.Co. Wm. Merrill sold to John Cheeseman who gave to his wife Rachel Cheeseman. She married second William Smith.
7 May 1743 William Smith of Sussex Co.Del. and wife Rachel Smith sold to James Hardy 100 acres.
9 May 1743 John Pollitt of Dorc.Co. sold to James Hardy part 2 tracts for 5 shillings LYONS FOLLY 100 acres, and FOLLY 50 acres.
29 July 1755 James Hardy of Worc.Co. sold 150 acres to Day Givans.
1783 tax- James Phillips 150 acres - Rewastico 100.

LYONS LOTT

Patented on 21 May 1683 John Lyon 100 acres.

Rent Rolls 1666-1723 possessed by James Givans 100 acres
1723 James Givans willed to son James Givans.
1735 Robert Givans willed 6 acres to son Robert Givans.
5 Oct.1743 James Givans s/o James sold to William Winder 6 acres.
8 Dec.1743 Benjamin Warrington sold to William Winder for 5 shillings all lands conveyed by James Givans to William Winder 117 acres of COMMONS and 86 acres of LYONS LOTT.
10 Dec.1743 James Givans sold to Robert Givans 8 acres.
6 Aug.1763 Ephraim King appointed to resurvey lands of William Givans orphan of Robert Givans, DEAR PASTURE & 16 acres of LYONS LOTT.
1 May 1770 William Givans of Boston, New England sold to Ephraim King 17 1/4 acres
9 Mar.1775 Ephraim King sold to William Whittington for 5 shillings 8 1/4 acres.
1783 tax - William Whittington 8 acres- Rewastico 100
1783 tax - William Winder 96 1/2 acres
4 Jan.1790 Samuel King sold to William Winder 15 acres that William Givans sold to Ephraim King his father.

MC DANIELS LUCK

Patented in 1761 by James McDaniel for 50 acres
1783 tax - James McDaniel 50 acres, Rewastico 100
1783 ADDTION TO MCDANIELS LUCK patented by Joseph Venables for 321 acres.
1788 Joseph Venables willed to grandson Samuel Venables, if no issue to nephew Joseph son of Benjamin Venables.
18 Dec.1788 Joseph Venables sold 17 acres of ADDITION to James MacDaniel Sr.
10 Dec.1788 Joseph Venables sold 51 acres to Thomas Badley of Sussex Co. Delaware of ADDITION
10 Dec.1788 Joseph Venables sold to William McDaniel 74 acres of MACDANIELS LUCK & ADDITION.
26 May 1797 Daniel Phillips sold to Nancy Robertson, William Robertson, Samuel Robertson, James Robertson heirs of James Robertson 89 3/4 acres of MacDANIELS LUCK & TULLYS ADDITION.
22 Sep.1804 James MacDaniel sold to Thomas Badley of Sussex Co.Del. 14 1/2 acres of ADDITION
1825 Elender Cooper willed to son Samuel Cooper ADDITION TO MACDANIELS LUCK.

MADDUX CHANCE

Patented in 1762 by Alexander Maddux for 50 acres
1763 Alexander Maddux willed 50 acres to sons Alexander Maddux and Ezekiel Maddux.
8 July 1769 Alexander Maddux sold 50 acres to Benjamin Hearn.
1783 tax - Benjamin Hearn, Rewastico 100
1786 HEARNS ADDITION TO MADDUX CHANCE patented by Benjamin Hearn for 94 acres.
1802 Benjamin Hearn willed to wife Sarah Hearn and to son Samuel Hearn lands unnamed.

MADDUX'S CONCLUSION

Patented in 1794 by John Maddux for 487 3/4 acres

4 May 1799 John Maddux with wife Lydia Maddux sold 28 acres to John Benston.
5 Feb.1803 John Maddux sold 4 acres to Thomas Humphries.

MADDUX DISCOVERY

Patented in 1825 by John Maddux for 11 1/2 acres.

MADDUX ENLARGEMENT

Patented in 1758 by Daniel Maddux for 9 acres.
7 July 1800 Daniel Maddux with wife Elizabeth Maddux sold to Daniel Ballard 136 1/2 acres of MADDUX ENLARGEMENT & MADDUX SECURITY.

MADDUX'S FANCY

Patented in 1759 by Alexander Maddux Jr. for 50 acres.
22 June 1763 Alexander Maddux sold 50 acres to Nathan Culver
25 Feb.1764 Nathan Culver sold 50 acres to William Stevens.
15 Dec 1769 William Stevens sold 50 acres to Henry Trader
5 Apr.1771 Henry Armatrader with wife Agnes Armatrader sold to William McClemmy 50 acres.
17 Aug.1774 William McClemmy mortgaged lands, goods and chattels to Zorobable King and Solomon Long purchased of Henry Trader, etc.
7 Apr.1792 John Leatherbury, sheriff sold to Joshua Hitch highest bidder, on behalf of Ann Dixon and William Wheatley administrator of Robert Dixon deceased, asignee against Gillis McClemmy, John Pope Mitchell and Benjamin Wailes heirs of William McClemmy 46 3/4 acres.
7 Apr.1792 Joshua Hitch Jr. sold to Levin Irving.
8 Sep.1792 Levin Irving sold to Thomas Byrd 35 1/4 acres of CONFUSION & MADDUX FANCY.
9 Feb.1793 Levin Irving sold to John Maddux 8 1/2 acres of MADDUX FANCY & LAST DISCOVERY.
1822 Thomas Byrd willed to son Benjamin Harvey Byrd.

MADDUX LUCK

Patentedon 29 Oct.1676 by William Maddux for 410 1/4 acres at head of Wicomico River on south west side of main road to Spring Hill Chapel.
9 June 1764 William Maddux sold 154 acres to Jonathan Shockley
4 Mar.1769 William Maddux Jr. sold to Jonathan Shockley, confirmation of original deed which did not contain whole intended.
18 Nov.1766 James Collins sold 4 1/2 acres to James Houston
22 Apr.1769 William Maddux sold to Joshua Hitch 151 acres and 7 acres of same.
20 May 1771 William Maddux of Worc.Co. sold to Joshua Hitch 229 acres.
19 Oct.1771 William Maddux with wife Elizabeth Maddux of Worc.Co. sold 147 acres to Jonathan Shockley of Somerset County. Other deed was voided.
28 Feb.1774 Jonathan Shockley and wife Elizabeth Shockley sold 147 acres to Henry Trader.
21 June.1785 William Maddux of Sussex Co.Del. sold 34 1/2 acres to William Stone, mortgage.
2 Jan.1786 Henry Trader and wife Elizabeth Trader sold to Benjamin Nutter 147 acres.

9 Aug.1803 John Wilkins, sheriff sold to Hugh Gemmill 247 acres per judgement against heirs of Joshua Hitch.
1801 resurveyed to HITCHES HARD LUCK.

MADDUX PATCH

Patented in 1792 by John Maddux for 12 acres

MAGDALENS CHOICE

Patented on 16 Apr.1695 by John Jenner for 100 acres.
Rent Rolls 1666-1723 possessed by Thomas Highway
19 Aug.1719 Abraham Highway and wife Margaret Highway sold to Robert Atkins. John Jenner died without disposition and it descended to his daughter Deborah Highway. James McKimmey and Deborah McKimmey his wife sold to Thomas Highway.
4 Nov.1761 William Atkins son of Robert Atkins sold to Jacob Christopher 81 acres.
4 Nov.1761 William Atkins sold to Adam Christopher 81 acres.
9 Mar.1765 Jacob Christopher sold to Stephen Horsey of Somerset County 19 acres with DUNKIRK & DURHAM.
7 Feb.1771 Stephen Horsey sold 19 acres to Samuel Horsey.
1783 tax - Stephen Toadvine 19 acres. Wicomico 100
1783 tax - Adam Christopher 71 acres.
14 Mar.1783 Samuel Horsey with wife Ann Horsey sold to Stephen Toadvine 19 acres.

MAGEES LOT

Patented on 8 July 1762 by David Magee, a resurvey of DAVIDS CHOICE for 247 acres.
6 Apr.1764 David Magee with wife Mary Magee sold to Richard Biglands 76 acres with SMITHS DISCOVERY.
8 Aug.1764 David Magee sold to Edmund Northern Nelms 50 acres.
8 Aug.1764 David Magee sold to George Parsons 30 acres.
3 June 1767 Edmund Northern Nelms sold to George Parsons 33 1/2 acres
20 Feb.1767 David Magee with wife Mary Magee sold to Isaac Handy 142 acres of MAGEES LOTT & SMITHS DISCOVERY
6 July 1770 Isaac Handy sold to Solomon Russell 160 acres of MAGEES LOTT & SMITHS DISCOVERY.
9 May 1778 Price Russell and wife Ann Russell sold to Josiah Russell.
1783 tax - James Trader 200 acres, Wic.100 Worc.Co.

MAIDENS CHOICE

Patented in 1759 by Sarah Johnson for 25 acres
8 Mar.1781 Sarah Johnson of Dorc.Co. sold 25 acres to James Phillips.
1783 tax- James Phillips 25 acres, Rewastico 100.

MAIDENHEAD

Patentedon 24 Oct.1676 by William Stevens who assigned to Daniel Clark for 300 acres.
1683 repatented by Rebecca Cox.
Rent Rolls 1666-1723 possessed by John Caldwell
22 Nov.1750 Joshua Caldwell mortgaged to Robert Jenkins Henry and John

Henry 300 acres.
1758 Joshua Caldwell son of John Caldwell willed to Thomas Savage.
23 June 1758 Robert Jenkins Henry and John Henry released mortgage of 300 acres to Thomas Savage.
22 June 1758 Thomas Savage sold to William Winder 300 acres.
1783 tax- Henry Handy 300 acres.
1792 William Winder willed to daughter Jane Ker and after her death to her sons Peter Handy and William Handy.

MAIDEN LAND

Patented in 1746 by George Dashiell for 170 acres.
1768 George Dashiell willed to daughter Sarah Walter use of lands in Nanticoke, unnamed and after death to grandson George Dashiell Walter.

MAIDEN LOTT

Patented on 4 May 1677 by Elizabeth Williams for 300 acres on the south side of barren Creek.
Rent Rolls 1666-1723 possessed by John Gillis
1720 John Gilis willed to son John 300 acres
3 Oct.1765 Thomas Gillis with wife Elizabeth Gillis sold 100 acres to Thomas Gillis.
23 Feb.1770 Thomas Gillis and wife Elizabeth Gillis sold to Thomas Glaster 100 acres.
25 Apr.1771 Joseph Gillis with wife Grace Gillis sold 100 acres to Thomas Gillis.
25 Apr.1771 Thomas Gillis with wife Elizabeth sold 100 acres to Joseph Gillis.
1783 tax - Joseph Gillis 100 acres, Nanticoke 100
1783 tax - Thomas Gillis 100 acres
1783 tax - Thomas Glaster 100 acres
22 Mar.1787 Joseph Gillis sold 1 acre to Lewis Daltrieu part called PINE LANDING on east side of Barren Creek.
1793 Joseph Gillis willed to son Littleton Gillis
1 May 1795 Joseph Gillis sold all to James Acworth.
22 Jan.1796 Joseph Gillis sold part to Charles Weatherly, no acres given.
22 June 1796 James Acworth sold part to Joseph Gillis
3 Sep.1799 George Handy, sheriff sold to John Huffington MAIDENS LOTT & SOON IN THE MORNING per judgement against James Acworth
12 Sep.1800 John Huffington sold to William Birkhead
31 Jan.1801 Charles Weatherly sold part to John Byrd.
1802 Arthur Dashiell willed part to son Henry Dashiell and to son Matthias Dashiell, balance of lands.
7 Nov.1803 Ezekiel Gillis with wife Ann Gillis sold 100 acres to Edward Hull.
29 Oct.1803 John Byrd with wife Margaret Byrd sold to John Moore
15 May 1804 Robert Leatherbury, sheriff sold to highest bidder Levin Farrington 120 acres of CHESTNUT RIDGE part of MAIDENS LOT per judgement against Ezekiel Gillis.
3 May 1806 William Birkhead sold to John Moore of Sussex Co.Del. 9 3/4 acres.
29 May 1807 Joseph Gillis sold to Levin Stewart 1 acre.
3 Feb.1809 John Glaster sold rights to Thomas Wright.

MAIDENS LOTT AND ADDITION

Patented on 7 Mar.1767 by Ann Collier a resurvey of COLLIERS CONTENTMENT for 150 acres in Nanticoke forge.
MAIDENS ADDITION patented 283 acres.
12 Mar.1776 Sussex Co.Delaware warrants to George Adams.

MALONES CHANCE

Patented in 1769 by Robert Malone for 115 1/2 acres

MALONES LOTT

Patented in 1762 by John Malone for 79 1/4 acres
16 Nov.1791 Peter Malone sold 2 acres to Elizabeth White widow of Isaac White.
26 July 1791 Stephen Malone sold to Peter Malone part.
1793 ADDITION patented by John Malone for 156 acres
5 Dec.1795 Peter Malone sold 20 acres to Obed Bayley of ADDITION

MALONES VENTURE

Patented in 1762 by John Malone for 20 3/4 acres.
1783 tax - Mary Malone 20 3/4 acres Wic.100
26 July 1791 Peter Malone sold to Stephen Malone.
26 July 1791 Stephen Malone sold part to Peter Malone, probably division of land.

MANLOVES ADVENTURE

Patented on 28 Nov.1673 by John Manlove.
10 Aug.1674 John Manlove with wife Elizabeth Manlove sold to John Ricketts 50 acres.
Rent Rolls 1666-1723 possessed by James Weatherly (he married Ann Manlove widow of Richard Acworth)
1705 James Weatherly sold 50 acres to John Gillis.
31 Mar.1761 Joseph Gillis gave to son George Gillis 50 cres.

MANLOVES GROVE

Patented on 5 Apr.1680 by Luke Manlove for 500 acres on the south side of the Nanticoke River
1707 Luke Manlove died in Dorcester Co.Maryland.
Rent Rolls 1666-1723 possessed by James Caldwell for 250 acres and George Hutchins 250 acres by the name of FIRST CHOICE.
1726/7 George Hutchins willed entire estate to son William Hutchins and daughter Mary Hutchins.
10 Apr.1775 Alice Manlove widow of Luke Manlove, of Kent Co.Delaware sold to brother John Mitchell heir of Robert Mitchell 500 acres.

MAREGLANTE

Patented on 12 Nov.1766 by Joseph Dashiell for 493 acres a resurvey of 366 acres of PARSONS CONQUEST.
1783 tax - Capt. Joseph Dashiell, Wic.100 Worc.Co.

22 Oct.1790 Zadock Sturgis, sheriff, per judgement against Benjamin F.A.C. Dashiell sold to Thomas Harwood of Annapolis 403 acres.
25 July 1796 Thomas Harwood with wife Margaret Harwood of Annapolis sold to Joshua Johnson and Isaac Hearn of Worc. Co. 403 acres.
1797 part resurveyed to PARTNERSHIP
7 Mar.1807 Isaac Hearn sold to Jonathan Parsons Sr. 13 1/2 acres
1808 Jonathan Parsons willed to son Jonathan Stevens Parsons.
1808 George Parsons willed to sons George and Elijah Parsons.

MARISH POINT

Patented on 11 May 1683 by James Weatherly for 200 acres
Rent Rolls 1666-1723 possessed by Richard Acworth 200 acres
1727 Richard Acworth gave to sons Richard, Charles Acworth and Thomas Acworth.
1759 Thomas Acworth gave to sons Charles Acworth, Train Acworth, William Acworth, James Acworth and Richard Acworth.
25 Sep.1759 Charles Acworth sold 75 acres to Joseph Weatherly except 13 acres conveyed to Mary Harris.
23 Nov.1759 Charles Acworth gave to James Acworth son of Thomas Acworth, brother of Charles 450 acres of ACWORTHS DELIGHT, ACWROTHS CHOICE, HOGG QUARTER, RIDGES, MARISH POINT.
20 June 1769 James Acworth sold to William Acworth 20 acres
1783 tax - Train Acworth, Rewastico 100- resurveyed to UNITED STATES.

MARLBOROUGH

Patented on 25 May 1688 by Edward Wheeler back from the south side of Wicomico River for 150 acres.
Rent Rolls 1666-1723 possessed by Peter Fitzgerald for orphan of Edward Wheeler.
1703 Edward Wheeler willed to sons Isaac Wheeler and John Wheeler.
Patented in 1762 by Daniel Townsend for 146 acres, could be a resurvey.

MARSH GROUND

Patented on 12 Nov.1723 by Christopher Nutter on the north side of the mouth of Quantico Creek.
Rent Rolls 1666-1723 possessed by Christopher Nutter
1728 Christopher Nutter willed lands at Quantico Creek to son William Nutter.
1783 tax- William Nutter Sr. 100 acres, Nanticoke 100
1783 William Nutter willed lands to sons William Nutter and Charles Nutter at Quantico, unnamed.
29 Aug.1793 Charles Nutter and William Nutter divided lands.
27 Aug.1806 Henry E. Bayley and wife Sarah Bayley sold to Charles Nutter.
1813 Charles Nutter son of William willed all lands to son Christopher Nutter owned by brother William Nutter, unamed.

MARSH HOOK

Patented in 1802 by William White of F. for 21 3/4 acres.

MARSH HOOK

Patented on 15 Dec.1679 by James Weatherly for 100 acres at bottom on a neck made by the Rewastico and Mamumquak creeks.
Rent Rolls 1666-1723 possessed by Charles Nutter for the orphans of William Piper.
James Weatherly sold 100 acres to William Piper.
28 May 1720 William Piper heir to Capt. William Piper sold to brother Christopher Piper 100 acres.
12 Feb.1728 Christopher Piper sold to James Hardy 240 acres of WEATHERLYS PURCHASE, ONCE AGAIN & MARSH HOOK
11 Mar.1736 Christopher Piper and wife Rachel Piper sold to James Hardy, confirmation of above deed.
22 June 1743 James Hardy and James Weatherly sold 240 acres of WEATHERLYS PURCHASE, ONCE AGAIN & MARSH HOOK, to James Train Jr.
1783 tax - Joseph Piper 75 acres   Rewastico 100
1783 tax - William Turpin 25 acres

MARSH POINT & ENLARGED

Patented on 15 July 1755 by Avery Morgan for 40 acres.
MARSH POINT ENLARGED patented on 3 June 1760 by Avery Morgan for 117 acres
24 Feb.1770 Avery Morgan son of Avery sold to John Aydelotte Sr. 1 1/2 acres of ENLARGED.
20 Feb.1770 Avery Morgan sold 36 acres to William Holland.

MARTINS CHOICE

Patented on 19 Sep.1753 by John Martin for 50 acres
8 Feb.1757 John Martin sold to John Hearn 50 acres
1762 resurveyed to CANAAN

MARTINS CONSOLIDATION

Patented on 1854 by Martin L.H. Maddux for 36 7/8 acres
1850 he is in Salisbury District.

MARTINS LOTT

Patented in 1774 by Luther Martin for 25 acres

MARYS CHOICE

Patented on 1 Dec.1688 by Thomas Humphries for 200 acres
18 Aug.1715 Thomas Humphries and wife Mary Humphries gave to daughter and her husband Richard Green 200 acres.
1763 Resurveyed to GREENS LUCK

MARYS FANCY

Patented in 1794 by Mary Kilby for 237 7/8 acres

MARYS TRAVEL

Patented in 1755 by Edmund Dority for 21 acres.
8 Mar.1776 Sussex Co.Del. warrents to Jonathan Green on the w/s of Little Creek Delaware.

MARYS VENTURE

Patented in 1785 by Henry Graham for 40 1/2 acres
8 Apr.1786 James Gunby of Sussex Co.Del. and wife Mary Gunby sold to Jacob Stayton of Dorcester Co.Md. 20 acres being part devised to Mary Graham wife of James Graham by her father Henry Graham.

MASSEYS FOLLY

Patented in 1754 by Thomas Massey for 13 acres
2 May 1776 resurveyed to Sussex Co.Delaware by Joseph Massey

MATTANGRETAR

Patented in 1796 by Henry Dulaney for 92 1/4 acres

MATTHEWS FOLLY

Patented in 1771 by John Nelms for 24 acres

McCLESTERS INHERITANCE

A resurvey of SWEETWOOD HALL for 80 acres
1720 Daniel McClester willed to brother John McClester 86 acres of McCLESTERS INHERITANCE part of SWEETWOOD HALL.
5 June 1721 Daniel McClester sold to John McClester Sr.80 acres.

McCLESTERS PURCHASE

see RUNCELL & YEARSLAND

McGEES ADVENTURE

Patented in 1822 by James Magee for 72 3/4 acres

McGEES FOLLY

Patented in 1833 by Robert J. H. King for 37 acres

MEADOW

Patented on 3 July 1741 by William Collins for 150 acres
17 Mar.1757 William Collins, yoeman sold to Andrew Collins Sr., on the east side of the Nanticoke River. 150 acres.

MEADOW

Patented in 1764 by William Douglas and Jonathan Vaughn for 10 acres.
13 Feb.1768 Jonathan Vaughn ironmaster with wife Ann Vaughan sold to Christopher Marshall of Philadelphia, William Wishart of same, Jemima Edwards widow, William Douglas of Worc.Co., Joseph Pennell, his

undivided part in Deep Creek and Nanticoke River DEEP CREEK FURNACE & NANTICOKE FORGE 5000 acres, no names.

MEADOW

Patented in 1783 by Josiah Polk for 122 acres
1784 Josiah Polk willed to sister Sinah Bayley 1/4rd part lands and mills near Vienna Ferry.
1802 Sinah Bayley willed to sons Thomas Bayley, Henry Bayley and Josiah Bayley lands devised by brother Josiah Polk, no name.

MEASLEYS BEGINNING

Patented on 10 Aug.1753 by John Measley for 87 acres
21 Aug.1755 John Measley sold to John Morris
1773 John Morris sold to son John Morris
1783 tax- Joshua Morris Wic.100 Worc.Co. with COLLINS CHANCE 124 acres

MECHANIC

Patented in 1805 by James Weatherly for 1 3/4 acres

MEECHES DESERT

Patented on 14 Sep. 1688 by John Meech for 200 acres.
31 Dec.1668 John Meech of Ann Arundel Co. sold to James Dashiell
1697 James Dashiell willed to son James.
Rent Rolls 1666-1723 possessed by Capt. James Dashiell
1708 James Dashiell willed 200 acres to son James
1735/7 James Dashiell gave part to son James and part to son Jesse Dashiell.
1773 Jesse Dashiell willed lands to wife Susannah Dashiell and to son James Dashiell, unnamed.
1783 tax - Susannah Dashiell 66 acres   Nanticoke 100
1783 tax - James Dashiell 131 acres
25 Oct.1784 James Dashiell gave 2 acres to George Dashiell and wife Rebecca Dashiell for life and then to their daughter Elizabeth Davis Whithear until she marries.

MEECHS HOPE

Patented on 14 Sep.1688 by Thomas Meech for 300 acres
18 Feb.1670 Thomas Meech sold to Alexander Jamison who bequeathed to two daughters Elizabeth Nesham wife of Benjamin Nesham and Margaret Serman wife of Thomas Serman.
10 Feb.1702 Peter Booth with wife Margaret Booth sold to Edward Serman.
Rent Rolls 1666-1723 possessed by the widow of Thomas Serman 150 acres and 150 acres by Benjamin Nesham son of Benjamin.
1706 Thomas Serman gave to son Thomas Serman orders to give his brother 150 acres of MEECHES HOPE at head of Tipiquin Creek.
17 Nov.1721 Benjamin Nesham with wife Mary Nesham sold 150 acres to William Vaughn, carpenter with 150 acres of RICH SWAMP.
25 Dec.1731 William Vaughn and wife Mary Vaughn sold to Thomas Serman 150 acres of MEECHS HOPE & RICH SWAMP.

28 Nov.1735 Thomas Serman and wife Elizabeth Serman sold to Benjamin Townsend 135 acres.
17 Feb.1738 Thomas Serman sold to William Dashiell 12 acres of MEECHS HOPE & YEARSLAND and 51 acres of YEARSLAND that he resurveyed to DASHIELLS PURCHASE.
2 Apr.1737 William Vaughn sold to Levin Dashiell 115 acres
8 July 1738 Benjamin Townsend sold 135 acres to Joseph Dashiell tract bought of Thomas Serman, unnamed.
22 Mar.1753 Levin Dashiell and wife Bridget Dashiell sold to Isaac Dashiell 115 acres with RICH SWAMP now called LEVEL LAND.
22 June 1757 Isaac Dashiell sold to Nehemiah Crockett 115 acres.
22 June 1760 Nehemiah Crockett with wife Alice Crockett sold to William Bounds 80 acres of CHANCE, part out of MEECHS HOPE.
18 June 1760 Nehemiah Crockett with wife Alice Crockett sold to George Dashiell son of Joseph Dashiell 115 acres that Isaac Dashiell sold to Nehemiah, no name.
18 June 1761 Nehemiah Crockett sold to Isaac Atkinson 50 acres of marsh formerly belonging to Thomas Dashiell, no name.
1783 tax- Joseph Dashiell, Nanticoke 100.

MEECHS RIGHT

Patented on 20 Apr.1667 by John Meech for 300 acres.
31 Dec.1669 John Meech of Ann Arundel Co.Md. ordered George Johnson to sell to James Dashiell
1697 James Dashiell willed to son James Dashiell 300 acres
1708/9 James Dashiell willed to son James.
Rent Rolls 1666-1723 possessed by Capt. James Dashiell on the west side of Wetipquin Creek.
1736/7 James Dashiell gave to son James and part to son Jesse Dashiell.
1773 Jesse Dashiell willed lands unnamed to son James Dashiell
1783 tax - James Dashiell 200 acres- Nanticoke 100
1783 tax - John Dashiell 116 acres.

MEETING HILL

Patented in 1777 by John Farlow for 202 acres
21 Dec.1793 John Farlow sold to Violetta Fooks 202 acres.
1802 Violetta Fooks willed to son Thomas Fooks.
8 Dec.1809 Billy Fooks, Jonathan Fooks, James Fooks, Thomas Fooks, Daniel Fooks agree to division of lands of Daniel Fooks, deceased.
8 Dec.1809 Thomas Fooks with wife Sarah Fooks sold to Billy Fooks.

MELALYS FOLLY

Patented in 1763 by Patrick McLally for 12 acres
1 Aug.1770 Patrick McLally sold to Benjamin Venables for 5 shillings 12 acres.
1783 tax - Joseph Venables 12 acres, Rewastico 100
1788 Joseph Venables willed to grandson Samuel Venables.

MELSONS ADDITION

Patented in 1773 by Daniel Melson for 50 acres

1783 tax - Daniel Melson Sr. Wic.100, Worc.Co.
1785 Daniel Melson willed to son Daniel
1798 MELSONS ADDITION ENGLARGED patented by Daniel Melson for 76 acres
1833 Elijah Melson willed to son Samuel Melson 50 acres and to son
Elijah Melson 25 acres of MELSONS ADDITION ENLARGED.

MELSONS LOTT

Patented in 1773 by Daniel Melson for 18 acres
5 Aug.1804 Joseph Melson of Sussex Co.Delaware sold to Benjamin Melson
of Worcester County, 18 acres.

MESSICKS CHANCE

Patented in 1741 by John Mezick for 100 acres
1759 part resurveyed to CHANCE by John Spicer
20 July 1771 George Mezick of Sussex Co.Del. son of John sold to
George Farrington 50 acres on the south east side of the Nanticoke
River.

MEZICKS CONCLUSION

Patented in 1804 by Aaron Mezick for 186 acres

MIDDLENECK

Patented on 17 Apr.1695 by William Curry for 200 acres
Rent Rolls 1666-1723 possessed by William Curry
1713 John Curry son of William Curry sold to Thomas Highway 200 acres.
13 Nov.1728 Robert Atkins and wife Elizabeth Atkins sold to Samuel
Davis 200 acres that Abraham Highway son of Thomas Highway who died
intestate sold to Robert Atkins.
1756 Samuel Davis willed to son Samuel 100 acres.

MIDDLE NECK

Patented on 16 Apr.1680 by Thomas Walker and Susanna Walker children
of Thomas Walker and wife Jane Walker for 400 acres
Rent Rolls 1666-1723 possessed by Thomas Walker and Capt. Nicholas
Evans who married Susanna Walker.
1728 Timothy Kennedy willed to son John Kennedy 200 acres of dwelling
plantation and to son Timothy Kennedy 200 acres, unnamed.
8 Oct.1741 Timothy Kennedy sold 100 acres to Esther Noble.
13 Mar.1750 Elisha Webb and wife Ann Webb sold 100 acres to George
Smith that Thomas Walker devised 400 acres to Timothy Kennedy who died
and lands fell to Ann Kennedy his daughter who married Elisha Webb.
1753 Timothy Kennedy willed to sister Ann Webb, then to her oldest
child, unnamed.
19 Aug.1758 part resurveyed to WHEEL OF FORTUNE
27 Aug.1762 George Smith of Worc.Co. sold to Thomas Noble 64 acres out
of MIDDLE NECK, part now called WHEEL OF FORTUNE
15 Oct.1768 Thomas Brooks and wife Ann Brooks (sister of Timothy
Kennedy Jr.) and James Willis with wife Mary Willis and Sarah Webb
daughter of Ann Webb sold 300 acres to John Nelms MIDDLE NECK at head
of the Wicomico River.

17 Oct.1805 Thomas Noble and wife Nancy Noble sold to James Smith.
1783 tax - Thomas Cox Sr. 48 acres and 98 acres.
12 Jan.1796 Archibald Smith with wife Mary Smith sold to George Slocomb of Dorcester Co. Md. at head of Rokiawalkin River 300 acres except part conveyed to Esther Noble by Timothy Kennedy.
18 Dec.1790 Thomas Harwood with wife Margaret Harwood of Annoplis sold to Purnell Johnson 400a. MILL LOT, MIDDLE NECK, DYKES CHOICE, SECURITY
11 Feb 1791 Purnell Johnson sold to Thomas Johnson 400 acres as above.
14 Sep.1792 Purnell Johnson, ELijah Johnson, William Hearn sold to Benjamin Johnson.
8 Sep.1792 Rebecca Cochran of Kent Co. Delaware widow of George SLocomb and husband David Cochran sold to George SLocomb.

MIDDLE NECK

Patented on 24 May 1688 by William Brereton for 300 acres near the head of the Wicomico River.
1690 William Brereton willed to sons Thomas Brereton and Henry Brereton (under 18).
Rent Rolls 1666-1723 claimed William Brereton, heir.
4 Oct.1779 David Crocker and wife Rebecca Crocker of Kent Co.Del. sold to Edmund Northern Nelms 300 acres, two miles from Salisbury Town.
17 Feb.1781 John Nelms sold to Archibald Smith 300 acres.
11 Mar.1802 Scott Brereton sold to William Pollitt of Worc.Co. his rights to 300 acres.
15 Mar.1806 William Pollitt and wife Sarah Pollitt sold to Kirk Gunby part.
15 Mar.1806 William Pollitt Sr. sold to Jacob Morris part taken off by COLLINS CHANCE 14 3/4 acres, part called THE FORK 7 3/4 acres and part called COME BY CHANCE 20 acres.
15 March 1806 William Pollitt with wife Sarah Pollitt sold part to Joshua Morris

MIDDLE RIDGE

Patented in 1826 by Hambleton Bratcher for 2 1/2 acres

MIDDLESEX

Patented on 30 Nov.1672 by Charles Hutchins who assigned to Robert Wilson for 300 acres.
1687 Robert Wilson willed all estate to wife Eliza Wilson
Rent Rolls 1666-1723 possessed by David Howard in right of the orphans of John Wilson.
1713 Andrew Wilson willed to cousin Thomas Wilson son of brother Thomas Wilson deceased, and then to pass to the nearest in blood of said Thomas Wilson.
12 Aug.1721 Thomas Wilson and wife Mary Wilson of Kent Co.Md. sold 300 acres to William Wallace of Somerset County.

MIDDLE TRACT

Patented in 1734 by Christopher Nutter and William Nutter for 100 acres.
6 Mar.1752 George Hardy and wife Sarah Hardy formerly relic of Christopher Nutter sold 50 acres to John Handy with NUTTERS ADVENTURE,

DELIGHT, ROSS, BOTTOM, NUTTERS CONTRIVANCE..
17 Sep.1781 Samuel King sold to Thomas Maddux 50 acres from father Ephraim King with DELIGHT & ROSS.
11 Sep.1781 Thomas Maddux sold same back to Samuel King.
1783 tax - William Nutter 100 acres- Rewastico 100
1783 William Nutter willed lands to sons William and Charles Nutter.
29 Aug.1793 William Nutter and Charles Nutter divided.
24 Aug.1806 Charles Nutter with wife Louisa Nutter sold to Henry E. Bayley 331 1/2 acres of ROSS, MIDDLE TRACT, DELIGHT, MONMOTH.
21 Oct.1808 Henry E. Bayley with wife Sarah Bayley sold to Thomas Mitchell same as above.

MIDFIELD

Patented on 29 Sep.1678 by Henry Morgan on the south side of Quantico Creek for 200 acres.
9 Jn.1685 Henry Morgan and wife Jane Morgan of New Castle Kent Co. Delaware sold 200 acres to John Marrett.
Rent Rolls 1666-1723 possessed by possessed by Nathaniel Abbott in right of the orphans of John Luckly
1734 Richard Rider willed to son Heathley Rider 200 acres.
29 Aug.1759 Richard Rider and wife Priscilla Rider mortgaged to Wilson Rider 200 acres.
Resurveyed in 1768 by John Rider for 201 acres.
3 Sep.1764 Peter Freeney and wife Elizabeth Freeney of Worc.Co. sold to John Rider of Somerset County their rights for 5 shillings, as John Luckly died intestate and left a daughter Elizabeth Freeney.
5 Oct.1767 John Rider and wife Margaret Rider sold 110 acres of WARWICK & MIDFIELD to Thomas Irving.
1783 tax - Heirs of John Rider
1783 tax - Thomas Irving
1784 Thomas Irving willed to son Joseph Irving 110 acres purchased of John Rider.
14 Sep.1789 Joseph Irving sold to Levin Irving.
12 Feb.1790 Thomas Moore and wife Mary Moore of Sussex Co.Del. sold to Charles Rider and Edward Austin, WARWICK, MIDFIELD, LEATHERBURYS FANCY formerly belonging to John Rider.
2 Feb 1791 Charles Serman and wife Sarah Serman sold to Edward Austin and Charles Leatherbury
19 Oct.1793 Charles Rider and Edward Austin sold to George James 132 acres of WARWICK & MIDFIELD.
22 Mar.1794 George Moore of Sussex Co.Del. and wife Elizabeth Moore sold all rights to Charles Rider.
8 Apr.1797 George Moore s/o George and wife Elizabeth Moore sold their rights to John Rider.
19 Jan 1799 Levin Irving son of Thomas Irving with wife Leah Irving sold to William Mezick.
15 Jan.1801 William Mezick and wife Sarah Irving sold to Thomas Cannon 15 3/4 acres of WARWICK & MIDFIELD.
1801 Charles Rider willed to wife Mary Rider part bought of the heirs of John Rider.
1818 William Mezick willed this land to be sold.
1843 John Taylor of William Taylor willed to daughter Mary Ann Bratten 1/3rd part of planatation, part of MIDFIELD & WARWICK and to granddaughter Ann Maria Brattan other 2/3rds part.

MIDLAND

Patented on 8 March 1761 by Jonathan Cathell for 80 acres
1772 Jonathan Cathell willed to son Jonathan Cathell.

MIGHT A HAD MORE

Patented on 9 Jan.1679 by Daniel Haste for 50 acres
Rent Rolls 1666-1723 possessed by Benjamin Wailes in right of his wife and coheir of Daniel Haste.
1701 Daniel Haste willed to daughter Elizabeth Haste
1726/9 Benjamin Wailes willed to son Joseph Wailes
1738 Joseph Wailes died intestate (wife Helena Wailes)
22 Mar.1758 Haste Wailes quitclaimed to brother Daniel Wailes devised by will of Joseph Wailes, TOSITER, FORTUNE, MIGHT A HAD MORE, JOSEPHS LOTT.

MIGHT HAVE HAD MORE

Patented on 10 Mar.1676 by James Jones for 400 acres in Nanticoke 100
26 Sep.1677 James Jones with wife Sarah Jones sold to kinsman Andrew Jones.
14 Mar.1680 Andrew Jones and wife Elizabeth Jones sold to Sampson Waters of Boston New England and Thomas Willin of Som.Co.
20 Jan.1685 Sampson Waters sold to Richard Crockett.
1682 Thomas Willin willed to daughter Eliza Willin 200 acres.
Rent Rolls 1666-1723 possessed by Richard Crockett 100 acres and Capt. Nicholas Evans 200 acres for Willin's orphans.
1738 Thomas Willin sold to John Shiles, part.
15 Apr.1745 Thomas Willin and wife Major Willin sold upper part to John Shiles 200 acres not formerly conveyed.
27 July 1763 Benjamin Huggins and wife Ann Huggins sold to William Rencher land that descended to Ann Huggins from death of John Shiles deceased, neice and coheir. no name or acres.
2 July 1764 William Rencher, Benjamin Huggins sold to Alice Waller and William Waller land that descended to Ann Huggins wife of Benjamin Huggins and mother to said Alice and William on death of John Shiles 100 acres.
4 June 1766 articles of Agreement- Bridget Chapley of Sor.Co. and John Span Conway of Som.Co. sold to Ann Huggins and William Waller part that John Shiles had became property of Bridget and Ann. no name.
13 Sep.1766 Bridget Chapley widow of Dorc.Co. give to daughter Susannah Conway of Som.Co. land that descended me from death of John Shiles.
20 Apr.1773 Ann Huggins sold to John Crockett.
5 Feb.1771 William Waller sold 194 acres to John Crockett
7 Mar.1771 William Waller mortgaged to Thomas Rencher and John Crockett, balance.
1783 tax - John Crockett 100 acres and 111 acres.
1783 tax - George Gale of Levin 200 acres.
28 Nov.1785 Levin Gale sold to John Span Conway and Susannah Conway his wife daughter of Bridget Chapley 100 acres, this is a division of land.
28 Nov.1785 John Crockett to Levin Gale Esq. division of land.
22 Dec.1788 Moses Pank with wife Elizabeth Pank sold to Benjamin Johnson SUNKEN GROUND, MIGHT HAVE HAD MORE, TAYLORS HILL.

27 Nov.1792 Benjamin Johnson sold to Moses Pank same as afsd.
3 Sep.1796 George Gale sold to John Crockett Sr. 110 acres, real estate of Levin Gale deceased.
13 Sep.1796 John Crockett Sr. sold to Shiles Crockett 110 acres.
13 Sep.1796 John Crockett and Shiles Crockett sold to John Span Conway 100 acres where Robert Crockett formerly lived conveyed Alice Waller wife of John Crockett by William Rencher and Benjamin Huggins.
6 Jan.1798 Shiles Crockett sold to George Robertson 110 acres.
8 Apr.1806 George Gale, Littleton Gale of Cecil Co.Md. sold to George Robertson. As Levin Gale deceased brother of George and Littleton mortgaged to George Robertson 10 acres. It was allotted to Robert Gale who died intestate with no issue and descended to his brothers and sisters George Gale, Littleton Gale, Levin Gale and Leah Wilson wife of Samuel Wilson.
2 Aug.1806 Leah Wilson sold to George Robertson 10 acres.
15 June 1810 George Robertson sold to George D. Atkinson 2 lots of LOWER FERRY now called WHITE HAVEN within the lines of MIGHT HAVE HAD MORE.
20 Mar.1810 George Robertson sold to George W. Jackson 10 acres as trustee of Elizabeth Ann Wilson Gale and Henry Gale minors and heirs of Levin Gale.
1829 George Robertson willed to daughter Sarah Anne Waters Dennis.

MIGHT HAVE HAD MORE ALS FINISH ALL

see NOBLE QUARTER

MILES END

Patented on 22 May 1688 by Edward Wright for 100 acres in Nanticoke near head of Barren Creek..
1 Aug.1710 Edward Wright sold to Richard Parremore 75 acres.
1 Aug.1721 Richard Parremore of Sussex Co.Del. sold to Edward Whitty of Somerset County. 75 acres
Rent Rolls 1666-1723 possessed by the widow of John Parremore 150 acres and 150 acres by John Lame.
2 June 1738 Jeremiah Wright sold to James Tully 300 acres on the south side of Barren Creek.
18 Nov.1762 John Smith of Worc.Co. sold to Joseph Venables of Somerset County 150 acres.
8 Mar.1765 Edward Wright am bound to make over 150 acres to Benjamin Venables and Jacob Smith.
1770 Resurveyed by Joseph Venables for 256 acres.
1783 tax- Joseph Venables 406 acres rewastico 100
1788 Joseph Venables with wife Nelly Venables sold to Joshua Bratten son of James Bratten and Mary Bratten.
1834 Joshua Bratten sold to the trustees one acre for schoolhouse and burying ground and preaching house.
1838 Joshua Bratten willed to son Joseph Bratten tract on Barren Creek Springs (unnamed.)
this became part of MARDELLA SPRINGS TOWN.

MILES LUCK & MILES GOOD LUCK

Patented in 1819 by John Miles of William Miles 31 1/4 acres of MILES LUCK
Patented in 1819 for 6 5/8 acres by John Miles of William Miles MILES

GOOD LUCK.

MILFORD

Patented in 1773 by Peter Gordy for 50 acres
1775 ADDITION TO MILFORD patented by Peter Gordy Jr. 323 1/2 acres
1783 tax - Peter Gordy 143 acres.
22 Oct.1790 Zadock Sturgis, sheriff sold to Thomas Harwood of Annapolis ADDITION TO MILFORD 180 acres per judgement against Benjamin F.A.C. Dashiell s/o Joseph Dashiell except dower of Susanna Dashiell widow of Joseph.
27 Apr.1797 Peter Gordy, Elisha Parker with wife Eleanor Parker, Samuel Parker with wife Hetty Parker, Benjamin Hearn son of Samuel Hearn and William Hearn of Sussex Co. Delaware sold to William Gordy all rights of ADDITION TO MILFORD.
1811 Johnson Dennis willed to grandson Littleton Dennis
1825 Obediah Disharoon sold to Jehu Parsons 180 acres of ADDITION TO MILFORD and 150 acres of same and 145 acres of same.
1823 John Parker of E. gave to son John T. Parker.

MILFORD

Patented in 1798 by Daniel Fooks, Billy Fooks, Jonathan Fooks for 203 acres
8 Dec.1809 Billy Fooks, Daniel Fooks and Jonathan Fooks sold to Peter Parsons of John Parsons, part.
1830 Jonathan Fooks of Daniel Fooks willed to daughter Henrietta Byrd 57 acres.
13 May 1833 Thomas Fooks of Sussex Co.Del. with wife Sally Fooks sold to Simon P. Parsons.

MILKMORE

Patented on 23 Oct.1696 by Samuel Fluellin for 50 acres on the north side of the mouth of the Wicomico River.
Rent Rolls 1666-1723 possessed by the widow Fluellin
1783 tax - Jane Fluellin 50 acres
13 July 1789 Samuel Fluellin sold 50 acres to George Robertson
26 Mar.1793 Gillis Polk surviving trustee of Ephraim King and Samuel Fluellin sold to Isaac Atkinson son of Isaac WOOLF QUARTER, FLUELLINS PURCHASE, MILKMORE, ADDN. TO PRICKLECOX HOLT, TICKNELL, etc.

MILL CHANCE

Patented on 26 Oct.1762 by Whittington Johnson for 9 acres
18 Apr.1776 Sussex Co.Delaware land warrants- John Houston

MILLERS LOT

Patented in 1793 by Isabella Miller for 39 acres

MILL FORK

Patented in 1760 by Joshua Robinson Jr. for 85 acres.
10 July 1776 Sussex Co.Del. land warrents Joshua Robinson Jr. of Baltimore Md.

MILL FRAME RIDGE

Patented in 1783 by Middleton Atkins for 25 acres
25 July 1795 Middleton Atkins sold to Purnell Johnson 25 acres.

MILL GROVE

Patented in 1795 by William Winder for 604 3/4 acres
1793 part of MILL GROVE patented by William Winder for 88 1/2 acres.
20 Feb.1802 William Winder sold to Isaac Eshum 166 9/10 acres
6 Dec.1806 Isaac Eshum sold to Eben Christopher 2 3/4 acres
1808 William Winder willed to son William Henry Winder
14 Oct.1809 William Henry Winder of Baltimore Md. sold part to James Laird, at Salisbury.
15 Sep.1810 James Laird with wife Dorothy Arietta Laird sold to John Huffman
15 Sep.1810 John Huffman and wife Catherine Huffman sold to James Laird.
15 Sep.1810 James Laird with wife Dorothy Arietta Laird sold to William Williams.

MILL LOTT

Patented on 3 June 1695 by Lambrook Thomas for 100 acres
Rent Rolls 1666-1723 possessed by Lambrook Thomas
1713 Lambrook Thomas willed to son and daughter Mary Cordrey wife of John Cordrey.
8 Apr.1730 Mary Cordrey wife of John Cordrey sold 100 acres to Levin Gale.
14 July 1742 Levin Gale sold to George Parris 100 acres.
18 Oct.1746 George Parris and wife Elizabeth Parris gave to Samuel Donnell and wife Elizabeth Donnell 100 acres.
27 Mar.1754 triparte- Samuel Donnell and wife Elizabeth Donnell sold to Isaac Handy and Henry Waggamen.
2 June 1783 Nathaniel Ramsey, comissioner to sell British property sold 61 1/4 acres to William Adams of MILL LOTT (could be other land)
9 Sep.1806 Lambert Hyland and Henry James Carroll surviving adminstrators of William Adams sold to Peter Dashiell on Tony Tank Creek.

MILL LOT

Patented in 1740 by Peter Calloway for 75 acres

MILL LOT

Patented on 23 July 1759 by Joseph Collins for 10 acres

MILL LOT

Patented on 1 Oct.1761 by George Vance for 20 acres

MILL LOT

Patented in 1762 by Nathan Culver for 2 acres

He repatented in 1770 for 65 acres.
1783 tax - John Culver 65 acres, Wic.100 Worc.Co.
1783 tax - Ebenezer Waller 2 acres, Rewastico 100
28 May 1785 Nathan Culver sold to James Weatherly Waller heir of Ebenezer Waller and Esme Marshall Waller son of William Cottman Waller and Thomas Waller PEACE & QUIETNESS with 22 acres of MILL LOT
22 Aug.1789 Nathan Culver sold 19 1/2 acres to William Elzey of POINT PATIENCE & MILL LOTT.
28 Nov.1789 Nathan Culver sold to Joshua Hitch Sr. 35 acres of PEACE & QUIETNESS, MILL LOTT and POINT PATIENCE
15 June 1799 William Hitch and John Hitch with wife Jean Hitch, sons of Joshua Hitch Jr. sold to Thomas Humphries.
13 Oct.1802 James Weatherly Waller sold to Esme Marshall Waller.

MILL LOT

Patented in 1770 by David Cathell for 327 1/2 acres.
22 Jan.1780 Jonathan Cathell sold 80 acres to Bela Cropper
26 Mar.1781 Daniel Cathell with wife Jane Cathell sold to Bela Cropper 80 acres.
1783 tax - John Cathell 11 acres, Wic.100. Worc.Co.
12 Mar.1796 James Perdue with wife Sarah Perdue sold to Aaron Mezick
1 Apr.1789 Bela Cropper with wife Mary Cropper sold to James Perdue 80 acres near head of Wicomico River.
1802 David Cathell willed to son Joshua Cathell 325 1/2 acres.
4 Nov.1805 Zachariah Parsons sold to Purnell Johnson 16 1/2 acres
16 Jan.1806 Zachariah Parsons with wife Abigail Parsons sold to Benjamin Brumbley 1 1/3 acres.
16 Jan.1806 Zachariah Parsons sold to Johnson Dennis 82 acres.
16 Jan.1806 Zachariah Parsons with wife Abigail Parsons sold to Jonathan Parsons of John Parsons 48 1/2 acres.
3 Jan.1831 James M. Cathell sold to Matthias O. Toadvine 1/8th part of mill and MILL LOT called ROACHES MILL.

MILL LOT

Patented in 1772 by Stephen Toadvine for 126 1/2 acres

MILL LOT

Patented in 1744 by William McBryde
18 Feb.1809 James Ritchie trustee to sell real estate of William McBryde sold to William Johnson Coulbourn 252 1/4 acres of PARKERS CHANCE, POPES FOLLY, MILL LOT, GIBBONS LIBERTY.

MILL LOTT

Patented on 2 Dec.1782 by Joseph Dashiell from RUM RIDGE for 19 acres.
1783 tax - Capt. Joseph Dashiell Wic.100 Worc.Co.
22 Oct.1790 Zadock Sturgis Esq, sheriff sold to Thomas Harwood of Annapolis per judgement against Benjamin F.A. C. Dashiell, except dower right of Susanna Dashiell widow of Joseph Dashiell
18 Dec.1790 Thomas Harwood with wife Margaret Harwood of Annapolis sold to Purnell Johnson of Worc.Co. part.
11 Feb.1791 Purnell Johnson sold to Thomas Johnson part.

14 Sep.1791 Purnell Johnson, Elijah Johnson and William Hearn sold to Benjamin Johnson.

MILL LOT

Patented in 1787 by William Polk for 16 acres

MILL LOT

Patented in 1799 by Eli Showell for 143 acres
12 Mar.1806 Eli Showell of Kent Co. Delaware with wife Sarah Showell sold to Hezekiah D. Shockley of Maryland, rights.

MILL LOT

Patented in 1807 by Abraham Taylor for 10 acres.

MILLRIGHTS GOOD INTENT

Patented on 20 Sep.1759 by George Parker in Wicomico Forest, for 30 acres
1765 George Parker willed lands to be sold.
21 Dec. 1793 Levi King of Sussex Co.Delaware impowered by John Parker conveyed to Jacob Evans.

MILL SECURITY

Patented in 1744 by John Caldwell for 70 acres. (this probably became part of Salisbury Town.)
1754 John Caldwell sold to William Venables
25 June 1774 William Venables Sr. sold to Gustavous Scott 20,504 sq.ft.
23 July 1774 William McClemmy sold to John Craig and William Dymock part, description
1775 William Venables sold to son John Venables part.
1783 tax - Abraham Gullett 1 acre, Wic.100
1783 tax - Dr. James Houston 1/2 acres
1783 tax - Hamilton Austin 1/2 acre
1783 tax - Stephen Christopher 3/4 acre
1783 tax - William Dymock 1 1/2 acre
1783 tax - William McBryde 1/4 acre
1783 tax - James McLeary 1/4 acre
1783 tax - John Nelms 1 acre
1783 tax - Richard Richards 1 acre
1783 tax - John Venables 30 acres
1783 tax - George Stevens 1/2 acre
1783 tax - Benjamin Riley 1/2 acre
1783 tax - Robert Dashiell 3/4 acre
30 Apr.1785 William Dymock with wife Hannah Dymock sold to John Mitchell of Sussex Co.Del. part that bounds landing place in Salisbury.
24 Oct.1786 John Venables sold to Dr. James Houston, land William Venables willed to him, no name or acres.
12 Dec.1788 Katharine Scroglimour sold to James Houston 2 acres willed Polly Venables by William Venables.
26 Apr.1791 Ezekiah Keen with wife Catherine Green of Dorc.Co.sold to

Catherine Howard of Somerset Co. 4 acres left by William Venables to Catherine Howard.
13 July 1791 Esme Bayley, Gillis Polk and William McBryde sold to William Winder Jr. - to sell real estate of John Mitchell late of Sussex Co.Del. for payment of debts 30 1/2 acres.
22 May 1793 John Denwood, sheriff sold to Dr. Robert Lemon part that William Venables willed to son John Venables. John Venables became insolvent and delivered his property to John Denwood, sheriff.
9 Aug.1794 William Jones with wife Ann Jones of St.Marys Co. sold to Robert Lemon. As Samuel Caldwell left to daughter Ann Caldwell who married William Jones adjacent PEMBERTONS GOOD WILL.
27 Sep.1794 William Jones of St. Marys Co. and wife Ann Jones daughter of Samuel Caldwell sold 33 1/2 acres to William Winder.
29 Mar.1806 Robert Lemon and wife Nancy Lemon sold to John Rider 1504 sq.ft.
11 Oct.1806 William Winder and William Hearn sold to Ebenezer Leonard part near Salisbury.
25 Mar.1808 William Winder sold to Ebenezer Leonard a lot.
1808 William Winder willed to son William Henry Winder
4 Apr.1809 William Hearn sold to Ebenezer Leonard for 5 shillings a lot.
29 Aug.1809 John Wilkins Esq, sheriff sold to John Rider per judgement against John Houston (aka CHANCE)
10 Mar.1810 Robert Lemon sold to John Rider MILL SECURITY near Salisbury.
30 June 1810 Robert Lemon and wife Nancy Lemon of Salisbury sold to Purnell Trader a lot.
18 Nov.1809 Robert Lemon with wife Nancy Lemon sold to Nancy Townsend of Worc.Co. part.

MILL SUPPLY

Patented in 1794 by John Cathell for 75 1/2 acres
15 Feb.1795 John Cathell sold to John Johnson and Joshua Johnson 52 acres
1808 John Cathell willed to son David Cathell.
1 May 1832 James M. Cathell brother of David Cathell sold to Jesse Fooks
1819 Charles Fooks son of Jesse willed to son Jesse Fooks part.

MILLS FRIENDSHIP

Patented in 1854 by John M. Mills for 266 7/8 acres.

MILLS PLEASURE

Patented in 1814 by Stephen Mills and Benjamin Mills for 59 1/2 acres resurveyed in 1840 by John M. Mills and L.M. Mills for 61 1/4 acres

MISFORTUNE

Patented in 1755 by Robert Collier Jr. for 21 acres.
1783 tax - Robert Collier Sr. 21 acres Nanticoke 100
25 Sep.1790 Douty Collier and wife Helena Collier sold to William Dashiell all interest. As Robert Collier willed plantation and small

piece adjacent to son Douty Collier and to daughter Nelly Dashiell wife of William Dashiell.
16 Mar.1793 Ebenezer Collier sold to William Dashiell lands of Robert Collier, no name.
28 Mar.1783 William Bounds with wife Bridget Bounds sold to William Dashiell lands of Robert Collier.
1844 Jacob Dashiell, negro willed to daughter Hester Dashiell 2 1/2 acres purchased of George Hopkins.

MISTRUST

Patented in 1788 by Elihu Mezick 2 acres
1788 Elihu Mezick willed to wife Margaret Mezick and after death to sons Elihu, John Mezick and Daniel Mezick.

MITCHELLS CHANCE

Patented in 1770 by Benjamin Mitchell for 131 1/2 acres

MITCHELLS FIRST PURCHASE

see WOODFIELDS

MOANEN

Patented on 20 Oct.1721 by William Polk for 100 acres on a branch of the Nanticoke River
Rent Rolls 1666-1723 possessed by William Polk.
10 June 1758 James Polk gave to son Joshua Polk 200 acres of DONNEGAL & MONANEN.
1783 tax - William Dutton 100 acres, Wicomico 100

MONMOUTH

Patented on 31 Oct.1674 by John Evans for 300 acres on the north side of Quantico Creek.
3 Apr.1676 John Evans sold to Jeremiah Webb
26 May 1684 Jeremiah Webb and wife Ann Webb sold to John Bowler 300 acres.
Rent Rolls 1666-1723 possessed by Oliver South in the right of one Webb in Northumberland Co. Virginia
28 June 1743 Day Scott mortgaged to James Bounds 75 acres at Rewastico Mill.
16 Sep.1755 Elizabeth Cathell wife of David Cathell daughter of Thomas Webb late of St.Stephens Parish, Northumberland Co.Va. sold 300 acres to Day Scott.
5 Dec.1758 George Day Scott son of Day Scott sold to John Nelson 150 acres
5 Dec.1758 George Day Scott sold to Joseph Holder 75 acres of 5 shillings.
23 Feb.1760 Joseph Holder and wife Isabell Holder sold 75 acres to Ephraim King.
16 May 1767 George Day Scott and wife Elizabeth Scott sold to Henry Gale 70 acres that Day Scott contracted for sale but willed to his son Matthew Scott. Release of part.
23 Feb.1773 Ephraim King sold 75 acres to Thomas Handy.
25 Oct.1775 Thomas Handy son of John Handy deceased sold part to

Ephraim King.
16 Nov.1782 Samuel King and wife Mary King gave bond to Matthew Kemp to make over CHELSEA & MONMOUTH and after his death to Eleanor Kemp. If no issue to revert to the heirs of Matthew Kemp.
1783 tax - Henry Gale 75 acres, Rewastico 100
1783 tax - Matthew Kemp 75 acres
1783 tax - James Nelson 100 acres.
1784 John Nelson willed part to son James Nelson and balance to son John Nelson.
1787 NELSONS ADDITION TO MONMOUTH pat. John Nelson 94 3/4 acres
1788 NELSONS ADDITION TO MONMOUTH pat. John Nelson for 204 acres.
23 Sep.1796 Samuel Wilson with wife Leah Littleton Wilson sold for 5 shillings to Eleanor Nelson wife of John Nelson CHELSEA & MONMOUTH.
23 Sep.1796 George Gale of Cecil Co. and Levin Gale with wife Leah Gale sold to Eleanor Nelson and John Nelson for 5 shillings all rights.
24 Jan.1798 Matthew Kemp sold all rights to John Nelson
22 Sep.1800 John Nelson with wife Eleanor Nelson gave part to son Francis Nelson.
13 Jan.1804 James Nelson with wife Esther Nelson sold to Augustus Cannon all except 63 3/4 acres and part of ADDITION 9 1/4 acres
17 Aug.1804 Henry Gale sold to John Gale, per agreement to divide the real estate of Capt. Henry Gale.
9 Nov.1804 John Nelson sold to Augustus Cannon MONMOUTH,ADDITION TO MONMOUTH & GALES DISCOVERY.
24 Aug.1806 Charles Nutter with wife Louisa Nutter sold to Henry E. Bayley 331 1/2 acres of ROSS, MIDDLE TRACT, DELIGHT, MONMOUTH.
21 Oct.1808 Henry E. Bayley with wife Sarah Bayley sold to Thomas Mitchell same as above.
9 Aug.1809 Daniel Ballard, sheriff sold to Alexander Stewart, per judgement against Augustus Cannon 156 3/4 acres of MONMOUTH, ADDN. TO MONMOUTH, GALES DISCOVERY and HARRIS LOTT.
9 Oct.1810 Daniel Wailes of Worc.Co. sold to John Stewart of Som. Co. his part of distribution of the real estate of Alexander Stewart, no name.
13 March 1818 Henry Gale sold to George Bounds MONMOUTH aka GEORGE GALES GENEROSITY in town of Quantico Mills 15906 sq.ft.
1 July 1818 George Gale sold to John Bounds of William Bounds lot in town of Quantico called MIDDLE LOTT or GALES GENEROSITY 148 sq.ft.
10 Nov.1841 John Austin sold to James Bounds 112 acres, parts of MONMOTH, CHELSEA & DELIGHT formerly belonging to Francis D. Nelson and Henry Gale.

MONMOUTH

Patented in 1754 by Thomas Moore for 760 acres

MONSHAM

Patented on 3 July 1683 by John Christopher
Rent Rolls 1666-1723 possessed by John Christopher
1748 John Christopher willed to son John plantation where I live, unnamed.
23 May 1772 John Christopher with wife Sarah Christopher sold 1 acre to Heber Whittingham.
1783 tax - John Christopher 93 acres, Wic.100, Worc.Co.

2 Aug.1800 John Stewart and wife Sarah Stewart sold part to Boardvine Bayley.
11 Feb.1802 Elizabeth White sold to Loudy Price.
31 Jan.1805 Elizabeth White sold 3 3/8 acres to Ezekiel Savage from her father John Christopher
11 Apr.1808 Ezekiel Savage and wife Jane Savage sold 1/2 acre to John Stanford.
1848 Sarah Stewart willed to grandson Robert James Stewart.

MONTREAL

Patented in 1763 by Horatio Taylor for 343 1/4 acres

MONTEREY

Patented in 1850 by Raymond Lamar and Jacob Lamar for 72 1/8 acres.

MOOREFIELDS

Patented in 1769 by Jacob Aires for 693 acres
24 July 1765 Jacob Aires sold 42 acres to Daniel McIntyre.
24 July 1765 Jacob Aires sold 193 1/2 acres to George Robertson.
29 Oct.1765 George Robertson sold 54 acres to John Evans.
1783 tax - Littleton Aires 456 acres Nanticoke 100
1783 tax - George Robertson 130 1/2 acres
1783 tax - Betty McIntyre widow of Daniel McIntyre. 42 1/2 acres
12 Nov.1785 John McIntyre son of Daniel sold all rights to George Aires.
1 Dec.1807 Littleton Aires sold to Isaac Atkinson 7 5/8 acres, a trade for PRICKLE COXHOLT.
14 Dec.1808 Benjamin Dashiell of James Dashiell, with wife Isabella Dashiell sold to Chaplin Conway 280 1/4 acres of MOOREFIELDS, EVANS SECOND CHANCE.
19 May 1809 Matthias D. Hopkins with wife Eleanor Hopkins sold to David Walston 20 acres.
29 Apr.1809 Samuel Robertson with wife Eleanor Robertson and Thomas Robertson sold for 5 shillings 14 1/4 acres to Elias Robertson.
6 May 1809 Elias Robertson with wife Eleanor Robertson sold to Samuel Robertson for 5 shillings 7 1/4 acres.
6 May 1809 Matthias D. Hopkins with wife Eleanor Hopkins sold to Samuel Robertson 17 acres 1 rod. 23 perches.
6 May 1809 Matthias D. Hopkins with wife Eleanor Hopkins sold to Elias Robertson 25 acres
6 May 1809 Samuel Robertson with wife Eleanor Robertson and Thomas Robertson sold to Matthias D. Hopkins 112 acres for 5 shillings.
2 May 1810 David Walston sold 10 1/4 acres to George Willin
2 May 1810 David Walston sold 10 1/4 acres to Henry Willin of Francis Willin.
1846 William Robertson willed to grandaughter Mary Absalom, where her father Henry Absalom lives. (1850 Tyaskin district)

MOORESFIELD and MOORES CHANCE

Patented by John Moore for 160 acres.
15 May 1759 Shadrack Driskell and wife Nelly Driskell of Worc.Co. sold

to Obediah Disharoon 160 acres of MOORESFIELD and resurveyed to MOORES CHANCE with 30 acres of vacancy added. John Moore willed to daughter Nelly Moore who married afsd. Shadrack Driskell.
13 Dec.1769 George Lane Moore sold 50 acres to Samuel Hearn of MOORES CHANCE.
1849 John Disharoon willed to son James Disharoon and part to daughter Mariah Fooks four chilcren, John Fooks, Elizabeth Fooks, Anthony Fooks and Letishay Fooks, 60 acres.

MOORES JOY

Patented on 13 July 1759 by John Lane Moore
22 Mar.1776 Sussex Co.Del. land warrants, pat. by Samuel Hearn.

MOORES LOT

Patented on 15 June 1759 by Joshua Moore for 353 acres
10 Feb.1763 Joshua Moore sold 86 acres to David Greer
10 Feb.1763 Joshua Moore sold to William Waller 120 acres
17 June 1769 William Waller sold 63 acres to James Waller with ROUND SAVANAH
25 June 1776 Sussex Co.Del. land warrants, pat. by George Greer

MOORES SECOND CHANCE

Patented in 1730 by John Moore for 50 acres
18 Oct.1737 John Moore and wife Mary Moore sold to Job Serman 50 acres between banks of Nanticoke and Wicomico Rivers.
18 Apr.1776 Sussex Co.Del.land warrants, to Job Serman

MOORES VENTURE

Patented in 1762 by William Moore for 27 1/4 acres
1783 tax - William Moore Jr. 27 1/2 acres, Rewastico 100
1788 William Moore willed to grandson Thomas Moore son of Levin Moore, in Leatherburys Neck.

MOORES DELIGHT

Patented in 1812 by Henry Moore for 20 3/4 acres

MORGANS VENTURE

Patented in 1740 by Joseph Morgan for 50 acres.
7 Sep.1770 David Owens sold to Nehemiah Stayton 21 acres, 86 perches.
14 Feb.1775 David Owens sold to William Gaskins 27 acres on the north east branch of the Nanticoke River.

MORE LOSS THAN GAIN

Patented in 1757 a resurvey from FAIR RIDGE and part of HAZARD by Joseph Dashiell for 185 acres near the mouth of the Nanticoke River.
1775 ADDITION patented Joseph Dashiell 53 \1/4 acres
1783 tax - John Jones 238 1/4 acres, Nanticoke 100
1788 Joseph Dashiell willed to grandson John Jones of Benjamin Jones

the tract ADDITION adjacent.
1832 John Jones son of Benjamin Jones and Elizabeth Dashiell Jones made a will. This land not mentioned.

MORRIS'S ADVENTURE

Patented in 1749 by Dennis Morris for 50 acres
5 Oct.1762 Dennis Morris of Sussex Co.Del. sold 50 acres to John Richardson.

MORRIS'S CONCLUSION

Patented in 1811 by Jacob Morris for 431 3/4 acres
Resurveyed in 1801 by Joshua Morris for 341 acres
20 Mar.1802 Joshua Morris of Worc.Co. sold to Eben Disharoon 24 1/2 acres with CHANCE & DISHAROONS ADVENTURE.
1819 Joshua Morris willed to wife Amelia Morris, on the west side of the road dividing Som.Co.and Worc.Co. 1/3 of and to granchildren William Gunby, Sarah Gunby, Mary A. Gunby and James Gunby 1/4th acre adjacent the lot of Jeptha Morris out of MORRIS CONCLUSION and balance to grandson Joshua Morris.

MORRIS'S DELIGHT

Patented on 26 Nov.1672 by Jenkins Morris for 300 acres near the Nanticoke.
13 Mar.1746 Florence Sullivan and wife Sarah Sullivan of Dorc.Co. sold 300 acres to Edward Kellum and John Huffington of Somerset County.
26 Nov.1801 Jonathan Huffington sold to William Russum 100 acres of MORRIS DELIGHT & ILL NEIGHBORHOOD & BARREN QUARTER.
This was resurveyed into ILL NEIGHBROHOOD.

MORRIS'S DESIRE

Patented in 1762 by Joseph Morris for 100 acres
17 Nov.1767 Joseph Morris sold to John Henry Carey 100 acres.

MORRIS DISCOVERY

Patented in 1794 by James Round Morris a resurvey of HUNGARY QUARTER
5 Aug.1798 Leah Morris, William Morris, Levin Winder, execs. of James Round Morris sold to Reubin Davis.
15 Aug.1798 Leah Morris, William Morris, Levin Winder execx. of James Round Morris sold to Stephen Townsend 46 1/4 acres of MORRIS DISCOVERY AND SAW MILL LOTT.
15 Aug.1798 same as above sold to Joshua Pollitt 48 3/8 acres.
17 Nov.1798 Reubin Davis with wife Sarah Davis and Stephen Davis sold to Jordan Parsons 8 acres with LAND DOWN
17 Nov.1798 Joshua Pollitt sold to Jordan Parsons 6 acres
15 Aug.1798 Reubin Davis sold to Leah Morris and William Morris executors of will of James Round Morris, part.

MORRIS DISCOVERY

Patented in 1812 by Joshua Morris

MORRIS'S FANCY

Patented in 1793 by Jacob Morris for 17 1/4 acres
15 June 1803 Jacob Morris sold part to John Morris son of Joseph Morris.
13 Mar.1804 John Morris sold to Jacob Morris son of Joseph Morris, part.

MORRIS'S FROLIC

Patented in 1803 by John Morris for 34 1/2 acres
1810 John Morris of Joseph Morris willed to sons Joseph and John H. Morris 26 acres.

MORRIS'S HUNDRED

Patented in 1806 by Jacob Morris for 361 acres

MORRISS LOTT

Patented on 17 May 1688 by Manasses Morris for 300 acres on branch of the Quantico.
3 May 1688 Manasses Morris and wife Elizabeth Morris sold 100 acres to William Elgate.
7 Dec.1720 Capt. Charles Ballard and wife Eleanor Ballard sold 200 acres to Solomon Wright that he purchased from Andrew Caldwell attorney for Manasses Morris.
9 July 1744 Solomon Wright with wife Sarah traded to Thomas Records 40 acres for same conveyed to William Wright of Solomon .
9 July 1744 Benjamin Records of Dorc.Co. and wife Elizabeth Records traded with Thomas Records of Som. Co. and wife Sarah Records MORRIS LOTT at branch of Quantico Creek for land in Dorc.Co. that formerly belonged to John Lame grandfather of Elizabeth Records and Sarah Records.
9 July 1744 Thomas Records and wife Sarah Records daughter of John Lame the younger sold to William Wright of Solomon Wright 100 acres that Manasses Morris conveyed to John Lame the elder grandfather of the wife of Thomas Records.
24 May 1751 Thomas Records and wife Sarah Records sold to Thomas Lankford 80 acres for 10 shillings.
20 Mar.1753 Henry Ballard and Solomon Wright and Thomas Records sold 200 acres to Charles Ballard.
25 Jan.1755 Thomas Lankford Jr. sold to Thomas Roberts 50 acres.
5 Apr.1757 Triparte agreement -Thomas Lankford and William Hayward and Henry Lowe, division of lands CHANCE, GOOD WILL & MORRIS LOTT near Quantico Branch adjacent that Thomas Lankford has the right from the will of his father Thomas Lankford.
17 Apr.1762 Thomas Records with wife Sarah Records sold 100 acres to Lame Records.
27 Mar.1769 Thomas Records and wife Sarah Records sold 100 acres to John Dorman.
13 Dec.1769 Henry Lowe sold to James Jones for 5 shillings part that Thomas Lankford had a right.
21 Oct.1769 Thomas Records and wife Elizabeth Records sold 170 acres to William Rencher.
1783 tax - Lame Records 183 acres

MORRIS'S LOTT

Patented on 16 Nov.1675 by Jenkins Morris for 100 acres who sold to Christopher Nutter.
Rent Rolls 1666-1723 possessed by Christopher Nutter 50 acres and Matthew Nutter 50 acres
3 Oct.1720 John Nutter of Sussex Co. Del. sold 100 acres to Christopher Nutter.
1729 Christopher Nutter willed to son Christopher and William Nutter lands, unnnamed.
2 Dec.1738 Christopher Nutter sold 100 acres to John Cox that Christopher Nutter the elder bought of Jenkins Morris.
27 Dec.1749 John Cox and wife Isabelle Cox sold to Hezekiah Dorman 100 acres.
6 Mar.1775 John Dorman sold 95 acres to William Winder.
1783 tax - John Dorman 43 acres
1783 tax - William Nutter Sr. 110 acres.
1783 William Nutter willed lands to son William.
17 Jun 1786 James Makemorie Jones and John Dorman sold to Levin Winder 30 acres.
5 Jan.1790 Jabez Tilghman with wife Ann Tilghman, lately Ann Dorman sodl 52 acres to William Done.
5 Jan.1793 William Nutter sold to William Done 52 acres, per partition with Jabez Tilghman.
27 Aug.1793 William Done with wife Ann Done sold 104 acres to William Cottman son of Joseph Cottman.

MORRIS'S LOT

Patented on 29 July 1794 by William Cottman for 112 acres
1796 William Cottman son of Joseph Cottman sold 104 acres to Levin Farrington
13 Sep.1808 Levin Farrington mortgaged to Farmers Bank of Md.

MORRIS'S PURCHASE

no patent found
26 Aug.1749 Jacob Morris with wife Rebecca Morris sold to James Smith 100 acres formerly purchased of John Leatherbury by Jacob Morris deceased. the whole containing 200 acres and divided by the will of Jacob Morris to sons Levin Morris and Jacob Morris.
22 Mar.1786 Joseph Morris s/o Jacob sold 10 acres to Martin Bowles.
1801 repatented by Jacob Morris for 98 acres.

MORRIS RESOLUTION

Patented in 1765 by Joseph Morris for 9 acres
1783 tax - Joseph Morris 9 1/2 acres, Wic.100 Worc.Co.
1786 Joseph Morris willed to son John Malone Morris 9 1/2 acres.
1810 John Morris of Joseph Morris willed 9 acres to sons Joseph and John H. Morris.

MORRIS VENTURE

Patented in 1774 by Joseph Morris for 4 acres

MOTHERTON

Patented in 1841 by Joseph S. Cottman for 665 5/8 acres

MOUNT ALEXANDER

Patented 16 Aug.1715 Tobias Burke for 105 acres, resurvey of parts of NOBLE QUARTER, LITTLE MONMOUTH & THE ADVENTURE.
19 Mar.1726 Tobias Burke and wife Hannah Burke sold to Thomas Dashiell 105 acres, on the west side of Shields Creek.
24 Dec.1732 Thomas Dashiell sold 105 acres to son Charles Dashiell.
9 Jan.1759 Thomas Dashiell s/o Thomas gave to son Josiah Dashiell 105 acres.
17 June 1743 Charles Dashiell and wife Elizabeth Dashiell traded with Josiah Dashiell MT ALEXANDER & FATHERS PURCHASE.
1 June 1765 Josiah Dashiell and wife Mary Dashiell sold 105 acres to Isaac Atkinson.
1783 tax - Elizabeth Atkinson 105 acres.

MOUNT CHARLES

Patented in 1750 by Jacob Carter for 50 acres
10 Sep.1769 Jacob Carter sold 50 acres to George Martin
Resurveyed to WHEEL OF FORTUNE

MOUNT CHARLES

Patented in 1756 by Jacob Spear for 66 acres
29 Jan.1770 Jacob Spear and wife Elizabeth Spear sold to Capt. Charles Dashiell 66 acres.
1783 tax - Charles Dashiell 61 acres
1800 Charles Dashiell willed to grandsons Charles and George Dashiell

MOUNT EPHRAIM

Patented in 1762 by Ephraim King for 467 1/2 acres
1777 Ephraim King willed to Mitchell Dashiell and William Donoho
21 Apr.1783 Samuel King traded to Mitchell Dashiell 82 1/2 acres for part of RECOVERY
1783 tax - Elizabeth King, Nanticoke 100
1783 tax - Samuel King 467 acres
1789 Mitchell Dashiell son of Thomas Dashiell willed to grandson Nicholson Collier and lands unnamed to daughter Peggy Nicholson wife of Isaac Nicholson.
26 July 1784 Samuel King with wife Mary King sold to John Stewart 997 3/4 acres of FISHERMANS QUARTER, HOG QUARTER, KINGS MISFORTUNE & MT. EPHRAIM.
25 Aug.1791 Nicholson Collier sold to Ephraim Wilson 82 1/2 acres
16 Nov.1795 Isaac Nicholson and wife Peggy Nicholson sold to Ephraim Wilson 78 acres of RECOVERY & MT. EPRHAIM that was willed to Peggy by her father Mitchell Dashiell.
28 Jan.1806 Ephraim Wilson son of George Wilson sold to Levin Farrington 78 acres of RECOVERY & MT. EPHRAIM.
21 Oct.1808 Ephraim Wilson of George Wilson with wife Esther Wilson and George D. Wilson with wife Amelia Wilson sold to Charles Jones 298

acres of RECOVERY, MT.EPHRAIM, WILSONS ADVENTURE, EPHRAIMS HOOK.

MOUNT HOPE

Patented on 2 Dec.1672 by William Wright for 150 acres.
8 Mar.1674 William Wright with wife Frances Wright sold to Oliver Haile 150 acres.
23 Aug.1679 Nehemiah Covington attorney for Oliver Haile sold to John Brown 150 acres.
20 Oct.1703 John Brown and wife Sarah Brown sold to William Bennett.
4 Aug.1713 Thomas Bennett and wife Catherine Bennett sold to Thomas Larramore 75 acres.
Rent Rolls 1666-1723 possessed by 75 acres William Bennett and 75 acres Thomas Larramore.
1719 Thomas Larramore sold 75 acres to Robert Collier.
19 Oct 1728 Thomas Larramore and wife Mary Larramore sold to Henry McCabe and wife Elizabeth McCabe their daughter.
19 Oct.1728 Thomas Larramore gave to Elias Venatson and his wife Catherine Venatson 65 acres.
1 Oct.1739 Elias Venatson and wife Catherine Venatson and Elias their son sold 130 acres to Daniel McIntyre.
1756 Robert Collier willed to son George Collier
21 Nov.1759 Daniel McIntyre and wife Elizabeth McIntyre sold 65 acres to Archibald Ritchie.
1783 tax - Delilah Ritchie widow of Archibald Ritchie 105 acres.
1783 tax - Robert Collier 45 acres
6 Feb.1801 Keturah Dashiell and Leah Dashiell sold to William Harris their claim to where grandfather Robert Collier had, no name.
2 Nov.1806 James Ritchie sold to Covington Cordrey part.
1823 John Jones of James willed to son Thomas Jones bought from James Willin.
17 Jan 1806 James Ritchie sold to Ebenezer Collier 92 1/2 acres

MT PLEASANT

Patented on 24 May 1684 by James Ingram for 150 acres near the main branch of the Wicomico River.
1682 James Ingram sold 150 acres to John Records.
13 Nov.1723 John Records Jr. son of John, with wife Susannah Records sold to William Carey.
1734 William Carey willed to sons Jonathan Carey and Thomas Carey.
10 Feb.1753 Jonathan Carey and Thomas Carey sold to George Wilson
26 Jan.1765 George Wilson sold to Benjamin Hitch 150 acres.
10 Feb.1752 Jonathan Carey and Thomas Carey sold 150 acres to George Wilson, confirmation of deed.
1 Aug.1770 Benjamin Hitch with wife Mary Hitch sold 50 acres to Thomas Price.
1783 tax - Benjamin Hitch 100 acres, Wic.100, Worc.Co.
1795 Ezekiel Gillis willed to son Joseph Dashiell Gillis if daughter Nelly Dashiell Gillis has no issue.
31 July 1802 Solomon Kibble Price and mother Patience Price sold to Jacob Morris 50 acres.
13 May 1803 Benjamin Hitch sold to Joseph Hitch 50 acres.
13 Sep.1809 Joseph Hitch of Pendleton Co.Ky. sold to John Hitch of Somerset Co.Md. 50 acres.

MT PLEASANT

Patented in 1801 by Robert Jones for 327 1/2 acres
1804 Robert Jones willed to wife Nelly Jones 220 acres and to son Robert Jones 132 acres.
1846 John Jones of Robert Jones willed to son Cyrus Jones.

MT SINAI

Patented in 1794 by Jenkins Kibble for 435 3/4 acres, a resurvey on HOG NECK
19 Feb.1800 Kibble Jenkins sold part to James Bennett.
4 Oct.1800 James Bennett sold 2 acres to William Crouch
4 Oc.1800 James Bennett sold to James Jones 5 7/8 acres in SHARPS POINT now called JAMES POINT.
1820 Benjamin Stevens willed to son Isaac Stevens 25 acres.
1830 Kibble Jenkins willed to George Willis son of Lotta Willis 70 acres.

MT TURSEY

Patented in 1758 by Thomas Fletcher for 57 acres
19 Aug.1766 Nathan Culver sold to Joseph Hitch 57 acres
10 Aug.1767 Joseph Hitch sold to Ezekiel Bell 57 acres
1783 tax - Ezekiel Bell 57 acres, Rewastico 100
Part resurveyed to SAW MILL SUPPLY 1765

MUIRS ADDITION TO SHARPS ADDITON

Patented on 15 Aug.1753 for 22 acres a resurvey of 15 acres by James Muir.

MUIRS ADVENTURE

Patented in 1734 by Adam Muir for 150 acres

MULBERRY LANDING

Patented in 1755 by Purnell Johnson out of PEMBERTON for 3 acres.
1759 Purnell Johnson sold to Isaac Handy
1760 Isaac Handy willed to son William Handy.
1783 tax- Elijah Johnson s/o Purnell Johnson 3 acres in Rewastico 100.
10 Mar.1787 Thomas Johnson sold to William Handy and Henry Handy to adjust lands called PEMBERTON & FRIENDS CHOICE, to determine lines of a parcel deeded by Purnell Johnson for 10 acres.
1817 Purnell Johnson willed to Purnell Johnson tract MULBERRY.

MULLINSFIELD

Patented on 24 May 1721 by John Roach for 50 acres
1726 John Roach willed to son William Roach 50 acres
1765 William Roach willed 50 acres to son Stephen Roach, after the death of son Levin Roach.
1769 ADDITION patented by Stephen Roach for 223 3/4 acres.
1783 tax - James Roach 50 acres of ADDN. TO MULLINSFIELD
13 Aug.1785 Levin Roach sold to Sarah Roach wife of James Roach for life, in consideration of her care of Levin and after her death to the

children she had by James Roach, Anne Roach, Matty Roach, Betsy Roach, Nelly Roach and Mary Bozman, all no acreage mentioned.
1808 John Cathell willed to son George Cathell.
2 June 1821 Levi Cathell sold to Ebenezer Leonard 25 acres. Levi trustee of John Cathell Sr. who devised lands to son George who died. It descended to brothers John Cathell Jr., David Cathell and James Martin Cathell. David Cathell died and John Jr. willed in 1820 his undivided half to be sold.

MUNSLEY

Patented on 26 June 1694 by William Elgate for 354 acres near Cottinghams Creek.
Rent Rolls 1666-1723 possessed by William Elgate 354 acres
1725 William Elgate willed to daughter Rebecca Bready 260 acres and balance to daughter Ann Hall (she married Thomas Hall)
19 Feb.1735 William Elgate sold to Levin Gale 11 acres laid out for a mill called Rokiawalkin Mill being part of MUNSLEY 1 acre.
1 Apr.1737 William Elgate sold to Levin Gale 100 acres.
1 Aug.1737 William Elgate with wife Catherine Elgate gave to daughter Catherine Driskell wife of Moses Driskell 150 acres part of 1/3rd of MUNSLEY & AVERS POLICY. They gave to daughter Rebecca Evans 150 acres.
13 Nov.1747 Moses Driskell and with Catherine Driskell, Ann Hall and Rebecca Evans (was Rebecca Bready) sold to William Murray that part that Levin Gale sold to William Murray 45 acres, that was never conveyed.
10 Mar.1770 Samuel Carter and wife Unice Carter and Sophia Bready alias Wright sold to Ezekiel Bell with BREADYS CHANCE 260 acres (this was called James Bready plantation and known as LONG POINT.
6 Apr.1790 William Driskell son of Catherine Driskell sold to William McBryde 150 acres.
7 July 1810 Sarah McBryde sold to John Rider
7 July 1810 John Rider sold to Sarah McBryde (division of lands.)

MURCKLE ISLAND

Patented on 21 Feb.1760 by Henry Hayman for 50 acres
8 Mar.1765 Henry Hayman with wife Mary Hayman sold to Levin Gunby 50 acres in Wicomico forest.
1767 resurveyed to LITTLEWORTH

MY ADDITION

Patented in 1762 by Obediah Disharoon for 50 acres

MY DELIGHT

Patented in 1729 by Robert Givans for 100 acres
1735 Robert Givans willed to son George Givans part of CYPRESS SWAMP and 100 acres adjacent, no name.

MY FORTUNE

6 Nov.1761 Whittington Draper of Kent Co in the government of New

Castle, Kent and Sussex sold to George Adams of Worc.Co. 300 acres on the south side of the Nanticoke River
11 Sep.1764 Whittington Draper sold same to George Adams, carpenter (confirmation of sale.)

MYRTLE MEADOW

Patented in 1774 by James Perdue for 50 acres
1797 ADDITION TO MYRTLE MEADOW patented to James Perdue for 97 1/4 acres.

MYRTLE RIDGE

Patented in 1771 by John Cathell for 161 3/4 acres
1772 James Cathell willed to grandsons Joshua Cathell and James Cathell sons of James.
27 Mar.1780 Joshua Cathell sold to Alexander Porter 91 3/4 acres.
1 Jan.1793 Betty Christopher sold to David Cathell 93 acres.
1821 ADDITION TO patented Solomon Townsend for 10 acres.
18 Mary 1824 Joshua Cathell of Kentucky sold to Levi Cathell
5 Feb.1820 Levi Cathell Jr. sold to Arthur Burroughs

NABOTH VINEYARD

Patented on 29 Sep.1763 by Naboth Dykes for 81 acres
1769 tax- William Dykes, 38 acres
4 Aug.1774 Naboth Dykes with wife Ann Dykes sold to Elijah Shockley 81 acres.
1783 tax - Elijah Shockley for 81 acres Wic.100 Worc.Co.
21 Jan.1809 Benjamin Johnson with wife Sarah Johnson sold to Matthew Jones 81 acres
8 Dec.1806 Capt. Elijah E. Shockley sold to Benjamin Johnson 81 acres
1810 Matthew Jones willed to daughter Nancy Jones 81 acres

NALZEY RENEWED

Patented in 1803 by Samuel Fletcher for 301 1/4 acres.

NANCYWAGAN

Patented in 1820 by William Bounds for 14 1/2 acres
24 Aug.1721 William Bounds of James Bounds, with wife Zipporah Bounds sold to John Nichols 14 1/2 acres on the north side of Rewastico Creek.

NANTES

Patented on 8 Sep.1682 by James Langstor for 100 acres who assigned to Julian Mezick
Rent Rolls 1666-1723 possessed by Julian Mezick for 100 acres
4 July 1710 Julian Mezick gave to sons John Mezick, Jacob Mezick, Joshua Mezick and Julian Mezick.
29 Aug.1746 Nehemiah Mezick of Som.Co. and John Mezick of Worc.Co. sold 50 acres to Elihu Mezick, bricklayer
1788 Elihu Mezick son of Jacob Mezick of Julian Mezick willed to wife Margaret Mezick 50 acres and then to sons Elihu Mezick, John Mezick and Daniel Mezick.

NANTICOKE FORGE AND DEEP CREEK FURNACE

19 June 1764 John Spicer sold to Jonathan Vaughan ironmaster, William Douglas, David McMurke, Persisor Frazier, Christopher Marshall druggist, of Philadelphia Pa. and John Chamberlin of Chester Co. Pa. SPICERS INHERITANCE 32 acres, SPICERS PLEASURE 50 acres, WARRIOR LOSS 100 acres, SANDY LOTT 100 acres, ALLENS MANOR 200 acres, SAW MILL SUPPLY 199 acres, DOUBLE PURCHASE 100 acres.
13 Feb.1768 Jonathan Vaughan ironmaster with wife Ann Vaughan of Ashton in Chester Co. Pa.sold to Christopher Marshall of Philadelphia, William Wishart merchant of same, Jemima Edwards widow, William Douglas of Worc.Co.and Joseph Pennell his undivided part in DEEP CREEK FURNACE & NANTICOKE FORGE 5000 acres.
19 Oct.1767 David McMurke of Philad. with wife Margery McMurke sold to Joseph Pennell of same his interest in the partnership of casting and making pig and bar iron and erecting grist mills, sand mills on the waters of Deep Creek and Nanticoke River in Worcester Co. or Sussex Co. Delaware the lands being in dispute between the counties. THE STONES 50 acres, 400 acres purchased of John Spicer, WOODLAND 50 acres, SUCESS & STOUGHTONS GOOD WILL 150 acres, 153 acres pur/o Daniel Kelly, 150 acres pur/o Samuel Petty, 5 acres pur/o Joseph Boyce, WILLINS ADVENTURE 150 acres, SWAINS CHOICE 50 acres, PLEASANT MEADOW 100 acres, BROWNS INHERITANCE, VENTURE, ALLENS MANOR, ADDITION 333 acres CHANCE, BANNISTERS ADDITION, BANNISTERS CONCLSUION, FORKED NECK in Nanticoke River.
19 Oct.1767 Persisor Frazier of Ashton Township Pa. with wife Mary Frazier sold to Christopher Marshall of Philadelphia hin interest in the iron works.
12 Nov.1772 Christopher Marshall of Philadelphia sold to Benjamin Marshall, Christopher Marshall Jr. and Charles Marshall his children 1/5th part of the iron works.

NANTWICK

Patented in 1726 by Joseph Venables for 300 acres
20 Mar.1733 Benjamin Venables and wife Ann Venables gave 300 acres to brother William Venables.

NARROW NECK

Patented on 7 May 1758 by Daniel Dykes for 50 acres at the branch of the Wicomico River.
1768 tax- heirs of Daniel Dykes.
1774 tax- Arthur Dykes 50 acres.

NECESSITY

Patented in 1761 by Joseph Freeman for 10 acres

NEGLECT

Patented in 1801 by Leah Murray Slemons, Francis McBryde, Hugh McBryde, Elizabeth McBryde, Samuel McBryde and Sally McBryde.
21 Jan.1809 James Ritchie sold to Sarah McBryde the real estate of William McBryde 154 acres KINGS, NEGLECT & pt.NEWBERRY

27 Dec.1809 James Ritchie as trustee to sell the land of William McBryde sold to Samuel Hilman, with part of DOWGATE.

NEGLECT

Patented in 1801 by George Jones for 406 acres

NEHEMIAHS LOTT

Patented in 1759 by Nehemiah Morris for 84 acres
18 Apr.1776 Sussex Co.Del. lands warrents, Nehemiah Morris.

NEEDLESS COST

Patented in 1743 by John Piper and Joseph Piper for 150 acres as resurvey of WEATHERLYS PURCHASE.
1783 tax - George Phillips 150 acres.
16 Oct.1835 James Bounds and Susan L. Weatherly sold to Joseph Harris 282 acres, part of WILTON, SALISBURY PLAIN, NEEDLESS COST the lands of the heirs of Elihu Jackson and heirs of Levin Wilson.

NEIGHBORS FOREWARNING

Patented in 1774 by Levin Wright for 100 acres
1775 Levin Wright willed to daughter Mary Wright 50 acres and to son William Wright 50 acres.
11 June 1808 William Wright son of Levin Wright sold to Huffington Nicholson of Sussex Co.Del. 50 acres.
23 Dec.1808 Richard Johnson and wife Mary Johnson sod 50 acres to Huffington Nicholson of Sussex Co.Del. willed Mary Johnson by her father Levin Wright.

NEIGHBORS VEXATION

Patented in 1760 by Henry Graham for 285 acres
1783 tax - Ann Huffington 155 acres, Rewastico 100
1783 tax - William Hitch 140 acres
21 Nov.1804 John Wilkins, tax collector sold to Isaac Kennerly property of William Hitch, taken for delinquent taxes.
1 Feb.1805 Isaac Kennerly sold to Richard Johnson
1857 Benjamin Gravener willed part to son Benjamin P. Gravener and part to son Clement J. Gravener, bought of Asa Graham and James Graham.
1857 Algenon Johnson willed to son Daniel Webster Johnson, on road from Bacon Quarter to Vienna Md.
(in 1850 he was in Barren Creek District)

NELMS ADDITION

Patented in 1786 by John Nelms for 80 acres

NELMS CHANCE

Patented in 1785 by John Nelms for 18 1/2 acres

NELMS DIFFICULTY

Patented in 1770 by Edward Ellis for 55 acres
23 May 1774 Edward Ellis sold to John Nelms 55 acres.
1783 tax - Samuel Howard 55 acres, Rewastico 100

NELMS MEADOW

Patented on 26 Nov.1762 by Joshua Nelms for 22 1/2 acres
5 Mar.1762 Joshua Nelms with wife Sarah Nelms sold to Joseph Dashiell son of George Dashiell 22 1/2 acres
22 Oct.1790 Zadock Sturgis, sheriff sold to Thomas Harwood of Annapolis 11 1/2 acres per judgement against Benjamin F.A.C. Dashiell son of Joseph Dashiell.
25 July 1796 Thomas Harwood with wife Margaret Harwood sold to Joshua Johnson and Isaac Hearn 22 1/2 acres.

NELMS SUPPORT

Patented in 1785 by John Nelms for 40 acres

NELSONS ADVENTURE

Patented in 1808 by James Nelson for 517 1/2 acres resurvey of SUNKEN GROUND.

NEVER OUT DONE

Patented in 1797 by Elizabeth Henderson for 4 1/2 acres
1783 tax - Benjamin Henderson 10 acres, Wic.100

NEVINS ADDITION

Patented in 1772 by James Nevin for 24 acres
15 Aug.1778 William McBryde executor of James Nevin sold to John Cathell 24 acres on road to Salisbury Town
22 Feb.1800 John Cathell sold to Stewart Shockley 24 acres

NEW ADDITION

Patented in 1761 by John Gupton for 18 acres
1783 tax - Ann Gupton 18 acres.
1819 Ann Gupton widow of John Gupton willed to son Peter Gupton

NEWBURY

Patented on 27 Nov.1688 by Alexander Price for 300 acres
Rent Rolls 1666-1723 possessed by the widow Rebecca Price.
28 June 1746 Alexander Thomas Russell and wife Ann Price Russell sold to Obediah Reed 100 acres for 5 shillings.
12 Aug.1748 Levin Hitch and wife Eve Hitch daughter of Christopher Price sold 100 acres that became right of Eve by the death of her brother Solomon Price.
18 Mary 1767 Thomas Stanford and wife Rachel Stanford and John Reed sold to Isaac Handy, William Venables, John Henry of Dorset Co. 3

acres for chapel of the Presbyterian congregation in Wicomico.
16 Oct.1769 John Reed and wife Mary Reed sold 100 acres to Thomas Stanford.
13 Oct.1778 John Reed of Worc.Co. sold to Henry Handy of Som. Co. 100 acres. (as Christopher Price left two sons and 3 daughters. Both sons died young and daughter Rachel married Obediah Reed who purchased of the other two daughters Ann Price who married Alexander Thomas Russell annd Eve Price who married Levin Hitch. Obediah Reed died intestate and left son John Reed. The widow Rachel Price married Thomas Stanford and she died intestate.)
20 Aug.1771 John Reed sold his share 100 acres to Thomas Stanford for 5 shillings.
20 Feb.1779 Henry Handy sold 100 acres to William McBryde
1802 Thomas Stanford Jr. son of William willed to brother William Stanford.
22 Sep.1780 William Stanford sold to William McBryde -division of lands.
1783 tax - Thomas Stanford 297 acres, Rewastico 100
21 Jan.1809 James Ritchie sold 79 acres to Sarah McBryde real estate of William McBryde.

NEW CAREY

Patented in 1734 by Michael Lynch for 50 acres
15 Mar.1739 Michael Lynch and wife Isabell Lynch sold 50 acres to George Vinson on the n/w side of the Wicomico River.
1783 tax - George Vinson 50 acres, Rewastico 100
11 Mar.1790 George Vincent willed to son Curtis Martin Vincent, lands unnamed.
12 Jan.1793 Curtis Martin Thomason devisee of George Vinson sold 50 acres to Benjamin Hearn.
1802 Benjamin Hearn willed to wife Sarah Hearn land where George Vincent formerly lived, no name.

NEW CASTLE

Patented on 16 Sep.1675 by Stephen Cannon who assigned to Joseph Thompson for 100 acres.
Rent Rolls 1666-1723 possessed by James Langrell on the south side of Oyster Creek, 100 acres
8 Aug.1720 George Langrell of Dorc.Co. Md. traded 175 acres of BLESS ISLAND in Dorc.Co. for NEW CASTLE, with William Hickman Jr.
1765 William Hickman willed to son William.
1770 resurveyed by Stephen Hickman for 107 acres
18 July 1768 Stephen Hickman of Frederick County sold 100 acres to James Windsor of OLD CASTLE & NEW CASTLE.
1783 tax - James Windsor 105 acres

NEW CASTLE

Patented on 5 Dec.1768 by Benjamin Hamblin for 150 acres
1810 Benjamin Hamblin willed 80 acres to daughter Hessey Hamblin, of HAMBLINS NEW CASTLE.
NEW CASTLE POINT, a resurvey patented in 1848 by John Hamblin for 188 acres. (in 1850 he is in the 3rd district of Worc.Co.)

NEW CASTLE UPON NANTICOKE

Patented in 1803 by James Dean for 110 3/4 acres

NEW ENGLAND

Patented on 22 Jan 1754 by Samuel Daley for 100 acres.
1783 tax - John Nelms 100 acres, Wic.100 Worc.Co.
25 July 1796 Thomas Harwood of Annapolis sold to Joshua Johnson and Isaac Hearn.
16 Mar.1799 William Daley with wife Keziah Daley sold to Samuel T. Parker 2 acres of NEW ENGLAND & COX'S NEGLECT
12 July 1800 Elizabeth Smith sold to Samuel T. Parker 1 acre.
1814 ADDITION TO NEW ENGLAND patented to William Daley for 167 1/2 acres.

NEW HAVEN

Patented on 10 Dec.1705 by Thomas Everton who assigned to William Whittington in a fork of the Rokiawalkin River at Meadow Branch for 1034 acres.
1720 William Whittington willed to kinsman Edward Bayley and Whittington Bayley sons of Richard Bayley of Acco.Co.Va. and his wife Ursulla Whittington.
19 Nov.1728 Whittington Bayley of Accoc.Co.Va. and wife Alice Bayley sold 517 acres to John Lecat, upper part.
1 Mar.1747 John Lecat of Acco.Co.Va. willed to son John 100 acres during life and after death to grandson Levin Lecat.
22 Feb.1752 John Lecat Jr. sold 100 acres to Benjamin Byrd that reverted to him after the death of Levin Lecat.
1752 Joseph Lecat and wife Ann Lecat of Acco. Co.Va. willed to friends John Huffington and his son Gilbert Huffington of Somerset Co. to sell 209 acres devised me by may father John Lecat and brothers John Lecat and Nathaniel Lecat, unnamed.
7 Aug.1750 Littleton Lecat son of John Lecat, with wife Francina Lecat of Acco.Co.Va. sold 208 acres to George Green of Som.Co.
5 Apr.1760 John Huffington and Gilbert Huffington sold 209 acres to John Elzey Jr.
13 Nov.1768 Tabitha Armatrader of Acco. Co.Va. widow and only daughter of Whittington Bayley sold to George Handy of Somerset Co. 517 acres.
20 Nov.1768 James Justice son of Ralph Justice deceased of Acco.Co.Va. sold to George Handy 323 acres devised by William Whittington to Whittington Bayley and Edmund Bayley.
1 Dec.1770 John Elzey Jr. and wife Mary Elzey sold to William McClemmy 209 acres
23 July 1774 William McClemmy sold to John Craig and William Dymock, mortgage.
17 Sep.1774 John Green sold 100 acres to Bable Green
7 Sep.1774 John Green son of George Green sold to William McClemmy 108 acres.
16 Nov.1774 William McClemmy sold 108 acres to Benjamin Byrd.
1782 George Handy willed to son Isaac Handy, part bought of James Justice.
1783 tax - Robert Anderson 100 acres, Rewastico 100
1783 tax - Benjamin Byrd 208 acres

1783 tax - Isaac Handy 498 1/2 acres
1783 tax - William McClemmy 207 acres
5 Aug.1786 Isaac Handy sold to William Horsey 1/2 of saw mill and 1 1/4 acres.
7 Apr.1792 John Leatherbury, sheriff sold to highest bidder Joshua Hitch 192 acres to satisfy debts of William McClemmy.
1792 Benjamin Byrd willed 50 acres to son Thomas Byrd
7 Apr.1792 Joshua Hitch Jr. sold to Levin Irving 192 acres.
5 May 1792 Joshua Townsend son of Barkley Townsend, with wife Isabell Townsend sold to Thomas Byrd all rights that John Green sold to Bable Green father of Isabell Townsend.
1 Mar.1794 William Caudrey and wife Betty Caudrey sold to Thomas Byrd all rights that Bable Green father of Betty had.
14 July 1798 Nancy Green daughter of Bable Green sold all rights to Thomas Byrd.
26 Sep.1810 William Handy and Edward G. Handy of Washington DC sold to Spencer Todd 40 acres, as trustees of the real estate of Isaac Handy.
5 Oct.1810 William Handy and Edward G. Handy of Washington DC sold part to Leah Irving.
26 Sep.1810 William Handy and Edward G. Handy sold part to Peter Dashiell.
26 Sep.1810 William Handy and Edward G. Handy sold 312 acres to Thomas Byrd of NEW HAVEN, CORKLAND & HANDYS CARE.
1821 Thomas Byrd willed to son Benjamin Harvey Byrd.

NEW HOLLAND

Patented on 20 Feb.1761 by Edmond Greenfield for 28 acres
23 Apr.1761 ADDITION patented Edmond Greenfield for 134 acres.
4 Aug.1762 Edmond Greenfield, shoemaker sold to Benjamin Savage, planter 100 acres.
15 Apr.1763 Edmond Greenfield sold to Alexander Thomas Russell 34 acres.
3 Mar.1763 Benjamin Savage sold to Alexander Thomas Russell 100 acres.
5 Oct.1772 Alexander Thomas Russell sold 150 acres to William Horsey and Isaac Horsey.
2 Sep.1774 Alexander Thomas Russell mortgaged to Price Russell 34 acres
9 May 1778 Josiah Russell of Frederick Co. and Price Russell with wife Ann Russell of Som.Co. sold to Col. William Hopewell of Worc.Co. 308 acres of ADDITON TO NEW HOLLAND, COXES CHOICE, HUNGARY QUARTER.
4 Feb.1786 Price Russell son of Alexander Russell, with wife Ann Russell sold to Isaac Horsey of Sussex Co.Delaware rights to fathers land, no name or acreage mentioned.

NEW HOLLAND & NEW HOLLAND RENEWED

Patented on 13 May 1685 by Cornelius Johnson for 600 acres on the southeast branch of the Wicomico River near Parsonburg.
Cornelius Johnson willed to William Jones.
13 Mar.1687 William Jones sold to Adam Hitch 300 acres of BEAVER DAMS 1/2 part of NEW HOLLAND.
20 Nov.1694 William Jones sold 1/2 to Nicholas Taylor.
1 Nov.1722 Joshua Curle Jr. of Elizabeth City Va. and wife Rosa Curle only daughter of Nicholas Taylor formerly of Somerset County but

lately of North Carolina sold to William Lingo of Accoc.Co.Va.
1726 NEW HOLLAND RENEWED patented William Lingo 600 acres.
1727 William Lingo willed to son Daniel Lingo 100 acres, to son Jacob Lingo 100 acres, son Richard Lingo 100 acres and son John Lingo 150 acres.
5 June 1733 Daniel Lingo with wife Mary Lingo and Rachel Lingo sold to John Perdue, cooper that William Lingo willed to Daniel Lingo 100 acres.
5 June 1733 John Lingo and wife Sarah Lingo with Rachel Lingo sold 150 acres to Edward McGlammery.
5 June 1733 Jacob Lingo with wife Urselly Lingo and Rachel Lingo widow of William Lingo sold 100 acres to Patrick Causey.
29 Oct.1740 Patrick Causey Sr. with wife Isabel Causey sold 50 acres to George Perdue.
20 Oct.1740 Patrick Causey Sr. with wife Isabel Causey sold 50 acres to Edward McGlammery.
3 Aug.1742 George Perdue sold for 5 shillings 50 acres to John Perdue.
1743 John Perdue Sr. willed 100 acres of dwelling plantation, unnamed, to son John Perdue.
10 Aug.1744 Patrick Causey and wife Isabel Causey sold to Richard Lingo 40 acres called PAGELE part of NEW HOLLAND.
2 Aug.1758 John McGlammery sold to Joshua Nelms of Northumberland Co.Va. 200 acres left by the will of William Lingo.
31 Mar.1746 Rachel Lingo of Accoc.Co.Va. relic of William Lingo sold 150 acres to Burnell Niblett of Worc.Co.
8 Aug.1753 John Perdue and wife Arcada Perdue sold 50 acres to John McGlammery.
5 Jan.1765 John Nelms sold 250 acres to George Dashiell son of George.
15 Feb.1766 John McGlammery of North Carolina sold to Joshua Nelms of Worc.Co. 50 acres.
21 Mar.1768 Richard Niblett nephew and heir of Burnell Niblett sold to Joseph Dashiell 150 acres.
12 Jan.1771 Levin Ruark and wife Elizabeth Ruark and Comfort Lingo and Comfort James sold 50 acres to George Vance.
1783 tax - George Lowe 50 acres, Wic.100
1783 tax - David McGee 50 acres
1783 tax - William Mills Jr. 75 acres
1783 tax - Joshua Sturgis Jr. 163 acres
1783 tax - Joseph Dashiell 250 acres and 150 acres of RENEWED
1783 tax - William Horsey for brother Isaac Horsey
1783 tax - Leah Perdue 80 acres of RENEWED.
14 Mar.1783 Comfort James sold to George Lowe 16 3/4 acres
19 July 1788 George Lowe sold to Joshua Johnson 16 3/4 acres.
22 Oct.1790 Zadock Sturgis, sheriff sold to Thomas Harwood of Annapolis, per judgement against Benjamin F.A.C. Dashiell 400 acres of NEW HOLLAND RENEWED.
2 Apr.1793 William Lowe sold to Joshua Johnson his rights.
25 July 1796 Thomas Harwood of Annapolis sold to Joshua Johnson and Isaac Hearn 400 acres of NEW HOLLAND or NEW HOLLAND RENEWED.
1797 part resurveyed to PARTNERSHIP
1 Feb.1806 Eli Perdue sold to John Kendal Hebrew Perdue 100 acres
12 Aug.1809 John Kendal Hebrew Perdue sold to Jonathan S. Parsons rights to NEW HOLLAND, EAGLE POINT & BEAVER DAM
1817 Joshua Johnson willed to son Joshua, RENEWED and to son James H. Johnson.

NEW IRELAND

Patented on 25 Nov.1685 by Lawrence Young for 500 acres on the south side of Deep Creek.
Rent Rolls 1666-1723 possessed by Richard Russell guardian of the orphans of Lawrence Young.
24 Apr.1765 James Hust, wheelwright, with wife Mary Hust sold to William Lightfoot 500 acres. Lawrence Young died intestate leaving son William Young who died without issue and another son Jehu Young who died without heir leaving Mary Hust daughter to William Young.

NEW PROVIDENCE

Patented on 24 Mar.1756 by Michael Leonard for 52 acres
13 Mar.1788 Benjamin Leonard sold 50 acres to Edmund Northern Nelms
4 Mar.1808 John Bounds with wife Nancy Bounds of Dorc.Co. sold to Ebenezer Lowe 72 1/2 acres NEW PROVIDENCE, GEORGES LOTT as Nancy is only heir of father Edmund Northern Nelms.

NEWMANS LOTT

Patented in 1808 by John Newman for 159 3/4 acres

NEWMANS MEADOW

Patented in 1766 by John Newman for 59 3/4 acres

NEW MEXICO

Patented in 1857 by Joshua Holloway for 27 acres.

NEW SCOTLAND

Patented on 27 Nov.1685 by William Laws for 400 acres
1703 William Laws willed land at Nanticoke to be sold.
1744 James Laws and wife Phillis Laws sold to John Handy 400 acres.
1745 John Handy willed to son John, bought of Francis Parsons that was alienated to me by James Laws 400 acres
1755 Charles Handy of Newport Rhode Island sold to Smith Snead of Acco.Co. Va. 400 acres.
6 Aug.1755 Smith Snead of Va. with wife Sophia Snead sold to Charles West of the same place 400 acres.

NEW YORK

Patented in 1774 by Joseph Anno for 54 acres
1794 Joseph Anno willed to sons William Anno and Joseph Anno, wife Nancy Anno, no lands mentioned in will.

NICHOLSONS LOTT

Patented on 23 Mar.1687 by Richard Nicholson for 100 acres that was part of VULCANS VINEYARD..
Rent Rolls 1666-1723 possessed by Richard Nicholson
1735 Richard Nicholson willed to son Joseph Nicholson part and parts

to sons James Nicholson and Richard Nicholson. [grandson]
19 Nov.1747 Richard Nicholson sold 150 acres to James Nicholson
10 Mar.1752 Richard Nicholson of Worc.Co. grandson of Richard sold to
George Parris of Som.Co. 100 acres of NICHOLSONS LOTT & VULCANS
VINEYARD.
16 June 1752 James Nicholson sold to Abraham Dean 110 acres of
NICHOLSONS LOTT & VULCANS VINEYARD.
4 July 1752 Abraham Dean sold same to Thomas Gillis
17 Mar.1752 George Parris sold to Henry Waggaman 100 acres
1 Mar.1753 Thomas Gillis and Abraham Dean sold to Henry Waggaman
11 Oct.1755 William Cannon of Dorc.Co. and wife Mary Cannon sold to
Henry Waggaman part conveyed by John Nicholson to son John who willed
to Mary Nicholson.
25 Jan 1758 Charles Nicholson and James Nicholson sold part to Henry
Waggaman.
1759 Henry Waggaman willed to son Henry Waggaman.
27 May 1776 Joseph Nicholson and wife Sarah Nicholson of Dorc.Co. sold
50 acres to Mary Waggaman wife of Henry Waggaman.
1783 tax - Charles Nicholson 100 acres, Rewastico 100
9 Nov.1797 Charles Nicholson Sr. sold for 5 shillings to Ross
Nicholson.
8 May 1804 George Handy, sheriff sold to highest bidder, James
Ballard, per court order to sell lands of Elijah Nicholson and Charles
Nicholson for debts, 100 acres.
16 July 1805 James Ballard sold 100 acres to Levin Ballard.
1821 Thomas Byrd willed to son Benjamin Harvey Byrd.
7 Oct.1806 Levin Ballard with wife Sarah Ballard and Charles Nicholson
sold 100 acres to Thomas Byrd.

NICHOLSONS SETTLEMENT

Patented in 1758 by John Fletcher for 140 acres
10 Nov.1767 John Fletcher sold 140 acres to James Fletcher
1783 tax - James Fletcher 140 acres, Rewastico 100
15 June 1789 James Fletcher of Sussex Co.Del. and wife Charlotte
Fletcher sold 140 acres to Benjamin Hearn with SAW MILL SUPPLY.

NIGHT

Patented on 29 Mar.1732 by Robert Ingram for 50 acres
6 Feb.1757 Robert Ingram, yoeman sold to Julian Mezick 50 acres.

NITHSDEAL (aka NETHERSDALE)

Patented in 1749 by William Murray for 289 acres a resurvey of marsh
and AVERYS POLICY.
31 Aug.1772 As Capt. William Murray died without male heir, Betty
Handy and Sarah McBryde his daughters divided the lands. William
McBryde took NEATHERSDALE and Betty Handy took VULCANS VINEYARD & HIGH
SUFFOLK.
1783 tax - William McBryde 289 acres, Rewastico 100.
1801 NEW NITHSDALE patented, a resurvey, by Sarah McBryde for 371 1/2
acres.
7 July 1810 Sarah McBryde sold to John Rider, probably a settlement of
boundaries since he returned to her on the same date.

1821 Thomas Byrd willed to daughter Sarah Ann Byrd.

NOBLE QUARTER

Patented on 8 Sep.1663 by John Taylor for 1000 acres. This patent voided and resurveyed by Nicholas Rice for 550 acres.
5 Jan.1677 Nicholas Rice willed to Richard Crockett and John Evans.
4 Nov 1679 Richard Crockett and John Evans agreed to divide lands. Also see IGNOBLE QUARTER.
Part of original tract resurveyed to Mt. Alexander
20 Sep.1729 Robert Crockett son of Richard Crockett gave to brother John Crockett.
15 Aug.1730 John Evans Sr. sold to Robert Crockett part.
15 Aug.1730 Robert Crockett s/o of Richard Crockett sold for 5 shillings 200 acres of NOBLE QUARTER & LITTLE MONMOUTH.
23 Jan.1732 John Evans sold to Edward Willin 25 acres of EDWARDS LOTT taken out of NOBLE QUARTER & LITTLE MONMOUTH.
6 May 1734 Robert Crockett for 5 shillings sold to Richard Crockett Fluellin son of Samuel Fluellin and Jane Fluellin his wife 50 acres called CROCKETTS PURCHASE.
8 Mar.1735 John Evans Sr. sold 70 acres to William Nelson
31 Mar.1738 Richard Crockett son of Robert Crockett, with wife Elizabeth Crockett sold to John Shiles.
2 July 1757 Nehemiah Crockett son of John Crockett with wife Elender Crockett sold to John Miles
1762 William Nelson willed to grandson William Atkinson 70 acres where I live bought of John Evans and 50 acres bought of John Evans Jr. and 25 acres bought of Thomas Dashiell.
1783 tax - John Willin 50 acres
1783 tax - Samuel Willin 50 acres
1783 tax - John S. Conway 261 acres.
(FINISH ALL alias MIGHT HAD MORE is part of NOBLE QUARTER.)
14 Apr.1798 Isaac Atkinson sold to Sarah Robertson 100 acres.
3 Nov.1801 Sarah Robertson sold 100 acres to Samuel Robertson.

NOBLE QUARTER

Patented in 1750 by Thomas Gillis for 632 acres.

NORTH AND SOUTH END OF SMITHS INDUSTRY

Patented in 1857 by Levin Smith and Henry I. B. Smith for 1198 3/4 acres.

NORTH DEN

Patented in 1738 by William Brown for 40 acres
23 Feb.1770 Robert Brown son of William sold to William Brown 40 acres with WILSONS MISTAKE
22 July 1791 John Brown sold to William Lloyd 40 acres
1783 tax - William Lloyd 40 acres, Rewastico 100.

NORTHS

Patented in 1825 by Edward North for 9 3/4 acres

1850 he lives in Tyaskin district.

NORTHS CONCLUSION

Patented in 1848 by Theodore North for 2 3/8 acres
1850 he is in Tyaskin district.

NORTHS SITUATION

Patented in 1752 for 281 acres by Edward North.
19 Nov.1735 John North s/o Edward sold to John Richardson and his wife Mary Richardson 200 acres of HORSEYS BALIWICK now resurveyed with vacancy to NORTHS SITUATION.
16 Dec.1766 Mary Richardson sold 25 acres to John North.
25 June 1778 Mary Richardson sold 280 acres to Alexander McLaughlin and his wife Mary McLaughlin for 5 shillings.
1783 tax - Alexander McLaughlin 436 acres
1783 tax - Joseph Morris 25 acres
1786 Joseph Morris willed to son John Malone Morris for 25 acres
22 Mar.1804 Samuel Covington and wife Matilda Covington sold to James Bounds 100 acres.
1809 William Bounds sold to John Covington
1810 John Morris willed to son Joseph Morris 25 acres.
13 Dec.1826 Samuel T. Bounds sold to William Whayland 30 1/2 acres.
13 Feb.1835 William Whayland and Polly Whayland sold to Samuel T. Bounds 30 1/2 acres.
25 Feb.1837 James Marcellas Goslee and wife Susan Goslee sold to Samuel T. Bounds 100 acres that fell at death of Samuel Covington to John R. Covington and his sister Elizabeth Goslee. John R. Covingtons part fell also to his sister.
27 Nov.1837 Samuel T. Bounds sold to Benjamin Davis part.

NORTH WALES

Patented on 24 Nov.1685 by Alexander Thomas for 400 acres
1695 Alexander Thomas willed to daughters Eliza Thomas and Frances Thomas.
Rent Rolls 1666-1723 possessed by John Bouger 200 acres and James Russell 200 acres who married the coheirs of Alexander Thomas.
19 Jan 1727 Adam Heath and wife Mary Heath sold to Edward Shores son of Edmund Shores of Dorc.Co. 200 acres the land that James Bouger and James Russell alienated to Adam Hitch.
19 July 1727 Edward Shores of Dorc.Co. sold 200 acres to Edward Willen.
19 Jan.1735 Timothy Atkinson gave to Nelson Waller and wife Ann Waller and to Bridget Renshaw sister 200 acres on the south side of Deep Creek opposite Seaforth Delaware.
23 Jan.1738 Edward Shores son of Edward sold 200 acres to John Moore Jr. of Quantico called SHORES LOTT.
24 Mar.1743 Edward Willin and wife Hannah Willin sold 100 acres to John Moore.
9 May 1744 John Moore and wife Mary Moore sold 200 acres to Adam Muir, called SHORES LOTT
17 Dec.1770 William Waller sold to Thomas Lightfoot, William Lightfoot, Abraham Mitchell, Walter Franklin and Samuel Franklin

company and owners of Pine Grove Furnace in Wor.Co. 200 acres.
1793 Ann Huggins, widow of Nelson Waller and widow of Benjamin Huggins appoints brother Thomas Rencher to sell NORTH WALES, in Sussex Co.Del. near Seaforth.

NORTH WALES

Patented in 1794 by John Huett for 200 acres
9 Sep 1740 John Huett Nutter sold 200 acres to James West
1749 James West willed 200 acres on Nanticoke River at mouth of Broad Creek to be sold.
2 Aug.1764 James West sold 200 acres to Nehemiah King.

NOTHING

Patented in 1774 by William Donoho for 32 acres
1783 tax - William Donoho 32 acres, Nanticoke 100
1785 William Donoho willed to daughter Rebecca Powell NOTHING BE IT.
22 Mar.1789 William Powell and wife Rebecca Powell sold 32 acres to Richardson Donoho.

NOVA FRANCIA

Patented on 27 Nov.1685 by Michael Disharoon for 300 acres.
1690 Michael Disharoon willed 100 acres each to sons John Disharoon, Lewis Disharoon and William Disharoon
Rent Rolls 1666-1723 possessed by William Disharoon and Lewis Disharoon

NOW OR NEVER

Patented in 1755 by Ezekiel Jackson for 4 1/2 acres

NOW OR NEVER

Patented in 1755 by Jacob Wright for 53 1/2 acres
1783 tax - Jacob Wright 53 1/2 acres, Rewastico 100
1796 Jacob Wright willed to sons Joseph Wright and Benjamin Wright.

NUTTERS ADVENTURE

Patented on 5 Dec.1670 by Christopher Nutter for 200 acres on the east side of Quantico Creek.
Another patent in 1672 for 550 acres by Christopher Nutter.
1702 Christopher Nutter willed to sons Christopher and Matthew Nutter jointly.
Rent Rolls 1666-1723 possessed by 275 acres and 100 acres Christopher Nutter and 274 acres and 100 acres by Matthew Nutter.
14 July 1700 John Nutter of Sussex Co.Del. appointed Robert Jones attorney to convey land.
3 Oct.1720 Robert Jones, attorney sold to Matthew Nutter 25 acres and to Christopher Nutter 200 acres and 550 acres out of another tract by same name in NUTTERS NECK and 25 acres to John Huett Nutter. If no heirs to brother Matthew Nutter.
16 Apr.1736 Matthew Nutter of Quantico sold 25 acres to John Huett Nutter.
6 Mar.1752 George Hardy and wife Sarah Hardy former relic of

Christopher Nutter sold 468 acres to John Handy.
12 Aug.1755 Huett Nutter son of John Nutter sold to Henry Lowe Jr. devised to John Nutter brother of Huett Nutter.
1772 Christopher Nutter willed to son Robert Nutter 200 acres NUTTERS LOTT?
11 Mar.1774 Henry Lowe and wife Esther Lowe sold to John Waters of Calvert Co. but now of Somerset Co part. of DORMANS DELIGHT & NUTTERS ADVENTURE.
24 May 1774 Thomas Smith of Sussex Co.Del. sold to John Waters NUTTERS NECK (Thomas Smith heir of John Nutter deceased)
24 May 1774 Thomas Smith of Sussex Co.Del. sold to John Waters 12 of all his land 200 acres of NUTTERS ADVENTURE, 50 acres of NUTTERS LOWER ADVENTURE. with SHILES CHOICE, DORMANS DELIGHT.
1783 tax - William Nutter 232 acres, Nanticoke 100
1783 tax - Samuel King, 468 acres and 50 acres.
1783 William Nutter willed to son William lands in NUTTERS NECK unnamed, if no issue to son Thomas Eccleston Nutter and also lands to son Charles Nutter.
31 Mar.1787 Francis Hutchins Waters son of John Waters sold to John Gale, that John Waters willed him after death of wife Elizabeth Waters now deceased.
29 May 1793 Charles Nutter and William Nutter divided.
27 Aug 1806 Henry E. Bayley and wife Sarah Bayley sold to Charles Nutter part.

NUTTERS CONTRIVANCE

Patented in 1734 by Christopher Nutter for 219 acres.
6 Mar.1752 George Hardy and wife Sarah Hardy former relic of Christopher Nutter sold to John Handy 219 acres.
1777 ADDITION TO NUTTERS CONTRIVANCE pat. Ephraim King for 361 3/4 acres.
1783 tax - Samuel King (ADDITION) 261 3/4 acres Rewastico 100
1777 Ephraim King willed to son Charles King lands on the south side of Quantico, unnamed.
1813 Charles Nutter willed to son Christopher Columbus Nutter, all land owned by brother William Nutter.
27 Aug.1806 Henry E. Bayley and wife Sarah Bayley sold to Charles Nutter.

OAK GROVE

Patented on 8 June 1721 by Daniel McClester for 200 acres.
Rent Rolls 1666-1723 possessed by Daniel McClester
1754 Neal McClester (brother of Daniel McClester) willed to nephew Samuel McClester son of John McClester.

OAK HALL

Patented on 21 Nov.1672 by Richard Acworth for 200 acres on the south side of Barren Creek.
Rent Rolls 1666-1723 possessed by James Weatherly
22 June 1748 Charles Acworth sold to Joseph Gillis 200 acres.
31 Mar.1761 Joseph Gillis gave to son George Gillis 200 acres.
1769 resurveyed by George Gillis to 960 acres.
1783 tax - William Gillis 960 acres, Rewastico 100

23 Nov.1787 John Denwood, high sheriff sold to Ezekiel Gillis 960 acres per judgement of Samuel Chase against Peter Waters and William Gillis.
27 Nov.1787 William Gillis sold 960 acres to Ezekiel Gillis.
18 Mar.1796 Charles Weatherly sold pt. to Joseph Gillis
11 Oct.1799 Joseph Gillis sold to Richard Minnish 9 5/8 acres.
12 Oct.1802 Ezekiel McClemmy Gillis, his son James Gillis infant and Samuel Gillis Holbrook infant grandson of Ezekiel Gillis only heirs of Ezekiel sold 100 acres to Levin Winder son of William Winder.
1802 Arthur Dashiell willed to son Levin Dashiell.
10 May 1803 Ezekiel McClemmy Gillis and Samuel Holbrook sold to John Byrd 575 acres. (Nelly Gillis married Samuel Holbrook guardian of infants.)
17 May 1803 Ezekiel McClemmy Gillis and children sold to John Byrd 100 acres.
3 Dec.1803 John Byrd with wife Margaret Byrd sold to William Russum 100 acres.
29 Oct.1803 John Byrd and wife Margaret Byrd sold to John Moore 575 acres.
3 Nov.1804 John Byrd and wife Margaret Byrd sold to John Moore of William Moore 9 5/8 acres.
1804 John Moore willed lands to be sold, unnamed.
8 Apr.1809 Brittingham Hull sold 200 acres to Edward Hull.
1879 Matilda Kennerly Dashiell wife of Charles Dashiell of Thomas Dashiell willed to son Orlando Dashiell 100 acres.

OAK RIDGE

Patented in 1777 by Henry Toadvine Jr. for 20 acres
6 Apr. 1779 Henry Toadvine sold to George Bayley
12 Nov.1779 George Bayley with wife Fanny Bayley sold to Arnold Toadvine 20 acres.
20 Apr.1787 Arnold Toadvine sold 20 acres to Nathan Culver.
8 Nov.1789 Nathan Culver sold 20 acres to Benjamin Shockley
1791 Benjamin Shockley willed to son Elijah Shockley

OLDBURY & OLDBURY RENEWED

Patented on 1 Apr.1681 by William Stevens who assigned to Francis Jenkins, 400 acres on the south side of the main branch of the Quantico.
Rent Rolls 1666-1723 possessed by Francis Jenkins
1708/10 Francis Jenkins willed lands to wife Mary Jenkins.
9 July 1710 Mary Jenkins widow of Francis Jenkins gave to Sarah Ballard eldest daughter of Charles Ballard. If no issue to Ann Ballard and Isabel Ballard sisters to Sarah and daughters of Charles Ballard (neices)
1767 articles of agreement, Charles Leatherbury to John Smith for 7 years.
15 Apr.1773 Charles Leatherbury released 400 acres to Robert Ballard and George Ballard, mortgage.
22 June 1773 Charles Leatherbury gave to son John Leatherbury 400 acres.
19 Apr.1774 Charles Leatherbury sold to George Ballard his rights from fathers estate not yet recieved, to pay his debts.

17 Nov.1774 George Ballard, shipwright leased to John Leatherbury, mariner 400 acres
1783 tax - John Leatherbury Jr. 400 acres, Wicomico 100
21 Sep.1787 John Leatherbury and John Anderson established lines.
7 Jan.1802 John Leatherbury sold to Arthur Dashiell Jr. mortgage.
3 Aug.1808 Eleanor Ballard widow of George Ballard (late Eleanor Leatherbury) sold rights to 400 acres to Peregrine Leatherbury.
15 Aug.1808 Samuel Rencher with wife Elizabeth Rencher (late Elizabeth Ballard) sold their rights to Peregrine Leatherbury, formerly property of Charles Leatherbury.
3 Aug.1808 Thomas Rencher and wife Priscilla Rencher (late Priscilla Ballard) sold their rights to Peregrine Leatherbury.
15 Aug.1808 Robert Venables and wife Sarah Venables (late Sarah Ballard sold rights to Peregrine Leatherbury.
1 Aug.1808 Joshua W. Langsdale and wife Matilda Langsdale (late Matilda Ballard) sold rights to Peregrine Leatherbury.
3 Aug.1808 Ann Ballard daughter of George Ballard sold rights to Peregrine Leatherbury.
19 Sep.1808 John Gray and wife Margarget Gray (late Margaret Ballard) sold rights to Peregrine Leatherbury
11 Apr.1810 Levin Ballard Esq, sheriff sold to Arthur Dashiell, per judgement against John Leatherbury.
OLDBURY RENEWED patented to Henry Dulaney for 507 7/8 acres.

OLD CASTLE

Patented on 20 Sep.1713 by William Hickman for 50 acres
Rent Rolls 1666-1723 possessed by William Hickman
18 July 1768 Stephen Hickman of Frederick County sold to James Windsor 50 acres with NEW CASTLE.
1783 tax - James Windsor 50 acres, Nanticoke 100

OLD HOUSE MARSH

see UNITED STATES.

ONCE AGAIN

Patented on 14 Dec.1679 by James Weatherly for 100 acres.
Rent Rolls 1666-1723 possessed by James Weatherly 100 acres.
28 May 1720 William Piper heir of Capt. William sold to brother Christopher Piper, that James Weatherly made over to Capt. William Piper.
12 Feb.1728 Christopher Piper sold to James Hardy 240 acres out of WEATHERLYS PURCHASE, ONCE AGAIN & MARSH HOOK.
11 Mar.1736 Christopher Piper and wife Rachel Piper sold to James Hardy same as above.
22 June 1743 James Hardy and James Weatherly sold 240 acres to James Train of WEATHERLYS PURCHASE, ONCE AGAIN & MARSH HOOK.
1783 tax - Joseph Piper 75 acres Nanticoke 100.
1783 tax - William Turpin 25 acres

ORPHANS LOTT

Patented on 13 May 1689 by Gabriel Cooper for 500 acres
Rent Rolls 1666-1723 possessed by Gabriel Cooper
13 Mar.1746 John Hardy and wife Margaret Hardy sold to Edward Collins

30 acres at head of Barren Creek taken up by Gabriel Cooper.
1748 Joseph Hardy willed to son Joseph Hardy 65 acres of dwelling plantation and balance to son Benjamin Hardy, no name.
20 Feb.1762 John Collins sold to Joseph Hardy 30 acres, formerly property of Edward Collins.
11 Apr.1763 Benjamin Hardy sold to Aaron Acar of Sussex Co.Del. 166 1/3 acres that he bought of Gabriel Cooper and wife Ann Cooper.
29 June 1763 Aaron Acar of Sussex Co.Del. sold to Custis Darby of Somerset County 100 acres.
29 June 1763 Aaron Acar sold 66 acres to William Phillips.
15 Aug.1765 George Hardy of Sussex Co.Del. sold 166 1/2 acres to William Tully that James Hardy uncle of George willed.
20 Sep.1765 Benjamin Hardy son of John Hardy sold to Joseph Hardy 83 acres.
2 July 1768 Custis Darby and wife Mary Darby of Dorc.Co. sold 100 acres to John Evans of Somerset County.
6 Apr.1770 Levin Cooper sold to Joseph Hardy.
7 June 1775 John Evans sold 100 acres to John Winright.
7 June 1775 John Winright sold 100 acres to Joseph Hardy.
28 Sep.1778 William Tully sold to William Turpin all BLACKWATER BRANCH 29 acres being part of ORPHANS LOTT.
1783 tax - William Turpin 37 acres, Rewastico 100.

ORKNEY

Patented in 1800 by Charles Badley for 497 3/4 acres
1816 Charles Badley willed to daughter Prissy Badley and her son Clement Badley.
1849 Mark Walker willed to grandson George W. Wright son of Levin Wright, on road from Barren Creek to the Delaware Line, and part to grandson Charles Walker.

OREGON

Patented in 1748 by Robert Walter for 176 1/2 acres

OUTLETT

Patented by Robert Givans for 100 acres.
1735 Robert Givans willed to son George Givans 100 acres adjacent Cypress Swamp, unnamed.
6 Nov.1745 George Givans sold to Jonathan Bell of Northampton Co.Va. 47 acres called BELLS GARDEN, with part of Cypress Swamp.
29 July 1755 Day Givans sold to James Hardy 22 acres.

OUTLETT

Patented in 1773 by Richard Mills who assigned to Isaac Horsey for 50 acres.
22 May 1782 William Horsey with wife Mary Horsey sold to Isaac Horsey, partition of lands.
1783 tax - William Horsey for brother Isaac Horsey, Wic.100

OUTLETT

Patented on 4 Jan. 1774 by Jacob Parker for 50 acres.
13 Mar.1785 Jacob Parker sold to William Beauchamp and wife Nancy Beauchamp 50 acres.
11 Oct.1785 William Beauchamp and wife Ann Beauchamp sold to Boaz Walston 50 acres.
12 Jan.1792 Boaz Walston sold to Elizabeth Trader 50 acres.
20 Dec.1806 Purnell Trader sold to Joshua Trader that mother Eliabeth Trader willed him.

OWENS CHANCE

Patented on 10 July by Only Owens for 37 acres in Wicomico Forrest at School House Ridge.
1783 tax - Only Owens 37 acres.
4 Mar.1797 Only Owens with wife Sarah sold to Jesse Fooks 37 acres.

OWENS VENTURE

see STAYTONS FOLLY

OYSTER ALLEN

Patented in 1806 by William Donoho for 5 1/2 acres
1823 William Donoho willed to son William R. Donoho.

PARIS

Patented on 18 July 1679 by John White who assigned to Peter Douty for 150 acres.
Rent Rolls 1666-1723 possessed by Peter Douty.
1798 Peter Douty willed to daughter Ann Collier wife of Robert Collier.
1775 Douty Collier son of Robert Collier willed to daughter Betty Collier.
1783 tax - William Bounds 46 1/4 acres, Nanticoke 100
1783 tax - Betty Handy 46 acres
1783 tax - Solomon Winright 46 1/2 acres
5 Dec.1785 William Bounds with wife Mary Bounds sold to Douty Bounds 46 3/4 acres with DOUTYS MISFORTUNE.
6 Dec.1785 Douty Bounds sold to William Bounds 46 3/4 acres.
26 Mar.1789 Solomon Winright and wife Bridget Winright sold to Betty Handy 8 1/4 acres.
7 June 1795 Solomon Winright, Levin Winright, Elizabeth Handy, William Bounds with wife Mary Bounds sold to John Crockett land of Ann Collier 8 acres.
7 June 1795 John Crockett sold 8 acres to Elizabeth Handy of DOUTYS MISFORTUNE & PARIS.
27 July 1799 George Handy sold to George Collier 7 3/8 acres of DOUTYS MISFORTUNE & PARIS.
22 Aug.1808 George Handy sold to George Collier 7 3/8 acres of DOUTYS MISFORTUNE & PARIS.
5 Nov.1808 George Collier and wife Martha Collier sold to Matthias Dashiell Hopkins 7 3/8 acres of DOUBTY MISFORTUNE & PARIS.
5 Nov.1808 Matthias Dashiell Hopkins and wife Eleanor Hopkins sold to James Walter 7 3/8 acres of DOUTYS MISFORTUNE & PARIS.

1827 James Walter with wife Sarah Walter gave part to daughter Dorothy Walter.

PARIS

Patented on 17 Jan.1715 by Thomas Waller for 100 acres at head of Barren Creek.
10 Nov.1755 Thomas Waller sold to John Waller Sr. 50 acres.
6 Apr.1758 John Waller sold to Richard Waller, blacksmith 30 acres.
10 Jan 1763 Thomas Waller Sr. sold 12 acres to son John Waller.
17 Feb.1764 Thomas Waller sold 30 acres to son John Waller
20 June 1764 John Waller son of Thomas Waller sold to Luke Huffington.
5 Nov.1764 Luke Huffington sold to Aaron Carter 30 acres.
12 Nov.1768 John Waller sold to Robert Pitt 52 acres of STEPNEY & PARIS.
26 Mar.1771 Ebenezer Waller sold to John Magee 52 acres of STEPNEY & PARIS.
10 Oct.1769 Aaron Carter sold to Thomas Waller 30 acres
26 May 1771 Thomas Waller grandson of Thomas sold to Zachariah Maddux 30 acres.

PARKERS ADDITION

Patented on 17 July 1760 by George Parker for 50 acres on branch of the Wicomico River.
1772 George Parker willed to wife Abigail Parker and after death to daughters Betty Parker, Nelly Parker, Sarah Parker and Elizabeth Parker.
1783 tax- Peter Gordy 25 acres Wic.100 Worc.Co.
26 Apr.1785 Stephen Dikes with wife Betty Dikes, Josiah Dennis and wife Nelly Dennis, John Dennis with wife Sarah Dennis, Leonard Gordy, wife Elizabeth Gordy sold to Peter Gordy, that George Parker father of wives patented 25 acres.

PARKERS CHANCE

Patented in 1759 by Jacob Parker for 50 acres.
1783 tax - Jacob Parker 50 acres, Wic.100 Worc.Co.

PARKERS CHANCE

Patented in 1788 by John Parker for 44 acres
1783 tax - John Parker of George Parker 40 acres.
5 July 1788 Levi King power of attorney for John Parker son of George Parker and Jacob Parker son of John Parker of Sussex Co.Del. sold to George Parker son of Elisha Parker of Worc.Co. 119 acres of ALDERBURY, WILTON & PARKERS CHANCE.

PARKERS DELIGHT

Patented 20 March 1756 Elisha Parker for 54 acres.
7 Sep.1760 PARKERS DELIGHT ENLARGED pat. Elisha Parker for 228 acres.

PARKERS FROST

Patented in 1767 by George Parker for 51 acres

PARKERS HARD FORTUNE

Patented on 17 July 1760 by George Parker Jr. a resurvey from TAYLORS ADVENTURE, for 113 acres.
1772 George Parker and wife Abigail Parker willed to daughters Nelly Parker, Sarah Parker, Betty Parker and Elizabeth Parker.
1783 tax - Peter Gordy 113 acres Wic.100 Worc.Co.(mar.Eleanor Parker)
26 Apr.1785 Stephen Dikes with wife Betty Dikes, Josiah Dennis with wife Nelly Dennis, John Dennis with wife Sarah Dennis, Leonard Gordy with wife ELizabeth Gordy sold to Peter Gordy.

PARKERS MISFORTUNE

Patented in 19 July 1768 by Levin Disharoon for 50 acres
9 Oct.1772 Levin Disharoon with wife Sarah Disharoon sold to Elisha Parker 50 acres.

PARKERS MISTAKE

Patented in 1759 by Moses Gordy Jr. for 50 acres.
5 Mar.1765 Moses Gordy Jr. sold 50 acres to Peter Gordy
1775 Peter Gordy willed to son John Gordy.
1783 tax - John Gordy 50 acres Wic.100 Worc.Co.

PARKERS SECURITY

Patented in 1770 by George Parker for 5 acres on main branch of Wicomico River.
12 Oct.1785 Benjamin Parker of Sussex Co.Del. with wife Jenny Parker sold to ELisha Parker of Worc.Co. Md.

PARRAMORES FIRST CHOICE

Patented on 2 Dec.1678 by John Parremore for 300 acres on the south side of Quantico Creek, near the head.
Rent Rolls 1666-1723 possessed by William Giles 300 acres Nanticoke 100.
1749 William Giles willed to son William 300 acres
11 Dec.1775 Isaac Giles and wife Elizabeth Giles sold to Ralph Moore 300 acres.
20 Mar.1784 Isaac Giles son of Jacob Giles sold all rights to John Leatherbury.
18 May 1784 Isaac Giles Jr. sold rights to John Leatherbury Sr.
6 Mar.1786 Ralph Moore and wife Mary Moore sold to Mary Bonnewell wife of Hall Bonnewell of Dorc.Co. 50 acres.
6 Ma.1786 Ralph Moore and wife Mary Moore sold to Sarah Moore wife of Levin Moore 50 acres.
18 May 1791 Ralph Moore leased for 7 years to James Anderson
9 Mar.1793 Michael Hall Bonnewell wife Mary Bonnewell of Kent Co. Del. sold to James Anderson her rights, that will come at the death of her parents Ralph Moore and Mary Moore.
25 Aug.1794 Ralph Moore and James Anderson sold to Charles Serman, Thomas Garrettson, William James ,Charles Rider, George Parker, Isaac Dashiell and Isaac Vinson trustees of the Methodist Society in

Quantico for a chapel, 1 acre.
1804 James Anderson willed to son James land purchased of Michael Hall Bonnewell.

PARREMORES FOLLY

Patented on 11 Aug.1732 by James Parremore for 50 acres.
12 Aug.1735 James Parremore Jr. and wife Rose Parremore sold to John Calloway Jr.
20 Apr.1743 James Parremore sold to John Williams Jr. 50 acres.

PARREMORES PLEASURE

Patented in 1767 by Stephen Parremore for 58 acres
19 June 1782 Samuel Parremore sold 58 acres to Thomas Bedsworth on the south side of Barren Creek.
1783 tax - Thomas Bedsworth 58 acres, Rewastico 100
1785 Thomas Bedsworth willed to wife Susanna Bedsworth dwelling plantation, after death to son William Bedsworth, unnamed.

PARSONS ADDITION

Patented in 1775 by George Parsons for 133 acres
1808 George Parsons willed to son Elijah Parsons part of ADDITION

PARSONBURG TOWN

was knows as JOHNSONS CROSS ROAD

PARSONS CONQUEST

Patented on 19 Sep.1762 by George Parsons for 850 acres a resurvey of THIRD CHOICE.
15 Feb.1765 George Parsons with wife Hannah Parsons sold to Joshua Nelms 375 acres.
5 March 1765 Joshua Nelms with wife Sarah Nelms sold 375 acres to Joseph Dashiell son of George Dashiell.
13 June 1770 part 366 acres resurveyed to MARGALANTE by Joseph Dashiell.
1783 tax - Jonathan Parsons 490 acres
1783 tax - William Parsons 10 acres
1783 repatented by George Parsons for 504 1/4 acres.
1792 William Parsons willed 10 acres to son Samuel Parsons.
2 Jan.1809 Samuel Parsons of William Parsons sold rights to William Parsons of William.
1808 Jonathan Parsons willed to sons Levin Parsons and Jonathan Stevens Parsons.

PARSONS GOOD LUCK

Patented in 1865 by Peter R. Parsons for 538 acres, 1 perch 12 rods.
1850 he is in 4th district HH#323 Worc.Co. with family.

PARSONS LOTT

Patented in 1760 by John Parsons for 50 acres.
1775 ADDITION patented by John Parsons for 392 1/2 acres

1783 tax - Johnson Parsons 206 acres, Acquango Worc.Co.
1783 tax - John Parsons Blizzard 40 acres of ADDITION
6 May 1785 John Parsons Sr. sold to John Parsons Blizzard 40 acres.
1805 John Parsons willed to son Jonathan Parsons 120 acres of ADDITION and to son Caleb Tingle Parsons 120 acres.

PARSONS OUTLETT

Patented in 1830 by Jonathan S. Parsons for 826 3/4 acres.
1848 Jonathan S. Parsons willed to Lydnam H. Mills son of Davis Mills.

PARTNERS CHOICE

Patented on 12 June 1682 by Christopher Nutter who assigned to William Keen.
27 May 1717 William Keen sold 300 acres to his son in law Edward McGlammery.
15 May 1722 William Keen and wife Tabitha Keen sold to Phillip Records 100 acres.
20 Nov.1722 William Keen with wife Ann Keen gave to daughter Sarah Keen 200 acres.
30 Nov.1723 William Keen and wife Margaret Keen sold 150 acres to Samuel Jackson.
Rent Rolls 1666-1723 possessed by William Keen 200 acres, Edmund McGlammery 200 acres, orphans of William Keen Jr. 200 acres.
1721 Edward McGlammery willed to sons George McGlammery and Edward McGlammery.
2 Aug.1723 George McGlammery son of Edward, batchelor sold to William Keen his grandfather 150 acres.
11 Sep.1725 Edward McGlammery sold 150 acres to William Moore.
23 Feb.1725 William Elgate and wife Sarah Elgate (was Sarah Keen) sold 200 acres to John Leatherbury.
18 Mar.1746 John Leatherbury sold 150 acres to William Evans.
28 Nov.1743 William Keen and Edward McGlammery the younger divided.
20 Jan.1749 William Evans sold 150 acres to Matthias Jones.
22 Aug.1751 William Moore sold to Joshua Morris 150 acres for 5 shillings.
31 July 1752 Matthias Jones with wife Temperance Jones sold 150 acres to Thomas Byrd.
1752 Thomas Byrd willed 150 acres to son Benjamin Byrd
17 Feb.1770 Phillip Records of Dorcester Co. sold to Thomas Records of Som.Co. 100 acres.
1783 tax - William Dorman Sr.50 acres- Rewastico 100
1783 tax - William Goddard 100 acres
1783 tax - Allen Howard 100 acres
1783 tax - Ebe Morris 100 acres
1783 tax - Elizabeth McLally 80 acres
1783 tax - Archelus Records 100 acres
1783 tax - Robert Brown 22 acres.
6 Nov.1783 Jonathan Bayley and wife Mary Bayley of Sussex Co.Del sold 150 acres to William Goddard of Som.Co. for 5 shillings per deed from William Keen to Samuel Jackson father of Mary Bayley.
23 Nov.1787 John Denwood sheriff sold at public sale to William Goddard on behalf of a judgement against Allen Howard, 50 acres.

22 Sep.1786 Fisher Roberts and wife Elizabeth Roberts sold their rights to James Moore 150 acres after the death of Margaret Johnson.
17 Sep.1794 William McLally sold to George Twilley son of John Twilley 80 acres.
23 Jan.1798 bond- James Moore and wife Mary Moore to John Reddish, to make over rights to him.
8 Sep.1810 Thomas Reddish and wife Nancy Reddish and Isabell Morris sold to Caleb Kennerly 158 acres of PARTNERS CHOICE, GODDARDS ADDITION & FOX HALL.

PARTNERS CHOICE

Patented on 22 Nov.1672 by William Green for 250 acres
Rent Rolls 1666-1723 possessed by William Green
5 Aug.1685 William Green of Dorc.Co. gave to daughter Elizabeth Green.
13 July 1721 William A. Robinson only son of Elizabeth Green sold 250 acres to Samuel Melson.
1739 Samuel Melson willed to wife Isabel Melson 1/3rd and to son Samuel Melson.
1757 Thomas Melson sold to John Huffington 80 acres.
1767 Thomas Melson sold 50 acres to Jacob Giles.
2 July 1774 Joseph Melson and wife Eunice Melson sold 80 acres to Benjamin Venables 80 acres.
1783 tax - Isaac Giles 50 acres
1783 tax - Eunice Giles 50 acres
8 Sep.1788 Isaac Giles Jr. sold to William Bowland 50 acres.

PARTNERS CONQUEST

Patented in 1809 by David Cordrey for 104 1/2 acres
1820 David Cordrey willed to friend Matthias Dashiell WILSONS CONQUEST.

PARTNERS GOOD LUCK

Patented in 1769 by Josiah Polk for 59 acres
23 Apr.1775 Susanna Dennis exec. of Littleton Dennis sold to Josiah Polk her interest 1/3rd in mills and CORKLAND & PARTNERS GOOD LUCK that he was in partnership with Josiah Polk and Gillis Polk.
1783 tax - Josiah Polk and Gillis Polk, Wicomico 100

PARTNERSHIP

Patented in 1759 by John Williams and Phillip Williams for 100 acres
10 Mar.1770 William Phillips sold 100 acres to John Williams 100 acres on th north side of Barren Creek.
17 Oct.1772 Robert Phillips sold to William Phillips 100 acres.
1777 Samuel Williams willed to sons David Williams and Esau Williams 100 acres.
1783 tax - David Williams 50 acres
1783 tax - Esau Williams 50 acres

PARTNERSHIP

Patented in 1763 by James Weatherly, a resurvey from ADDITION, for 527 acres.

1764 Joseph Weatherly willed to cousin John Weatherly and to James
Weatherly, Charles Weatherly and Jesse Weatherly ADDITION that I
conveyed to their father James, since resurveyed to PARTNERSHIP
31 Jan.1770 John Weatherly sold to Richard Waller all rights.
2 Aug.1771 Richard Waller and John Weatherly sold to William Winder 95
acres and 52 acres.
23 Nov.1779 Charles Weatherly, James Weatherly, John Weatherly and
Jesse Weatherly sold to William Winder.
23 Nov.1779 John Weatherly, Charles Weatherly, Jesse Weatherly sold to
James Weatherly 93 /34 acres.
25 Nov.1779 James Weatherly sold 164 acres to John Weatherly for 10
shillings.
1783 tax - Jesse Weatherly 55 acres- Rewastico 100
1783 tax - James Weatherly 93 1/2 acres
1783 tax - William Winder 228 acres
1783 tax - John Weatherly 181 acres
27 Apr.1798 Jesse Weatherly son of James Weatherly and wife Sarah
Weatherly sold to Levin Winder 170 acres of PARTNERSHIP & WEATHERLYS
LOTT.

PARTNERSHIP

Patented in 1759 by Alexander Thomas Russell for 15 acres
1 May 1773 Alexander Thomas Russell sold to his son Price Russell all
his land, unnamed.
1783 tax - Price Russell 15 acres, Nanticoke 100

PARTNERSHIP

Patented in 1771 by William Truitt s/o Littleton Truitt for 350 acres.
4 Apr.1771 William Truitt son of Littleton Truitt with wife Ann Truitt
sold to Thomas Tyre 106 acres.
4 Apr.1774 William Truitt sold to William Richardson son of William 50
acres.
4 Apr.1774 William Truitt sold to Matthew Richardson son of William
Richardson 50 acres
4 Apr.1774 William Truitt sold to Samuel Richardson 68 acres.
4 Apr.1774 William Truitt sold to Jesse Brattan 55 1/2 acres
1774 William Richardson willed to brother Joseph Richardson 50 acres.
11 May 1775 Thomas Tyre with wife Keziah Tyre sold to Jesse Davis 100
acres.
3 Mar.1784 Joseph Richardson sold to Matthew Richardson 50 acres
9 Sep.1786 Jesse Davis sold to Annanias Davis 106 acres
5 May 1798 Samuel Richardson sold to Jesse Bratten 60 acres of
PARTNERSHIP & GUM SWAMP.

PARTNERSHIP

Patented in 1776 by Henry Handy for 25 3/4 acres
1807 Thomas W. Handy petitioned the court to see the real estate of
brother Henry Handy who died intestate 25 3/4 acres.

PARTNERSHIP

Patented in 1797 by Richard Acworth for 266 1/2 acres
3 Dec.1795 Richard Acworth mortgaged to Robert Venables.

PARTNERSHIP

Patented in 1797 by Joshua Johnson and Isaac Hearn for 499 1/2 acres a resurvey of NEW HOLLAND RENEWED, MARGALENTE, FATHERS ADVICE and vacancy.
10 Mar.1798 Isaac Hearn sold to Joshua Johnson 460 acres.
7 Mar.1798 Joshua Johnson sold to Isaac Hearn, division of land.

PARTNERSHIP

Patented on 13 Sep.1800 by Jacob Evans for 296 acres
23 Sep.1809 Jacob Evans sold to Abisha Davis 88 acres

PARTNERSHIP

Patented in 1848 by William Wright, Levin Wright and Joseph Wright.
1850 they are in Barren Creek area.

PARTNERHIP

Patented in 1851 by Levin P. White and Elijah Holloway for 1197 acres 1 perch and 23 rods.
1850 in Salisbury district.

PARTNERSHIP

Patented in 1864 by Isaac S. Brittingham and James P. Dennis for 46 acres.

PASTURAGE

Patented on 20 Oct.1715 by James Train for 60 acres
Rent Rolls 1666-1723 possessed by James Train
3 Ma.1764 Isaac Hardy of Worc.Co. son of James Hardy and Eliza Train Hardy sold to Matthew Dorman.
1783 tax - William Dorman 60 acres, Rewastico 100.

PASTURAGE

Patented on 25 Nov.1721 by Jacob Mezick for 45 acres
Rent Rolls 1666-1723 possessed by Jacob Mezick
9 Mar.1731 Jacob Mezick and wife Elizabeth Mezick sold 22 1/2 acres to Nehemiah Mezick, lower part.
29 Aug.1746 Nehemiah Mezick and John Mezick sold to Elihu Mezick, bricklayer 22 1/2 acres
1751 Jacob Mezick willed 1/3rd to wife Elizabeth Mezick and all lands to son Jacob Mezick, no name.
1783 tax - Elihu Mezick 22 1/4 acres, Nanticoke 100
1783 tax - Mary Mezick 22 1/4 acres
1788 Elihu Mezick son of Jacob willed to wife Margaret Mezick 20 acres and to sons Elihu, John Mezick and Daniel Mezick.

PASTURAGE

Patented on 14 Dec.1681 by James Weatherly for 50 acres on the south side of Rewastico Creek, north side of Lyons Creek.

Rent Rolls 1666-1723 possessed by James Weatherly
10 Dec.1679 James Weatherly made over to daughter Sarah Twilley wife of Robert Twilley 50 acres.
16 Nov.1724 Ann Twilley daughter of Robert Twilley and Sarah Twilley, sold 50 acres to William Farrington.
23 Feb.1725 William Farrington and wife Sarah Farrington (was Sarah Twilley) sold to Robert Givans 7 acres now called BEGINNING.
1735 Robert Givans willed to son Robert 7 acres of BEGINNING
1756 William Farrington willed to sons George Farrington and Robert Farrington 293 acres of WEATHERLYS PURCHASE, SLIPE, PASTURAGE.
17 Aug.1758 Robert Farrington sold all interest to Ephraim King.
27 June 1759 George Farrington sold to Samuel Wilson 146 1/2 acres of PASTURAGE, SLIPE & WEATHERLYS PURCHASE.
8 Feb.1760 George Farrington sold 146 1/2 acres of same to Ephraim King.
1777 Ephraim King willed lands purchased of George Farrington and Robert Farrington in Rewastico, unnamed, to son Samuel King.
1783 tax- Samuel King 45 acres
1787 Samuel King willed to daughter Lucretia Jones and her mother Elizabeth King land devised by father Ephraim King, unnamed.
1 Aug.1801 Charles Nutter sold to William Bounds 484 2/8 acres of WEATHERLYS PURCHASE,CLOVER FIELDS, PASTURAGE & SLIPE conveyed to Charles Nutter by David Wilson.

PASTURAGE

Patented on 8 Sep.1719 by John Lame for 50 acres one mile above Barren Creek mouth against lower end of Vienna.
Rent Rolls 1666-1723 possessed by John Lame.
1740 Thomas Records married Sarah Lame daughter of John Lame
3 May 1763 Lame Records, Thomas Records and Sarah Records sold to Joshua Weatherly and Edward Kellum 50 acres.
1783 tax - Josiah Polk and Gillis Polk 50 acres
1783 ADDITION patented for 278 acres by John Gillis and James Polk.

PASTURAGE

Patented on 20 Oct.1705 by James Makemorie and William Winright for 260 acres.
8 June 1734 James Makemorie sold 260 acres to Cannon Winright.
27 Jan.1755 James Winright son of Cannon Winright, with wife Nelly Winright sold 130 acres to Cannon Winright for 5 shillings.
1783 tax - James Winright 130 acres, Nanticoke 100.
1795 James Winright willed to grandson Levi Selby son of Henry Selby and Rebecca Selby deceased, 265 acres except 30 acres sold to Elihu Larramore, to daughter Sarah Mezick wife of George Mezick use of 75 acres. After her death to grandson Benjamin Mezick son of George Mezick.
27 June 1796 William Winright, Solomon Winright, Nancy Winright, Jane Winright and James Riggin (married Betty Winright) of Worc.Co. sold 100 acres to Henry Walston.
1 Dec.1800 David Walston sold to Chaplin Conway 100 acres.
29 Mar.1803 Chaplin Conway with wife Ann Conway sold to William Robertson for 5 shillings 19 1/2 acres of FLUELLING NEGLECT, HANDYS CHANCE & PASTURAGE.

PASTURAGE

Patented in 1764 by Matthew Dorman and wife Leah Farrington Dorman for 607 1/2 acres.

PEA HILL

Patented 2 Apr.1760 by William Burk for 12 acres.

PEA PATCH

Patented on 7 Oct.1761 by David Smith for 50 acres
8 Nov.1769 Isaiah Smith sold to Elizabeth Smith 50 acres, at Long Hill in Wicomico Forrest.
6 May 1773 Henry Trader with wife Elizabeth Trader sold to Peter Gordy 50 acres.
16 Oct.1784 Peter Gordy sold to Elisha Pennewell 50 acres.

PEACE

Patented in 1802 by William Bedsworth for 110 acres.

PEACE & PLENTY

Patented in 1785 by Patrick Causey for 25 acres
21 Mar.1795 Patrick Causey sold to Benjamin Fooks 25 acres.
PEACE & PLEANTY ENLARGED patented in 1796 by Benjamin Fooks for 41 1/2 acres
12 Mar.1808 Benjamin Fooks sold to Samuel Powell 8 1/4 acres
11 Apr.1809 Benjamin Fooks with wife Hannah Fooks sold to Outten Toadvine 277 acres of FORT NECK,FOOKS COST, LONG ACRES,PEACE & PLENTY ENLARGED.

PEACE AND QUIETNESS

Patented in 1765 by Nathan Culver for 255 acres, part a resurvey from DENWOODS DEN
23 May 1774 Nathan Culver sold 9 1/2 acres to Charles Nicholson
1783 tax - Charles Nicholson 9 1/2 acres, Rewastico 100
1783 tax - Thomas Hitch Sr. 36 acres
1783 tax - John Maddux 15 acres
1783 tax - Ebenezer Waller 20 acres
24 Sep.1784 Nathan Culver sold 24 acres to John Maddux
28 May 1785 Nathan Culver sold to James Weatherly Waller heir of Ebenezer Waller deceased and Esme Marshall Waller son of William Cottman Waller and Thomas Waller 22 acres with tract MILL LOTT
10 Sep.1787 Nathan Culver sold to Nancy Nelms of Salisbury 217 1/s4 acres of POINT PATIENCE & PEACE & QUIETNESS.
28 Nov.1789 Nathan Culver sold to Joshua Hitch Sr. 35 acres of POINT PATIENCE,PEACE & QUIETNESS, MILL LOTT.
11 July 1795 Robert Lemon and wife Nancy Lemon of Salisbury Town sold to James Weatherly Waller 217 1/4 acres of PEACE & QUIETNESS & POINT PATIENCE.
15 June 1799 William Hitch and John Hitch sons of Joshua Hitch sold to Thomas Humphries Jr.
10 May 1800 James Weatherly Waller sold 13 1/8 acres to Curtis Hitch.

13 Oct.1802 James Weatherly Waller sold to Esme Marshall Waller 1/6th part of lands and mills.
11 Oct.1803 James Weatherly Waller with wife Ann Waller sold to Esme Marshall Waller 2/3rds of saw and grist mill
13 Sep.1803 James Weatherly Waller sold to Thomas Humphries 4 3/4 acres.
10 Sep.1803 James Weatherly Waller sold to Jesse Maddux 1 acre.
7 Oct.1806 Levin Ballard and wife Sarah Ballard and Charles Nicholson sold to Thomas Byrd 9 1/2 acres.
21 Oct.1810 Esme Marshall Waller sold to Curtis Hitch 23 acres.

PEACE IS BEST

Patented in 1833 by Stephen Wright for 111 5/8 acres
1843 Stephen Wright willed to daughters Eliza Wright and Catherine Moore, lands at Nanticoke River, unnamed.

PECHINGO RIDGE

Patented on 20 Nov.1681 by Owen McGraugh who assigned to James Weatherly for 250 acres.
Rent Rolls 1666-1723 apportains to the orphan of Thomas Acworth.
5 Nov.1741 Thomas Acworth sold 250 acres to Richard Parker between Rewastico and Quantico Branchs of Nanticoke River.
8 Mar.1745 Richard Parker sold to Robert Allen 250 acres
5 Sep.1747 Richard Parker and wife Mary Parker sold to John Fritz of Dorc.Co. 250 acres.
4 Mar.1763 triparte- Edward Fritz of Maiden Bradley in County of Wilts in Great Britain, brother and devisee of John Fritz late of Dorc.Co. deceased, Zachariah Bayley of Frame Selwood in Somerset County Great Brittian and wife Mary Bayley daughter of Edward Fritz and also devisee, sold to John Henry of Dorc.Co. Md., Levin Farrington of Som. Co. and Nehemiah King, Samuel Wilson and Levin Wilson 250 acres (there were 3 separate entries for his land)
16 Nov.1771 George Farrington of Worc.Co. sold 250 acres to William Winder.
1783 tax - William Winder 261 acres
This was resurveyed to FARRINGTONS PURCHASE.

PEMBERTON

Patented on 29 Sep.1680 by Thomas Pemberton for 900 acres
27 June 1705 Thomas Pemberton of Sussex Co.Delaware sold to William Whittington 900 acres.
Rent Rolls 1666-1723 possessed by William Whittington
14 Mar.1722 William Whittington with wife Elizabeth Whittington sold 900 acres to Joseph Pemberton, late of the island of Nevis.
21 Nov.1726 Joseph Pemberton of Sussex Co.Del. sold to Isaac Handy 900 acres.
1732 Isaac Handy resurveyed to 970 acres.
18 May 1741 William Hitch son of William, Adam Hitch, Elgate Hitch and Samuel Hitch sold 2 acres to Isaac Handy
20 Nov.1750 Isaac Handy sold to son George Handy, mariner 350 acres.
1760 Isaac Handy willed to son William Handy 270 acres and balance of

to son Henry Handy.
7 July 1754 PEMBERTONS ADDITION patented by Henry Johnson for 50 acres.
1775 William Handy and Henry Handy repatented to 900 acres.
1783 tax - Henry Handy 350 acres, Wicomico 100
1783 tax - William Handy 270 acres
1783 tax - John Adams Jr. 37 acres.
5 Jan.1782 George Handy and Henry Handy settled dispute of boundaries of land in Handys Neck with SURVEYORS MISTAKE, HANDYS MEADOW & PEMBERTON.
10 Mar.1787 Thomas Johnson sold to William Handy and Henry Handy, as Elijah Johnson and William Johnson (now dead)brothers to Elijah and Thomas Johnson heir of William Johnson on 22 June 1785 conveyed to George Gale and John Gale and William Adams, to adjust lines of PEMBERTON & FRIENDS ADVICE and to determine lines of a parcel deeded by Purnell Johnson to Isaac Handy for 10 acres called MULBERRY LANDING.
17 July 1802 Henry Handy sold 450 acres to William Winder.
18 Nov.1808 John Byrd and wife Margaret Byrd (was Margaret Handy wife of William Handy) sold her dower rights to son William Smith Handy.
18 Nov.1808 William Smith Handy with wife Phoebe Handy mortgaged to Thomas Hooper of Worc.Co.
1858 HANDYS LAST ADDITION TO PEMBERTON patented by John Parsons for 437 acres.

PEMBERTONS GOODWILL
(sight of Salisbury Town)

Patented on 3 Sep.1683 by John Winder for 700 acres.
Rent Rolls 1666-1723 possessed by John Winder 350 acres and belongs to William Winder in Virginia.
1698 John Winder willed to son William Winder.
1703 William Winder of Northumberland Co. Va. willed to brother John Winder.
1716 John Winder willed 100 acres to London Walston and 200 acres to John Stewart.
20 May 1720 John Stewart of Kent Co.Del. and Sarah Stewart sold his share to Daniel Lingo.
9 May 1731 Daniel Lingo sold 100 acres to John Carr.
1 May 1731 Peter Hack of Cumberland Co.Va. appoints John Tunstall attorney for obligation of William Winder of Va. deceased. William Winder bound to Peter Hack for 1/2 of 700 acres at head of Wicomico River. To the behalf of grandson Tunstall Hack of Peter Hack.
1762 Patent 426 acres by William Winder.
8 Nov.1767 William Winder sold 1/2 acre to Aaron Ready.
4 Nov.1762 William Winder sold 3 acres to John Nelms.
19 Nov.1771 William Winder sold 1/4 acres to Henry Trader in Salisbury Town.
21 Mar.1772 William Winder Sr. sold to William Handy and Isaac Handy 17771 sq.ft., pat of a lot.
18 Nov.1772 Capt. William Winder and Alexander Thomas Russell of Worc.Co. sold to John Nelms 3/4 acre in Salisbury Town.
12 Dec.1772 Henry Trader sold 1/4 a. to John Nelms.
20 June 1774 Aaron Ready of Worc.Co. sold to Gustavous Scott of Somerset Co. 1/2 acre.

1783 tax - John Nelms 10 acres
1783 tax - Thomas Skinner 1/2 acre
1783 tax - John Winder Sr. 130 acres
15 Apr.1794 John Winder of Northampton Co.Va. sold to Martin Luther Haynie 74 3/4 acres
28 Mar.1794 James Round Morris, Leah Morris, Levin Handy, Nancy Handy, Ephraim Wilson and Jane Wilson sold 74 3/4 acres to Martin Luther Haynie.
23 July 1794 William Winder, Levin Winder, Richard Henry Handy sold 84 acres to Martin Luther Haynie.
13 Feb.1795 James R. Morris with wife Leah Morris, Levin Handy, Nancy Handy, Ephraim Wilson and Jane Wilson sold to Levin Handy formerly of Rhode Island all rights.
15 Nov.1795 John Winder of Northampton Co.Va. sold to Levin Handy 357 acres.
2 Apr.1796 Martin Luther Haynie sold 3 acres to Samuel Parr
6 Mar.1796 Martin Luther Haynie sold 3 acres to Samuel Parr
6 Feb.1796 Martin Luther Haynie sold to Andrew Gilchrist 3 lots,lot #2 1/2 acre and 1/4 acre and 1 acre.
2 Apr.1796 Martin Luther Haynie sold to George Robertson 2 acres.
12 Mar.1796 Martin Luther Haynie sold to Joseph Brittingham lot #7, 1 acre
12 Mar.1796 Martin Luther Haynie sold to Purnell Johnson lot #13.
12 Mar.1796 Martin Luther Haynie sold to John Hearn lot #4
12 Mar.1796 Martin Luther Haynie sold to John Knipshitt lots #15 and #16, 2 acres.
2 Apr.1796 John Knipshitt sold to Thomas Lane lot #16
20 Dec.1796 Andrew Allen Gilchrist sold to John Knipshitt lot #3
15 Oct.1796 Andrew Allen Gilchrist sold to Joseph Brittingham 1 acre
28 Jan 1797 Andrew Allen Gilchrist with wife Nancy Gilchrist sold to Thomas Handy Gillis lot #2, 1/2 acre
15 Nov.1797 Martin Luther Haynie of Kent Co. sold to Esme Bayley 3 1/2 acres lots #5,#6,#9,#10 two acres.
13 Sep.1797 Thomas Handy Gillis sold to John Knipshitt for 5 shillings lot #2
13 May 1797 John Houston and wife Nancy Houston sold to Benjamin Disharoon lot in Salisbury called CHANCE
19 July 1797 Benjamin Disharoon sold to John Houston, same as above.
19 July 1798 John Houston and wife Nancy Houston quitclaimed to Benjamin Disharoon all rights to lot called CHANCE.
1799 Esme Bayley willed to son Josiah Bayley, part.
19 July 1800 Martin Luther Haynie sold 2 acres to William Wright
28 June 1800 Martin Luther Haynie sold to Samuel Parr lot #32.
9 Apr.1802 Levin Handy sold to John Umsted one lot.
22 July 1802 Martin Luther Haynie sold to William James 6 acres of 3 lots #18,#19,#20.
18 Sep.1802 John Cutler of Worc.Co. sold to Charles Winright lot #23 near Salisbury.
15 Jan.1803 John Umsted sold to Nancy Chattam during life and at her decease to her son William Parks Chattam, one lot.
24 Sep.1803 John Umsted with wife Betsy Dashiell Umsted sold to Samuel Hopkins 1 rod 7/16 poles, a lot.
4 Aug.1804 Levin Pollitt , sheriff per judgement against Levin Handy sold to Peter Dashiell 228 1/2 acres.
7 Jan.1804 Levin Handy with wife Nelly Handy sold to Charles Dashiell

1/2 acre lot.
29 Sep.1804 William Vance and wife Letty Vance sold to John Gould lot #22
18 Aug.1804 Martin Luther Haynie sold to James Smith 6 acres, lots #30 and #35
16 Nov.1804 Martin Luther Haynie sold to Thomas Vance lot #17 2 acres.
1 Aug.1804 Joseph Brittingham and wife Polly Brittingham, tailor, sold to Samuel Daley of Worc.Co. lot #7 1 acre and lot #8 1 acre.
20 Oct.1804 John Knipshitt and wife Amelia Knipshitt sold to Littleton Hitch 1 acres
12 Jan.1805 Nelly Handy sold her rights to Peter Dashiell
27 July 1805 Peter Dashiell sold to John Houston 228 1/2 acres.
26 Jan.1806 Samuel Hopkins sold to Mary James 1 rod 5 7/16 poles,lot.
15 Mar.1806 William Vance released mtg. to William Winder on lots #23,#24,#25.
8 Apr.1806 John Winder of Northampton Co. Va. heir of William sold all interest to William Winder of Som.Co.
17 May 1806 Esther Buly sold to James Smith of Samuel Smith purchased by Charles Winright and sold to Esther.
9 Sep.1806 Levin Winder, Richard Henry Handy, Hetty W. Winder, Josiah Polk coheirs of William Winder sold to William Winder, coheir.
17 May 1806 William Vance sold to Esther Buly 1/2 acre lot #22
27 May 1806 Molly Daley sold to William Daley for 5 shillings lots #7 and #8
8 Aug.1806 John Winder of Northampton Co. Virginia sold to William Winder of Somerset County Md. rights.
9 Sep.1806 Levin Winder, Richard Henry Handy, Hetty W. Winder and Josiah Polk coheirs of William Winder sold to coheir William Winder
13 Oct.1806 Purnell Johnson sold two acres to Nelly Handy.
11 Oct.1806 George Robertson sold 2 acres to Nelly Handy
25 Dec.1806 William Winder Esq. attorney sold to Dr. Thomas Winder Handy, as Henry Handy mortgaged to William Winder 450 acres with other tracts.
17 Apr.1807 Richard Henry Handy, Thomas Winder Handy heirs of William Winder sold rights to William Winder cohier.
17 Apr.1807 Leah Morris, Richard Henry Handy and Thomas Winder Handy sold to William Winder, cohier of William Winder.
4 June 1807 William Henry Handy with wife Gertrude Handy, George Dashiell with wife Esther Dashiell, William W. Handy and George D.S. Handy of Baltimore Co. heirs of William Winder sold rights to William Winder.
21 May 1807 Polly Wilson sold to John Houston 347 acres
8 Aug.1807 John Houston sold to George Parsons Sr. 137 acres
14 Nov.1807 William Winder sold to John Houston 228 1/2 acres
14 Nov.1807 William Winder sold to George Parsons 138 acres
1808 William Winder willed to son William Henry Winder part.
9 Mar.1808 Robert Leatherbury, sheriff sold to Samuel Williams heir of George Williams of Sussex Co.Del. per judgement against Thomas Lowe lots #16 & #17.
17 Feb.1810 John Freeney sold to John Rider 18 1/4 acres
6 June 1810 Thomas Handy Gillis, and wife Nelly Gillis of Washignton DC sold to David Prior of Som. Co. that Joseph Gillis died intestate leaving eight children lot #6. As Levin Irving died intestate leaving issue Nelly Gillis, William H. Irving, Handy H. Irving and Leah Irving.

10 Feb.1810 James Smith with wife Nelly Smith sold 1/2 acre to Whitty Cox.
1811 Stephen Davis willed 1/2 lot to be sold.
7 Oct.1812 Nelly Gillis Handy sold 5 acres to John Houston

PEMBRIDGE

Patented on 7 June 1688 by John Bounds for 300 acres
1700 John Bounds willed to son William Bounds
Rent Rolls 1666-1723 possessed by William Bounds
11 Sep.1764 Jehu Bounds sold 300 acres to George Adams.
14 Aug.1783 James Houston sold to Henry Banks 50 acres.
4 Feb.1797 Henry Banks sold to Benjamin Johnson and John Johnson 50 acres.

PEMBROOK

Patented in 1784 by James Houston for 50 acres
1783 tax - Dr. James Houston 50 acres, Wic.100, Worc.Co.

PENNEWELLS CHOICE

Patented in 1782 by Elisha Pennewell for 40 1/2 acres

PETER

Patented in 1760 by James Robertson Jr. for 50 acres
1783 tax - James Robertson 50 acres, Rewastico
1783 ADDITION TO PETER patented for 74 1/2 acres by James Robertson
1814 James Robertson willed to half nephew George Bole, sisters child and 1/2 to the wife of Charles Venables Robertson.

PETERS CHOICE

Patented in 1763 by Peter Gordy for 190 acres
1771 PETERS CHOICE ENGLARGED patented for 293 acres by Peter Gordy.
1783 tax - William Gordy 100 acres
1783 tax - Peter Gordy 195 acres
1783 tax - Daniel Melson 30 acres
1785 Daniel Melson willed to son Daniel, lands unnamed.
27 Apr.1797 Peter Gordy sold all rights to William Gordy.
29 May 1798 William Gordy sold to Daniel Melson 17 acres of ENLARGED
16 Mar.1799 William Gordy sold to Benjamin Melson 50 acres
1804 William Gordy willed to son William 100 acres and to son Samuel Gordy 100 acres, unnamed.
3 Aug.1805 Stephen Mitchell sold to William Gordy 129 acres
9 Nov.1809 William Gordy with wife Eliza Gordy sold part to Betty Gordy.

PETERS LOTT

Patented in 1754 by Peter Gordy for 50 acres
23 feb.1760 Peter Gordy sold 50 acres to Peter Gordy Jr.
3 Apr.1755 ADDITION TO PETERS LOTT, pat. Peter Gordy 50 acres.
26 Aug.1762 resurveyed by Peter Gordy for 190 acres in Wicomico Forrest.

PETERS LOTT

Patented in 1795 by Ezekiel Bell for 167 1/2 acres

PETERS SWAMP

Patented in 1817 by William Russum for 40 acres.
1818 William Russum willed to son William.

PHARSALIA

Patented on 18 July 1679 by John White who assigned to Mark Manlove for 600 acres at head of Rewastico Creek.
20 June 1682 Mark Manlove sold to Francis Jenkins
Rent Rolls 1666-1723 possessed by Francis Jenkins
1708 Francis Jenkins willed to wife Mary Jenkins 400 acres.
1720 John Henry and wife Mary Henry (was widow Mary Jenkins) sold to James Caldwell Sr.
12 July 1721 James Caldwell Jr. son of James sold to Patrick Donelson.
31 Mar.1738 William Moore and wife Elizabeth Moore and John Moore and wife Tabitha Moore sold to Isaac Moore 100 acres now called ISAACS BEGINNING. (that they purchased of James Caldwell and Jane Caldwell)
9 Apr.1744 George McKean of Brunswick Co.Va. sold to Thomas Roberts 107 acres of FOWERFIELD & PHARSALIA, that Patrick Donelson his grandfather left him.
5 May 1744 Patrick McKean sold to Thomas Roberts 107 1/2 acres of PHARSALIA and FLOWERFIELD.
14 Feb.1745 James Caldwell and Isaac Moore sold 91 acres to Hugh Henry part called PRISCILLA.
2 June 1745 William Dashiell sold 175 acres to Robert Kirby of Northampton Co.Va. with GOOD LUCK
1752 George Dashiell willed to sons William Dashiell and Mitchell Dashiell.
20 Aug.1755 Robert Kirby sold to Isaac Dashiell 175 acres.
23 Mar.1758 Isaac Dashiell and wife Henrietta Dashiell sold to Mitchell Jones 125 acres with tract GOOD LUCK
12 Jan 1768 John Henry son of John, with wife Sarah Henry sold to Mitchell Jones.
1768 Mitchell Dashiell willed to son George Dashiell lands left by father on Rewastico.
1783 tax - George Dashiell 175 acres
1783 tax - Esther Jones 275 acres
1783 tax - Fisher Roberts 30 acres
1783 tax - Beauchamp Hull 91 acres
15 Jan.1795 Isaac Henry and wife Dorothy Henry sold to Benjamin Jones 56 1/4 acres of HENRYS CONCLUSION & PHARSALIA
15 Jan.1795 Benjamin Jones sold to Isaac Henry- to establish lines.
3 Mar.1795 George Dashiell son of Mitchell Dashiell sold to Robert Dashiell.
1795 Thomas Roberts willed to son William Roberts.
12 Feb.1798 Benjamin Jones son of Mitchell Jones, sold to George Robertson 300 acres of PHARSAILA, GOOD LUCK, HENRYS CONCLSUION and part of PHARSALIA conveyed by Isaac Henry.
12 Jan.1799 Esther Jones widow of Mitchell Jones sold her interest to Shiles Crockett.

9 Mar.1799 Robert Dashiell Sr. and wife Isabella Dashiell sold to
Arthur Dashiell, left by will of Mitchell Dashiell.
26 Oct.1803 William Roberts with wife Sarah Roberts sold to Joshua
Roberts and Levin Taylor FLOWERFIELD and PHARSALIA bought by Thomas
Roberts.

PHILADELPHIA

Patented in 1776 by Jacob Evans for 50 acres
13 Sep.1791 Jacob Evans sold to Daniel Fooks 50 acres.
1783 tax - Daniel Fooks 50 acres.
1783 tax - Jonathan Fooks, ADDITION TO PHILIADELPHIA 400 acres
1803 ADDITION TO PHILADELPHIA pat. Jonathan Fooks 1443 acres
8 Apr.1806 Jonathan Fooks sold to Daniel Fooks 117 acres
7 Apr.1805 Jonathan Fooks of Daniel Fooks sold to William Jones 52 acres.
7 Apr.1805 Jonathan Fooks of Daniel Fooks sold to Jonathan Fooks of
Jonathan, 108 acres
8 Dec.1809 Billy Fooks, Jonathan Fooks, James Fooks, Thomas Fooks and
Daniel Fooks, division of lands of Daniel Fooks deceased.
1825 SECOND ADDN. TO PHILADELPHIA Jonathan Fooks 98 3/4 acres.
1830 Jonathan Fooks willed to son James Minos Fooks ADDITIION and
SECOND ADDN.TO PHILADELPHIA except 75 acres where William Parsons
lives.

PHILLIPS ADDITION

Patented on 17 Apr.1695 by Roger Phillips for 25 acres taken out of
HORSEYS BALIWICK.
Rent Rolls 1666-1723 possessed by Richard Phillips son of Roger.
4 Dec. 1695 Roger Phillips sold to Phillip Ascue
3 July 1708 Phillip Ascue and wife Grace Ascue sold to Thomas Brown.
20 Dec.1721 William Serman and wife Sarah Serman sold 12 1/2 acres to
Roger Phillips.
1 Feb.1739 Richard Phillips son of Richard sold to Roger Kellett and
wife Eunice Kellett 12 1/2 acres
26 Apr.1746 Thomas Phillips sold to Roger Kellett and wife Eunice
Kellett 107 acres and 12 1/2 acres of marsh adjacent being land left
to Sarah Phillips by Roger Phillips.
7 Dec.1800 John Webb mortgaged to John Dashiell Sr.
17 Dec.1801 John Dashiell and wife Elizabeth Dashiell released
mortgage
4 Oct.1805 John Webb and wife Hetty Webb sold to John Dashiell.

PHILLIPS DESIRE

Patented on 7 May 1760 by Jacob Phillips for 50 acres
2 May 1771 Jacob Phillips sold to Daniel Melson 50 acres
1785 Daniel Melson willed to son Daniel Melson
24 Mar.1804 Joseph Melson of Sussex Co.Delaware sold to Jesse Davis of
Worc.Co. 50 acres.
14 Sep.1809 Jesse Davis with wife Ruth Davis and Benjamin Melson sold
to William Layfield 50 acres.

PHILLIPS FAREWELL

Patented in 1792 by Rhoda Phillips for 906 1/2 acres

PHILLIPS FOLLY

Patented on 27 Apr.1762 by Moses Driskill for 100 acres
1764 resurveyed to DRISKILLS HAZZARD.

PHILLIPS LOT

see WHITE OAK SWAMP

PICK AND CULL

Patented on 10 June 1734 by John Moore at Nanticoke
11 Oct.1755 John Moore sold to Isaac Calloway 100 acres, at Little Creek.
1 Sep.1760 Isaac Calloway sold to John Crouch
6 Apr.1773 Robert Crouch sold 100 acres to William Polk
3 Mar.1776 Sussex Co.Del. land warrants, William Polk

PIGG PENN

Patented in 1744 by Joseph Rowle for 50 acres
1783 tax - John Romner 50 acres, Rewastico
1849 Mark Waller willed to grandson George W. Wright son of Levin Wright.

PICK POCKET

Patented in 1845 by Thomas Robertson for 4 1/2 acres.

PIG POINT

Patented in 1788 by William Dryden for 8 acres.

PILCHARDS DESIRE

Patented in 1774 by William Pilchard for 50 acres
26 Nov.1784 John Pilchard sold to Benjamin Shockley 50 acres.
1791 Benjamin Shockley willed to son Noble Shockley
25 Jan.1800 Noble Shockley with wife Livecia Shockley sold to George Truitt son of John Truitt, 50 acres.

PINA ISLAND

Patented in 1725 by William Layfield for 25 acres

PINE NECK

Patented by Isaac Ingram for 100 acres
13 Jan.1744 Isaac Ingram with wife Margaret Ingram sold to Thomas Collins, at head of the Nanticoke River.

PINE LANDING

see MAIDENS LOTT

PINE NECK

Patented in 1775 by John Richardson for 311 acres
1783 tax - John Richardson Wic.100 Worc.co. 261 acres

PINE SWAMP

Patented in 1786 by Robert Stanford for 26 acres
3 Oct.1795 Robert Stanford of Columbia Co. Georgia and attorney John Harris Hayman sold to Joshua Stanford of Som. Co. 12 acres.
10 Oct.1795 Robert Stanford of Columbia Co.Ga. sold to George Pollitt 6 acres.
1 Nov.1802 Joshua Stanford with wife Mary Stanford sold to Outten Toadvine 12 acres.

PINEY BEAVER DAM

Patented on 24 Aug.1762 by Peter Parsons for 45 acres
1762 Peter Parsons willed to wife Martha Parsons all lands, then to son Joshua Parsons 45 acres.
1783 tax - Martha Parsons 45 acres, Acquango 100 Worc.Co.
13 July 1801 John Bennett, Peter Bennett of Kent Co. Delaward sold to James Round of Worc.Co.
5 Dec.1803 James Round with wife Tabitha Round sold to Joshua Holloway of Joshua 18 1/2 acres

PINEY FIELDS

Patented in 1802 by Ephraim Dykes for 240 acres.

PINEY GROVE

Patented in 1756 by Dorothy McClure for 45 acres
1776 Dorothy McClure willed to cousin Benjamin McClellan
1783 tax - Benjamin McClellan 45 acres, Rewastico
25 May 1795 Benjamin McClellan with wife Bridget McClellan sold to Hudson Lowe 7 3/4 acres and 1/8 acres of SAW MILL SUPPLY
25 May 1795 Benjamin McClellan and wife Bridget McClellan sold to Thomas Humphries 10 3/4 acres of PINEY GROVE & SAW MILL SUPPLY
1802 Hudson Lowe willed lands unnamed to son Samuel Lowe.

PINEY GROVE

Patented in 1760 by John Houston for 100 acres
8 Mar.1776 Sussex Co.Delaware land warrants, John Houston.

PINEY HILL

Patented in 1769 by Isaac Vinson for 23 acres
1783 tax - Isaac Vinson 23 acres, Rewastico
1805 Isaac Vinson willed to wife Mary Vinson 100 acres
1808 Mary Vinson willed to Samuel Moore.

PINEY ISLAND

Patented in 1765 by Joseph Collins and Jonathan Bell for 152 1/2 acres probably a resurvey of part of PINEY ISLAND, see below.
1783 tax - John Thorns 132 1/2 acres

PINEY ISLAND

Patented in 1759 by Samuel Acworth for 25 acres

6 Dec.1762 2nd. patent by Thomas Acworth for 29 acres
1761 Samuel Acworth willed to son Ephraim Acworth
16 Nov.1763 Thomas Acworth sold to Joseph Collins 29 acres.
1783 tax - Sarah Acworth 19 acres, Rewastico

PINEY MARSH

14 Apr.1743 Richard Crockett and wife Elizabeth Crockett of Som.Co. sold to Adam Muir of Dorc.Co. CROCKETTS PETITION, DELIGHT and 150 acres of PINEY MARSH.
19 Apr.1754 PINEY MARSH ADDITION 20 acres patented by James Muir
1765 Richard Crockett willed to son Richard 1/2 and to son John Crockett 1/2.

PINEY RIDGE

Patented on 20 Oct.1763 by Peter Gordy Jr. for 50 acres
16 Oct.1784 Peter Gordy sold to Elisha Pennewell 50 acres.

PIPING HILL

Patented on 13 Apr.1762 by John Brattan for 50 acres
1783 tax - Job Truitt 50 acres, Acquango 100
1785 Job Truitt willed to daughters Leah Truitt and Mary Truitt.

PITTSBURGH

Patented in 1784 by John Dennis for 40 acres.
8 Oct.1785 William Dennis sold to Benjamin Shockley of Jonathan Shockley 40 acres.
7 Sep.1799 Charles Shockley sold his 1/6th part of land of Benjamin Shockley, to Betsy Shockley
23 Jan.1808 Benjamin Shockley of Benjamin sold to Billy Fooks, part
1831 ADDITION TO PITTSBURGH patented to John Brown for 245 acres

PLAGUE WITHOUT PROFIT

Patented in 1800 by Elias Bayley for 11 acres
1817 Elias Bayley willed to son Isaiah Bayley 10 acres of PLAGUE

PLAIN DEALING

There were a number of patents under this name.
Patented in 1765 by John Reddish for 50 acres
1770 ADDITION TO PLAIN DEALING patented to John Reddish.
Patented in 1791 by John Reddish for 41 1/4 acres.
4 Jan.1772 John Reddish and wife Joanna Reddish sold to Hiron Reddish 27 1/2 acres and 13 acres of ADDITION
1783 tax - Hiron Reddish 50 acres.
1783 tax - John Reddish Sr. 222 acres with ADDITION
10 Apr.1798 John Reddish and wife Rhoda Reddish sold to John Reddish 27 acres and 13 acres of ADDITION.
3 Nov.1806 Richard Ingersol and Richard Bennett sold to Benjamin Johnson of Worc.Co. PLAIN DEALING & ADDITION TO PLAIN DEALING
24 Sep.1808 John Reddish sold to Benjamin Johnson 75 1/2 acres
19 Aug.1809 John Reddish of Worc.Co. sold to Benjamin Johnson 16 1/2

acres and 75 1/2 acres of ADDITION.

PLANTATION

Patented in 1788 by David Wallace for 1 1/4 acres

PLEASANT GREEN

Patented in 1746 by Jonathan Bayley for 50 acres

PLEASANT GROVE

Patented in 1761 by Thomas Robins for 50 acres

PLEASANT GROVE

Patented on 15 May 1762 by Jonathan Dyer for 9 acres
9 Oct.1767 Jonathan Dyer sold to Parker Selby 9 acres, in Wicomico forrest.
1770 resurveyed by Parker Selby to 150 acres
8 Oct.1802 George Selby heir of Parker sold to Marshall Smiith 150 acres, in Wicomico forest.

PLEASURE

Patented on 7 Sep.1753 by James Jones for 50 acres
27 Jan.1762 James Jones sold 50 acres to Samuel Jackson Bayley
25 Oct.1765 Samuel Jackson Bayley and wife Sarah Bayley sold 50 acres for 5 shillings to Davis Bayley with BAYLEYS CHOICE.

PLUMPTON SALTASH

Patented on 15 Dec.1715 by Thomas Cox Sr. on the south side of the main branch of the Wicomico River for 563 acres.
17 Jan 1723 Thomas Cox sold to Lewis Disharoon and wife Jane Disharoon and to Levin Disharoon his grandson.
1724 Thomas Cox willed to grandsons Hill Cox and Thomas Cox 50 acres and grandchildren Archibald Smith and Sarah Ann Smith 200 acres.
29 July 1729 Jeremiah Wright and wife Lydia Wright and Thomas Cox and wife Elizabeth Cox sold to John Carr 100 acres, that Matthew Swain willed to his daughter Lydia Wright that he purchased of Thomas Cox.
9 Nov.1730 John Carr and wife Catherine Carr sold to Daniel Lingo 100 acres.
50 acres resurveyed to SWANNS LUCK
17 Apr.1734 Daniel Lingo and wife Margaret Lingo sold to Catherine Carr 50 acres of SWANS LUCK out of 100 acres of PLUMPTONS SALTASH.
1737 Bryan Ready and wife Catherine Ready (aka Catherine Carr) sold to Joseph Leonard 40 acres
4 Feb.1754 Hill Cox and Thomas Cox sold to Robert Handy 80 acres of WILTON & PLUMPTON SALTASH
4 Feb.1754 Hill Cox sold 39 acres to Thomas Cox for 10 shillings.
11 Aug.1760 Lydia Wright sold to Levin Turner and Elizabeth Disharoon 200 acres that Thomas Cox sold to Lewis Disharoon.
13 May 1763 Hill Cox sold 28 acres to George Parker Sr.
1765 George Parker willed to wife Sarah Parker 100 acres purchased from Hill Cox and after her death to son John Parker, unnamed.

11 May 1772 Levin Hobbs and wife Elizabeth Hobbs sold 100 acres to James Buchannan
1783 tax - Thomas Cox Sr. 30 acres.
1783 tax - Cox Clarkson 50 acres
1783 tax - John Parker of George Parker 35 acres
1783 tax - Archibald Smith 100 acres
1783 tax - John Smith 100 acres
1783 tax - Joseph Leonard 40 acres
1783 tax - John Nelms 10 acres
13 Feb.1787 Levin Turner and Samuel Turner of Worc.Co. sold 102 1/4 acres to Joseph Leonard of Somerset Co.
9 June 1788 Robert Parsons and wife Sarah Parsons of Sussex Co.Del. sold to John Nelms, Noah Nelms and Peter Nelms of Som.Co. 10 acres with TATUMS HABITATION & SWANS LUCK.
23 Nov.1797 Archibald Smith with wife Esther Smith sold to John Byrd 200 acres and 19 perches.
10 May 1806 John Byrd and wife Margaret Byrd sold to Thomas Byrd Sr. 200 acres, 19 perches.
18 Mar.1808 William Hearn as attorney of Archibald Smith sold to George Parker 2 1/2 acres and 4 5/8 acres.

POINT COMFORT

Patented in 1746 by John Taylor for 50 acres

POINT LARRAMORE

Patented in 1804 by James Larramore for 14 acres
1830 James Larramore willed lands unnamed to sons James Larramore, William Larramore and daughter Louise Mary Riall wife of George Riall.

POINT LOOK OUT

Patented in 1782 by James Perdue for 22 1/2 acres
1783 tax - James Perdue of John Perdue 22 1/2 acres Wic.100 Wor.Co.

POINT MARSH

Patented on 9 Sep.1720 by Richard Crockett on the north side of the Wicomico River.
Rent Rolls 1666-1723 possessed by Richard Crockett
1726 Richard Crockett willed lands unnamed to son John Crockett
1783 tax - John S. Conway 4 1/2 acres, Nanticoke 100

POINT MARSH

Patented on 8 Dec.1703 by John McClester for 200 acres
Rent Rolls 1666-1723 possessed by John McClester
26 Apr.1743 Samuel McClester son of John McClester gave 100 acres to brother George McClester.
1783 tax - Sarah McClester 160 acres
1783 tax - John Sterling 40 acres
28 June 1790 John Sterling and wife Rachel Sterling sold to Jesse Hughes and wife Sarah Hughes 200 acres (Rachel and Sarah were

daughters of George McClester.)

POINT OF MARSH

Patented on 13 Mar.1766 by Thomas Dashiell for 9 1/4 acres between CHANCE & DASHIELLS LOTT on the north side of Wicomico Creek.
1771 Thomas Dashiell willed lands to son William Dashiell
1783 tax - William Dashiell 9 1/4 acres

POINT NOBLE

Patented in 1807 by Robert Lemon for 6 1/2 acres
18 Nov.1809 Dr. Robert Lemon and wife Nancy Lemon sold to Joshua Linnard, blacksmith, all.

POINT PATIENCE

Patented on 20 May 1689 by William Elgate for 143 acres on the west most side of the main branch of the Wicomico River
Rent Rolls 1666-1723 possessed by Andrew Caldwell
5 Sep.1717 Andrew Caldwell, carpenter, of Kent Co. Del. with wife Margaret Caldwell sold to George Dashiell 143 acres.
6 July 1722 George Dashiell Jr. with wife Mary Dashiell sold to Bryan Snee 143 acres.
6 Dec.1733 Bryan Snee gave to friend Samuel Hall 143 acres.
8 Sep.1768 Samuel Hall sold to Nathan Culver 143 acres.
10 Sep.1787 Nathan Culver Sr. sold to Nancy Nelms of Salisbury 217 1/2 acres of PEACE & QUIETNESS & POINT PATIENCE.
1783 tax - Nathan Culver 26 acres, Rewastico
1783 tax - Elijah Vinson 112 acres.
22 Aug.1789 Nathan Culver sold to William Elzey 19 1/2 of POINT PATIENCE & MILL LOTT.
28 Nov.1789 Nathan Culver sold to Joshua Hitch Sr. 35 acres of PEACE & QUIETNESS, MILL LOTT, POINT PATIENCE.
11 July 1795 Robert Lemon and wife Nancy Lemon of Salisbury Town sold to James Weatherly Waller 217 1/4 acres of PEACE & QUIETNESS & POINT PATIENCE.
21 Jan.1797 James W. Waller sold 9 1/4 acres to Curtis Hitch
11 Oct.1803 James W. Waller with wife Ann Waller sold to Esme Marshall Waller.
5 Sep.1804 William Elzey of Sussex Co.Del. sold to Curtis Hitch, POINT PATIENCE & MILL LOTT, no acreage mentioned.

POLEHAMBLETON

Patented on 21 May 1689 by John Huett for 300 acres on the south arm of the Wicomico River.
2 Mar.1725 Alexander Leckie and wife Ann Leckie sold 100 acres to William Hayman.
14 June 1733 William Hayman and wife Mary Hayman sold 100 acres to James Ruark.
8 Mar.1753 James Ruark with wife Elizabeth Ruark sold 100 acres to John Jenkins.
12 Mar.1772 Rachel Jenkins widow of John, Thomas Lamberson with wife Leah Lamberson, Patey Truitt with wife Rachel Truitt, William Gault

with wife Mary Gault daughters of John Jenkins and Rachel sold to Joseph Dashiell 300 acres.
1783 tax - Joseph Dashiell 100 acres.
9 Nov.1805 Benjamin Dashiell sold to George Winright 100 acres

POLKS ADDITION

Patented in 1820 by Whittington Polk for 34 1/2 acres

POLKS CONCLUSION

Patented 7 Aug.1752 by John Polk for 1372 acres, a resurvey of LABOUR, POLKS CHANCE, JOHNS VENTURE, NANTICOKE POINT, etc.
2 May 1761 John Polk with wife Jane Polk sold to James Polk 400 acres.

POLKS DISAPPOINTMENT

Patented in 1819 by Joseph Richards for 17 1/2 acres

POLKS FANCY

Patented in 1803 by Josiah Polk for 4 1/8 acres

POLLITTS ADDITION

Patented on 10 Oct.1767 by George Pollitt for 45 1/2 acres.
30 June 1798 George Pollitt sold to John Cathell 4 acres
1823 Patented for 18 acres by Levin Pollitt

POLLITTS CRAFT

Patented in 1786 by William Pollitt for 15 acres

POLLITTS FINDING

Patented in 1770 by William Pollitt for 42 acres

POLLITTS MILL LOT

Patented in 1801 by William Pollitt for 14 3/4 acres

POLLITTS TRYAL

Patented in 1814 by Joshua Morris for 12 1/4 acres

POLLITTS VICTORY

Patented in 1749 by William Pollitt for 198 acres

POOR CHANCE

Patented in 1747 by Joseph Hust for 50 acres
19 mar.1752 Joseph Hust sold 50 acres to Arthur Hickman
21 Nov.1754 Arthur Hickman with wife Sabrah Hickman sold 40 acres to Robert Walter, being part of tract PURCHASE.

1783 tax - Robert Walter 40 acres, Nanticoke 100.

POOR CHANCE

Patented on 30 Sep.1762 by William Venables for 50 acres near head of the Wicomico River
1783 tax - John Venables 50 acres Wic.100, Worc.Co.

POOR CHANCE

Patented on 10 June 1718 by James King for 50 acres on the east side of the road to Broad Creek from the head of the Wicomico River.
30 Oct.1765 Nehemiah King heir at law to James King sold to Robert King 50 acres.
10 Apr.1776 Sussex Co.Del.land warrants, Robert King.

POOR CHOICE

Patented in 1761 by Andrew Spear for 86 acres
10 Mar.1770 Andrew Spear with wife Betty Spear sold 86 acres to Charles Davis at Barren Creek.
18 July 1773 Charles Davis sold 75 /12 acres to Ahab Coston
14 Nov.1772 Levin Fletcher and Charles Davis sold to David Dutton free mulatto part of POOR CHANCE & CROOKED CHANCE 60 acres.
4 Mar.1775 Ahab Coston sold 31 acres to David Dutton
11 Mar.1775 Ahab Coston sold to William Mills 30 acres
11 Mar.1775 Ahab Coston sold to William Mills 3 acres.
1777 part resurveyed to HONEST PURCHASE.
1848 ADDITION TO POOR CHOICE patented by Edward Fowler for 15 3/4 acres (in 1850 he is in Salisbury District.)

POORFIELDS

Patented on 11 Apr.1689 by James Ingram for 150 acres back in the woods from the south side of the Wicomico River.
19 Nov.1747 Isaac Ingram of Wroc.Co. eldest son of Abrahm Ingram who was the son of James Ingram sold 150 acres to Benjamin Mitchell.
27 Nov.1756 Benjamin Mitchell with wife Mary Mitchell sold 150 acres to Robert Hopkins.
21 June 1759 Robert Hopkins sold 21 acres to Constant Disharoon.
1783 tax - Constant Disharoon.
1790 resurveyed by Constant Disharoon to 152 1/4 acres.
2 Aug.1794 Horatio Hopkins sold balance of to Joshua Disharoon.
1795 Constant Disharoon willed 29 1/2 acrs to daughter Milla Stanford and then to grandson Constant D. Stanford.

POOR HILL

No Patent found
2 June 1800 John Phillips sold to john Downing 31 acres in Wicomico Forest
1792 ADDITION TO POOPR HILL patented by John Phillips for 25 acres

POOR HILL

Patented in 1857 by John R. Downing for 6 acres

POOR MANS CHANCE

Patented on 10 July 1760 by William Davis Jr. for 25 acres
1767 William Davis willed to son Spencer Davis 25 acres
1783 tax - Spencer Davis 25 acres, Wic.100 Worc.Co.
1809 Spencer Davis willed to sons Levin Davis and William Davis.

POOR MANS HYPOCRACY DECEIVED

Patented on 18 July 1760 by Benjamin Handy for 80 acres.
14 June 1792 Haste Handy sold 80 acres to Gabriel Slocomb.
13 May 1800 Gabriel Slocomb with wife Catherine Slocomb of Dorc.Co. sold to Marcellus Slocomb of same 80 acres.
17 Nov.1807 Sarah Slocomb widow of Marcellus Slocomb of Dorc. Co. and Barzilla Slocomb, guardian, sold rights to William Bassett.
1832 William Bassitt willed to daughters Mary Brittingham, Sally Brittingham, Rachel Adkins and Betsy Davis.

POOR PROSPECT

Patented in 1802 by Esme Merrill for 10 1/2 acres

POOR QUARTER

Patented on 23 Mar.1689 by Cornelius Anderson for 150 acres.
Cornelius Anderson made over to Thomas Wilson his soled heir and executor
13 Oct.1729 Thomas Wilson of Cedar Creek Sussex Co.Del. sold to George Goddard of Somerset Co. 150 acres
23 Jan.1732 George Goddard sold to James Fullerton second son to Sarah Howjean 150 acres.
Repatented in 1764 by Alexander Fullerton for 265 1/2 acres
28 Oct.1765 Alexander Fullerton gave to son John Fullerton.
1783 tax - James Anderson 50 acres Wic.100 Worc.Co.
1783 tax - Obed Stanford 110 acres.
20 Mar.1788 Stephen Magee with wife Margaret Magee sold to Nicholas Reddish 1/4 acres.
20 Mar.1788 Stephen Magee with wife Peggy Magee sold to James Anderson 69 acres.

POOR RIDGE

Patented on 25 Apr.1763 by Robert Davis son of William Davis for 50 acres
1768 Robert Davis willed 50 acres to grandson Robert Kelley.

POPLAR HILL

Patented in 1741 by John Dennis Hudson for 200 acres

POPLAR NECK

Patented on 10 Oct.1730 by Josiah Quartermus for 200 acres
10 Nov.1766 James Quartermus sold 50 acres to Ephraim Vaughan
1773 Ephraim Vaughan willed to son James Vaughan, if no heir to Ephraim Vaughan.

POPLAR NECK

Patented in 1774 by Daniel Fooks for 50 acres
1783 tax - Daniel Fooks 50 acres, Acquango 100
1793 Daniel Fooks willed to sons Daniel Fooks and James Fooks.

POPLAR RIDGE

Patented on 11 Oct.1728 by Samuel Melson for 150 acres
1739 Samuel Melson willed to sons Joseph Melson and Benjamin Melson
13 July 1774 Joseph Melson with wife Esther Melson sold 75 acres to Phillip Wingate at a branch of Broad Creek on the north side of the Nanticoke River.
1771 Benjamin Melson willed to son Joseph Melson, on road from Broad Creek to Luestown, and to sons William Melson and Jesse Melson
1757 Phillip Wingate willed 75 acres to son Phillip.
4 July 1776 Sussex Co.Del. land warrants, William Melson

PORTERS BEGINNING

Patented on 15 Apr.1763 by William Porter for 50 acres.
8 June 1768 Samuel Porter and William Porter sold to Edward Ellis 50 acres.
2 Feb.1771 Edward Ellis with wife Rachel Ellis sold to John Trader 50 acres.
6 Mar.1780 John Trader with wife Rachel Trader sold to William McBryde.
25 Apr.1791 William McBryde with wife Sarah McBryde sold to Joshua Dorman 75 acres of PORTERS BEGINNING & GIBBONS LIBERTY.

PORTERS ISLAND

see SARAHS SECURITY

PORTERS INVENTION

Patented in 1810 by William L. Porter for 212 3/8 acres

PORTERS MEADOWS

Patented in 1770 by McKimmea Porter for 17 1/2 acres
1783 tax - McKimmea Porter 17 1/2 acres, Rewastico 100
1790 McKimmea Porter willed to son Levi Porter, if no issue to daughters Elizabeth Porter, Gatta Porter and Leah Porter.
11 June 1810 Levi Porter with wife Hetty Porter sold to Joshua Brattan land devised by father McKimmea Porter, no name of land.

POTOMACK

Patented in 1750 by John Phillips for 35 acres
4 Mar.1758 John Phillips Sr. sold to John Phillips Jr. 35 acres

POVERTY

Patented in 1784 by Isaac Moore for 166 1/2 acres

POWELLS MEADOW

Patented in 1800 by Levin Powell for 2 acres

POWELLS NECK

Patented in 1749 by Gabriel Powell for 50 acres
1807 Gabriel Powell willed to grandson John Powell of Elijah Powell 50 acres, unnamed.

PRESTON

Patented on 28 Apr.1695 by Thomas Pollitt for 250 acres
Rent Rolls 1666-1723 possessed by Thomas Pollitt
PRESTONS ADDITION patented in 1728 for 125 acres by Henrietta Boulve and Ann Boulve.
22 Feb.1762 repatented by Thomas Pollitt for 320 acres, was in right of Hannah Dixon who died intestate without heirs and became escheated.
1 Dec.1764 Stephen Garland, escheat of land of Samuel Davis PRESTONS ADDITION granted Henrietta Boulve and Ann Boulve who died intestate 125 acres.
2 Jan.1766 Stephen Garland sold to Thomas Dashiell, sheriff, 125 acres at head of Wicomico River on behalf of a prisoner in jail.
19 Aug.1767 Thomas Pollitt with wife Betty Pollitt sold to James Thompson, blacksmith 320 acres.
6 Oct 1772 James Thompson sold 8 acres to William Horsey and Josiah Russell
26 Aug.1775 Josiah Russell sold to Isaac Horsey and William Horsey 8 acres.
22 May 1782 William Horsey sold to Isaac Horsey of Sussex Co.Delaware 8 acres partition of lands. .
1783 tax - Leah Thompson 300 acres, Wic.100
1784 ADDITION TO PRESTIN(PRESTON) patented by James Thompson for 433 3/4 acres.
6 Nov.1793 Robert Graham sold to William McBryde 99 1/2 acres, mortgage.
4 Mar.1794 Sarah McBryde administratrix of William McBryde sold to Moses Dryden 99 1/2 acres of ADDITION TO PRESTON
23 Nov.1795 Moses Dryden sold rights to Edward Hammond.
4 Mar.1797 William A. Winder with wife Nancy Winder sold to David Cathell all rights
4 Mar.1797 David Cathell and wife Nancy Cathell only child of James Thompson sold to William H. Winder ADDITION TO PRESTON 433 3/4 acres.
9 June 1797 George Purnell, sheriff, sold to Isaac Ewing 102 acres with saw mill per judgement against Robert Graham.
13 June 1800 Isaac Ewing sold to David Cathell 102 acres
1802 David Cathell willed to son James Thompson Cathell 400 acres of ADDITION TO PRESTON
8 May 1824 Joshua Cathell sold to James Disharoon of Worc.Co. his right that descended to him at the death of brother James T. Cathell.

PREVENTION

Patented on 18 May 1688 by James Weatherly for 90 acres
Rent Rolls 1666-1723 possessed by James Weatherly

23 Nov.1779 Charles Weatherly, James Weatherly, John Weatherly, Jesse Weatherly sold to William Winder
1783 tax - James Weatherly 58 acres, Rewastico 100
1783 tax - William Winder 12 acres

PREVENTION

Patented in 1773 by Henry Lowe for 6 acres
1783 tax - Henry Lowe 6 acres, Wicomico 100

PRICKLE COCKSHOLT

Patented on 6 July 1686 by George Collins for 75 acres.
Rent Rolls 1666-1723 possessed by the widow Fluellin that her husband Samuel Fluellin purchased from George Collins.
1760 ADDITION patented by Samuel Fluellin for 297 acres
1766 Samuel Fluellin willed to son John Fluellin, ADDITION
11 May 1761 Samuel Tull sold to William Winright 136 1/2 acres of ADDITION TO PRICKLECOKCHOLT.
13 June 1764 Samuel Fluellin sold 8 1/2 acres to Isaac Atkinson
19 Mar.1770 Richard Crockett Fluellin son of Samuel Fluellin deceased sold 297 acres to Ephraim King.
1783 tax - Jane Fluellin 1 acres
1783 tax - Elizabeth Atkinson 8 1/2 acres of ADDITION
1783 tax - William Winright 136 1/2 acres of ADDITION
13 Nov.1792 William Winright and wife Elizabeth Winright sold 25 /14 acres to Daniel Foreman for 5 shillings of ADDITION.
26 Mar.1793 Gillis Polk surviving trustee of Ephraim King and Samuel Fluellin sold to Isaac Atkinson son of Isaac, ADDITION TO PRICKLECOCKSHOLT, FLUELLINS SETTLEMENT, TICKNELL, MILKMORE, etc.
1 Dec.1807 Isaac Atkinson exchangedd with Littleton Aires 7 5/8 acres for MOOREFIELDS.

PRISCILLA

see PHARSALIA

PRISCILLAS DELIGHT

Patented in 1748 by Priscilla Dunn for 118 acres

PRIVILEDGE

Patented in 1705 by Peter Douty for 50 acres
19 Jan 1709 Peter Douty willed to Peter Furbush son of John Furbush
16 Mar.1729 Peter Furbush sold to John Larramore 50 acres.
9 Mar.1747 Levin Larramore and mother Mary Larramore sold 50 acres to Teague Dickerson.
22 Aug.1764 John Furbush and John Dougherty sold to Teague Dickerson.

PRIVILDEGE

Patented in 1748 by Henry Lowe for 1 acres
1783 tax - Henry Lowe, 1 acres, Wic.100

PRIVILEDGE

Patented in 1767 by John Dougherty for 39 acres
1783 tax - John Dougherty 39 acres, Nanticoke 100

PRIVILEDGE

Patented in 1775 by John Sterling for 19 1/2 acres

PRIVILEDGE

Patented in 1782 by Samuel King for 76 1/2 acres
1783 tax - Samuel King 76 1/2 acres- Rewastico 100

PRIVILEDGE

Patented in 1798 by Matthias Miles for 44 1/2 acres.

PRIVILEDGE

Patented in 1815 by Richard Bennett for 5 3/4 acres

PROMISE

see LAND OF PROMISE

PROMISE LAND

Patented in 1851 by William Laws for 723 acres, 25 perches

PROPERTY

Patented in 1783 by Jacob Morris for 29 1/2 acres

PROSPECT

Patented in 1803 by John McClester for 455 1/2 acres
1825 John McClester willed to son James Robert John McClester.
1825 James R. J. McClester Fountain willed to George Washignton Fountain all rights. If wife Ann Fountain has a child all legacies voided.

PROSPECT HILL

Patented on 13 Aug.1796 by Benjamin F.A.C. Dashiell for 52 3/4 acres part of Wicomico Marsh formerly sold to Col. Joseph Dashiell, resurveyed to one tract.
14 Mar.1804 James Bennett sold to William Sturgis, carpenter lots 11 and 26.
7 Mar.1807 James Bennett sold to William Black lots 34 & 36 and 2 perches.
24 June 1807 James Bennett sold to John Field lots 32 and 33.
24 Feb.1810 James Bennett and wife Jane Bennett sold to Levin Disharoon and Thomas Disharoon 305 perches.
1812 James Bennett willed to be sold bought of Benjamin F.A.C. Dashiell.

PROSPECT HILL

Patented in 1814 by Emanuel Walker for 11 3/4 acres

PROSPERITY

Patented on 10 May 1758 by John Willis for 50 acres in the woods from the Wicomico River.
1761 Nathaniel Willis willed to son John Willis 50 acres.
7 Aug.1765 John Willis sold to James Davis 50 acres.
2 Dec.1767 James Davis with wife Sabra Willis sold to John Willis 50 acres.
2 Apr.1791 David Willis sold to Sarah Mears 50 acres.
7 Oct.1797 Sarah Mears sold to John Shockley 50 acres.
8 Jan.1810 Peter Dashiell sold to John Nelms of Baltimore.
19 May 1808 Robbert Nairn, sheriff sold to Peter Dashiell 50 acres per judgement against John Willis.

PROVIDENCE

Patented on 14 Mar.1753 by Joseph Marshall for 100 acres.
17 Aug.1763 Joseph Marshall, blacksmith sold to John Mitchell and John Holston Jr. 100 acres.

PROVIDENCE

Patented in 1765 by Thomas Willin for 42 1/2 acres.

PRYERS HARD FATE

Patented in 1790 by David Prior for 183 1/2 acres
5 Feb.1803 David Prior sold to Henry Banks 43 1/4 acres

PRYERS CHANCE

Patented in 1791 by David Prior for 12 1/2 acres

PUNCH BOWL

Patented in 1753 by Abraham Dean for 1 acres

PURCHASE

Patented on 12 June 1720 by James Parremore for 50 acres
Rent Rolls 1666-1723 possessed by James Parremore
1740 James Parremore willed to son Isaac Parremore 50 acres, unnamed.
1765 Isaac Parremore willed to son James Parremore 50 acres where I live.
1783 tax - James Parremore 50 acres, Rewastico 100
17 Mar.1797 James Parremore Sr. sold 7 1/2 acres to Robert Dorman.

PURCHASE

Patented on 15 Oct.1706 by John Caldwell for 134 acres on the north side of the main branch of the Wicomico River.

7 APr.1739 James Givans sold to James Train 16 acres.
10 Dec.1743 James Givans sold to James Hardy 16 acres
4 Nov.1743 James Givans sold 16 acres to William Giles Jr.
1772 William Giles willed to Leah Duncan LARGEE.
10 Sep.1760 Thomas Savage sold to Joseph Hitch 134 acres of PURCHASE patented John Caldwell.
1783 tax - William Harris 16 acres, Rewastcio 100
1783 tax - William Dorman 16 acres.

PURCHASE

Patented in 1766 by William Houghan for 269 1/2 acres
22 Sep.1767 William Houghan and wife Sarah Houghan of Kent Co.Del (she spinster executrix of Joseph Collins late of Worc.Co. Sarah was the only heir of David Harris late owner of the orignial tract HARRIS CHANCE) sold to John Collins 269 1/2 acres.
10 Oct.1782 John Collins of Sussex Co.Del. sold to George Wilson 45 acres, at Quantico Creek.
1783 tax - George Wilson 45 acres
10 Oct.1782 John Collins of Sussex Co.Del. sold to Benjamin Hearn of Somerset County Maryland 25 acres.

PUZZLE

Patented on 2 Aug.1762 by Randall Smulling for 50 acres
17 Aug.1798 John Scarbrough and Peter Smulling sold to Robert Dukes 50 acres.

PUZZLE

Patented in 1747 by John Williams for 100 acres
10 Mar.1758 John Williams and wife Charity Williams sold to William Toadvine 100 acres.

PUZZLE

Patented on 25 Mar.1748 by John Short for 100 acres
22 Dec.1769 Jonathan Short with wife Elizabeth Short sold to Adam Short on the south east side of the Nanticoke River.

PUZZLE

Patented on 9 May 1760 by Nehemiah Stayton for 72 acres
4 Feb.1775 Nehemiah Stayton with wife Sarah Stayton sold to William Laws.

PUZZLE

Patented in 1805 by Jonathan Waller for 91 acres

PUZZLESOME

Patented in 1848 by Willin Wright, Joseph Wright and Levin Wright for 77 3/4 acres

PUZZLE TO FIND

Patented in 1801 by Jesse Covington for 7 acres

QUADRANT

Patented in 1795 by Robert Dorman for 92 1/4 acres
17 Mar.1797 Robert Dorman sold 7 1/2 acres to James Parremore
1799 Robert Dorman willed to son Hamilton Dorman.
1813 Hamilton Dorman willed to brother Henry Dorman all land willed me by father Robert Dorman.

QUACKAM

Patented in 1774 by William McBryde
12 Mar.1806 Eli Showell of Kent Col. Deleware with wife Sarah Showell sold to Hezekiah D. Shockley of Maryland, rights.

QUANTICO

Patented in 1766 by Henry Lowe for 27 acres
11 Mar.1774 Henry Lowe son of Henry with wife Esther Lowe sold to John waters late of Calvert Co., now of Somerset Co. 64 acres of QUANTICO, and TUBMANS LOTT.
1783 tax - John Waters 27 acres.
1784 John Waters willed to son Francis Hutchins Waters plantation in Quantico Creek, unnamed.
31 Mar.1787 Francis Hutchings Waters sold to John Gale.

QUANTICO TOWN

Town was taken out of tract MONMOUTH
20 Feb.1779 John Gale sold for 5 shillings to Henry Gale 12 acres at Quantico Mill being part of WARRINGTON and 15 acres formerly belonging to Elizabeth McGinnis.
13 Mar.1818 Henry Gale sold to James Bounds 15,906 sq.ft. of MONMOUTH or GEORGE GALES GENEROSITY in town of Quantico Mill.
1 July 1819 George H. Gale sold to John Bounds of William Bounds middle lot 148 ft.
1828 Sarah Gale willed to sister Mary Judah (married William Judah of Baltimore) two lots in Quantico Mills.
8 Dec.1840 James Bounds sold to Priscilla Carey and Freeborn Garrettson of Dorc.Co. lot per deed from Henry Gale.(Freeborn Garrettson and Priscilla Garrettson children of Thomas Garrettson)
1843 John Taylor of William Taylor willed to grandchildren Samuel W. Phillips, John M. Phillips, George Phillips and Sarah A.E.L. Phillips 1/2 of house and lot purchased of Henry Gale.
2 Jan.1845 Eleanor Bounds widow of John Bounds gave to the Vestry of Spring Hill lot 76 sq. perches.
26 Sep.1846 James Bounds sold to James E. Bounds 3/4 acre house and lot conveyed by Dr. John Austin.
1855 Henry W. White willed to wife Eliza Ann White house bought of John Taylor

QUARTER LANDS

see HIGH SUFFOLK, LAST CHOICE, HITCHES CHOICE, MADDUX LUCK, WILSONS DISCOVERY & FATHERS NEGLECT.

QUAIKESON NECK

Patented on 1 Dec.1688 by James Weatherly for 500 acres
Rent Rolls 1666-1723 possessed by James Weatherly
7 May 1746 James Weatherly and William Weatherly sold to Ezekiel Jackson 100 acres now called CHANCE.
27 Feb.1746 John Weatherly and William Weatherly sold 214 acres to Isaac Cooper.
28 Apr.1750 Joseph Weatherly and John Weatherly sold 100 acres to Benjamin Wailes, cabinetmaker, for 5 shillings.
20 Nov.1753 Isaac Cooper sold 50 acres to Morgan Cordrey.
17 Aug.1764 John Weatherly sold to Zebulon Wright 180 acres.
18 June 1765 John Weatherly and Joseph Weatherly sold to Henry Graham 42 acres.
23 June 1768 John Weatherly son of James Weatherly sold to Henry Graham 100 acres.
1 Feb.1780 Ezekiel Jackson of Sussex Co.Del. sold to Joshua Humphries 100 acres, with CHANCE
1783 tax - Daniel Cordrey 50 acres Rewastico 100.
1783 tax - Abraham Smith 100 acres
1783 tax - Ezekiel Graham 50 acres
1783 tax - John Anderson 65 acres
1783 tax - Alice Wright 180 acres
1783 tax - John Ansley 180 acres
14 Mar.1794 Lewis Graham son of Ezekiel Graham and Elizabeth Darby widow of Ezekiel Graham sold 50 acres to Benjamin Jones, purchased by Henry Graham father of Ezekiel Graham.
18 Mar.1796 Elizabeth Brown and James Acworth sold 50 acres to John Jones of Dorc.Co.
13 June 1800 Isaac Ewing sold to David Cathell 50 acres
28 Sep.1803 George Lowe of Sussex Co.Del. sold 192 5/8 acres to John Walker of Somerset County.
11 Apr.1804 John Jones with wife Elizabeth Jones sold to John Walker of Sussex Co.Delaware.
1830 Thomas Dougherty and wife Amy Dougherty sold 180 acres to George Bounds.

QAIAKESON NECK

Patented on 19 Oct.1738 by Henry Dorman for 50 acres
24 Jan.1755 Henry Dorman sold to Joshua Dorman 50 acres.
26 Apr.1791 Joshua Dorman sold 50 acres to William McBryde
6 Nov.1793 William McBryde sold to Robert Graham 50 acres.
6 Nov.1793 Robert Graham sold to William McBryde, mortgage.
4 Mar.1794 Sarah McBryde sold to Moses Dryden 50 acres
28 Feb.1794 Robert Graham sold rights to Moses Dryden
23 NOv.1795 Moses Dryden sold to Edward Hammond 50 acres.
9 June 1797 George Purnell Esq. sheriff sold to Isaac Ewing 50 acres per judgement as Robert Graham had part with saw mill and he was in debt to James Ewing.

QUIET ENTRANCE

Patented on 9 Sep.1713 by Andrew Caldwell 100 acres.
11 June 1718 Andrew Caldwell sold 100 acres to John Cotton.

31 Dec.1728 John Cotton of Kent Co. Del. with wife Agnes Cotton sold 100 acres to John Gray Jr.
26 Dec.1748 John Gray willed to Allen Gray 100 acres
7 Dec.1752 Allen Gray sold 100 acres to Nehemiah Hitch
24 Feb.1757 Nehemiah Hitch sold 100 acrs to Joseph Ellis.

RACE GROUND

Patented on 28 Jan.742 by Thomas Walker for 100 acres
6 Feb.1762 Thomas Walker son of Thomas sold to Jonathan Dolbe 100 acres.

RACE GROUND LOT

Patented in 1792 by John Pope Mitchell for 27 3/4 acres a resurvey of part of MILL SECURITY
6 Apr.1801 John Pope Mitchell sold to Peter Chaille
13 June 1801 Peter Chaille with wife Scarborough Chaille sold to John Gunby, John Bishop, Zadock Sturgis, McKimmey Porter, and Ephraim King Wilson
18 Dec.1801 Zadock Sturgis, sheriff sold to John Gunby.
18 Dec.1801 John Gunby, Zadock Sturgis, John Bishop, Ephraim King Wilson, McKimmey Porter sold to James Fooks.
15 Oct.1803 James Fooks of Jesse Fooks, and Jesse Fooks sold to George Dashiell, lot
13 June 1804 George Dashiell with wife Sally Dennis Dashiell sold to William Parsons 1/2 acres
2 Feb.1805 George Dashiell with wife Sally sold to Thomas Hooper part.
4 June 1805 Jesse Fooks with wife Rebecca Fooks, and James Fooks of Jesse with wife Sabra Fooks sold to William Nelson part.
28 June 1806 James Fooks of Jesse Fooks with wife Sabra Fooks sold to Rachel Fooks 9000 sq.ft.
25 Sep.1807 Thomas J. Winder with wife Harriet Winder sold to Smith Horsey, part.

RACOON RIDGE

Patented in 1792 by William Layfield for 25 acres

RADBURN

Patented on 3 Dec.1688 by Thomas Wilson for 140 acres.
Rent Rolls 1666-1723 possessed by Thomas Wilson
1752 John Wilson son of Thomas Wilson willed 145 acres to daughter Ann Robertson.
17 May 1752 John Wilson son of Thomas Wilson and John Huffington and John Kellum 140 acres, triparte agreement..
17 Aug.1753 John Wilson sold to William Robinson 140 acres.
1783 tax - Daniel Darby 140 acres, Rewastico
3 Dec.1802 Gideon Bradley and wife Priscilla Bradley sold to Isaac Kennerly 3 1/2 acres.

RAGLINS ADDITION

Patented on 27 Aug.1762 by David Raglin for 20 acres.
28 Mar.1785 David Raglin of Kent Co.Delaware sold to Jacob Morris of

Somerset County Md. 20 acres.
15 June 1803 Jacob Morris sold to John Morris son of Joseph Morris, part.
13 Mar.1804 John Morris sold to Jacob Morris son of Joseph Morris, part.

RALPHS DELIGHT

Patented on 18 Nov.1758 by Thomas Ralph
5 Nov.1764 Thomas Ralph sold to brother William Ralph 20 acres
8 Jan.1765 Thomas Ralph sold 20 acres to brother William Ralph

RALPHS PREVENTION

Patented on 23 May 1688 by Thomas Ralph on the north side of Wicomico Creek for 9 acres..
22 June 1750 George Gale brother and executor of Levin Gale and Leah Gale only child of Levin, sold to Henry Lowe
1761 Henry Lowe willed to son Tubman Lowe dwelling plantation purchased of the heirs of Levin Gale, unnamed.
9 Mar.1773 Henry Lowe mortgaged to James Dickenson and William Hayward of Talbot Co.Md. 9 acres.
1783 tax - Henry Lowe 9 acres.

RALPHS PROPERTY

Patented in 1758 by Thomas Ralph for 46 acres
5 Nov.1764 Thomas Ralph sold to brother William Ralph
8 Jan 1765 Thomas Ralph sold to William Ralph 46 acres,same as above.

RALPHS PURCHSE

see TRULOCK GRANGE

RALPHS VENTURE

Patented in 1732 by Thomas Ralph for 100 acres
1743 Thomas Ralph willed to daughter Susanna Serman 100 acres of THE VENTURE
4 Oct.1758 another patent for 12 acres by Thomas Ralph
1783 tax - Charles Serman 100 acres.
4 Mar.1797 Charles Serman sold 100 acres to Charles Rider
1801 Charles Rider willed to son Thomas Rider, bought of Charles Serman.
19 Mar.1804 Thomas Rider sold to John Gale, division of boundaries
29 mar.1804 John Gale sold to Thomas Rider. same
13 Feb.1804 James Rider son of Charles Rider sold to John Taylor 8 3/4 acres.
13 Feb.1804 Thomas Rider of Sussex Co.Del. sold to John Taylor 13 1/2 acres with saw mill on same land.
8 Apr.1806 Thomas Rider and wife Priscilla Rider of Sussex Co.Del. sold to John Rider 78 acres that Charles Rider willed to son Thomas except 9 acres he willed to son James Rider.

RAMAS

Patented on 20 Oct.1725 by William Polk for 100 acres
1739 William Polk willed to daughter Elizabeth Polk

31 Jan.1742 John Williams and wife Elizabeth Williams (Elizabeth Polk)
of Somerset. Co. sold to John Laws of Worc.Co. 100 acres

RAPHO

Patented on 20 May 1695 by William Alexander Jr. for 200 acres
Rent Rolls 1666-1723 possessed by William Alexander
1732 William Alexander willed 200 acres to son Moses Alexander where
father William lived, unnamed.
21 Mar.1739 Moses Alexander, blacksmith sold 200 acres to Rencher
Roberts.
6 Mar.1754 Rencher Roberts sold to William Davis 100 acres.
1767 William Davis willed to son Spencer Davis 100 acres.
1773 Rencher Roberts willed 100 acres to son John Roberts.
1783 tax - John Roberts 100 acres, Wic.100
1783 tax - Patience Davis widow of William Davis 100 acres.
10 Feb.1798 Spencer Davis sold to Isaac Vinson 9 1/2 acres.
1809 Spencer Davis willed to sons Levin Davis, Spencer Davis and
William Davis 100 acres.

RAYMONDS CHANCE

Patented on 14 May 1714 by Jonathan Raymond for 69 acres on the north
side of a branch of Wicomico Creek below the mill dam.
Rent Rolls 1666-1723 possessed by Jonathan Raymond
14 Oct.1724 Jonathan Raymond with wife Judith Raymond mortgaged to
Thomas Gillis 69 acres.
9 May 1735 Resurveyed and renewed.

READEN

Patented on 6 Oct.1761 by David Hale for 100 acres
15 Jan.1768 David Hale resurveyed to 293 acres.
4 June 1770 David Hale Sr. sold to James Perdue 58 acres six miles
from the head of the Wicomico River.
19 Oct.1770 David Hale sold to John Nelms 100 acres
1783 tax - Mary Hale 131 acres of ADDITION TO READEN
4 Nov.1795 John Hale and Mary Hale sold to James Perdue son of John
Perdue 135 acres.
1844 ADDITION TO READEN patented Robert H. Parsons for 7 acres
1853 ADDITION TO READEN patented to Isaac H. Parsons 7 acres
(1850 they are in the 4th district of Worc.Co.Md.)

RECORDS DELIGHT

Patented by Ann Records for 561 acres
16 Feb.1758 Ann Records sold to Joshua McDowell 100 acres
20 Feb.1759 Ann Records sold 1 acre to Samuel Calloway
5 Sep.1754 John Records of Sussex Co.Del. son of John of Som. Co. sold
to Ann Records widow of John Records part that John willed to his son
John.
17 Feb.1763 John Records son of John sold his rights to Joseph Foreman
that John Records devised to children Jonah Records, Charity Records,
John Records and Betty Records. After decease of Jonah and Betty it
fell to son John.

26 Jul 1764 Ann Records spinster sold to Elizabeth Records and Charity Records 223 acres for 5 shillings.
17 July 1766 Ann Records sold right of dower to Joseph Foreman.
22 Sep.1766 Josiah Records, James Quartermus, Elizabeth Quartermus and Charity Records sold to Joseph Foreman 561 acres for 5 shillings.
26 Sep.1768 Joseph Foreman Jr. of Som.Co. sold to John Fall of New York City (mortgage)

RECORDS FOLLY

Patented in 1766 by John Goddard Jr. for 48 1/2 acres

RECOVERY

Patented on 23 Nov.1681 by John Tarr on the south side of Wetipquin Creek who assigned to Peter Calloway and George Andrews for 288 acres
1703 George Andrews with wife Frances Andrews sold 182 acres to Thomas Larramore.
15 Sep.1726 Thomas Larramore Sr. sold 288 acres to Thomas Larramore Jr.
28 Oct.1752 John Beard son of Lewis Beard, with wife Rachel Beard sold 5 1/2 acres to Samuel Fluellin that Lewis Beard purchased of John Larramore.
1766 Samuel Fluellin willed to son Samuel land bought of John Beard, unnamed.
17 May1771 Samuel Fluellin sold to Ephraim King 5 1/2 acres
1777 Ephraim King willed to Richard Crockett Fluellin and Samuel Fluellin land purchased of Samuel Fluellin, unnamed.
1783 tax - Elijah Larramore 189 acres, Nanticoke 100
1783 tax - Samuel King 3 1/2 acres
1794 ADDITION TO RECOVERY patented to Elijah Larramore for 294 3/4 acres.
3 Aug.1799 Samuel Fluellin sold to Covington Cordrey
19 Dec.1799 James Larramore sold to Elihu Mezick 288 acres
19 Dec.1799 Elihu Mezick sold to James Larramore 288 acres
7 Sep.1809 James Larramore with wife Louisa Larramore sold to James Mezick 71 1/2 acres and 12 1/2 acres of ADDITION.

RECOVERY

Patented on 8 Dec.1676 by Thomas Brereton a resurvey from CLOSEFORK on the south side of Quantico Creek for 500 acres who conveyed to George Dashiell.
Rent Rolls 1666-1723 possessed by George Dashiell
1733 George Dashiell willed to Mitchell Dashiell and part to son Robert Dashiell.
1755 patent for GRANDFATHERS CARE granted Esther Dashiell being combined lands of IMPROVEMENT & RECOVERY 548 1/2 acres.
31 Mar.1764 tripart agreement between Henry Lowe Jr. with wife Esther Lowe and George Day Scott and William Hayward from Robert Dashiell father of Esther,devised by grandfather George Dashiell, 372 acres.
20 June 1764 triparte agreement, same as above. 40 acres.
1783 tax - Mitchell Dashiell 167 acres, Nanticoke 100
21 Apr.1783 Mitchell Dashiell sold to Samuel King for 5 shillings devised by grandfather George Dashiell 82 1/2 acres a trade for Mt Ephraim.

16 Nov.1795 Isaac Nicholson with wife Peggy Nicholson daughter of
Mitchell Dashiell sold to Ephraim Wilson 78 acres of RECOVERY & MT.
EPHRAIM.
17 June 1800 Tubman Lowe son of Henry Lowe sold to Frederick A.C.
Dashiell 600 acres of RECOVERY, IMPROVMENT, GRANDFATHERS CARE, LOWES
MEADOW & VENTURE PRIVILEDGE.
28 Jan.1806 Ephraim Wilson sold to Levin Farrington 78 acres of
RECOVERY & MT. EPHRAIM.
21 Oct.1808 Ephraim Wilson son of George Wilson with wife Esther
Wilson, George D. Wilson with wife Amelia Wilson sold to Charles
Jones.

REDDISHES LOTT

Patented on 17 May 1760 by Nicholas Reddish for 50 acres
1770 ADDITION patented Nicholas Reddish for 29 1/4 acres.
1783 tax - Nicholas Reddish 50 acres and ADDITION 29 1/4 acres
1794 Nicholas Reddish willed to wife Nancy Reddish manor plnatation
1/3rds unnamed. and to son Nicholas Reddish ADDITION TO REDDISHES
LOTT.
15 Mar.1803 John Wilkins sheriff sold to James Anderson Sr. lands of
George Revel, for debts 72 acres of LOTT & 11 acres of ADDITION TO
REDDISHES LOTT
5 Feb.1803 Thomas Reddish sold to Henry Banks 50 acres REDDISHES LOTT
& 29 1/4 acres of ADDITION.
1 Mar.1806 Henry Banks sold to William Anderson 40 acres.

REMANENT

Patented in 1814 by Reuben Davis for 7 acres

RETIREMENT

Patented in 1797 by Samuel Godman for 167 acres
4 June 1799 Samuel Godman of Annapolis with wife Anne Godman sold to
John Sprigg of Ann Arundel Co. 167 acres
13 Oct.1807 John Brewer of Annapolis, trustee of Samuel Fodman sold
for debts to Lewis Duvall and Francis T. Clements of same 167 acres

RHODES CHANCE

see SHANTAVANNA & WARRINGTON

RHOADES LOT

Patented in 1688 for 100 acres by John Rhoads out of part of COXS
DISCOVERY
11 June 1764 John Rhoads, blacksmith sold to Thomas Kennerly 100 acres
25 Feb.1769 Thomas Kennerly sold 100 acres to Ephraim Vaughan
1773 Ephraim Vaughan willed to son Levin Vaughan 100 acres bought of
Thomas Kennerly
1776 this was probably resurveyed to Sussex Co.Del. with COXES
DISCOVERY.

RHODEE

Patented on 1 Feb.1682 by Thomas Pemberton who assigned to John
Singleton for 350 acres
Rent Rolls 1666-1723 possessed by Robert Dashiell by marrying the

daughter of Daniel Haste who was entitled to the land.
1701 Daniel Haste willed to Robert Dashiell 350 acres, unnamed.

RICELAND

Patented on 8 Sep.1663 by Nicholas Rice for 1000 acres.
5 Jan 1677 Nicholas Rice willed to Richard Crockett and John Evans 1000 acres.
4 Nov.1679 Richard Crockett and John Evans divided the lands.
Rent Rolls 1666-1723 possessed by Capt. Nicholas Evans to who it descended by the oath of his father John Evans who was possessed with the right.
1723 Nicholas Evans willed to son John Evans and part to daughter Sarah Evans.
19 Apr.1736 John Huett Nutter eldest son of Ann Leckie dec'd who was Ann Huett daughter of Rev. John Huett sold to Levin Gale
1750 resurveyed by Capt. Thomas Gillis for 1035 acres
1783 tax - John Evans of Nicholas Evans 32 acres.
24 Mar.1787 John Evans of Nicholas Evans sold to Levin Gale, Henry Jackson and John Stewart his equity.

RICH HILL

Patented in 1857 by John R. Downing for 92 acres

RICH ISLAND

Patented on 2 July 1762 by Nathaniel Morris for 10 acres

RICH LAND

Patented in 1728 by William Polk for 200 acres
27 Aug.1739 William Polk gave to son David Polk 200 acres, on branch of the Nanticoke River.
29 Nov.1760 David Polk with wife Betty Polk sold to William Laws 200 acres
23 Sep.1767 William Laws sold to John Mitchell 1 1/2 acres.

RICH NECK

Patented on 25 June 1767 by William Brittingham for 32 acres
5 Nov.1790 Jeremiah Brittingham son of William sold to William Whittington, rights

RICH POINT

Patented in 1785 by William Bethards for 20 acres
14 Mar.1791 William Bethards sold to Zachariah Parsons 20 acres.

RICH QUARTER

Patented in 1791 by John Reddish for 11 1/4 acres

RICH QUARTER

Patented in 1798 by Joshua Disharoon for 143 acres

RICH RIDGE

Patented on 2 Oct.1713 by Robert Givans for 200 acres who assigned to John Gillis
Rent Rolls 1666-1723 possessed by John Gillis
1720 John Gillis willed to sons Thomas Gillis and Ezekiel Gillis
21 June 1737 Thomas Gillis with wife Priscilla Gillis sold to Geroge Oliver 30 acres on broad from Barren Creek Mill to Broad Creek on Horekill Road.
13 Ocr.1742 Ezekiel Gillis of Ann Arundel Co. sold 100 acres to Jonathan Bayley
7 Dec.1742 Thomas Gillis sold 70 acres to Peter Magee.
1762 Peter Magee willed to son John Magee 75 acres.
2 Jan.1769 John Magee son of Peter sold to John Henry 70 acres
6 Apr.1771 John Henry with wife Sarah Henry sold 70 acres to Jacob Gordy of Worc.Co.
25 June 1776 Sussex Co. Delaware land warrants by Daniel Kenicken.

RICH SWAMP

Patented on 26 Mar.1711 by Joseph McClester and wife Isabel McClester
Rent Rolls 1666-1723 possessed by Joseph McClester.
1720 Joseph McClester sold 150 acres to Benjamin Nesham
17 Nov.1721 Benjamin Nesham with wife Mary Nesham sold to William Vaughan, carpenter 150 acres with MEECHES HOPE.
28 Nov.1735 Thomas Serman with wife Elizabeth Serman sold to Benjamin Townsend 135 acres of MEECHES HOPE & RICH SWAMP.
1783 tax - Joseph Dashiell Jr. 115 acres.

RICH SWAMP

Patented in 1782 by Matthew Richardson for 20 acres

RICHARDS HOG YARD

Patented in 1754 by Richard Blizzard for 50 acres
1783 tax - Rackliffe Blizzard 50 acres, Acquango 100, Worc.Co.
3 Oct.1789 Daniel Fooks sold to John Farlow part 50 acres by power of attorney from Rackliffe Blizzard.
21 Dec.1793 John Farlow sold to Benjamin Fooks 50 acres.
8 Dec.1809 Billy Fooks, Jonathan Fooks, James Fooks and Thomas Fooks sold to Daniel Fooks, division of lands of Daniel Fooks deceased.
1830 Jonathan Fooks of David Fooks willed to daughter Henrietta Byrd 16 2/3 acres

RICHARDSONS ADDITION

see CASTOWAY

RICHARDSONS DISCOVERY

Patented in 1791 by John Richardson for 61 1/2 acres

RICHARDSONS DISCOVERY

Patented in 1799 by Richardson Donoho for 122 3/4 acres

RICHARDSONS GRIEF

Patented in 1770 by John Twilley for 18 acres
6 Feb.1810 Horatio Stayton with wife Mary Stayton sold to Isaac Henry 27 3/8 acres of CASTOWAY & RICHARDSONS GRIEF.

RICHARDSONS LUCK

Patented in 1816 by Richardson Donoho for 58 acres
Another patent for 73 3/4 acres by Richardson Donoho
1783 tax - Richardson Donoho 72 1/2 acres, Nantcioke 100
1823 William Donoho willed to son Alexander Donoho, in Wetepquin Neck.
RICHARSONS HARD LUCK

RIDERS CONSOLATION

Patented in 1803 by John Rider for 14 1/4 acres

(The) RIDGES

Patented in 1738 by Richard Acworth for 100 acres
1727 Richard Acworth willed to sons Richard Acworth, Charles Acworth and Thomas Acworth.
25 Sep.1769 Charles Acworth sold to Mary Harris 25 acres
25 Sep.1759 Charles Acworth sold to James West 25 acres
23 Nov.1759 Charles Acworth son of Thomas Acworth gave to James Acworth his brother 450 acres of ACWORTHS DELIGHT, ACWORTHS CHOICE, RIDGES, HOG QUARTER & part OF MARSH POINT.
20 June 1769 James Acworth sold to William Acworth 20 acres
10 June 1769 James Acworth sold to brother Richard Acworth 10 acres
1783 tax - Train Acworth 40 acres, Rewastco 100
1783 tax - Richard Acworth 10 acres
1783 tax - Mary Harris 25 acres
1783 tax - James West 10 acres
1792 Train Acworth willed to son Train 10 acres
1797 Robert Venables gave to wife Amelia Venables (Amelia Acworth daughter of William Acworth)
1848 Train Acworth gave to daughter Priscilla Francis Acworth.

RISE

Patented in 1798 by John Anderson for 15 acres

RIVER LANDING

see BOTTOM OF THE NECK

RIVER TRACT

Patented in 1788 by Elihu Mezick for 26 1/4 acres
1783 tax - Elihu Mezick 26 acres, Nanticoke 100.
1788 Elihu Mezick willed to wife Margaret Mezick 26 acres of THE RIVER SIDE tract.
4 July 1799 John Mezick sold to Elihu Mezick 135 acres of END OF STRIFE, LEES SITUATION, THE GORE, RIVER TRACT.

ROACH'S CONCLUSION

Patented on 20 Aug.1762 by William Roach for 45 acres
1765 William Roach willed 45 acres to son Stephen Roach
1819 Joshua Morris willed to son Jeptha Morris 40 1/2 acres bought of Stephen Roach
27 Oct.1821 Levi Cathell trustee to sell the real estate of John Cathell Jr. sold part to James Toadvine
1822 James Toadvine willed to daughter Catherine Toadvine bought of the estate of John Cathell, unnamed and to daughters Harriett Toadvine and Mary Ann Toadvine, part of the same.

ROACHES MILL

see MILL LOTT

ROADS MISFORTUNE

Patented on 9 Oct. 1760 by John Carmichael for 10 acres
1783 tax - Rachel Carmichael 10 acres, Rewastico
1796 John Carmichael willed to brother Levin Carmichael lands on the north side of WARRINGTON, no name or acreage.
1 Mar.1805 Levin Carmichael sold to Nathan Rhoads 10 acres.

ROBERSONS HILL

Patented in 1849 by William Taylor for 78 acres

ROBERTSONS SWAMP

Patented in 1791 by James Robertson for 71 1/4 acres

ROBERTS FIRST CHOICE

Patented on 6 Aug.1760 by William Roberts for 50 acres
20 Sep.1767 ADDITION TO ROBERTS FIRST CHOICE patent by William Roberts for 282 acres
3 Nov.1785 William Roberts s/o William with wife Elizabeth Roberts sold to John Pope Mitchell 1/2 acre.

ROBERTS LOT

Patented in 1752 by Robert Walter for 25 acres
1783 tax - Robert Walter, Nanticoke 100
1788 Robert Walter willed lands to son Daniel Walter, unnanamed.

ROBERTS SECURITY

Patented in 1765 by Robert Banks for 391 1/2 acres a resurvey of SARAHS SECURITY
1768 Robert Banks willed to sons Robert and Thomas Banks
1771 Thomas Banks willed to brother Henry Banks all left me by the death of father and will be left me by mother, unnamed lands.
1776 Isaiah Banks willed to brother Robert Banks
1783 tax - Robert Banks 301 acres
1789 Robert Banks willed to son Warren Banks, if no issue to sons Robert or Sterling Banks.

1799 Warren Banks gave 100 acres to daughter Polly Banks and balance to son Gabriel Banks.
10 Oct.1801 Nancy Banks sold to Samuel Hilman of Worc.Co. rights of dower lands of late husband Warren Banks who sold to William Beard or Henry Banks, 50 acres.
1826 Gabriel Banks willed to nephews Richard Taylor, William Taylor and son Emery Banks.

ROBERTSONS BEGINNING

Patented in 1849 by William Taylor for 8 5/8 acres

ROBERTSONS DELIGHT

Patented in 1792 by John Robertson for 300 acres
14 Mar.1794 John Robertson Sr. sold 1/2 acres to James Badley of Sussex Co.Delaware.
1799 John Robertson willed dwelling plantation to son John, unnamed.
14 Mar.1794 John Robertson Sr. sold 1/2 acre to Gideon Badley of Sussex Co.Delaware
14 Mar.1794 John Robertson sold 1/2 acre to Thomas Walker
14 Mar.1794 John Robertson sold to Ephraim Walker 1/2 acre
14 Mar.1794 John Robertson sold to Matthew Walker 1 1/2 acres
14 May 1794 John Robertson sold to Henry Walker 8 1/4 acres
26 Sep.1794 John Robertson sold 57 1/4 acres to son William Robertson
20 Mar.1795 John Robertson sold 10 acres to Thomas Connerly
2 May 1779 Henry Walker with wife Esther Ann Walker sold 8 1/4 acres to Solomon Robertson
6 June 1800 James Badley of Sussex Co.Del. sold to James Badley of same 1/2 acre
1800 John Robertson willed to son Isaac Robertson.
14 Apr.1803 Isaac Robertson sold to Jacob Allen 1 1/2 acres 25 sq.perches.
1817 Thomas Connerly willed 10 acres to son John Connerly
1822 Benjamin Melson willed to son Elijah Melson 101 acres of ROBERTS DELIGHT
1831 George Bennett willed to son Hamilton B. Bennett 1 1/2 acres
This is the sight of SHARPTOWN.

ROBERTSONS HARDSHIP

Patented in 1816 by John Robertson for 40 1/2 acres

ROBERTSONS RETREAT

Patented in 1820 by John Robertson for 16 3/4 acres

ROBINS ADDITION

Patented on 6 May 1763 Bowdin Robins for 25 acres

ROBINS MILL LOTT

Patented in 1798 by James B. Robins for 254 acres
28 Jan.1802 James B. Robins with wife Elizabeth late Elizabeth Horsey,

sold to Ebenezer Christopher, Jonathan Noble, Stewart Shockley and Major Dorman with tract adjacent, unnamed, 300 acres.
9 Jan.1802 Ebenezer Christopher, Jonathan Noble, Major Dorman, Stewart Shockley sold to James B. Robins with OUTLETT 300 acres.
16 July 1803 Stewart Shockley with wife Nelly, Major Dorman with wife Sarah Dorman, Jonathan Noble with wife Nancy Noble, sold to Ebenezer Christopher 80 acres.
16 July 1803 Ebenezer Christopher with wife Polly Christopher, Stewart Shockley with wife Nelly Shockley and Jonathan Noble with wife Nancy Noble sold to Major Dorman 86 acres.
8 Apr.1809 Major Dorman with wife Sarah Dorman sold to Benjamin White 86 acres.

ROBINS PARTNERSHIP

Patented in 1777 by Bowdin Robins for 357 acres.

ROBINSONS LOTT

Patented in 1734 by Robinson Lingo for 75 acres
2 Apr.1756 Robinson Lingo sold to Thomas Butler on the east side of the head of the Wicomico River in Davis Neck, 75 acres
1 Sep.1769 Peter Calloway sold to John Richardson 75 acres land of Thomas Butler, per judgement against.

ROKIAWALKIN MILL

see tr. MUNSLEY
1735 William Elgate sold to Levin Gale 10 acres laid out for a mill being part of MUNSLEY now 1 acres, the whole 11 acres.
14 July 1743 Levin Gale sold to George Parris
17 Mar.1752 George Parris sold to Henry Waggaman grist mill
ROKIAWALKIN MILL alias PARRIS MILL.

ROMNEY

Patented in 1782 by William Winder for 203 1/2 acres
1808 William Winder willed to son William Henry Winder

ROOKS ADVENTURE

Patented in 1746 by John Wooten for 141 acres
18 Mar.1769 John Wooten Sr. sold to John Wooten Jr. 41 acres.

ROSS

Patented on 6 Dec.1678 by John Evans for 50 acres on the north side of Quantico Creek. Assigned to Alexander Thomas
1695 Alexander Thomas willed lands to daughters Eliza Thomas and Frances Thomas
Rent Rolls 1666-1723 possessed by James Russell and John Bouger by marrying the coheirs of Alexander Thomas.
6 Mar.1752 George Hardy and wife Sarah Hardy former relic of Christopher Nutter sold to John Handy 25 acres.
10 Sep.1759 Ephraim King and wife Ann King sold to Samuel King, property that became right of Ann by the death of her brother

Christopher Nutter that was not conveyed by Ann to her son Thomas Handy.
11 Sep.1781 Samuel King sold to Thomas Maddux 50 acres had from father Ephraim King.
11 Sep.1781 Thomas Maddux sold to Samuel King, all.
1783 tax - William Nutter Sr. 30 acres, Rewastico
29 May 1793 William Nutter and Charles Nutter divided land.
26 Apr.1805 Priscilla Bond sold to Levin Farrington
24 Aug.1806 Charles Nutter with wife Louisa Nutter sold to Henry E. Bayley 331 1/2 acres of ROSS, MIDDLE TRACT, DELIGHT & MONMOUTH.
21 Oct.1808 Henry E. Bayley with wife Sarah Bayley sold to Thomas Mitchell 331 1/2 acres of above.
Part resurveyed to HANDYS CARE

ROTTERDAM

Patented in Dec.1688 by Cornelius Johnson for 400 acres
Rent Rolls 1666-1723 possessed by Cornelius Johnson in Dorchester Co.
1689 Cornelius Johnson willed to Margaret Jones daughter of William Jones, William Jones Jr. and David Jones, estate.
9 Dec.1717 Cornelius Johnson sold to Edmund Huggins
20 Nov.1728 John Huggins of Bath Co. North Carolina, weaver son of Edmund Huggins appointed Jacob Mezick to make over to John Mezick, part.
4 Apr.1732 John Huggins late of Som.Co. son of Edmund Huggins sold 150 acres to John Mezick
1 Feb.1739 John Mezick sold 150 acres to Richard Phillips.
31 May 1773 John Phillips s/o Richard sold to Sarah McClester and Rachel McClester daughters of George McClester that father gave bont to George McClester of 150 acres.
2 Apr.1776 Sussex Co. Delaware land warrants to John Ellegood in Broad Creek 100.

ROUND POND

Patented in 1742 by James O'Neal for 100 acres
1761 Charles Tindell willed to son Charles 100 acres.

ROUND POND & ROUND POND ENLARGED

Patented on 9 Sep.1728 for 100 acres by John Huffington
Rent Rolls 1666-1723 possessed by John Huffington
25 July 1725 John Huffington, planter sold 100 acres to William Taylor.
2 Sep.1762 ROUND POND ENLARGED patented by John Houston for 860 acres.
24 Oct.1765 John Houston sold to James Windsor 134 acres.
1768 John Houston willed to son John 50 acres and to grandson Leonard Houston 200 acres of ENLARGED and to daughter Sally Minor Houston 50 acres and to son Robert Houston 100 acres.
1770 William Taylor willed to son James Taylor 170 acres, to son Abraham Taylor 117 acres and balance to son Isaac Taylor
part resurveyed to TAYLORS ADDITION
1783 tax - Abraham Taylor, (resurvey) Rewastico 100
1791 Abraham Taylor willed to son Abraham MILL POND left by father William Taylor.

ROUND SAVANAH

Patented in 21 Mar.1757 by Thomas Waller for 153 acres
21 Mar.1757 Thomas Waller sold 25 acres to Isaac Jones
8 Feb.1759 Thomas Waller sold 19 1/2 acres to Outerbridge Horsey.
8 Feb.1759 Thomas Waller sold to William Waller 9 acres.
16 Aug.1759 Thomas Moore sold to Outerbridge Horsey.
8 Feb.1759 Thomas Waller sold 50 acres to William Gray
8 Feb.1759 Thomas Waller sold 25 acres to John McDowell
4 Apr.1760 Isaac Jones sold to William Waller 25 acres.
20 May 1761 Thomas Waller sold to John McDowell 20 acres.
20 Aug.1761 Thomas Waller sold to Joshua Waller 5 acres
17 June 1769 William Waller sold to son James Waller 25 acres.
17 Jan 1770 Joshua Waller sold 5 acres to Zephaniah Waller.
1 Apr.1771 Zephaniah Waller sold 5 acres to Revel Wharton
29 Feb.1772 Revel Wharton with wife Mary Wharton sold 5 acres to Levin Ellis.
17 Apr.1776 Sussex Co. Delaware land warrants by Levin Ellis and James Waller.
1785 Outerbridge Horsey willed to son Lazarus Horsey lands on Broad Creek out of the Nanticoke River.

ROUND SWAMP

see WHITTY S CONTRIVANCE

ROUND THE CREEK

Patented in 1774 by Thomas Lloyd for 31 acres

ROYAL EXCHANGE

Patented in 1763 by Charles Dean for 445 acrs
6 Nov.1777 Ephraim Dean son of Charles Dean of Dorc.Co. sold 100 acres to Lazarus Huffington of Som.Co.
1778 William Badley willed to son William 143 acres.
1783 tax - Levin Huffington 100 acres
1783 tax - Elizabeth Badley 143 acres
1783 tax - John Robertson 113 acres
1783 tax - James Dean 80 acres
1783 182 1/2 acres resurveyed to DEANS VENTURE
4 Jan 1788 William Dean and Levi Dean and Noble Dean of Dorc.Co. sold to James Dean of Som.Co.
13 Nov.1787 James Dean son of James Dean with wife Susanna Dean of Som.Co., William Dean of Dorc.Co. sold to Jonathan Waller of Dorcester Co. 94 acres.
4 Jan.1788 William Dean of Dorc.Co. sold to Wilson Badley 100 acres
4 Jan.1788 William Dean and Noble Dean of Dorc.Co. sold 43 acres to Wilson Badley
3 Oct.1789 James Dean sold to John Robertson 113 acres devised James by William Dean and Levi Dean.
16 Oct.1807 William Waller of Washington Co.Ga.sold to Isaac Phillips of Sussex Co.Del. 94 acres with DEANS CHANCE sold by James Dean and wife Susanna Dean to Jonathan Waller of Som.Co.

ROYAL RANGE

Patented in 1803 by Thomas Walker for 43 1/4 acres

RUARKS ADVENTURE

Patented in 1853 by Major T. Ruark for 88 1/8 acres
1850 he is in Salisbury District.

RUARKS PURCHASE

Patented in 1836 by William T. Ruark for 76 1/8 acres
1850 he is in Salisbury District.

RUARKS VENTURE

Patented in 1850 by William T. Ruark for 4 1/2 acres

RUBICON

Patented in 1816 by Jonah Bayley for 148 acres

RUM RIDGE

Patented on 1 Apr.1680 by Thomas Walker for 300 acres who assigned to Thomas Cox at head of the Wicomico River.
1681 Thomas Cox sold to John Frizzell
Rent Rolls 1666-1723 possessed by James Watts who owns, rent not paid.
1721 Samuel Handy willed to son Ebenezer Handy and to son Benjamin Handy.
1735 Ebenezer Handy willed to son Benjamin Handy 300 acres.
7 Mar.1755 Benjamin Handy son of Ebenezer Handy sold to George Smith, that John Frizzell sold to William Wallace who sold to John Watts who gave to sons John and Spencer Watts and from them to Samuel Handy who willed to Ebenezer Handy 40 acres.
1772 John Handy willed to son Haste Handy, where I Live.
2 Dec.1782 Joseph Dashiell resurveyed to MILL LOTT assigned from Joshua Hill.
1783 tax - Joseph Dashiell for Haste Handy 260 acres, Wic.100 Worc.Co.
14 June 1792 Haste Handy sold to Gabriel Slocomb.
12 Aug.1795 George Smith son of Andrew Smith sold to Seth Smith and Isaac Vincent 40 acres with ALDERBURY.
13 Apr.1800 Gabriel Slocomb of Dorcester Co. sold to Marcellus Slocomb 250 acres.
17 Nov.1807 Sarah Slocomb widow of Marcellus Slocomb of Dorc.Co.and Barzilla Slocomb guardian of John Slocomb, Barzilla Slocomb, Marcellus Slocomb, Nelly Slocomb, Gabriel Slocomb sold to William Bassett of Worcester Co. all rights.
1832 William Bassett willed to daughters Mary Brittingham, Sarah Brittingham, Rachel Adkins and Betsy Davis.

RUNNINGMEAD

Patented in 1850 by David G. O'Dell and John E. Scott for 268 acres, 30 perches.

RUNSELL

Patented on 2 Nov.1671 by Samuel Jackson for 100 acres on the east side to Tipiquen Creek.
14 Jan 1673 Samuel Jackson sold to John Bounds.
Rent Rolls 1666-1723 possessed by William Bounds viz John Bounds.
1686 John Bounds gave to John Bounds Jr.
1 Feb.1725 James Bounds son of John who was the son of John Bounds with wife Ann Bounds sold to Joseph McClester now called McCLESTERS PURCHASE 100 acres.
1729 repatented 120 acres by Joseph McClester.
3 Mar.1731 Joseph McClester sold to William Dashiell and his wife Isabella Dashiell.
1745 William Dashiell resurveyed to DASHIELLS PURCHASE.

RUSSELLS LIBERTY

Patented in 1746 by Alexander Thomas Russell for 78 acres
2nd patent 1769 by Alexander Thomas Russell for 173 acres
1 May 1773 Alexander Thomas Russell sold all lands to son Price Russell, unnamed.
1783 tax - Price Russell 173 acres
15 Jan.1801 James Russell sold to Thomas Cannon 36 3/8 acres

RUSSUMS CONVENEINCY

Patented in 1801 by William Russum for 52 3/4 acres

RUSSUMS DISCOVERY

Patented in 1797 by William Russum for 46 1/2 acres
1819 William Russum willed to son Joseph Russum.

RUSSUMS HARD BARGAIN

Patented in 1795 by William Russum.
1 Mar.1805 Levi Russell sold to Charles Rhoads AGEULOW, LARGEE, RUSSELLS HARD BARGAIN.
1831 Eli Bennett willed to brothers Turpin Bennett and Levin Bennett
1833 Turpin Bennett willed torother Eli Bennett and Levin Bennett son of Joshua Bennett 220 acres

RYANS CHANCE

see DOUBLE PURCHASE

RYANS GRAVE

Patented in 1730 by Joseph Parremore for 50 acres
8 Mar.1734 Joseph Parremore and wife Isabelle Parremore sold 50 acres to Edward Calloway at a branch of the Wicomico River.
29 July 1755 Edward Calloway of Sussex Co.Del. with wife Elizabeth Calloway sold to Bryan Ready of Worc.Co. 50 acres.
1764 Bryan Ready willed to son John Ready 50 acres.
6 Apr.1776 Sussex Co.Delaware land warrants, pat. Aaron Ready.

RYE PLAINS

Patented in 1788 by Esme Bayley for 249 1/2 acres
1799 Esme Bayley willed to son Henry Bayley in Rockawalkin
27 Feb.1807 Henry E. Bayley with wife Sarah Bayley sold to Thomas Mitchell 272 acres.
21 Oct.1808 Thomas Mitchell with wife Nancy Mitchell sold to John Byrd 272 1/2 acres.
1822 Thomas Byrd willed to son John Byrd.

SAFETY

Patented in 1725 by John Shiles for 50 acres
15 Apr.1745 John Shiles sold to Thomas Willin
13 June 1746 Thomas Willin sold 23 acres to Daniel McIntyre SHILES SAFETY.
12 June 1764 Thomas Willin with wife Elizabeth Willin sold to son Robert Willin balance.
2 Sep.1772 Robert Willin sold to Daniel McIntyre for 5 shillings 9 1/4 acres.
1783 tax - Betty McIntyre 9 1/2 acres
1783 tax - Willin McIntyre 23 acres
12 Nov.1785 John McIntyre son of Daniel sold to George Aires, all rights.
20 June 1786 Charles Willin with wife Elinor Willin, Robert Willin with wife Ann Willin sold rights to George Aires.

SAILORS DELIGHT

Patented in 1772 by Nathaniel Thrift for 1 1/2 acres
8 Apr.1806 John Winder of Northampton Co.Va. heir of William Winder sold to William Winder of Somerset Co., coheir.
9 Sep 1806 Levin Winder, Richard Henry Handy, Hetty W. Winder and Josiah Polk coheirs of William Winder, sold to William Winder.
17 Apr.1807 Richard Henry Handy and Thomas Winder Handy heirs of William Winder sold all rights to William Winder
4 June1807 William Henry Winder with wife Gertrude Winder, George Dashiell with wife Esther Dashiell, William W. Handy and George D.S. Handy of Baltimore Co. heirs of William Winder sold all rights to William Winder.
1810 possessed by Dr. Robert Lemon
1816 ADDITION 1/8th acre patented by Robert Lemon.

ST. ALBANS

Patented on 18 June 1674 by William Woodgate who assigned to Richard Townsend, 200 acres, Nanticoke 100.
Rent Rolls 1666-1723 possessed by widow of John Aylward.
2 Dec.1726 John W. Barkley and wife Ann Barkley sold 140 acres to John Rider of Dorc.Co.Md.
27 Sep.1733 Hororable Col. John Rider of Dorc.Co. sold to Alexander Adams. 140 acres
21 Apr.1753 Alexander Adams sold to John Barkley and wife Ann Barkley 140 acres.
7 Dec.1757 John Barkley Sr.,bricklayer sold to Aylworth Barkley 60

acres of ST ALBANS & 160 acres of STANAWAY.
13 Dec.1757 Aylworth Barkley,bricklayer with wife Ann Barkley sold 60 acres to Teague Dickerson for 5 shillings.
15 Mar.1768 John Barkley sold to Samuel McClester Sr. 100 acres
1783 tax - Henry Barkley 20 acres
1783 tax - Levi Dickerson 60 acres
1783 tax - John McClester 100 acres
1783 tax - Samuel Townsend 20 acres
11 Apr.1776 Charles Barkley sold to John Barkley 20 acres.
10 Aug.1784 Isaac Dickerson son of Levi Dickerson sold to Thomas Smith 60 acres that Teague Dickerson gave to son Levi Dickerson.
8 June 1788 James Dashiell of Stepney Parish sold to Henry Wallace Barkley.
8 June 1788 Henry Wallace Barkley sold to James Dashiell, same as above, a reset of boundaries.
28 APr.1798 Henry W. Barkley sold 20 acres to Thomas Smith
1797 Samuel Townsend willed to wife Nelly Townsend 20 acres.
6 Jan.1810 John McClester with wife Betsy McClester sold 1 acres to Samuel Gordan.
1825 John McClester willed to James R.J.McClester Fountain
1829 James Robert JohnMc. Fountain willed to George Washington Fountain
1853 Stephen Nutter willed to daughter Sarah Priscilla Nutter 1 acre.

ST GERMAINS

Patented on 8 Oct.1700 by Peter Douty for 50 acres
Rent Rolls 1666-1723 possessed by Peter Douty
1709 Peter Douty willed to daughter Ann Collier wife of Robert Collier.
28 Mar.1800 George Handy sold 50 acres to Levin Winright
28 Mar.1800 Levin Winright sold to George Handy.

ST GYLES

Patented on 10 Sep.1688 by William Giles between Quantico and Rewastico branches for 200 acres
1709 George Betts willed to son-in-law John Irving and his wife Francis Irving 200 acres
25 Sep.1734 Ebenezer Cottman traded 10 acres to James Caldwell for FIRST CHOICE.
4 May 1782 Ebenezer Waller sold to Everton Kennerly 200 acres.
5 July 1782 Ebenezer Moore of Granville Co.N.C. sold to Everton Kennerly his claim.
1783 tax - Everton Kennerly 120 acres
1783 tax - Ellender McClennan 50 acres
25 Aug.1786 George Young son of Jonathan Young of Worc.Co. sold to Everton Kennerly his rights.
18 Feb.1787 John Smith with wife Mary Smith sold to Fisher Roberts 150 acrs of ST.GILES, GOOD LUCK, FIRST CHOICE
28 Feb.1787 Fisher Roberts with wife Elizabeth Roberts sold 150 acres of FIRST CHOICE, ST.GILES, GOOD LUCK, to Everton Kennerly
15 Jan.1791 Robert Venables and wife Amelia Venables sold 300 acres of FIRST CHOICE & ST. GILES formerly property of James Caldwell Sr. grandfather of Amelia Venables to Everton Kennerly.

15 Jan.1791 Robert Dashiell with wife Mary Caldwell Dashiell sold 300 acres of ST. GILES & FIRST CHOICE to Everton Kennerly.

ST KITTS

Patented in 1759 by Thomas Hearn for 50 acres
1762 Thomas Hearn willed 50 acres to son John Hearn
18 June 1768 Joseph Hitch and wife Jemimah Hearn Hitch sold to Samuel Haynie 16 1/2 acres
14 Mar.1772 Francis Disharoon and wife Sarah Hearn Disharoon sold to Samuel Haynie for 5 shillings 1/3rd part
9 Sep.1774 Ann Hearn sold to Samuel Haynie 16 1/2 acres her 1/3 part not conveyed before by sisters with HEARNS VENTURE.

SALEM

Patented on 25 Apr.1674 by George Layfield on the northeast branch of the Nanticoke River for 800 acres
Rent Rolls 1666-1723 possessed by Samuel Layfield heir to George Layfield.
10 Aug.1721 Thomas Layfield a mere relation to George Layfield heir, with Catherine Layfield his wife sold to James Polk 800 acres

SALEM

see LITTLE BELEAN & SLIGO

SALLY

Patented in 1804 by John Graham for 410 acres a resurvey from LONG ACRE
4 June 1808 John Graham sold 410 acres to Samuel Acworth
1821 Samuel Acworth willed to son William Harris Acworth 327 1/2 acres.
1843 Elizabeth Moore widow of Samuel Acworth and widow of Henry Moore gave to children of son John L. Moore.
19 May 1836 John L. Moore sold 327 1/2 acres to William A.D. Bounds near Green Hill where John Moore now resides.
5 May 1840 William A.D. Bounds with wife Temperance Bounds sold to Elizabeth Acworth 327 1/2 acres.

SALISBURY TOWN

Taken out of tract PEMBERTONS GOOD WILL- these entries are for the town.
23 Apr.1764 William Winder sold to Alexander Thomas Russell 1/2 acre in Salisbury Town.
26 May1770 William Winder sold a lot to James Buchannan
1 Mar.1771 William Winder sold a lot to Joseph Dashiell
21 Mar.1771 William Winder sold lot 1/4 acre to Elijah Vinson
1774 Samuel Davis willed to daughter Mary Davis house and lot.
1775 John Nelms patented SALISBURY 2 1/2 acres
24 Sep.1776 John Craig, inholder sold to William Tharp of city of Philadelphia lot near Salisbury Town that John Craig and William Dommock purchased from William McClemmy (mortgage?)

20 Aug.1778 Gustavous Scott of Dorc.Co. sold to William Ewing house and lot conveyed by William Venables to Adam Ready deceased, who conveyed to Gustavous Scott.
6 Apr.1779 Doctor John Venables sold to Dr. James Houston, lot
6 Apr.1780 Dr. John Venables sold to Hamilton Austin 1 lot.
1782 George Handy willed to son Isaac Handy house and lot.
20 May 1782 Isaac Horsey with wife Mary Horsey of Sussex Co.Del.sold to William Horsey and wife Elinor Horsey of Somerset County, lot.
23 Nov.1784 Dr. John Venables sold to James Mackey, lot
1786 William Horsey per will had a storehouse and lot.
13 Nov.1787 Jacob White with wife Ally White, James Clark and wife Betsy Clark (formerly Betsy Buchannan) all of Sussex Co.Del. sold to James Buchannan lots left to John Handy by his grandfather John Caldwell and sold by him to James Buchannan deceased, 41 sq.ft and 10525 sq.ft and another small lot.
1788 Hambleton Austin willed to daughters Hetty Austin, Nelly Austin and sister Betty Austin house and lot.
3 May 1788 Dr. John Venables sold lot to Dr. James Houston
1790 Isaac Horsey willed to son Isaac house and lot.
5 June 1790 George Robertson with wife Sarah Robertson sold to Jane Handy lot that James Mackey died seized of leaving widow Sarah Mackey now wife of George Robertson.
1792 William Winder had warehouse and lot near the bridge.
15 Feb.1792 John Leatherbury, sheriff sold to Robert Smyly lot on behalf of Ann Dixon, William Wheatley administrator of Robert Dixon against Gillis McClemmy, John Pope Mitchell and Benjamin Wailes.
4 Feb.1794 Robert Smyly sold to Purnell Johnson lot on Water Street
14 Mar.1795 Benjamin Wilson and Charles Vetch sold to Francis Nelms, lot.
25 May 1795 John Pope Mitchell of Worc.Co. sold to Mary Kennedy lot 1/4 acre called CHANCE pat. him on 7 Nov.1792
19 May 1798 Comissioneers to sell Stepney Parish lands sold lot #5 to William Anderson.
19 July 1799 Robert Dashiell and Peter Dashiell sold to Christopher Williams of city of Baltimore house and lots in Salisbury.
25 Feb.1800 Levin Ballard, sheriff sold to James Smith lot 5/16th acre per judgement against Nathaniel Horsey.
10 Jan.1801 Martin Luther Haynie sold to John Cutler lot #23.
6 Apr.1801 Eli Vinson son of Elijah Vinson sold to William Caldwell lot 1/4 acre
25 May 1801 Isaac Horsey son of William Horsey sold to Outerbridge Horsey devised by father who purchased of John Scott near Salisbury Town.
25 May 1801 Outerbridge Horsey sold to Isaac Horsey son of William Horsey same as above.
10 Jan.1801 Martin Luther Haynie sold to William Vance 25 acres
13 May 1801 William Stone, Francis Hutchins Waters, William Waters, William Done, George Robertson and Tubman Lowe of Parish of Stepney sold lot 1/4 acres to James Ritchie.
6 Oct.1801 Christopher Williams of Baltimore, mariner sold to Margaret Bulger of same lot
21 Oct.1801 William Wright with wife Elizabeth Wright sold to John Botham lot #21, 2 acres.
15 Dec.1801 Margaret Bulger of Baltimore sold to John Moore houses and lots.

16 June 1801 Tubman Lowe, John Nichols, etc. comissioners to sell real estate of Stepney Parish sold lot #4 to William Stone.
6 Nov.1802 Comissioners afsd sold lot #6 to William James.
14 Oct.1801 Martin Luther Haynie sold to John Freeney 6 lots of 3 acres each lots numbers 26,27,28,29,30,31.
7 Aug.1802 Martin Luther Haynie sold to William Vance 3 acres and lot #24
29 Jan.1803 John Knipshitt with wife Nelly Knipshitt sold to John Gould of Alexandria Va. PEMBERTONS GOOD WILL lots #2 and #3.
9 Mar.1803 Benjamin Dashiell son of Joseph Dashiell sold to William James lots and 23 acres that Joseph agreed to convey to Thomas Skinner and heirs and as Thomas Skinner on 26 May 1795 sold 23 acres to Phillip Hughes who sold to Rev. George Dashiell who sold to William James, confirmation of sale.
1803 Samuel Smyley willed lands in Salisbury to be sold.
26 Jan.1803 Martin Luther Haynie sold to Eli Collins lot #22
16 Apr.1803 Charles Winright sold to William Vance of Worc.Co. #23
12 Feb.1803 Martin Luther Haynie sold to John Gould of Alexandria Va. lot #1
13 Apr.1803 Charles Winright sold to Esther Bewdly lot #23
8 Oct.1803 Samuel Parr sold to John Knipschitt 1 acre
10 Dec.1803 Isaac Horsey and William Horsey of Kent Co.Del. heirs of Isaac Horsey, sold to William Handy 1 acres
24 Sep.1803 Elijah Coulbourn of Worc.Co. with wife Hetty Coulbourn sold to Isaac Hearn lot that descended from Hamilton Austin to daughters Nelly Austin and Hetty Sturgis Austin, afsd. Hetty.
13 Mar.1804 James Denson and wife Polly Denson sold to Isaac Denson 1/2 acre.
1 May 1804 William Stone, Tubman Lowe, William Done comissioners to sell lands of Stepney Parish sold to William Nelson lot #3.
18 Feb 1804 Jonathan Pollitt, constable sold lot #22, goods of Eli Collins to William Vance, 3 acres.
9 June 1804 William Vance sold to William Winder lot #24 2 acres, lot #23 2 acres and lot #25 3 acres.
97 July 1804 William Anderson sold to John Rider land laid off for Stepney parish
21 Nov.1804 William Nelson and wife Rebecca Nelson sold to Mary James lot #3.
11 Dec.1804 James B. Robins and wife Eliabeth Robins and Littleton Robins with wife Martha Robins sold a lot to William Patrick.
16 Mar.1805 The vestrymen of Stepney Parish sold to James Ritchie lots #3 & #4, 4050 sq.ft.
16 Mar.1805 The vestrymen of Stepney Parish sold lot to Isaac Hearn.
5 Nov.1805 Benjamin Disharoon sold to Samuel Gordon and James Gordon a lot.
13 Sep.1805 John Moore with wife Peggy Moore sold lot to John Gould.
29 Mar.1806 John Jones, Benjamin Shiles Crockett, John Dashiell of Jesse Dashiell, Jonathan Waller vestrymen of Stepney Parish sold parcel to John Cathell.
4 Oct.1806 Robert Lemmon sold lot to Isaac Hearn
14 Mar.1807 Isaac Hearn with wife Nancy Hearn of Worc.Co. sold to William Hearn of Somerset County 2 lots.
22 Aug.1807 Noah Nelms of Baltimore City sold to George Parker, Jesse Townsend, John Rider, William Patrick, William Leonard, William Brewington, Joseph Leonard Jr., James Parker and George Brewington,

trustees of Methodist Epis. Ebenezer Chappel, a lot.
10 Aug.1808 Vestrymen of Stepney Parish sold to John Rider lot 4535 sq.ft.
29 Mar.1809 Outerbridge Horsey of Delaware sold 2 lots to James Powell, property of William Horsey deceased.
22 July 1809 Trustees of Methodist Epis. Chappel of Necessity sold to Samuel James, John J. James and John W.D.F. James, a lot.
8 Aug.1809 Capt. Henry R. Graham, US Army with wife Charlotte A.H. Graham (lately Charlotte Winder daughter of William Winder) sold to Rev. James Laird 1/2 of mills and lot at Salisbury.
29 July 1809 William H. Winder sold to Boaz Walston lots #23,24,25.
29 Aug.1809 John Wilkins sold to John Rider lot per judgement against John Houston.
6 Sep.1809 Jesse Green of Sussex Co.Del. sold to Benjamin Disharoon 1/3pt. of 3 lots bought from Samuel Laferty.
28 Oct.1809 Robert Lemon sold lot to John Rider
1 Oct.1809 John Rider sold lot to William Patrick
28 Oct.1809 Robert Lemon sold lot to James Powell
10 Oct.1809 William H. Winder son of William of Baltimore Md. sold to Stephen Davis and Jehu Parsons of Som.Co. lot.
7 Aug.1810 John Cathell of Worc.Co. sold to John Rider lot.
27 Apr.1810 Nancy Townsend of Worc.Co. sold lot to James Powell.
22 Sep.1810 William Handy and Edward G. Handy sold lands of Isaac Handy deceased sold to Josiah Bayley of Dorc.Co. on Handys Mill pond at Salisbury 43 5/8 acres.
27 Apr.1810 James Powell with wife Priscilla Powell sold lot to Nancy Townsend.
30 June 1810 Robert Lemon with wife Nancy Lemon sold lot MILL SECURITY adjacent Salisbury to Purnell Trader.
5 Oct.1810 Samuel Gordon and James Gordon released mortgage on lot of Benjamin Disharoon.
12 Aug.1810 James Buchannan of Caroline Co.Md. sold to Benjamin Disharoon, lots.
11 June 1810 Thomas Dashiell, constable sold to John W.B. Parsons lot per judgement against Levin Parsons
9 Oct.1810 William Handy and Edward G. Handy trustees to sell real estate of Isaac Handy sold lot to Jehu Bounds.
9 Nov.1816 Nancy Bounds and Francis Smith sold to Jehu Bounds part of lower end of lot sold by William Venables to Capt.Robert Handy
1816 John Johnson willed to son Benjamin Johnson house and lot
1817 Joshua Johnson willed to son George P. Johnson house and lot
21 May 1819 Daniel Davis, executor of Jehu Bounds sold to highest bidder Peter Bell lot.
1824 Sampson Davis willed to daughter Henrietta Davis lot purchased of James Powell.
4 Apr.1826 Thomas J. Bounds of Worc.Co. sold to Charles Rider part that Benjamin Wilson and Charles Hitch sold to Francis Nelms in 1795.
1826 William Hearn willed to daughter Julia Ann Hearn house in Salisbury now occupied by Jacob Morris purchased of Peter Dashiell.
1833 Thomas Hooper willed to wife Sally Hooper house and lot
1837 Wilson Rider willed to wife Henrietta Rider 1/3rd house and lot
1844 Mary Walker willed to grandaughter Mary Jane Cathell house and lot bought of the heirs of James Smith
1846 Isaiah Smith willed to daughter Sally A.T. Smith lot purchased of Purnell Johnson formerly property of Levin Hitch.

1848 Jonathan Parsons willed to William S. Parsons son of Jehu Parsons lot purchased of Henry White.
1853 James Wilson willed lot to be sold.

SALISBURY PLAIN

Patented on 28 Nov.1672 by Isaac Noble for 200 acres
4 Sep.1676 Isaac Noble and wife Mary Noble sold 200 acres to Christopher Nutter.
2 May 1683 Christopher Nutter with wife Mary Nutter sold 200 acres to William Piper.
Rent Rolls 1666-1723 possessed by Charles Nutter in right of the orphans of William Piper.
1783 tax - Agnes Piper 200 acres, Rewastico 100
13 Nov.1800 David Wilson sold to Charles Nutter 623 acres on Rewastico Creek willed by Major Ephraim King and Henry Steele.
13 Sep.1808 Levin Farrington mortgaged to Farmers Bank of Md.
16 Oct.1835 James Bounds and Susan L. Weatherly sold to Joseph Collins 282 acres of WILTON,SALISBURY PLAIN, NEEDLESS COST the lands of the heirs of Elihu Jackson and the heirs of Levin Wilson.

SALLYS LOT

Patented in 1774 by William Darby for 39 acres
17 Jan.1794 Levin Bennett and wife Betsy Bennett and Sally Darby heirs of William Darby sold to Isaac Wright 10 3/4 acres of WILLIAMS ADVENTURE & SALLYS LOTT
19 Mar.1796 Levin Bennett and wife Elizabeth Bennett sold to Levin Taylor 29 3/4 acres.

SALLOP

Patented on 23 Nov.1672 by John Windsor for 250 acres.
Rent Rolls 1666-1723 possessed by William Giles Jr.
1751 William Giles Jr. willed 250 acres to son William.
1772 William Giles willed to son William Jr. 250 acres, not ever to be sold.
11 Sep.1775 Isaac Giles with wife Elizabeth Giles sold 250 acres to Ralph Moore.
1783 tax - Ralph Moore 250 acres, Nanticoke 100
20 Mar.1784 Isaac Giles son of Jacob Giles sold to John Leatherbury his rights.
18 May 1784 Isaac Giles Jr. sold his interest to John Leatherbury
6 Mar.1786 Ralph Moore,with wife Mary Moore sold to Mary Bonnewell wife of Hall Bonnewell of Dorc.Co. all of SALLOP
6 Mar.1786 Ralph Moore with wife Mary Moore sold to Sarah Moore wife of Levin Moore, part.
18 May 1791 Ralph Moore leased for 7 years to James Anderson 600 acres of SALOP, PARRAMORES CHOICE or GILES FOLLY.
9 Nov.1791 Ralph Moore and wife Mary Moore and James Moore sold to James Anderson, description, no acreage given.
9 Mar.1793 Michael Hall Bonnewell with wife Mary Bonnewell of Kent Co.Del. sold to James Anderson that Mary Bonnewell at the death of her parents Ralph Moore and Mary Moore died siezed.
25 Aug.1794 Ralph Moore and James Anderson sold 1 acre to the trustees of the Methodist Society for a chapel of PARRAMORES FIRST CHOICE,

GILES FOLLY or SALLOP
1804 James Anderson willed to son James land bought of Michael Hall Bonnewell..
1822 George Walters willed to wife Eleanor Walters, part.

SAMPSONS BEGINNING

Patented in 1850 by William Adkins for 65 3/4 acres

SAMUELS ADDITON

Patented in 1865 by Samuel M. Riley for 187 acres, 1 perch, 20 rods.

SAMUELS ADVENTURE

Patented see SMITHS ADVENTURE

SAMUELS ADVENTURE

Patented in 1727 by John Caldwell for 59 acres who assigned to Peter Samuels.
16 Aug.1753 Peter Samuels sold 59 acres to Andrew Collins.
14 Sep.1769 Andrew Collins sold to John Collins, yoeman 59 acres.
1773 Andrew Collins willed to son John Collins 50 acres.

SAMUELS CHANCE

Patented in 1800 by Samuel Pollitt for 193 acres

SAMUELS LOTT

Patented on 23 Oct.1696 by Richard Samuels for 200 acres in a neck between Nanticoke and Wicomico Rivers.
Rent Rolls 1666-1723 possessed by Richard Samuels.
1709 Richard Samuels willed 200 acres to son Richard.
1732 Richard Samuels of Stepney Parish willed 140 acres to son Peter Samuels. At decease to his son Robert Samuels by his first wife (part has been conveyed to Stephen Hopkins and daughter Elizabeth Hopkins his wife.)
1732 Peter Samuels willed 140 acres to daughters Mary Samuels and Sarah Samuels.
6 Nov.1750 Elijah Riall with wife Mary Riall of Dorc.Co. (Mary Samuels d/o Peter)and Sarah Samuels of Som. Co. sold to Stephen Hopkins.
1783 tax - Nelly Hopkins 70 acres, Nanticoke 100
1783 tax - Robert Hopkins 150 acres
25 Mar.1805 William Mezick and wife Sarah Mezick sold to David Hopkins, Eleanor Hopkins, George Hopkins and Stephen Hopkins 151 acres of SAMUELS LOTT & WARE.
3 Apr.1805 David Hopkins of Stephen Hopkins, Eleanor Hopkins and George Hopkins of Stephen Hopkins, sold their interest to Jesse Hughes.
17 Jan.1805 Richard Hopkins, John Hopkins, Samuel Hopkins sons of Robert Hopkins sold to David Hopkins
20 June 1806 Eleanor Hopkins sold for 5 shillings to Jesse Hughes.
18 July 1808 James Hopkins with wife Polly Hopkins sold to Jesse Hughes, part between them.

18 July 1808 David Hopkins with wife Mary Ann Hopkins sold to Jesse Hughes 58 3/4 acres a resurvey by David Hopkins called TROUBLE FOR LITTLE.

SAND HILLS

Patented in 1782 by Andrew Adams for 150 3/4 acres.
13 Apr.1791 Andrew Adams with wife Mary Adams, Boardvine Bayley, Elias Bayley with wife Ann Bayley sold to Obed Bayley for 5 shillings 80 3/4 acres.

SAND RIDGE

Patented in 1694 by John Taylor for 100 acres
17 Feb.1790 Thomas Goslee and Stephen Tully sold all to John Jenner
31 Aug.1793 John Jenner with wife Easter Jenner sold 1/2 to John Reddish
31 Aug.1793 John Jenner with wife Easter Jenner sold 1/2 to James Knight.
22 Oct.1801 James Knight with wife Eliza Knight, Peter Manlove with wife Sarah Manlove, John Reddish with wife Rhoda Reddish sold all rights to William Brereton, conveyed by John Jenner to James Knight.
1 Dec.1801 Elzey Davis with wife Mary Davis (late Mary Knight) sold to William Brereton with FISHWATERS STUDY.

SANDERS FOLLY

Patented in 1742 by Peter Calloway for 73 acres

SANDY HILL

Patented in 1770 by Jonathan Pollitt for 200 acres
1783 tax - Jonathan Pollitt, Rewastico
12 Nov.1796 Jonathan Pollitt sold to Stephen Pollitt 200 acres.
1882 Lewis Pollitt willed to son Lewis Asbury Pollitt.

SANDY HILL

Patented in 1748 by Nehemiah Hearn for 75 acres
1760 Nehemiah Hearn willed to son Thomas Hearn, 75 acres
1783 tax - Thomas Hearn 75 acres
20 Oct.1786 Thomas Hearn sold to Elijah Hearn 20 acres for 8 shillings.
1789 Elijah Hearn willed to son William Hearn.

SANDY PLAIN

19 Dec.1782 Nathaniel Ramsey of the comission to sell confiscated property sold 736 acres to William Winder.
6 Apr.1791 William Winder gave 15 acres to son William Jr.
1783 tax - William Winder Jr. 686 acres, Wic. 100
1792 William Winder willed to son John Winder.
28 Mar.1794 James R. Morris, Leah Morris, Levin Handy, Nancy Handy, Ephraim Wilson, Jane Wilson sold all interest to William Winder Jr.
20 Nov.1794 John Whittington Round and Peggy Winder Round of Worc.Co. sold all interest to William Winder.
4 Dec.1798 John Winder of Northampton Co.Va. gave to Thomas Jones

Winder lands William Winder willed him and lands Levin Winder of William sold him, no name or acreage.
15 June 1799 Dr. Thomas Jones Winder sold to Thomas Lane 160 1/4 acres.
15 June 1799 Dr. Thomas Jones Winder sold 100 1/4 acres to Samuel Williams
15 June 1799 Dr. Thomas Jones Winder sold to Joseph Furbush 126 1/4 acres.
17 May 1800 Thomas Lane sold to Jesse Fooks 160 1/4 acres
1801 Jesse Fooks of Wor.Co. sold to Joshua Disharoon 160 1/4 acres
12 Sep.1801 William Winder sold to Thomas Lowe 19 1/2 acres
17 Sep.1801 Thomas Lane with wife Nelly Lane sold to Joshua Disharoon 16 1/4 acres
7 Dec.1801 Thomas Lane, blacksmith with wife Nelly Lane sold to Thomas Jones Winder for 5 shillings 19 1/8 acres.
5 Jan.1799 William Winder sold to Samuel Williams of Worc.Co. 186 1/2 acres for 10 shillings.
8 Apr.1806 John Winder of Northampton Co.Va. coheir of William Winder sold to William Winder coheir all equity.
9 Sep.1806 Levin Winder, Richard Henry Handy, Hetty W. Winder and Joseph Polk sold to William Winder coheir of William Winder, to settle estate.
17 Apr.1807 Leah Morris, Richard Henry Handy, Thomas Winder Handy. heirs of William Winder sold to other heir William Winder.
17 Apr.1807 Richard Henry Handy and Thomas Winder Handy heirs of William Winder sold all rights to William Winder coheir.
4 June 1807 William Henry Winder with wife Gertrude Winder, George Dashiell with wife Esther Dashiell, William W. Handy and George D.S. Handy of Baltimore Co. heirs of William Winder sold to William Winder all rights.
8 Oct.1808 William Williams Sr. sold 3/4 acre 9 perches to Joseph Furbush.
1808 William Winder willed to son William Henry Winder.
26 Aug.1809 William H. Winder son of William, with wife Gertrude Winder of Baltimore sold 44 acres to Joshua Disharoon.
1834 Samuel Williams willed that son Samuel sell this land.

SANKY ISLAND

Patented on 15 Dec.1679 by James Weatherly for 100 acres on an island at the north side of the mouth of Rewastico Creek.
Rent Rolls 1666-1723 possessed by James Weatherly
1751 James Weatherly willed to son John Weatherly
1735 William Weatherly son of James willed to sons Joseph Weatherly, Elijah Weatherly, Richard Weatherly, Nathan Weatherly and William Weatherly.
18 Nov.1756 James Weatherly and John Weatherly sold 38 acres to Joseph Weatherly.
6 Oct.1759 James Weatherly, John Weatherly, Joseph Weatherly with wife Patience Weatherly sold 100 acres to Ephraim King.
23 Feb.1773 Ephraim King sold 100 acres to Thomas Handy
25 Oct.1775 Thomas Handy son of John Handy sold to Ephraim King 100 acres
1783 tax - William Horsey 33 /13 acrees
1783 tax - Isaac Horsey 33 1/3 acres

1783 tax - William McBryde 33 1/2 acres.
1790 Isaac Horsey willed lands and marsh to son Isaac Horsey.

SARAHS CHOICE

Patented in 1759 by Stephen Seady for 50 acres.
1770 Stephen Seady willed lands to wife Sarah Seady, after her death to son Burton Seady
1783 tax - Sarah Seady 50 acres
19 Apr.1788 Sarah Scady, Leah Scady, Major Dorman with wife Sarah Dorman, Selby Dakes with wife Dinah Dakes sold to Jesse Fooks 50 acres
1809 John Fooks willed to daughter Rachel Noble Fooks and her son George Noble Fooks.

SARAHS LOTT

Patented in 1808 by Sarah Jones for 3 acres

SARAHS NECK

Patented on 18 Apr.1680 by John Winder who assigned to Phillip Carter for 100 acres
Rent Rolls 1666-1723 possessed by David Shehee
1729 David Shehee willed estate to wife Sarah Shehee and her children David Shehee and Margery Shehee
5 Nov.1748 William Toadvine of Worc.Co. with wife Miriam Toadvine (formerly Miriam Watts dau/o John Watts and Ann Watts) and Isaac Tull, carpenter with wife Winifred Tull (Winifred Watts d/o John) sold to Henry Lowe 250 acres of DOWGATE & SARAHS NECK.

SARAHS SECURITY

Patented in 1729 by Sarah King and Joseph Wailes for 350 acres
2 Dec.1745 Capell King with wife Sarah King sold to Francis Allen 350 acres patented Sarah wife of Capell. Joseph Wailes died before division.
3 Mar.1748/9 Francis Allen sold to Robert Banks of Northampton Co.Va.
1765 probably resurveyed to ROBERTS SECURITY 391 1/2 acres.

SATSIFIED

Patented in 1789 by Constant Disharoon for 74 acres
1795 Constant Disharoon willed 74 aces to daughter Milla Stanford and after death to grandson Constant Disharoon Stanford.

SAVAGES SECURITY

Patented on 11 July 1762 by Benjamin Savage for 40 acres and repatented on 17 March 1763
13 Jan.1792 Benjamin Savage sold to Boaz Walston 103 1/2 acres of SAVAGES PURCHASE, SAVAGES SECURITY, END OF STRIFE
2 July 1808 Boaz Walston with wife Bathsheba Walston sold to James Walker Bayley Perdue 103 1/2 acres, same as above.
1823 John Parker of E. willed to daughter Elizabeth Parsons and daughter Sarah Parsons.

SAVANAH LOT

Patented in 1761 by William Lloyd for 15 acres
1783 tax - William Lloyd 15 acres, Rewastico

SAW MILL LOTT

Patented on 4 Apr.1755 by Joseph Marshall for 118 acres
17 Aug.1763 Joseph Marshall sold 118 acres to John Mitchell and John Holston.

SAW MILL LOTT

Patented on 3 June 1753 by William Winder for 26 acres
1791 resurveyed by William Winder for 166 acres from HUNGARY QUARTER
22 Oct.1791 William Winder gave to daughter Leah Morris, part
22 Nov.1793 James Round Morris with wife Leah Morris sold to Joshua Pollitt 105 3/4 acres.
3 May 1794 Joshua Pollitt with wife Sally sold to Francis Gurley for 5 shillings 7 3/4 acres, of resurvey.
15 Aug.1798 Leah Morris, William Morris, Levin Winder executors of James Round Morris sold to Stephen Townsend 46 1/4 acres of MORRIS DISOCOVERY, SAW MILL LOTT.
15 Aug.1798 Leah Morris, William Morris, Levin Winder sold to Joshua Pollitt 48 2/8 acres of SAW MILL LOTT, MORRIS DISCOVERY
14 Aug.1803 Leah Morris daughter of William Winder, Levin Winder sold to George Dashiell 26 acres and 11 1/2 acres
15 Oct.1803 Col. George Dashiell with wife Sally Dashiell sold to James Fooks of Jesse Fooks 26 acres and 11 1/2 acres.
4 June 1805 James Fooks with wife Sabra Fooks sold to Joshua Pollitt 7 1/2 acres.
8 Apr.1806 John Winder of Northampton Co.Va. coheir of William Winder of Som.Co. sold to coheir William Winder all interest.
9 Sep.1806 Levin Winder, Richard Henry Handy, Hetty W. Winder and Josiah Polk sold to coheir William Winder of William.
17 Apr.1807 Richard Henry Handy and Thomas Winder Handy sold to William Winder all rights.
4 July 1807 William Henry Winder with wife Gertrude Winder, George Dashiell with wife Esther Dashiell, William W. Handy and George D.S. Handy of Baltimore sold rights to William Winder.
1808 William Winder willed to son William Henry Winder.
5 Oct.1810 Leah Irving sold to William Handy real estate of Isaac Handy.
5 Oct.1810 William Handy and Edward G. Handy of Washington D.C. sold to Leah Irving, trustees to sell real estate of Isaac Handy, mills and lands, Small lott and New Haven, etc.

SAW MILL SUPPLY

Patented in 1765 by Nathan Culver for 367 acres a resurvey from MT.TURRSEY
12 Dec.1767 Nathan Culver sold to Thomas Lankford.
1774 part resurveyed to JAMES FORTUNE 96 acres.
22 June 1757 Nathan Culver sold to Thomas Humphries 100 acres
17 Nov.1767 Nathan Culver sold 54 acres to Benjamin McClellan
12 Dec.1767 Nathan Culver sold 50 acres to Thomas Lankford.

25 Jan.1782 Nathan Culver sold to Thomas Humphries, reconfirmation of 1767 sale, altered plat.
25 Jan.1782 Nathan Culver sold 16 acres to James Fletcher
31 Dec.1782 Nathan Culver sold 45 acres to Benjamin Hearn
1783 tax - Benjamin Hearn 55 acres
1783 tax - John Johnson 40 acres
1783 tax - Levin Huffington 110 acres
1783 tax - Benjamin Lankford 50 acres
1783 tax - Mary Lankford 40 acres
1783 tax - James Fletcher 16 acres
1783 tax - Benjamin McClellan 55 acres
1783 tax - Joshua Nicholson 50 acres.
29 Sep.1788 John Johnson sold 30 acres to Rachel Johnson.
1789 Benjamin Lankford sold to John Lankford
11 Aug.1789 John Johnson sold to Benjamin Hearn 10 acres
25 May 1795 Benjamin McClellan with wife Bridget McClellan sold to Thomas Humphries 10 3/4 acres oof PINEY GROVE & SAW MILL SUPPLY
25 May 1795 Benjamin McClellan with wife Bridget McClellan sold to Hudson Lowe 1/8 acre.
23 Mar.1796 Robert Jones with wife Ann Jones of Sussex Co.Del. sold 11 acres to John Johnson of Som.Co.
14 Dec.1799 John Johnson sold 24 //34 acres to Benjamin Hearn.
1802 Hudson Lowe willed lands unnnamed to son Samuel Lowe.
10 Nov.1804 triparte Thomas Humphries of Hancock Co.Georgia sold to George Parker of Md. and Thomas Humphries Jr. with Joseph Humphries and Curtis Hitch attorneys to acknowledge deed 100 acres. Signed in Georgia in the presence of Henry Turner, Elisha Parker, Levi Matthews and William Parker.
16 Mar.1805 George Parker sold 100 acres to Ezekiel Bell
8 Apr.1806 John Winder of Northampton Co. Va. sold to William Winder coehir of William Winder of Somerset County
13 Jan.1810 John Johnson sold 2 /34 acres to Samuel Lowe.

SAW PIT LANDING

29 July 1793 Nathaniel Ramsey, comissioner to sell confiscated real estae sold to Isaac Handy eldest son of George Handy deceased, as George had 124 3/4 acres that he willed to Isaac, as Isaac Handy paid the debt.
24 Jan 1789 Isaac Handy sold to Edmund Northern Nelms of Worc.Co. 124 3/4 acres on the south side of the Wicomico River.

SAW PITT RIDGE

Patented in 1776 by John Gordy for 50 acres

SCOTCH IRELAND

Patented on 6 Dec.1688 by Edward Craig for 300 acres in a fork of Deep Creek Branch.
24 Dec.1731 William Craig of Sussex Co.Del. son of Edward Craig, sold to David Shockley of Som.Co. 300 acres that Edward late of Sussex Co. patented.
1754 David Shcokley willed to daughter Amely Rathbone, begotten by me of Mary Rathbone, 200 acres and to daughter Love Rathbone 100 acres.

28 Apr.1774 William Mezick and wife Amely Mezick and Love Cranfield widow of Isaiah Cranfield sold to Luke Huffington 300 acres that David Shockley willed Amely and Love.

SCOTLAND

Patented in 1788 by Samuel Miles for 437 acres

SCOTLAND

Patented in 1774 by Archibald Smith for 4 acres

SCOTTS ADVENTURE

Patented in 1840 by George D. Scott for 1 acre

SCOTTS CHANCE

Patented in 1765 by Windom Scott for 160 acres
1772 Windom Scott willed lands to wife Comfort Scott and son Michael Scott, unnamed.
8 Oct.1768 Windom Scott sold 80 acres to Luke Mezick
28 Nov.1772 Luke Mezick of Dorchester Co. sold 80 acres to Thomas Culver of Worc.Co.
31 Oct.1774 Thomas Culver carpenter, with wife Catherine Culver sold to Charles Vaughan 80 acres.
3 Feb.1775 Michael Scott sold 80 acres to Charles Vaughan.
1783 tax - Charles Vaughan 160 acres, Rewastico
11 Mar.1782 Zorobable King, Jesse Walston and Solomon Long purchased 20 acres from Charles Vaughan, with FRIENDS ADVENTURE.
11 Dec.1792 John Denwood sheriff, per court order on behalf of Gustavous Scott against Charles Vaughan sold to Charles Badley, SCOTTS CHANCE, FRIENDS ADVENTURE, no acres mentioned.
17 June 1794 Charles Badley sold to David Gray and Levin Gray for 5 shillings 150 acres of SCOTTS CHANCE, FRIENDS ADVENTURE.
16 Jan.1803 David Gray sold to Charles Badley.
1843 Polly Cooper (Polly Badley)widow of Samuel Cooper willed to son Severn B. Cooper, at Barren Creek near Mardella Springs.

SCOTTS CHOICE

Patented in 1740 by William Scott for 150 acres

SCOTTS DISCOVERY
Patented in 1840 George D. Scott for 6 acres.

SCOTTS FOLLY

Patented in 1766 by William Scott for 247 acres

SCUFFLE

Patented in 1801 by William Bounds for 134 acres

SEAMANS FANCY

Patented in 1805 by Hugh Gemmill for 5 acres

SECOND ADDITION

Patented in 1775 by John Waters for 14 1/2 aacres

SECOND ADDITION

Patented in 1836 by William Summers for 5 1/4 acres

SECOND ATTEMPT

Patented in 1806 by Boardvine Bayley for 9 3/4 acres

SECOND CHANCE

Patented in 1715 by William Whittington for 100 acres

SECOND CHOICE

Patented on 23 Apr.1675 by Samuel Smith of Northumberland Co. Va.for 300 acres who conveyed to Peter Presley with SMITHS ADVENTURE
5 Aug.1706 Peter Presley of St.Stevens Parish, Northumberland Co.Va. gave to Jonathan Raymond and wife Judith Raymond part of 500 acres at head of Wicomico Creek.
13 May 1721 Peter Presley of Northumberland Co.Va. sold to Thomas Gillis 500 acres of SECOND CHOICE & SMITHS ADVENTURE.
14 Oct.1724 Jonathan Raymond mortgaged to Thomas Gillis 15 acres with 69 acres of RAYMONDS CHANCE.

SECOND CHOICE

Patented in 1725 by John Holland for 72 acres

SECOND CHOICE

Patented on 10 May 1760 by William Spicer for 50 acres in Deep Creek forrest.
31 Mar.1764 William Spicer with wife Lydia Spicer sold to Zachariah Harris 10 acres
9 Nov.1764 William Spicer sold to John Johnson, on Nanticoke River 50 acres.

SECOND CHOICE

Patented on 12 Feb.1764 by John Hearn for 50 acres
5 Feb.1767 John Hearn with wife Elizabeth Hearn sold 50 acres to George Davis
24 Mar.1774 George Davis sold to Elijah Smith 50 acres, in Wicomico Forrest.

SECOND PURCHASE

see FORKED NECK, 250 acres

SECOND PURCHASE

Patented on 15 July 1695 by Daniel Haste for 300 acres.
27 Jan. 1701 Daniel Haste willed to daughters Sarah Haste and Elizabeth Haste.
Rent Rolls 1666-1723 possessed by Benjamin Wailes 150 acres and 150 acres by Robert Dashiell.
11 July 1714 Robert Dashiell and wife Sarah Dashiell with Benjamin Wailes and wife Elizabeth Wailes sold to Michael Disharoon 300 acres.
1755 Michael Disharoon Jr. son of Michael sold to David Jenkins 100 acres of upper part for 5 shillings.
1773 David Jenkins willed to son David 100 acres and 100 acres to son Littleton Jenkins, unnamed.
1783 tax - William Disharoon 150 acres.
11 July 1789 William Disharoon sold to William Crouch 50 acres
26 July 1792 William Disharoon with wife Betsy Disharoon sold 42 acres to James Bennett
4 Oct 1800 William Crouch sold all to James Bennett
6 Feb.1806 Littleton Jenkins with wife Betsy Jenkins sold to Samuel Bassett land left him by father, 100 acres.
5 Sep.1810 Benjamin Disharoon sold to Stephen Roach.
25 Sep.1810 Stephen Roach with wife Nancy Roach of Worc.Co. sold to Benjamin Disharoon 107 1/4 acres with WOULD HAVE MORE.

SECOND PURCHASE

Patented in 1733 by Charles Polk for 400 acres

SECURITY

Patented in 1732 by Samuel Fluellin for 50 acres
1783 tax - Samuel Fluellin 50 acres Nanticoke 100
13 July 1789 Samuel Fluellin sold to George Robertson 50 acres.
26 Mar.1793 Gillis Polk surviving trustee of Ephraim King and Samuel Fluellin brother of Richard Crockett Fluellin sold to Isaac Atkinson son of Isaac with CLEAR OF CANNON SHOTT, WOOLF QUARTER, etc.

SECURITY

Patented in 1735 by John Stevens for 213 acres.

SECURITY

Patented in 1738 by Matthias Gale for 2 acres

SECURITY

Patented on 15 Sep.1747 by John Williams for 100 acres
6 Nov.1754 John Williams, yoeman sold to Littleton Williams 100 acres back in woods from Nanticoke River.

SECURITY

Patented on 2 May 1750 by John Phillips for 51 acres.
8 Jan.1758 John Phillips sold to Edmund Hitchens 51 acres

13 Jan.1761 Edmund Hitchens resurveyed to SECURITY ENLARGED, 561 acres.

SECURITY

Patented in 1760 by William Kibble for 191 1/2 acres
1783 tax - Betty Kibble 113 acres, Wic.100
1783 tax - heirs of John C. Kibble 100 acres
15 Oct.1793 John Kilby of North Carolina, eldest son of Christopher Kilby and wife Mary Kilby of Som.Co. deceased sold to Elizabeth Bounds of Som.Co. land on north side of Wicomico Creek where John Kibble lives which descended to John Kibble from his mother 100 acres.
11 March 1802 James Bounds sold to George Kibble 100 acres being lands Elizabeth Bounds mother of James bought of John Kilby.

SECURITY

Patented in 1764 by Samuel Davis for 1120 acres a resurvey of DAVIS ADDITION
resurveyed to 1626 acres by Samuel Davis
18 Oct.1765 Samuel Davis sold to Daniel Dykes 110 acres for 5 shillings
18 Oct.1765 Samuel Davis sold to James Davis for 5 shillings 94 acres
18 Oct.1765 Samuel Davis sold to Hezekiah Carey 33 acres
4 Mar.1771 Hezekiah Carey sold 33 acres to Levin Carey
5 Aug.1772 Samuel Davis with wife Sarah Davis sold to Stephen Beauchamp 100 acres.
22 Apr.1782 Saul Davis heir of Samuel Davis sold 100 acres to John Taylor.
1783 tax - Samuel Davis 73 acres, Wic.100, Worc.Co.
1786 Daniel Dykes sold to Benjamin Johnson, part.
4 Nov.1786 Saul Davis sold to Charles Roach 100 acres, no name.
4 Nov.1786 Saul Davis sold to Joseph Dashiell 100 acres, as Samuel Davis died leaving daughters Mary Davis and Sarah Davis and son Powell Davis all since dead without issue.
5 June 1787 Stephen Beauchamp with wife Rachel Beauchamp sold to Benjamin Dashiell heir of Joseph Dashiell 100 acres purchaed from Samuel Davis.
18 Dec.1790 Thomas Harwood of Annapolis with wife Margaret Harwood sold to Purnell Johnson and Thomas Johnson 10 acres.
22 Oct.1790 Zadock Sturgis, sheriff sold to Thomas Harwood of Annapolis per judgement against Benjamin F.A.C. Dashiell son of Joseph Dashiell 10 acres.
11 Feb.1791 Purnell Johnson sold 10 acres to Thomas Johnson.
14 Sep.1792 Purnell Johnson, Elijah Johnson, William Hearn sold to Benjamin Johnson 10 acres.
13 Sep.1794 Thomas Taylor and Mary Taylor sold to Sarah Orman 100 acres.
8 July 1797 Benjamin Dashiell sold to Benjamin Johnson 100 acres.
5 Jan.1805 Eben Disharoon with wife Hetty Disharoon, Aaron Mezick with wife Ann Mezick, Patty Disharoon, Matthew Jones with wife Frankey Jones, Molly Disharoon sold to James Fooks of Thomas Fooks 65 acres.
17 Oct.1807 Sarah Disharoon of Francis Disharoon sold to James Fooks 1/6th part.
8 Jan.1810 Peter Dashiell sold to John Nelms of Baltimore.

SECURITY

Patented to Daniel Maddux for 310 acres.
1773 SECURITY ENLARGED patented to Hezekiah Maddux for 270 acres
1783 tax - Hezekiah Maddux -Enlarged 236 acres, Wic.100, Worc.Co.
1822 Elijah Melson willed to son Elijah SECURITY ENLARGED.

SETTLEMENT

Patented on 20 Dec.1741 by John Taylor for 100 acres
8 June 1770 Charles Bannister sold to John Houston that John Taylor willed to son John who absconded himself from justice. Charles Bannister attached as creditor, 100 acres.

SHADWELL

Patented on 30 Nov.1672 by Charles Hutchins for 300 acres in Nanticoke 100 who assigned to John Pearce.
14 Feb.1683 John Pearce and wife Elizabeth Pearce sold to Robert Collier 150 acres.
Rent Rolls 1666-1723 possessed by Robert Collier 150 acres, Sidney Brown 150 acres.
1702 Robert Collier willed to son Robert 200 acres.
3 July 1724 Robert Collier sold to William Stevens 120 acres and tract adjacent now called STEVENS INHERITANCE.
1 Jan.1728 Robert Collier sold to Richard Dunn 20 acres with LATE DISCOVERY.
1 Sep.1728 George Langrell of Dorc.Co. sold to Richard Dunn 100 acres. that Robert Collier and wife Ann Collier sold to George.
13 Dec.1763 Thomas Stevens sold to Benjamin Mezick 50 acres.
2 Mar.1764 Nicholas Dunn sold 50 acres to Thomas Dunn
1773 Benjamin Mezick willed 50 acres to son George Mezick
1783 tax - Richard Dunn 100 acres
1783 tax - Elizabeth Handy 24 acres
1783 tax - Benjamin Mezick 50 acres
1783 tax - Solomon Winright 12 acres
1783 tax - William Bounds 124 acres
6 July 1785 William Dunn son of Nicholas Dunn sold to Richard Dunn son of Thomas Dunn 100 acres of SHADWELL & late discovery.
15 Nov.1792 George Mezick son of Benjamin Mezick sold to Richard Dunn 23 1/4 acres of SHADWELL & BEWDLY.
1795 William Walter willed to son John Walter, on Broad Creek.

SHANDY

Patented in 1792 by William Winder Jr. for 1 1/2 acres

SHANTAVANAH

Patented on 25 Apr.1722 by James Givans for 200 acres.
1723 James Givans willed to son John Givans 200 acres
15 Sep.1740 John Givans with wife Mary Givans sold to Daniel Rhoads 200 acres with 10 acres of WARRINGTON now called RHOADS CHANCE.
16 Mar.1768 Daniel Henderson and Daniel Rhoads sold to John Phillips 158 acres with WARRINGTON, HENDERSONS CHOICE.

1773 William Russell willed lands to sister Leah Russell and brother James Russell.
1783 tax - Thomas Russell 42 acres, Rewastico 100
1783 tax - Jacob Rhoads 138 acres
18 Feb.1768 Daniel Henderson and Daniel Rhoads sold 42 acres to William Russell.
5 June 1783 John Phillips sold 158 acres to Jacob Rhoads.
1787 Jacob Rhoads willed to son Nathan Rhoads upper part where I live and to son Charles Rhoads lower part next to Thomas Russell.
1791 Thomas Russell willed to son Levin Russell 42 acres and 10 acres of marsh, part of SHANTAVANAH.
14 Sep.1795 Jesse Russell with wife Eleanor Russell sold 42 acres to Thomas Russell.

SHARPES CHANCE

No patent found under this name.
7 Nov.1744 John Sharp of Worc.Co. sold to John Collins 100 acres, near head of Nanticoke River.
7 Aug.1753 William Sharp of Worc.Co. son of John Sharp sold to Thomas Waller Jr. of Somerset Co. 50 acres.
26 Oct 1757 Thomas Waller mortgaged to Outerbridge Horsey with HOGG PALACE, LOGSGATE HILL.
17 Mar.1757 Thomas Waller Jr. mortgaged to Thomas Moore.
16 Aug.1758 Thomas Moore sold to Outerbridge Horsey mortgaged.
1785 Outerbridge Horsey willed to son Lazarus Horsey, on Broad Creek.

SHARPES ADDITION

Patented in 1761 by George Sharp for 5 acres.

SHARPTOWN

First Settlement on the southern Bank of the Nanticoke River in the mid 1700's.
1849 William Gravener willed to son Urias Gravener, 2 acres and house in Sharptown.
1850 this is in the Barren Creek District.

SHAVE THE BALD FRIAR

Patented in 1785 by George Sharp for 290 3/4 acres
1783 tax - George Sharp 54 acres
1783 tax - George Disharoon 72 acres
1784 George Sharp willed to friend George Disharoon per bond of conveyance.
9 Apr.1787 Daniel Sharp and Cyrus Sharp sold to George Disharoon for 5 shillings 87 acres.
19 Mar.1796 Stephen Disharoon son of George sold to Cyrus Sharp 87 acres since resurveyed to ADDITION TO LITTLE EDEN.
1802 Cyrus Sharp willed lands to brothers William Sharp and Daniel Sharp, unnamed.
31 Mary 1810 Daniel Sharp with wife Rebecca Sharp sold to James Bennett.

SHEPPARDS CROOK

Patented on 12 Dec.1730 by John Records for 150 acres
1744 John Records willed to son Phillip 50 acres.
3 Mar.1767 Thomas Records sold to Joseph Cannon 70 acres.
1 Aug.1767 Phillip Records sold to Joseph Cannon 50 acres.
12 Jan.1771 Joseph Records sold to Joseph Cannon 11 acres.

SHEPPARDS CROOK

Patented in 1804 by William Huffington for 43 1/2 acres

SHEROODANS DESIRE

Patented in 1728 by Daniel Sherrodan for 20 acres.
31 July 1764 Elizabeth Sherrodan and Sarah Sherrodan daughters of William Sherrodan sold to Joseph Dashiell Sr. for 5 shillings 20 acres land that Daniel Sherrodan grandfather took up on the north side of Wetpquin Creek.
19 Aug.1772 Joseph Dashiell sold son George Dashiell.
1783 tax - George Dashiell 20 acres.

SHIELDS HIS CHOICE

Patented on 21 Sep 1676 by Alice Shields for 200 acres on the north side of Quantico Creek.
Rent Rolls 1666-1723 possessed by Christopher Nutter 110 acres, Matthew Nutter 110 acres.
3 Oct.1720 John Nutter of Sussex Co.Del. appointed Robert Jones attorney to convey lands to Christopher Nutter and Matthew Nutter laid out for Thomas Shields and part to John Huett Nutter, if no issue to brother Matthew Nutter.
16 Apr.1736 Matthew Nutter of Quantico sold to John Huett Nutter
1740 John Nutter of Sussex Co.Del. willed to heirs, sister Betty Smith, Cousin David Smith and Mary Smith children of sister Betty, Mary Nutter daughter of Christopher Nutter and brother-in-law John Smith, uncle Christopher Nutter.
24 May 1774 Thomas Smith of Sussex Co.Del. sold to John Waters late of Calvert Co., now of Som.Co. 1/2 of all lands SHILES CHOICE, DORMANS DELIGHT, NUTTERS ADVENTURE, NUTTERS LOWER ADVENTURE.
1783 tax - John Waters 110 acres, Rewastico 100
1784 John Waters willed plantation in Quantico Creek to wife Elizabeth Waters and after her death to son Francis Hutchins Waters.
31 Mar.1787 Francis Hutchins Waters son of John Waters sold to John Gale

SHIELLS FOLLY

Patented on 20 Sep.1700 by James Dashiell and Thomas Dashiell for 1225 acres.
1710 resurveyed and found to be 1350 acres.
1713 James Dashiell willed to sons James, Jesse Dashiell, Winder Dashiell and Benjamin Dashiell, equal rights.
7 June 1722 Thomas Dashiell Sr. gave to James Dashiell 650 acres.
6 Sep.1735 Thomas Dashiell sold to Isaac Handy 300 acres now called HANDYS PASTURE.

22 Mar.1753 Levin Dashiell son of Thomas Dashiell with wife Bridget Dashiell sold to Isaac Dashiell 100 acres
1755 Thomas Dashiell willed to sons Henry Dashiell, Thomas Dashiell and Levin Dashiell 350 acres.
22 June 1757 Thomas Dashiell sold 25 acres to William Nelson
8 Sep.1758 Nehemiah Crockett sold 25 acres to John Robertson for 15 shillings part that he purchased of Isaac Dashiell.
22 June 1758 Nehemiah Crockett sold 40 acres to Jacob Aires.
27 Aug.1768 Josiah Dashiell sold 75 acres to Thomas Dashiell.
7 Aug.1768 Josiah Dashiell s/o Thomas Dashiell sold to Thomas Dashiell 12 acres.
1773 Jesse Dashiell willed to wife Susannah Dashiell lands and to son James Dashiell, unnamed lands.
1783 tax - Littleton Aires 40 acres Nanticoke 100
1783 tax - John Douglas 25 acres
1783 tax - John Dashiell 20 acres
1783 tax - Mary Dashiell 128 acres
1783 tax - James Dashiell 32 1/2 acres
1783 tax - Henry Handy 15 acres
1783 tax - Betty Handy 15 acres
1783 tax - Susannah Dashiell 16 acres
1783 tax - Jane Dashiell 65 acres

SHIELDS MEADOW

Patented on 4 Dec.1701 by John Shields for 60 acres
Rent Rolls 1666-1723 possessed by John Shields
15 Apr.1745 John Shields sold to Thomas Willin 60 acres
22 Feb.1755 Thomas Willin gave to son Levin Willin 60 acres
20 Mar.1765 Levin Willin sold to Isaac Atkinson 60 acres.

SHILES MISTAKE

Patented in 1765 by Daniel McIntyre for 30 acres
1773 Daniel McIntyre willed to wife Elizabeth McIntyre, after her death to son William McIntyre
1783 tax - Betty McIntyre 30 acres, Nanticoke 100

SHILES RIDGE

Patented in 1749 by John Moore for 75 acres
5 Nov.1769 John Moore sold to George Lane Moore 75 acres
25 Mar 1771 George Lane Moore and wife Mary Moore sold to James Layton of Dorcester County 75 acres.

SHILES VENTURE

Patented in 1741 by Thomas Shiles for 100 acres

SHINGLE LANDING

8 Apr.1749 Abraham Dean, merchant sold 14 acres to Clement Dashiell of STRAWBERRY PLAIN known as SHINGLE on the south side of Broad Creek part of 25 acres from the Nanticoke Indians.
23 Aug.1753 Clement Dashiell sold to Abraham Dean.

22 Feb.1755 Abraham Dean sold 14 acres to Henry Lowe.

SHINGLE POINT

Patented on 15 March 1784 by John Lamberson for 20 acres
9 Apr.1784 John Lamberson sold 20 acres to William Morris son of Thomas Morris
25 Oct.1799 William Morris sold to Charles Hammond 20 acres
23 Dec.1810 William Morris sold to Charles Hammond,20 acres

SHOCKLEYS BEGINNING

Patented on 2 Oct.1762 by James Noble Jr. for 50 acres
6 June 1770 James Noble Jr. with wife Elizabeth Noble sold to David Adams, 50 acres.
1 Oct.1784 David Adams with wife Leah Adams sold to Benjamin Dennis 50 acres.
19 Oct.1802 Benjamin Dennis sold to James Dennis 50 acres.

SHOCKLEYS CHANCE

Patented in 1755 by John Shockley Jr. for 95 acres
1762 resurveyed to SHOCKLEYS SECURITY

SHOCKLEYS OUTFIELD

Patented in 1786 by Elijah Shockley for 48 acres
4 Sep.1786 Elijah Shockley with wife Sarah Shockley sold 48 acres to Jonathan Shockley.
28 Feb.1791 Jonathan Shockley son of John Shockley sold to Jesse Fooks 48 acres.
9 Dec.1797 Jesse Fooks sold to John Shockley of John 48 acres.
18 Sep.1798 John Shockley sold to Moses Pank 48 acres.
19 May 1808 Robert Nairn, sheriff sold to Peter Dashiell per judgement against John Shockley 50 acres.
8 Jan.1810 Peter Dashiell sold to John Nelms.

SHOCKLEYS PRIVILEDGE

Patented in 1806 by Elijah Shockley for 27 acres in Wicomico Forest
1783 tax - Elijah Shockley 27 acres, Wic.100 Worc.Co.
7 Mar.1807 Elijah E. Shockley sold to John Johnson of Benjamin Johnson

SHOCKLEYS SECOND CHOICE

Patented on 8 Dec.1757 by John Shockley Jr. for 75 acres
Second patent in 1773 by John Shockley for 323 acres.
4 Sep.1786 Jonathan Shockley sold to Elijah Shockley 190 acres
15 June 1792 Elijah Shockley sold to John Richardson 24 1/2 acres
28 Sep.1792 Elijah Shockley sold to Eli Shockley 11 acres
18 oct.1794 Elijah Shockley sold 23 acres to Eli Shockley
19 Nov.1796 Thomas Covington Shockley of Hancock Co.Georgia sold to John Shockley son of Elijah of Worc.Co. 132 acres.
12 Nov.1796 Catherine Smith sold all rights to John Shockley
28 Feb.1801 Eli Shockley with wife Elizabeth Shockley sold to Elijah

Shockley that John Shockley willed to Jonathan Shockley, part.
3 Nov.1806 Elijah Shockley sold to John Richardson 20 1/2 acres.

SHOCKLEYS SECURITY

Patented on 6 Apr.1762 by John Shockley for 338 acres a resurvey of SHOCKLEYS CHANCE.
2 Aug.1769 John Shockley with wife Elizabeth Shockley sold to Elijah Shockley 90 acres.
1771 John Shockley willed lands unnamed to son Jonathan Shockley
1783 tax - John Shockley 60 acres
1783 tax - David MaGee 130 acres
4 Sep.1786 Jonathan Shockley with wife Elizabeth sold to John Shockley 68 acres.
5 Feb.1791 Jonathan Shockley sold to John Richardson 24 acres.
10 Feb.1791 Jonathan Shockley sold to John Shockley 11 1/2 acres
28 feb.1791 Jonathan Shockley sold to Jesse Fooks, part.
9 Dec.1797 Jesse Fooks sold to John Shockley of John, part
9 Dec.1797 John Richardson sold part to John Shockley of John.
18 Sep.1798 John Shockley son of John sold part to Moses Pank
23 July 1803 Moses Pank sold to John Shockley of John, part.
8 Jan.1810 Peter Dashiell sold to John Nelms of Baltimore 552 acres of SSHOCKLEYS PROSPERITY, SHOCKLEYS OUTFIELD, SECURITY & FOLLY.

SHORES LOT

see NORTH WAILES.

SHORTS LUCK

Patented on 17 Oct.1760 by Eli Short for 50 acres.
22 Jan.1754 repatented by John Short for 55 acres
2 Nov.1768 Jonathan Short sold to John Willis, blacksmith 55 acres that John Short willed to Jonathan.
15 Oct.1776 Sussex Co.Del. land survey pat. by John Willis

SIDNEY

Patented on 5 July 1677 by William Stevens who assigned to Thomas Rowe, John Evans and Richard Crockett for 50 acres.
1688 John Evans willed to son John, one half of SIDNEY
Rent Rolls 1666-1723 possessed by Richard Crockett by right of survivorship 50 acres.
1783 tax - George Gale son of Levin Gale 16 acres, Nanticoke 100
14 Dec1808 Chaplin Conway with wife Ann Conway sold to Tubman Willin 64 3/4 acres of SIDNEY, EVANS SECOND CHANCE
14 Dec.1809 Chaplin Conway with wife Ann Conway sold to Mansfield Street for 5 shillings 90 acres of EVANS SECOND CHANCE & SIDNEY.

SILVER STREAM

Patented on 14 Mar.1763 by Nehemiah Tilghman for 108 acres
11 Dec.1771 Nehemiah Tilghman sold to Levi Noble 30 acres
1775 Nehemiah Tilghman willed to be sold.
1783 tax - John White 30 acres, Acquango 100.
1 Dec.1791 Joseph Tilghman sold rights to Charles Townsend.
25 Mar.1791 Joseph Tilghman executor of Nehemiah sold to Charles

Townsend 40 acres.
5 Mar.1791 Charles Townsend sold 40 acres to Henry Kelly.

SKINNERS FANCY

Patented in 1821 by Thomas Skinner, Mary Skinner, William Skinner and Peter Skinner for 719 1/4 acres.
1829 John Horsey willed 18 acres to wife Susan Horsey.

SKINNERS RETREAT

Patented in 1791 by Thomas Skinner for 19 3/4 acres

SLEMONS EXPERIMENT

Patented in 1807 by John B. Slemons for 100 acres
1832 John B. Slemons willed to sons Robert W. Slemons and James McCree Slemons, where I now reside.

SLIGO

see LITTLE BELEAN

SLIM CHANCE

Patented in 1794 by James Dickenson for 33 acres

SLIPE

Patented on 14 Dec.1679 by James Weatherly for 50 acres between Rewastico and the south west side of Lyons Creek.
Rent Rolls 1666-1723 possessed by James Weatherly 50 acres
13 Feb.1724 James Weatherly and wife Elizabeth Weatherly and William Weatherly with wife Charity Weatherly sons of James, sold to James Train, upper part called NOT YET MADE OVER.
1756 William Farrington willed to son George Farrington
17 Aug.1758 Robert Farmington sold to Ephraim King all his interest in WEATHERLYS PURCHASE & SLIPE
8 Feb.1760 George Farrington sold to Ephraim King upper part of SLIPE,WEATHERLYS PURCHASE, PASTURAGE 146 1/2 acres.
1777 Ephraim King willed land purchased of Robert Farrington and George Farrington in Rewastico to son Samuel King, unnamed.
1783 tax - Samuel King 25 acres- Rewastico 100
1783 tax - James Train 25 acres
1787 Samuel King willed lands from father Ephraim King to Lucretia Jones and her mother Elizabeth King.

SLIPE

Patented in 1776 by Henry Handy for 19 1/2 acres

SLIPE

Patented in 1818 by Levin Miller for 4 acres. He repatented the same in 1833.

SLOCOMBS LOTT

Patented in 1784 by George Slocomb for 289 1/4 acres

SMALL ACQUISITION

Patented in 1807 by George Robertson for 95 1/4 acres

SMALL ADDITION

Patented in 1771 by Benjamin Polk for 6 1/4 acres

SMALL ADDITION

Patented in 1764 by James Twilley for 183 acres

SMALL ADDITION

Patented in 1769 by George Dashiell for 33 acres
16 Feb.1802 George Dashiell with wife Elizabeth Dashiell and son Robert Dashiell sold to Ichabod Dashiell 151 1/2 acres of DASHIELLS FOLLY, EASOMS CHANCE, SMALL ADDITION
18 Mar.1805 Ichabod Dashiell with wife Priscilla Dashiell sold to Alexander Stewart, same as above.

SMALL ADDITION

Patented in 1782 by Arthur Denwood for 3 1/2 acres
1783 tax - Arthur Denwood 3 1/2 acres, Nanticoke 100

SMALL ADDITION

Patented in 1784 by Henry Davis for 102 1/4 acres
10 Dec.1804 Henry Davis of Kent Co. Delaware sold to Robert Davis now of Kent Co. 52 1/4 acres
20 May 1807 Robert Davis of Kent Co.Del. sold to James Round of Worc.Co. 50 acres.

SMALL ADDITION

Patented in 1801 by Jonathan Huffington for 17 1/2 acres

SMALL ADDITION

Patented in 1802 by George Miles for 8 1/4 acres

SMALL ADDITION

Patented in 1808 by Nathan Cahoon for 13 1/4 acres

SMALL CHANCE

Patented on 10 Sep.1755 by Benjamin Calloway for 6 acres
23 Feb.1760 Benjamin Calloway sold to David Greer 6 acres

SMALL CHANCE

Patented on 9 Nov.1765 by Thomas Dashiell for 5 acres at head of Tipiquin Creek.
2 Aug.1768 Thomas Dashiell sold 5 acres to Richard Crockett Fluellin
1783 tax - Elizabeth Atkinson 5 acres, Wic.100 Worc.Co.
26 Mar.1793 Gillis Polk surviving trustee of Ephraim King and Samuel Fluellin brother of Richard C. Fluellin sold to Isaac Atkinson son of Isaac.

SMALL HOPES

Patented in 1763 by Andrew Spear for 50 acres
21 Apr.1770 Andrew Spear sold 36 acres to William Martin of Worc.Co.
18 July 1773 Charles Davis sold to Ahab Coston 14 acres
11 Mar.1776 Ahab Coston sold 14 acres to William Martin
1788 William Martin willed lands unnamed to wife Mary Martin.

SMALL LOTT

Patented on 21 Oct.1676 by Samuel Jackson for 100 acres on the south side of Quantico Creek.
1687 Samuel Jackson willed to son Jonathan Jackson
Rent Rolls 1666-1723 possessed by Jonathan Jackson s/o Samuel
14 Oct.1738 Jonathan Jackson with wife Rachel Jackson sold for 5 shillings to Thomas Jackson part of ABERGAVENY & SMALL LOTT.
14 Jan.1745 Thomas Jackson with wife Sarah Jackson sold to John Leatherbury of Acco. Co.Va.
1783 tax - Charles Leatherbury 100 acres.

SMALL LOTT

Patented in 1758 by Jonathan Summers for 4 acres

SMALL LOTT

Patented in 1768 by Richard Small for 6 1/2 acres
1783 tax - Benjamin Atkinson 6 1/2 acres, Nanticoke 100

SMALL LOTT

Patented in 1765 by William Vickers for 13 1/2 acres

SMALL LOTT

Patented in 1787 by John Robertson for 10 1/2 acres

SMALL SPOT OF GROUND

Patented in 1761 by James Robertson for 10 acres
1783 tax - John Robertson 10 acres, Rewastico 100
ADDITION patented 1792 by John Robertson for 34 1/2 acres
1799 John Robertson willed to son Eli Robertson.

SMITHS ADDITION

Patented in 1857 by Levin S.H. Smith and Henry I.B. Smith for 364 3/4 acres.

SMITHS ADVENTURE

Patented in 1666 by Samuel Smith of Northumberland Co. Va. for 10000 acres. Samuel Smith sold to Peter Presley of Northumberland Co.Va. 500 acres.
6 Mar.1718 William Brereton, planter with wife Diana Brereton sold to Alexander Adams, rector, 160 acres in fork of Wic.Creek and Passerdyke Creeks.
3 Nov.1719 All goods of William Brereton, one moity of SMITHS ADVENTURE per judgement, sheriff to deliver to John Caldwell.
13 May 1721 Peter Presley of Northumberland Co.Va. sold to Thomas Gillis of Som. Co. 500 acres of SMITHS ADVENTURE & SECOND CHOICE.
26 Oct.1728 William Brereton sold to Alexander Adams 150 acres part of SMITHS ADVENTURE, BRERETSONS CHANCE & MILES END except part sold 1718 to John Waltham of 100 acres.
28 Oct.1765 Rev. Alexander Adams gave to son Andrew Adams 160 acres.
1783 tax - Andrew Adams
1783 tax - William Brereton
1799 Joseph Brereton gave to brother Scott Brereton
14 Apr.1807 Scott Brereton sold to Stephen Taylor 25 1/4 acres.
1813 William Brereton gave to son John Brereton lot from Scott Brereton now in possession of Andrew Adams.
1817 Andrew Adams willed to nephew Andrew son of John Adams.

SMITHS CHANCE

Patented on 2 Nov. 1768 by Archibald Smith for 408 1/2 acres.
1 Apr.1775 Archibald Smith with wife Mary Smith of Worc.Co. sold 22 acres to Joseph Dashiell for 5 shillings.
1 Apr.1775 Archibald Smith with wife Mary Smith sold 20 acres to John Noble, two miles from Salisbury.
1783 tax - Thomas Skinner 23 acres
1783 tax - Thomas Cox Sr. 98 acres
12 Jan.1786 Archibald Smith with wife Mary Smith sold 227 acres to George Slocomb of Dorcester Co.Md.
1793 John Smith willed to Joshua Smith son of brother Archibald Smith.
4 Apr.1804 Thomas Noble sold all interest to James Smith
19 Oct.1805 Thomas Noble with wife Nancy Noble sold to James Smith.

SMITHS CHOICE

Patented on 21 Jan.1748 by George Smith son of Andrew Smith for 50 acres
1753 Andrew Smith Sr. willed to son Andrew 50 acres.
6 Oct.1787 George Smith son of Andrew Smith sold to Nancy Nelms 50 acres.
2 Aug.1788 Nancy Nelms sold to Elisha Parker 30 acres.

SMITHS COW BELLS

Patented in 1857 by Levin S. H. Smith and Henry I.B. Smith for 96 3/4

acres
1857 ADDITION patented to same for 25 acres, Worc. Co.

SMITHS DEFENSE

Patented on 3 May 1763 by George Smith for 221 acres a resurvey of COVINGTONS CHOICE.

SMITHS DELIGHT

Patented on 29 Aug.1745 by David Smith for 100 acres
8 Mar.1757 David Smith, yoeman sold to Job Smith on the east side of the Nanticoke River, north side of Deep Creek.

SMITHS DISCOVERY

Patented on 7 May 1758 by Moses Smith for 371 acres a resurvey of DOG DOWN BOTTOM
3 Aug.1763 Moses Smith sold to David Magee 171 acres
6 Apr.1764 David Magee with wife Mary Magee sold to Richard Biglands 76 acres.
21 Aug.1765 David Magee with wife Mary Magee sold to William Caldwell 100 acres.
20 Feb. 1767 David Magee sold to Isaac Handy 142 acres of MAGEES LOTT & SMITHS DISCOVERY
6 July 1770 Isaac Handy sold same as above to Solomon Russell
9 May 1778 Price Russell sold to Josiah Russell 300 acres of MAGEES LOTT, SMITHS DISCOVERY & DAVIS CHOICE.
1783 tax - Richard Biglands 76 acres Wic.100 Worc.Co.
1783 tax - John Caldwell 100 acres
8 oct.1794 John Caldwell sold to John Biglands 85 acres.
8 Sep.1798 John Biglands sold to Isaac Henry 100 acres.
23 Oct.1801 Levin Pollitt, sheriff sold to William Biglands per judgement against John Biglands 100 acres.

SMITHS ENDING

Patented on 1 Oct.1762 by George Smith for 53 acres on a branch of the Wicomico River.
3 June 1767 George Smith son of Andrew Smith sold to William Davis 13 acres
1767 William Davis willed 13 acres to son Spencer Davis
1783 tax - James Townsend 50 acres
14 Sep.1793 Spencer Davis sold 13 acres to Elisha Parker
1809 Spencer Davis willed to sons Levin Davis, Spencer and William Davis.
1 Nov.1806 Dr. Robert Lemon with wife Nancy Lemon sold to Elisha Parker

SMITHS GOOD LUCK

Patented in 1794 by George Smith for 37 1/2 acres
28 Mar.1793 George Smith sold to George Parker 27 1/2 acres

SMITHS LAST CHOICE

Patented on 24 Feb.1763 by Moses Smith for 40 acres
1783 tax- Col. Joseph Dashiell for Moses Claywell, Wic.100, Worc.Co. 40 acres

SMITHS LOTT

Patented on 1 July 1739 by David Smith for 100 acres
5 Nov.1741 David Smith sold to Robert Dukes 100 acres of a resurvey on the north side Deep Creek.
29 Mar.1764 Robert Dukes sold to John Spicer 100 acres
29 June 1764 John Spicer sold 69 acres to Jonathan Vaughan and Company of Pennnsylvania
1769 I William Spicer quitclaim to Jonathan Vaughan and Company of Deep Creek Furnace all claim.

SMITHS LUCK

Patented in 1797 by Archibald Smith for 43 1/2 acres

SMITHS MEADOW

Patented on 10 Oct.1809 by Archibald Smith for 56 1/2 acres
18 Mar.1809 William Hearn by power of attorney of Archibald Smith sold for 5 shillings to George Parker 56 1/4 acres

SMITHS NECK

Patented in 1742 by Francis Newbold for 75 acres

SMITHS PROJECT

Patented in 1767 by George Smith for 2 acres

SMITHS SMALL CHANCE

Patented in 1786 by Levin Smith for 30 acres
2 Aug.1788 Levin Smith sold to Nancy Nelms 30 acres
1 Nov.1806 Dr. Robert Lemon with wife Nancy Lemon sold to Samuel Hearn 173 1/3 acres of LEMONS FANCY, SMITHS SMALL CHANCE.

SMITHS TRIAL

Patented in 1795 by Moses Smith for 39 acres

SMITHS VENTURE

Patented in 1753 by Obediah Smith for 100 acres

SMOCKS PURCHASE

Patented in 1786 by Parker Selby for 138 acres
1791 Parker Selby willed 138 acres to Henry Parker.
9 Apr.1798 Henry Parker sold to John Dennis of Johnson Dennis 83 1/2 acres.

SNOW HILL

Patented in 1763 by Richard Waller for 75 acres
20 Mar.1800 Richard Waller sold to Eli Vinson 92 1/2 acres of SNOW
HILL, VICTORY OF WISDOM, ADDN. TO WILLIAMS GREEN
17 Mar.1800 Richard Waller sold to Esme Marshall Waller for 5
shillings 41 1/4 acres of SNOW HILL, VICTORY OF WISDOM, and ADDITION
TO WILLIAMS GREEN.
13 Oct.1804 Eli Vinson Jr. with wife Comfort Vinson sold to Henry
White of Worc.Co.

SOLOMONS DELIGHT

Patented in 1734 by Solomon Wright for 100 acres
1783 tax - Elizabeth Wright 100 acres, Rewastico 100
11 June 1808 William Wright son of Levin Wright sold to Huffington
Nicholson of Sussex Co.Delaware, from grandfather Solomon Wright.

SOLOMONS SECURITY

Patented in 1743 by Solomon Hitch for 21 acres

SONS CHOICE

Patented on 7 Dec.1678 by John Manlove for 50 acres
Rent Rolls 1666-1723 possessed by the heir of Thomas Acworth.
(Thomas Acworth son of Richard Acworth and Ann Manlove Acworth)
23 Nov.1779 Richard Acworth sold 50 acres to William Winder
1783 tax - William Winder, 50 acres, Rewastico 100
8 Apr.1806 Elijah Reed of Worc.Co. heir of Zachariah Reed and Obediah
Reed sold to William Winder
29 Mar.1806 Henry Davis and wife Martha Davis and Adam Brattan with
wife Elizabeth Bratten sold to Elijah Reed brother of Martha and
Elizabeth.

SOON IN THE MORNING

Patented on 3 Mar.1798 by Arthur Dashiell for 448 3/16th acres a
resurvey of several tracts.
3 Sep.1799 George Handy, sherriff, sold to John Huffington MAIDENS
LOTT & SOON IN THE MORNING, per judgement against James Acworth.
1802 Arthur Dashiell willed to son Levin Dashiell.
12 Sep.1800 John Huffington sold to William Birkhead
3 Mar.1806 William Birkhead sold his interest to John Moore of Sussex
Co.Delaware.
30 June 1830 George Dashiell son of Levin Dashiell sold his part to
Martha Holt.

SOUND SIDE

Patented in 1773 by Henry Lowe for 12 acres

SOUTH WALES

Patented on 16 May 1689 by John Huett for 200 acres
Rent Rolls 1666-1723 disclaimed by heirs apparent and Capt. Nicholas
Evans who married Huetts widow.
31 May 1731 Alexander Leckie and wife Ann Leckie and Joseph Johnson

with wife Susannah Johnson sold 200 acres to Huett Nutter.
3 June 1768 Huett Nutter sold 200 acres to Nehemiah Hearn
6 Oct.1772 Nehemiah Hearn sold to Joseph Foreman
2 May 1776 Sussex Co.Delaware. warrants surv. for Joseph Foreman.

SPENCES CHOICE

Patented on 17 Mar.1673 by David Spence for 250 acres
1678 David Spence willed to sons David and Alexander Spence.
Rent Rolls 1666-1723 apportains to James Spence at North Carolina
2 Mar.1752 Sylvester Welch and William Pickman surviving heirs of David Spence of Northumberland Co.Va. sold 125 acres to Purnell Johnson of Somerset County.
6 Apr.1752 James Spence of Pasquetank North Carolina sold 125 acres to Isaac Handy, that David Spence and Alexander Spence died in North Carolina and willed part to James Spence.
4 Jan.1755 Isaac Handy and Purnell Johnson partitioned.
1778 Purnell Johnson willed to son Elijah Johnson 170 acres and balance to son William Johnson.
1785 William Johnson willed to brother Thomas Johnson if he returns, if not to brother Purnell Johnson.
1783 tax - Elijah Johnson 76 acres, Rewastico 100
1783 tax - James Bennett 125 acres
9 Feb.1793 Purnell Johnson of Worc.Co and William Hearn of Som. Co. gave to Elijah Johnson and William Purnell Johnson son of Elijah Johnson, that Thomas Johnson deceased had. He died intestate. Purnell Johnson representative of Sarah Hearn late Sarah Johnson sister of Purnell and Elijah Johnson became equally entitled.
1817 Purnell Johnson willed to Purnell Johnson land conveyed by William Purnell Johnson to his mother Annie Dashiell (widow of Purnell Johnson and Thomas Dashiell)

SPORTING FIELD

Patented in 1821 by William N. Lankford for 4 1/2 acres

SPORTING HALL

Patented in 1773 by Henry Lowe for 55 1/2 acres

SPRING HILL

Patented on 3 Mar.1680 by William Stevens for 1000 acres who assigned to Francis Jenkins.
Rent Rolls 1666-1723 possessed by Honorable Francis Jenkins.
1708 Francis Jenkins willed to wife Mary Jenkins 800 acres
(she married 2nd. John Henry and 3rd John Hampton.)
28 Nov.1738 Mary Hampton gave to the vestry of Stepney Parish 2 acres for a few therein.
1744 Mary Hampton willed to son John Henry
1781 John Henry willed to son Rider Henry
1783 tax - John Henry 1000 acres Rewastico 100
4 June 1787 John Henry of Dorcester Co. sold to Charlotte Winder sister of John Henry for her lifetime.
8 Aug.1809 Rider H. Winder sold to John W. Henry of Dorc.Co. that John

Henry willed to him, one moity.
18 Aug.1809 John Henry of Dorc.Co. sold to Hugh Henry of same 40 5/8 acres.

SPRY

Patented in 1794 by Elihu Mezick and Covington Mezick for 587 acres
19 Dec.1799 Elihu Mezick sold 12 acres to Samuel Larramore
19 Dec.1799 Elihu Mezick sold part to Covington Mezick
19 Dec.1799 Covington Mezick sold pt. to Elijah Mezick
25 July 1810 Levin D. Collier, Stephen Wright and Methia Wright sold to Ephraim K. Harris 3 1/2 acres with WESTON & CHANCE.
1828 Covington Mezick willed to son Levin W. Mezick SPRY being part of STRIFE, to corner of land sold to Samuel Jarman by Elihu Mezick out of SPRY and to wife Sarah Mezick 50 acres and son Joshua Mezick 50 acres.

STAINS

Patented on 10 Apr.1680 by Col. William Stevens for 850 acres
Rent Rolls 1666-1723 possessed by Samuel Layfield heir to George Layfield who bought the right.
19 Aug.1730 Thomas Layfield and wife Catherine Layfield sold 425 acres to William Hearn.
1741 William Hearn willed to son Elijah Hearn 175 acres and to son Isaac Hearn 150 acres.
21 Sep.1745 Thomas Hearn sold 125 acres to Nehemiah Hearn, sadler for 10 shillings
11 Dec.1745 Thomas Hearn sold 150 acres to George Henry for 10 shillings.
1760 Nehemiah Hearn willed to son Elisha Hearn 125 acres.
13 Dec.1753 I Thomas Hearn sell to William Hearn Jr. 150 acres
1762 Thomas Hearn willed to James Hearn son of William Hearn 150 acres out of tract near Coxes Branch.
19 May 1766 George Hearn of Worc.Co. sold 150 acres to Joseph Scroggin
19 May 1766 Elisha Hearn son of Nehemiah Hearn sold to Elijah Hearn 116 acres of STAINS & FAIRFIELDS.
1772 John Scroggin willed 150 acres to son Joseph Scroggin
4 Apr.1774 Elijah Hearn Jr. sold to Elijah Hearn Sr. his interest
12 Mar.1774 James Hearn sold 118 acres to Elijah Hearn for 10 shillings.
1783 tax - John Scroggin 130 1/2 acres- Rewastico
1783 tax - Elijah Hearn 523 1/2 acres
1783 tax - Elijah Hearn 37 acres ADDN. TO STAINS, resurv. from FAIRFIELDS.
1789 Elijah Hearn willed to son William Hearn 175 acres and 150 acres and 80 1/4 acres and 37 acres of ADDITION TO STAINS, and to daughter Joanna Townsend 118 acres.
1793 Joseph Scroggin willed 150 acres to brother Phillip Scroggin
3 Dec.1794 Phillip Scroggin with wife Polly Scroggin sold to John Dashiell.
1818 John Dashiell son of Jesse Dashiell willed to son George Dashiell 140 acres.

STAND OFF

Patented in 1789 by Constant Disharoon for 50 acres
1795 Constant Disharoon willed lands to daughter Milla Stanford,

4 Aug.1810 Milla Stanford sold 50 acres to Eben Disharoon
1815 Eban Disharoon willed to son Matthias Hopkins Disharoon
1850 Matthias Hopkins Disharoon is in the Salisbury District.

STANFORDS FINDING

Patented in 1746 by Joseph Stanford for 50 acres
25 Jan.1754 Joseph Stanford sold 50 acres to William Stanford at head of Wicomico Creek.
12 Apr.1771 Thomas Stanford with wife Rachel Stanford and William Stanford sold 50 acres to Levin Gunby of Worc.Co.
6 Apr.1772 Joseph Stanford gave to Jonathan Stanford 11 1/2 acres
6 Apr.1772 Joseph Stanford and Thomas Stanford sold 38 1/2 acres to Levin Gunby.
1783 tax - Levin Gunby 38 1/2 acres
1783 tax - Jonathan Stanford 11 1/2 acres
7 Mar.1786 Jonathan Stanford sold 11 1/2 acres to David Brown
18 Feb.1792 Jonathan Stanford of Columbia Co. Georgia by his attorney Robert Stanford of the same place sold to Joshua Stanford of Maryland 8 1/2 acres.
6 Mar.1797 David Brown sold 11 1/2 acres to Joshua Stanford.
3 Nov.1802 Joshua Stanford sold to John Cathell 131 1/4 acres of LITTLE NECK, ADDN. TO LITTLE NECK, STANFORDS FINDING & GREEN BRIAR
6 Nov.1802 Joshua Stanford sold to William Pollitt of Worc.Co., part.
28 Oct.1806 Tubman Lowe, attorney to sell the real estate of Levin Gunby deceased sold to Kirk Gunby 50 acres.

STATONS ADVENTURE

Patented in 1805 by Mary Stayton and Horatio Stayton for 303 1/2 acres
1800/2 Horatio Stayton willed to wife Mary Stayton and to all my children.
1828 Sally McCready Stayton willed to Sally Ann Stayton Vance and Mary Storks Vance 1/2 of tract left by father Horatio Stayton. if they die to heirs of Rosannah Vance wife of David Vance, land unnamed.

STATONS CHANCE

Patented on 10 Dec.1740 by James Stayton
1742 James Stayton of Dorc.Co. Md. willed to son Thomas Stayton 90 acres of CHANCE.
3 Oct.1758 Thomas Stayton with wife Keziah Stayton sold to John Laws Jr. 90 acres.

STANNAWAY

Patented on 16 Nov.1675 by Joseph Aylward for 300 acres
Rent Rolls 1666-1723 possessed by widow of John Aylward
2 Dec.1726 John W. Barkley and wife Ann Barkley sold to John Rider of Dorc.Co. 160 acres, with ST. ALBANS.
10 Nov.1729 Willoby James with wife Mary James sold 100 acres to John Phipps that John Barkley sold to David Evans late.
27 Sep.1733 Hon. Col. John Rider of Dorc.Co. with wife Ann Rider sold 160 acres to Alexander Adams.
21 Apr.1753 Alexander Adams sold to John Barkley Jr. and wife Ann Barkley 150 acres at Nanticoke Point.

4 Feb.1767 John Barkley sold to Rachel Barkley widow of Abraham
Barkley and her son Joseph Barkley 62 3/4 acres.
1783 tax - Henry Barkley 40 acres. Nanticoke 100
8 June 1788 James Dashiell of Stepney Parish sold to Henry Wallace
Barkley ST ALBANS, STANAWAY, FAIR MEADOW.
8 June 1788 Henry Wallace Barkley sold to James Dashiell same as above
1795 Rachel Barkley willed land from John Barkley to grandson Absalom
Barkley son of Joseph Barkley
6 May 1805 Jonathan Barkley of Som.Co. and James Barkley of Dorc.Co.
sold for 5 shillings to Gowan White and Bridget White.
20 Apr.1810 Jonathan Barkley sold 69 acres to Abraham Barkley Jr.
1854 Isaac Barkley willed to son Isaac Barkley land bought of Esme
Barkley.

STAVE YARD

Patented in 1811 by Mezick Winright, Nancy Winright, Isaac Dickerson,
Jenny Winright and Sally Winright for 173 acres

STAYTONS FOLLY

Patented by James Stayton on a branch of the Nanticoke River 60 acres
aka HAZZARD
ADDITION TO STAYTONS FOLLY patented James Stayton 23 acres.
1742 James Stayton of Dorc.Co. willed to son Joseph Stayton
7 June 1768 Joseph Stayton sold to Nehemiah Stayton 24 acres
7 Sep.1770 Nehemiah Stayton sold to David Owens 10 acres, 8 perches
called OWENS PURCHASE.
4 Feb.1775 Nehemiah Stayton with wife Sarah Stayton sold to William
Laws 50 acres.
7 Sep.1770 David Owens sold to Nehemiah Stayton 10 acres 86 perches.

STAYTONS NECESSITY

Patented in 1811 by Horatio Stayton for 2 1/4 acres.

STEPNEY

Patented in 1739 by John Huett Nutter for 100 acres
12 May 1740 John Huett Nutter and wife Ann Nutter sold 100 acres to
Thomas Waller.
10 Nov.1755 Thomas Waller sold 60 acres to son Richard Waller
26 Apr.1762 Thomas Waller Sr. willed to wife Mary Waller and to all
his children.
10 Jan.1763 Thomas Waller Sr. sold to son John Waller 40 acres.
12 Nov.1768 John Waller sold to Robert Pitts 52 acres of STEPNEY &
PARISH
26 Mar.1771 Ebenezer Waller sold to John Magee 52 acres of STEPNEY &
PARISH that John Waller sold to Robert Pitts.
18 Apr.1776 Sussex Co.Del. land warrent, Richard Waller Sr.
2 Apr.1803 Benjamin Wailes sold to William Horsey ADDITION TO STEPNEY
in Sussex Co.Delaware with Wicomico Co.lands.

STEPHENS CONCLUSION

Patented in 1787 by Stephen Disharoon for 106 1/2 acres.

STEPHENS FOLLY

Patented in 1770 by Stephen Adams for 13 1/2 acres

STEVENS CONQUEST

Patented on 6 June 1665 by Richard Stevens for 300 acres
Rent Rolls 1666-1723 possessed by Richard Stevens
1713 Richard Stevens willed to son Isaac Stevens at age 18 100 acres and to grandson Jonathan Bounds the balance.
1728 Isaac Stevens died intestate leaving wife Ann Stevens and daughter Rebecca Stevens.
1783 tax - Thomas Collins 244 acres, Wic.100 Worc.Co.
13 July 1792 Thomas Collins Sr. with wife Rebecca Collins sold to Thomas Collins Jr.
13 July 1792 Thomas Collins Jr. sold to William Collins son of William 41 1/2 acres.
29 June 1798 Thomas Collins sold 5 acres to George Kibble.
27 Feb.1738 William Collins sold 300 acres to Samuel T. Bounds that descended him from father William Collins.
26 Feb.1840 Samuel T. Bounds and wife Anne Bounds sold 300 acres to Robert Jones of George Jones of Robert Jones.
1841 Levin Morris willed to daughter Eliza Ann Morris, purchased of Robert Jones of George Jones and his brother Charles Jones.

STEPHENS SECURITY

Patented in 1761 by Stephen Phillips for 150 acres
4 June 1766 Stephen Phillips sold to Benjamin Hearn 66 acres.
3 Mar.1766 Stephen Phillips sold to Daniel Melson 83 acres
17 Apr.1770 Benjamin Hearn sold to Hezekiah Maddux 66 acres.
1783 tax - Daniel Melson Sr. 70 acres
1785 Daniel Melson willed 50 acres to son Daniel
1822 Elijah Melson willed 64 acres to son Elijah Melson

STEVENS LOTT

Patented in 1737 by Richard Stevens for 73 acres
19 Oct.1756 Stephen Stevens son of Richard sold to Joseph Morris 73 acres.
ADDITION TO STEVENS LOTT pat. Joseph Morris for 162 acres.
11 May 1762 Joseph Morris with wife Elizabeth Morris sold 162 acres to John Caldwell.
1775 John Caldwell willed to wife Mary Caldwell land purchased of Joseph Morris, during lifetime.
27 Mar.1777 Spencer Caldwell of Dobbs Co. North Carolina sold 162 acres to Jones Bounds of Somerset Co.Md.
1783 tax - Jones Bounds 167 acres, Wicomico 100
1791 SECOND ADDITION TO STEVENS LOTT patented by Jones Bounds for 205 1/4 acres.
13 Feb.1835 Samuel T. Bounds with wife Ann Bounds sold 43 acres to William Whayland.

STEVENS CHOICE

Patented in 1728 by Steven O'Dear Jr. for 50 acres

STEVENS CONCLUSION

Patented in 1815 by Levi Stevens for 309 acres
1832 Levi Stevens willed to son Davis Stevens.

STEVENS INHERITANCE

see SHADWELL

STEVENS FOLLY

Patented on 11 Apr.1760 by Joseph Dashiell a resurvey of CONTENTION 63 1/2 acres.
26 Sep.1774 Joseph Dashiell with wife Susannah Dashiell sold to George Dashiell 63 1/2 acres
6 Nov.1775 George Dashiell with wife Rosy Dashiell sold to Thomas Collins (mortgage)
1783 tax - Thomas Collins 22 acres
1783 tax - George Dashiell 20 acres
18 Dec.1789 George Dashiell sold to William McBryde 30 acres, mortgage for bond.
28 May 1791 George Dashiell son of George, with wife Rosey Dashiell sold to John Stewart 38 1/4 acres.
28 May 1791 William McBryde released mtg. to George Dashiell.

STEVENS LOTT

Patented in 1775 by Stephen Stevens for 14 3/4 acres
1816 Joshua Donoho willed to son Fillmurroh Donoho left by my father and to son Joshua Donoho STEPHENS LOTT.

STEVENTON

Patented on 16 June 1694 by Stephen Tully for 85 acres
Rent Rolls 1666-1723 possessed by Stephen Tully
3 Feb.1742 William Austin with wife Elizabeth Austin sold 85 acres to Charles Harris, on main branch of Quantico Creek.
2 July 1768 Nehemiah Harris sold 85 acres to Benjamin Gillis
14 Mar.1772 Benjamin Gillis with wife Esther Gillis sold to John Nelson now called on resurvey HARD FORTUNE
1769 resurveyed to HARD FORTUNE

STEWARTS MISTAKE

Patented in 1800 by George Twilley for 103 1/2 acres

STITCH HILL

Patented in 1807 by Thomas Jones for 76 acres
1803 Thomas Jones willed to sons John Jones and Tubman Jones, at Wicomico.

STILLEYS ISLAND
see DEANS CHANCE

STILLEYS PRIVILEDGE

Surveyed by John Stilley- no patent found
30 July 1769 John Stilley sold 50 acres to John Cordrey, near Broad Creek with CALLOWAYS DELIGHT
18 Apr.1776 Sussex Co.Delaware land warrants, by John Cordrey.

STONES

Patented on 26 June 1722 by Charles Tindell for 50 acres on the north side of a branch of Deep Creek
1761 Charles Tindell willed 50 acres to son Elijah Tindell
29 June 1764 Elijah Tindell sold to Jonathan Vaughan, William Douglas, David McMurke, Persisor Frazier, Christopher Marshall and John Chambers of Pennsylvania 50 acres
This is part of Nanticoke Furnace land purchased by Jonathan Vaughan and company.

STONEY BRANCH

Two patents for this land, in 1727 by Jonathan Vaughan for 137 acres and in 1728 by John Caldwell 137 acres.

STOP THE GAP

Patented in 1770 by Isaac Serman for 12 1/2 acres

STOPAGE

Patented in 1762 by Richard Acworth for 5 acres
5 Dec.1772 Richard Acworth sold to John Sterling son of Aaron Sterling
1783 tax - Aaron Sterling 5 acres, Rewastico 100

STRAWBERRY PLAIN
see SHINGLE LANDING

STRAIGHTS

Patented on 19 Sep.1759 by George Parker, millright 20 acres.
21 Dec.1793 John Parker of Green Co. Georgia sold to Solomon Mitchell of Worc.Co. 30 acres in Wicomico Forest. He appointed Levi King of Sussex Co.Delaware to convey.
6 Oct.1795 Solomon Mitchell sold to Walker Evans 20 acres

STRIFE

Patented on 9 Aug.1718 by Abraham Ingram for 200 acres
Rent Rolls 1666-1723 possessed by Abraham Ingram
8 Nov.1743 Abraham Ingram with wife Elinor Ingram sold to Adam Muir 200 acres
19 Nov.1764 James Muir of Dorc.Co. Del. sold to Job Smith of Sussex Co.Del. at Gravelly Branch.

STRIFE

Patented in 1775 by Samuel Ingersol for 4 1/2 acres

1782 Henry Toadvine willed to son Purnell Toadvine, bought of Jesse Fooks 4 1/2 acres
21 Nov.1783 Samuel Ingersol sold to William Toadvine 4 1/2 acres.
1783 tax - Mary Toadvine 4 1/2 acres, Wic.100 Worc.Co.

STRIFE

Patented in 1783 by John Bradford for 433 acres.
13 Oct 1779 John Bradford with wife Sarah Bradford sold to William Hammond 100 acres.
6 Oct.1791 John Bradford wold to William Morris 50 acres.
6 Oct.1791 William Hammond with wife Nelly Hammond sold 50 acres to William Morris
6 Oct.1791 William Hammond sold to Samuel Magee 50 acres.
24 May 1794 John Bradford sold to Cornelius Morris 40 acres.
13 May 1796 William Morris of Thomas Morris sold to David Bridell 15 acres.
22 June 1798 John Bradford sold to William Baynum 240 acres.
29 Oct.1798 William Morris son of Thomas Morris, with wife Aikada Morris sold to John Lamberson 50 acres.
13 Oct.1799 William Baynum sold to Cornelius Morris 24 acres
8 Sep.1800 William Baynum sold 50 acres to Henry Magee.

STRIP NOT ENDED YET

Patented in 1772 by Jacob Mezick for 9 acres

SUCESS

Patented on 10 Nov.1730 by William Waller for 100 acres
20 Aug.1755 William Mitchell son of Isaac Mitchell heir at law to William Waller will sold to William Conway, at head of Deep Creek.
13 Aug.1767 William Conway with wife Eve Conway sold to Jonathan Vaughan and Company
Site of Nanticoke and Deep Creek Furnaces.

SUFFOLK

Patented on 10 Oct.1677 by Thomas Walker for 200 acres
Rent Rolls 1666-1723 possessed by Thomas Walker who sold to Alexander Adams
31 Jan.1751 Alexander Adams, rector of Stepney Parish gave to son William Adams 200 acres.
5 June 1763 William Adams with wife Leah Adams sold 200 acres to George Handy, aka BRIMLOW.

SUIT YOURSELF

Patented in 1792 by Eli Vinson for 47 acres
20 July 1794 Eli Vinson sold 27 1/4 acres to James Selby of Ezekiel Selby
12 July 1800 Eli Vinson sold 18 acres to William Hearn

SUMMERFIELD

Patented by Thomas Pemberton who assigned to John Roach for 500 acres

Rent Rolls 1666-1723 possessed by John Roach Jr.
1726 John Roach willed to son Stephen Roach 200 acres and to wife 300 acres, after her death to son William Roach.
1765 William Roach willed to son Stephen Roach part and to son James Roach part.
11 May 1765 memorandum, John Roach willed to son William Roach and son Stephen Roach, they agree to divide.
1766 Stephen Roach willed to son Charles Roach
12 Nov.1779 Charles Roach sold 90 acres to Stephen Roach for 20 shillings.
19 Nov.1779 Charles Roach sold to Stephen Roach 110 acres.
1783 tax - James Roach 150 acres, Wic.100
1783 tax - Stephen Toadvine 100 acres
13 May 1795 Stephen Roach sold to John Ingersol 110 acres
26 Aug.1803 John Ingersol sold to Outten Toadvine 110 acres.
1804 William Toadvine willed land purchased of Polly Roach to be sold.
1808 John Cathell willed to son George Cathell, per bonds from Betty Roach, Nelly Roach for lands that fell them by death of their father James Roach.
1819 Joshua Morris willed to wife Amelia Morris and to son Jeptha Morris bought of Stephen Roach.
27 Oct.1821 Levi Cathell trustee to sell land of John Cathell Jr. sold to James Toadvine.
1822 James Toadvine willed to son Purnell Toadvine, bought of Jeptha Morris, and to daughter Catherine Toadvine land bought of the estate of John Cathell, and to daughters Harriett Toadvine and Mary Ann Toadvine, land.

SUNKEN GROUND

Patented in 1759 by David Hopkins for 21 acres
1783 tax - Stephen Hopkins 21 acres
13 May 1829 James M. Cathell with wife Elizabeth Cathell sold to William Taylor

SUNKEN GROUND

Patented on 10 Apr.1677 by James Jones for 500 acres
1677 James Jones with wife Sarah Jones devised to cousin Andrew Jones
1684 Andrew Jones died with no issue.
Rent Rolls 1666-1723 possessed by Capt. Evans who bought from Howell Jones heir to James Jones. The remainder by Mary Day who claims 350 acres purchased of Howell Jones.
1723 Nicholas Evans gave to daughter Rachel Collier
19 Apr.1736 John Huett Nutter eldest son of Ann Leckie dec'd who was Ann Huett daughter of Rev. John Huett sold pt. to Levin Gale.
9 Apr. 1742 Daniel Cordrey with wife Rachel Cordrey sold to Levin Gale all interest in tract AKAM 200 acres, part of JONES HOLE & SUNKEN GROUND.
1742 Levin Gale sold to Day Scott, formerly sold to Edward Day of Accoc.Co.Va. part of AKAM being part of SUNKEN GROUND.
1752 part resurv. to AKAM by Levin Gale.
1753 Day Scott willed to son George Day Scott GREEN HILL being part of SUNKEN GROUND.
13 Dec.1755 Day Scott sold to Thomas Williams 450 acres of LAST CHOICE & SUNKEN GROUND 392 acres.
17 Oct.1761 Thomas Williams sold 392 acres to George Day Scott s/o Day

Scott, probably a release of mortgage.
12 Oct.1775 James Taylor of Caroline Co. Va. sold to George Day Scott his rights, no acreage mentioned.
1783 tax - George Day Scott 268 acres, Nanticoke 100
1783 tax - John Holbrook 250 acres.
2 Dec.1788 Moses Pank with wife Elizabeth Pank sold to Benjamin Johnson SUNKEN GROUND, MIGHT HAVE HAD MORE & TAYLOR HILL in Som.Co.
2 May 1791 Thomas Williams of David Williams sold to William Davis with LAST CHOICE, devised by Thomas Williams his grandfather.
28 May 1792 William Davis sold to Thomas Williams of David Williams.
27 Nov.1792 Benjamin Johnson of Worc. Co. sold to Moses Pank, all.
1796 George Day Scott willed lands to Dr. Ware Cheney, unnamed.
7 Jan. 1800 Thomas Williams, John Gale, Amelia Gale sold to James Nelson 540 1/2 acres of SUNKEN GROUND & LAST CHOICE.
1801 James Nelson willed to son Ephraim Nelson 200 acres and to son James T. Nelson 200 acres unnamed land.
7 Apr.1802 Ware Cheney sold to Francis Ware Hayes all interest.
7 Apr.1802 Francis Ware Hayes sold to Ware Cheney, all interest.

THE SUPPLY

Patented on 25 June 1679 by William Elgate for 25 acres
Rent Rolls 1666-1723 possessed by Joseph Venables who purchased
15 Sep. 1743 Benjamin Venables, Elgate Hitch, Thomas Byrd, Ann Hall, Rebecca Evans, Moses Driskell sold 25 acres to Jonathan Stott.
10 Feb.1762 Jonathan Stott sold 25 acres to Christopher Piper.
13 Jan.1767 Christopher Piper sold to Esme Bayley of Worc.Co. 25 acres.

THE SUPPLY

Patented 7 July 1683 by Isaac Foxcroft for 750 acres
Rent Rolls 1666-1723 possessed by Rebecca Waters widow of Sampson Waters in New England but left to management of James Dashiell (he married Mary Waters d/o Sampson and Rebecca Foxcroft Waters.
2 Mar.1717 Obediah Wakefield and John Wakefield both of Boston Mass. sold to Peter Bowden s/o John Bowden late of Northampton Co.Va. 1/2.
23 Aug.1729 Peter Bowden and wife Susanna Bowden of Northampton Co.Va. sold to Capell King 1 moity at Nanticoke River and Quantico Creek.
1783 tax - Thomas Layfield 91 acres Wicomico 100
1783 tax - John Layfield 80 acres

THE SUPPLY

Patented in 1812 by Spencer Walker for 27 acres

SUPPORT

Patented in 1738 by Jacob Morris for 50 acres
22 Nov.1758 Jacob Morris of Sussex Co.Del. sold 50 acres to Alexander Chain of Somerset County.
1783 tax - Alexander Chain 50 acres
24 Oct.1795 Isaiah Chain with wife Sarah Chain sold 50 acres to George Marshall.
1812 Robert Morris willed to son John Morris, purchased of George

Marshall.

SUPPORT

Patented in 1747 by Thomas Gillis for 138 acres
15 Feb.1760 Thomas Gillis sold to Levin Gillis 138 acres
24 Oct.1793 Ezekiel Gillis sold 42 acres to George Handy.

SUPPORT

Patented in 1760 by Elijah Hearn for 100 acres
1783 tax - Elijah Hearn 20 acres, Rewastico 100
1789 Elijah Hearn willed 20 acres to son William Hearn, bought of Thomas Hearn, being part of SAND HILL.

SUPPORT

Patented in 1771 by Samuel Ingersol for 213 acres. Purchased of the comissioners to sell confiscated British property in Wicomico Manor, at the head of the Wicomico River.
20 June 1794 William James sold to Stephen Toadvine rights that Samuel Ingersol sold him before his death
13 May 1795 John Ingersol son of Samuel who died intestate, sold to Stephen Toadvine 213 acres.
29 Mar.1796 Whittington White and wife Tabitha White a child of Samuel Ingersol sold rights to Stephen Toadvine.

SUPPORT

Patented in 1774 by George Smith for 5 acres

SUPPORT

Patented in 1775 by George Howard for 13 acres

SUPPORT

Patented in 1777 by William Winder for 143 acres

SUPPORT

Patented in 1809 by Aaron Sterling for 6 1/2 acres

SURVEYORS MISTAKE

Patented in 1752 by George Handy for 30 acres
10 Sep.1759 George Handy sold 15 acres to Isaac Handy
1760 Isaac Handy willed to son Henry Handy, deeded me by son George Handy
5 Jan.1782 settlement of dispute of title, by George Handy and Henry Handy.
1783 tax - Henry Handy 15 acres, Rewastico 100

SUSANNAHS INHERITANCE

No patent found

1 May 1731 Joseph Johnson of Charles Co.Md. and wife Susannah Johnson sold to Huett Nutter bequeathed Susannah by father Col. Nicholas Evans deceased. Adjacent land of Alexander Leckie and Ann Leckie his wife whereon John Huett Nutter father of Ann and Susannah lately lived, now called SUSANNAHS INHERITANCE.

SWAINS CHOICE

Patented on 17 Oct.1760 by William Swain for 50 acres
29 June 1764 William Swain and wife Mariah Swain sold to Jonathan Vaughan and Company of Pennsylvania, prop. of iron Furnace at DEEP CREEK or NANTICOKE

SWANNS LUCK

Patented in 1734 by Catherine Carr for 50 acres a resurvey of part of PLUMPTON SALTASH.
9 Nov.1730 John Carr and wife Catherine Carr sold to Daniel Lingo 50 acres
18 Aug.1733 Daniel Lingo with wife Margaret Lingo sold to John Carr 50 acres
17 Apr.1734 Daniel Lingo with wife Margaret sold to Catherine Carr 50 acres.
8 June 1788 Robert Parsons with wife Sarah Parsons of Sussex Co.Del. sold 50 acres to John Nelms, Noah Nelms and Peter Nelms of Som.Co.

SWEET HOPE

Patented in 1795 by Betty Handy for 84 1/2 acres

SWEETWOOD HALL

Patented on 23 Oct.1696 by John McClester for 400 acres near Nanticoke point
Rent Rolls 1666-1723 possessed by John McClester
4 Nov.1719 John McClester sold 80 acres to Daniel McClester.
1720 Daniel McClester willed to brother John McClester 86 acres of MC CLESTERS INHERITANCE, part of SWEETWOOD HALL.
5 June 1721 Daniel McClester sold 80 acres to John McClester Sr.
1743 Daniel McClester willed to eldest brother John 86 acres and to brother Neal McClester balance of estate.
1783 tax - John McClester 400 acres, Nanticoke 100

SWORD

Patented in 1817 by John Nicholson for 2 3/8 acres

SWORD

Patented in 1805 by William Lankford for 8 1/4 acres

TABLE LANDS

Patented in 1826 by William Laws for 100 acres

TARGET HILL

Patented on 19 Aug.1762 by John Parsons for 50 acres
1783 tax - Johnson Parsons 50 acres, TARGET HILL RIDGE
1795 John Parsons willed to son John Parsons
1822 John Parsons of John, willed to son John Parker Parsons.

TARRKILL

9 Oct.1766 Cornelius English sold 45 1/2 acres to Isaac Collins
1776 Sussex Co.Del. land Warrents, Little Creek 100 Isaac Collins.

TARRKILL RIDGE

Patented in 1782 by Jarman Bethards for 50 acres
1782 Jarman Bethards willed 50 acres to son Samuel Bethards, unnamed land.
5 Mar.1783 William Jarman Bethards sold to Samuel Bethards 50 acres.

TARKILL HUMMOCK

Patented on 5 Oct.1683 by Richard Wilson for 30 acres in Nanticoke 100.
Rent Rolls 1666-1723 possessed by David Howard in right of the orphans of John Wilson.
12 Oct.1721 Thomas Wilson and wife Mary Wilson of Kent Co.Md. sold 30 acres to William Wallace of Somerset County.

TAT AGAIN

Patented in 1795 by Benjamin Wailes for 139 acres

TATUMS HABITATION

Patented in 1730 by John Tatum for 40 acres
9 June 1788 Robert Parsons with wife Sarah Parsons of Sussex Co.Del. sold to John Nelms, Noah Nelms and Peter Nelms of Som.Co. 40 acres.

TAYLORS ADDITION

Patented on 26 Feb.1755 by William Taylor for 50 acres, a resurvey of part of COMMONS.
9 Apr.1759 William Taylor sold 50 acres to John Badley
31 July 1765 John Badley sold to Dean Badley 50 acres.
1783 tax - James Taylor 117 1/2 acres. Rewastico 100
1783 tax - Abraham Taylor 117 acres a resurvey of ROUND POND
1783 tax - Heirs of Isaac Taylor 142 acres.
2 Sep.1785 Ezekiel Taylor sold to Sarah Marshall Skinner daughter of Benjamin Atkinson 50 acres between Rewastico and Quantico Rivers. Appeared Elizabeth Taylor widow of William Taylor and released her dower rights.
(note there must be more patents by this name)
1792 Abraham Taylor willed to sons Abraham and Loudy Taylor
1796 John Grumble willed to son John Grumble (wife Temperance Grumble)
3 June 1803 Abraham Taylor with wife Molly Taylor sold 100 acres to

Horatio Taylor with TOWER HILL & KINNEYENGTON.
3 June 1803 Abraham Taylor with wife Molly Taylor sold to Ebenezer Taylor
30 Nov.1805 Benjamin Taylor with wife Nancy Taylor sold 25 acres to Horatio Taylor
16 Oct.1807 Horatio Taylor with wife Betsy Taylor sold to Thomas Darby 46 5/8 acres.
1 Nov.1808 Louther Taylor with wife Heather Taylor of Baltimore sold to William Jones merchant of Same 117 acres that Abraham Taylor willed to sons Abraham Taylor and Louther Taylor.(see TOWER HILL)
17 May 1810 Louther Taylor of Kent Co. Del. sold to Horatio Taylor of Som.Co. as Bartholomew Taylor and Abraham Taylor of Bracken Co. Kentucky appointed Louther attorney to sell lands.

TAYLORS ADVICE

Patented in 1749 by Bowden Robins for 150 acres
24 Aug.1801 Joyce Handy daughter of William Handy and granddaughter of Bowden Robins sold 150 acres to David Walston.
24 Apr.1802 David Smith Walston with wife Polly Walston sold to Boaz Walston 150 acres.
2 July 1808 Boaz Walston with wife Bathsheba Walston sold 150 acres to Billy Fooks.

TAYLORS ADVENTURE

Patented on 2 Nov.1730 by Thomas Taylor for 100 acres.
23 Feb.1760 John Taylor sold to George Parker all, that Thomas Taylor who died intestate had. His eldest son Solomon Taylor died at non age and John Taylor is heir.
17 July 1760 George Parker Jr. resurveyed to PARKERS HARD FORTUNE in Wicomico Forrest.

TAYLORS BOG

Patented in 1794 by Jesse Taylor for 22 1/4 acres

TAYLORS CHANCE

Patented in 1773 by Abraham Taylor for 100 acres

TAYLORS CHANCE

Patented in 1760 by Nehemiah Taylor and Abraham Taylor for 100 acres.
1783 tax - Bartholomew Taylor 100 acres, Rewastico 100
21 Sep.1796 Bartholomew Taylor sold all to Isaac Kinney, all resurveyed to ANNAN

TAYLORS CHANCE

Patented in 1734 by William Taylor for 50 acres.
5 Nov.1742 William Taylor sold 50 acres to John Badley
1776 John Badley willed to son Gideon Badley

TAYLORS DELIGHT

Patented in 1818 by Matthias C. Taylor for 169 1/2 acres

TAYLORS HILL

Patented on 3 June 1683 by John Gladstean for 200 acres.
1702 John Panter gave to cousin Catherine Laws and her children
Rent Rolls 1666-1723 possessed by Robert Laws by gift from John Panter who purchased from John Gladstean.
1745 Robert Laws gave to son William Laws in Dorc.Co.Md. 200 acres
2 Dec.1788 Moses Pank and wife Elizabeth Pank sold to Benjamin Johnson
27 Nov.1792 Benjamin Johnson of Worc.Co. sold to Moses Pank

TAYLORS INTENT

Patented in 1767 by James Taylor for 50 acres
1783 tax - James Taylor 50 acres, Rewastico 100
1788 James Taylor willed to son Levin Taylor

TAYLORS LAST PIECE

Patented in 1850 by William Taylor for 2 1/2 acres

TAYLORS LUCK

Patented in 1850 by William Taylor for 26 7/8 acres

TAYLORS POINT

Patented in 1749 by John B. Taylor for 1 11/16 acres
1850 he is in Barren Creek area

TAYLORS PURCHASE

Patented on 11 July 1762 by John Taylor for 50 acres
1783 tax - John Taylor Sr. Wic.100. Worc.Co. 50 acres
20 May 1783 Clement Holliday and Nathaniel Ramsey comissioners to sell British confiscated property to William Williams, 50 acres
1771 repatented by William Williams for 50 acres
22 Apr.1809 John Driskell sold to Shephard Johnson 10 3/4 acres.

TAYLORS TRAVEL

Patented in 1801 by Eben Taylor for 10 1/2 acres

TAYLORS VENTURE

Patented in 1730 by Thomas Taylor for 100 acres

TERRAPIN TOWN

see BELLAIN

THIRD CHOICE

Patented on 2 Nov. 1738 by George Parsons for 100 acres
1762 Resurveyed to PARSONS CONQUEST

THIRD CHOICE

Patented on 20 Oct.1769 by Daniel Fooks for 46 acres

THIS AND MORE

Patented in 1808 by William Fleming for 6 1/4 acres

THIS OR NONE

Patented in 1782 by Andrew Adams for 19 1/2 acres
1783 tax - Andrew Adams, Wic.100, 50 acres

THIS OR NONE

Patented in 1789 by Thomas Stanford for 21 3/4 acres
1791 Thomas Stanford willed to son Constant Disharoon Stanford.

THOMAS'S CONCLUSION

Patented in 1762 by Thomas Stanford for 150 acres
13 Apr.1771 Thomas Stanford with wife Rachel Stanford and William Stanford sold to Levin Gunby of Worc.Co. 75 acres
6 Apr.1772 Joseph Stanford and Thomas Stanford sold to Levin Gunby 68 acres of THOMAS CONCLUSION & STANFORDS FINDING
28 Oct.1806 Tubman Lowe, attorney to sell real estate of Levin Gunby sold to Kirk Gunby 181 1/2 acres THOMAS CONSLUSION, ADDITION & STANFORDS FINDING.

THOMAS'S COURT

Patented on 31 Oct.1687 by John Gordon for 500 acres
1 Sep.1756 Thomas Gordon of Sussex Co.Del.sold to Charles Perry of same, 500 acres.
1768 Isaac Calloway willed to son Edward Calloway 54 acres, to son Isaac Calloway 100 acres and part to son Louther Calloway.
19 Mar.1776 Sussex Co.Del. land warrent to Simon Kollock.

THOMAS SPOT

Patented in 1801 by Thomas Dashiell of Thomas, 8 acres
25 Aug.1804 Josiah Sterling with wife Mattty Sterling sold to Thomas Dashiell of Thomas that John Hopkins son of George Collier Hopkins land conveyed to Thomas Dashiell by Peter Body and wife Frances Body on 26 Feb.1707 and resurveyed by him.

THOMPSONS TRAP

Patented in 1740 by Charles Thompson for 78 acres

TICKNELL

Patented on 23 June 1676 by Leonard Jones for 100 acres about two miles from Wetpquin Creek near Tyaskin
10 June 1684 Leonard Jones with wife Jane Jones sold 100 acres to Samuel Fluellin and Thomas Larramore
Rent Rolls 1666-1723 possessed by 50 acres Thomas Larramore, 50 acres by the widow of Samuel Fluellin
1731 Thomas Larramore willed to son John Larramore

1738 John Larramore willed to son Levin Larramore, all real estate, lunnamed.
14 Aug.1750 triparte, Levin Larramore sold to Benjamin Wailes 50 acres. Jacob Aires to sue Wailes for land.
1766 Samuel Fluellin willed lands to son Richard Fluellin, unnamed.
19 Mar.1770 Richard Crockett Fluellin s/o Samuel sold 50 acres to Ephraim King.
1783 tax - Charles Fluellin 50 acres, Nanticoke 100
26 Mar.1793 Gillis Polk, surviving trustee of Ephraim King and Samuel Fluellin, sold to Isaac Atkinson son of Isaac.

TIMBER GROVE

Patented in 1735 by Nicholas Evans for 100 acres
1783 tax - John Evans of Nicholas 52 1/2 acres, Nanticoke 100
1783 tax - Joshua E. Moore 27 acres
1783 tax - George Gale of Levin Gale 20 acres
28 Apr.1784 John Evans of Nicholas Evans sold to Joshua Evans Moore 27 acres
23 Nov.1786 John Evans of Nicholas sold to George Gale son of Levin Gale 76 3/4 acres of TROY & TIMBER GROVE.
24 Mar.1787 John Evans of Nicholas sold to Levin Gale, Henry Jackson and John Stewart, his equity
10 July 1792 Henry Jackson and John Stewart surviving partners of Levin Gale sold to Levin Dashiell Sr.

TIMBER LOTT

Patented in 1783 by William Pollitt for 153 acres.
9 Apr.1792 William Pollitt sold to Jacob Morris 32 acres
1784 Ebenezer Waller willed to son Ebenezer Cottman Waller, TIMBER LOT
15 June 1802 Jacob Morris sold to John Morris son of Joseph Morris TIMBER LOTT, COME BY CHANCE, FORK, MORRIS FANCY, etc.
13 Mar.1804 John Morris sold to Jacob Morris son of Joseph Morris, part.
17 Oct 1803 James Weatherly Waller sold to Ebenezer Cottman Waller for 5 shillings
19 Oct.1804 Ebenezer Cottman Waller with wife Nancy Waller sold to John Dashiell 267 acres of TIMBER LOT & CLOWLETT.
15 Mar.1806 William Pollitt with wife Sarah Pollitt sold to Joshua Morris 4 3/4 acres.
1806 John Dashiell patented TIMBER LOTT 42 acres
24 Sep.1808 George Parker sold to Joshua Trader 16 1/4 acres.

TIMBER PURCHASE

Patented in 1794 by George Parker for 214 acres

TIMBER RIDGE

Patented in 1755 by Benjamin Piper for 50 acres

TIMBER TRACT

Patented in 1738 by Elias Nutter for 100 acres

TIMBER TRACT

Patented in 1738 by Samuel Coulbourn for 50 acres

TIT FOR TAT

Patented in 1759 by Nathaniel Willis for 50 acres
1761 Nathaniel Willis willed to son Elijah Willis
14 Feb.1765 Elijah Willis, yoeman sold to Joseph Marshall, blacksmith 50 acres, near head of Wicomico Creek.
1 Mar.1765 John Willis sold to John Shockley 50 acres
1773 John Shockley willed lands unnamed to son Jonathan Shockley
28 Feb.1791 Jonathan Shockley son of John sold to Jesse Fooks 50 acres
9 Dec.1797 Jesse Fooks sold to John Shockley s/o John 50 acres
18 Sep.1798 John Shockley sold to Moses Pank 50 acres.

TIT FOR TAT

Patented in 1763 by George Wailes and John Wailes for 30 acres
1783 tax - George Wailes 15 acres, Rewastico 100
1783 tax - John Wailes 15 acres
1797 John Wailes willed to son Benjamin Wailes, on Back Water Branch.

TIT FOR TAT

Patented in 1808 by McMurray Johnson for 13 acres

TOADVINES ADDITION

Patented by Thomas Toadvine for 34 /34 acres
1771 Thomas Toadvine willed land to son Stephen Toadvine, not named.

TOADVINES ADVENTURE

Patented in 1771 by Henry Lurten for 70 acres a resurvey from Wicomico Manor
20 May 1783 Clement Holliday and Nathaniel Ramsey comissioners to sell confiscated property sold 70 acres to Henry Lurten
1783 tax - Henry Lurten 70 acres, Wic.100
15 Oct.1795 Henry Lurton with wife Sabra Lurten sold to Stephen Baine 70 acres
1 Nov.1797 Stephen Baine sold to Samuel Williams 70 acres
10 Mar.1798 Samuel Williams of Worc.Co. sold to Stephen Baine.

TOADVINES CHOICE

Patented on 23 July 1760 by George Toadvine for 20 acres in Wicomico forrest.
5 Aug.1772 John Toadvine with wife Ann Toadvine sold 5 acres to John Cathell.
Resurveyed and patented by Thomas Toadvine in 1775 for 69 acres
6 Apr.1779 Henry Toadvine sold to George Bayley 60 acres
12 Nov.1779 George Bayley with wife Fanny Bayley sold to Arnold Toadvine 69 acres.
1783 tax - Arnold Toadvine 69 acres

20 Apr.1787 Arnold Toadvine sold to Nathan Culver 60 acres
5 Nov.1789 Nathan Culver sold to Benjamin Shockley 60 acres
1791 Benjamin Shockley willed to son Jonathan Shockley 69 acres.
3 Apr.1801 Jonathan Shockley sold to Jethro Morris all rights.

TOCITER

Patented on 5 Oct.1677 by John White for 150 acres, who assigned to Daniel Haste
Rent Rolls 1666-1723 possessed by Benjamin Wailes who married Elizabeth Haste, coheir of Daniel Haste, 150 acres
1701 Daniel Haste willed to daughter Elizabeth w/o Benjamin Wailes.
1726 Benjamin Wailes willed 150 acres to son Joseph Wailes
1736 Joseph Wailes willed to sons Daniel Wailes and Haste Wailes, dwelling plantation, unnamed.
22 Mar.1758 Haste Wailes quitclaimed to brother Daniel Wailes all rights.

TONY'S PLANK

Patented in 1808 by Peter Dashiell a resurvey from CHESTNUT LOTT for 171 acres.
14 Mar.1807 Peter Dashiell sold to William Williams Jr. 15 acres, 6 perches.
21 Feb.1807 Peter Dashiell sold 5 acres to William Williams Sr. of CHESTNUT LOTT.

TOSSWANDOCK

Patented on 3 June 1682 by William Stevens who assigned to Charles Nutter at head of Nanticoke River, 130 acres
1702 Christopher Nutter willed to son Charles Nutter 130 acres and balance to son William Nutter.
9 Nov.1756 Ann Handy gave to son Thomas Handy, in Nutters Neck.
23 Feb.1773 Thomas Handy and wife Sarah Handy sold to Ephraim King.
Charles Nutter willed to sons Christopher and William Nutter and Ann Nutter the daughter of Christopher who married John Handy and had issue Thomas Handy who died intestate.
1777 Ephraim King willed to son Samuel King lands on the south side of Quantico, If he dies to Levin Gale, unnamed. land.

TOWER HILL

Patented on 9 Sep.1718 by Edward Kellum for 100 acres.
Rent Rolls 1666-1723 possessed by Edward Kellum
27 July 1739 Edward Kellum gave to grandson Gilbard Huffington son of John Huffington 100 acres
9 Apr.1759 Gilbard Huffington sold to Isaac Taylor
1765 resurveyed by Isaac Taylor to 960 acres
20 Aug.1767 Isaac Taylor sold 55 1/2 acres to Abraham Taylor
20 Aug.1767 Isaac Taylor sold to William Badley 35 acres
20 Aug.1767 Isaac Taylor sold to James Robertson Jr. 55 1/2 acres
20 Aug.1767 Isaac Taylor sold to William Lord 67 acres
20 Aug.1767 Isaac Taylor sold to William Badley 23 1/2 acres
20 Apr.1772 Isaac Taylor and wife Aseney Taylor sold 318 acres to John Robertson for 20 shillings.
1773 James Taylor patented TAYLORS ADDN. TO TOWER HILL 10 acres

1778 William Badley willed to sons James Dean Badley and son Eli Badley 23 1/2 acres.
1788 James Taylor willed to sons Joshua Taylor and Levin Taylor.
1783 tax - Abraham Taylor 55 acres, Rewastico 100
1783 tax - Heirs of Isaac Taylor 305 1/2 acres
1783 tax - John Lord 67 acres
1783 tax - Charles Badley 24 acres
1783 tax - Elizabeth Badley 113 1/2 acres
1783 tax - John Robertson 229 acres
1783 tax - James Robertson 55 1/2 acres
1789 ROBERTSONS ADDITION TO TOWER HILL patented James Robertson for 80 3/4 acres.
1791 Abraham Taylor willed to son Loudy Taylor 1/2 and to son Abraham Taylor 1/2 of 50 acres.
24 July 1795 Horatio Taylor sold 100 acres to Ebenezer Taylor
3 July 1803 Abraham Taylor with wife Molly Taylor sold to Horatio Taylor part.
3 June 1803 Abraham Taylor with wife Molly sold part to Ebenezer Taylor
3 July 1803 Abraham Taylor and wife Molly Taylor sold to Ebenezer Hill and Isaac Kinney.
1 Nov.1808 Louther Taylor with wife Heather Taylor of Baltimore sold to William Jones merchant of same, 117 acres.
17 May 1810 Louther Taylor of Kent Co.Del. sold to Horatio Taylor of Somerset Co 216 1/2 acres of TAYLORS ADDN. KENNINGTON, TOWER HILL, GLADSTONES ADVENTURE & HARDSHOP that Bartholomew Taylor and Abraham Taylor of Bracken Co. Kentucky appointed Louther attorney to sell.
1843 Polly Badley Cooper widow of Samuel Cooper willed to sons Martin Cooper and Severn Cooper.
1 Mar.1859 Robert Billings and Mary Billings of Sangamon Co.Ill sold to James Rhoads of Sussex Co.Del. formerly possessed by James Dean, adjacent lands of Samuel Weatherly. Robert Billings married by 1837 Mary Dean of Baltimore Co.Md.

TOWER HILL

Patented on 23 Mar.1687 by Manus Morris for 150 acres.
Rent Rolls 1666-1723 possessed by no one per accounts of Alexander Carlysle
25 Sep.1773 Adam Carlylse of Cumberland Co. Great Britian son of Alexander Carlylse sold 50 acres to Josiah Polk.

TOWER HILL

Patented on 19 Jan.1767 by Nathaniel Waller for 50 acres
8 Nov.1769 Nathaniel Waller sold to John Parsons 50 acres
12 Jan.1772 John Parsons sold 50 acres to Thomas McClish

TOWER HILL

Patented in 1760 by George Sharp for 600 acres
1784 George Sharp willed to sons Daniel Sharp 100 acres and balance of lands to Cyrus Sharp, unnamed, plantation.
1783 tax - George Sharp 160 acres, Wic. 100

TOWER HILL

Patented in 1769 by John Anderson for 35 acres

TOWNSENDS BEGINNING

Patented in 1790 by Barkley Townsend for 25 acres
1795 Barkley willed land to son Joshua Townsend, no name
1791 ADDITION TO TOWNSENDS BEGINNING patented to Thomas Waller for 95 acres.

TOWNSENDS SITUATION

Patented in 1749 by Benjamin Townsend for 306 acres
10 June 1750 Benjamin Townsend sold 53 acres to Teague Dickerson
1751 Benjamin Townsend willed to son Samuel Townsend 306 acres and if no issue to daughter Mary Townsend.
1783 tax - Samuel Townsend 203 acres Nanticoke 100
1783 tax - Levi Dickerson 53 acres
1797 Samuel Townsend willed to wife Nelly Townsend, aka HARTFORD, after death to Thomas Smith, all lands.
26 Apr.1799 James Dean with wife Mary Dean sold to James Smith
1837 Samuel Dickerson willed part, a lot, to free negro Hannah Nutter.

TOWN SUPPORT

Patented in 1792 by William McBryde for 34 1/2 acres
8 Sep.1798 John Biglands sold to Isaac Henry 34 acres.

TRADERS PURCHASE

Patented in 1812 by Joshua Trader for 34 1/2 acres

TRAINS LOT

Patented in 1738 by James Train for 85 acres
3 Mar.1764 Isaac Hardy of Worc.Co. heir of James Hardy and Eliza Train Hardy, sold to Matthew Dorman, all interest.
1783 tax - William Dorman 80 acres
13 Sep.1808 Levin Farrington mortgaged to the Farmers Bank of Maryland.

TRANQUILITY

Patented in 1811 by James Disharoon for 309 1/2 acres
1832 James Disharoon willed to son John Disharoon, part.

TRAVERSE CONSOLIDATED

Patented in 1800 by Joseph Leonard for 627 1/8 acres.

TRIANGLE

Patented in 1833 by Willin Wright for 4 /5th an acre in Barren Creek
1849 Willin Wright willed lands and mills to sons Isaac K. Wright, Clement M. Wright and Beauchamp A. Wright

TRIFALDI

Patented in 1785 by William Winder for 56 1/4 acres
6 June 1786 William Winder Sr.sold for 5 shillings 28 3/4 acres to Eli Vinson
13 Oct.1804 Eli Vinson with wife Comfort Vinson sold to Henry White of Worc.Co.

TROUBLE

1680 part of CRAMBOURNE

TROUBLE

Patented in 1805 by William Dashiell for 243 acres
18 Dec.1805 William Dashiell with wife Mary Dashiell mortgaged to Douty Bounds.
18 Dec.1806 William Dashiell and Douty Bounds sold 243 acres to William Harris.
1808 William Harris willed lands, unnamed to son William
1840 John Turner willed to wife Polly Turner, at Nanticoke Point.

TROUBLE FOR LITTLE

Patented in 1801 by David Hopkins, a resurvey from SAMUELS LOTT for 66 1/4 acres
18 July 1808 David Hopkins with wife Mary Ann Hopkins sold to Jesse Hughes.

TROUBLESOME

Patented on 10 Nov.1688 by John Richins for 200 acres near the head of Barren Creek. John Richins died and his widow married William Limbree. They sold to John Wheeeler.
Rent Rolls 1666-1723 possessed by John Wheeler
17 Sep.1715 John Wheeler with wife Ann Wheeler sold 1/2 to Thomas Wood.
29 Apr.1733 Thomas Wood sold 100 acres to William Polson.
2 July 1734 James Rawley with wife Mary Rawley of Dorcester Co. gave to friend William Young 100 acres.
23 Dec. 1770 Patience Records and Levin Polson sold all rights to Joseph Venables.

TROY

Patented on 21 Mar.1680 by John Evans for 50 acres
Rent Rolls 1666-1723 possessed by Capt. Nicholas Evans son of John, 50 acres
9 May 1782 John Evans of Nicholas sold to Levin Gale 40 acres
1783 tax - John Evans of Nicholas 30 acres, Nanticoke 100
1783 tax - George Gale of Levin Gale 20 acres
24 Mar 1787 John Evans of Nicholas Evans sold to Levin Gale, Henry Jackson and John Stewart, his equity.
10 July 1792 Henry Jackson and John Stewart surviving partners of Levin Gale sold to Levin Dashiell Sr.
11 Feb.1806 Thomas Jones of Thomas with wife Ann Jones lately Ann Evans, sold 48 acres to Alexander Stewart.

TRUITTS LOT

Patented on 8 Aug.1768 by Littleton Truitt for 50 acres
1783 tax - Littleton Truitt, Aquango 100, Worc.Co.
24 June 1786 Littleton Truitt sold to Thomas Truitt 50 acres.

TRUELOCK GRANGE

Patented on 23 Mar.1672 by Phillip Ascue for 250 acres
Phillip Ascue with wife Lydia Ascue sold to John Evans.
1 Feb.1675 James Jones attorney for John Evans sold 250 acres to Alexander Thomas.
1695 Alexander Thomas willed to Ganer Waller 100 acres and to daughters Elizabeth Thomas and Frances Thomas. Elizabeth married James Russell and Frances married James Boucher.
Rent Rolls 1666-1723 possessed by 100 acres Thomas Ralph Jr., 75 acres John Boucher, 75 acres, James Russell
May 1720 James Boucher with wife Frances Boucher sold to Thomas Ralph of Quantico 88 acres.
17 Apr.1740 James Russell Sr. gave to James Russell Jr. 65 1/2 acres
6 Jan.1745 James Russell son of James, cooper sold to Alexander Thomas Russell 62 1/2 acres called GOOD LUCK
1743 Thomas Ralph Jr. willed to daughter Mary Goslee
29 Feb.1772 Levin Goslee sold 37 1/2 acres to Wilson Rider, called RALPHS PURCHASE, at Quantico Creek.
1 May 1773 Alexander Thomas Russell sold all his land to son Price Russell, no names.
1783 tax - Levin Goslee 137 1/2 acres
1783 tax - Price Russell 75 acres
1783 tax - Charles Rider 200 acres
1784 Wilson Rider (wife Charity Rider daughter of Thomas Ralph) willed to son Charles 27 1/2 acres called RALPHS PURCHASE.
1801 Charles Rider willed 37 acres to wife Mary Rider.
1843 John Taylor of William Taylor willed to grandaughter Ann Maria Bratten.

TRYAL

Patented on 20 Dec.1741 by John Boyce for 100 acres on east side of the Nanticoke River
31 Aug.1749 John Boyce sold to Daniel Boyce 100 acres
1755 Daniel Boyce willed to son Joseph Boyce 100 acres.

TRYALL

Patented in 1774 by William Lloyd for 4 1/2 acres
1796 William Lloyd willed lands to wife Martha Lloyd, after her death to son Edward Lloyd, unnamed

TRYAL

Patented in 1812 by Solomon Evans for 6 1/4 acres

TUBMANS LOT

Patented in 1766 by Henry Lowe for 37 3/4 acres

11 Mar.1774 Henry Lowe with wife Esther Lowe sold to John Waters of Calvert Co.now of Somerset, lands from father Henry.
1783 tax - John Waters 37 1/2 acres, Rewastico 100
1784 John Waters willed dwelling plantation to wife Elizabeth Waters, then to son Francis Hutchins Waters.
31 Mar.1787 Francis Hutchins Waters sold to John Gale

TULLS KNAVERY

Patented in 1773 by Nathaniel Willis for 95 acres.
6 June 1774 John Willis brother of Nathaniel Willis, sold to Joseph Dashiell 95 acres.
22 Oct.1777 Joseph Dashiell sold to James Houston, merchant, 95 acres
26 Apr.1783 Joseph Dashiell sold to James Houston 95 acres
15 Aug.1783 James Houston sold to Henry Banks 95 acres.
1783 tax - Dr. James Houston and Henry Banks, Wic.100, Worc.Co.
4 Feb.1797 Henry Banks sold to Benjamin Johnson and John Johnson 95 acres.

TULLS PURCHASE

Patented in 1785 by Patrick Causey for 33 acres who assigned to Stephen Tull.

TULLYS ADDITION

Patented in 1774 by William Tully for 177 acres.
20 Oct.1777 William Tully sold to John Winright of Sussex Co.Delaware 73 acres
20 Mar.1779 John Winright of Sussex Co.Del. sold 73 acres to Thomas Badley.
26 Apr.1776 Sussex Co.Delaware land warrants, William Tully.
1796 John Grumble willed to son John
26 Aug.1797 Daniel Phillips sold to Nancy Robertson, William Robertson, Saul Robertson and Nelly Robertson heirs of James Robertson deceased, with McDANIELS LUCK.

TULLY CHOICE

Patented in 1734 by James Tully for 100 acres
5 Nov.1742 James Tully sold to Samuel Badley on the southast side of Barren Creek, 50 acres now called BADLEYS PURCHASE.
1796 John Grumble (wife Temperance Grumble) willed to son John.

TURKEY COCK HILL

Patented on 6 June 1683 by Manasses Morris for 150 acres
1 May 1688 Manasses Morris with wife Elizabeth Morris sold to Phillip Carter.
Rent Rolls 1666-1723 possessed by William Giles Jr. 150 acres
1783 tax - Mary Moore 100 acres
1783 tax - William Moore Sr. 50 acres
1788 William Moore Jr. gave to wife Rachel Moore part.
28 Oct.1793 William Moore sold 10 acres to Elijah Humphries
28 May 1799 William Moore sold to John Moore 40 acres
8 Oct 1799 William Moore sold to John Moore 100 acres.

29 Oct.1803 John Moore with wife Margaret Moore sold to John Byrd 287 3/4 acres of WOODYARD, TICKFIELD & all TURKEY COCK HILL.

TURKEY HALL

Patented on 20 Apr.1695 by Phillip Ascue for 116 acres
Rent Rolls 1666-1723 possessed by Phillip Ascue
13 Dec.1728 Phillip Ascue sold 116 acres to Alexander Adams.

TURKEY RIDGE

Patented on 19 July 1745 by George Dashiell for 83 acres
1748 George Dashiell willed to son Benjamin Dashiell
21 Mar.1760 Joseph Dashiell with wife Martha Dashiell sold to John Malone 83 acres.
1783 tax - Mary Malone 83 3/4 acres
26 July 1791 Peter Malone sold to Stephen Malone
26 July 1791 Stephen Malone sold to Peter Malone. Probably division of lands.

TURKEY TRAP

Patented on 29 Mar.1732 by Thomas Adams for 200 acres
1735 Thomas Adams willed to son David 100 acres and to son Thomas 100 acres. (David Adams died intestate, no issue)
31 Jan.1753 Phillip Adams the younger son of Abraham Adams who was son of Thomas Adams, cordwinder sold to Samuel Adams 100 acres.
17 Mar.1770 Caleb Balding, merchant with wife Sarah Balding sold to William Venables Sr. devised by will of Samuel Adams.
25 June 1777 Sussex Co.Delaware land warrants, Thomas Adams.

TURKEY TRAP RIDGE

Patented in 1746 by Joseph Ellis for 50 acres
13 Oct.1759 Joseph Ellis sold to Alexander Adams 50 acres
1769 Alexander Adams willed to son Andrew Adams.
1763 Samuel Adams sold to Caleb Balding

TURNERS ADDITION

Patented in 1841 by John Turner for 205 3/8 acres
1850 he is in Tyaskin District

TURNERS CHOICE

Patented on 21 July 1732 by Samuel Turner for 68 acres
1761 Archibald Smith with wife Turner Smith willed to son Samuel Smith 68 acres.
Repatented on 16 June 1763 by Solomon Smith for 130 acres
1783 tax - Betty Smith 130 acres, Wic.100, Worc.Co.
5 Apr.1774 Solomon Smith sold to Samuel Smith 130 acres.

TURNERS DELIGHT

Patented on 20 Apr.1762 by Zadock Turner for 50 acres

1783 tax- Zadock Turner 50 acres, Wic.100. Worc.Co.
3 Oct.1795 Zadock Turner sold to Benjamin Shockley 50 acres.
7 Sep.1799 Charles Shockley sold to Porter Parsons 50 acres
1815 Porter Parsons willed to Peter Parsons of Porter Parsons part.

TURNSTILE

Patented on 19 July 1679 by William Stevens who assigned to John Brown for 300 acres.
Rent Rolls 1666-1723 possessed by Peter Douty 150 acres, Thomas Larramore 150 acres
1709 Peter Douty gave to Ann Collier wife of Robert Collier part and to Thomas Collier residue. If no issue to Ann Dashiell daughter of James Dashiell.
23 Dec.1723 Thomas Collier and wife Ann Collier sold to John Robertson, carpenter, his part.
2 Apr.1727 John Robinson, carpenter with wife Mary Robinson sold to Robert Henderson, 1 moity.
19 Oct.1728 Thomas Larramore with wife Mary Larramore gave 10 acres to Henry McCabe and wife Elizabeth McCabe that he purchased of John Brown being part of the moity that John Brown sold to Peter Douty for love of his daughter Elizabeth McCabe.
19 Oct.1728 Thomas Larramore gave to Elias Venatson and wife Catherine Venatson, his daughter and to descend to grandson Elias Venatson and sons and daughters of Elias. 65 acres
1731 Thomas Larramore willed to son John Larramore 75 acres.
1748 Edward Willin willed to son Charles Willin 1/2
21 Nov.1759 Daniel McIntyre with wife Elizabeth McIntyre sold 65 acres to Thomas Willin Sr. that he purchased of Elias Venatson.
19 Aug.1761 Daniel Henderson sold to Archibald Ritchie 5 acres, that Robert Henderson bought of John Robertson, no name.
1775 Douty Collier son of Robert Collier gave to daughter Betty Collier.
19 Aug.1761 Daniel Henderson sold to James Winright 95 acres.
1783 tax - James Winright 95 acres
1783 tax - James Willin 95 acres
1783 tax - Henry Cordrey 70 acres
1783 tax - Delilah Ritchie w/o Archibald Ritchie 15 acres.
1783 tax - Elizabeth Handy 26 1/4 acres.
2 Nov.1785 Covington Cordrey sold part to Douty Cordrey
13 Apr.1793 John Willin son of Robert Willin sold to Henry Cordrey, that Thomas Larramore Sr. gave to daughter Catherine Venetson who sold to Daniel McIntyre who sold to Thomas Willin Sr.
1794 James Winright willed to wife Eleanor Winright and daughters Nancy Winright and Jane Winright where I live except part dau-in-law Ann Winright wife of James Winright lives, to her. After their deaths to grandson Levi Selby son of Henry Selby and Rebecca Selby, deceased.
1797 Henry Cordrey willed to son Covington Cordrey, lands unnamed.
28 Mar.1800 Levin Winright sold to George Handy
28 Mar.1800 George Handy sold to Levin Winright
6 Feb.1802 Isaac Atkinson and James Larramore sold 83 acres to John Jones for 5 shillings.
(also see BETTYS ENLARGEMENT, FISHERMANS QUARTER & CALLOWAYS ADDITION)

TWIFORDS BEGINNING

see COW QUARTER, & ADDITION

TWIFORDS SUPPORT

Patented in 1783 by John Twiford for 73 1/2 acres
25 June 1796 John Twiford of Dorcester Co. sold to Isaac Easum for 73 1/2 acres.
17 Oct.1801 Isaac Easum with wife Mary Easum sold to Isaac Kennerly
1857 Benjamin Gravener willed to daughters Maria Phillips wife of Roger Phillips, & Elizabeth Bennett wife of James Bennett.

TWILLEYS GOOD LUCK

Patented in 1847 by Robert Twilley for 66 5/8 acres in Tyaskin

TWILLEYS RIDGE

Patented in 1749 by William Winder for 134 acres
1783 tax - William Winder 134 acres, Rewastico 100

TYBURN

Patented in 1774 by John Parsons for 50 acres
1783 tax - John Parsons 50 acres, Acquanto 100, TYBURN HILL
1795 John Parsons willed to son William Parsons
1825 ADDITION patented by William Parsons for 413 3/4 acres
1824 ADDITION patented by William Parsons for 405 3/4 acres

UNIAKS CHANCE

Patented in 1739 by William Dulaney for 50 acres

UNION

Patented in 1794 by Francis Hutchins Waters for 562 acres
10 Nov.1804 Thomas Humphries of Hancock Co.Georgia sold to George Parker of Som.Co. 10 3/4 acres with SAW MILLS SUPPLY
16 Mar.1805 George Parker sold to Ezekiel Bell 10 3/4 acres.

UNION

Patented in 1793 by Benjamin Hearn for 156 acres
26 Nov.1796 Benjamin Hearn sold to Benjamin McClellan 156 acres.

UNITY UNTO GLASGOW

is part of TROUBLE and also DAINTRY

UNITED STATES

Patented in 1796 by William Acworth for 1018 1/2 acres, Rewastico, a resurvey from MARISH POINT
1783 tax - Train Acworth 273 acres
1783 tax - Nathan Culver 300 acres

28 Nov.1789 Nathan Culver sold to Joshua Hitch Sr. part.
2 Jan.1796 Robert Dashiell with wife Polly Dashiell, Robert Venables with wife Milky Dashiell heirs of William Acworth sold to John Tully 300 acres of WEATHERLYS ADDITION & UNITED STATES.
28 Apr.1798 Robert Dashiell Jr. with wife Mary Dashiell sold to Amilcah Venables wife of Robert Venables, that William Acworth father of Mary and Amilcah possessed at Barren Creek at Boat Landing, 10 acres of OLD MARSH HOUSE being part of UNITED STATES.
10 Apr.1802 Robert Dashiell, seaman and wife Polly Dashiell sold 227 1/2 acres to John Robertson part of WEATHERLYS ADDITION & UNITED STATES.

VAINE

Patented in 1762 by Daniel McIntyre a resurvey from END OF STRIFE for 33 acres
3 Sep.1771 Daniel McIntyre sold to Robert Willin 33 acres for 5 shillings
20 June 1786 Charles Willin with wife Elinor Willin, Robert Willin with wife Ann Willin sold to George Aires, in Nanticoke

VANCES NEGLECT

Patented in 1806 by William Brereton
6 Jan.1798 William Brereton with wife Sarah Brereton sold to William Daley 80 acres.
8 Sep.1798 William Brereton sold to Margaret Parsons 230 acres.

VENABLES MISTAKE

Patented in 1741 by William Venables for 100 acres
20 July 1743 William Venables with wife Mary Venables sold to George Parris 100 acres, north side of Wicomico River
17 Mar.1752 George Parris sold to Henry Waggaman 100 acres.

VENABLES PRETENSIONS

Patented in 1766 by Benjamin Venables for 95 acres
1783 tax - Joseph Venables son of Benjamin, 60 acres, Rewastico
1788 Joseph Venables willed to nephew Joseph son of Benjamin Venables.
5 Oct.1797 Levin Ballard, sherrif sold to William Russum, to satsify judgement against Thomas Venables grandson of Benjamin Venables.
29 Oct.1798 Thomas Venables sold to Jonathan Waller of Sussex County Delaware, no acreage given.

VENISON PASTURE

Patented in 1741 by John Gale for 506 acres
1783 tax - Elizabeth Gale 506 acres, Nanticoke 100

VENTURE

Patented on 17 July 1678 by Magdalen Westlock for 100 acres
Rent Rolls 1666-1723 possessed by Nathaniel Abbott in right of the orphans of John Leckie 200 acres.
1734 Richard Rider willed to son Wilson Rider 200 acres.

1784 Wilson Rider willed to son Charles Rider 200 acres of WESTLOCKS VENTURE
1801 Charles Rider willed to wife Mary Rider.

VENTURE

Patented on 20 July 1679 by Thomas Bloyes who assigned to William Wright for 50 acres
Rent Rolls 1666-1723 possessed by widow of William Wright
1700 Levin Denwood sold to Thomas Dashiell 50 acres
20 Jan.1741 Thomas Dashiell gave to son Charles Dashiell, granted William Wright and purchased of Levin Denwood.
1783 tax - Solomon Shockley 50 acres, Wic.100
1813 Solomon Shockley willed lands unnamed to sons Thomas Shockley and Elijah Shockley.

VENTURE

Patented on 2 Nov.1682 by Samuel Jackson for 300 acres
1687 Samuel Jackson willed lands to sons Samuel and Daniel Jackson, no name
Rent Rolls 1666-1723 possessed by Jonathan Jackson

VENTURE

Patented in 1757 by Edward Willey for 35 acres

VENTURE

Patented in 1761 by William Byrd for 50 acres
1783 tax - Jesse Byrd 50 acres, Rewastico

VENTURE

Patented in 1761 by Thomas Connerly for 50 acres
1783 tax - Thomas Connerly 50 acres, Rewastico
1817 Thomas Connerly willed to son John Connerly

VENTURE

Patented in 1760 by John Robertson for 50 acres
1783 tax - John Robertson 50 acres, Rewastico
1784 ADDITION TO patented by John Robertson for 90 1/2 acres
1800 John Robertson willed to son Alexander Robertson 50 acres, ADDITION TO VENTURE
28 Mar.1800 John Robertson Sr. sold to Thomas Walker 12 3/8 acres of ADDITION TO VENTURE.

VENTURE

Patented in 1761 by Thomas Humphries for 50 acres
1771 Thomas Humphries willed to son William Humphries
1783 tax - Phillis Humphries widow of Thomas, 50 acres, Rewastico
18 Sep.1789 William Humphries sold to Ezekiel Bell 50 acres

VENTURE

Patented on 7 May 1760 by Thomas Records for 50 acres
3 Mar.1767 Thomas Records sold to Joseph Cannon 50 acres

VENTURE

Patented in 1766 by Thomas Records for 23 acres
1768 Thomas Records willed to wife Sarah Records and children
1783 tax - George Tull 23 acres, Rewastico
18 June 1808 Thomas R. Tull sold to John Byrd 51 1/4 acres of VENTURE & GOOD LUCK.
1810 Lame Records son of Thomas Records willed to daughters Betty Records, Polly Records and Phillip Records 23 acres purchased of Thomas R. Tull.

VENTURE

Patented in 1761 by Richard Waller for 35 1/2 acres
1783 tax - James Pritchett 35 1/2 acres, Rewastico
16 Oct.1804 Benjamin Waller son of Richard Waller with wife Mary Whittington Waller sold to John Dashiell
1 Mar.1808 John Dashiell sold to Eli Vinson 18 1/4 acres of VENTURE, BALLY BUGIN & ANYTHING.

VENTURE

Patented in 1813 by John Hayman for 16 1/4 acres

VENTURE

Patented in 1815 by Thomas Bevans for 20 acres

VENTURE PRIVILEDGE

Patented on 13 June 1721 by George Dashiell for 250 acres on Quantico Creek.
1733 George Dashiell willed to sons Thomas Dashiell, Robert Dashiell, Mitchell Dashiell, William Dashiell and to grandson Mitchell Dashiell. Not to be sold.
1783 tax - William Dashiell Sr. 62 1/2 acres, Nanticoke 100
1783 tax - Mitchell Dashiell 62 1/2 acres
1783 tax - Henry Lowe 62 1/2 acres
1789 Mitchell Dashiell willed to grandson George Dashiell Wilson son of Ephraim Wilson.
17 June 1700 Tubman Lowe son of Henry Lowe sold to Frederick A.C. Dashiell 600 acres of RECOVERY, VENTURE PRIVILEDGE, LOWES MEADOW,etc.

VENTURE SMITH

Patented in 1741 by John Smith for 80 acres
25 Jan.1762 John Smith Sr. sold to John Smith Jr. 80 acres

VERDANT RETREAT

Patented in 1821 by Jesse Hughes for 624 1/2 acres

VEXATION

Patented on 8 Mar.1746 by Jarrad Wyley for 50 acres
8 June 1753 Jarrad Wyley of Worc Co. sold to John Scarborough Jr. on road from Broad Creek Bridge to the head of the Wicomico River.
22 Mar.1764 John Scarborough Jr. of Worc.Co. sold 50 acres to Charles Moore.
23 Jan.1775 Charles Moore sold 50 acres to Isaac Cooper
18 Apr.1776 Sussex Co.Delaware warrants, Isaac Cooper.

VICTORY

Patented in 1765 by Thomas Pollitt for 1 acre, 1 rod, 31 perches.

VICTORY OF WISDOM OVER HAYNIES ADVERSARY

Patented in 1771 by Samuel Haynie, a resurvey of HAYNIES VENTURE for 607 1/2 acres in Rewastico.
1783 tax - Richard Haynie 100 acres
1783 tax - Judiah Haynie 287 1/2 acres
1783 tax - Richard Waller 50 acres
1783 tax - James Pritchett 100 acres
1783 tax - Thomas Waller 50 acres
3 Oct.1795 John Moore of Sussex Co.Del. sold to Richard Waller son of Richard and to Joshua Lingo son of William Lingo 100 acres for 5 shillings.
7 Nov.1796 Levin Moore of Sussex Co.Del. sold to Thomas Byrd 25 acres
20 Mar.1800 Richard Waller sold to Eli Vinson for 5 shillings 92 1/2 acres of SNOW HILL, VICTORY OF WISDOM & ADDITION TO WILLIAMS GREEN.
17 Mar.1800 Richard Waller sold to Esme Marshall Waller for 5 shillings 41 1/4 acres, same as above.
13 Oct.1804 Eli Vinson with wife Comfort Vinson sold to Henry White of Worc.Co. 324 1/2 acres.
8 Aug.1806 Henry White with wife Catherine White sold to Benjamin White 152 acres.

VINSONS LUCK

Patented in 1800 by Isaac Vinson for 266 3/4 acres
1821 Thomas Byrd willed to son Benjamin Harvey Byrd.

VINSONS SLIPE

Patented in 1812 by Isaac Vinson for 4 acres

VULCANS VINEYARD

Patented on 6 Apr.1666 by Thomas Cottingham for 300 acres.
7 Sep.1671 Thomas Cottingham with wife Mary Cottingham sold to William Coulbourn.
26 July 1681 William Coulbourn with wife Margaret Coulbourn sold 300 acres to John Outten who sold to Richard Nicholson.
Rent Rolls 1666-1723 possessed by Richard Nicholson who purchased from Thomas Cottingham.
1735 ~~Joseph~~ Nicholson willed part to sons Joseph, James Nicholson and grandson Richard Nicholson.

2 Aug.1745 James Nicholson sold to William Murray 29 1/4 acres
19 Nov.1747 Richard Nicholson sold to James Nicholson 150 acres he has as heir at law to Richard Nicholson.
10 Mar.1752 Richard Nicholson of Worc.Co. sold 100 acres to George Parris of Som. Co. mariner.
17 Mar.1752 George Parris sold to Henry Waggaman 100 acres of VULCANS VINEYARD & NICHOLSONS LOTT.
16 June 1752 James Nicholson sold to Abraham Dean 110 acres.
4 July 1752 Abraham Dean sold to Thomas Gillis 110 acres.
1 Mar.1753 Thomas Gillis and Abraham Dean sold to Henry Waggaman.
11 Oct.1755 William Cannon of Dorc.Co. and wife Mary Cannon sold to Henry Waggaman part conveyed by John Nicholson to his son John Nicholson and wife Mary Nicholson.
25 Jan.1758 Charles Nicholson and James Nicholson sold to Henry Waggaman.
1759 Henry Waggaman willed to son William Elliott Waggaman
31 Aug.1774 Betty Handy and William McBryde with wife Sarah McBryde. As Capt. William Murray, father of Betty and Sarah afsd had 289 acres of NITHSDALE 29 acres and VULCANS VINEYARD & HIGH SUFFOLK in Rokiawalkin. He died with no male heir. This is a division of land and William McBryde to have VULCANS VINEYARD, 29 acres
1783 tax - William McBryde 29 acres, Rewastico
1783 tax - George Waggaman 100 acres
1783 tax - Henry Waggaman 100 acres.
12 Sep.1808 Daniel Ballard Esq. sheriff sold to Josiah Bayley of Dorc.Co. per judgement against Henry Waggaman
12 Sep.1808 Josiah Bayley with wife Ann H. Bayley of Dorc.Co. sold to John Rider.

WAILES RETREAT

Patented in 1796 by Benjamin Wailes for 261 1/4 acres.
1 Nov.1800 Benjamin Wailes sold to William Horsey son of Wiiliam Horsey that due him 261 1/4 acres and 1/2 of mill bought of Denwood Turpin.
2 Apr.1803 Benjamin Wailes sold to William Horsey 261 acres.
5 Jan.1805 Dr. William Horsey of Dover Delaware sold to John Wailes GOLDS DELIGHT & WAILES RETREAT.

WAINRIGHTS HARD LUCK

Patented in 1851 by George Winright for 420 acres

WINRIGHTS PLEASURE

Patented in 1763 by James Winright for 25 acres
1794 James Winright willed to wife Eleanor Winright and to daughters Nancy Winright and Jane Winright. After their deaths to Levi Selby grandson, son of Henry Selby and Rebecca Selby.

WALES

Patented on 22 May 1683 by William Stevens for 50 acres, who assigned to John Lyon. On the north side of Rewastico Creek.
7 May 1743 William Smith of Sussex Co.Delaware with wife Rachel Smith sold to James Hardy 200 acres of LYONS FOLLY & WALES. John Lyon sold

to Robert Bowdith who conveyed to William Merrill of Dorc.Co. who
conveyed to John Cheeseman who gave to wife Rachel Cheeseman who
married William Smith.
9 May 1743 John Pollitt of Dorc.Co. sold for 5 shillings to James
Hardy 200 acres of LYONS FOLLY & WALES.
29 July 1755 John Hardy of Worc.Co. sold 50 acres to Day Givans.

WAILES CHOICE

Patented in 1760 by George Wailes for 100 acres
1788 George Wailes willed to son John Irving Wailes 100 acres and to
son George land in my resurvey from WAILES CHOICE 100 acres.

WALKERS FOLLY

No patent found
1766 Thomas Walker willed 50 acres to son Emanuel Walker
18 Apr.1776 Sussex Co.Del.land warrents Emanuel Walker
21 Aug.1795 Emanuel Walker of Sussex Co.Del. sold 5 acres to John
Twiford of Worc.Co.
28 June 1802 Dennis Morris and Ann Starling Morris of Sussex Co.Del.
sold to Bartholomew Twiford of Dorc.Co. land entitled to as heirs of
Sally Twiford daughter of John Twiford, 5 acres WALKERS FOLLY

WALKERS NEST EGG

Patented by Jesse Walker for 11 acres
17 Sep.1794 Benjamin Venables with wife Ann Venables sold 11 acres to
George Twilley son of John Twilley with WHITE HALL, in Barren Creek

WALLACES ADVENTURE

Patented on 19 Mar.1694 by James Wallace for 200 acres
Rent Rolls 1666-1723 possessed by George Smith
7 Mar.1768 Samuel Carter with wife Eunice Carter and Zebulon Wright
and wife Sophia Wright of Som.Co. sold to Ezekiel Bell 200 acres near
fork of Wicomico River.
9 Apr.1776 Ezekiel Bell and wife Phillis Bell sold to William Parsons
200 acres, near Salisbury Town.
1792 William Parsons willed to son Samuel Parsons 200 acres
2 Jan.1809 Samuel Parsons of William, sold to William Parsons of
William, rights.

WALLACES VENTURE

Patented in 1761 by John Wallace for 705 acres
7 Sep.1764 William Walker with wife Ann Walker sold to Hugh Porter and
wife Elizabeth Porter (settlement of boundaries) As Ann and Eliabeth
are coheirs of John Wallace.
1788 Hugh Porter willed to wife Sarah Ann Porter and after death to
grandson Francis Porter.
15 May 1792 William Walker with wife Ann Walker gave to son William
Walker Jr. all interest. If no issue to heirs of Winder Walker.
1783 tax- Hugh Porter 454 acres.
16 Mar.1810 Francis Porter with wife Ann Porter sold 8 acres to John
Donoho.
1783 tax - Henry Walker 30 acres, Rewastico.

WALLBROOK

Patented on 4 May 1688 by Edward Fowler for 260 acres
Rent Rolls 1666-1723 possessed by Thomas Fowler heir of Edward.
5 Oct.t1726 John W. Evans and wife Mary Evans sold to Aaron Lynn 260 acres
14 June 1749 Aaron Lynn, merchant sold to Robert Swan 1009 acres with CARTERS LOTT & AARONS FOLLY

WALLERS FANCY

Patented in 1761 by Richard Waller for 100 acres
1783 tax - Thomas Waller 100 acres, Rewastico

WALLERS MEADOW

1783 tax - Ebenezer Waller 20 acres in Rewastico
1784 Ebenezer Waller willed to son Ebenezer Cottman Waller.
17 Oct.1803 James Weatherly Waller sold to Ebenezer Cottman Waller for 5 shillings his interest in CLOVE LOTT, WALLERS MEADOW & TIMBER LOTT.

WALTERS CHANCE

Patented in 1743 by John Walter for 50 acres
17 June 1746 John Walter gave to brother Robert Walter 50 acres
1783 tax - Robert Walter Sr. 50 acres, Nanticoke 100
1800 repatented by Daniel Walter for 161 3/4 acres

WARDS FOLLY

Patented in 1770 by John Ward for 12 acres

WARE

Patented on 13 June 1674 by William Woodgate who assigned to Richard Samuels 300 acres.
Rent Rolls 1666-1723 possessed by Richard Samuels 300 acres
1709 Richard Samuels willed to son Richard and wife Isabell Samuels, and land to son Peter Samuels.
10 Nov.1729 Richard Samuels with wife Ann Samuels gave 16 acres to daughter Ann Phipps wife of John Phipps, NEW ENGLAND out of tract WARE.
15 Aug.1730 Peter Samuels with wife Hannah Samuels sold 140 acres to John Hopkins, now called HOPKINS GIFT.
1732 Richard Samuels willed plantation to daughter Martha Samuels, unnamed.
18 Oct.1757 Martha Wallace widow and Richard Samuel Wallace sold 145 acres to John Gupton mariner, part that Richard Samuels gave to daughter Martha Samuels.
19 May 1760 John Gupton with wife Ann Gupton sold 143 acres to Stephen Hopkins.
1771 Stephen Hopkins willed part to son Stephen.
1783 tax - David Hopkins 70 acres
1783 tax - Robert Hopkins 65 acres
1783 tax - Nelly Hopkins 10 acres

1783 tax - Isaac Bartley 23 1/2 acres
1783 tax - Ezekiel Maddux 2 1/4 acres
26 Aug.1783 Levi Dickerson sold to William Cooper 50 acres that fell him by fathers will.
29 Sep.1805 George Willin sold 60 acres to William Willin
25 Mar.1805 William Mezick and Sarah Mezick sold to David Hopkins, George Hopkins, Stephen Hopkins 151 acres of SAMUELS LOTT & WARE.
3 Apr.1805 David Hopkins of Stephen, Eleanor Hopkins, George Hopkins of Stephen Hopkins sold to Jesse Hughes their interest.
17 Jan.1805 Richard Hopkins with wife Sarah Hopkins, John Hopkins with wife Leah Hopkins, Isaac Hopkins with wife Martha Hopkins, Samuel Hopkins with wife Jamima Hopkins sold to David Hopkins WARE & SAMUELS LOT in Nanticoke, as sons of Robert Hopkins.
11 Feb.1806 Isaac Dickerson sold 8 1/2 acres to Samuel Dickerson.

WAREHOUSE ISLAND

Patented in 1760 by Joseph Venables for 4 acres
1783 tax - Joseph Venables, Rewastico
1788 Joseph Venables willed to Joshua Bratten son of James Bratten and Mary Bratten and part to Benjamin Venables and Richard Venables sons of William Venables.

WARRINGTON

Patented on 28 Feb.1680 by Thomas Halsey for 200 acres
13 Sep.1719 Jane Halsey daughter of Thomas sold to James Givans 200 acres.
1723 James Givans of Rewastico willed to son John Givans 20 acres and to daughter Sarah Givans 190 acres.
10 Sep.1740 John Givans with wife Mary Givans sold to Daniel Rhoads 10 acres now called RHOADS CHANCE.
4 Nov.1743 Thomas Smith with wife Sarah Smith daughter of James Givans sold to William Farrington 190 acres.
1756 William Farrington willed to daughter Rachel Carmichael 190 acres
1783 tax - Rachel Carmichael 190 acres, Rewastico
1783 tax - Jacob Rhoads 10 acres.
18 Feb.1768 Daniel Henderson and Daniel Rhoads sold 10 acres to John Phillips.
5 June 1783 John Phillips sold to Jacob Reed 10 acres.
1796 John Carmichael willed to brother Levin Carmichael and sister Prissy Carmichael and Lear Adkins.
7 Sep.1801 Levin Carmichael sold to Henry Wilson 176 1/4 acres
11 Apr.1803 Levin Carmichael with wife Elizabeth Carmichael sold to Henry Wilson WARRINGTON, ADDITION TO WARRINGTON, LYONS DEN.total 231 1/2 acres.
1801 ADDITION TO WARRINGTON patented Levin Carmichael 198 1/2 acres
14 Apr.1803 Henry Wilson with wife Sally Wilson sold to Edward Hull 53 5/8 acres of WARRINGTON & ADDITION.
1 Mar.1805 Levin Carmichael sold to Nathaniel Rhoads 13 3/4 acres
8 Aug.1806 Levin Carmichael sold to Henry Wilson 189 4/8 acres of ADDITION
8 Aug.1806 Henry Wilson with wife Catherine Wilson sold to James Walton 44 1/4 acres of WARRINGTON & ADDITION.

4 Sep.1807 Henry Wilson and wife Catherine Wilson sold to Eleanor Handy 132 1/2 acres of LYONS DEN, WARRINGTON, GREENS DISCOVERY.

WARMINGTON

Patented on 4 Apr.1680 by Gilbert Jones for 50 acres.
18 Sep.1684 Gilbert Jones and wife Jane Jones sold 50 acres to John Marrett.
Rent Rolls 1666-1723 possessed by James Jones.
1740 Jonathan Jackson willed to son Joshua Jackson.
1756 WARMINGTONS ADDITON patented for 50 acres
14 Jan.1745 Joshua Jackson with wife Sarah Jackson sold to John Leatherbury, shpiwright of Acco.Co.Va. 15 acres left Joshua by father.
1783 tax - Samuel Jackson 85 acres
10 may 1788 Samuel Jackson with wife Patience Jackson sold to James Anderson 35 acres.
27 Feb.1790 James Anderson sold to Douty Collier for 5 shillings 1/3rd part WARMINGTONS ADDITION.
20 Dec.1805 Jonathan Jackson son of Samuel Jackson sold to James Anderson.

WARRIORS LOTT

Patented on 1 July 1745 by John Spicer for 100 acres
29 June 1764 John Spicer sold to the partnership of Nanticoke Furnace and Broad Creek Furnace 100 acres.
19 Oct.1767 Persisor Frazier of Ashton Township, Chester Pennsylvania and wife Mary Frazier sold interest to Christopher Marshall of Philadelphia, druggist, William Wishart of Philadelphia and Jemima Edwards widow, in iron works.
12 Nov.1772 Christopher Marshall of Philadelphia gave to his children his 1/5th part of Iron Works Furnace in Deep Creek and Nanticoke River with lands in Dorc.Co. and Sussex Co.Del.

WARWICK

Patented on 14 Sep.1674 by John Squire for 200 acres.
1678 John Squire with wife Edelia Squire sold to Gilbert James.
13 June 1681 Gilbert James and wife Jean James sold to Peter Lowe 200 acres.
15 Apr.1708 Edward James with wife Eleanor James heir of Gilbert James sold to Henry Hayman interest.
14 Oct.1709 Henry Hayman sold to Jonathan Jackson 100 acres
4 Aug.1713 Jonathan Jackson sold 100 acres to Thomas Ralph
27 Oct.1732 Thomas Ralph and wife Elizabeth Ralph of Quantico sold 100 acres to William Richardson
1739 Jonathan Jackson willed to son Joshua Jackson 100 acres.
14 Jan.1745 Joshua Jackson and wife Sarah Jackson sold 100 acres to John Leatherbury, shipwright of Accomack County Virginia.
18 June 1750 Benjamin Richardson son of William Richardson sold to Wilson Rider 100 acres.
3 Oct.1767 Jonathan Jackson sold 100 acres to John Rider.
5 Oct.1767 John Rider with wife Margaret Rider sold to Thomas Irving 110 acres of WARWICK & MIDFIELD.
1783 tax - Charles Leatherbury 100 acres
1783 tax - Heirs of John Rider 35 acres

1783 tax - Thomas Irving
1784 Thomas Irving willed to son Joseph Irving 25 1/2 acres.
14 Sep.1789 Joseph Irving son of Thomas sold to Levin Irving, sold all
12 Feb.1790 Thomas Moore and wife Mary Moore of Sussex Co.Del. sold to Charles Rider and Edward Austin, all interest.
19 Oct.1793 Charles Rider and Edward Austin sold 132 acres of WARWICK & MIDFIELD to George James.
19 Jan.1799 Levin Irving son of Thomas Irving, with wife Leah Irving sold to William Mezick
15 Jan.1801 William Mezick with wife Sarah Mezick sold to Thomas Cannon 15 3/4 acres of WARWICK & MIDFIELD.
27 July 1810 Thomas Jones with wife Nelly Jones sold to Levin D. Collier 16 1/4 acres
1818 William Mezick willed this land to be sold.
1843 John Taylor willed to daughter Mary Ann Brattan 1/3rd and to granddaughter Ann Maria Bratten 2/3rds.
1850 Jesse Leatherbury willed to half brother George W. Hitch

WATERMELLON

Patented by Samuel Hearn for 39 acres
20 Apr.1770 Samuel Hearn sold 39 acres to John Freeney of Worc.Co.
8 Mar.1776 Sussex Co.Delaware land warrants by John Freeney.

WATSONS DISCOVERY

Patented in 1762 by John Watson for 100 acres.
18 Mar.1767 David Cathell with wife Elizabeth Cathell sold to George Disharoon 100 acres
12 Dec.1767 George Disharoon and wife Sarah Disharoon sold 40 acres to Francis Disharoon
1783 tax - Francis Disharoon 40 acres, Wic.100
1783 tax - George Disharoon 60 acres
9 Jam.1796 Stephen Disharoon son of George sold 58 1/2 acres to Joshua Morris.

WEALTH

Patented in 1753 by Abraham Heath for 13 acres

WEATHERLYS ADDITION

Patented in 1762 by Joseph Weatherly for 85 acres
6 Apr.1774 John Weatherly and Joshua Weatherly sold 85 acres to William Acworth for 5 shillings.
1783 tax - Train Acworth 85 acres, Rewastico
2 Jan.1796 Robert Dashiell with wife Polly Dashiell and Robert Venables with wife Milkey Venables sold to John Tully (Polly and Milkey daughters of William Acworth) 300 acres of WEATHERLYS ADDN. & UNITED STATES.
10 Apr.1803 Robert Dashiell, seaman with wife Polly Dashiell sold 227 1/2 acres of WEATHERLYS ADDN. & UNITED STATES.

WEATHERLYS ADVENTURE

Patented on 4 Apr.1680 by James Weatherly for 300 acres on northmost

branch of Quantico
Rent Rolls 1666-1723 possessed by James Weatherly 300 acres
14 May 1731 James Weatherly and William Weatherly sons of James sold to John Lankford 100 acres
Rent Rolls 1731 John Lankford 100 acres
1760 Ebenezer Cottman willed to grandson Nathan Cottman son of daughter Sarah Lowe 200 acres.
4 May 1782 Ebenezer Waller son of Richard Waller and Mary Cottman Waller, sold to Everton Kennerly part.
5 July 1782 Ebenezer Moore of Granville Co.N.C.son of Mary Cottman, daughter of Ebenezer Cottman, sold his claim to Everton Kennerly
1783 tax - Nicholas Cantwell 100 acres, Rewastico
1783 tax - Nathan Lowe 164 acres.
18 Feb.1784 William Lowe heir of Sarah Lowe sold to Everton Kennerly his rights.
22 Apr.1784 Nathan Cottman with wife Mary Cottman sold 200 acres to John Anderson.
26 May 1791 John Anderson sold 200 acres to Lambert Hyland.

WEATHERLYS CONTRIVANCE

Patented on 12 Apr.1681 by James Weatherly for 300 acres
1 Sep.1697 James Weatherly made over to Richard Acworth 150 acres
Rent Rolls 1666-1723 possessed by by heir of Thomas Acworth son of Richard 150 acres, James Weatherly 150 acres.
12 July 1721 Richard Acworth sold 150 acres to Abraham Taylor
1783 tax - William Taylor Jr. Rewastico 100
9 Mar.1784 Richard Acworth Jr. sold 10 acres to Levin Winder.
7 Dec.1784 Richard Acworth sold 150 acres to John Hobbs.
1784 William Taylor willed to son Ezekiel Taylor 100 acres and to son John Taylor 50 acres.
20 Aug.1797 John Hobbs, Jesse Dorman with wife Margaret Dorman sold to John Nelson 80 acres
20 May 1797 John Hobbs and John Nelson sold to Jesse Dorman and wife Margaret Dorman 80 acres.
14 Apr.1801 John Taylor sold to James Russell 50 acres
8 Apr.1806 Elijah Reed of Worc.Co. heir of Zachariah Reed and Obediah Reed sold to William Winder with ACWORTHS DELIGHT, SONS CHOICE
29 Mar.1806 Henry Davis with wife Martha Davis and Adam Brattan with wife Elizabeth Brattan sold to Elijah Reed brother of Martha and Elizabeth.
8 Apr.1806 Elijah Reed sold to John Nelson
31 Dec.1807 John Taylor of Ezekiel Taylor sold to John Taylor of William Taylor bought of Abraham Taylor.
1825 Richard B. Porter willed tract purchased from Charles Horsey to three children, Mary Forcett Porter, John Beard Porter, Richard Porter.

WEATHERLYS CONVIENCY

Patented on 6 Nov.1699 by James Weatherly for 200 acres
Rent Rolls 1666-1723 possessed by James Weatherly
18 June 1765 John Weatherly and Joseph Weatherly sold to Henry Graham 200 acres
26 Oct.1803 Lewis Graham sold 44 acres to John Jones.
11 Apr.1804 John Jones, with wife Elizabeth Jones sold to John Walker

of Sussex Co. Delaware 44 acres.

WEATHERLYS LOT

Patented in 1755 by James Weatherly 75 acres
1761 James Weatherly willed to sons James, Charles Weatherly and Jesse Weatherly
1783 tax - Jesse Weatherly, Rewastico 100
27 Apr.1798 Jesse Weatherly s/o James Weatherly, with wife Sarah Weatherly sold to Levin Winder 170 acres of WEATHERLYS LOTT & PARTNERSHIP.
Repatented in 1798 by Levin Winder for 99 3/4 acres

WEATHERLYS MARSHES

Patented in 1728 by James Weatherly and William Weatherly for 136 acres.
1731 James Weatherly willed to son John Weatherly
19 Mar.1767 James and William Weatherly sold to Ephraim King
23 Feb.1773 Ephraim King sold to Thomas Handy 100 acres
25 Oct.1775 Thomas Handy son of John Handy sold to Ephraim King
1783 tax - William Horsey 45 1/3 acres, Rewastico 100
1783 tax - Isaac Horsey 45 1/3 acres
1783 tax - William McBryde 45 1/2 acres

WEATHERLYS POND

Patented in 1762 by William Winder for 10 acres
1764 Joseph Weatherly willed to Charles Weatherly 2 acres
1783 tax - William Winder 10 acres, Rewastico.

WEATHERLYS PURCHASE

Patented on 28 Nov.1672 by James Weatherly for 750 acres.
James Weatherly made over 260 acres to Capt. William Piper.
Rent Rolls 1666-1723 possessed by James Train 225 acres, Charles Nutter in right of the orphans of William Piper 200 acres. James Weatherly 325 acres.
William Piper heir of William sold to Christopher Piper 240 acres.
31 Oct.1702 James Weatherly gave to daughter Sarah Twilley wife of Robert Twilley 250 acres.
16 Nov.1724 Ann Twilley daughter of Robert and Sarah sold 250 acres to William Farrington.
12 Feb.1728 Christopher Piper sold to James Hardy for 5 shillings 240 acres out of WEATHERLYS PURCHASE, ONCE AGAIN & MARCH HOOK.
11 Mar.1736 Christopher Piper with wife Rachel Piper sold to James Hardy same as above.
22 June 1743 James Hardy and James Weatherly sold afsd, to James Train Jr. 240 acres.
1756 William Farrington willed to sons George Farrington and Robert Farrington.
1743 part 150 acres resurveyed to NEEDLESS COST
17 Aug.1758 Robert Farrington sold to Ephraim King his interest, from father and mother.
27 June 1759 George Farrington son of William Farrington sold to

Samuel Wilson 146 /12 acres.
8 Feb.1760 George Farrington sold to Ephraim King 146 1/2 acres SLIPE, PASTURAGE, WEATHERLYS PURCHASE.
1777 Ephraim King willed to son Samuel King all lands purchased of George Farrington in Rewastico.
1783 tax - James Train 302 acres
1783 tax - William Dorman 250 acres
1783 tax - James Parremore 18 acres
1783 tax - Agnes Piper 33 /12 acres-a resurvey to CLOVERFIELDS
1783 tax - William Turpin 113 acres
1783 tax - George Phillips 150 acres a resurv. of this & NEEDLESS COST.
21 Aug.1801 Charles Nutter with wife Louise Nutter sold to William Bounds 482 2/8 acres of WEATHERLYS PURCHASE, PASTURAGE, SLIPE, CLOVERFIELDS.
13 Sep.1808 Levin Farrington mortgaged to Farmers Bank of Maryland.
19 Feb.1857 Marcellus Weatherly sold to Martha Jane Knowles daughter of Wilson Knowles of Sussex Co.Delaware.

WEATHERLYS RIDGE

Patented on 15 Dec.1679 by James Weatherly for 200 acres
Rent Rolls 1666-1723 possessed by James Weatherly
21 May 1744 William Weatherly son of William sold to Solomon Hitch 100 acres for 15 shillings
1764 Joseph Weatherly willed to sons Constantine Weatherly and John Weatherly, land, no name.
18 Nov.1756 James Weatherly and John Weatherly sold 100 acres for 10 shillings to Joseph Weatherly.
1783 tax - John Waller 100 acres, Rewastico
1783 tax - Constantine Weatherly 100 acres
16 Sep.1791 Constantine Weatherly shipcarpenter with wife Elizabeth Weatherly sold to William Winder. Devised by father and brother John Weatherly provided that Constantine deliver to John Weatherly exec. of late Sarah Weatherly, now Sarah Skinner land given to John Waller for conveyance.
19 May 1791 Sarah Skinner late widow of John Weatherly divided lands.
1791 resurveyed 125 acres to CONSTANTINES DELIGHT.

WEATHERLYS RESERVE

Patented on 16 Dec.1679 by James Weatherly for 300 acres
Rent Rolls 1666-1723 possessed by James Weatherly.
22 Mar.1724 William Weatherly son of James, with wife Charity Weatherly sold to James Parremore 300 acres
2 Feb.1747 James Parremore sold 32 acres to James Hardy, now called HARDYS ADDTION
29 July 1755 James Hardy sold 36 acres to Day Givans.
1756 William Farrington willed 225 acres to Leah Dorman
20 Feb.1763 James Parremore mortgaged to William Farrington 250 acres left by father James Parremore, except graveyard.
1783 tax - James Phillips, 32 acres.
28 July 1783 Thomas Parremore son of James Parremore Jr. of James sold to Matthew Dorman 250 acres.

1783 Matthew Dorman willed to son George Dorman, if no issue to son
Matthew Dorman, to sons William Dorman and Robert Dorman 25 acres.
1783 Isaac Coulbourn (wife Comfort Coulbourn) willed to daughter Mary
Coulbourn purchased of Thomas Parramore where Matthias Dorman lives.
25 Dec.1806 William Dorman son of Matthew Dorman sold to Robert Selby
all rights.
1 June 1810 Robert Selby sold to Robert Twilley all lands purchased of
William Dorman at Rewastico and Barren Creek, no name or acreage.

WELCOME

see DOUBLE PURCHASE 1679

WESSLINGTON

Patented in 1813 by Thomas Bayley for 454 1/2 acres

WESTERN FIELDS

Patented on 4 June 1680 by Robert Ridgley for 1400 acres
1680 Robert Ridgley of St. Marys Co.Md. willed to son William Ridgley.
Rent Rolls 1666-1723 possessed by no one, belongs to son of Robert
Ridgley.
24 Apr.1762 Charles Carroll sold 1400 acres to Benjamin Venables, that
James Carroll of Ann Arundel Co. willed in 1728 to be sold.
11 Nov.1762 Hugh Henry willed to Isaac Henry 150 acres, he to pay to
other children.
17 Mar.1763 Benjamin Venables and wife Ann Venables sold to Sarah
Henry widow of Rev. Hugh Henry and Isaac Henry, James Henry and Hugh
Henry all sons of Hugh Henry who purchased of Benjamin Venables 150
acres.
23 June 1763 Benjamin Venables gave to son William Venables 300 acres
23 June 1763 Benjamin Venables gave to son Benjamin Jr. 300 acres
23 Apr.1764 Benjamin Venables sold to John Turville 50 acres.
1783 tax - Joseph Venables 300 acres Rewastico
1783 tax - Benjamin Venables 600 acres
1783 tax - Rachel Venables 300 acres
1783 tax - Esther McClennan 50 acres
1783 tax - Beauchamp Hull 150 acres
1788 Joseph Venables willed to nephew Joseph of Benjamin Venables
escept 100 acres my father willed to Betty Bozman and Joseph Weatherly
son of Constantine Weatherly and Betty Weatherly.
1788 Richard Acworth gave to sister Esther Acworth
25 June 1785 Joseph Venables sold 153 1/2 acres to Isaac Henry
17 Mar.1786 Constantine Weatherly with wife Elizabeth Weatherly sold
to Joseph Austin part devised to Elizabeth Bozman now Elizabeth afsd.
by grandfather Benjamin Venables.
21 Mar.1783 Thomas Venables sold to Lewis Daltrieu 160 acres
16 May 1793 John Parsons of Sussex Co.Del. sold to Arthur Dashiell all
rights that Edward Austin sold to Richard Acworth who willed to siste
Esther Acworth. She died no issue and 1/4th part became right of John
Parsons.
16 Aug.1793 Thomas Venables mortgaged to James Nelson
28 Sep.1793 George Parsons with wife Jessey Parsons of Sussex Co.Del.
sold his 1/4th part to Arthur Dashiell
29 Mar.1794 Edward Austin sold 100 acres to John Dashiell

3 Oct.1794 John Dashiell of Jesse Dashiell sold 100 acres to Benjamin Jones for 5 shillings.
17 Sep.1794 George Twilley son of John Twilley sold 50 acres to Benjamin Venables where mother Eleanor McClennan now lives.
9 May 1795 Benjamin Jones sold 100 acres to John Dashiell of Jesse Dashiell.
13 Jan.1795 James Nelson made over rights to William Russum
24 June 1795 John Dashiell with wife Eleanor Dashiell sold 100 acres to Benjamin Jones.
5 Oct 1797 George Robertson, sheriff sold to William Russum 171 acres per judgement against Thomas Venables, to satisfy debts.
29 Oct.1798 Thomas Venables sold to Jonathan Waller of Sussex Co.Del., part.
28 Sep.1798 Benjamin Jones sold to Arthur Dashiell 100 acres
13 Apr.1800 Benjamin Venables with wife Anna Venables and James Russell with wife Polly Russell sold 33 acres to Charles Venables.
7 Nov.1801 Stephen Wright, Belitha Wright with wife Mary Ann Wright sold to Levin D. Collier 116 1/8 acres
26 Nov.1801 Constantine Weatherly with wife Elizabeth Weatherly sold to William Russum, parcels Joseph Bozman died possessed.
7 Oct.1805 Benjamin McClennan sold to William Andrews wife's dower interest.
21 Nov.1807 Joseph Venables with wife Sarah Venables sold 160 acres to Benjamin Venables, to revert to Joseph if Benjamin has no heirs.
10 Nov.1809 Robert Venables and John Venables sold all interest to Levin Crockett
6 June 1810 John Venables sold to Matthias Dashiell 28 1/4 acres
2 Mar.1810 John Venables sold to brother Charles Venables, part.
12 Oct.1810 Robert Venables with wife Sarah Venables sold to Shiles Crockett 13 1/4 acres
1826 Loudy Goslee willed to wife Elizabeth Goslee
1828 William Phillips willed to son Peregrine Phillips.

WESTLOE NECK

Patented on 9 Dec.1676 by John Span for 533 acres on the south side of Quantico.
1670 Phillip Shapleigh sold to Thomas Brereton of Northumberland Co.Va. 533 acres.
20 Apr.1672 Thomas Brereton of Little Winicomico in Northumberland Co. Va. for bond I bear unto John Span youngest son of Richard Span, deceased and wife Grariana Brereton 533 acres at Quantico Creek.
Rent Rolls 1666-1723 possessed by George Betts 300 acres, 233 acres by orphans of Capt. Thomas Winder in Virginia.
1709 George Betts gave to daughter Mary Betts 300 acres.
19 Aug.1761 Triparte Agreement, Mary Benston sold to George Dashiell son of James Dashiell and William Hayward 300 acres, which was conveyed by Dorothy Span to George Betts father of Mary Benston.
1783 tax - Phillip Graham 300 acres.
1 Nov.1790 Phillip Covington with wife Priscilla Covington exchanged lands with Robert Graham for BETTS PRIVILEDGE
1 Nov.1790 Robert Graham sold 300 acres to Benjamin Venables
1 Nov.1790 Benjamin Venables sold to Robert Graham 300 acres
25 Jan.1794 Robert Graham sold to Edward Austin 280 acres.
5 June 1798 Edward Austin with wife Mary Austin sold to John Gale 300

acres, bond against claim of wife's dower by widow of Robert Graham.
20 Apr.1802 Elizabeth Elliott, Daniel Jones, George Dashiell with wife Polly Dashiell sold to John Gale 50 acres, as heirs of mother Mrs. Jones.

WESTON

Patented on 12 Mar 1680 by John Reed for 200 acres
Rent Rolls 1666-1723 possessed by John Reed 200 acres
10 Jan.1791 James Reed and wife Elizabeth Reed sold 6 1/4 acres to George Furbush
19 Apr.1798 James Reed with wife Betty Reed sold 191 acres to David Dutton
1798 David Dutton willed to be sold.
2 Aug.1803 George Furbush sold to Andrew Scott.
1 Dev.1804 Belitha Wright with wife Mary Ann Wright sold to Stephen Wright land devised to Matthew Wright and Mary Ann Dutton, now Mary Ann Wright by will of David Dutton.
8 Apr.1806 Andrew Scott sold to Richardson Donoho 4 acres, property of James Reed
1 Aug.1806 Samuel Larramore of Thomas Larramore sold to Levin D. Collier.
25 July 1810 Levin D. Collier, Stephen Wright and Methia Wright sold 116 acres to Ephraim K. Harris
7 Apr.1810 Stephen Wright, shipwright, sold to Delaney Wright 101 acres of WESTON, HOG RIDGE, CHANCE

WETEPKEWANT

Patented on 1 July 1664 by Stephen Horsey for 600 acres
Rent Rolls 1666-1723 possessed by no such land so hath been returned
1754 Stephen Horsey willed to friend George McClester lands on Tipqueen in Nanticoke River with sons Stephen Horsey and Revell Horsey, to divide equally, they to give Robert Collier a small moity of said lands where he lives.

WETIPQUIN

Patented in 1842 by Isaac D. Jones for 528 1/4 acres

WHARF OF SALISBURY

Patented in 1771 by William Adams and William Horsey for 1 acre
1786 William Horsey willed to son William, storehouses and lots in Salisbury.

WHAT YOU PLEASE

Patented on 1 Dec.1688 by William Keen for 300 acres
Rent Rolls 1666-1723 possessed by Joseph Venables 250 acres, John Goslee for 50 acres
1718 Joseph Venables willed to son Benjamin Venables.
3 Apr.1738 Benjamin Venables sold 25 acres to John Hardy taken up by William Keen except 1/2 acre where meeting house stands.
15 Sep.1753 Benjamin Venables, Elgate Hitch, Thomas Byrd, Ann Hall, Rebecca Evans, Moses Driskell sold to Jonathan Stott the balance.
1755 John Goslee willed to wife Joanna Goslee lands, after death to

son William Goslee, unnamed lands.
1755 part resurveyed to BELLAIN
10 Feb.1762 Jonathan Stott sold to Christopher Piper for 2 shilings.
13 Jan.1767 Christopher Piper sold to Esme Bayley
23 Jan.1770 Henry Dorman with wife Sarah Dorman sold 12 acres to Stephen Redden
1779 William Goslee son of John Goslee sold to Esme Bayley
19 Mar.1782 Joseph Morris Jr. sold to George Dashiell 29 acres
1783 tax - George Dashiell
1783 tax - George Bayley 57 acres
1783 tax - Stephen Baine
19 Mar.1788 George Dashiell sold 29 acres to Mills Bayley

WHAT YOU PLEASE

see COCKLAND

WHAT YOU PLEASE

Patented on 9 Sep.1718 by William Calloway for 50 acres
Rent Rolls 1666-1723 possessed by William Calloway
1758 William Calloway willed to son Moses Calloway 50 acres
1758 Moses Calloway willed to sons Moses Calloway and Clement Calloway
4 July 1776 Sussex Co.Delaware resurvey to Northwest Fork 100 by Charles Brown.

WHAT YOU PLEASE

Patented in 1754 by Christopher Piper for 50 acres
5 Aug.1762 Christopher Piper with wife Mary Piper sold to Ezekiel James 50 acres.
1783 tax - George James 50 acres

WHAT YOU PLEASE

Patented on 14 Nov.1768 by Joshua Holloway for 256 acres a resurvey of EVENING CHANCE.

WHEEL OF FORTUNE

Patented on 19 May 1758 by George Smith for 304 acres a resurvey of MIDDLE NECK & MT. CHARLES
27 Aug.1762 George Smith of Worc.Co. sold 64 acres to Thomas Noble of Somerset County.
8 Aug.1764 George Smith son of George sold to Archibald Smith 240 acres.
1775 George Smith willed lands to be sold to pay debts. Any surplus to be divided equally between children Benjamin Smith, George Smith, Archibald Smith Elijah Smith and Mary Parker wife of Jacob Parker, wife Catherine Smith.
1783 tax - William Martin 150 acres
1783 tax - William Rose 30 acres
1783 tax - Archibald Smith 100 acres
1783 tax - John Nelms 15 acres
7 Aug.1792 George Martin sold 305 acres to Ezekiel Bell, mortgage.
11 Nov.1801 Thomas Noble with wife Nancy Noble 13 3/4 acres to Hugh Oliphant.

29 May 1803 Thomas Noble with wife Nancy Noble sold 4 acres to Hugh Oliphant.
4 Apr.1804 Thomas Noble sold to James Smith, all interest.
19 Oct.1805 Thomas Noble with wife Nancy sold all to James Smith.
1842 Richard Waller willed to sons James Waller, Alfred Waller, Esme Waller and William Waller.

WHEEL OF FORTUNE

Patented in 1793 by Mary Stayton for 591 acres.

WHETSTONE

Patented on 19 Mar.1680 by Phillip Carter for 350 acres.
Rent Rolls 1666-1723 possessed by Phillip Carter, 350 acres
1715 Phillip Carter willed to wife Mary Carter, and to Sarah Acworth Jr 100 acres and balance to John Records Sr.
1744 John Records gave to son Thomas Records 150 acres.
24 Aug.1759 Ann Records sold for 10 shillings 100 acres to Thomas Records that John Records willed wife Ann to sell.
1772 ADDITION TO WHETSTONE patented Archelus Records
1783 tax - Esme Bayley 200 acres, escheated to CONTENTMENT
1783 tax - Archelus Records, ADDITION
11 Mar.1797 Archelus Records sold 8 acres to Elijah Humphries.

WHAT YOU PLEASE

Patented on 22 Nov.1672 by John Craycroft who assigned to William Green for 250 acres.
Rent Rolls 1666-1723 possessed by William Green 250 acres
1 Mar.1755 Robert Brown sold to John Brown 50 acres on the north side of Barren Creek.
1783 tax - Robert Brown resurvey
1783 tax - Joseph Hust, resurvey to ILL NEIGHBORHOOD
1792 resurveyed to BROWNS CONCUSION 269 3/4 acres

WHITE CHAPPELL

Patented on 20 Nov.1685 by Edward Wright 300 acres
Rent Rolls 1666-1723 possessed by John Lame 300 acres
1704 Thomas Serman son of Edward Serman willed to sons Peter Serman and William Serman, 300 acres.
1711 Peter Serman willed to mother Margaret Booth wife of Peter Booth 150 acres.
19 Apr.1731 Thomas Serman with wife Eliza Serman and William Serman with wife Sarah Serman sold to Neal McClester, 300 acres alienated by Edward Wright to Thomas Serman father of afsd.
1751 Neal McClester willed to nephew Samuel McClester son of brother John McClester, near Barren Creek.
1757 resurveyed to 502 acres.
1 Aug.1775 Josiah Bayley sold 1 acre to John Adams
13 Aug.1775 Josiah Bayley sold 100 acres to Andrew Adams, his rights.
1783 tax - John Adams Sr. 1 acre, Wicomico 100
1783 tax - Andrew Adams
1783 tax - John McClester 300 acres Rewastico 100.

1725 John McClester willed to Samuel Gordon.

WHITE CLAY

Patented in 1783 by Adam Christopher for 30 acres
1783 tax - Adam Christopher 30 acres, Wic.100 Worc.Co.
1796 Adam Christopher willed lands, unnamed to sons Eben Christopher, Tubman Christopher and George Christopher.

WHITE HALL

Patented in 1783 by Benjamin Venables for 432 1/2 acres
1782 Benjamin Venables willed to grandson Benjamin son of William Venables on north side of Barren Creek.
17 Sep.1794 Benjamin Venables son of Benjamin with wife Ann Venables sold to George Twilley son of John Twilley 431 1/2 acres, in Barren Creek.
1838 Thomas Daugherty with wife Ann Daugherty sold 61 acres to George W. Bounds.
2 Dec.1847 George W. Bounds with wife Rachel Bounds sold 1 acre and 51 perches to Luther Kennerly, WHITE HALL or HARD FORTUNE.

WHITE HALL

Patented in 1795 by William Polk for 897 1/2 acres
19 Mar.1803 William Polk sold all to Samuel Sims.

WHITE HILL

Patented in 1762 by John Robertson for 50 acres
1783 tax - John Robertson, 50 acres Rewastico
1800 John Robertson willed 50 acres to son Solomon Robertson.

WHITE MOUNTAINS

Patented in 1753 by William Jones for 46 acres
17 Apr.1753 William Jones, housecarpenter sold 46 acres to Nicholas Fountain.
1743 ADDTION TO WHITE MOUNTAINS, resurveyed by Nicholas Fountain for 243 acres with part of FOUNTAINS CHOICE.
1779 Nicholas Fountain willed to son Steven Fountain plantation, unnamed, after death to grandson Belitha Nicholson.
1784 ADDITION patented to Steven Fountain for 197 acres
1783 tax - Steven Fountain 100 acres, Acquango 100 Worc.Co.
1783 tax - David Briddle 100 acres,
23 July 1785 Steven Fountain with wife Judah Fountain sold to Wiliam Morris 65 acres of ADDITION
7 Mar.1787 Stephen Fountain sold to Richard Powders 52 acres ADDITION
14 Sep.1792 Belitha Nicholson sold to William Morris son of Thomas Morris, rights
25 Oct.1799 William Morris sold to Charles Hammond 186 acres
23 Dec.1801 William Morris with wife Catherine Morris sold all to Charles Hammond.
2 Apr.1803 John Culver with wife Ibby Culver sold to William Dixon all rights, late property of Richard Powders.

24 July 1803 Nathan Culver of Hancock Co. Georgia with wife Nancy Culver formerly Nancy Powders, sold to brother John Culver of Maryland.
11 Feb.1804 William Dixon of Nathaniel Dixon,with wife Leah Dixon and Pierce Powell sold to Jethro Morris, had from Richard Powders.
22 Nov.1806 The heirs Richard Powders sold to Thomas Wimbro, rights. Signed Ibby Culver, Pierce Powell.

WHITE OAK LINE

Patented in 1759 by Alexander Russell for 35 acres
1 May 1773 Alexander Thomas Russell sold to son Price Russell all his lands, no name.

WHITE OAK SWAMP

Patented in 1773 by Peter Gordy Jr. for 50 acres
20 Aug.1825 Obediah Disharoon sold to Jehu Parsons 50 acres

WHITE OAK SWAMP

Patented in 1738 by Robert Givans for 200 acres
29 Aug.1740 Robert Givans sold to Jacob Bounds 23 acres at head of Broad Creek now called BOUNDS ADDITION for 10 shillings.
19 Aug.1740 Robert Givans sold to John Phillips 90 acres
19 Aug.1740 Robert Givans sold 87 acres to Robert Houston
17 Feb.1743 John Phillips sold to Jarrad Wyley 90 acres now called PHILLIPS LOTT
4 Mar.1745 Robert Houston sold 87 acres to Phillip Wingate in Parsons Neck
8 June 1753 Jarrad Wyley sold 90 acres to John Scarborough Jr.
15 July 1755 Jarrad Wyley with wife Martha Wyley sold to Erasmus Drinkle, merchant, 90 acres.
1757 Phillip Wingate willed to son Thomas Wingate 87 acres and to son John Wingate 60 acres
4 Mar.1763 John Scarborough sold to Thomas Wingate 90 acres.

WHITE PLAINS

Patented in 1815 for 403 1/2 acres by Richard Bennett, a resurvey.
31 May 1810 Daniel Sharp with wife Rebecca Sharp sold to James Bennett, SHAVE THE BALD FRIAR, HOUND RIDGE, ADDITION, part of GOOD INTENT owned by Cyrus Sharp deceased, included in a resurvey called WHITE PLAINS 364 2/3 acres.

WHITELY REGULATION

Patented in 1787 by William Whitely for 565 1/2 acres

WHITEMARSHES DELIGHT

Patented on 18 Feb.1664 by Richard Whitemarsh for 300 acres
3 July 1669 Richard Whitemarsh with wife Elizabeth Whitemarsh of Northampton Co. Va. sold to William Waters, who assigned to John Lyon.
15 Nov.1690 John Lyon of Nanticoke River in Dorcester County sold to James Givans.

Rent Rolls 1666-1723 possessed by 150 acres Robert Givans, 150 acres, James Givans. by the name of GIVANS LOTT
1723 James Givans willed to son James.
1735 Robert Givans willed to son Robert 150 acres
2 Nov.1743 James Givans sold to John Gale 20 acres from will of father, no name.

WHITES ADVENTURE

Patented in 1755 by John White for 50 1/2 acres

WHITES DESIRE

Patented in 1749 by Archibald White for 11 acres

WHITES INDUSTRY

Patented on 12 March 1762 by Henry White for 70 1/2 acres

WHITES SECURITY

Patented in 1757 by John White for 66 acres

WHITEFIELD

Patented on 2 Apr.1680 by William Stevens who assigned to Thomas Walker and Susanna Walker children of Thomas Walker and Jane Walker 700 acres
Rent Rolls 1666-1723 possessed by Thomas Walker and Nicholas Evans who married Susannah Walker.
1748 Alexander Maddux guarantees bond to brother William Maddux part of WHITEFIELD which by death of father Lazarus Maddux was to be divided.
1763 Alexander Maddux willed to wife Elizabeth Maddux 138 acres, after death to sons Joseph Maddux, Zachariah Maddux and William Maddux. To son Alexander 50 acres on north side of WHITEFIELD.
1 Sep.1764 William Maddux sold 8 acres to Isaac Covington
1767 agreement of division of land between William Maddux and Alexander Maddux sons of Lazarus Maddux.
1 Sep.1757 Alexander Maddux Sr. sold 63 acres to Alexander Jr
1 Sep.1767 Alexander Maddux sold 63 acres to Hezekiah Maddux
1 Sep.1767 Alexander Maddux sold 63 acres to Zephaniah Maddux.
14 May 1768 Isaac Covington sold to John Nelms 111 acres of COVINGTONS CHOICE & WHITFIELD.
31 Mar.1770 William Maddux sold 140 acres to Isaac Maddux
26 Jan.1771 Alexander Maddux, Zephaniah Maddux, Hezekiah Maddux, Joshua Maddux heirs of Alexander Maddux, sold to Benjamin Hearn 289 acres.
1783 tax - Isaac Maddux 130 acres, Rewastico
1783 tax - John Maddux 130 acres
13 Mar.1794 Benjamin Hearn sold to John Maddux and Henry Maddux, no acreage given.
13 Mar.1794 John Maddux and Henry Maddux sold to Benjamin Hearn, probably settlement of boundaries.
9 Feb.1798 George Puzey sold to Elzey Maddux rights to land that Lazarus Maddux died seized.

1799 WHITEFIELD patented by Hezekiah Maddux 14 acres, Worc.Co.
1805 Hezekiah Maddux willed to son Wilson Maddux.

WHITE FIELD

Patented on 4 Dec.1757 by John Calloway for 50 acres
8 Apr.1765 John Calloway sold to John Houston

WHITTINGTONS CHANCE

Patented on 26 June 1706 by William Whittington for 300 acres.
14 Mar.1722 William Whittington and wife Elizabeth Whittington sold 300 acres to Joseph Pemberton late of the Island of Nevis.
21 Nov.1726 Joseph Pemberton of Sussex Co.Del. sold to Isaac Handy 300 acres.
8 Jan.1734 Isaac Handy sold 268 acres to William Stevens.
25 Apr.1764 William Stevens with wife Margaret Stevens sold to George Handy 150 acres.
1823 ADDITION TO patented by Levi Stevens for 165 3/4 acres
1832 Levi Stevens willed to son William Stevens

WHITTYS CONTRIVANCE

Patented to Thomas Shiles 100 acres
1574 Thomas Shiles of Wicomico gave land 100 acres to son John Shiles.
Rent Rolls 1666-1723 possessed by 86 acres by Thomas Dashiell and 14 acres by John Shiles.
14 Dec.1731 Thomas Dashiell gave to son Charles Dashiell 100 acres.
17 June 1743 Charles Dashiell sold 36 acres to Thomas Willin, at a place called ROUND SWAMP.
17 June 1743 Charles Dashiell sold to Stephen Winright 50 acres.
15 Apr.1745 John Shiles sold to Thomas Willin 14 acres.
1763 Stephen Winright gave to son Cannon Winright 50 acres.
30 June 1764 Thomas Willin with wife Elizabeth Willin sold to Thomas Willin Jr.
22 Aug.1771 Evans Winright and Cannon Winright sold 50 acres to Thomas Rencher
1783 tax - Thomas Rencher 50 acres, Wic.100
1783 tax - John Evans of John 50 acres, Nanticoke 100
8 June 1784 Samuel Willin son of Thomas Willin sold 36 acres to John Evans of John.

WHITTYS INVENTION

Patented on 7 Apr.1666 by Richard Whitty for 300 acres.
4 June 1672 Richard Whitty and wife Elizabeth Whitty sold 300 acres to John Winder.
Rent Rolls 1666-1723 possessed by James Makemorie who purchased of Thomas Winder son of John Winder.
1738 James Makemorie willed to grandson James Makemorie Jones 150 acres and to son James Makemorie 250 acres.
1768 George Dashiell willed to grandaughter Peggy Nicholson daughter of Joseph Nicholson land Matthew Cannon deeded him being part of trs. WHITTYS INVENTION & DEDFORD.
26 Nov.1778 Price Russell with wife Ann Russell and Arthur Dorman with wife Rebecca Dorman partition of 300 acres. Ann and Rebecca daughters

of James Makemorie.
17 Apr.1780 Price Russell sold to William Russell part.
25 Apr.1800 Rebecca Carey sold to James Russell 13 1/2 acres.
13 Dec.1808 Thomas Cannon sold to Francis James and wife Louisa James 89 1/2 acres.
13 Dec.1808 Francis James with wife Louisa James sold to Thomas Cannon.

WHITTYS LATER INVENTION

Patented on 10 Apr.1666 by Richard Whitty for 300 acres.
4 June 1672 Richard Whitty with wife Elizabeth Whitty sold 300 acres to John Winder.
Rent Rolls 1666-1723 possessed by James Makemorie 100 acres, John Winder 200 acres
1738 James Makemorie willed to grandson James Makemorie Jones 150 acres and to son James Makemorie 250 acres of WHITTYS INVENTION & WHITTYS LATER INVENTION.
23 APr.1764 Matthew Cannon with wife Mary Cannon sold 200 acres to George Dashiell for 5 shillings.
26 Nov.1778 Price Russell and wife Ann Russell and Arthur Dorman with wife Rebecca Dorman partitioned.
16 Sep.1805 Mary Cannon sold all interest to Thomas Cannon.

WICOMICO MANOR

Patented for 600 acres by Henry Harford.
1771 Tenants claimed. They obtained an order from Lord Baltimore's revenue officer to surveyor of Somerset Co. to resurvey with contiguous vacancy so the tenants could buy the lands he lived on. Confiscated in 1783. Sight of the town of Fruitland. Tenents who resurveyed to other names were -
Joseph Dashiell 452 acres
Elijah Austin 104 acres - to AUSTINS SECURITY
Henry Lurton 70 acres- to TOADVINES ADVENTURE
Smullin Layfield 84 acres - to ADVENTURE
William Williams 50 acres- to WILLIAMS CHOICE
Edward Serman 122 acres- to FOUNTAINS FROLIC
George Sockwell 33 1/2 acres- to GALES FROLIC
Samuel Williams 72 acres- to GUM SWAMP
John Nelms 65 1/4 acres- to CONCLUSION
Joshua Sturgis 409 1/2 acres- to ADDITION
James Hill 65 acres.
also see INDIAN LOTT
31 Mar.1800 Underwood Roberts sold to Isaac Serman and Betty Serman part of WICOMICO MANOR

WICOMICO BRIDGE

4 Aug.1672 Samuel Smith of Wicotomaco of Northumberland Co.Va. appoints Richard Whitty to adknowledge a deed of gift to William Brereton and his now wfe Sarah Brereton, son in law, land on Wicomico River, WICOMICO BRIDGE, that bounds SMITHS ADVENTURE a full half of lands.

WIDOWS CRUSE

Patented in 1849 by James Fairfax Dashiell for 77 1/8 acres

WILD CAT RIDGE

Patented on 27 Mar.1761 by William Turner Davis for 67 acres
29 Nov.1775 Turner Davis of Bladen Co. North Carolina sold to Samuel Davis of Worc.Co. 22 /12 acres
22 Jan.1763 resurveyed to DAVIS ADVANTAGE.

WILEYS FROLIC

see INCLOSED

WILL HAVE MORE

Patented in 1762 by Constant Disharoon for 100 acres
1795 Constant Disharoon willed 100 acres to grandson John Stanford.

WILLIAMS ADVENTURE

Patented in 1769 by William Darby for 36 acres
1783 tax - Sarah Darby 36 acres, Rewastico
17 Jan.1794 Levin Bennett and wife Betsy Bennett and Sally Darby heirs of William Darby sold to Isaac Wright 10 3/4 acres of WILLIAMS ADVENTURE & SALLYS LOTT
25 Oct.1799 Lewis Graham and wife Sally Graham sold to Levin Taylor 28 1/8 acres

WILLIAMS CHANCE

Patented in 1723 by William Carey for 100 acres
1734 William Carey willed to son Levin Carey 100 acres
7 Mar.1755 Levin Carey gave to son Thomas Carey 50 acres
3 Nov.1761 Thomas Carey gave to Levin Carey 50 acres
1783 tax - Levin Carey 100 acres
1791 Levin Carey willed lands unnamed to wife Lidy Carey.
14 May 1795 Levin Carey son of Levi sold to Samuel Carey 59 acres
8 Apr.1796 Josiah Mitchell sold to Thomas Whaley 70 acres
9 Feb.1796 Josiah Mitchell with wife Hessey Mitchell sold to Solomon Carey 30 acres
24 Oct.1795 Samuel Carey with wife Rachel Carey sold to Samuel Pollitt rights, at head of Tony Tank Creek.
26 Oct.1795 Samuel Carey sold rights to John Ingersol.
29 June 1799 Solomon Carey sold to Thomas Whaley 30 acres.
1823 Seth Whaley willed to grandson James Whaley
1850 REPATENTED by James Whaley 100 acres.

WILLIAMS CHOICE

Patented on 5 oct.1758 by William Parsons for 50 acres
1783 tax - William Parsons 50 acres
1783 ADDITION TO WILLIAMS CHOICE patented by William Parsons for 250 acres.
1792 ADDITION TO WILLIAMS CHOICE patented William Parsons for 300 acres

2 Jan.1809 Samuel Parsons of William Parsons sold to William Parsons of William with ADDITION TO WILLIAMS CHOICE.

WILLIAMS CHOICE

Patented on 17 Sep.1756 by William Driskell for 50 acres
17 Feb.1768 William Driskell with wife Rosanna Driskell (daughter of John Christopher) sold to Benjamin Johnson 50 acres
1783 tax - Benjamin Johnson 50 acres, Wic.100, Worc.Co.

WILLIAMS CHOICE

Patented in 1762 by William Dykes for 100 acres
10 July 1762 Daniel Dykes assigned to William Dykes 100 acres.
repatented in 1776 by William Dykes for 469 acres
12 May 1776 William Dykes with wife Naomi Dykes sold to William McBryde for 5 shillings 129 acres
1783 tax - William McBryde 129 acres, Wic.100 Worc.Co.
11 Feb.1785 William Dykes sold to John Tilghman 32 acres.
13 Mar.1789 William Dykes sold to Elijah Christopher 50 acres.
13 Mar.1789 William Dykes and Sarah Dykes sold to Charles Harris 50 acres.
29 Mar.1796 Benjamin Dennis with wife Polly Christopher Dennis and Elijah Christopher sold to Charles Harris 50 acres.
21 Oct.1809 Daniel Dykes son of William Dykes sold to Belitha Christopher and Henry White, all rights.
1802 William Dykes willed to son Daniel Dykes

WILLIAMS DISCOVERY ON TAYLORS ADDITION

Patented in 1850 by William Taylor for 151 acres in Barren Creek.
1857 William Taylor willed to son Anthony M. Taylor

WILLIAMS GREEN

Patented in 1748 by William Waller for 50 acres
ADDITION patented in 1799 by Esme Marshall Waller
20 Mar.1800 Richard Waller sold to Eli Vinson for 5 shillings 92 1/2 acres of SNOW HILL, VICTORY OF WISDOM etc, ADDITION TO WILLIAMS GREEN
17 Mar.1800 Richard Waller sold to Esme Marshall Waller 41 1/4 acres of above.
13 Oct.1804 Eli Vinson with wife Comfort Vinson sold to Henry White, ADDITION TO WILLIAMS GREEN.
8 Aug.1806 Henry White with wife Catherine White sold part to Benjamin White
27 Oct.1810 Esme Marshall Waller sold to Hetty Kellum, Henrietta Kellum, Patience Kellum and William Kellum 100 acres of CLOVELOTT, WILLIAMS GREEN, WALLERS CONCLUSION.

WILLIAMS LOT

Patented in 1762 by Daniel McIntyre for 29 acres
1772 Daniel McIntyre willed to wife Elizabeth McIntyre and after death to son Willin McIntyre
1783 tax - Betty McIntyre 20 acres, Nanticoke 100

16 Dec.1788 Willin McIntyre sold 9 acres to Levin Willin for 9 acres
1 May 1810 Daniel McIntyre Jr. with wife Elizabeth McIntyre sold to Henry Willin 70 acres of ADDITION TO FINISH ALL & part WILLIAMS LOT

WILLIAMS LOT

Patented on 23 Aug.1768 by William Truitt for 4 1/2 acres

WILLIAMS LOT

Patented in 1796 by William Russum for 66 acres
26 Nov.1801 William Russum sold to William Wilson 60 acres

WILLIAMS PURCHASE

Patented in 1791 by William Bethards for 50 acres
ADDITION patented in 1807 by William Bethards for 80 acres

WILLIAMS SECURITY

Patented in 1831 by William Parsons for 302 acres

WILLINGS ADDITION

Patented in 1791 by Levin Willin for 25 acres
1797 Levin Willin willed to wife Nancy Willin plantation, after death to sons Alexander Willin and and Chaplin Willin

WILLINS ADVENTURE

Patented on 18 Mar. 1746 by Charles Willin for 50 acres
4 Sep.1769 Thomas Willin son of Charles Willin who died intestate, with wife Eleanor Willin sold to Andrew Collins, yoeman 50 acres.

WILLINS MISTAKE

Patented in 1786 by Robert Willin and Charles Willin for 43 1/2 acres
20 June 1786 Charles Willin with wife Eleanor Willin, Robert Willin and wife Ann Willin sold to George Aires 31 acres out of DANIELS CHANCE, HOGS QUATTER, WILLINS MISTAKE, SAFETY, VAIN, DANIELS PRIVILEDGE for 5 shillings.
27 Feb.1787 Charles Willin sold to George Willin 11 1/2 acres of HOGG QUARTER, WILLINS MISTAKE.
3 May 1800 Charles Willin sold to George Willin 17 3/4 acres

WILSONS DISCOVERY

Patented on 1 Dec.1688 by James Weatherly for 500 acres.
25 Jan.1737 James Weatherly son of James sold to John Kibble 150 acres called DELIGHT.
18 Feb.1737 James Weatherly son of James sold to John Knight 100 acres called HAPHAZARD.
18 Mar.1738 James Weatherly sold 100 acres to Peter Magee.
5 Oct.1743 Peter Magee sold 100 acres to Peter Quinton
5 Oct.1743 John Kibble sold to Peter Quinton 75 acres of DELIGHT now

called BEGINNING
22 Mar.1764 Thomas Price and wife Patience Price sold to William Kennerly part called DELIGHT, 75 acres.
26 Mar.1774 James Weatherly and Richard Waller sold 150 acres to Joshua Parremore of Dorcester County.
1783 tax - Thomas Cordrey 75 acres, Rewastico
1783 tax - Jesse Parremore 149 1/4 acres
1783 tax - Jacob Quinton 100 acres
1783 tax - John Vicass 100 acres
1783 tax - William Kennerly 75 acres
1784 Jacob Quinton willed to mother 100 acres and to Thomas Cordrey 25 acres.
1788 Thomas Cordrey willed to son Henry Cordrey 75 acres, if no issue to son Salathiel Cordrey
15 Apr.1790 ADDITION patented by James Knight for 234 3/4 acres.
8 Aug.1799 James Knight of City of Washington sold to Benjamin Hersey of Fairfax Co.Va. ADDITION 132 3/4 acres.
2 Oct.1798 Benjamin Hersey of Fairfax Co.Va. sold to William Whann of Georgetown, Montgomery Co.Md. 132 3/4 acres.
20 Sep.1799 William Whann of Montgomery Co. sold to Amos Alexander and Benjamin Hersey of Fairfax Co. Va. 132 3/4 acres
2 June 1803 James Knight of the City of Washington sold to William Haslett Smith and Matthew Steene trading firm of Smith & Steene of Baltimore Co. mortgage 234 3/4 acres of WILSONS DISCOVERY & ADDITION.
1857 Benjamin Gravener willed to son Benjamin P. Gravener on road from Bacon Quarter to Vienna.
1858 Algenon Johnson willed to wife Elizabeth Johnson

WILSONS DISCOVERY

Patented in 1761 by George Wilson for 100 acres
26 oct.1765 George Wilson sold 100 acres to Joshua Hitch
1783 tax - Joshua Hitch 100 acres, Rewastico
1801 resurveyed to HITCHES HARD LUCK

WILSONS GOOD LUCK

Patented in 1773 by George Wilson for 38 1/4 acres
1783 tax - Benjamin Lankford 19 1/2 acres a resurvey of Mt.Tuzzy
1783 tax - George Wilson Sr. 16 acres, Rewastico
1789 Benjamin Lankford willed to son Thomas Lankford 19 1/2 acres.

WILSONS LOT

Patented on 3 Dec.1688 by Thomas Wilson for 200 acres
Rent Rolls 1666-1723 possessed by Thomas Wilson
1722 Thomas Wilson willed to granddaughter Mary Wilson daughter of son Thomas 100 acres, unnamed.
1742 John Wilson son of Thomas willed to cousin Mary Wilson Taylor 100 acres left by father's will.
17 Mar.1752 triparte- John Wilson son of Thomas sold to John Huffington and John Kellum 200 acres. Mortgage
17 Aug.1753 John Wilson sold to Benjamin Venables 99 acres on the south side of Barren Creek.
18 Feb.1769 Nathan Culver with wife Mary Culver sold 100 acres to

David Wilson
1783 tax - Joseph Venables 200 acres
1788 Joseph Venables willed to grandson Samuel Venables.
10 Dec.1788 Ephraim Wilson sold to Joseph Venables 100 acres
100 acres resurveyed to BATCHELORS CHOICE.

WILSONS MEADOW

Patented in 1773 by George Wilson for 9 acres
1783 tax - George Wilson 9 acres, Rewastico.

WILSONS MISTAKE

Patented on 1 Nov.1688 by James Weatherly for 200 acrs
28 July 1729 James Weatherly son of James, with wife Elizabeth Weatherly sold to Henry Carter 200 acres.
9 Mar.1729 Henry Carter with wife Margaret Carter sold to William Brown 200 acres
23 Feb.1770 Robert Brown eldest son of William Brown deceased sold to William Brown 100 acres.
1 Mar.1755 William Brown sold 200 acres to William Brown Jr.
1783 tax - Elizabeth Brown 200 acres Rewastico 100

WILTON

Patented on 23 Oct 1676 by James Cox for 550 acres
Rent Rolls 1666-1723 possessed by Thomas Cox 550 acres
13 July 1724 Thomas Cox sold to Ebenezer Handy 100 acres out of ALDERBURY and WILTON
1724 Thomas Cox willed to son Thomas and part to daughter Lydia Cox of the balance not sold to Ebenezer Handy.
10 May 1749 Hill Cox heir at law of Thomas Cox sold to Thomas Cox 50 acres
5 Feb.1754 Hill Cox and Thomas Cox sold to Robert Handy s/o Ebenezer Handy 80 acres of WILTON & PLUMPTONS SALTASH.
6 Apr.1751 Lydia Wright daughter of Thomas Cox sold to Jeremiah Wright 380 acres of WILTON & ALDERMANBERRY
20 Sep.1752 Lydia Wright widow of Jeremiah Wright and Jeremiah Wright eldest s/o Lydia sold to Lewis Disharoon 200 acres of WILTON & ALDERMANBERRY an agreement with John Handy to recover money owed from Lewis Disharoon.
1 Apr.1757 John Handy sold to Samuel Brereton for 5 shillings 215 acres of WILTON & ALDERMANBERRY
17 Oct.1758 John Handy of Kent Co.Del. sold to John Brereton of Somerset County 157 acres.
1764 Levin Disharoon son of Lewis Disharoon and Jane Cox Disharoon willed to daughters Mary Disharoon, Sarah Disharoon, Rebecca Disharoon, Jane Disharoon, Elizabeth Disharoon and Eunice Disharoon 200 acres.
1783 tax - John Brereton 157 acres, Wic.100
1783 tax - William Brereton 72 acres
1783 tax - James Brereton 130 acres with ALDERMANBERRY
1783 tax - Thomas Cox 50 acres
1783 tax - Ebenezer Handy 19 acres

23 May 1786 James Brereton gave to sons William Smith Brereton, James Brereton, Joshua Brereton, Joseph Brereton all lands, unnamed.
1797 Thomas Cox willed to sons John Cox and Aaron Cox.
5 July 1788 Levi King attorney for John Parker s/o George Parker and Jacob Parker son of John of Sussex Co.Del. sold to George Parker son of Elisha Parker of Worc.Co. 119 acres of ALDERBERRY, WILTON, PARKERS CHANCE.
16 Oct.1835 James Bounds and Susan L. Weatherly sold to Joseph C. Harris 282 acres part of WILTON, SALISBURY PLAIN, NEEDLESS COST, the lands of the heirs of Elihu Jackson and heirs of Levin Wilson.

WILTON

Patented on 6 Nov.1678 by Christopher Nutter for 100 acres
21 May 1683 Christopher Nutter and wife Mary Nutter sold to William Piper 100 acres.
Rent Rolls 1666-1723 possessed by Charles Nutter in right of the orphans of Capt. William Piper
1783 tax - Joseph Piper 100 acres, Rewastico
14 May 1801 John O. Twiford of Accoc.Co.Va. with wife Anna Twiford sold to Levin Farrington of Somerset Co. 1/4th part of lands of Joseph Piper deceased.
27 Jan.1803 John Stevens sold to Levin Farrington 50 acres, per right of Joseph Piper deceased.
13 Sep.1808 Levin Farrington mortgaged to Farmers Bank of Maryland.

WINDERS ADDTION

Patented on 9 Nov.1748 by Winder Dashiell on the east side of Wetipquin Creek for 102 acres.
1779 Winder Dashiell willed lands to son John Dashiell.
4 May 1771 George McGlemmy and William Winder sold to Samuel Ingersol 50 acres of WINDERS ADDN. & 50 acres of DORMANS CHANCE.
18 Dec.1789 George Dashiell sold to William McBryde 1/2. resurveyed to CONCLUSION 102 acres.

WINDERS CHOICE

Patented in 1765 by William Winder
8 Feb.1772 William Winder sold to Samuel Ingersol 50 acres
6 Aug.1772 John Toadvine with wife Ann Toadvine sold to John Cathell 9 acres of WINDERS CHANCE.
5 Nov.1778 I William Winder give bond to William McBryde and Charles Phillips of Som.Co. and Cecil Co., part 200 acres except 58 acres sold George McClemmy.
1808 William Winder willed to son William Henry Winder 20 acres
8 Apr.1806 John Winder of Northampton C. Va. coheir of William Winder sold all interest to William Winder of Som.Co., coheir.
9 Sep.1806 Levin Winder, Richard Henry Handy, Hetty W. Winder and Josiah Polk coheirs of William Winder sold to William Winder coheir, to settle estate
17 Apr.1807 Richard Henry Handy and Thomas Winder Handy sold rights to William Winder, coheir.
4 June 1807 William Henry Winder with wife Gertrude Winder, George

Dashiell with wife Esther Dashiell, William W. Handy and George D.S. Handy of Baltimore Co. sold all rights to William Winder
27 Oct.1809 William H. Winder of Baltimore City sold to Sarah McBryde from grandfather William Winder who left to children John Winder, William (father of afsd), Leah Winder and to the childrne of his his daughters Prissy Wilson (Jane Gemill and Polly Slemons) and Esther Polk, 284 acres.
18 Apr.1810 Rev. John R. Slemons with wife Polly Slemons sold all rights to Sarah McBryde for one dollar.

WINDSOR

Patented in 1685 by George Goddard for 100 acres
16 June 1704 George Goddard sold 50 acres to Griffith Jones.
16 Aug.1709 George Goddard sold 60 acres to Alexander Carlylse who conveyed on same date back to him.
1720 Griffith Jones of Albarmarle Co. N.C. sold to William Alexander
1732 William Alexander willed to son Liston Alexander tract 90 acres bought of Griffith Jones, unnamed.
1737 Liston Alexander gave lands unnamed to William Alexander son of Moses Alexander and to sister Agnes Alexander and heirs.

WINDSORS PLEASURE

Patented in 1814 by James Windsor for 26 acres

WINRIGHTS PROMISE

2 June 1759 Levin Winright sold to John Houston that William Winright willed to son Levin, part 50 acres.

WINTER QUARTER

Patented in 1734 by Moses Gordy for 50 acres
16 Apr.1737 Moses Gordy sold to Jeremiah Morris 50 acres
5 Mar.1743 Jeremiah Morris sold to Moses Gordy 50 acres
8 Mar.1748 Moses Gordy sold to Samuel Hall 50 acres
1768 Samuel Hall willed to son John Hall
1783 tax - John Hall 30 acres, Wic.100 Worc.Co.

WOLCOTES MANOR

Surveyed in 1674 by Lord Baltimore for 6000 acres
1783 this was confiscated property
24 Oct.1795 James Dean sold to Levi Dean part.
25 Jan.1806 Levi Dean with wife Margaret Dean, mother Elizabeth Dean sold to Thomas Badley with DEANS VENTURE
24 Jan.1806 Noble Dean of Dorc.Co. sold his interest to Thomas Badley.

WOLF PITT

Patented in 1796 by Jonathan Parsons 555 1/4 acres
1808 Jonathan Parsons willed to son Levin Parsons.

WOLF PIT HILL

Patented on 21 Aug.1761 by Jacob Spear for 42 acres
10 Mar.1770 Jacob Spear sold 42 acres to Levin Fletcher
1783 tax - Levin Fletcher 42 acres, Rewastico
19 Nov.1791 Levin Fletcher with wife Betty Fletcher sold 42 acres to Arthur Dashiell
19 Dec.1804 Arthur Dashiell with wife Esther Dashiell sold to James Donoho.

WOLF PIT RIDGE

Patented on 5 March 1768 by Benjamin Dashiell for 50 acres on the south side of Quantico Creek.
1783 tax - Mitchell Dashiell 50 acres
1789 Mitchell Dashiell son of Thomas Dashiell willed to grandson Nicholas Collier
5 Aug.1791 Ephraim Wilson, Esther Wilson, Isaac Nicholson, Peggy Nicholson and Nicholas Collier, Betty Collier and Nancy Collier sold 50 acres to William Bounds.
20 Dec.1803 John Gale sold to William Bounds and Douty Bounds under bond of dispute of lands with William Winder and Samuel Smith to convey all interest to 33 1/4 acres deeded John Gale on 1 Jan.1794.

WOLF RIDGE

Patented in 1758 by Peter Gordy for 50 acres.
3 Au.1805 Stephen Mitchell sold to William Gordy 34 acres

WOLFS QUARTER

Patented on 5 June 1688 by William Wright for 100 acres
Rent Rolls 1666-1723 possessed by Sarah Wright widow of William.
19 Jan.1709 Bloyce Wright son of William Wright and Sarah Wright sold to Peter Douty 50 acres.
1709 Peter Douty willed to Peter Furbush 50 acres
16 Mar.1729 Peter Furbush sold to John Larramore 50 acres.
9 Mar.1757 Levin Larramore and mother Mary Larramore sold to Teague Dickerson 50 acres.
22 Aug.1764 John Furbush sold to John Douty and Teague Dickerson 100 acres.
1783 tax - Samuel Fluellin 50 acres, Nanticoke 100
1783 tax - Abendego Green 50 acres
13 July 1789 Samuel Fluellin sold 100 acres to George Robertson
26 Mar.1793 Gillis Polk surviving trustee of Ephraim King and Samuel Fluellin brother of Richard C. Fluellin sold to Isaac Atkinson s/o Isaac.
4 May 1804 Isaac Atkinson sold to Samuel Dickerson.

WOLF TRAP RIDGE

Patented on 22 Nov.1701 by William Whittington who assigned to James Dashiell, for 50 acres
Rent Rolls 1666-1723 possessed by James Dashiell
1708 James Dashiell willed to son James 50 acres
1736 James Dashiell willed to son Winder Dashiell

1777 Winder Dashiell willed estate to wife Ann Dashiell and then to son John Dashiell.
1783 tax - John Dashiell 50 acres.
1786 resurveyed 14 1/2 acres to CONCLUSION by John Dashiell

WOLF TRAP NECK

Patented on 23 Nov.1673 James Dashiell for 50 acres
1697 James Dashiell willed to son James
Rent Rolls 1666-1723 possessed by James Dashiell
28 Oct.1672 resurveyed to DISCOVERY by Jesse Dashiell.

WOODFIELD

Patented on 2 Apr.1682 by Thomas Walker and Susanna Walker for 350 acres.
1680 Thomas Walker willed to son Thomas plantation on Wicomico River, wife Jane Walker, daughter Susanna Walker.
15 Sep.1733 Thomas Walker of Stepney parish and Sarah Walker his wife sold 100 acres to Isaac Mitchell taken out of a patented Thomas Walker and Susanna Walker now called MITCHELLS FIRST CHOICE
1 Dec.1731 Thomas Walker with wife Sarah Walker sold 100 acres to Ralph Lowe FIRST CHOICE out of WOODFIELD.
22 Mar.1744 Isaac Mitchell sold 100 acres to Richard Phillips.
4 Apr.1745 Richard Wallace sold to Ralph Lowe 169 acres left by will of Thomas Walker at Rewastico
19 Aug.1760 Ralph Lowe and wife Ann Lowe sold 100 acres to John Gupton of WOODFIELD & CASSOWAY
21 Jan.1769 Ralph Lowe and wife Ann Lowe, George Lowe and Robert Lowe sold 107 acres to Joshua Cottman
11 Feb.1775 John Lowe and wife Tabitha Lowe sold 119 1/2 acres to Benjamin Dashiell.
1783 tax - Charles Davis 100 acres, Rewastico
1783 tax - Jeanne Gupton 56 acres
1783 tax - Isaac Henry 119 acres
1783 tax - George Phillips 107 acres
22 May 1784 Charles Davis sold to Isaac Henry part of WOODFIELD called HENRYS MEADOW taken up by Hugh Henry father of Isaac that Charles Davis purchased and agreed to quitclaim to him.
29 Aug.1796 Benjamin Dashiell with wife Mary Dashiell of Baltimore Md. sold to Isaac Henry 121 1/4 acres.
1819 Ann Gupton willed to son Peter Gupton.

WOODGATE DOCK

Patented on 19 Mar.1672 by William Woodgate for 100 acres
1 Aug.1673 William Woodgate sold to James Chissell
10 June 1687 James Chissell with wife Abigail Chissell sold to John McClester 100 acres.
Rent Rolls 1666-1723 possessed by Capt. John McClester
1783 tax- John McClester 100 acres, Nanticoke 100

WOODSTOCK

Patented on 15 June 1679 by Robert Twilley for 200 acres

Rent Rolls 1666-1723 possessed by William Langsden 200 acres granted in 1681
1708 William Langsden willed to sons John Langsden, Spear Langsden and William Langsden.
1735 John Langsden willed to wife Mary Langsden.
1 Dec.1741 Spear Langsden gave interest to William Langsden
1 Dec.1741 John Langsden sold to Dicola Beaks 1/3 part.
12 June 1742 John Langsdale sold to William Langsdale all rights to that surveyed by Robert Twilley
12 June 1741 William Langsdale and John Langsdale sold 100 acres to Robert Twilley.
10 May 1760 John Langsdale sold to Daniel Short for 10 shillings 50 acres patented John 29 Feb.1724
2 June 1764 James Twilley and wife Mary sold 80 acres to Arthur Dashiell.
27 Mar.1769 James Twilley with wife Mary Twilley sold 20 acres to George Twilley.
5 Dec.1769 Arthur Dashiell resurveyed 81 acres to DASHIELLS CHANCE
1783 tax - John Langsdale 95 acres, Rewastico
1783 tax - George Twilley 20 acres
19 Jan.1798 Richard Goslee and wife Eleanor Goslee of Sussex Co.Del. sold to Arthur Dashiell Jr. all lands of John Langsdale, no name.
29 Apr.1803 Henry Langsdale son of John Langsdale sold to Esther Langsdale widow of John that he purchased as highest bidder of Henry Langsdale on 19 Apr.1803 60 acres. John Langsdale died intestate and left issue William Langsdale, John Langsdale, Henry Langsdale, Eleanor Langsdale, Elizabeth Langsdale, Joshua Whittington Langsdale, James Huett Langsdale and Robert Langsdale.

WOODVINE LOT

Patented in 1804 by James Dashiell and Ichabod Dashiell for 676 3/4 acres.
11 Dec.1803 Ichabod Dashiell and wife Priscilla Dashiell and Thomas Jones with wife Anna Jones, division of lands as Priscilla and Ann were granddaughters of Levin Dashiell and daughters of John Evans of Nicholas Evans.
10 Dec.1804 Thomas Jones of Thomas and wife Ann Dashiell Jones sold to George Robertson 192 acres.
18 Mar.1805 Alexander Stewart sold to Priscilla Dashiell during her life as single widow of William Francis Dashiell and Ichabod Dashiell her son.
18 Mar.1805 Priscilla Dashiell and Ichabod Dashiell sold to Alexander Stewart, land adjacent LONG HILL, no name.
20 March 1805 Ichabod Dashiell with wife Priscilla Dashiell sold to George Robertson 47 acres, 3 rods, 29 perches.
3 June 1806 Robert Leatherbury, sheriff to sell lands of Thomas Jones in right of his wife Ann D. Jones sold to George Aires Jr.
21 Sep.1807 Ichabod Dashiell with wife Priscilla Dashiell and Thomas Jones and wife Ann D. Jones sold to George Robertson.
27 Jan.1808 George Robertson sold to Thomas Jones and wife Ann Dashiell Jones.
1 July 1810 Thomas Jones and wife Ann Dashiell Jones sold to Sarah Evans for 5 shillings daughter of Levin Dashiell.

WOOD YARD

Patented in 1765 by John Kellum for 349 1/2 acres
1771 John Kellum willed to son Edward Kellum, to sell
2 Mar.1774 Edward Kellum sold 185 1/2 acres to Levin Follin of Dorcester County
1783 tax - Levin Follin 155 acres, Rewastico 100

WOOD YARD

Patented in 1766 by William Moore for 350 acres a resurvey of CROSS
1783 tax - William Moore Sr. 200 acres
1783 tax - William Moore son of William 85 acres
1783 tax - James Moore 55 acres
1783 tax - Aaron Sterling 35 acres
1783 tax - Beauchamp Hull 40 acres
1788 William Moore willed to wife Rachel Moore and to son James Moore part of lands unnamed.
29 Oct.1803 John Moore with wife Margaret Moore sold to John Byrd 287 3/4 acres of WOOD YARD, TICKFIELD & TURKEY COCK HILL.

WOOLHOPE

Patented on 6 June 1688 by George Collins for 75 acres
Rent Rolls 1666-1723 possessed by William Winright
1734 James Makemorie sold to Cannon Winright 75 acres
27 Jan.1755 James Winright and wife Nelly Winright sold 75 acres to Cannon Winright.
1783 tax - William Winright 55 acres, Nanticoke 100.
22 June 1796 William Winright, Solomon Winright, Nancy Winright and Jane Winright and James Riggin sold 64 acres to Henry Walston
1 Dec.1800 Chaplin Conway sold to George Aires Sr. 44 acres
1 Dec.1800 David Walston sold to Chaplin Conway 64 acres with PASTURAGE.

WORCESTER SIDE

Patented on 22 Jan.1754 by Robert Handy for 70 acres
1765 Robert Handy willed to son Ebenezer Handy 70 acres
1783 tax - Ebenezer Handy 70 acres.
21 Dec.1805 William Daley sold to Thomas Layfield, all.

WORST IS PAST

Patented in 1753 by Jonathan Stott for 132 1/2 acres
10 Feb.1762 Jonathan Stott sold 132 1/2 acres to Christopher Piper
13 Jan.1767 Christopher Piper sold to Esme Bayley of Worc.Co.
1783 tax - Esme Bayley, Rewastico, 132 1/2 acres

WOULD HAVE HAD MORE

Patented on 29 Apr.1680 by John Richardson for 50 acres
1783 tax - William Disharoon 50 acres, Wic.100, Worc.Co.
1792 William Disharoon willed friend James Bennett to sell.
9 Nov.1793 James Bennett sold to Elizabeth Disharoon 32 1/2 acres
5 Sep.1810 Benjamin Disharoon sold to Stephen Roach

25 Sep.1810 Stephen Roach with wife Nancy Roach sold to Benjamin Disharoon 8 acres with SECOND PURCHASE.

WRIGHTS ADVICE

Patented 16 June 1734 by George Clifton for 50 acres
1 July 1738 George Clifton with wife Mary Clifton sold 50 acres to George Goddard.

WRIGHTS CHOICE

Patented on 19 July 1689 by William Wright for 100 acres
Rent Rolls 1666-1723 possessed by the relict of William Wright 100 acres.
10 Jan.1719 Bloyce Wright heir of William sold to brothers William Wright and Solomon Wright
7 Dec.1720 Solomon Wright and wife Sarah Wright sold to Capt. Charles Ballard 127 1/2 acres of WRIGHTS CHOICE & WRIGHTS VENTURE, EASON.
1723 Charles Ballard willed land at Wicomico to son Charles, unnamed.
25 Jan.1734 William Wright and wife Judith Wright sold to William Nelson. Confirmed 6 Jan.1753 by Solomon Wright.
15 Sep.1742 Henry Ballard son of Charles Ballard sold to Isaac Handy.
25 Jan.1742 agreement of division of Cannon Winright to William Nelson.
1783 tax - Elizabeth Atkinson 50 acres, Nanticoke 100
1783 tax - James Winright 25 acres

WRIGHTS CONCLUSION

Patented in 1807 by John Dashiell for 1 1/8 cares

WRIGHTS ENLARGEMENT

Patented in 1771 by William Wright for 60 acres
23 Oct.1778 Isaiah Wright with wife Sarah Wright sold to Samuel Parker 60 acres
23 Oct.1778 Samuel Parker sold to Eli Showell 50 acres. back in woods from Salisbury Town.
12 Mar.1806 Eli Showell of Kent Co. Delaware sold to Hezekiah D. Shockley.

WRIGHTS VENTURE

Patented on 5 June 1688 by William Wright for 105 acres
10 July 1709 Bloyce Wright with wife Sarah Wright, heir of William sold to brothers William and Solomon Wright
7 Dec.1720 Solomon Wright and wife Sarah Wright sold 50 acres to Charles Ballard
25 Jan.1735 William Wright and wife Judith Wright sold part to William Nelson
15 Sep.1742 Henry Ballard s/o Charles Ballard sold to Isaac Handy 52 1/2 acres.

WRINGTON

Patented on 29 Nov.1672 by Samuel Sims for 200 acres who asssigned to Benjamin Cottman.

Rent Rolls 1666-1723 possessed by Benjamin Nesham by marrying the widow of Benjamin Cottman.
17 Sep.1728 Benjamin Cottman sold 100 acres to William Serman
3 Mar.1742 William Serman sold to John Gale for 5 shillings 12 acres
12 Nov.1743 William Serman sold 100 acres to John Gale.
20 Feb.1779 John Gale sold for 5 shillings to Henry Gale 100 acres.

WYLES FROLICK

see INCLOSED

WYLES VENTURE

Patented in 1747 by Jarrad Wyley for 72 acres

YEARS LAND

Patented on 27 Nov.1672 by John Bounds for 150 acres
Rent Rolls 1666-1723 possessed by John Bounds 150 acres
1700 John Bounds willed to sons William Bounds, John Bounds, James Bounds and daughter Ann Young.
1 Feb.1725 James Bounds with wife Ann Bounds sold part to Joseph McClester
26 Dec.1729 John Collins sold to Levin Dashiell, tract sold Collins by Jonathan Bounds
1731 Joseph McClester assigned to William Dashiell and Isabella Dashiell his wife.
2 May 1731 Jonathan Bounds with wife Frances Bounds sold to John Collins, turner.
22 Mar.1753 Levin Dashiell and wife Bridget Dashiell sold to Isaac Dashiell 100 acres.
18 Mar.1767 John Bounds sold to Jonathan Bounds 150 acres
1783 tax - William Bounds 75 acres
1783 tax - John Dority 37 acres, ADDITION to YEARS LAND.
25 June 1791 William Bounds sold to Isaac Nicholson 11 acres.
9 June 1794 Isaac Nicholson sold 11 acres to John Howard
10 Oct.1809 Robert Stewart of Baltimore sold to Alexander Stewart of Somerset County.
2 Nov.1809 John Stewart, James Evans and wife Elizabeth Evans, formerly Elizabeth Stewart, Nancy Stewart and Matty Stewart sold to Alexander Stewart.
1820 Douty Bounds sold 3 3/4 acres to William Arvey, on road from Quantico to Wetipquin.

YORK

Patented in 1760 by Thomas Hearn Jr. for 50 acres
25 Sep.1764 Thomas Hearn sold to Robertson Lingo 50 acres
1772 Robertson Lingo willed to son John Lingo 150 acres, unnamed.
25 Apr.1795 Elijah Lingo sold to George Waller, millwright of Sussex Co.Del. that was willed to heirs of William Lingo son of Robertson Lingo.

Abbott,Nathaniel:.........271,413
Absalom,Henry:.................281
Absalom,Mary:..................281
Acar,Aaron:....................306
Acworth,Amelia:................348
Acworth,Ann Manlove:..........385
Acworth,Ann:.................2,137
Acworth,Beauchamp:.............113
Acworth,Betsy:.................177
Acworth,Charles:.2,3,9,64,206,264
:..............................348
Acworth,Elizabeth:.....3,4,156,358
Acworth,Ephraim:...........5,9,326
Acworth,Esther:................426
Acworth,Henry:...5,12,156,231,237
Acworth,James:...2,3,5,31,206,262
:....................340,348,385
Acworth,John:................5,156
Acworth,Kittury:.................5
Acworth,Mary:........3,31,177,206
Acworth,Priscilla Francis:....348
Acworth,Priscilla:.............113
Acworth,Richard:2,3,4,5,65,81,137
:139,184,206,240,263,264,303,313
:...........348,385,392,423,426
Acworth,Samuel:...5,9,156,325,326
:..............................358
Acworth,Sarah:..........5,326,430
Acworth,Thomas:..2,3,9,90,206,264
:...........317,326,348,385,423
Acworth,Train:.2,9,42,113,206,258
:....................264,348,412,422
Acworth,William Harris:.......358
Acworth,William:.2,3,4,42,206,264
:..................348,412,413,422
Adams,Abraham:.................410
Adams,Alexander:...6.27,73,97,124
:133,138,140,157,215,356,382,388
:..........................393,410
Adams,Andrew:6,73,195,217,364,382
:....................401,410,430
Adams,Ann:......................6
Adams,Betty:...............126,186
Adams,David:...............377,410
Adams,Elizabeth:...............146
Adams,George:...46,97,157,182,263
:.........................290,321
Adams,Jacob:...................110
Adams,John Whittingham:.......195
Adams,John:..........6,318,382,430
Adams,Josiah:..................217
Adams,Leah:........133,138,377,393
Adams,Louisa:..................217
Adams,Mary:....................364
Adams,Morgan:...................11

Adams,Nathan:..............126,186
Adams,Phillip:.................410
Adams,Rebecca:.................212
Adams,Samuel:....27,124,212,410
Adams,Stephen:.................390
Adams,Sumner:.............5,6,11
Adams,Thomas:..................410
Adams,William:.78,133,138,169,195
:196,200,201,217,275,318,393,428
Addison,Jacob:...................6
Adkins,Betsy:..................150
Adkins,Betty:..................224
Adkins,David:..................108
Adkins,Elijah:.................108
Adkins,Ephraim:................116
Adkins,Hannah:.................108
Adkins,Henry J.:...............116
Adkins,Hunter:.................108
Adkins,Joseph:.................108
Adkins,Lear:...................420
Adkins,Mary:...............151,224
Adkins,Middleton:..............108
Adkins,Milby:........108,151,224
Adkins,Nimrod:.......108,150,224
Adkins,Rachel:........189,332,354
Adkins,Sarah:..................108
Adkins,Stanton:................108
Adkins,Stephen:................108
Adkins,William H.:.............116
Adkins,William:......108,250,363
Aires,Aaron:....................33
Aires,Betsy:....................34
Aires,Betty:....................12
Aires,George:12,34,99,100,132,207
:........281,356,413,438,445,446
Aires,Isaac:....................34
Aires,Jacob:.12,85,99,281,376,402
Aires,Littleton:..34,78,81,99,122
:...............181,281,335,376
Aires,Sally E.:................181
Aires,Sarah E.:.................78
Aires,Sarah Elligood:.........122
Alexander,Agnes:...............442
Alexander,Amos:................439
Alexander,Elizabeth:............28
Alexander,Henry:...............155
Alexander,John:.................28
Alexander,Liston:..............442
Alexander,Moses:...........343,442
Alexander,William:.........343,442
Allen,Betty:..............152,247
Allen,Francis:.................366
Allen,Hugh:.....................24
Allen,Jacob:...................350
Allen,Joseph:..........152,166,247

Allen,Robert:..................317
Allen,William Davis:..152,166,247
Allen,William:........152,182,247
Alpha,Joseph:..............3,4,198
Alpha,Mary:................4,198
Anderson,Cornelius:..16,58,77,332
Anderson,Ignatius:.............217
Anderson,Isaac:.............16,79
Anderson,James:.1,15,16,65,79,116
:126,164,309,310,332,345,362,363
:..............................421
Anderson,John H.:..........67,185
Anderson,John:..15,16,21,22,62,79
:157,184,185,191,305,340,348,406
:..............................423
Anderson,Joshua:............16,79
Anderson,Margaret:..............79
Anderson,Maria:................185
Anderson,Robert:...........79,295
Anderson,Thomas:...............184
Anderson,William:..79,120,242,257
:....................345,359,360
Andrews,Frances:...............344
Andrews,George:................344
Andrews,William:...........165,427
Ann,Mary:......................428
Ann,Sarah:.................87,238
Anno,Joseph:...................298
Anno,Nancy:....................298
Anno,William:..................298
Ansley,John:...................340
Argo,Alexander:.................91
Armatrader,Agnes:..83,240,252,260
Armatrader,Henry:..83,240,252,260
Armatrader,Tabitha:...........295
Arvey,William:.................448
Ascue,Grace:..........7,213,323
Ascue,Lydia:...............213,408
Ascue,Phillip:...7,212,213,323,408
:..............................410
Atkins,Elizabeth:..............269
Atkins,Middleton:..............275
Atkins,Robert:......122,123,261,269
Atkins,William:.......122,123,261
Atkinson,Benjamin:.15,127,184,185
:....................240,381,398
Atkinson,Elizabeth:19,139,209,210
:..................286,335,381,447
Atkinson,George D.:........36,273
Atkinson,George:...............145
Atkinson,Isaac:...19,55,72,90,139
:145,209,249,268,274,281,286,300
:....335,371,376,381,402,411,443
Atkinson,John:.................240
Atkinson,Priscilla:........72,145

Atkinson,Timothy:..........77,301
Atkinson,William:..........125
Austin,Ann:...................30
Austin,Betty:................359
Austin,Edward:..38,45,160,164,243
:...............271,422,426,427
Austin,Elijah:........20,216,435
Austin,Elizabeth:............391
Austin,George:........41,180,250
Austin,Hambleton:............359
Austin,Hamilton:......277,359,360
Austin,Harris:...............121
Austin,Hetty Sturgis:........360
Austin,Jane:.............69,110
Austin,Jesse:................127
Austin,John:...69,110,162,203,280
:............................339
Austin,Joseph:........41,250,426
Austin,Mary:.............160,427
Austin,Matthias:.............203
Austin,Nancy:................216
Austin,Nelly:............359,360
Austin,Polly:.................20
Austin,Priscilla:.........30,180
Austin,Prissey:..............216
Austin,Prissy:................20
Austin,Richard:..............169
Austin,Sarah:................121
Austin,William:..........127,391
Avery,John:...................20
Avery,Sarah:..................20
Aydelotte,John:..............265
Aylward,John:............356,388
Aylward,Joseph:..............388
Bacon,Dudson:.........92,140,244
Bacon,Elizabeth:..............92
Badley,Adah:.................169
Badley,Azariah:...............22
Badley,Charles:...155,168,192,306
:........................369,405
Badley,Clement:..............306
Badley,Dean:...21,107,168,192,398
Badley,Eli:...............23,405
Badley,Elijah:................22
Badley,Elizabeth:......65,353,405
Badley,Ephraim:..20,21,23,155,169
Badley,George:................21
Badley,Gideon:...1,22,177,192,350
:............................399
Badley,James Dean:.....43,65,405
Badley,James:..........23,25,350
Badley,John W.:...............22
Badley,John:21,23,108,168,192,398
:............................399
Badley,Mary:.................192
Badley,Milly:.................20
Badley,Polly:............155,369
Badley,Prissy:...............306
Badley,Samuel:............22,409
Badley,Severn:............23,155
Badley,Thomas:..22,108,259,409,442
Badley,William:.23,65,108,353,404
:............................405
Badley,Wilson:...............353
Bagwell,John:.................37
Bagwell,Tabitha:..............37
Bailey,Esme:..................78
Baine,Ann:...................148
Baine,Duncan:................148
Baine,Stephen:........148,403,429
Baker,Isaac:..................24
Baker,John:...................34
Balding,Caleb:........52,85,410
Balding,Sarah:...............410
Ballard,Ann:.................305
Ballard,Charles:..124,284,304,447
Ballard,Daniel:50,160,194,260,280
:............................417
Ballard,Eleanor:.........284,305
Ballard,Elizabeth:........79,305
Ballard,George:.......184,304,305
Ballard,Henry:........124,284,447
Ballard,Isabel:..............304
Ballard,James:...............299
Ballard,Levin:.79,126,225,299,305
:........................317,359,413
Ballard,Margaret:............305
Ballard,Matilda:.............305
Ballard,Priscilla:...........305
Ballard,Robert:..............304
Ballard,Sarah:....299,304,305,317
Ballard,,Levin:..............299
Banister,Charles:............149
Banks ,Henry:................409
Banks,Emery:.................350
Banks,Gabriel:...............350
Banks,Henry:46,54,120,159,161,186
:187,214,233,321,337,345,349,350
:............................409
Banks,Isaac:.................191
Banks,Isaiah:........186,233,349
Banks,Mary:..................214
Banks,Nancy:.................350
Banks,Polly:.................350
Banks,Priscilla:.............186
Banks,Robert:..46,186,214,349,366
Banks,Sarah:..................11
Banks,Sterling:..............349
Banks,Thomas:................349
Banks,Warren:............349,350
Bannister,Charles:........64,373
Barkley,Abraham:.............389
Barkley,Absalom:.............389
Barkley,Ann:.........356,357,388
Barkley,Aylworth:......26,356,357
Barkley,Charles:......136,194,357
Barkley,Esme:................389
Barkley,Henry W.:............357
Barkley,Henry Wallace:.136,357,38
Barkley,Henry:........136,357,389
Barkley,Isaac:...............389
Barkley,James:...............389
Barkley,John W.:.........356,388
Barkley,John:..26,136,194,207,356
:....................357,388,389
Barkley,Jonathan:........104,389
Barkley,Joseph:..............389
Barkley,Nancy:................26
Barkley,Rachel:..............389
Barnard,Joseph S.:...........256
Bartlett,Hannah:.............249
Bartlett,Pascoe:..........70,249
Bartlett,Sarah:..............249
Bartlett,Thomas:..............70
Bartley,Isaac:...............420
Bashaw,Andrew:...............159
Bashaw,Ann:..................204
Bashaw,Eleanor:..............204
Bashaw,Giles:............203,204
Bashaw,Graves:...............216
Bashaw,Jarrett:..........203,204
Bashaw,Joyles:...........203,204
Bashaw,Mary:.............159,216
Bashaw,Thomas:...........203,204
Bashaw,William:..........203,204
Bassett,Alice:...............116
Bassett,Benjamin:............205
Bassett,Betsy:...............205
Bassett,Elizabeth:...........204
Bassett,John:........116,183,205
Bassett,Samuel:..............371
Bassett,William:...28,116,189,204
:........................332,354
Bayley,Alice:................295
Bayley,Ann H.:...............417
Bayley,Ann:...............50,364
Bayley,Benjamin:....23,24,130,222
Bayley,Boadvine:..........24,43
Bayley,Boardvine:..23,131,281,364
:............................370
Bayley,Davis:.............23,327
Bayley,Edmund:...............295
Bayley,Edward:...............295
Bayley,Elias:...24,30,170,224,326
:............................364

Bayley,Esme:35,42,49,78,91,84,109
:133,146,158,200,201,204,278,319
:............356,395,429,430,446
Bayley,Fanny:..........198,304,403
Bayley,George:..23,77,127,130,131
:............170,198,304,403,429
Bayley,Henry E.:43,84,110,118,146
:........264,271,280,303,352,356
Bayley,Henry:.....133,146,267,356
Bayley,Isaiah:......23,130,170,326
Bayley,Jackson:.................23
Bayley,James Walker:..........130
Bayley,Jonah:.................354
Bayley,Jonathan:..126,311,327,347
Bayley,Josiah:..49,50,187,204,226
:............267,319,361,417,430
Bayley,Lesh:...................23
Bayley,Littleton:.............170
Bayley,Mary:...........77,311,317
Bayley,Mills:.............198,429
Bayley,Newton:.............23,170
Bayley,Obed:23,24,131,143,263,364
Bayley,Polly:..................24
Bayley,Richard:..............295
Bayley,Robins:............23,170
Bayley,Samuel Jackson:.23,190,222
:..........................228,327
Bayley,Samuel:.................23
Bayley,Sarah:23,43,84,110,118,264
:........271,280,303,327,352,356
Bayley,Sinah:...49,78,201,204,267
Bayley,Stephen:.............23,30
Bayley,Tabitha:..............150
Bayley,Thomas Biffen:.........150
Bayley,Thomas:.109,146,204,267,42
Bayley,Whittington:..........295
Bayley,Zachariah:.............317
Baynum,William:..............393
Beaks,Dicola:.................445
Beale,Thomas:..................34
Beard,Elisah:......161,242,243
Beard,James:32,87,161,190,242,252
Beard,Jarvis:.............40,143
Beard,John:.31,39,40,51,72,90,142
:............................344
Beard,Lewis:.31,32,39,142,245,344
Beard,Molly:.................161
Beard,Rachel:....32,39,40,142,344
Beard,Rebecca:................39
Beard,Sarah:.................242
Beard,Thomas:............161,242
Beard,William:.......161,242,350
Beauchamp,Ann:...............307
Beauchamp,Edmund:.............32
Beauchamp,Marcy:..............32

Beauchamp,Nancy:.............21,307
Beauchamp,Rachel:.............372
Beauchamp,Stephen:............372
Beauchamp,William:.........21,307
Bedsworth,Susanna:...........9,310
Bedsworth,Thomas:....9,12,237,310
Bedsworth,William:...9,12,237,310
:............................316
Bell,Anna M.:..............35,36
Bell,Ezekiel:...35,45,288,289,322
:............368,412,414,418,429
Bell,Isaac:....................35
Bell,Jacob:...........68,128,239
Bell,John H.:..................35
Bell,John:................35,249
Bell,Jonathan:........97,306,325
Bell,Judah:................68,239
Bell,Newell:..............35,249
Bell,Peter:...........35,47,361
Bell,Phillis:................418
Benjamin,Hetty:..............113
Bennett,Betsy:...........362,436
Bennett,Catherine:...........287
Bennett,Dorothy:..134,135,136,143
Bennett,Edward:37,100,101,125,135
:........................136,143
Bennett,Eli:.........15,243,355
Bennett,Elisha:...............37
Bennett,Elizabeth:..29,37,100,101
:............................362,412
Bennett,George:....68,108,143,350
Bennett,Hambleton E.:........143
Bennett,Hamilton B.:.........350
Bennett,James:..10,16,19,37,39,67
:..95,96,143,173,189,195,206,214
:224,248,288,336,371,374,386,412
:........................432,446
Bennett,Jane:................336
Bennett,Jean:................143
Bennett,John:........100,141,325
Bennett,Jonathan N.:..........37
Bennett,Joshua:.15,29,101,243,355
Bennett,Levin:.15,28,29,30,36,100
:........101,179,243,355,362,436
Bennett,Littleton:...........126
Bennett,Peter:...............325
Bennett,Richard:.36,37,58,116,326
:........................336,432
Bennett,Sarah:...........125,136
Bennett,Thomas:..............287
Bennett,Turpin:......15,243,355
Bennett,William:..134,136,143,248
:............................287
Benson,Thomas:.........7,37,213
Benston,George:..............163

Benston,Henry:................214
Benston,James:................214
Benston,John:.................260
Benston,Mary:.................427
Benston,Rebecca:..............163
Benston,Thomas:...............213
Betharde,Elizabeth:...........220
Bethards,Henry S.:............220
Bethards,Jarman:.....219,220,398
Bethards,Martha:..............220
Bethards,Mary:................117
Bethards,Samuel:..........220,398
Bethards,William Jarman:..220,398
Bethards,William:.116,117,346,438
Betts,Bridget:................150
Betts,Francis:.................38
Betts,George:......38,150,357,427
Betts,Mary:...................427
Bevans,John:..................177
Bevans,Thomas:.............71,415
Bevans,William:................52
Bewdly,Esther:................360
Biggans,John:..................38
Bigland,Richard:..............86
Biglands,John:..383,14,93,195,406
Biglands,Richard:......17,261,383
Biglands,William:..........81,383
Billings,Mary:................405
Billings,Robert:..............405
Bird,Elgate:...................88
Bird,Thomas:...............42,86
Birkhead,William:41,42,49,262,385
Bishop,John:..................341
Black,Charles William:........37
Black,Sarah:...................37
Black,William:................336
Blizard,Richard:..............42
Blizzard,John Parsons:.......311
Blizzard,Rackliffe:...........347
Blizzard,Richard:.............347
Bloodsworth,John:..........66,185
Bloodsworth,Margaret Lucas:....66
Bloodsworth,Margaret:........185
Bloyes,Thomas:...........124,414
Bluett,John:.................247
Bluett,Miarian:..............247
Boardman,Francis:........203,246
Boardman,Graves:.....203,204,247
Boardman,Samuel:.........246,247
Boardman,Susannah:...........204
Body,Frances:................401
Body,Peter:................55,401
Bole,George:.................321
Bond,Priscilla:......110,164,352
Bond,William B.:.............164

Bond,William:..............110
Bonnewell,Hall:..........309,362
Bonnewell,Marv:......164,309,362
Bonnewell,Michael Hall:..164,309
:.................310,362,363
Booth,George:..............61,92
Booth,John:....................61
Booth,Margaret:..........267,430
Booth,Peter:.............267,430
Booth,William:................61
Boston,Henry:........66,190,252
Boston,Nancy:........66,190,252
Botham,John:.................359
Boucher,Frances:.........173,408
Boucher,James:...........173,408
Boucher,John:................408
Boucher,Thomas:..............173
Bouger,James:............53,301
Bouger,John:.............176,351
Bouger,Mary:..................53
Boulve,Ann:..................334
Boulve,Henrietta:............334
Bounds,Ann:......221,355,390,448
Bounds,Anne:.................390
Bounds,Bridget:..............279
Bounds,Doubty:...............103
Bounds,Douty:..66,119,238,251,407
:......................443,448
Pounds,Eleanor:..............339
Bounds,Elizabeth:............372
Bounds,Frances:..............448
Bounds,George W.:.....44,191,431
Pounds,George Washington:....243
Bounds,George:.......175,280,340
Bounds,Hester:...............228
Bounds,Jacob:.............44,432
Pounds,James E.:.............339
Bounds,James H.:.............228
Bounds,James:...44,45,65,66,69,73
:110,134,168,228,279,280,290,292
:...301,339,355,362,372,441,448
Bounds,Jehu:........17,87,321,361
Bounds,Jesse:.................44
Bounds,John:..14,17,45,93,124,134
:..162,168,280,298,321,339,355,4
:..............................8
Bounds,Jonathan:...25,44,51,66,90
:...................124,390,448
Bounds,Jones:............243,390
Bounds,Joseph:.......17,27,76,124
Bounds,Magaret:...............44
Bounds,Mary:.........119,238,307
Bounds,Matilda:............44,66
Bounds,Nancy:14,87,93,134,162,298
:............................361

Bounds,Peggy:.................66
Bounds,Rachel:...........191,431
Bounds,Richard Stevens:....25,51
Bounds,Richard:...161,228,229,242
:............................243
Bounds,Samuel T.:........301,390
Bounds,Sarah:.................90
Bounds,Tabitha:...............17
Bounds,Temperance:...........358
Bounds,Thomas J.:............361
Bounds,Train A.:..............17
Bounds,William A.D.:.........358
Bounds,William Richard:......228
Bounds,William:.27,44,45,65,66,73
:119,160,161,168,171,228,229,238
:242,243,251,268,279,280,290,301
:307,315,321,339,355,369,373,425
:........................443,448
Bounds,Zipporah:.............290
Bowden,John:........28,225,395
Bowden,Peter:.......28,225,395
Bowden,Susanna:.........225,395
Bowditch,Ann:..............4,113
Bowditch,Joanna:..........4,113
Bowditch,Robert:...........4,113
Bowdith,Robert:..........258,418
Bowdoin,John:..............37,88
Bowdoin,Peter:.......28,37,38,88
Bowdoin,Susanna:...........38,88
Bowdoin,Susannah:.............28
Bowen,John:...................57
Bowen,Luke:...................57
Bowland,William:.........181,312
Bowler,John:.................279
Bowles,Martin:.........242,285
Bowman,John:.............152,247
Bowman,William:..............211
Boyce,Daniel:............182,408
Boyce,John:..................408
Boyce,Joseph:.....46,182,291,408
Boyce,William:...............256
Bozman,Elizabeth:............426
Bozman,John:.................214
Bozman,Joseph:...............427
Bozman,Mary:.................289
Bozman,Sarah:................214
Bozman,William:..............214
Bradford,John:...............393
Bradford,Sarah:..............393
Bradley,Ann:..................75
Bradley,Ely:.................129
Bradley,Gideon:..............341
Bradley,James:.............75,76
Bradley,Jesse A.D.:..........108
Bradley,Jesse:................16

Bradley,Priscilla:...........341
Bradley,Sarah:................76
Bradley,William:..............75
Brady,Francis:...............254
Bratcher,Hambleton:..........270
Brattan,Adam:..........4,385,423
Brattan,Ann Maria:...........271
Brattan,Elizabeth:.........4,423
Brattan,Jesse:............45,313
Brattan,John:................326
Brattan,Joshua:........3,139,333
Brattan,Mary Ann:............422
Bratten,Ann Maria:...........422
Bratten,Anna Marie:..........408
Bratten,Elizabeth:...........385
Bratten,James:.......221,273,420
Bratten,Jesse:...........186,313
Bratten,Joshua:......221,273,420
Bratten,Mary Ann:............271
Bratten,Mary:............221,273
Bready,James:................289
Bready,Rebecca:......45,108,289
Bready,Sophia:............45,289
Brereton,Diana:..............382
Brereton,Grariana:...........427
Brereton,Henry:...............73
Brereton,James:.......14,440,441
Brereton,John:...........382,440
Brereton,Joseph:.........382,441
Brereton,Joshua:.............441
Brereton,Nancy:..............144
Brereton,Samuel:..........14,440
Brereton,Sarah:..........413,435
Brereton,Scott:..........270,382
Brereton,Thomas:...73,229,248,270
:........................344,427
Brereton,William Smith:......441
Brereton,William:.144,222,270,364
:................382,413,435,440
Brewer,John:.................345
Brewington,George:...........360
Brewington,James:.............14
Brewington,Sarah:........151,224
Brewington,Smith:.........71,161
Brewington,William:14,93,151,224
:............................360
Briddell,Benjamin:...........153
Briddle,David:...............431
Bridell,David:...............393
Bridell,Elihu:...............151
Brinkley,William:.............41
Brittingham,Isaac S.:........314
Brittingham,Jarman:.......27,46
Brittingham,Jeremiah:........346
Brittingham,John:.........34,183

Brittingham,Joseph:...223,319,320
Brittingham,Mary:.189,223,332,354
Brittingham,Polly:............320
Brittingham,Sally:........189,332
Brittingham,Sarah:........189,354
Brittingham,Truitt:.........27,46
Brittingham,William:......203,346
Broadwater,Caleb:.............177
Broadwater,William:...........177
Brooks,Ann:...................269
Brooks,Thomas:................269
Broughton,John:...............149
Brown,Betsy:..........139,201,202
Brown,Charles:................429
Brown,David:..............223,388
Brown,Edward:.........139,201,202
Brown,Elizabeth:......202,340,440
Brown,George:..................24
Brown,James:............15,47,226
Brown,John W.:.................47
Brown,John:.47,74,181,223,226,287
:.................300,326,411,430
Brown,Robert:..47,168,300,311,430
:.............................440
Brown,Sarah:...........15,47,287
Brown,Sidney:.................373
Brown,Thomas:...47,94,133,213,223
:.............................323
Brown,William:.....47,147,300,440
Brumble,John:..................99
Brumbley,Benjamin:............276
Buchannan,Betsy:..............359
Buchannan,James:..328,358,359,361
Bulger,Margaret:..............359
Buly,Esther:..................320
Burbage,Elias:................167
Burbage,Samson:...............167
Burbage,Thomas:...........88,167
Burkum,Elizabeth:.............184
Burk,William:.................316
Burke,Hannah:.............139,286
Burko,Tobias:.............139,286
Burkum,John:..................184
Burkum,Lucy:..................184
Burkum,Robert:................184
Burkum,Roger:.............157,184
Burroughs,Arthur:.............290
Burroughs,Asher:..............255
Burroughs,Joshua:.............255
Butler,Thomas:................351
Byrd,Benjamin H.:..........87,147
Byrd,Benjamin Harvey:.112,260,296
:.........................299,416
Byrd,Benjamin:....111,295,296,311
Byrd,Catherine:...........126,225
Byrd,Elgate:..................126
Byrd,Henrietta:21,192,214,255,347
Byrd,Jesee:...................181
Byrd,Jesse:...............186,414
Byrd,John:.50,75,76,78,88,103,105
:133,138,143,154,169,201,262,304
:........318,328,356,410,415,446
Byrd,Margaret:...76,78,88,103,105
:.............201,262,304,318,328
Byrd,Polly:....................85
Byrd,Sarah Ann:...........187,300
Byrd,Sarah:........108,126,181,186
Byrd,Thomas:...49,50,83,87,88,109
:126,180,181,186,187,225,260,296
:299,300,311,317,328,356,395,416
:.............................428
Byrd,William:.................414
Cahoon,Benjamin:...............50
Cahoon,Betsy:.................153
Cahoon,Lanta:..................50
Cahoon,Nathan:................380
Cahoon,Peter:.................153
Cahoon,Sally:.................153
Caldwell,Andrew:......284,329,340
Caldwell,Ann:.................278
Caldwell,Elizabeth:...........157
Caldwell,Elverton:............112
Caldwell,James:16,120,141,142,173
:.................237,263,322,357
Caldwell,Jane:................322
Caldwell,John Joshua:.........262
Caldwell,John:..18,24,25,51,60,72
:110,112,157,173,209,225,228,233
:234,235,261,262,277,337,338,359
:............363,382,383,390,392
Caldwell,Joshua:..18,25,51,60,112
:.................157,235,256,261
Caldwell,Margaret:...18,24,51,329
Caldwell,Mary:............174,390
Caldwell,Patrick:.............174
Caldwell,Rachel:...............51
Caldwell,Robert:....18,51,92,112
Caldwell,Samuel:.......35,249,278
Caldwell,Sarah:...............235
Caldwell,Spencer:.............390
Caldwell,William:.....235,359,383
Calloway,Ann Peter:............52
Calloway,Ann:.................221
Calloway,Benjamin:...52,53,86,380
Calloway,Clammond:............221
Calloway,Clement:.............429
Calloway,Ebenezer:.........52,67
Calloway,Edward:.........355,401
Calloway,Elizabeth:...........355
Calloway,Isaac:......52,324,401
Calloway,Isaiah:..............197
Calloway,John:...52,67,86,171,183
:.........................310,434
Calloway,Joseph:...........17,86
Calloway,Joshua:...........86,171
Calloway,Levin:...........171,244
Calloway,Louther:.............401
Calloway,Matthew:.............221
Calloway,Moses:...........221,429
Calloway,Peter:.52,86,183,275,344
:.........................351,364
Calloway,Priscilla:............86
Calloway,Rachel:...............86
Calloway,Samuel:.....52,53,86,343
Calloway,Sarah:................86
Calloway,Thomas:...............52
Calloway,William:.........221,429
Campbell,William:.............220
Cannady,Hugh:..................54
Cannon,Allie:..................56
Cannon,Augustus:...54,160,194,232
:.........................233,280
Cannon,Cloe:..................232
Cannon,Ebenezer:..............146
Cannon,Elijah:.............55,146
Cannon,Frances:...............119
Cannon,James:..............55,146
Cannon,John:...................55
Cannon,Joseph:........55,375,415
Cannon,Judith:................119
Cannon,Mary:54,98,109,232,233,245
:.....................299,417,435
Cannon,Matthew:98,109,245,434,435
Cannon,Matthias:...............98
Cannon,Sarah:.................253
Cannon,Stephen:..54,55,56,119,122
:.........................127,294
Cannon,Thomas:...54,55,98,109,232
:.............233,253,271,355,422,435
Cannon,William:...........299,417
Cannon,Wingate:...............146
Cantwell,Nicholas:............423
Carberry,Thomas:..............121
Carbury,Thomas:...............121
Cardiff,Christopher:..........158
Carey,Edward:..................56
Carey,Henry M.:...............115
Carey,Hezekiah:.57,82,153,209,230
:.............................372
Carey,John Henry:........17,57,283
Carey,Jonathan:...............287
Carey,Joshua:.................115
Carey,Levin:....56,57,244,372,436
Carey,Lidy:...............244,436
Carey,Priscilla:..............339

Carey,Rachel:................436
Carey,Rebecca:...............435
Carey,Richard:................56
Carey,Samuel:............244,436
Carey,Solomon:...............436
Carey,Thomas:.56,57,76,89,209,244
:........................287,436
Carey,William:...........287,436
Carlylse,Adam:......7,116,211,405
Carlylse,Alexander:.7,211,405,442
Carlylse,William:............116
Carlysle,Alexander:..........116
Carmean,Louther:.............242
Carmichael,Elizabeth:....258,420
Carmichael,John:.3,64,256,258,349
:............................420
Carmichael,Levin:...4,258,349,420
Carmichael,Prissy:...........420
Carmichael,Rachel:.......349,420
Carr,Catherine:..........327,397
Carr,John:...........318,327,397
Carroll,Charles:.............426
Carroll,Henry James:.........275
Carroll,James:...............426
Carter,Aaron:................308
Carter,Eunice:...............418
Carter,George:................57
Carter,Henry:................440
Carter,Isaac:................205
Carter,Jacob:................286
Carter,John:.................205
Carter,Margaret:.............440
Carter,Mary:.................430
Carter,Phillip:......366,409,430
Carter,Samuel:........45,289,418
Carter,Sarah:................205
Carter,Unice:.............45,289
Cathell,Clement:.............121
Cathell,Daniel:..........228,276
Cathell,David:..59,60,104,105,121
:147,149,163,222,224,276,278,279
:............289,290,334,340,422
Cathell,Elizabeth:..1,279,394,422
Cathell,George:...175,181,217,289
:............................394
Cathell,Haste:...............121
Cathell,James M.:....276,278,394
Cathell,James Martin:....175,289
Cathell,James T.:............334
Cathell,James Thompson:......334
Cathell,James:1,59,60,104,163,222
:........................223,290
Cathell,Jane:................276
Cathell,John:..60,104,149,150,175
:181,217,222,223,224,250,253,276
:278,289,290,293,330,349,360,361
:................388,394,403,441
Cathell,Jonathan:.121,163,228,272
:............................276
Cathell,Joshua:59,104,175,222,276
:........................290,334
Cathell,Josiah:..............163
Cathell,Levi:..60,104,121,147,163
:........175,217,289,290,349,394
Cathell,Mary Jane:...........361
Cathell,Matty:............60,163
Cathell,Nancy S.:............163
Cathell,Nancy:............60,334
Cathell,Rebecca:.........147,163
Cathell,Thomas:..............121
Cathell,William:.............121
Catherwood,Robert:...........158
Caton,Thomas:............21,184
Caudrey,Abraham:.............252
Caudrey,Betty:...............296
Caudrey,John:.............78,252
Caudrey,William:.............296
Causey,Isabel:............32,297
Causey,Patrick:32,123,297,316,409
Cave,Benjamin:...............129
Cave,Henry:..................129
Cave,John:...................129
Chaille,Peter:...............341
Chaille,Scarborough:.........341
Chain,Alexander:...........6,395
Chain,Isaiah:..............6,395
Chain,Sarah:...............6,395
Chamberlain,John:.............46
Chamberlin,John:.............291
Chambers,John:........60,61,392
Chambers,Mary:................61
Chambers,Nancy:...............61
Chambers,Peggy:..............119
Chambers,Rachel:..........61,119
Chambers,Richard:............223
Chambers,Sarah:..............223
Chapell,Thomas:..............234
Chapley,Bridget:.............272
Chapman,John:.................64
Chapman,Paris:................64
Chapman,Rebecca:..............64
Chase,Samuel:................304
Chattam,Francis:.........49,58,116
Chattam,James:...............243
Chattam,John:26,49,58,116,223,243
Chattam,Josiah:...............58
Chattam,Nancy:...............319
Chattam,Priscilla:...........243
Chattam,William Parks:.......319
Cheeseman,John:..........258,418
Cheeseman,Rachel:........258,418
Chenev,Ware:.........182,229,395
Chissell,Abigail:............444
Chissell,James:..............444
Christopher,Adam:......5,261,431
Christopher,Belitha:.........437
Christopher,Benjamin:.118,119,208
Christopher,Betty:....59,222,290
Christopher,Eben:......5,275,431
Christopher,Ebenezer:........351
Christopher,Elijah:.......29,437
Christopher,Elizabeth:...119,208
Christopher,George:........5,431
Christopher,Hannah:......119,208
Christopher,Jacob:...122,123,261
Christopher,John:.1,46,71,280,281
:............................437
Christopher,Joseph:..118,119,208
Christopher,Matthias:........111
Christopher,Polly:...........351
Christopher,Sarah:...........280
Christopher,Stephen:.........277
Christopher,Tubman:........5,431
Clark,Betsy:.................359
Clark,Daniel:................261
Clark,Edward:.............72,134
Clark,James:.................359
Clark,Joanna:..................4
Clark,John:...................72
Clark,Rebecca:.............4,113
Clarkson,Cox:................328
Clay,John:....................72
Claywell,Moses:..............384
Clements,Francis T.:.........345
Clifton,George:..............447
Clifton,Mary:................447
Clowes,John:.................129
Cochran,David:...............270
Cochran,Rebecca:.............270
Collier,Ann:..55,119,163,238,247
:............263,307,357,373,411
Collier,Betsy C.:.............87
Collier,Betsy:........66,190,252
Collier,Betty:.79,119,307,411,443
Collier,Douty:39,65,66,79,119,126
:........136,238,278,279,411,421
Collier,Ebenezer:...41,74,119,250
:........................279,287
Collier,Elizabeth:.........56,88
Collier,Esme:.................66
Collier,Francis:....66,87,190,252
Collier,George Betts:...13,74,122
:............................229
Collier,George:..55,74,79,119,120
:........122,162,163,238,287,307

Collier,Helena:.............279
Collier,James:............74,122
Collier,John F.:...............69
Collier,John:.......55,162,238
Collier,Levin D.:...45,63,387,422
:......................427,428
Collier,Martha:..55,74,79,120,162
:........................163,307
Collier,Mary Evans:...........56
Collier,Mary:............74,122
Collier,Nancy:...............443
Collier,Nicholas E.:......87,238
Collier,Nicholas Evans:.56,87,229
:...........................238
Collier,Nicholas:............443
Collier,Nicholson:...........286
Collier,Priscilla:............56
Collier,Rachel:........13,229,394
Collier,Rebecca:..............56
Collier,Robert:.28,39,65,66,67,74
:..88,99,119,122,126,152,230,241
:278,279,287,307,357,373,411,428
Collier,Thomas:......6,74,247,411
Collier,William:..............67
Collins,Andrew:75,221,226,266,363
:...........................439
Collins,Charles:..............75
Collins,Edward:........17,305,306
Collins,Eli:.................360
Collins,Elizabeth:............75
Collins,George:....75,220,335,446
Collins,Isaac:...............398
Collins,James:........166,228,260
Collins,John:.9,17,30,63,64,66,94
:169,231,252,254,306,338,363,374
:...........................448
Collins,Joseph:.9,30,75,77,94,167
:........254,275,325,326,338,362
Collins,Margaret:......9,75,77,167
Collins,Rachel:...............75
Collins,Rebecca:.............390
Collins,Samuel:..........17,234
Collins,Sarah:...........77,231
Collins,Solomon:............169
Collins,Tabitha:.............222
Collins,Thomas:......324,390,391
Collins,Timothy:..............76
Collins,William:..221,222,243,266
:...........................390
Connerly,John:...........350,414
Connerly,Thomas:..221,248,350,414
Conway,Ann:...132,144,188,315,378
Conway,Chaplin:...132,144,187,188
:..............281,315,378,446
Conway,Eve:..................393

Conway,John S.:......141,300,328
Conway,John Span:........272,273
Conway,John:.................212
Conway,Span:.................272
Conway,Susannah:.............272
Conway,William:..............393
Cooksey,John:................183
Cooper,Abraham:........33,192,193
Cooper,Ann:..................306
Cooper,Elender:..............259
Cooper,Elijah:...............214
Cooper,Gabriel:........33,305,306
Cooper,Isaac:...33,85,125,178,190
:..................191,340,416
Cooper,James:................214
Cooper,Jane:.................214
Cooper,Joan:.................214
Cooper,John:..............33,191
Cooper,Levin:........33,192,306
Cooper,Martin:......169,192,405
Cooper,Mary:.................192
Cooper,Nancy:.................33
Cooper,Polly Badley:.........405
Cooper,Polly:...155,169,192,369
Cooper,Samuel:..33,83,168,169,191
:..............192,259,369,405
Cooper,Severn B.:.....155,192,369
Cooper,Severn:..........169,405
Cooper,Silas:.............85,89
Cooper,Thomas:...33,83,85,168,191
:...........................192
Cooper,William:...........33,420
Cope,David:..................183
Cope,John:................15,183
Cope,Jonathan:...............227
Cope,Margaret:...............183
Cope,Phoebe:.................183
Cope,William:................131
Copes,Elizabeth:..............77
Copes,Thomas:.................77
Corby,David:.................238
Corby,Edward:.............87,238
Corby,Matthew:...............238
Corby,Sarah Ann:..........87,238
Cordrey,Covington:...12,40,51,143
:..................287,344,411
Cordrey,Daniel:.13,56,229,340,394
Cordrey,David:........158,229,312
Cordrey,Douty:...............411
Cordrey,Elizabeth:............33
Cordrey,Henry:......12,33,411,439
Cordrey,Jacob:............87,204
Cordrey,John:.51,52,78,87,200,275
:...........................392
Cordrey,Mary:................275

Cordrey,Morgan:......78,200,340
Cordrey,Rachel:.....12,56,229,394
Cordrey,Salathiel:...........439
Cordrey,Thomas:.........159,439
Corkill,Henry:...............196
Corkwell,Henry:..............205
Costin,Ahab:..................25
Coston,Abigail:..............127
Coston,Ahab:.........127,331,381
Coston,Jacob:.................88
Coston,Matthias:..............21
Cottingham,Charles:..........230
Cottingham,John:.............243
Cottingham,Mary:.............416
Cottingham,Thomas:...........416
Cottingman,Thomas:............20
Cottman,Mary:................423
Cottman,Ann:.................141
Cottman,Arminta:..........35,36
Cottman,Benjamin:38,59,61,141,447
:...........................448
Cottman,Bridget:.............233
Cottman,Ebenezer:....141,357,423
Cottman,Hester:..............102
Cottman,James:................35
Cottman,John:................225
Cottman,Joseph S.:...........286
Cottman,Joseph:......61,102,285
Cottman,Joshua:..........59,444
Cottman,Lazarus:.............195
Cottman,Mary:.............61,423
Cottman,Nathan:..............423
Cottman,Susannah:.............59
Cottman,William:61,89,102,144,195
:.......................222,285
Cotton,Agnes:............180,341
Cotton,John:........180,340,341
Coulbourn,Comfort:...........426
Coulbourn,Elijah:............360
Coulbourn,Hetty:.............360
Coulbourn,Isaac:...78,137,200,426
Coulbourn,Margaret:..........416
Coulbourn,Mary:..............426
Coulbourn,Samuel:............403
Coulbourn,William J.:........154
Coulbourn,William Johnson:167,276
Coulbourn,William:........240,416
Covington,Abraham:............89
Covington,Isaac:......89,163,433
Covington,Jane:..............252
Covington,Jesse:.............338
Covington,John R.:...........301
Covington,John:......89,252,301
Covington,Mary:..............252
Covington,Matilda:...........301

Covington,Nehemiah:....75,252,287
Covington,Phillip:...38,74,75,122
:............................427
Covington,Priscilla:....38,75,427
Covington,Samuel:..89,213,257,301
Covington,Thomas:..............89
Cox,Aaron:..................92,441
Cox,Allen:.....................105
Cox,Ann:.......................251
Cox,Elizabeth:.................327
Cox,George:.....................93
Cox,Hill:..............14,327,440
Cox,Isabelle:..................285
Cox,James:.....................440
Cox,John:..........92,251,285,441
Cox,Lydia:.....................440
Cox,Moses:..................87,88
Cox,Rebecca:.........93,157,261
Cox,Southv:.....................87
Cox,Thomas:.13,14,86,87,92,93,105
:157,187,270,327,328,354,382,440
:..............................441
Cox,Whitty:.............86,87,321
Craig,Edward:..................368
Craig,John:...........277,295,358
Craig,William:.................368
Cranfield,Isaiah:..............369
Cranfield,Love:................369
Crawford,Esther:...............230
Crawford,George:...........152,247
Crawford,Henry:..........1,69,230
Crawford,John:.............152,247
Craycroft,John:................430
Crocker,David:.................270
Crocker,Rebecca:...............270
Crockett,Alice:66,139,217,218,268
Crockett,Benjamin Shiles:.....360
Crockett,Charles:...............11
Crockett,Elender:..............300
Crockett,Elizabeth:94,110,300,326
Crockett,John:119,248,272,273,300
:....................307,326,328
Crockett,Levin:................427
Crockett,Nehemiah:.66,139,217,248
:....................268,300,376
Crockett,Richard:...11,94,110,139
:....157,272,300,326,328,346,378
Crockett,Robert:..125,249,273,300
Crockett,Shiles:..174,273,322,427
Croney,James:...................94
Croney,Margaret:................94
Crookshank,Charles:.......152,247
Cropper,Bela:..................276
Cropper,Mary:..................276
Crouch,Ann:................95,205

Crouch,Elizabeth:..............115
Crouch,Isaac:..................205
Crouch,John:...52,115,200,205,324
Crouch,Mary:....................95
Crouch,Robert:......52,95,115,324
Crouch,William:............288,371
Culver,Aaron:...................40
Culver,Catherine:.............369
Culver,Ebe:....................153
Culver,George:.............23,121
Culver,Ibby:..........153,431,432
Culver,John:...40,153,276,431,432
Culver,Mary:...............40,439
Culver,Moses:..............40,190
Culver,Nancy:............153,432
Culver,Nathan:...29,75,83,111,153
:175,196,199,224,240,260,275,276
:288,304,316,329,367,368,404,412
:....................413,432,439
Culver,Thomas:........97,180,369
Cunningham,Daniel:.............27
Curle,Joshua:..................296
Curle,Rosa:....................296
Curry,John:....................269
Curry,William:.................269
Cutler,John:..............319,359
Dakes,Daniel:...................71
Dakes,Dinah:..............133,366
Dakes,Selby:..............133,366
Dale,Jacob:...................209
Dale,James:...................209
Dale,John:....................209
Dale,Joshua:..................209
Dale,Mary:....................209
Daley,Keziah:..........93,105,295
Daley,Molly:..................320
Daley,Samuel:............295,320
Daley,William:.93,105,295,320,413
:.............................446
Daltrieu,Lewis:........47,262,426
Darby,Benjamin:................29
Darby,Custis:.................306
Darby,Daniel:.................341
Darby,Elizabeth:..............340
Darby,Mary:...........28,100,306
Darby,Sally:.............362,436
Darby,Sarah:.........28,100,436
Darby,Thomas:......28,100,101,399
Darby,Walter:..............28,100
Darby,William:.28,100,101,362,436
Dashiell,Alice:...............119
Dashiell,Ann:...61,81,113,255,411
:.............................444
Dashiell,Anney:................65
Dashiell,Annie:..........156,386

Dashiell,Arthur:..49,62,80,95,100
:101,102,103,130,165,166,174,198
:215,236,237,240,241,262,304,305
:........323,385,426,427,443,445
Dashiell,Asa:.................237
Dashiell,Benjamin F.A.C.:.112,138
:........264,276,293,297,336,372
Dashiell,Benjamin Fred.A.:....179
Dashiell,Benjamin J.:..........69
Dashiell,Benjamin:...59,69,84,113
:132,175,240,281,330,360,372,375
:....................410,443,444
Dashiell,Betty:..........8,56,79,80
Dashiell,Bridget:..44,268,376,448
Dashiell,Cadmus:..............255
Dashiell,Chapman:..............47
Dashiell,Charles:.8,47,51,117,139
:.217,218,251,286,304,319,414,43
Dashiell,Christopher:......17,120
Dashiell,Clement:..61,102,173,174
:.............................376
Dashiell,Daniel J.:...........103
Dashiell,Edgar J.:............103
Dashiell,Eleanor:.............427
Dashiell,Elizabeth:.17,41,101,124
:....139,213,247,257,286,323,380
Dashiell,Esther:....95,179,218,320
:........344,356,365,367,442,443
Dashiell,Etamus:..............162
Dashiell,Frederick A.C.:..257,345
:.............................415
Dashiell,Frederick Augustus:..179
Dashiell,George H.:...........166
Dashiell,George :8,25,32,37,41,43
:..44,47,51,52,56,61,73,79,80,84
:,90,101,102,103,109,124,130,138
:....141,162,173,174,198,218,238
Dashiell,George:..250,256,262,267
:268,286,293,297,310,320,322,329
:341,344,356,360,365,367,375,380
:385,387,391,410,415,427,428,429
:....................434,435,441
Dashiell,Haste:.......185,227,255
Dashiell,Henny:...............102
Dashiell,Henrietta:...102,174,322
Dashiell,Henry:.61,66,103,119,141
:................142,241,262,376
Dashiell,Hester:..............279
Dashiell,Ichabod:.101,124,140,380
:.............................445
Dashiell,Isaac:.44,61,102,113,128
:........174,268,309,322,376,448
Dashiell,Isabella:.69,174,281,323
:........................355,448
Dashiell,Jacob:...........162,279

Dashiell,James Fairfax:.......436
Dashiell,James:17,28,32,37,41,103
:113,136,162,196,225,227,240,251
:255,267,268,281,357,375,376,389
:........395,411,427,443,444,445
Dashiell,Jane:48,66,67,80,142,255
:.............................376
Dashiell,Jesse:22,113,135,196,251
:267,268,360,375,376,387,427,444
Dashiell,John:..18,22,25,65,73,81
:101,102,113,115,135,162,193,195
:196,213,230,247,257,268,323,360
:376,387,402,415,426,427,441,444
:.............................447
Dashiell,Joseph:...18,44,61,79,84
:101,103,112,123,130,136,138,175
:182,188,189,196,238,256,263,268
:274,276,282,287,293,297,310,330
:336,347,354,358,360,372,375,382
:............384,391,409,410,435
Dashiell,Josiah:61,74,102,139,174
:.....................183,286,376
Dashiell,Keturah:............287
Dashiell,Leah:...............287
Dashiell,Levi:............66,141
Dashiell,Levin:...44,46,62,64,166
:201,268,304,376,395,402,407,445
:.............................448
Dashiell,Louther:..........61,102
Dashiell,Margaret:.........67,185
Dashiell,Martha:.............410
Dashiell,Mary C.:..............4
Dashiell,Mary Caldwell:...142,358
Dashiell,Mary:...4,17,48,59,66,80
:...139,195,286,329,376,407,413,
:.............................444
Dashiell,Matilda Kennerly:....304
Dashiell,Matilda:.............67
Dashiell,Matthias:..49,61,102,103
:....176,198,227,255,262,312,427
Dashiell,Mitchell:286,322,323,344
:.....................345,415,443
Dashiell,Nancy Ann:...........82
Dashiell,Nancy:........81,113,128
Dashiell,Nelly:........39,135,279
Dashiell,Orlando:............304
Dashiell,Peter:...11,49,70,86,134
:226,242,275,296,319,320,337,359
:............361,372,377,378,404
Dashiell,Polly:.......413,422,428
Dashiell,Priscilla:41,101,140,380
:.............................445
Dashiell,Rebecca:.........41,267
Dashiell,Robert:,4,16,36,49,61,66
:67,69,87,88,101,102,124,134,142

:174,176,179,185,195,202,218,227
:255,277,322,323,344,345,346,358
:........359,371,380,413,415,422
Dashiell,Rosey:..............391
Dashiell,Rosy:...........102,391
Dashiell,Rufus:..............162
Dashiell,Sally Dennis:.......341
Dashiell,Sally:.......61,102,367
Dashiell,Sarah:..........227,371
Dashiell,Susanna:....112,274,276
Dashiell,Susannah:.113,267,376,39
Dashiell,Thomas:32,33,41,48,55,62
:.80,100,102,119,139,156,163,164
:189,217,222,286,300,304,329,334
:361,375,376,381,386,401,414,415
:........................434,443
Dashiell,William Francis:.255,445
Dashiell,William:8,39,56,66,74,79
:.99,103,174,185,222,227,255,268
:278,279,322,329,355,407,415,448
Dashiell,Winder:65,81,113,375,441
:.........................443,444
Daugherty,Ann:...............431
Daugherty,John:...............41
Daugherty,Thomas:............431
Davenport,Stephen:...........169
Davis,Abisha:........106,107,314
Davis,Ann:...................106
Davis,Annanias:..............313
Davis,Benjamin:..........106,301
Davis,Betsy:.........189,332,354
Davis,Bridget:...........246,247
Davis,Charles:..25,95,199,331,381
:.............................444
Davis,Daniel:.......11,43,235,361
Davis,Delitha:...............105
Davis,Elijah:................235
Davis,Elizabeth:.........105,235
Davis,Elzey:.............144,364
Davis,George:.............30,370
Davis,Henrietta:.............361
Davis,Henry:.......4,380,385,423
Davis,Hezekiah:..............105
Davis,James:..105,106,253,337,372
Davis,Jesse:.........106,313,323
Davis,John B.:...............107
Davis,John:..11,58,66,105,106,183
:............208,209,216,235,246
Davis,Joshua:................255
Davis,Kesiah:................105
Davis,Levin:.......43,332,343,383
Davis,Martha:......4,183,385,423
Davis,Mary:...105,112,144,358,364
:.............................372
Davis,Patience:...........43,343

Davis,Patty:.................106
Davis,Phillip:...............208
Davis,Powell:................372
Davis,Rencher:...............235
Davis,Reuben:...2,106,216,235,345
Davis,Reubin:................283
Davis,Robert:............332,380
Davis,Ruth:..................323
Davis,Sampson:...........150,361
Davis,Samuel:.105,106,112,171,208
:.....................269,358,372,436
Davis,Sarah:..112,235,246,283,372
Davis,Saul:.......105,112,120,372
Davis,Seymore:...............112
Davis,Sophia:................105
Davis,Spencer:.43,178,332,343,383
Davis,Stephen:.58,216,235,283,321
:.............................361
Davis,Thomas:..19,105,106,222,235
Davis,Turner:................105
Davis,Walker:............105,171
Davis,William Turner:.....105,436
Davis,William:.43,105,152,238,246
:.............247,332,343,383,395
Day,Edward:...........92,107,394
Day,George:..................394
Day,Mary:....................394
Day,Sarah:...................215
Dayley,William:..............203
Dean,Abraham:..34,337,376,377,417
Dean,Charles:......107,108,169,353
Dean,Elizabeth:..........108,442
Dean,Ephraim:................353
Dean,James:24,107,108,123,149,205
:........215,295,353,405,406,442
Dean,Levi:.........107,108,353,442
Dean,Levin:..................108
Dean,Margaret:...........108,442
Dean,Mary:...........194,405,406
Dean,Noble:........108,353,442
Dean,Susanna:............107,353
Dean,William:............107,353
Dennis,Affradozy:............111
Dennis,Annanias:.............111
Dennis,Benjamin:.........377,437
Dennis,Betty:................192
Dennis,Elizabeth Leah:........180
Dennis,Henry:................192
Dennis,James P.:.............314
Dennis,James:........111,140,377
Dennis,John Upshur:..........180
Dennis,John:......308,309,326,384
Dennis,Johnson:......274,276,384
Dennis,Josiah:...........308,309
Dennis,Littleton:18,51,86,251,274

:................................312
Dennis,Nelly:................308,309
Dennis,Polly Christopher:.......437
Dennis,Sarah Anne Waters:.......273
Dennis,Sarah:................308,309
Dennis,Susanna:..............86,312
Dennis,Thomas:..................194
Dennis,William:.............192,326
Denson,Eliza A.F.:..............103
Denson,Isaac:................86,360
Denson,James:...................360
Denson,Polly:...................360
Denwood,Arthur:.............162,380
Denwood,George:.................111
Denwood,John:.155,185,278,304,311
:...............................369
Denwood,Levin:........111,129,414
Denwood,Thomas:.................111
Derrickson,James:...............163
Derrickson,John C.:.............163
Derrickson,Levin:............22,106
Deverix,Ann:....................170
Deverix,John:...................170
Dickenson,Harriett:..............50
Dickenson,James:............342,379
Dickenson,John:.................112
Dickenson,Joshua:................64
Dickerson,Isaac:26,90,112,357,389
:...............................420
Dickerson,Leah:.............112,148
Dickerson,Levi:26,112,357,406,420
Dickerson,Rebecca:...............90
Dickerson,Samuel:.....406,420,443
Dickerson,Teague:..26,112,148,335
:.......................357,406,443
Dickerson,William Winright:.....90
Dikes,Betty:................308,309
Dikes,Stephen:..............308,309
Disharoon,Amelia J.:............114
Disharoon,Benjamin:...319,360,361
:.......................371,446,447
Disharoon,Betsy:................371
Disharoon,Constant:80,174,175,212
:.......................331,366,387,436
Disharoon,Eben:65,114,228,283,372
:...............................388
Disharoon,Ebenezer:..............65
Disharoon,Elizabeth:..327,440,446
Disharoon,Eunice:...............440
Disharoon,Francis:..65,78,114,195
:.............197,228,358,372,422
Disharoon,George:10,77,78,114,173
:.......................248,374,422
Disharoon,Hetty:................372
Disharoon,James:...80,159,175,282

:...........................334,406
Disharoon,Jane:......13,14,327,440
Disharoon,Jean:.................158
Disharoon,John:...13,77,80,93,158
:....159,173,175,248,282,302,406
Disharoon,Joshua:..80,142,212,331
:...........................346,365
Disharoon,Levin:...80,210,244,309
:...........................327,336,440
Disharoon,Lewis:.13,14,14,158,210
:...........................302,327,440
Disharoon,Margaret:........93,158
Disharoon,Marv:........80,159,173
Disharoon,Matthias Hopkins:...388
Disharoon,Michael:.....45,302,371
Disharoon,Molly:..........228,372
Disharoon,Newton:.............173
Disharoon,Obediah:.77,212,274,282
:...........................289,432
Disharoon,Patty:..........228,372
Disharoon,Rebecca:............440
Disharoon,Sarah Hearn:........358
Disharoon,Sarah:..197,228,248,309
:...........................372,422,440
Disharoon,Stephen:...10,77,78,114
:...........................173,248,389,422
Disharoon,Thomas:.............336
Disharoon,Tomlinson:...........77
Disharoon,Waitman:.............80
Disharoon,William:.80,159,173,371
:...............................446
Dixon,Ambrose P.:..............57
Dixon,Ambrose:................115
Dixon,Ann:................260,359
Dixon,Frances Todd:...........115
Dixon,Frances:................115
Dixon,Hannah:.................334
Dixon,Huett N.:...............115
Dixon,Isaac:..........101,114,115
Dixon,Leah:...............153,432
Dixon,Nathaniel:......115,153,432
Dixon,Outerbridge:........115,153
Dixon,Risdon:.............115,181
Dixon,Robert:.............260,359
Dixon,Samuel:.................115
Dixon,William Dashiell:.......115
Dixon,William:....115,153,431,432
Dobson,Eleanor:...............129
Dobson,Elenor:................129
Dolbe,Jonathan:...............341
Dommock,William:..............358
Done,Ann:.....................285
Done,Elizabeth Bayley:........204
Done,John:....................204
Done,Juliet Henrietta:........204

Done,Leah Bayley:.............204
Done,Patience:................204
Done,William:.........285,359,360
Donelson,Janet:................53
Donelson,Patrick:.........146,322
Donnell,Elizabeth:............275
Donnell,Samuel:...............275
Donoho,Alexander:....208,233,348
Donoho,Fillmurroh:............391
Donoho,Filmurroh:...............5
Donoho,James:..............95,443
Donoho,John:..................418
Donoho,Joshua:......5,117,248,391
Donoho,Richardson:..17,27,165,172
:.......................302,347,348,428
Donoho,William D.:..............5
Donoho,William R.:........208,307
Donoho,William:.57,89,129,150,208
:....233,244,246,286,302,307,348
Dority,Edmund:................266
Dority,John:..................448
Dorman,Ann:...................285
Dorman,Arthur:............434,435
Dorman,Catherine:...............5
Dorman,David:.................207
Dorman,Frances:...............117
Dorman,George:................426
Dorman,Hamilton:..............339
Dorman,Henry:....198,339,340,429
Dorman,Hezekiah:..............285
Dorman,Jesse:.................423
Dorman,John:31,62,117,179,213,228
:...................247,284,285
Dorman,Joshua:......167,333,340
Dorman,Leah Farrington:.......316
Dorman,Leah:..................425
Dorman,Levin:.................114
Dorman,Major:......68,133,351,366
Dorman,Margaret:..............423
Dorman,Matthew:..8,81,117,231,314
:...................316,406,425,426
Dorman,Matthias:..........118,426
Dorman,Nancy:.............179,247
Dorman,Rebecca:..........434,435
Dorman,Robert:.....5,337,339,426
Dorman,Sarah:.133,198,351,366,429
Dorman,William:.8,311,314,338,406
:...........................425,426
Dorsey,Betty:.................143
Dorsey,Talman:................143
Dougherty,Amy:................340
Dougherty,Jesse:..............104
Dougherty,John:...112,148,335,336
Dougherty,Robert:.............148
Dougherty,Thomas:.............340

Douglas,John: 129,376
Douglas,William: ...46,177,242,266
: 291,392
Douty,John: 443
Douty,Peter:39,54,119,148,307,335
: 357,411,443
Downing,John R.: 331,346
Downs,Ann: 40
Downs,George: 41
Downs,Jacob: 121
Downs,John: 121
Downs,Mary: 41
Downs,Robert: 40,120,121
Draper,Whittington: 289,290
Drinkle,Erasmus: 432
Driscoll,Dennis: 110,111
Driskell,Catherine: 20,289
Driskell,Cathrine: 20
Driskell,Dennis: 88,111,149
Driskell,Elizabeth: 121
Driskell,James: 88,111,149
Driskell,John: 490
Driskell,Kathryn: 108
Driskell,Moses:.20,42,109,121,289
: 395,428
Driskell,Nelly: 281
Driskell,Rosanna: 437
Driskell,Shadrack: 281,282
Driskell,Shardrack: 88
Driskell,William:...20,88,121,133
: 289,437
Driskill,Moses: 121,324
Drummond,Richard: 37
Drummond,Scarborough: 37
Dryden,Joshua: 197
Dryden,Moses: 334,340
Dryden,William: 324
Dukes,Robert: 338,384
Dulaney,Dennis: 78,200,248
Dulaney,Henry:.78,131,201,266,305
Dulaney,William: 412
Dulany,Henry: 79
Dullahide,Thomas: 170
Duncan,Charles: 67,68,154,205
Duncan,Esther: 165
Duncan,James McLaughlin: 116
Duncan,Josiah: 154
Duncan,Kesiah: 154
Duncan,Leah:..127,164,184,237,338
Duncan,Levi: 68
Duncan,Margaret: 166
Duncan,Martha: 28,154
Duncan,Thomas: 154
Dunn,Joseph: 227
Dunn,Nicholas: 241,373

Dunn,Priscilla: 335
Dunn,Richard:...41,55,185,241,250
: 373
Dunn,Thomas: 41,373
Dunn,William: 241
Durham,Richard: 123
Duskey,Moses: 171
Dutton,David:19,63,95,208,331,428
Dutton,Mary Ann: 63,208
Dutton,William: 279
Duvall,Gabriel: 114,219
Duvall,Lewis: 345
Dyer,Jonathan: 327
Dykes,Ann: 290
Dykes,Arthur: 71,291
Dykes,Daniel:.112,123,291,372,437
Dykes,Ephraim: 71,325
Dykes,Naboth: 290
Dykes,Naomi: 437
Dykes,Sarah: 437
Dykes,Stephen: 113
Dykes,William: 290,437
Dymock,Hannah: 277
Dymock,William: 93,277,295
Easum,Benjamin: 36,124
Easum,Isaac: 412
Easum,Mary: 412
Eckley,Joseph: 146
Eckley,Susanna: 146
Edge,Nehemiah: 125
Edwards,Jemima: 266,291
Edwards,Jemimah: 177
Elgate,Ann: 20
Elgate,Catherine: 20,289
Elgate,Hannah: 20
Elgate,Rebecca: 20
Elgate,Sarah: 20,186,311
Elgate,William:.20,42,108,155,186
: 225,284,289,311,329,351,395
Ellegood,John: 352
Ellegood,Sarah: 122
Ellegood,William: 126,186
Ellingsworth,Elizabeth: 127
Ellingsworth,Josiah: 149
Ellingsworth,Richard: 127
Ellingsworth,William:32,40,85,143
Elliott,Daniel: 127
Elliott,Elizabeth: 428
Ellis,Amey: 52
Ellis,Ann: 16
Ellis,Edward:..89,125,128,137,293
: 333
Ellis,Elijah: 128
Ellis,Esther: 128
Ellis,Francis: 52

Ellis,Joseph: 127,128,341,410
Ellis,Levin: 353
Ellis,Rachel: 128,137,333
Ellis,Sarah: 16
Ellis,Stephen: 127,128
Ellis,William: 16
Elzey,Arnold: 61
Elzey,Elizabeth: 169
Elzey,Francis: 168,169
Elzey,John: 46,252,295
Elzey,Margaret: 61
Elzey,Mary: 295
Elzey,Peter: 168,169
Elzey,William: 276,329
English,Cornelius: 398
English,James: 131,233
English,Thomas: 233,237
English,William: 118
Ennals,Joseph:..13,51,112,168,219
: 238
Ennals,William: 131
Ennis,Elijah: 123
Esham,Charles: 227
Esham,Martha: 227
Eshum,Isaac: 275
Evans,Ann: 138,245,407
Evans,Betty: 142
Evans,David: 388
Evans,Elizabeth: 17,46,448
Evans,Jacob: 277,314,323
Evans,James: 17,46,142,448
Evans,John W.: 419
Evans,John:.63,67,118,125,131,132
:138,140,154,163,166,230,245,249
:279,281,300,306,346,351,378,402
: 407,408,434,445
Evans,Joshua: 238
Evans,Lemuel: 49
Evans,Mary: 163,419
Evans,Nicholas:...13,56,58,98,118
:138,154,166,200,229,245,269,272
:346,385,394,397,402,407,433,445
Evans,Prisa: 98
Evans,Rachel: 200
Evans,Rebecca:20,42,45,59,109,289
: 395,428
Evans,Sarah: 140,346,445
Evans,Solomon: 131,408
Evans,Susanna: 138
Evans,Walker: 392
Evans,William Riley: 49
Evans,William: 311
Everton,Thomas: 295
Ewing,Isaac: 334,340
Ewing,James: 340

459

Ewing,William: 359	Fluellin,Richard C.:55,90,381,443	:150,171,192,228,253,268,274,323
Fall,John: 344	Fluellin,Richard Crockett:..40,72	:........................ 347,372
Fallon,Barnaby: 68	:.90,142,145,335,344,371,381,402	Fooks,Violetta: 137,268
Farlow,Benjamin: 137	Fluellin,Richard: 72,402	Fooks,William:147,148,149,150,209
Farlow,Daniel: 137	Fluellin,Samuel:39,40,51,55,63,72	:........................ 250,253
Farlow,David: 137	:..85,90,142,143,145,274,300,335	Footman,John W.: 50
Farlow,George: 41,96,137	:........ 344,371,381,401,402,443	Foreman,Daniel: 335
Farlow,John: 137,268,347	Fodman,Samuel: 345	Foreman,Joseph: ...125,343,344,386
Farlow,William: 97,122	Follin,Levin: 38,446	Fortune,Betty: 106
Farnel,ELizabeth: 176	Fooks,Ann: 147	Fountain,George W.: 336,357
Farnel,Thomas: 176	Fooks,Anne: 150,253	Fountain,James R.J.Mc.: 357
Farrington,Charlotte: 110	Fooks,Anthony: 282	Fountain,James.R.R.Mc: 336
Farrington,Emmy: 110	Fooks,Benjamin:...147,149,150,192	Fountain,Judah: 152,431
Farrington,George:250,269,315,317	:.............. 252,253,316,347	Fountain,Nicholas: 153,431
:.................. 379,424,425	Fooks,Betsy: 248	Fountain,Stephen: 152,431
Farrington,Levin:...71,73,110,138	Fooks,Billy:77,96,192,214,268,274	Fountain,Steven: 431
:164,195,262,285,286,317,345,352	:................ 323,326,347,399	Fountain,Tabitha: 153
:.............. 362,406,425,441	Fooks,Charles:....147,150,160,278	Fowler,Arthur: 153
Farrington,Robert:....315,379,424	Fooks,Daniel:..96,137,141,192,250	Fowler,Edward:....117,132,331,419
Farrington,Sarah: 315	:............ 274,323,333,347,400	Fowler,Isaac: 153
Farrington,William:...315,379,420	Fooks,David: 255,347	Fowler,Jesse: 153
:...................... 424,425	Fooks,Delila: 209	Fowler,John: 8,132
Fassitt,William: 183	Fooks,Elizabeth: 282	Fowler,Jonathan: 153
Fergusson,Robert: 121	Fooks,George Noble: 366	Fowler,Thomas: 419
Field,John: 336	Fooks,George: 44,66,121,133	Foxcroft,Isaac: 28,225,395
Figgs,Thomas: 140	Fooks,Handy: 77	Foxcroft,Rebecca: 28,225
Figgs,William: 140,169	Fooks,Hannah: 147,150,316	Foy,Adam: 154
Finch,Elizabeth: 33	Fooks,Henny: 150	Franklin,Samuel: 301
Finch,James: 33,86	Fooks,James M.: 147	Franklin,Walter: 301
Finch,John: 33	Fooks,James Minos:...... 96,192,323	Frazier,Mary: 291,421
Finch,Margaret: 33	Fooks,James:83,96,147,149,171,192	Frazier,Persisor:..46,177,291,392
Fitchwater,Ambrose: 143	:216,220,228,253,268,323,333,341	:............................. 421
Fitzgerald,Henry: 257	:...................... 347,367,372	Freeman,Joseph: 291
Fitzgerald,Peter: 264	Fooks,Jesse:...92,121,133,147,183	Freeney,Elizabeth: 27,271
Fleming,Phillip: 191	:209,216,219,253,254,278,307,341	Freeney,John:48,75,76,155,196,320
Fleming,William: 401	:....365,366,367,377,378,393,403	:......................... 360,422
Fletcher,Betty: 95,117,443	Fooks,John: 121,282,366	Freeney,Joshua:....48,155,177,190
Fletcher,Charlotte: 299	Fooks,Jonathan:...21,82,92,96,192	Freeney,Peter: 27,271
Fletcher,Clement Bell: 59	:........ 214,255,268,274,323,347	French,William: 152,247
Fletcher,Elizabeth: 249	Fooks,Joseph: 147,150,253	Fritz,Edward: 317
Fletcher,Esther: 51,59	Fooks,Leah: 228,253,254	Fritz,John: 317
Fletcher,George: 59,134	Fooks,Letishay: 282	Frizzell,John:.91,159,216,222,354
Fletcher,James:....93,210,299,368	Fooks,Mariah: 248,282	Fullerton,Alexander: 58,332
Fletcher,John: 51,59,299	Fooks,Mary: 147,149,209,253	Fullerton,Charles: 145
Fletcher,Levin:.94,95,117,331,443	Fooks,Nancy: 148	Fullerton,James: 332
Fletcher,Mary: 59	Fooks,Rachel Noble: 366	Fullerton,John: 332
Fletcher,Samuel: 290	Fooks,Rachel: 92,183,209,341	Furbush,George: 62,428
Fletcher,Sarah: 59	Fooks,Rebecca: 341	Furbush,John: 148,335,443
Fletcher,Thomas:35,59,110,217,249	Fooks,Ritchie: 83	Furbush,Joseph: 365
:.............................. 288	Fooks,Sabra: 341,367	Furbush,Peter: 335,443
Flint,John: 145,157,215	Fooks,Sabrey: 216	Furrs,John: 54
Flint,Thomas: 145,157,215	Fooks,Sabrough: 137	Gale,Amelia: 152,238,247,395
Fluellin,Charles: 402	Fooks,Sally: 150,274	Gale,Anne Maria: 160
Fluellin,Jane: 274,300,335	Fooks,Sarah: 137,252,268	Gale,Elizabeth Ann Wilson: 273
Fluellin,John: 90,145,335	Fooks,Thomas:...46,96,137,147,149	Gale,Elizabeth: 160,413

Gale,George H.:................339
Gale,George:..12,13,20,69,111,160
:164,237,254,272,273,280,318,342
:......................378,402,407
Gale,Henry:.68,69,110,161,215,273
:.....................279,280,339
Gale,James:........................13
Gale,John:...12,39,91,111,118,152
:160,161,227,237,238,247,251,280
:303,313,339,342,375,395,409,413
:...........427,429,433,443,448
Gale,Leah:........69,111,290,342
Gale,Levin:,6,9,12,13,19,69,73,84
:111,160,164,182,229,254,272,273
:275,285,289,342,346,351,378,394
:......................402,404,407
Gale,Littleton:...160,164,254,273
Gale,Matthias:...6,13,111,160,371
Gale,Milcah:...................160
Gale,Robert:....................273
Gale,Sarah:.....................339
Gale,Susan:....................110
Game,Betty:....................162
Game,Daniel:....................89
Game,Jeremiah:...................89
Game,Samuel:....................89
Garland,Stephen:...............334
Garrettson,Freeborn:...........339
Garrettson,John A.:............254
Garrettson,Priscilla:..........339
Garrettson,Thomas:164,254,309,339
Gaskins,William:...............282
Gasteneau,Job:.................168
Gault,Charlotte:................27
Gault,David:....................27
Gault,Mary:....................330
Gault,William:.................329
Geddes,Robert:.................151
Gemill,Jane:...................442
Gemmill,Ann:...................202
Gemmill,Hugh:,133,137,139,155,201
:.....................202,261,370
Gemmill,Jane:..............137,139
Gibbons,John:..................251
Gibbons,Mary:..................251
Gilchrist,Andrew Allen:........319
Gilchrist,Andrew:..............319
Gilchrist,Nancy:...............319
Giles,Elizabeth:..164,165,309,362
Giles,Eunice:..............165,312
Giles,Ganer:...................258
Giles,Isaac:...12,164,165,237,309
:......................312,362
Giles,Jacob:..164,165,309,312,362
Giles,John:....................105

Giles,Mary:....................165
Giles,Thomas:..................165
Giles,William:.69,127,164,165,184
:....237,258,309,338,357,362,409
Gillis,Ann:.............71,98,262
Gillis,Benjamin:...........190,391
Gillis,Elizabeth:..............262
Gillis,Esther:.............190,391
Gillis,Ezekiel McClemmy:.......304
Gillis,Ezekiel:71,166,262,287,304
:.......................347,396
Gillis,George:..62,67,166,263,303
Gillis,Grace:..................262
Gillis,James:..................304
Gillis,John:...62,115,166,262,263
:.......................315,347
Gillis,Joseph:30,62,70,71,111,166
:............262,263,303,304,320
Gillis,Levin:..................396
Gillis,Littleton:...........71,262
Gillis,Nelly Dashiell:.........287
Gillis,Nelly:..................320
Gillis,Priscilla:..............347
Gillis,Samuel:.................304
Gillis,Sarah:...................67
Gillis,Thomas Handy:.......319,320
Gillis,Thomas:.8,84,91,98,115,118
:166,167,213,262,299,300,343,346
:............347,370,382,396,417
Gillis,William:........159,303,304
Givan,James:....................12
Givans,Ann:.....................64
Givans,Davy:..9,97,167,219,258,306
:.......................418,425
Givans,George:..12,97,219,237,289
:..............................306
Givans,Hiram:..................167
Givans,James:12,80,81,168,183,237
:........259,338,373,420,432,433
Givans,Jane:...................183
Givans,John:...............373,420
Givans,Margaret:............12,237
Givans,Martha:.................183
Givans,Mary:...........146,373,420
Givans,Robert:.7,44,51,97,109,145
:146,167,168,172,219,249,259,289
:............306,315,347,432,433
Givans,Sarah:..................420
Givans,Solomon:............88,167
Givans,Thomas:..............97,219
Givans,William:..7,64,109,237,259
Gladstean,John:............168,400
Glass,Alice:...................195
Glass,Christopher:.............195
Glaster,John:..................262

Glaster,Thomas:................262
Goddard,Francis Lane:..........107
Goddard,George:...107,170,218,332
:......................442,447
Goddard,John:..92,107,170,218,344
Goddard,Thomas:................170
Goddard,William:.......77,218,311
Godman,Anne:...................345
Godman,Samuel:.................345
Gold,Edward:..............40,171,172
Goldsmith,William:..............34
Gordan,Samuel:.................357
Gordey,Moses:..................111
Gordon,James:..............360,361
Gordon,John:...................401
Gordon,Samuel:....177,360,361,431
Gordon,Thomas:6,53,57,169,176,177
:..............................401
Gordy,Aaron:....................52
Gordy,Betty:......45,154,177,321
Gordy,Eli:.....................140
Gordy,Eliza:......45,154,177,321
Gordy,Elizabeth:...............308
Gordy,Elizabeth:...............309
Gordy,Hannah:..................217
Gordy,Jacob:...................347
Gordy,John P.:..................54
Gordy,John:....45,140,217,309,368
Gordy,Leonard:.............308,309
Gordy,Moses:..111,140,150,177,178
:.......................309,442
Gordy,Nathan:...........22,30,217
Gordy,Peter:...45,113,140,177,245
:252,274,308,309,316,321,326,432
:..............................443
Gordy,Samuel:..................321
Gordy,William:.45,113,154,177,190
:.....................274,321,443
Goslee,Daniel:..................68
Goslee,Eleanor:............236,445
Goslee,Elizabeth:..........301,427
Goslee,Hannah:.................179
Goslee,James Marcellas:........301
Goslee,James:..................179
Goslee,Joanna:.................428
Goslee,John:..........179,428,429
Goslee,Joseph:............179,209
Goslee,Josiah:.................179
Goslee,Leah:...................179
Goslee,Levin:..................408
Goslee,Loudy:..................427
Goslee,Mary:...................408
Goslee,Matthew:............179,246
Goslee,Richard:...179,236,246,247
:..............................445

Goslee, Samuel Boardman: 204
Goslee, Samuel: 179,204,247
Goslee, Sarah: 179
Goslee, Susan: 301
Goslee, Tabitha: 246
Goslee, Thomas: 179,204,364
Goslee, William: 429
Goslin, Daniel: 125,136
Goslin, Elizabeth: 125,136
Gould, John: 320,360
Gover, Samuel: 182
Graham, Asa: 292
Graham, Benjamin: 180
Graham, Betsy: 66,87,190,252
Graham, Charlotte A.H.: 230,361
Graham, Elizabeth: 38
Graham, Ezekiel: 53,134,340
Graham, Henry R.: 230,361
Graham, Henry: .134,256,266,292,340
: 423
Graham, James: 266,292
Graham, John:66,87,190,252,256,358
Graham, Levin: 30
Graham, Lewis: ...29,30,101,340,423
: 436
Graham, Mary: 75,252,266
Graham, Nancy: 66,190,252
Graham, Phillip: ...38,66,80,87,190
: 238,252,427
Graham, Priscilla: 75
Graham, Robert: ...38,75,87,122,252
: 334,340,427,428
Graham, Sally: 436
Graham, Sarah:.29,38,66,87,101,252
Graham, William:.75,87,122,190,252
Grant, Elizabeth: 250
Grant, John: 250
Gravener, Benjamin P.: 292,439
Gravener, Benjamin: ...180,292,412
Gravener, Clement J.: 292
Gravener, Louder: 28
Gravener, Mary: 28
Gravener, Phillip: 28
Gravener, Urias: 374
Gravener, William: 374
Gray, Allen: 180,341
Gray, David: ...123,155,180,193,369
Gray, John: 180,305,341
Gray, Joseph: 158
Gray, Levin: 155,369
Gray, Margaret: 305
Gray, Sinah: 96
Gray, Siner: 142
Gray, William: 155,256,353
Green, Abendego: 90,443

Green, Bable: 295,296
Green, Catherine: 277
Green, Elizabeth: 184,312
Green, Ezekiah: 277
Green, Ezekiel: 25,131,184
Green, George: 295
Green, Isaac: 184
Green, Jesse: 361
Green, John: 184,295,296
Green, Jonathan: 266
Green, Nancy: 296
Green, Rachel: 4
Green, Richard: 184,265
Green, Samuel: 4,183,184
Green, Sophia: 184
Green, William:.20,182,184,207,312
: 430
Greenfield, Edmond: 296
Greer, David: 161,282,380
Greer, George: 282
Griffin, John: 190
Griffin, Oliver: 190
Griffith, Martin: 1
Griffith, Salathiel: 1,229,247
Griffith, Samuel: 44
Grudman, Richard: 246
Grumble, John:3,33,125,185,258,398
: 409
Grumble, Temperance: ...125,185,398
: 409
Gullett, Abraham: 277
Gunby, David: 95
Gunby, Elizabeth: 95
Gunby, James: 186,266,283
Gunby, John: 341
Gunby, Kirk:..10,65,95,204,270,388
: 401
Gunby, Levin:10,95,250,289,388,401
Gunby, Mary A.: 283
Gunby, Mary: 204,266
Gunby, Nathaniel: 48
Gunby, Sabra: 250
Gunby, Sarah: 283
Gunby, Stephen: 95
Gunby, William: 283
Gupton, Ann: 293,419,444
Gupton, Jeanne: 59,444
Gupton, John: ...59,168,293,419,444
Gupton, Peter: 293,444
Gurley, Eleanor: 58
Gurley, Francis: 58,367
Hack, Peter: 318
Hack, Tunstall: 318
Hackett, John: 225
Haile, Oliver: 287

Haines, David: 186
Haines, Francis: 186
Haines, Martha: 186
Hale, David: 343
Hale, Mary: 343
Hall, Ann:...20,42,108,109,186,289
: 395,428
Hall, Elizabeth: 167
Hall, John: 171,187,442
Hall, Joshua: 57,77
Hall, Moses: 182
Hall, Phoenix: 57,116,157
Hall, Robert: 182
Hall, Samuel: 329,442
Hall, Spence: 182
Hall, Thomas:...20,182,186,187,289
Hall, William: 77
Halsey, Jane: 420
Halsey, Thomas: 420
Hamblin, Benjamin: 294
Hamblin, Hessey: 294
Hamblin, John: 163,294
Hamblin, Maddux: 187
Hambury, Thomas: 255
Hammond, Charles:..102,152,153,377
: 431
Hammond, Edward: 334,340
Hammond, Nelly: 393
Hammond, William: 393
Hampton, John: 386
Hampton, Mary: 172,217,386
Hancock, John: 187
Handy, Ann: 19,110,187,404
Handy, Benjamin:...13,14,57,58,188
: 189,332,354
Handy, Betty:..119,144,188,200,299
: 307,376,397,417
Handy, Charles: 298
Handy, Comfort: 76
Handy, Ebenezer:..13,14,93,187,189
: 210,354,440,446
Handy, Edward G.:..86,187,296,361
: 367
Handy, Eleanor:139,184,201,202,258
: 421
Handy, Elizabeth:...79,119,144,187
: 188,307,373,411
Handy, George D.S.:320,356,365,367
: 442
Handy, George W.: 139
Handy, George:66,68,86,110,119,124
:137,144,149,187,188,189,239,256
:262,295,299,307,317,318,357,359
: 368,385,393,396,411,434
Handy, Gertrude: 320

Handy,Haste:...58,188,189,257,332
:............................354
Handy,Henry:...124,156,189,262,288
:...294,313,318,320,376,379,396
Handy,Isaac:.45,66,86,124,144,156
:187,188,189,209,261,275,288,293
:295,296,317,318,359,367,368,375
:............383,386,396,434,447
Handy,Issac:................361
Handy,James:................182
Handy,Jane:............218,359
Handy,John:..13,14,34,35,43,45,58
:..68,70,93,110,187,188,189,210
:256,270,279,298,303,351,354,359
:................365,404,424,440
Handy,Joyce:................399
Handy,Levin:.35,50,70,126,139,146
:....164,187,201,202,256,319,364
Handy,Margaret:........78,201,318
Handy,Martha:..................58
Handy,Mary:....................34
Handy,Nancy:..........319,361,364
Handy,Nelly Gillis:...........321
Handy,Nelly:..........202,319,320
Handy,Peter:..................262
Handy,Phoebe:..........79,201,318
Handy,Richard Elizabeth:......257
Handy,Richard Henry:..133,137,139
:....201,202,319,320,356,365,367
:............................441
Handy,Robert:.118,187,327,361,440
:............................446
Handy,Samuel:........34,35,256,354
Handy,Sarah:..............110,404
Handy,Thomas R.:..............221
Handy,Thomas Robins:...........76
Handy,Thomas W.:..............313
Handy,Thomas Winder:..320,356,365
:........................367,441
Handy,Thomas:19,34,68,110,124,156
:....187,189,279,352,365,404,424
Handy,William Smith:78,79,201,318
Handy,William W.:..69,320,356,365
:........................367,442
Handy,William:...76,78,86,156,187
:188,189,200,201,262,288,296,317
:............318,360,361,367,399
Handy:........................361
Hangline,Isabel:..............132
Hangline,William:.............132
Hanson,Alexander Contee:...54,120
Hardeknight,James:............190
Hardeknight,Mary:.............190
Hardeknight,Susanna:..........190
Hardy,Benjamin:...............306

Hardy,Charles:..............26,98
Hardy,Eliza Train:.......8,81,406
Hardy,Elizabeth:............25,26
Hardy,George:...26,43,270,302,303
:........................306,351
Hardy,Isaac:8,25,26,81,97,314,406
Hardy,James:8,25,26,81,97,258,265
:305,306,314,338,406,417,418,424
:............................425
Hardy,John:.26,98,231,305,306,418
:............................428
Hardy,Joseph:................306
Hardy,Margaret:...............305
Hardy,Mary:....................26
Hardy,Robert:...............25,26
Hardy,Samuel:..............26,98
Hardy,Sarah:...43,270,302,303,351
Hardy,Susanna:.................97
Hardy,William:..............25,26
Harford,Henry:................435
Haris,Spencer:................167
Harris,Abihu:.................237
Harris,Alse:...................62
Harris,Amelia:................127
Harris,Charles:......14,391,437
Harris,David:.................338
Harris,Ephraim K.:....63,387,428
Harris,Eunice:................127
Harris,Isaac:............179,208
Harris,James:..............66,144
Harris,John:..............62,132
Harris,Joseph C.:.............441
Harris,Joseph:................292
Harris,Kezia:.................132
Harris,Levin:.................127
Harris,Mary:.......2,3,264,348
Harris,Nancy:..................96
Harris,Nehemiah:..............391
Harris,Phillip:...............231
Harris,Richard:...............127
Harris,Sinah:.................167
Harris,Solomon:........62,194,237
Harris,Spencer:............88,167
Harris,William:.62,66,132,194,237
:................287,338,407
Harris,Zachariah:.............370
Harrison,Elizabeth:.......158,195
Harrison,Joseph:..............195
Harrison,Patience:............195
Harrison,Solomon:.........158,195
Harrison,William:.........158,195
Harwood,Margaret:.112,264,276,293
:............................372
Harwood,Thomas:19,112,138,264,270
:........274,276,293,295,297,372

Haste,Daniel:...16,98,151,185,226
:...........227,272,346,371,404
Haste,Elizabeth:...16,151,272,371
:............................404
Haste,Sarah:........16,185,227,371
Hastings,Agnes:...............197
Hastings,Daniel:..............196
Hastings,Hezekiah:....76,196,197
Hastings,John:.................39
Hastings,Joshua:..........75,196
Hastings,Robert:...............39
Hastings,William:......76,197,225
Hatheley,Catherine:..........163
Hatheley,Judith:.............163
Hatheley,William:............163
Hatton,Esther:................182
Hatton,John C.:...............181
Hatton,John Cheney:...........182
Hayes,Francis Ware:.......229,395
Hayman,Charles:.................9
Hayman,Henry:.......58,158,289,421
Hayman,James:.................195
Hayman,John Harris:...........325
Hayman,John:..................415
Hayman,Joshua:................195
Hayman,Margaret:..............195
Hayman,Mary:..............289,329
Hayman,Nicholas:..............158
Hayman,Rachel:................195
Hayman,Revel:...............9,240
Hayman,Sarah:...............9,240
Hayman,William B.:............195
Hayman,William Brown:.......9,240
Hayman,William:...158,180,195,329
Haynie,Judiah:................416
Haynie,Martin Luther:.319,320,359
:............................360
Haynie,Richard:.......155,218,416
Haynie,Samuel:.......197,358,416
Haynie,William:............32,226
Hayward,George:..........126,225
Hayward,William:...62,179,284,342
:........................344,427
Haywood,David:.................46
Haywood,John:........45,46,120
Haywood,Sarah:................120
Hearn,Ann:................197,358
Hearn,Benjamin G.:...........197
Hearn,Benjamin:.36,45,177,178,197
:239,259,274,294,299,338,368,390
:........................412,433
Hearn,Betty Day:..............58
Hearn,Betty:..................54
Hearn,Clement:................193
Hearn,Ebenezer:..............144

Hearn,Elijah:...22,48,116,135,206
:................241,364,387,396
Hearn,Elisha:............135,387
Hearn,Elizabeth:..........30,370
Hearn,Isaac:19,54,138,245,251,264
:............293,295,314,360,387
Hearn,Isarc:..................297
Hearn,James:...............54,387
Hearn,Jemima:.................197
Hearn,Jemimah:................358
Hearn,John:.30,54,105,172,193,197
:....245,251,252,265,319,358,370
Hearn,Julia Ann:..............361
Hearn,Lovey:...................54
Hearn,Nancy:..............54,360
Hearn,Nehemiah:58,135,364,386,387
Hearn,Peter G.:................22
Hearn,Peter Gordy:.............54
Hearn,Peter:...............22,54
Hearn,Polly:...........45,113,177
Hearn,Samuel:..45,113,177,259,274
:.........................282,422
Hearn,Sarah:..135,156,197,239,259
:..........................294,386
Hearn,Solomon:................193
Hearn,Tabitha:.................22
Hearn,Thomas:.124,197,358,364,387
:.........................396,448
Hearn,William:...25,45,79,112,113
:156,193,201,206,270,274,277,278
:328,360,361,364,372,384,386,387
:.........................393,396
Heath,Abraham:................422
Heath,Adam:...................301
Heath,Jacob:..................199
Heath,James:..................199
Heath,Josiah W.:..............241
Heath,Mary:...............199,301
Heath,Smith:..............197,246
Heath,William:................197
Henderson,Benjamin:.......143,293
Henderson,Daniel:.198,373,374,411
:.............................420
Henderson,Elizabeth:......143,293
Henderson,Isaac:..........143,144
Henderson,Jenkins:............143
Henderson,John:...............143
Henderson,Lemuel:.............143
Henderson,Robert:.............411
Henderson,Taby:...............143
Hendy,John:....................58
Henry,Dolly:..................198
Henry,Dorothy:............198,322
Henry,Elizabeth:..............155
Henry,George:.................387

Henry,Hugh:...199,322,387,426,444
Henry,Isaac:...59,100,155,195,198
:....199,322,348,383,406,426,444
Henry,James:..................426
Henry,John W.:................386
Henry,John:24,155,172,183,262,293
:...............317,322,347,386,387
Henry,Mary:...................322
Henry,Rider:..................386
Henry,Robert Jenkins:...24,94,155
:.........................261,262
Henry,Robert:.................183
Henry,Sarah:..........322,347,426
Hersey,Benjamin:..............439
Hertz,Edward:...............7,213
Hickman,Arthur:...............330
Hickman,Jean:.................194
Hickman,Jonathan:.....136,194,199
Hickman,Sabrah:...............330
Hickman,Stephen:..........294,305
Hickman,William:......136,294,305
Highway,Abraham:..........261,269
Highway,Deborah:..............261
Highway,Margaret:.............261
Highway,Thomas:.........1,261,269
Hill,Ebenezer:................405
Hill,Frederick:........30,195,202
Hill,James:93,111,116.201,210,435
Hill,Joshua:..................354
Hill,Thomas:..................111
Hill,William:.................116
Hilman,Esther:................154
Hilman,Ezekiel:................74
Hilman,George:.................46
Hilman,James 1.:..............240
Hilman,John:...............45,201
Hilman,Joshua:....46,201,239,240
Hilman,Samuel:.46,120,240,292,350
Hilman,William:...........46,239
Hitch,Adam:78,184,200,296,301,317
Hitch,Amelia:.................226
Hitch,Andrew Elliot:..........112
Hitch,Ann:.....................78
Hitch,Anne:...................200
Hitch,Benjamin:...............287
Hitch,Betsy:..............128,180
Hitch,Betty:..................202
Hitch,Catherine:......126,186,225
Hitch,Charles:................361
Hitch,Curtis:.128,180,316,317,329
:.............................368
Hitch,Elgate:..42,78,109,200,317
:.........................395,428
Hitch,Elias:..............111,213
Hitch,Eva:....................200

Hitch,Eve:....................293
Hitch,Ezekiel:........128,180,202
Hitch,George W.:..............422
Hitch,George:..............64,239
Hitch,Hannah:.....126,184,186,225
Hitch,Isaac:..................78,201
Hitch,Jane:...............146,202
Hitch,Jean:......10,64,97,239,276
Hitch,Jemima:.................197
Hitch,John:..10,64,97,139,146,148
:181,200,201,202,224,226,239,276
:.........................287,316
Hitch,Joseph:...64,78,197,239,287
:.........................288,338,358
Hitch,Joshua:..10,64,78,83,97,128
:139,146,200,201,202,224,227,228
:229,239,240,260,276,296,316,329
:.........................413,439
Hitch,Laban:..................202
Hitch,Levin:......4,113,293,294,361
Hitch,Littleton:..............320
Hitch,Louther:........127,128,180
Hitch,Marsalas B.:............112
Hitch,Mary:78,139,200,261,202,287
Hitch,Mercy:..................200
Hitch,Molly:..........139,201,202
Hitch,Nancy:..........139,201,202
Hitch,Nehemiah:...111,200,213,341
Hitch,Peggy:..........139,201,202
Hitch,Polly:..................122
Hitch,Rebecca:..............4,113
Hitch,Robert:.........78,200,201
Hitch,Sally:..................201
Hitch,Samuel:........78,200,317
Hitch,Sarah Ellegood:......78,201
Hitch,Sarah:...78,111,181,201,213
Hitch,Solomon:........200,385,425
Hitch,Spencer:................200
Hitch,Thomas:.111,200,201,202,316
Hitch,William E.:......139,201,202
Hitch,William Elgate:..78,122,126
:.........................201,202
Hitch,William:...10,64,97,112,139
:183,200,201,202,224,239,276,292
:.........................316,317
Hitchens,Edmund:..........371,372
Hobbs,Absalom:.................61
Hobbs,Ann:.....................61
Hobbs,Benjamin:...............224
Hobbs,Betsy:..............162,203
Hobbs,Elizabeth:......213,224,328
Hobbs,George:..................61
Hobbs,John:...............185,423
Hobbs,Levin:..................328
Hobbs,Marcellus:..161,162,203,224

Hobbs, Matthias: 162,203,224
Hobbs, Nelly: 203
Hobbs, Thomas: 213
Holbrook, Alice: 133
Holbrook, John: .93,102,222,238,395
Holbrook, Patience: 102,222
Holbrook, Samuel: 304
Holbrook, Thomas: 133
Holder, Esther: 166
Holder, Isabell: 279
Holder, James: 166
Holder, John: 53,93,210
Holder, Joseph: 93,210,279
Holland, Ann: 133
Holland, John: 133,370
Holland, William: 265
Holliday, Clement:11,30,81,153,186
: 400,403
Hollis, William: 210
Holloway, Elijah: 211,246,314
Holloway, John: 211
Holloway, Joseph: 108
Holloway, Joshua: ..50,132,150,151
: 153,186,298,325,429
Holloway, Mary: 151
Holloway, Priscilla: 108
Holston, Jane: 250
Holston, John: 337,367
Holston, Thomas: 250
Holt, Martha: 166,385
Hooper, Sally: 361
Hooper, Thomas: .79,201,318,341,361
Hopewell, Nancy: 216
Hopewell, William: 91,216,296
Hopkins, David:363,364,394,407,419
: 420
Hopkins, Eleanor: ..50,55,74,80,113
:120,142,162,163,281,307,363,420
: 0
Hopkins, Elizabeth: 40,194,363
Hopkins, George C.: 56,65
Hopkins, George Collier:65,162,239
: 401
Hopkins, George: ...162,279,363,420
Hopkins, Horatio: 331
Hopkins, Isaac:.56,113,132,211,212
: 420
Hopkins, Jemima: 420
Hopkins, Jane: 56,149
Hopkins, John:47,56,68,142,166,191
: 194,363,401,419,420
Hopkins, Leah: 420
Hopkins, Levi: 56,140,212
Hopkins, Martha: 132,420
Hopkins, Mary Ann: 364

Hopkins, Matilda: 132
Hopkins, Matt: 162
Hopkins, Matthias D.:74,80,120,140
: 211,281
Hopkins, Matthias Dashiell:..55,74
: 79,113,120,162,163,307
Hopkins, Matthias: 34
Hopkins, Nelly: 363,419
Hopkins, Polly: 363
Hopkins, Richard: 40,363,420
Hopkins, Robert: ...149,194,212,331
: 363,419,420
Hopkins, Samuel: 319,320,420
Hopkins, Sarah: 420
Hopkins, Stephen:40,56,194,211,363
: 394,419,420
Hopkins, William: .35,50,70,166,191
: 256
Horner, Levin: 41,250
Horseman, E. L.: 152
Horseman, John: 152
Horseman, Thomas: 63
Horsey, Ann: 122,123,261
Horsey, Charles: 423
Horsey, Eleanor: 159
Horsey, Elinor: 138,169,359
Horsey, Elizabeth: 350
Horsey, George Wailes: 214
Horsey, Isaac: ...70,81,107,133,138
:159,169,296,297,306,334,359,360
: 365,366,424
Horsey, John: 142,184,379
Horsey, Lazarus: ...206,251,353,374
Horsey, Mary: ...133,138,159,169,306
: 359
Horsey, Nathaniel: 359
Horsey, Nelly: 214
Horsey, Outerbridge: ...206,251,353
: 359,361,374
Horsey, Revel: 428
Horsey, Samuel: 122,123,261
Horsey, Sarah: 22
Horsey, Smith: 341
Horsey, Stephen:.1,2,19,46,122,123
: 212,261,428
Horsey, Susan: 142,184,379
Horsey, William: ...133,138,159,165
:169,172,214,296,297,306,334,359
: 360,361,365,389,417,424,428
Hough, Edward: 213
Houghan, Sarah: 338
Houghan, William: 338
Houston, James: .57,166,214,230,250
: 260,277,321,359,409
Houston, John:53,67,94,274,278,319

:320,321,325,352,361,373,434,442
Houston, Leonard: 352
Houston, Nancy: 67,319
Houston, Rhoda: 94
Houston, Robert: 77,352,432
Houston, Sally Minor: 352
Howard, Allen: 311
Howard, Catherine: 278
Howard, David: ...46,87,134,214,270
: 398
Howard, Edward: 31
Howard, Eleanor: 46,214
Howard, George: 64,396
Howard, Gillis: 141
Howard, John: 448
Howard, Joseph: 193
Howard, Samuel: 128,293
Howjean, Sarah: 332
Hudson, John Dennis: 332
Huett, Ann: 229,346,394
Huett, John:.84,85,229,302,329,346
: 385,394
Huffington, Angelo: 30,191,243
Huffington, Ann: 134,292
Huffington, Gilbard: 404
Huffington, Gilbert: 295
Huffington, Isaac: 190
Huffington, James: 47,53,191
Huffington, Jesse: 53
Huffington, John:..27,29,47,53,100
:190,191,199,218,262,283,295,312
: 341,352,385,404,439
Huffington, Jonathan:27,53,191,218
: 283,380
Huffington, Joshua: 191
Huffington, Lazarus:.24,81,127,184
: 215,240,353
Huffington, Levin:.190,224,227,243
: 353,368
Huffington, Luke: 308,369
Huffington, Mary: 24,127,149
Huffington, Matildah: 227
Huffington, Richard: 24,149,250
Huffington, Sarah: 53,127,191
Huffington, Thomas:.24,107,149,194
: 195,215
Huffington, William: 375
Huffman, Catherine: 275
Huffman, John: 275
Hugg, Jane: 214
Hugg, Joanna: 157,215,234,235
Hugg, Thomas: 157,214,215,234
Huggins, Ann: 272,302
Huggins, Benjamin: 272,273,302
Huggins, Edmund: 26,27,352

Huggins,John:................352
Hughes,Jesse:6,12,215,219,328,363
:.................364,407,415,420
Hughes,John:..................132
Hughes,Josiah:............194,212
Hughes,Peggy Hopkins:.........212
Hughes,Peggy:.................194
Hughes,Phillip:...............360
Hughes,Sarah:............6,12,328
Hull,Beauchamp:.3,206,322,426,446
Hull,Brittingham:.........215,304
Hull,Edward:........71,262,304,420
Hull,Elizabeth:................98
Hull,Richard:..............98,210
Humphries,Amelia A.:..........231
Humphries,Amelia:.............182
Humphries,Ann:................204
Humphries,Archellus:..........149
Humphries,Archelus R.:........182
Humphries,Archelus:...........231
Humphries,Charles W.:.....149,182
Humphries,Charles:............231
Humphries,Dorothy:............182
Humphries,Elijah:..35,204,231,409
:.............................430
Humphries,Ezekiel:........34,204
Humphries,Jacob:..............181
Humphries,Joseph:.149,149,181,182
:.........................231,368
Humphries,Josephus:...149,182,231
Humphries,Joshua:..62,148,149,181
:.................182,204,231,340
Humphries,Margaret W.:149,182,231
Humphries,Mary:............34,265
Humphries,Phillis:....148,231,414
Humphries,Sarah McBryde:......231
Humphries,Sarah:..............204
Humphries,Thomas:..10,34,42,64,73
:..76,97,115,116,128,148,149,168
:180,181,211,216,224,230,231,239
:260,265,276,316,317,325,367,368
:.........................412,414
Humphries,William:........204,414
Hurt,David:...................247
Hust,James:.......158,218,257,298
Hust,Joseph:........27,218,330,430
Hust,Mary:................257,298
Hutchins,Charles:..68,194,270,373
Hutchins,Francis:.............375
Hutchins,George:...........34,263
Hutchins,Margaret:.............34
Hutchins,Mary:................263
Hutchins,William:.............263
Hutchison,Charles:.............68
Hyland,Lambert:62,184,185,275,423

Ingersol,Catherine:...........253
Ingersol,John:191,254,394,396,436
Ingersol,Mary:............253,254
Ingersol,Rebecca:.............254
Ingersol,Richard:......58,116,326
Ingersol,Samuel:..117,253,254,392
:.....................393,396,441
Ingram,Abraham:...............392
Ingram,Abraham:...............331
Ingram,Agnes:.................212
Ingram,Ann:...................219
Ingram,Charity:...............182
Ingram,Elinor:................392
Ingram,Isaac:.....212,219,324,331
Ingram,Jacob:.........182,212,219
Ingram,James:.............287,331
Ingram,John:..................231
Ingram,Margaret:..............324
Ingram,Robert:............217,299
Inslev,John:..............194,220
Insley,Valentine:..........11,123
Irving,Francis:...............357
Irving,Handy H.:..............320
Irving,John:..................357
Irving,Joseph:.....98,245,271,422
Irving,Leah:...98,137,245,271,296
:.....................320,367,422
Irving,Levin:.67,68,83,98,137,141
:202,240,241,245,260,271,296,320
:.............................422
Irving,Sarah:..............98,271
Irving,Thomas:..26,98,245,271,421
:.............................422
Irving,William H.:............320
Jackson,Alice:.................41
Jackson,Betty:.............76,154
Jackson,Daniel:............98,414
Jackson,Elihu:...25,75,76,154,222
:.....................292,362,441
Jackson,Elizabeth:...75,76,96,222
Jackson,Ezekiel:....62,75,302,340
Jackson,George W.:............273
Jackson,Henry:.....65,346,402,407
Jackson,Hugh:.................149
Jackson,Isaac B.:.............222
Jackson,James:................222
Jackson,John:.................154
Jackson,Jonathan:.1,65,76,381,421
Jackson,Joseph:............96,222
Jackson,Joshua:............41,421
Jackson,Noah:.................154
Jackson,Patience:..........65,421
Jackson,Rachel:.............1,381
Jackson,Samuel:..1,65,98,255,311
:.................355,381,414,421

Jackson,Sarah McB.:...........149
Jackson,Sarah:........1,41,381,421
Jackson,Thomas:..........1,98,381
James,Comfort:............223,297
James,Edward:.................421
James,Eleanor:................421
James,Ezekiel:..23,26,109,223,429
James,Francis:.......26,223,435
James,George:..26,223,271,422,429
James,Gilbert:................421
James,Jean:...................421
James,John J.:................361
James,John W.D.F.:............361
James,Levin:..................223
James,Louisa:.................435
James,Mary:..........320,360,388
James,Richard:.................30
James,Samuel:.................361
James,Thomas:..................26
James,Unice:...............26,223
James,William:253,254,309,319,360
:.............................396
James,Willoby:................388
Jamison,Alexander:............267
Jarman,Samuel:................387
Jarrett,Graves:...........203,204
Jarrett,James:................203
Jarrett,Mary:.................203
Jarrett,Richard:..............203
Jeasman,George:...............224
Jefferson,Richard:.............27
Jenkins,Betsy:................371
Jenkins,David V.:.............181
Jenkins,David Vance:..........181
Jenkins,David:............205,371
Jenkins,Francis:...28,149,205,225
:.....................304,322,386
Jenkins,Jarvis:....95,172,186,205
Jenkins,John:.....95,208,329,330
Jenkins,Jonathan:.........154,214
Jenkins,Joseph:........95,96,142
Jenkins,Kibble:.......173,206,288
Jenkins,Leah:..............96,142
Jenkins,Littleton:........205,371
Jenkins,Mary:.....225,304,322,386
Jenkins,Rachel:............95,329
Jenkins,Rebecca:..............181
Jenner,Easter:................364
Jenner,John:..149,166,225,261,364
Jessup,John:...................19
Johnson,Affradozi:............156
Johnson,Alexander:............150
Johnson,Algah:.................14
Johnson,Algenon:..........292,439
Johnson,Amelia:.................8

Johnson,Ann:....................226
Johnson,Arthur:.................6
Johnson,Benjamin:..29,42,45,57,58
:106,112,116,121,123,152,156,171
:214,228,270,272,273,277,290,321
:325,361,372,377,395,400,409,437
Johnson,Cornelius:......91,296,352
Johnson,Daniel Webster:........292
Johnson,Elijah:........112,156,186
Johnson,Elijah:................270
Johnson,Elijah:...277,298,318,372
:..............................386
Johnson,Elizabeth:......58,176,439
Johnson,Esther:................226
Johnson,George P.:.............361
Johnson,George:...........226,268
Johnson,Henry Blair:...........229
Johnson,Henry:.................318
Johnson,James H.:..............297
Johnson,Jesse:.............227,248
Johnson,John:.106,171,214,239,278
:........321,361,368,370,377,409
Johnson,Joseph:............385,397
Johnson,Joshua:.19,82,138,264,278
:..............293,295,297,314,361
Johnson,Littleton:.............226
Johnson,Margaret:......126,186,312
Johnson,Mary:..................292
Johnson,McMurray:..........248,403
Johnson,Phillis:...............106
Johnson,Purnell:8,112,206,250,270
:275,276,277,288,318,319,320,359
:..........................361,372,386
Johnson,Rachel:................368
Johnson,Richard:...............292
Johnson,Samuel:................156
Johnson,Sarah:156,231,261,290,386
Johnson,Shephard:..............400
Johnson,Shepherd:..............226
Johnson,Susannah:..........385,397
Johnson,Thomas:...8,9,112,141,156
:...176,226,270,276,288,318,372,
:...............................86
Johnson,Whittington:...........274
Johnson,William Purnell:..156,206
:..............................386
Johnson,William:..156,174,226,318
:..............................386
Jones,Andrew:..32,125,229,272,394
Jones,Ann D.:..............140,445
Jones,Ann Dashiell:............445
Jones,Ann:.............278,368,407
Jones,Anna:....................445
Jones,Benjamin:.22,32,101,135,174
:185,196,198,282,283,322,340,427

Jones,Benjmain:................135
Jones,Charles:....131,286,344,390
Jones,Cyrus:...................288
Jones,Daniel:..............93,428
Jones,David:...................352
Jones,Dorcas:..........69,225,226
Jones,Ebenezer:................229
Jones,Elizabeth Dashiell:......283
Jones,Elizabeth Winder:........229
Jones,Elizabeth:...93,229,272,340
:..............................423
Jones,Esther:..............174,322
Jones,Ezekiel:..................23
Jones,Frankey:............228,372
Jones,George P.:................11
Jones,George:.............292,390
Jones,Gilbert:.................421
Jones,Griffith:................442
Jones,Howell:.............229,394
Jones,Isaac D.:................428
Jones,Isaac:......227,228,229,353
Jones,Jacob:....................68
Jones,James Makemorie:.62,285,434
:..............................435
Jones,James Makaorie:...........15
Jones,James:...13,41,62,69,93,120
:125,159,227,228,229,252,272,284
:..............288,327,394,408,421
Jones,Jane:...........228,401,421
Jones,Jesse:...................48
Jones,John:..32,34,40,101,102,120
:164,185,208,227,228,229,282,283
:....287,288,340,360,391,411,423
Jones,Joshua:.........225,226,228
Jones,Leonard:..........32,40,401
Jones,Levin D.:............54,233
Jones,Lucretia:....73,233,315,379
Jones,Marcellas:...............251
Jones,Marcellus:...............103
Jones,Margaret:................352
Jones,Martha:..............93,158
Jones,Mary:........38,74,102,122
Jones,Matthew:....106,228,290,372
Jones,Matthias:................311
Jones,Mitchell:.......174,198,322
Jones,Nancy:..............163,290
Jones,Nathan:..................106
Jones,Nelly:..........41,288,422
Jones,Nicholas:.................77
Jones,Phillip:........38,74,75,122
Jones,Prisey:.............120,227
Jones,Purnell Johnson:.........106
Jones,Robert:.117,118,164,182,227
:............288,302,368,375,390
Jones,Samuel B.D.:.............228

Jones,Samuel:............28,67,68
Jones,Sarah:..159,229,272,366,394
Jones,Susan:....................98
Jones,Susannah:............98,194
Jones,Temperance:..............311
Jones,Thomas:41,64,98,140,158,171
:194,206,229,287,364,391,407,422
:..............................445
Jones,Tubman:..................391
Jones,William:...42,60,91,208,228
:...278,296,323,352,399,405,431
Jones.,Benjamin:...............196
Joseph,William:................157
Judah,Mary:....................339
Judah,William:.................339
Justice,James:.................295
Justice,Ralph:.................295
Keen,Ann:..................249,311
Keen,John:.....................170
Keen,Margaret:.................311
Keen,Mary:.................211,230
Keen,Richard:....................6
Keen,Sarah:....................311
Keen,Tabitha:..................311
Keen,William:..35,70,211,230,249
:...........................311,428
Kellett,Eunice:........213,247,323
Kellett,Robert:................257
Kellett,Roger:........213,247,323
Kelley,Robert:.................332
Kellum,Edward:12,30,53,70,231,237
:.............283,315,404,446
Kellum,Henrietta:...............73
Kellum,Hetty:..............73,437
Kellum,Jane:...................176
Kellum,John:.4,5,12,30,70,100,113
:......231,232,237,341,439,446
Kellum,Patience:...........73,437
Kellum,Priscilla:..........12,237
Kellum,Richard:................176
Kellum,William:............73,437
Kelly,Daniel:..........44,85,291
Kelly,Henry:...................379
Kemp,Eleanor:..................280
Kemp,Elinor:....................69
Kemp,John:.....................163
Kemp,Matthew:..........69,244,280
Kemp,Rebecca:...................69
Kenicken,Daniel:...............347
Kennedy,Ann:...................269
Kennedy,John:..................269
Kennedy,Luther:................191
Kennedy,Mary:..................359
Kennedy,Nancy:..................67
Kennedy,Priscilla:......5,113,232

Kennedy,Timothy:..........269,270
Kennerly,Caleb:59,154,168,170,312
Kennerly,Everton:.141,142,174,357
:......................358,423
Kennerly,Henry:................69
Kennerly,Isaac:...114,227,232,234
:..................292,341,412
Kennerly,Joseph:..............142
Kennerly,Juliann:.............170
Kennerly,Luther:..........232,431
Kennerly,Thomas:...........92,345
Kennerly,William:.......3,120,439
Kenny,Isaac:..................193
Ker,Jane:.................155,262
Kersey,Patrick:............32,123
Kibble,Betty:.................372
Kibble,George:.225,233,247,372,39
Kibble,Hannah:................135
Kibble,Jenkins:...............288
Kibble,John C.:...............372
Kibble,John:...43,103,134,372,438
Kibble,Richard:...............134
Kibble,Ursly:.................134
Kibble,William:43,103,134,135,372
Kilby,Christopher:............372
Kilby,John:...............149,372
Kilby,Mary:...............265,372
Kimmey,Henry:.................232
Kimmey,Jane:..................129
Kimmey,Solomon:...............224
King,Ann:.........110,164,351,352
King,Capell:..16,28,38,88,176,225
:...............227,255,366,395
King,Charles:.................303
King,Elizabeth:73,233,286,315,379
King,Ephraim:...3,7,19,39,40,55,68
:...72,73,90,109,110,142,145,164
:176,207,227,233,254,259,271,274
:279,280,286,303,315,335,344,351
:352,362,365,371,379,381,402,404
:.....................424,425,443
King,James:...................331
King,Levi:........277,309,392,441
King,Levin:................34,35
King,Louther:.................204
King,Mary:..19,69,118,120,205,208
:.....................233,280,286
King,Meriam:..................233
King,Nehemiah:...34,35,75,302,317
:.............................331
King,Phillip:.................233
King,Priscilla:...............149
King,Robert J. H.:............266
King,Robert:..........75,149,331
King,Samuel:7,19,43,69,73,110,143
:164,166,208,233,254,259,271,280
:286,303,315,336,344,351,352,379
:.........................404,425
King,Sarah:........16,176,255,366
King,Southy:...................95
King,Zorobable:83,155,240,260,369
Kinikin,James:................234
Kinikin,William:..............234
Kinney,Isaac:......16,112,399,405
Kinney,Joshua:................112
Kinney,Milly:..................16
Kinney,Samuel:................232
Kinney,William:...........112,232
Kirby,Robert:.............174,322
Kirkpatrick,David:............168
Kirkpatrick,Jane:.............168
Knight,Eliza:.............143,364
Knight,James:.....143,144,364,439
Knight,John:..................438
Knight,Jonathan:..............235
Knight,Joshua:............143,144
Knight,Mary:..............144,364
Knipschitt,John:..............360
Knipshitt,Amelia:.............320
Knipshitt,John:.....319,320,360
Knipshitt,Nelly:..............360
Knowles,Martha Jane:..........425
Knowles,Wilson:...............425
Knox,James:....................46
Kollock,Simon:................401
Laferty,Samuel:...............361
Laird,Dorothy Arietta:....230,275
Laird,James:..........230,275,361
Lamar,Jacob:..................281
Lamar,Raymond:................281
Lamberson,John:...127,223,377,393
Lamberson,Leah:...............329
Lamberson,Mary:...............223
Lamberson,Thomas:.............329
Lamberson,Zedekiah:...........187
Lane,John:........273,284,315,430
Lane,Sarah:...................315
Landon,Arthur:................235
Lane,Nelly:...................365
Lane,Thomas:..............319,365
Langeake,Francis:......56,78,200
Langeake,George:...............56
Langeake,Judah:................56
Langeake,Stephen:.............200
Langeake,William:..........78,200
Langrell,George:..........294,373
Langrell,James:...............294
Langsdale,Eleanor:....130,236,445
Langsdale,Elizabeth:......236,445
Langsdale,Esther:.....130,236,445
Langsdale,Henry:......130,236,445
Langsdale,Huett:..............236
Langsdale,James Huett:........445
Langsdale,James:..............236
Langsdale,John:...130,232,236,445
Langsdale,Joshua W.:......236,305
Langsdale,Joshua Whittington:.445
Langsdale,Joshua:.............236
Langsdale,Matilda:............305
Langsdale,Robert:.....235,236,445
Langsdale,Spear:..............232
Langsdale,Whittington:........236
Langsdale,William:........236,445
Langsden,John:................445
Langsden,Mary:................445
Langsden,Spear:...............445
Langsden,William:.............445
Langstor,James:...............290
Lank,Cannon:..................133
Lank,Francis:..........30,78,200
Lank,George:...............78,200
Lank,Mary:.....................51
Lank,Stephen:..................78
Lank,Thomas:...................51
Lank,William:..................78
Lankford,Benjamin:.96,236,368,439
Lankford,Ephraim:.............236
Lankford,Hiram:...............236
Lankford,John:........62,368,423
Lankford,Judea:................62
Lankford,Mary:.........96,236,368
Lankford,Phillip:.............232
Lankford,Sarah:................96
Lankford,Thomas Cuby:..........96
Lankford,Thomas:62,96,222,236,284
:.........................367,439
Lankford,William N.:..........386
Lankford,William:.............397
Larramore,Elihu:..............315
Larramore,Elijah:.............344
Larramore,James:..205,328,344,411
Larramore,John:.74,85,148,335,344
:.................401,402,411,443
Larramore,Levin:74,85,148,335,402
:.............................443
Larramore,Louisa:.............344
Larramore,Mary:...148,287,335,411
:.............................443
Larramore,Samuel:.........387,428
Larramore,Thomas:...55,85,287,344
:.................401,411,428
Larramore,William:............328
Lawrence,Sarah:................55
Laws,Alexander:...........140,178
Laws,Anne:....................176

Laws,Catherine:..............400
Laws,Elijah:..........82,97,241
Laws,James:..................298
Laws,Jane:....................84
Laws,John:......68,140,176,343,388
Laws,Phillis:................298
Laws,Robert:.............84,400
Laws,William:47,48,82,161,193,209
:241,298,336,338,346,389,397,400
Lawson,Leah:.................242
Lawson,Molly:................242
Lawson,Richard:..............242
Lawson,Sarah:................242
Layfield,Catherine:....27,358,387
Layfield,George:...27,159,358,387
Layfield,John:...............395
Layfield,Robert:..........71,242
Layfield,Samuel:......27,358,387
Layfield,Smullen:.........11,225
Layfield,Smullin:............435
Layfield,Solomon:.........14,242
Layfield,Thomas:..14,27,93,160,358
:...................387,395,446
Layfield,William:..83,217,242,256
:....................323,324,341
Layton,Henry:................141
Layton,James:............177,376
Layton,John:.................141
Layton,Thomas:...............180
Layton,William:.....156,213,242
Leary,Charles:...............131
Leatherbury,Charles:..184,242,243
:........251,271,304,305,381,421
Leatherbury,Eleanor:.........305
Leatherbury,Jesse:...........422
Leatherbury,John:..83,125,126,127
:134,136,143,164,215,240,242,243
:248,260,285,296,304,305,309,311
:...................359,362,381,421
Leatherbury,Margaret:.........50
Leatherbury,Mary:.............37
Leatherbury,Peregrine:.......305
Leatherbury,Robert:71,262,320,445
Leatherbury,Sarah:...........242
Leatherbury,Thomas:..........243
Lecat,Ann:...................295
Lecat,Francina:..............295
Lecat,John:..................295
Lecat,Joseph:................295
Lecat,Levin:.................295
Lecat,Littleton:.............295
Lecat,Nathaniel:.............295
Leckie,Alexander:..84,98,245,329
:........................385,397
Leckie,Ann:.84,98,229,329,346,385

:........................394,397
Leckie,John:.................413
Lecompte,John:...............234
Lecompte,Samuel:..........54,145
Lemmon,Robert:...............360
Lemon Robert:................383
Lemon,Nancy:...14,278,316,329,361
:........................383,384
Lemon,Robert:...14,22,278,316,329
:....................356,361,384
Leonard,Benjamin:............298
Leonard,Ebenezer:........278,289
Leonard,Isaac:................11
Leonard,John:.............93,210
Leonard,Joseph:..87,91,93,210,244
:...............327,328,360,406
Leonard,Leah:.............93,210
Leonard,Michael:.............298
Leonard,William J.:...........19
Leonard,William:.............360
Lewis :.......................14
Lewis,Arthur:................235
Lewis,Elizabeth:.............173
Lewis,James:.............223,235
Lewis,Jesse:.................235
Lewis,John:..................173
Lewis,Thomas:................235
Lewis,Zadock:................235
Libby,John:...................41
Lightfoot,Thomas:............301
Lightfoot,William:.......298,301
Limbree,William:.............407
Lingo,Ann:................32,123
Lingo,Comfort:...............297
Lingo,Daniel:......297,318,327,397
Lingo,Elijah:............124,448
Lingo,Jacob:..............79,297
Lingo,John:......124,246,297,448
Lingo,Joshua:............124,416
Lingo,Margaret:..........327,397
Lingo,Mary:..................297
Lingo,Rachel:................297
Lingo,Richard:...............297
Lingo,Richardson:.............32
Lingo,Robertson:...18,123,124,196
:...................245,246,448
Lingo,Robinson:..............351
Lingo,Sarah:.................297
Lingo,Smith:..........18,196,246
Lingo,Urselly:...............297
Lingo,William:...124,297,416,448
Linnard,Joshua:..............329
Little,Charles:................7
Littleton,Minos Covington:....27
Littleton,Thomas:.............27

Livingston,George:.........2,46
Livingston,Samuel:.............2
Livingston,Stephen:............1
Livingston,Susan:..............2
Livingston,Todd:..........46,148
Lloyd,Ann:....................40
Lloyd,Edward:............40,408
Lloyd,James:.................167
Lloyd,Jane:.............232,237
Lloyd,John:..................232
Lloyd,Martha:................408
Lloyd,Peggy:.............111,232
Lloyd,Thomas:.....109,111,146,353
Lloyd,William:111,231,232,300,367
:...........................408
Long,Solomon:..83,155,240,260,369
Lord,John:...........177,219,405
Lord,William:............177,404
Lowe,Ann:.................59,444
Lowe,Charles:................139
Lowe,Ebenezer:...........162,298
Lowe,Esther:34,62,118,120,179,227
:................303,339,344,409
Lowe,George:.......59,297,340,444
Lowe,Henry:...8,17,34,62,77,86,94
:114,118,120,134,135,146,179,181
:185,213,227,246,247,257,284,303
:335,339,342,344,345,366,377,385
:...................386,408,409,415
Lowe,Hudson:........51,75,325,368
Lowe,John:................58,444
Lowe,Levin:...................51
Lowe,Nathan:.................423
Lowe,Peter:..................421
Lowe,Ralph:......5,59,183,257,444
Lowe,Robert:..............59,444
Lowe,Samuel:.............325,368
Lowe,Sarah:..................423
Lowe,Tabitha:................444
Lowe,Thomas:.............320,365
Lowe,Tubman:...10,120,135,179,247
:257,342,345,359,360,388,401,415
Lowe,William:............297,423
Lowes,Henry:..................60
Lucas,Esther:................185
Lucas,James:..................85
Lucas,Jane:...............59,185
Lucas,Margaret:..............185
Lucas,Martha:................185
Lucas,Thomas:................249
Luckly,John:.................271
Lumm,Edward:.................163
Lurten,Henry:................403
Lurten,Sabra:................403
Lurton,Henry:................435

Lynch,Isabell:..............294
Lynch,Michael:...............294
Lynn,Aaron:................1,419
Lyon,John:........258,417,432
Lyon,Margery:................258
MacDaniel,James:.............259
Mackey,James:................359
Mackey,Sarah:................359
Maddox,Wilson:................54
Maddux,Alexander:....259,260,433
Maddux,Betty:.................89
Maddux,Daniel:........89,260,373
Maddux,Elizabeth:....256,260,433
Maddux,Elzey:................433
Maddux,Ezekiel:..........259,420
Maddux,Henry:................433
Maddux,Hezekiah:...54,178,252,373
:...................390,433,434
Maddux,Isaac:................433
Maddux,Jesse:................317
Maddux,John:89,93,137,239,241,255
:............259,260,261,316,433
Maddux,Joseph:...............433
Maddux,Joshua:...............433
Maddux,Lazarus:..............433
Maddux,Lydia:................260
Maddux,Martin L.H.:..........265
Maddux,Thomas:...........271,352
Maddux,William:....52,255,260,433
Maddux,Wilson:...........178,434
Maddux,Zachariah:........308,433
Maddux,Zephaniah:............433
Magee,Arbhibald Nelly:.......162
Magee,David:.............105,261
MaGee,David:.................378
Magee,David:.................383
Magee,Davis:.........161,162,203
Magee,George:.................91
Magee,Henry:.................393
Magee,James:.............117,266
Magee,John:..82,91,92,233,308,347
:............................389
Magee,Margaret:......233,332
Magee,Mary:..............261,383
Magee,Milbourn:..........161,203
Magee,Milby:.................224
Magee,Nelly:.............161,203
Magee,Peggy:.................332
Magee,Peter:........91,347,438
Magee,Rueben:................117
Magee,Samuel:.............82,393
Magee,Sarah:..................91
Magee,Stephen:...............332
Maglamery,Edward:............133
Maglamery,Elijah:............133

Maglamery,Geoge:.............117
Maglamery,George:....117,140,215
Maglamery,John:...........36,133
Maglamery,Levin:.............133
Maglamery,Sarah:.............133
Makemorie,Ann:...............221
Makemorie,James:29,30,221,315,434
:........................435,446
Makemorie,Mary:...............29
Malone,Elizabeth:............171
Malone,Frances:..........179,247
Malone,George:....102,103,171,179
Malone,John:.............170,263
Malone,Levi:.................103
Malone,Mary:.............263,410
Malone,Peter:.....144,179,263,410
Malone,Robert:....170,171,179,263
Malone,Sarah:................144
Malone,Simon:............103,179
Malone,Stephen:.......171,263,410
Malone,William:...102,171,179,247
Manlove,Alice:...............263
Manlove,Ann:...........2,139,263
Manlove,Boaz:................178
Manlove,Elizabeth:...........263
Manlove,John:......138,139,263,385
Manlove,Jonathan:............139
Manlove,Luke:................263
Manlove,Manuel:..............227
Manlove,Mark:................322
Manlove,Peter:...........143,364
Manlove,Rachel:..............139
Manlove,Sarah:...........144,364
Manlove,William:.............141
Maria ,Ann:..................408
Marine,Ann:...................24
Marine,Charles:...............24
Marine,Mary:..................24
Marine,William:...........24,249
Marine,Zorobable:.............24
Marrett.John:............258,421
Marsh,Paul:..................229
Marshall,Benjamin:.......242,291
Marshall,Betsy:...............16
Marshall,Charles:........242,291
Marshall,Christopher:..46,177,242
:................266,291,392,421
Marshall,George:........6,161,395
Marshall,Joseph:.15,67,94,218,337
:............................367
Marshall,Rachel:..............16
Marshall,Thomas:.............102
Martin,George:...........286,429
Martin,John:.............144,265
Martin,Luther:...............265

Martin,Mary:.................381
Martin,Nancy:.............96,193
Martin,William:..........381,429
Marvel,David:................168
Marvel,Hannah:...............211
Marvel,John:.................211
Marvel,Phillip:..............168
Marvel,Robert:...........168,187
Marvel,Thomas:...............168
Marvell,David:...........191,192
Marvell,Robert:..........191,192
Marvell,Thomas:......168,191,192
Massey,Joseph:...............266
Massey,Purnell:...............60
Massey,Thomas:...............266
Matthews,Elijah:.............241
Matthews,John:...............172
Matthews,Levi:...............368
Matthews,Sarah:..............172
McAllen,Eleanor:.............172
McBryde,Elizabeth:........42,291
McBryde,Francis:.............291
McBryde,Hugh:................291
McBryde,Sally:...............291
McBryde,Samuel:..............291
McBryde,Sarah:.20,21,50,54,76,167
:182,200,201,234,289,291,294,299
:............333,334,340,417,442
McBryde,Willen:..............120
McBryde,William:.1,20,42,54,70,76
:102,120,150,158,167,187,191,200
:201,233,276,277,278,289,291,292
:293,294,299,333,334,339,340,366
:............391,406,417,424,437,441
McCabe,Elizabeth:........287,411
McCabe,Henry:............287,411
McClellan,Benjamin:...216,325,367
:........................368,412
McClellan,Bridget:.......325,368
McClellan,Joseph:........172,216
McClemmy,George:.............441
McClemmy,Gillis:.........260,359
McClemmy,Thomas:.............216
McClemmy,William:...10,83,240,260
:................277,295,296,358
McClennan,Benjamin:......165,427
McClennan,Eleanor:...........427
McClennan,Ellender:..........357
McClennan,Esther:............426
McClester,Betsy:.............357
McClester,Daniel:....266,303,397
McClester,George:5,12,182,328,329
:........................352,428
McClester,Isabel:.........41,347
McClester,James Robert J.:...336

McClester,John:.5,6,11,12,136,182
:266,303,328,336,357,397,430,431
:...........................444
McClester,Joseph:.8,28,41,347,355
:...........................448
McClester,Neal:...182,303,397,430
McClester,Rachel:..............352
McClester,Samuel:5,12,182,303,328
:...........................357,430
McClester,Sarah:..........328,352
McClish,Thomas:................405
McClure,Dorothy:...............325
McCree,James:...............45,161
McDaniel,Edward:................33
McDaniel,James:...33,150,193,259
McDaniel,Margaret:............150
McDaniel,William:..............259
McDowell,John:............161,353
McDowell,Joshua:..............343
McGee,David:..................297
McGinnis,Elizabeth:...........339
McGlammery,Edmund:............311
McGlammery,Edward:........297,311
McGlammery,George:............311
McGlammery,John:..............297
McGlemmy,George:..............441
McGrath,John:..................56
McGrath,Levin:.................56
McGraugh,Owen:................317
McGregor,William:.............209
McGunis,Daniel:................68
McGunis,Elizabeth:.............68
McIntyre,Betty:99,103,130,189,281
:......................356,376,437
McIntyre,Daniel:...99,100,103,130
:140,141,189,281,287,356,376,411
:......................413,437,438
McIntyre,Elizabeth:........99,103
McIntyre,ELizabeth:...........130
McIntyre,Elizabeth:...130,141,189
:............287,376,411,437,438
McIntyre,John:.....99,100,281,356
McIntyre,Willen:..............146
McIntyre,William:..99,100,103,130
:..........................141,376
McIntyre,Willin:..141,189,218,356
:......................437,438
McKean,George:............146,322
McKean,Patrick:...........146,322
McKimmey,Deborah:.............261
McKimmey,James:...............261
McKimmey,Sarah:................89
McKimmey,Solomon:..............89
McLally,Elizabeth:............311
McLally,Patrick:..............268
McLally,William:..............312
McLaughlin,Alexander:.........301
McLaughlin,Mary:..............301
McLeary,James:................277
McMurke,David:........46,291,392
McMurke,Margery:..............291
McMurray,Ann:.................162
McMurray,Nancy:...............162
McMurray,Rebecca:.............162
McNeal,John:..................128
McNeal,Matilda:...............128
McNeal,William:...........128,129
McWilliams,James:..............12
Mears,Robert:..................95
Mears,Sarah:..............95,337
Measley,John:.................267
Mechan,Deborah:...............149
Meech,John:...............267,268
Meech,Thomas:.................267
Meek,Jacob:...................170
Meek,Sarah:...................170
Melson,Benjamin:...30,269,321,323
:......................333,350
Melson,Daniel:..9,172,197,268,269
:......................321,323,390
Melson,Elijah:....269,350,373,390
Melson,Esther:................333
Melson,Eunice:............159,312
Melson,Hannah:............151,224
Melson,Isabel:................312
Melson,Jesse:.................333
Melson,John:..............150,224
Melson,Joseph:159,269,312,323,333
Melson,Mary:..................159
Melson,Samuel:........269,312,333
Melson,Sary:..................159
Melson,Thomas:................312
Melson,William:...............333
Melton,Ann:...................234
Melton,John:..................234
Melton,Richard:...............234
Merrill,Esme:.................332
Merrill,William:......166,258,418
Messick,Benjamin:..............45
Messick,John:..................45
Methven,Thomas:...............256
Mezick,Aaron:...11,22,182,228,269
:.......................276,372
Mezick,Amely:.................369
Mezick,Ann:...............228,372
Mezick,Benjamin:..........315,373
Mezick,Bridget:................41
Mezick,Covington:85,87,89,129,238
:...........................387
Mezick,Daniel:.89,127,129,178,244
:......................279,290,314
Mezick,Eleanor:................98
Mezick,Elihu:..89,127,129,178,217
:224,243,244,279,290,314,344,348
:...........................387
Mezick,Elijah:................387
Mezick,Elizabeth:..89,218,224,314
Mezick,George:........269,315,373
Mezick,Jacob Elizabeth:.......218
Mezick,Jacob:..89,127,129,140,217
:............224,290,314,352,393
Mezick,James:40,41,89,143,224,344
Mezick,John:11,89,127,129,178,244
:............269,279,290,314,348,352
Mezick,Joseph:................129
Mezick,Joshua:............290,387
Mezick,Julian:............290,299
Mezick,Leah:...................89
Mezick,Levin W.:......89,129,387
Mezick,Levin William:.........127
Mezick,Luke:..............258,369
Mezick,Margaret:..127,129,178,243
:................279,290,314,348
Mezick,Martha W. Handy:.......245
Mezick,Martha W.Handy:.........98
Mezick,Martha Washington Handy:..
:............................09
Mezick,Mary:..............127,314
Mezick,Nehemiah:......127,290,314
Mezick,Newton Willis:..........85
Mezick,Sarah Ann:..........87,238
Mezick,Sarah:.315,363,387,420,422
Mezick,William:98,109,245,271,363
:......................369,420,422
Milbourn,Ralph:........87,190,252
Milbourn,Sarah:.......66,87,190,252
Miles,Elizabeth:..............143
Miles,George:.................380
Miles,John:...............273,300
Miles,Levin:..................143
Miles,Matthew:.................15
Miles,Matthias:........80,142,336
Miles,Samuel:..............63,369
Miles,William:................273
Miller,Isabella:..............274
Miller,Levin:.................379
Mills,Ann:................232,237
Mills,Benjamin:...............278
Mills,Davis:..................311
Mills,John M.:................278
Mills,L.M.:...................278
Mills,Lydnam H.:..............311
Mills,Patty:..............232,237
Mills,Richard:......91,92,219,306
Mills,Selby:...............25,211

Mills,Stephen:................278
Mills,William Washington:.232,237
Mills,William:......25,211,297,331
Minnish,Richard:..............304
Mister,Charles:..............29,30
Mister,Marmaduke:................29
Mitchell,Abraham:...............301
Mitchell,Alexander:............150
Mitchell,Benjamin:.....39,279,331
Mitchell,George:.................41
Mitchell,Hessey:................436
Mitchell,Isaac:........209,393,444
Mitchell,Isabel:.................41
Mitchell,John Pope:.21,67,171,260
:....................341,349,359
Mitchell,John:.21,182,263,278,337
:............................346,367
Mitchell,Joseph:................39
Mitchell,Joshua:...........21,171
Mitchell,Josiah:..........209,436
Mitchell,Marv:.............39,331
Mitchell,Nancy:................356
Mitchell,Polly:.................67
Mitchell,Robert:..........176,263
Mitchell,Rufus:.................21
Mitchell,Solomon:..............392
Mitchell,Stephen:......85,321,443
Mitchell,Thomas:...85,110,271,280
:........................352,356
Mitchell,William:.........204,393
Moore,Adam:....................158
Moore,Ann:..................51,234
Moore,Benjamin:.................35
Moore,Betsy:...............76,196
Moore,Catherine:...............317
Moore,Charles:.................416
Moore,Ebenezer:........141,357,423
Moore,Elijah:..........75,76,196
Moore,Elizabeth:..197,271,322,358
Moore,George Lane:...177,282,376
Moore,George:..........52,53,271
Moore,Henry:..............282,358
Moore,Isaac:...75,122,197,322,333
Moore,James:.35,95,98,136,164,242
:....................312,362,446
Moore,John L.:.................358
Moore,John Lane:...............282
Moore,John:..17,86,95,103,143,171
:176,177,226,262,281,282,301,304
:322,324,358,359,360,376,385,409
:.........................410,416
Moore,Joseph:..............182,228
Moore,Joshua E.:...............402
Moore,Joshua Evans:.......240,402
Moore,Joshua:.............233,282

Moore,Levin:.......164,282,309,362
Moore,Margaret:........143,410,446
Moore,Mary:.28,35,100,164,177,181
:243,271,282,301,309,312,362,376
:..........................409,422
Moore,Nelly:...................282
Moore,Newbold:.................122
Moore,Peggy:...................360
Moore,Priscilla:...............165
Moore,Rachel:.............409,446
Moore,Ralph:...28,100,164,309,362
Moore,Richard K.:..............165
Moore,Samuel:..............86,325
Moore,Sarah:.......103,164,309,362
Moore,Tabitha:.................322
Moore,Thomas:..85,183,243,251,271
:...............280,282,353,374,422
Moore,William:..92,95,127,136,143
:........282,304,311,322,409,446
Morgan,Avery:..................265
Morgan,Henry:..................271
Morgan,Jane:...................271
Morgan,Joseph:.............47,282
Morris,Aikada:.................393
Morris,Amelia:.........77,283,394
Morris,Ann Eliza:..............233
Morris,Ann Starling:.......90,417
Morris,Annaliza:...............103
Morris,Catherine:..57,102,153,431
Morris,Cornelius:..........82,393
Morris,Dennis:.........90,283,418
Morris,Ebe:....................311
Morris,Edward:.................160
Morris,Eliza Ann:..............390
Morris,Elizabeth:.146,284,390,409
Morris,Isabell:................312
Morris,Isabella:..........154,170
Morris,Jacob:76,77,79,104,146,148
:230,242,270,283,284,285,287,336
:............341,342,361,395,402
Morris,James R.:...........319,364
:..........................367
Morris,James Round:...216,283,319
:..........................367
Morris,James:..................30.217
Morris,Jenkins:...........283,285
Morris,Jeptha:........283,349,394
Morris,Jereniah:...............442
Morris,Jethro:.88,152,153,167,404
:..........................432
Morris,John Boucher:...........216
Morris,John H.:...171,233,247,257
:..........................284,285
Morris,John M.:................247
Morris,John Malone:...171,247,285
:..........................301

Morris,John:..76,77,79,90,104,146
:148,171,230,243,247,257,267,294
:...............285,301,342,395,402
Morris,Joseph:...76,79,90,104,146
:148,170,171,172,198,230,242,247
:257,283,284,285,301,342,390,402
:..........................429
Morris,Joshua:..43,65,76,77,78,82
:.90,114,148,153,173,230,267,270
:....283,311,330,349,394,402,422
Morris,Leah:..216,283,319,320,364
:..........................365,367
Morris,Levin:......103,233,285,390
Morris,Manasses:..........127,284,409
Morris,Manus:..................405
Morris,Mary:...................76
Morris,Morris:.................172
Morris,Nathaniel:..............346
Morris,Nehemiah:...............292
Morris,Priscilla:..............195
Morris,Robert H.:..............242
Morris,Robert:146,242,243,247,395
Morris,Samuel:.................76
Morris,Thomas:...57,82,88,102,152
:.................153,167,377,393
Morris,Warren Jones:...........103
Morris,William P.:........148,230
Morris,William Winder:.........216
Morris,William:..57,82,90,102,115
:152,153,209,216,283,367,377,393
:..........................431
Morris:........................418
Morrow,August:.................258
Morse,John:....................107
Muir,Adam:..27,94,110,288,301,326
:..........................392
Muir,James:...........288,326,392
Murray,Polly:..................161
Murray,Thomas:.................161
Murray,William:20,200,201,289,299
:..........................417
Murtre,David:..................177
Murray,Elizabeth:..............168
Nairn,Mary:.....................30
Nairn,Polly:..............20,216
Nairn,Robert:20,30,82,216,217,337
:..........................377
Neal,Esther:...................204
Nelms,Ann Eliza:................58
Nelms,Edmond Northern:.93,161,162
Nelms,Edmund Northern:134,261,270
:..........................298,368
Nelms,Edward Northern:....172,235
Nelms,Francis:............359,361
Nelms,Jeremiah:.................48

Nelms,John:..17,48,58,81,89,91,97
;128,208,239,252,266,269,270,277
;292,293,295,297,318,319,328,337
;343,358,372,377,378,397,398,429
:..........................433,435
Nelms,Joshua:......138,293,297,310
Nelms,Nancy:...91,134,208,210,316
:..................... 329,382,384
Nelms,Moah:........328,360,397,398
Nelms,Peter:...........328,397,398
Nelms,Sarah:..........138,293,310
Nelson,Almira:.................69
Nelson,Ann:...................209
Nelson,Benjamin:..............215
Nelson,Cyrus:..................69
Nelson,Eleanor:.............69,280
Nelson,Ephraim:...............395
Nelson,Esther:........160,194,280
Nelson,Francis D.:......69,110,280
Nelson,Francis:............69,280
Nelson,Hetty:..................69
Nelson,Horatio:................69
Nelson,James T.:..............395
Nelson,James:.160,194,237,238,280
:...............293,395,426,427
Nelson,John:.12,68,69.110,124,125
;126,136,160,190,194,215,218,233
:............237,279,280,391,423
Nelson,Rebecca:...............360
Nelson,Samuel:.................69
Nelson,William:...125,130,209,300
:.................341,360,376,447
Nesham,Benjamin:...38,267,347,448
Nesham,Elizabeth:.............267
Nesham,Marv:..............267,347
Nevin,James:..................293
Newbold,Francis:.......27,160,384
Newbold,John:..................27
Newbold,Rachel:................27
Newman,Ann:...................123
Newman,John:......44,103,123,298
Newman,Sarah:..................44
Niblett,Burnell:..............297
Niblett,Richard:..............297
Nichols,Eve:..............78,200
Nichols,Henry:.................36
Nichols,John:............290,360
Nichols,Richard:..........78,200
Nicholson,Ann:............75,122
Nicholson,Belitha:........152,431
Nicholson,Charles:.11,299,316,317
:............................417
Nicholson,Elijah:.............299
Nicholson,Elizabeth:......85,127
Nicholson,Ephraim:............345

Nicholson,Henry:..........85,127
Nicholson,Huffington:.....292,385
Nicholson,Isaac:......286,443,448
Nicholson,James:..181,216,241,299
:.......................416,417
Nicholson,John:...17,38,74,75,120
:.................122,221,397,417
Nicholson,Jonathan:........96,222
Nicholson,Joseph:.109,162,298,299
:.......................416,434
Nicholson,Joshua:..96,222,257,368
Nicholson,Levin:..............38
Nicholson,Mary:17,120,122,299,417
Nicholson,Nehemiah:........74,122
Nicholson,Peggy:..109,162,286,345
:.......................434,443
Nicholson,Phillip:.............75
Nicholson,Priscilla:.......38,122
Nicholson,Richard:298,299,416,417
Nicholson,Roger:....61,62,127,241
Nicholson,Ross:..............299
Nicholson,Sarah:..........62,299
Nicholson,Thomas:.........96,222
Niven,James:...................1
Noble,Elizabeth:.............377
Noble,Esther:............269,270
Noble,Isaac:.................362
Noble,James:.............153,377
Noble,John:................6,382
Noble,Jonathan:........83,160,351
Noble,Levi:..................378
Noble,Mary:..................362
Noble,Nancy:..270,351,382,429,430
Noble,Thomas:.269,270,382,429,430
North,Edward:...........300,301
North,Esther:................41
North,John:......41,58,59,250,301
North,Theodore:.............301
Nutter,Ann:..........229,389,404
Nutter,Benjamin:..145,153,157,260
Nutter,Charles N.:..........118
Nutter,Charles:...19,43,73,94,110
;118,195,217,234,264,265,271,280
;303,315,352,362,404,424,425,441
Nutter,Christopher Columbus:43,84
Nutter,Christopher:..19,43,70,110
;117,118,164,264,270,285,302,303
:....311,351,352,362,375,404,441
Nutter,Elias:...............402
Nutter,Hannah:..............406
Nutter,Huett:..84,118,168,303,386
:...........................397
Nutter,John Huett:..84,85,118,229
:........302,346,375,389,394,397
Nutter,John:...19,117,118,285,302

:.....................303,375
Nutter,Louisa:.73,110,195,217,271
:.........................280,352
Nutter,Louise:..............425
Nutter,Mary:........20,362,375,441
Nutter,Matthew:...117,118,285,302
:...........................375
Nutter,Nancy:................93
Nutter,Phillis Dykes:........171
Nutter,Phillis:.............171
Nutter,Robert:..............303
Nutter,Sarah Priscilla:.....357
Nutter,Sarah:................84
Nutter,Stephen:.............357
Nutter,Thomas Eccleston:....303
Nutter,William:..19,43,84,110,118
;187,234,264,270,271,285,303,352
:...........................404
O'Dear,Steven:..............391
O'Dell,David G.:............354
O'Neal,James:.......9,60,254,352
Okey,John:..................170
Okey,Mary:..................170
Oliphant,Ann:...............230
Oliphant,George:.........121,161
Oliphant,Hugh:..........429,430
Oliphant,James:..............93
Oliphant,Margaret:..........161
Oliphant,Matthew:.........93,230
Oliphant,William:....93,217,233
Oliver,Geroge:..............347
Orman,Sarah:............228,372
Osborn,John:................250
Osborne,John:...............250
Outten,John:................416
Outten,Obed:................176
Owens,Betty:................129
Owens,David:............282,389
Owens,Eleanor Robertson:....101
Owens,Elizabeth:.............17
Owens,James:................178
Owens,Joshua:...............223
Owens,Kesia:................178
Owens,Only:.................307
Owens,Robert:...........140,178
Owens,Samuel:...........140,178
Owens,Violetta:.............223
Owens,William:.17,120,178,205,255
Paca,William:...........157,158
Pank,Elizabeth:.....272,395,400
Pank,Moses:...272,273,377,378,395
:.......................400,403
Panter,John:............169,400
Parker,Abigail:.........308,309
Parker,Ann:..............37,150

473

Parker,Anne:..................82
Parker,Avres:.................108
Parker,Beniamin:..............309
Parker,Bettv:.............308,309
Parker,Billy:.................151
Parker,Charles:............70,150
Parker,Eleanor:45,113,177,274,309
Parker,Elijah:.................22
Parker,Elisha P.:.............251
Parker,Elisha:.................14
Parker,ELisha:.................21
Parker,Elisha:..21,45,109,113,151
:175,177,178,187,210,239,248,251
:.........................274,308
Parker,ELisha:................309
Parker,Elisha:.309,368,382,383,44
Parker,Elizabeth:.........308,309
Parker,Georoe:.14,22,37,48,76,116
:154,196,241,277,308,309,327,328
:360,368,383,384,392,399,402,412
:.............................441
Parker,Henry:.................384
Parker,Hettv:..45,113,177,203,274
Parker,Jacob:..1,14,21,22,151,307
:.....................308,429,441
Parker,James:.................360
Parker,Jenny:.................309
Parker,John T.:...............274
Parker,John:...14,105,130,151,191
:251,274,277,308,327,328,366,392
:.............................441
Parker,Marv:........22,151,317,429
Parker,Nelly:.............308,309
Parker,Richard:...............317
Parker,Sampson:................42
Parker,Samuel T.:...83,93,203,295
Parker,Samuel Turner:.162,203,224
Parker,Samuel:45,71,82,83,113,177
:.........................274,447
Parker,Sarah:..14,196,308,309,327
Parker,Unice:.................108
Parker,William:...........220,368
Parks,Elizabeth:...........13,229
Parks,Moses:...............13,229
Parr,Samuel:..............319,360
Parramore,Marv:.................3
Parramore,Stephen:..............3
Parramore,Thomas:.............426
Parremore,Eleanor:............107
Parremore,Isaac:..............337
Parremore,Isabelle:...........355
Parremore,James:..137,232,310,337
:.........................339,425
Parremore,Jesse:..............439
Parremore,John:......61,95,273,309
Parremore,Joseph:...107,173,355
Parremore,Joshua:............439
Parremore,Matthew:............61
Parremore,Richard:...........273
Parremore,Rose:..............310
Parremore,Samuel:............310
Parremore,Stephen:...........310
Parremore,Thomas:....137,173,425
Parris,Elizabeth:............275
Parris,George:275,299,351,413,417
Parsons,Abigail:......21,127,276
Parsons,Allison C.:..........188
Parsons,Ann:.................220
Parsons,Benjamin:.............48
Parsons,Betsy:...............220
Parsons,Caleb Tingle:........311
Parsons,Catherine:...........220
Parsons,Charles:..............70
Parsons,Elijah:..........264,310
Parsons,Elizabeth:130,151,251,366
Parsons,Francis:.............298
Parsons,George H.:...........163
Parsons,George:.82,87,115,116,153
:...157,261,264,310,320,400,426
Parsons,Hannah:..........208,310
Parsons,Henry:...........22,199
Parsons,Isaac H.:............343
Parsons,James:...............223
Parsons,Jehu:...15,58,274,361,362
:............................432
Parsons,Jessey:..............426
Parsons,John Albert:.........220
Parsons,John J.:.............151
Parsons,John S.:.............124
Parsons,John Selby:..........220
Parsons,John W.B.:...........361
Parsons,John:...21,50,127,169,170
:171,192,220,235,274,310,311,318
:................398,405,412,426
Parsons,Johnson:.........311,398
Parsons,Jonathan S.:..32,297,311
Parsons,Jonathan Stevens:..53,264
Parsons,Jonathan:21,22,53,223,264
:............276,310,311,362,442
Parsons,Jordan:....81,87,235,283
Parsons,Joshua:..............325
Parsons,Leah:.................22
Parsons,Levin:....22,310,361,442
Parsons,Margaret:............413
Parsons,Martha:.....50,150,325
Parsons,Mary:................170
Parsons,Molly:................48
Parsons,Nancy:...............109
Parsons,Peter R.:............310
Parsons,Peter:..21,50,150,151,170
:..........196,220,274,325,411
Parsons,Porter:...........50,411
Parsons,Priscilla:............31
Parsons,Robert H.:...........343
Parsons,Robert:....49,328,397,398
Parsons,Samuel:36,119,310,418,437
Parsons,Sarah:251,328,366,397,398
Parsons,Simon P.:............274
Parsons,Simon Peter:.........220
Parsons,Sophia:..............116
Parsons,William S.:..........362
Parsons,William:.31,36,48,109,119
:129,150,151,192,208,224,310,323
:........341,412,418,436,437,438
Parsons,Zachariah:.50,108,220,276
:............................346
Parsons,Zephaniah:...........220
Passwater,Jonas:..............58
Passwater,Thomas:.............58
Patison,Archibald:.......152,247
Patrick,William:.........360,361
Pearce,Elizabeth:............373
Pearce,John:.............246,373
Peasev,Elizabeth:............122
Peasey,John:.................122
Pemberton,Elizabeth:.........134
Pemberton,Joseph:........317,434
Pemberton,Thomas:.134,231,317,345
:............................393
Pennell,Joseph:......242,266,291
Pennewell,Elisha:..82,316,321,326
Pepper,John:..................70
Perdue,Arcada:...............297
Perdue,Benjamin:.........36,211
Perdue,Eli:..............151,297
Perdue,Elijah S.W.:.......32,124
Perdue,George L.:............197
Perdue,George:.......124,129,297
Perdue,Hannah:...............224
Perdue,James W. B.:..........124
Perdue,James W.B.:............32
Perdue,James Walker B.:......366
Perdue,James:.18,32,36,82,123,124
:151,197,208,211,217,223,224,246
:................276,290,328,343
Perdue,John K.H.:.........32,124
Perdue,John Kendal Hebrew:...297
Perdue,John:32,36,123,124,129,140
:....151,197,211,215,297,328,343
Perdue,Kendal H.:............124
Perdue,Leah:.................297
Perdue,Mary:.................215
Perdue,Sabrough Fooks:........32
Perdue,Sarah:............223,276
Perdue,Susanna:..............151

Perkins,John:..............250
Perkins,Marian:............246
Perkins,Simon:.............246
Parkinson,Daniel:..........28
Parkinson,John:............28
Perry,Charles:......6,57,401
Peterson,Peter:.............8
Petty,Samuel:.............291
Peyton,Robert:.............96
Peytons,Major:.............96
Philips,James:............231
Phillips,Absalom:.........176
Phillips,Asa:.............233
Phillips,Charles:.....180,441
Phillips,Daniel:......259,409
Phillips,Dorothy:...........1
Phillips,Elizabeth:...191,241
Phillips,George:59,73,241,292,339
:.....................425,444
Phillips,Henry:.......156,180
Phillips,Isaac:.23,31,107,109,121
:.........................353
Phillips,Jacob:.......178,323
Phillips,James:12,156,167,231,232
:.............237,258,261,425
Phillips,John M.:.........339
Phillips,John:..29,31,101,109,158
:159,176,198,207,218,331,333,352
:.........371,373,374,420,432
Phillips,Joshua:...........23
Phillips,Maria:...........412
Phillips,Mary:............184
Phillips,Peregrine:..144,148,427
Phillips,Rachel:......232,237
Phillips,Rhoda:.......159,323
Phillips,Richard:.125,136,213,746
:.................247,323,352,444
Phillips,Robert:..........312
Phillips,Roger:.1,184,213,246,247
:.....................323,412
Phillips,Samuel W.:.......339
Phillips,Sarah A.E.L.:....339
Phillips,Sarah:.......213,323
Phillips,Stephen:.........390
Phillips,Thomas:..184,213,247,323
Phillips,William:...28,40,144,148
:.................191,306,312,427
Phippen,Belitha:..........245
Phipps,Ann:...............419
Phipps,John:..........388,419
Pickman,William:..........386
Pilchard,John:............324
Pilchard,William:.........324
Pincher,Ann:..............182
Pinkney,Ninian:...........166

Piper,Agnes:.......73,362,425
Piper,Benjamin:...........402
Piper,Christopher:.25,26,28,42,68
:.70,109,265,305,395,424,429,446
Piper,John:...........73,292
Piper,Joseph:..73,265,292,305,441
Piper,Mary:...............109,429
Piper,Matthew:.............68
Piper,Rachel:..25,26,265,305,424
Piper,William:265,305,362,424,441
Pitt,Robert:..............308
Pitts,Robert:.............389
Polk,Benjamin:............380
Polk,Betty:...............346
Polk,Charles:......67,68,371
Polk,David:.49,94,152,204,247,346
Polk,Elizabeth:.......342,343
Polk,Esther:..............442
Polk,Gillis:..55,72,73,86,90,145
:158,204,274,278,312,315,335,371
:.................381,402,443
Polk,James:49,116,117,204,211,279
:.................315,330,358
Polk,Jane:................330
Polk,John:......157,174,234,330
Polk,Joseph:..............365
Polk,Joshua:.......78,117,279
Polk,Josiah:49,54,62,79,86,96,116
:126,152,182,200,204,211,225,233
:247,267,312,315,320,330,356,367
:.................405,441
Polk,Mary:................238
Polk,Nancy:.......67,116,204,211
Polk,Priscilla:.......157,234
Polk,Rebecca:..........54,233
Polk,Whittington:.........330
Polk,William Winder:..152,247
Polk,William:..49,52,54,79,96,152
:157,174,204,232,233,234,238,247
:........277,279,324,342,346,431
Pollitt,Betty:............334
Pollitt,George:.......325,330
Pollitt,John:.........258,418
Pollitt,Jonathan:.....104,360,364
Pollitt,Joshua:58,139,201,202,216
:.....................283,367
Pollitt,Levin:.59,111,222,223,319
:.....................330,383
Pollitt,Lewis Asbury:.....364
Pollitt,Lewis:............364
Pollitt,Sally:........202,217
Pollitt,Samuel:31,147,210,244,363
:.........................436
Pollitt,Sarah:..79,82,139,201,202
:.....................270,402

Pollitt,Stephen:..........364
Pollitt,Thomas:.70,79,154,210,334
:.........................416
Pollitt,William:..........217
Pollitt,William:10,20,30,31,70,76
:..77,82,147,148,162,209,216,217
:.............226,270,330,388,402
Polson,Levin:.............407
Polson,William:...........407
Porter,Alexander:....30,59,290
Porter,Ann:...............418
Porter,Elizabeth:.....333,418
Porter,Francis:...........418
Porter,Gatta:.............333
Porter,Hetty:.........3,139,333
Porter,Hugh:..............418
Porter,John Beard:........423
Porter,Leah:..............333
Porter,Levi:........3,139,238,333
Porter,Mary Forcett:......423
Porter,McKimmea:....139,238,333
Porter,McKimmey:.......2,3,341
Porter,Richard B.:........423
Porter,Richard:...........423
Porter,Samuel:............333
Porter,Sarah Ann:.........418
Porter,William L.:........333
Porter,William:.......208,333
Powders,Nancy:........153,432
Powders,Richard:...153,431,432
Powell,Elijah:............334
Powell,Gabriel:.......160,334
Powell,James:.............361
Powell,John:..............334
Powell,Levin:.............334
Powell,Perch:.............153
Powell,Pierce:........153,432
Powell,Priscilla:.........361
Powell,Rebecca:.....150,246,302
Powell,Samuel:............316
Powell,William:...........302
Presley,Peter:.....60,370,382
Price,Adam:...............200
Price,Alexander:..........293
Price,Ann:................294
Price,Christopher:....293,294
Price,Eve:................294
Price,John:...............200
Price,Loudy:..............281
Price,Mary:...............200
Price,Molly:..............242
Price,Patience:.......287,439
Price,Rachel:.............294
Price,Rebecca:............293
Price,Samuel:..............16

Price,Sarah:...................16
Price,Solomon Kibble:........287
Price,Solomon:................293
Price,Thomas:........245,287,439
Price,William:...............242
Prideaux,Joshua:.............209
Prior,David:.........212,320,337
Pritchard,David:..............86
Pritchett,James:.........415,416
Purnell,Elisha L.:...........163
Purnell,George:........8,334,340
Purnell,Jesse:...............198
Purnell,Thomas:..............117
Puzey,George:................433
Quartermus,Elizabeth:........344
Quartermus,Isaiah:.......172,207
Quartermus,James:....207,332,344
Quartermus,John:..............95
Quartermus,Josiah:...........332
Quartermus,Patrick:......176,207
Quartermus,Sarah:............207
Quatermass,Patrick:...........55
Quigley,John:................251
Quinton,Anslee:...............57
Quinton,Dixon:................57
Quinton,Jacob:...............439
Quinton,Peter:...............438
Quinton,Phillip:..............57
Racey,James:.................247
Raglate,Andrew:..............155
Raglin,David:.......79,104,341
Raglin,Elizabeth:.............79
Raglin,Michael:...............79
Rain,Arcada:.................183
Rain,Caleb:..................183
Rain,Elizabeth:..............183
Rain,John:...................183
Rain,Matthew:................183
Rain,Nanny:..................183
Ralph,Elizabeth:.............421
Ralph,George:................173
Ralph,Jane:...................84
Ralph,John:..................235
Ralph,Mitchell:..............173
Ralph,Sarah:.............17,173
Ralph,Thomas:..84,155,156,160,173
:..................342,408,421
Ralph,William:........17,173,342
Ramsey,Barnet:...............150
Ramsey,Nathaniel:...8,11,20,30,81
:...119,153,186,275,364,368,400.
:............................403
Rathbone,Amely:..............368
Rathbone,Love:...............368
Rathbone,Mary:...............368

Rawley,James:............221,407
Rawley,Mary:.................407
Rawley,William:..............221
Ray,Polly:...................146
Raymond,Jonathan:........343,370
Raymond,Judith:..........343,370
Rayne,Caleb:..................34
Rayne,John:................33,34
Ready,Aaron:.............318,355
Ready,Adam:..................359
Ready,Bryan:.............327,355
Ready,Catherine:.............327
Ready,Cornelius:..........12,237
Ready,John:..............232,355
Records,Alexander:....85,227,229
Records,Amelia:...............85
Records,Ann:...84,174,343,344,430
Records,Anna:.................85
Records,Archelus:..85,154,174,311
:............................430
Records,Benjamin:............284
Records,Betty:.......174,343,415
Records,Charity:.............344
Records,Elizabeth:.......284,344
Records,Euphrosina:...........85
Records,John:..95,146,168,174,287
:..................343,375,430
Records,Jonah:...............343
Records,Joseph:...........84,375
Records,Josiah:..............344
Records,Lame:..85,174,294,315,415
Records,Mary:.................85
Records,Patience:.........64,407
Records,Phillip:.....311,375,415
Records,Phillis:.............174
Records,Polly:...........174,415
Records,Sarah:.85,154,284,315,415
Records,Susannah:............287
Records,Thomas;85,154,174,284,311
:..............315,375,415,430
Records,William:..............23
Redden,Mary:.................198
Redden,Stephen:..........198,429
Redding,Charles:..........61,84
Reddish,Elizabeth:........58,91
Reddish,Hiram:.........58,91,116
Reddish,Hiron:...............326
Reddish,Joanna:..............326
Reddish,John:..58,106,116,121,144
:..............312,326,346,364
Reddish,Nancy:...154,170,312,345
Reddish,Nicholas:........332,345
Reddish,Rebecca:.............116
Reddish,Rhoda:.......144,326,364
Reddish,Thomas:..154,170,312,345

Redman,Mary:.............135,143
Redman,Walter:...........135,143
Reed,Betty:..........63,208,428
Reed,Elijah:..........4,385,423
Reed,Elizabeth:..............428
Reed,Hezekiah:.......63,207,208
Reed,Jacob:...4,57,63,183,207,420
Reed,James:.....57,63,129,208,428
Reed,John:...4,63,140,183,207,293
:........................294,428
Reed,Judah:..................207
Reed,Martha:.............183,207
Reed,Mary:...........57,129,294
Reed,Obediah:..4,293,294,385,423
Reed,Zachariah:.......4,385,423
Rencher,Elizabeth:...........305
Rencher,John:..................?
Rencher,Priscilla:...........305
Rencher,Samuel:..139,201,202,239
:........................255,305
Rencher,Thomas:.9,139,201,202,218
:..........239,272,302,305,434
Rencher,William:.9,62,272,273,284
Renshaw,Bridget:.............301
Revel,George:............123,345
Revel,Samuel:................123
Rhoads,Charles:12,198,237,355,374
Rhoads,Daniel:..81,99,198,373,374
:............................420
Rhoads,Isaac:............129,130
Rhoads,Jacob:..99,109,198,374,420
Rhoads,James:................405
Rhoads,John:..............92,345
Rhoads,Nathan:.......198,349,374
Rhoads,Nathaniel:............420
Riall,Elijah:................363
Riall,George:................328
Riall,Hetty Ann:.............132
Riall,Louise Mary:...........328
Riall,Mary:..................363
Riall,William:...............132
Rice,Nicholas:...........300,346
Richards,Alexander:...........85
Richards,Ann:................134
Richards,Elizabeth:......120,170
Richards,Henry:..............120
Richards,John:...........134,170
Richards,Joseph:.............330
Richards,Katherine:...........85
Richards,Phillip:............170
Richards,Richard:............277
Richardson,Angelo:...........235
Richardson,Benjamin:......59,421
Richardson,Elizabeth:.........39
Richardson,George:............35

Richardson,John:39,58.173.239,283
:.......301,324,347,351,377,378
Richardson,Joseph:.........313
Richardson,Mary:....58,59,239,301
Richardson,Matthew:.......313,347
Richardson,Samuel:........186,313
Richardson,Sarah:............59
Richardson,William:....82,313,421
Richins,John:................407
Ricketts,John:..............95,263
Rider,Ann:...................388
Rider,Charity:...............408
Rider,Charles:.55,160,176,243,271
:........309,342,361,408,414,422
Rider,Cleanor:...............228
Rider,Heathley:..............271
Rider,Henrietta:.............361
Rider,James:..............55,342
Rider,John:20,21,50,67,75,163,176
:196,228,243,271,278,289,299,320
:....348,356,360,361,388,417,421
Rider,Margaret:...........271,421
Rider,Mary:...........271,408,414
Rider,Nelly:..............76,196
Rider,Priscilla:..160,176,271,342
Rider,Richard:...........271,413
Rider,Thomas:.....160,176,243,342
Rider,Wilson:.271,361,408,413,414
:...........................421
Ridgley,Elizabeth:............34
Ridgley,Martha:..............246
Ridgley,Robert:34,213,246,256,426
Ridgley,William:.............426
Rigby,Elizabeth:.............168
Rigby,Levin:.................168
Rigg,Anna:...................155
Riggin,Benjamin:.............228
Riggin,James:........315,446
Riggin,Jonathan:......147,163,166
Riggs,Joseph:................195
Riggs,Sarah:.................195
Riley,Benjamin:..............277
Riley,Samuel M.:.............363
Ritchie,Archibald:.......287,411
Ritchie,Betsy:...............132
Ritchie,Delilah:.........287,411
Ritchie,James:..16,38,120,132,134
:167,234,276,287,291,292,294,359
:............................360
Rixon,John:..................120
Roach,Alice:.................253
Roach,Anna:..................181
Roach,Anne:..................289
Roach,Betsy:.................289
Roach,Betty:.............181,394

Roach,Charles:.......191,372,394
Roach,Isaac:.............252,253
Roach,James:..174,181,288,289,394
Roach,John:...252,253,288,393,394
Roach,Levin:.................288
Roach,Mary Bozman:...........181
Roach,Mary:..................143
Roach,Matty:.............181,289
Roach,Nancy:.............371,447
Roach,Nelly:.........181,299,394
Roach,Polly:.................394
Roach,Sarah:.................288
Roach,Stephen:143,191,288,349,371
:..................394,446,447
Roach,William:...174,288,349,394
Roberts,Elizabeth:141,142,174,312
:........................349,357
Roberts,Fisher:..141,142,146,174
:....................312,322,357
Roberts,John:........253,254,343
Roberts,Joshua:..........146,323
Roberts,Rachel:..........253,254
Roberts,Rencher:.............343
Roberts,Reuben:..............126
Roberts,Sarah:...........146,323
Roberts,Tabitha:.............254
Roberts,Thomas:..146,284,322,323
Roberts,Underwood:....253,254,435
Roberts,William:..146,254,322,323
:............................349
Robertson,Alexander:......13,414
Robertson,Ann:...........100,341
Robertson,Charles Venables:..321
Robertson,Eleanor:.......204,281
Robertson,Elendor:...........101
Robertson,Eli:............43,381
Robertson,Elias:..........36,281
Robertson,George:..13,145,164,174
:198,204,218,273,274,281,319,320
:....322,359,371,380,427,443,445
Robertson,Isaac:.............350
Robertson,Jacob:.............221
Robertson,James:...13,101,114,177
:..221,259,321,349,381,404,405,
:............................409
Robertson,John:.36,43,114,205,215
:217,221,248,255,350,353,376,381
:........404,405,411,413,414,431
Robertson,Joshua:.............43
Robertson,Mary:..........164,254
Robertson,Nancy:.........259,409
Robertson,Nelly:.............409
Robertson,Phillis:...........255
Robertson,Robert:............102
Robertson,Samuel:.101,144,180,249

:....................259,281,300
Robertson,Sandy:..........43,155
Robertson,Sarah:.....249,300,359
Robertson,Saul:..............409
Robertson,Solomon:...215,350,431
Robertson,Thomas:....111,281,324
Robertson,William S.:........155
Robertson,William:100,144,188,259
:................281,315,350,409
Robins,Bowden:...............399
Robins,Bowdin:........76,350,351
Robins,Eliabeth:.............360
Robins,Elinor:................76
Robins,James B.:..115,165,350,351
:............................360
Robins,John:..................76
Robins,Littleton:.........81,360
Robins,Martha:............81,360
Robins,Mary:..................01
Robins,Thomas:...............327
Robinson,Betty:...............82
Robinson,David:..............251
Robinson,John:...........171,411
Robinson,Joshua:.............274
Robinson,Mary:...........251,411
Robinson,Samuel:..............71
Robinson,Sarah:..............195
Robinson,William A.:.........312
Robinson,William:............341
Rogers,Amelia:...............164
Rogers,Charles:..............164
Roldolphus,William:...........61
Rolle,Joseph:............168,169
Romner,John:.................324
Rook,Edward:..................31
Rose,William:................429
Round,James:.............325,380
Round,John Whittington:......364
Round,Tabitha:...............325
Round,William:................80
Rounds,James:................151
Rousebey,John:................40
Rowe,Thomas:.................378
Rowle,Joseph:............191,324
Rowley,James:................169
Ruark,Elizabeth:.........297,329
Ruark,Ezekiel:...............147
Ruark,James:.................329
Ruark,Levin:..............89,297
Ruark,Major T.:..............354
Russell,Alexander Thomas:..91,105
:173,216,257,293,294,296,313,318
:................355,408,432
Russell,Alexander:...........432
Russell,Ann Price:...........293

Russell,Ann:..105,261,296,434,435
Russell,Anne:...............91,216
Russell,Eleanor:..............374
Russell,Hetty:..................4
Russell,James:.54,173,176,258,301
:....351,355,374,408,423,427,435
Russell,Jesse:..............258,374
Russell,Josiah:91,105,216,261,296
:.......................334,383
Russell,Leah:................374
Russell,Levi:........12,237,355
Russell,Levin:...............374
Russell,Polly:...............427
Russell,Price:.91,105,162,216,257
:296,313,355,383,408,432,434,435
Russell,Richard:.............298
Russell,Solomon:.........261,383
Russell,Thomas:....12,190,237,374
Russell,William:.........374,435
Russum,Joseph:........15,88,355
Russum,Robert C.:............218
Russum,Robert:.............20,27
Russum,William P.:...........218
Russum,William:15,20,27,53,88,134
:158,218,243,258,283,304,322,355
:....................413,427,438
Ruttledge,Edward:.............58
Saints,John:..................31
Sampson,Richard:.........68,154
Samuels,Ann:.............40,419
Samuels,Hannah:.............194,419
Samuels,Isabell:.............419
Samuels,Martha:.............419
Samuels,Mary:................363
Samuels,Peter:....149,194,363,419
Samuels,Richard:...40,136,146,194
:...................196,363,419
Samuels,Robert:..............363
Samuels,Sarah:...............363
Sangstor,James:...............55
Savage,Benjamin:......130,296,366
Savage,Eleanor I.:...........135
Savage,Ezekiel:..............281
Savage,Jane:.................281
Savage,Joseph:...............135
Savage,Thomas:...24,25,51,171,262
:...........................338
Savage,Iorobable:............130
Scady,Leah:..............133,366
Scady,Sarah:.................133
Scady,Stephen:...............133
Scarborough,Ann:..............37
Scarborough,Bennett:..........37
Scarborough,Charles:..........37
Scarborough,Elizabeth Ann:....37

Scarborough,Henry:............37
Scarborough,John:.........416,432
Scarborough,Winifred:.........37
Scarbrough,John:.............338
Schockley,Betsy:.............192
Scott,Alice:..................92
Scott,Andrew:........51,205,428
Scott,Comfort:............80,369
Scott,Day:...13,87,92,106,107,118
:........162,182,237,238,279,394
Scott,Elizabeth:...133,138,169,279
Scott,George D.:..........19,369
Scott,George Day.:...........179
Scott,George Day:.182,229,279,344
:.......................394,395
Scott,Gustavous:..277,318,359,369
Scott,John E.:...............354
Scott,John:.......133,138,169,359
Scott,Matthew:...............279
Scott,Michael:............80,369
Scott,William:...............369
Scott,Windom:............80,369
Scroggin,Ann:.................75
Scroggin,Betsey:..............18
Scroggin,Betsy:..............193
Scroggin,Elizabeth:..........196
Scroggin,Eunice:....18,22,135,193
Scroggin,John:..18,22,135,150,193
:...........................387
Scroggin,Joseph:18,51,135,193,196
:...........................387
Scroggin,Phillip Jenkins:.....18
Scroggin,Phillip:.....150,193,387
Scroggin,Polly:.......18,193,387
Scroggin,Robert:...75,135,150,196
Scroggin,Samuel:..............18
Scroggin,Sarah:..............135
Scroglimour,Katharine:.......277
Seady,Burton:................366
Seady,Sarah:.................366
Seady,Stephen:...............366
Selby,Ezekiel:........18,193,393
Selby,George:................327
Selby,Henry:...40,145,315,411,417
Selby,James:..........18,193,393
Selby,Leah:..................205
Selby,Levi:....40,145,315,411,417
Selby,Mary:..............18,193
Selby,Parker:............327,384
Selby,Rebecca:.40,145,315,411,417
Selby,Robert:................426
Seon,John:....................34
Seon,Thomas:..................34
Serman s,Levinah:............142
Serman,Betty:........253,254,435

Serman,Charles:...160,176,243,271
:........................309,342
Serman,Edward:.39,153,267,430,435
Serman,Eliza:................430
Serman,Elizabeth:........268,347
Serman,George:...............221
Serman,Grace:................221
Serman,Isaac:..39,125,136,221,254
:........................392,435
Serman,Isbell:................39
Serman,Job:..................282
Serman,Levinah:...............96
Serman,Margaret:.............267
Serman,Peter:................430
Serman,Rebecca:..............221
Serman,Samuel:...............253
Serman,Sarah:.243,246,271,323,430
Serman,Susanna:..........160,342
Serman,Thomas:103,267,268,347,430
Serman,William:...184,246,323,430
:...........................448
Shapleigh,Phillip:...........427
Sharp,Cyrus:...10,154,173,214,248
:...................374,405,432
Sharp,Daniel:..10,173,214,374,405
:...........................432
Sharp,George:........205,374,405
Sharp,Hannah:................205
Sharp,John:..............180,374
Sharp,Rebecca:.10,173,214,374,432
Sharp,William:........10,173,374
Shearman,Culett:..............63
Shearman,Thomas:..............63
Shehee,David:............120,366
Shehee,Margaret:.............120
Shehee,Margery:..............366
Shehee,Sarah:............120,366
Sherrodan,Daniel:............375
Sherrodan,Elizabeth:.........375
Sherrodan,Sarah:.............375
Sherrodan,William:...........375
Shields,Alice:...............375
Shields,John:................376
Shields,Thomas:..............375
Shiles,John:..118,141,199,207,217
:...........247,272,300,356,434
Shiles,Thomas:.207,217,249,376,43
Shockley,Benjamin:.77,152,153,192
:........199,304,324,326,404,411
Shockley,Betsy:..............326
Shockley,Betty:...............77
Shockley,Charles:..77,192,326,411
Shockley,David:..........368,369
Shockley,Eli:............152,377
Shockley,Elijah E.:......290,377

Shockley,Elijah John:........378
Shockley,Elijah:.18,21,82,152,230
:............290,304,377,378,414
Shockley,Elizabeth:...158,195,260
:........................377,378
Shockley,Hezekiah D.:...57,82,115
:....................277,339,447
Shockley,Isaac:................117
Shockley,John:152,180,199,253,337
:....................377,378,403
Shockley,Jonathan:.77,158,260,326
:................377,378,403,404
Shockley,Livecia:..............324
Shockley,Nelly:................351
Shockley,Noble:................324
Shockley,Richard:..........180,181
Shockley,Sampson:..............152
Shockley,Samuel:............21,82
Shockley,Sarah:....82,153,180,377
Shockley,Saul:..................82
Shockley,Solomon:..............414
Shockley,Stewart:........293,351
Shockley,Thomas Covington:....377
Shockley,Thomas:...............414
Shockley,Zilpah:...............152
Shores,Alice:..................221
Shores,Betsy:..................211
Shores,Edmund:.................301
Shores,Edward:.................301
Shores,John:...................221
Short,Adam:....................338
Short,Daniel:..................445
Short,Eli:.....................378
Short,Elizabeth:...............338
Short,John:................338,378
Short,Jonathan:............338,378
Short,Shadrack:................121
Showcraft,Isaiah:...............37
Showell,Eli:57,82,115,277,339,447
Showell,Sarah:......57,115,277,339
Simpson,Drummond:..............183
Sims,Samuel:...............431,447
Sims,Smith:....................161
Singleton,John:................345
Skinner,Benjamin:..............215
Skinner,Mary:..................379
Skinner,Peter:.................379
Skinner,Sarah Marshall:....15,398
Skinner,Sarah:.................425
Skinner,Thomas:...127,184,319,360
:........................379,382
Skinner,William:...............379
Slattery,Bartholomew:..........27
Slattery,William:..............27
Slemons,Albert:............13,42

Slemons,Clara E.:...............42
Slemons,Clara:..................13
Slemons,Francis M.:...........234
Slemons,Francis Marion:.....13,42
Slemons,James McCree:.........379
Slemons,John B.:.........13,42,379
Slemons,John R.:.............442
Slemons,John:.................149
Slemons,Leah Murray:..........291
Slemons,Polly:................442
Slemons,Robert W.:............379
Slocomb,Barzilla:.....189,332,354
Slocomb,Catherine:........189,332
Slocomb,Gabriel:..188,189,257,332
:.............................354
SLocomb,George:................270
Slocomb,George:.......270,380,382
Slocomb,John:.............189,354
Slocomb,Marcellus:....189,332,354
Slocomb,Nelly:............189,354
Slocomb,Sarah:........189,332,354
Small,Richard:.................381
Smiith,Marshall:...............327
Smith,Abraham:........190,191,340
Smith,Andrew:..1,14,48,71,116,134
:161,162,178,210,241,252,354,382
:.............................383
Smith,Archibald:.21,22,88,161,162
:203,270,327,328,369,382,384,410
:.............................429
Smith,Bathsheba:................54
Smith,Benjamin:.........21,22,429
Smith,Betty:..............375,410
Smith,Catherine:..........377,429
Smith,Charleton:..............169
Smith,David:.48,53,54,167,178,316
:....................375,383,384
Smith,Deborah:................161
Smith,Elijah:22,30,54,178,252,370
:.............................429
Smith,Elizabeth:.1,48,116,169,241
:.........................295,316
Smith,Esther:..............88,328
Smith,Francis:................361
Smith,George:13,14,21,22,31,53,89
:.97,134,161,162,178,210,252,269
:....354,382,383,384,396.418,429
Smith,Henry I.B.:.........300,382
Smith,Henry:...................91
Smith,Isaac:..................212
Smith,Isaiah:...48,54,178,316,361
Smith,Jacob:..................273
Smith,James:.53,71,83,270,320,321
:.............359,361,382,406,430
Smith,Jannet:.................178

Smith,Job:................383,392
Smith,John:..62,83,88,91,126,142
:169,174,180,201,258,273,304,328
:................357,375,382,415
Smith,Joseph:..................78
Smith,Joshua:......88,162,203,382
Smith,Levin S.H.:.............382
Smith,Levin:......21,158,300,384
Smith,Lovey:...................48
Smith,Mandy:...................48
Smith,Mary:6,21,31,53,142,158,174
:............212,270,357,375,382
Smith,Moses:.......53,116,383,384
Smith,Nelly:..................321
Smith,Obediah:................384
Smith,Patience:................21
Smith,Peggy:..................212
Smith,Polly:..............194,212
Smith,Rachel:.............258,417
Smith,Sally A.T.:.............361
Smith,Sally:...................22
Smith,Samuel:.320,370,382,410,435
:.............................443
Smith,Sarah Ann:..............327
Smith,Sarah:..................420
Smith,Seth:....14,178,210,235,354
Smith,Solomon:.........21,82,410
Smith,Thomas:...26,82,113,118,212
:............303,357,375,406,420
Smith,Turner:.................410
Smith,William Haslett:........439
Smith,William:.14,144,212,258,417
:.............................418
Saulling,Peter:...............338
Saulling,Randall:.............338
Sayley,Robert:.................57
Sayley,Samuel:................360
Savly,Robert:.................359
Snead,Smith:..................298
Snead,Sophia:.................298
Snee,Bryan:...................329
Sockwell,Esther:..........154,214
Sockwell,George:..............242
Sockwell,Samuel:..........154,214
South,Oliver:.................279
Southern,Edward:......203,212,213
Southern,George:..............203
Southern,Mary:........203,212,213
Span,Dorothy:.................427
Span,John:....................427
Span,Richard:.................427
Spear,Andrew:..25,117,250,331,381
Spear,Betty:..........25,117,331
Spear,Elizabeth:.......47,117,286
Spear,Henry:...........25,69,117

479

Spear,Jacob:........47,117,286,443
Spear,Thomas:................117
Spence,Alexander:............386
Spence,David:................386
Spence,James:................386
Spicer,Alexander:........152,247
Spicer,John:......219,291,384,421
Spicer,Lydia:................370
Spicer,William:...219,239,370,384
Sprigg,John:.................345
Squire,Edelia:...............421
Squire,John:.................421
Stanford,Amelia:.............175
Stanford,Constant D.:........331
Stanford,Constant Disharoon:...80
:........................366,401
Stanford,David:..........249,250
Stanford,John:....206,249,281,436
Stanford,Jonathan:..77,78,223,388
Stanford,Joseph:.........388,401
Stanford,Joshua:..181,250,325,388
Stanford,Judah:..............121
Stanford,Lotty:..............121
Stanford,Mary:...............325
Stanford,Milla:80,174,331,387,388
Stanford,Obed:...............332
Stanford,Patience:...........249
Stanford,Rachel:......293,388,401
Stanford,Robert:......121,325,388
Stanford,Sarah:..............249
Stanford,Stephen:............121
Stanford,Thomas:..206,249,293,294
:........................388,401
Stanford,William:.249,294,388,401
Stanton,Ann:.................123
Stanton,John:................123
Starling,Ann:................418
Staton,Grace:................176
Staton,James:................176
Staton,Nehemiah:.........209,282
Staton,Sarah:................209
Stayton,Horatio:...59,172,198,216
:....................348,388,389
Stayton,Jacob:...............266
Stayton,James:...........388,389
Stayton,Joseph:..............389
Stayton,Keziah:..............388
Stayton,Mary:......59,348,388,430
Stayton,Nehemiah:........338,389
Stayton,Sally McCready:....59,388
Stayton,Sarah:...........338,389
Stayton,Thomas:..............389
Steele,Henry:........182,195,362
Steene,Matthew:..............439
Stephens,William:.........83,240

Sterling,Aaron:.31,54,159,231,392
:........................396,446
Sterling,John:..6,10,12,31,64,159
:....................231,328,336,392
Sterling,Josiah:.....33,55,80,401
Sterling,Mary:...............159
Sterling,Matilda:........33,55,80
Sterling,Matty:..............401
Sterling,Rachel:........6,12,328
Sterling,Travis:.............159
Stevens,Abigail:.......98,134,170
Stevens,Agnes:...............152
Stevens,Ann:..........90,134,390
Stevens,Benjamin:............288
Stevens,Davis:...............391
Stevens,Elizabeth:...........163
Stevens,Ephraim:.............225
Stevens,Frances:..............93
Stevens,George:..............277
Stevens,Hannah:..............134
Stevens,Isaac:.90,134,170,288,390
Stevens,James:...............181
Stevens,John:...63,93,134,371,441
Stevens,Levi:............391,434
Stevens,Margaret:........249,434
Stevens,Rebecca:.............390
Stevens,Richard:90,98,134,170,205
:........................231,390
Stevens,Sarah:...............134
Stevens,Stephen:......3,5,390,391
Stevens,Thomas:...........41,373
Stevens,William A.Dashiell:...225
Stevens,William:...19,33,53,58,59
:100,109,126,132,141,142,149,151
:152,163,181,182,184,185,199,207
:225,245,249,260,261,304,373,378
:....386,387,404,411,417,433,434
Stewart,Alexander:...13,17,46,101
:124,160,194,208,233,255,280,380
:....................407,445,448
Stewart,Ann:.............225,226
Stewart,Elizabeth:.....17,46,448
Stewart,John Cottman:....225,226
Stewart,John:...17,46,102,114,143
:160,194,208,233,255,280,281,286
:........318,346,391,402,407,448
Stewart,Levin:...............262
Stewart,Matty:.........17,46,448
Stewart,Nancy:.........17,46,448
Stewart,Rebecca:.............255
Stewart,Robert James:........281
Stewart,Robert:........17,46,448
Stewart,Sarah:...........281,318
Stewart,William:........17,46,124
Stilley,Fountain:............169

Stilley,Grace:................51
Stilley,John:...51,83,169,234,392
Stillev,Margaret:............169
Stone,Betty:.................201
Stone,Henry:.................201
Stone,John Witmer:...........166
Stone,William Murray:....166,201
Stone,William:125,166,201,260,359
:............................360
Storey,Joanna:.............4,113
Storey,Mary:...............4,113
Stott,Jonathan:42,109,395,429,429
:............................446
Strawbridge,William:.........122
Street,Mansfield:........132,378
Sturgis,Esther:..............216
Sturgis,John:.....8,10,91,158,216
Sturgis,Jonathan:............216
Sturgis,Joshua:8,10,91,92,158,216
:........................297,435
Sturgis,William:........8,10,336
Sturgis,Zadock:22,112,138,175,264
:............274,276,293,297,341,372
Sudler,Robert:................96
Sullivan,Florence:...........283
Sullivan,Sarah:..............283
Summers,Jonathan:............381
Summers,William:.............370
Swain,Mariah:................397
Swain,Matthew:...............327
Swain,William:...........232,397
Swan,Robert:...............1,419
Talbot,George:...............150
Talbot,John:.............142,149
Tarr,John:...................344
Tatum,John:..................398
Taylor,Abraham:80,141,168,169,192
:193,234,251,277,352,398,399,404
:........................405,423
Taylor,Alexander:.............77
Taylor,Anthony M.:...........437
Taylor,Aseney:...............404
Taylor,Bartholomew:16,169,192,234
:............................399
Taylor,Benjamin:.............399
Taylor,Betsy:................399
Taylor,Delitha:..............105
Taylor,Eben:.................400
Taylor,Ebenezer:.....234,399,405
Taylor,Elizabeth:............398
Taylor,Ezekiel:....45,141,398,423
Taylor,George:.................8
Taylor,Heather:..........399,405
Taylor,Horatio:...123,169,192,234
:....................281,399,405

Taylor,Isaac:.....147,398,404,405
Taylor,James:...29,92,352,395,398
:.................400,404,405
Taylor,Jesse:................399
Taylor,John B.:..............400
Taylor,John W.:..............69
Taylor,John:45,55,151,160,228,271
:300,328,339,342,364,372,373,399
:.............400,408,422,423
Taylor,Joshua:..............77,405
Taylor,Levin:.146,220,323,362,400
:....................405,436
Taylor,Loudy:............398,405
Taylor,Louther:...169,192,234,399
:...........................405
Taylor,Mary Wilson:.......29,439
Taylor,Mary:..............228,372
Taylor,Matthias C.:.......208,399
Taylor,Molly:.169,192,234,398,399
:...........................405
Taylor,Nancy:................399
Taylor,Nehemiah:.............399
Taylor,Nicholas:.............296
Taylor,Richard:..............350
Taylor,Roger:.................77
Taylor,Samuel:...............105
Taylor,Sarah:................142
Taylor,Solomon:..............399
Taylor,Stephen:..............382
Taylor,Thomas:.77,151,228,372,399
:...........................400
Taylor,Walter:...........208,212
Taylor,William:64,141,142,147,168
:193,220,245,339,349,350,352,394
:.......398,399,400,408,423,437
Tennis,Joshua:...............242
Tennis,Sarah:................242
Tharp,William:...............358
Thomas,Alexander:.173,176,301,351
:...........................408
Thomas,Eliza:........176,301,351
Thomas,Elizabeth:........173,408
Thomas,Frances:...173,176,301,351
:...........................408
Thomas,Lambrook:.............275
Thomas,Levin:................250
Thomas,Nicholas:..............61
Thomas,William:...............11
Thomas:......................213
Thomason,Curtis Martin:...239,294
Thompson,Charles:........197,401
Thompson,James:..............334
Thompson,Joseph:.............294
Thompson,Leah:...............334
Thorns,Jacob:................204

Thorns,John:.................325
Thorns,Stephen:..............204
Thrift,Nathaniel:............356
Tilghman,Ann:................285
Tilghman,Elijah:..............52
Tilghman,Jabez:..............285
Tilghman,John:...............437
Tilghman,Joseph:.........230,378
Tilghman,Nehemiah:...........378
Timmons,Benjamin:............183
Timmons,Christina:...........195
Timmons,Esther:..............183
Timmons,John:................195
Timmons,Joseph:.........183,223
Timmons,Littleton:...........241
Timmons,Mary:................223
Tindell,Charles:...71,114,219,352
:...........................392
Tindell,Elijah:.......71,114,392
Tindell,Samuel:...............71
Toadvine,Alice:...............18
Toadvine,Ann:............403,441
Toadvine,Anne:...............230
Toadvine,Anthony Roach:.......20
Toadvine,Arnold:..198,199,304,403
:...........................404
Toadvine,Catherine:...175,349,394
Toadvine,Eleanor:............158
Toadvine,Ezekiel:..............1
Toadvine,George:.........181,403
Toadvine,Harriett:....175,349,394
Toadvine,Henry:.1,18,63,64,72,147
:163,175,191,198,253,254,304,393
:...........................403
Toadvine,Isaac:..............198
Toadvine,James:20,175,198,217,223
:.......................349,394
Toadvine,John:....181,230,403,441
Toadvine,Joshua:..............1
Toadvine,Juliet Amanda:.......58
Toadvine,Mary Ann:....175,349,394
Toadvine,Mary:175,191,198,230,253
:...........................393
Toadvine,Matthias 0.:........276
Toadvine,Miriam:.........120,366
Toadvine,Outten:..147,150,191,253
:...................316,325,394
Toadvine,Priscilla:......150,191
Toadvine,Purnell:..58,149,253,393
:...........................394
Toadvine,Sarah:..............181
Toadvine,Stephen:.122,123,150,191
:....253,254,261,276,394,396,403
Toadvine,Thomas:.............403
Toadvine,William:.120,150,175,191

:........230,253,338,366,393,394
Todd,Phillip:................107
Todd,Robert S.:...............72
Todd,Spencer:........86,187,296
Townsend,Barkley:.178,182,235,296
:...........................406
Townsend,Benjamin:194,268,347,406
Townsend,Brickhouse:..........49
Townsend,Charles:........378,379
Townsend,Daniel:.............264
Townsend,Isabell:............296
Townsend,James:..........210,383
Townsend,Jeremiah:............49
Townsend,Jesse:..............360
Townsend,Joanna:.............387
Townsend,John:................49
Townsend,Joseph:.............222
Townsend,Joshua:....14,93,296,406
Townsend,Luke:................49
Townsend,Mary:...........194,406
Townsend,Nancy:..........278,361
Townsend,Nelly:..............406
Townsend,Richard:............356
Townsend,Samuel:......194,357,406
Townsend,Solomon:............290
Townsend,Stephen:....116,283,367
Townsend,William Barkley:....182
Trader,Eliabeth:.............307
Trader,Elizabeth:..22,151,224,260
:.......................307,316
Trader,Henry:..93,178,217,240,252
:...................260,316,318
Trader,James:............105,261
Trader,John:.................333
Trader,Joshua:..22,48,116,307,402
:...........................406
Trader,Purnell:....22,278,307,361
Trader,Rachel:...............333
Train,Eliza:.................314
Train,James:...7,8,81,149,252,265
:....305,314,338,379,406,424,425
Travis,Matthew:..............132
Travis,Priscilla:............132
Trehearn,John:............93,210
Trotter,George:...............57
Truitt,Ann:..................313
Truitt,Arcada:...............192
Truitt,Benjamin:..........27,46
Truitt,George:...........192,324
Truitt,James:.........70,209,235
Truitt,Job:...........90,192,326
Truitt,John:.................324
Truitt,Leah:.................326
Truitt,Littleton:........313,408
Truitt,Mary:.................326

481

Truitt,Nancy: 106
Truitt,Outten: 96,193
Truitt,Patev: 329
Truitt,R.K.: 181
Truitt,Rachel: 329
Truitt,Riley: 70,235
Truitt,Samuel: 106
Truitt,Thomas: 70,235,408
Truitt,William: 313,438
Tucker,George: 34
Tucker,Mary: 34
Tull,Benjamin: 246,247
Tull,Elizabeth: 31
Tull,Esther: 85
Tull,George: 223,415
Tull,Isaac: 120,366
Tull,James: 167
Tull,Mary: 246
Tull,Nancy: 85
Tull,Richard: 223
Tull,Samuel: 85,111,335
Tull,Sarah: 223
Tull,Solomon: 31
Tull,Stephen: 409
Tull,Thomas R.: 415
Tull,Thomas: 240
Tull,Winifred: 120,366
Tully,Anna: 33
Tully,Benjamin: 68
Tully,Daniel: 81
Tully,Edward: 68
Tully,James: 33,273,409
Tully,Jane: 125,135
Tully,John Richard: 126
Tully,John: 68,135,143,413,422
Tully,Joseph: 3,135,143
Tully,Mary:68,125,126,135,136,143
Tully,Richard:...43,68,91,125,126
:136
Tully,Sarah: 3
Tully,Stephen:.68,125,135,364,391
Tully,William: 40,60,306,409
Tunstall,John: 318
Turner,Abigail: 22,151
Turner,Henry: 14,22,151,368
Turner,John: 194,233,407,410
Turner,Levin: 327,328
Turner,Polly: 407
Turner,Samuel: 205,328,410
Turner,William: 157
Turner,Zadock: 410,411
Turpin,Denwood: 165,417
Turpin,Grace: 116
Turpin,Joshua: 115,116
Turpin,Solomon: 176

Turpin,William:60,265,305,306,425
Turville,John: 426
Twiford,Ann: 225
Twiford,Anna: 73,441
Twiford,Bartholomew: 90,418
Twiford,Isabella: 132
Twiford,John O.: 73,225,441
Twiford,John:..90,107,132,135,136
:143,412,418
Twiford,Sally: 90,418
Twiford,William: 90,199
Twilley,Ann: 315,424
Twilley,George:.61,62,165,172,240
:312,391,418,427,431,445
Twilley,James: 61,380,445
Twilley,John:..17,165,172,175,312
:348,418,427,431
Twilley,Mary: 61,445
Twilley,Robert:.4,113,315,412,424
:426,444,445
Twilley,Sarah: 315,424
Tyre,Keziah: 313
Tyre,Thomas: 313
Umsted,Betsy Dashiell: 319
Umsted,John: 319
Underwood,Anthony: 91,246
Underwood,Martha: 91,246
Vance,David: 59,388
Vance,George: 172,203,275,297
Vance,Letty: 320
Vance,Margaret: 203
Vance,Mary Storks: 59,388
Vance,Rosannah: 59,388
Vance,Sally Ann Stayton:...59,388
Vance,Sally: 203
Vance,Thomas: 320
Vance,William: 320,359,360
Vanderwolf,Cornelius: 221
Vaughan,Ann: 266,291
Vaughan,Charles: 369
Vaughan,Edward: 149
Vaughan,Ephraim: 332,345
Vaughan,James: 332
Vaughan,Jon.: 219
Vaughan,Jonathan:.219,291,384,392
:393,397
Vaughan,Levin: 345
Vaughan,William: 347
Vaughn,Charles: 155
Vaughn,Ephraim: 92
Vaughn,Jethro: 92
Vaughn,Jonathan: 46,177,266
Vaughn,Levin: 94
Vaughn,Mary: 267
Vaughn,Nathaniel: 92

Vaughn,William: 92,267,268
Venables,Amelia:..4,5,142,348,357
Venables,Amilcah: 413
Venables,Ann:..35,165,249,291,418
:426,431
Venables,Anna: 427
Venables,Benjamin:33,35,42,47,109
:144,165,172,193,212,249,259,268
:273,291,312,395,413,418,420,426
:427,428,431,439
Venables,Betsy: 144
Venables,Charles:..85,165,191,427
Venables,Elizabeth: 165
Venables,James: 243
Venables,John:120,150,165,277,279
:331,359,427
Venables,Joseph:..15,35,42,47,144
:193,212,221,243,249,259,268,273
:291,395,407,413,420,426,427,428
:440
Venables,Joshua: 243
Venables,Mary: 243,413
Venables,Milkey: 422
Venables,Nelly: 273
Venables,Polly: 277
Venables,Purkins: 247
Venables,Rachel: 426
Venables,Richard: 47,420
Venables,Robert:..4,5,142,165,206
:305,313,348,357,413,422,427
Venables,Samuel:...15,243,259,268
:440
Venables,Sarah: 305,427
Venables,Thomas: 413,426,427
Venables,William:...35,47,120,158
:249,277,278,291,293,331,361,410
:413,420,426
Venatson,Bridget: 126
Venatson,Catherine: 287,411
Venatson,Charles: 212
Venatson,Elias:...126,212,287,411
Vetch,Charles: 359
Vicass,John: 439
Vickers,William: 381
Vincent,Brittana: 192
Vincent,Curtis Martin: 294
Vincent,Elijah: 112
Vincent,Ephraim: 192
Vincent,George: 68,239,294
Vincent,Isaac:.86,111,112,235,354
Vincent,Mary: 86
Vincent,Samuel: 110
Vinson,Ann: 18,193
Vinson,Bridget: 86
Vinson,Comfort:.25,51,385,407,416

:...........................437
Vinson,Eli:..18,25,51,193,197,359
:........385,393,407,415,416,437
Vinson,Eliiah:..51,86,329,358,359
Vinson,Elisha:................69
Vinson,George:........142,239,294
Vinson,Isaac:...14,86,111,210,309
:....................325,343,416
Vinson,Jesse:.................172
Vinson,Leah:..................210
Vinson,Mary:..............96,325
Vinson,Matthias:..........86,203
Waggaman,George:......34,50,417
Waggaman,Henry:.34,50,217,299,351
:.........................413,417
Waggaman,Mary:................299
Waggaman,Sarah:................50
Waggaman,William Elliott:..50,417
Waggamen,Henry:...............275
Wailes,Benjamin:.16,75,85,151,165
:172,229,230,260,272,340,359,371
:........389,398,402,403,404,417
Wailes,Betsy:..................99
Wailes,Betty:..................99
Wailes,Daniel:..66,99,151,160,162
:.............194,230,273,280,404
Wailes,Eleanor T.:.............72
Wailes,Elizabeth:..........75,371
Wailes,George:.23,151,172,403,418
Wailes,Haste:.....151,230,272,404
Wailes,Helena:............172,272
Wailes,John Irving:....23,172,418
Wailes,John:......165,172,403,417
Wailes,Joseph:..66,99,151,230,272
:.........................366,404
Wailes,Levin:.............165,172
Wailes,Mary:..................172
Wailes,William:...........135,172
Wainright,Cannon:..............56
Wainright,Eleanor:.............56
Wainright,Hambleton:...........36
Wainright,James:...............56
Wainright,Mary:................56
Wainright,Solomon:.............56
Wainright,Stephen:.............56
Wakefield,John:..28,37,88,225,395
Wakefield,Obediah:...28,37,88,225
:.............................395
Walker,Ann:...................418
Walker,Charles:...............306
Walker,Eleanor:................59
Walker,Emanuel:........43,337,418
Walker,Ephraim:...............350
Walker,Esther Ann:............350
Walker,George D.:..............38

Walker,Henry:.............350,418
Walker,James:..................72
Walker,Jane:......58,269,433,444
Walker,Jesse:................418
Walker,John:.........229,340,423
Walker,Mark:..................306
Walker,Mary:..................361
Walker,Matthew:...............350
Walker,Rebecca:................59
Walker,Sarah:............200,444
Walker,Spencer:...........114,395
Walker,Susanna:58,138,269,433,444
Walker,Susannah:..............433
Walker,Thomas:..6,37,45,58,59,75
:133,138,157,200,252,269,341,350
:........354,393,414,418,433,444
Walker,William:...............418
Walker,Winder:................418
Wallace,Agnes:.................53
Wallace,David:................327
Wallace,Elizabeth:.............53
Wallace,Esther:................51
Wallace,Henry:................357
Wallace,James:.........53,85,418
Wallace,John:.................418
Wallace,Katherine:.............53
Wallace,Martha:...............419
Wallace,Matthew:......157,234,235
Wallace,Richard Samuel:.......419
Wallace,Richard:........51,53,444
Wallace,Thomas:................53
Wallace,William:8,171,190,270,354
:.............................398
Waller,Alfred:................430
Waller,Alice:............272,273
Waller,Ann:.......141,301,317,329
Waller,Benjamin:18,25,193,197,415
Waller,Daniel:.................99
Waller,Ebenezer C.:............35
Waller,Ebenezer Cottman:72,73,402
:.............................419
Waller,Ebenezer:...72,141,276,308
:........316,357,389,402,419,423
Waller,Eleanor:...............131
Waller,Esme Marshall:..73,131,276
:........316,317,329,385,416,437
Waller,Esme:..................430
Waller,Gamer:.................173
Waller,Ganer:.................408
Waller,George:.......11,124,448
Waller,James W.:..............329
Waller,James Weatherly:73,276,316
:................317,329,402,419
Waller,James:........282,353,430
Waller,John:.........308,389,425

Waller,Jonathan:...33,107,148,338
:................353,360,413,427
Waller,Joshua:................353
Waller,Mark:..................324
Waller,Mary Whittington:18,25,193
:.............................415
Waller,Mary:..................389
Waller,Nancy:.............73,402
Waller,Nathaniel:.........94,405
Waller,Nelson:............301,302
Waller,Polly:.................197
Waller,Priscilla:.............107
Waller,Richard:.2,18,25,60,86,131
:141,193,197,238,308,313,384,385
:389,415,416,419,423,430,437,439
Waller,Thomas:.86,206,251,276,308
:....316,353,374,389,406,416,419
Waller,William Cottman:...144,276
:.............................316
Waller,William:...107,206,272,282
:...........301,353,393,430,437
Waller,Zephaniah:.............353
Walston,Bathsheba:....130,366,399
Walston,Boaz:22,53,54,105,130,192
:................307,361,366,399
Walston,David Smith:...31,205,399
Walston,David:.76,281,315,399,446
Walston,Henry:........258,315,446
Walston,Jesse:............155,369
Walston,London:...............318
Walston,Polly:................399
Walter,Ann Maria Dorothy:..55,120
Walter,Daniel:.....38,194,349,419
Walter,Dorothy:...............308
Walter,George D.:..............38
Walter,George Dashiell:....41,262
Walter,George:.................41
Walter,James:3,4,33,55,74,120,162
:....................163,307,308
Walter,John:..............373,419
Walter,Littleton Robertson:33,163
Walter,Robert:..38,49,75,122,306
:................330,331,349,419
Walter,Sarah:.......33,55,262,308
Walter,Thomas:................185
Walter,William:...............373
Walters,Eleanor:..............363
Walters,George:...............363
Waltham,John:.................382
Walton,James:.................420
Waples,Elizabeth:.............254
Waples,Margaret:..............254
Waples,Paul:..................254
Waples,William:...............254
Ward,Frances:..................30

483

Ward,James:..................30,52
Ward,John:...................419
Warner,Isaac:................27
Warner,William:..............27
Warrington,Benjamin:........81,259
Waters,Ann:..................94
Waters,Edward:...............185
Waters,Elizabeth:.118,120,303,409
Waters,Francis Hutchins:..118,227
:........303,339,359,375,409,412
Waters,John:..118,120,227,303,339
:......................370,375,409
Waters,Littleton:............185
Waters,Marv:..........28,225,395
Waters,Peter Hack:...........185
Waters,Peter:............185,304
Waters,Rebecca Foxcroft:......395
Waters,Rebecca:..............395
Waters,Richard:..............118
Waters,Sampson:..28,37,88,225,272
:............................395
Waters,Spencer:..............129
Waters,William:........359,432
Watson,Charles Levin:........153
Watson,John:.................422
Watson,Joyce:................153
Watson,Levin:................152
Watson,William:..........152,153
Watts,Ann:...............120,366
Watts,James:.................354
Watts,John:...120,246,247,354,366
Watts,Miriam:............120,366
Watts,Spencer:...............354
Watts,Winifred:.......120,247,366
Weatherly,Benjamin:..........248
Weatherly,Betty:.............426
Weatherly,Charity:.......379,425
Weatherly,Charles:.2,7,53,134,158
:....218,238,262,304,313,335,424
Weatherly,Constant:..........4
Weatherly,Constantine:.5,50,70,83
:......................425,426,427
Weatherly,Elijah Richard:........5
Weatherly,Elijah:.......2,4,7,365
Weatherly,Elizabeth:50,83,379,425
:......................426,427,440
Weatherly,James:..2,3,4,5,7,33,62
:.99,113,139,156,263,264,265,267
:303,305,312,313,314,315,317,334
:335,340,365,379,422,423,424,425
:......................438,439,440
Weatherly,Jesse:..2,7,238,313,335
:............................424
Weatherly,John:...2,3,4,5,7,50,66
:139,238,313,335,340,365,422,423

:......................424,425
Weatherly,Joseph:..2,4,7,42,50,70
:159,264,313,340,365,422,423,424
:......................425,426
Weatherly,Joshua:..2,3,42,315,422
Weatherly,Marcellus:......159,425
Weatherly,Nathan:............365
Weatherly,Patience:..........365
Weatherly,Richard:...........365
Weatherly,Sarah:..156,313,424,425
Weatherly,Susan L.:...292,362,441
Weatherly,William:..5,340,365,379
:......................423,424,425
Webb,Ann:................269,279
Webb,Callebra:...............214
Webb,Elisha:.................269
Webb,Hetty:..............257,323
Webb,Jeremiah:...............279
Webb,John:....213,214,247,257,323
Webb,Sarah:..................269
Webb,Thomas:.................279
Welch,Sylvester:.............386
Wells,Thomas:................69
West,Abigail:................184
West,Charles:................298
West,James H.:............62,166
West,James:.....3,157,184,302,348
West,Mary:...................157
West,Roger:..................157
West,Sarah:..................62
Westlock,Magdalen:...........413
Whaland,William:.............196
Whalen,Thomas:...............43
Whaley,James:................436
Whaley,Nathaniel:......18,196,246
Whaley,Seth:..........68,154,436
Whaley,Thomas:...............436
Whann,William:...............439
Wharton,Mary:.............31,353
Wharton,Revel:...............353
Wharton,William:.............31
Whayland,Polly:..............301
Whayland,William:........301,390
Wheatley,William:............260
Wheeeler,John:...............407
Wheeler,Ann:.................407
Wheeler,Edward:..............264
Wheeler,Isaac:...............264
Wheeler,John:............264,407
White,Ally:..................359
White,Archibald:.............433
White,Asa:...................103
White,Benjamin:....25,351,416,437
White,Bridget:...............389
White,Catherine:...25,207,254,416

:............................437
White,Charles:...............207
White,Eliza Ann:.............339
White,Elizabeth:......103,263,281
White,George:................39
White,Gowan:.............132,389
White,Henry W.:..............339
White,Henry:.25,51,82,362,385,407
:......................416,433,437
White,Isaac:.................263
White,Jacob:.................359
White,John:2,38,61,71,170,207,307
:..................322,378,404,433
White,Levin P.:..........223,314
White,Michael:...............39
White,Peter:.................254
White,Priscilla:.............39
White,Tabitha:.......253,254,396
White,Thomas:................196
White,Whittington:220,253,254,396
White,William:39,63,71,82,207,231
:............................264
White,Mrixam:................31
Whitely,William:.............432
Whitemarsh,Elizabeth:........432
Whitemarsh,Richard:..........432
Whithear,Elizabeth Davis:....267
Whittingham,Heber:...........280
Whittington,Elizabeth:...317,434
Whittington,Joshua:..........168
Whittington,Matthias:.....45,168
Whittington,Ursulla:.........295
Whittington,William:.15,17,96,168
:170,199,259,295,317,346,370,434
:............................443
Whitty,Edward:...............273
Whitty,Elizabeth:........434,435
Whitty,Richard:......67,73,434,435
Wilkins,John:.139,201,202,236,239
:..................261,278,292,345,361
Willen,Edward:...............301
Willey,Edward:...............414
Willey,Elizabeth:............67
Willey,John Alexander:....67,95
Willey,John:.............27,67
Williams,Amelia:.............87
Williams,Betty:..............87
Williams,Charity:............338
Williams,Charles:............141
Williams,Christopher:........359
Williams,David:....87,238,312,395
Williams,Edward:.............258
Williams,Elizabeth:......262,343
Williams,Esau:...............312
Williams,George:.............320

Williams,John:..16,92,114,131,205
:....244,247,310,312,338,343,371
Williams,Levin:.............13
Williams,Littleton:..........371
Williams,Mary:.......13,125,258
Williams,Michael:............137
Williams,Nathaniel:..........137
Williams,Phillip:............312
Williams,Planner:........153,247
Williams,Richard:........257,259
Williams,Samuel:37,76,186,312,320
:.......................365,403
Williams,Thomas:...87,238,394,395
Williams,Walter:.............137
Williams,William:..70,153,275,365
:...................400,404,435
Williamson,David:............252
Willin,Alexander:............438
Willin,Ann:....99,100,207,356,413
Willin,Betty:................218
Willin,Chaplin:..........210,438
Willin,Charles:.12,99,100,141,356
:...................411,413,438
Willin,Edward:125,249,300,301,411
Willin,Eleanor:.......99,207,438
Willin,Elinor:.......100,356,413
Willin,Eliza:................272
Willin,Elizabeth:.....207,356,434
Willin,George:.12,207,209,210,281
:.......................420,438
Willin,Hannah:...........125,301
Willin,Henry:................438
Willin,James:........199,287,411
Willin,John:......217,218,300,411
Willin,Levin:..99,207,209,210,376
:............................438
Willin,Major:............199,272
Willin,Mary:.................218
Willin,Nancy:............210,438
Willin,Priscilla:............130
Willin,Robert:.99,100,132,140,207
:............210,356,411,413,438
Willin,Samuel:113,130,141,199,218
:.......................300,434
Willin,Thomas:.78,130,199,207,209
:210,217,218,272,337,356,376,411
:.......................434,438
Willin,Tubman:...........132,378
Willin,William:..........194,420
Willis,Benjamin:..............18
Willis,Betty:.................18
Willis,David:................337
Willis,Elijah:...............403
Willis,Elizabeth:............203
Willis,Esther:................85

Willis,George:...........206,288
Willis,James:................269
Willis,John:...18,203,337,378,403
:............................409
Willis,Levi:..................89
Willis,Levin:.................85,89
Willis,Lotta:............206,288
Willis,Mary:.................269
Willis,Nathaniel:..18,203,337,403
:............................409
Willis,Richard:..............146
Willis,Sabra:................337
Willis,William:..............175
Wilson,Amelia:.......131,286,345
Wilson,Andrew:...............270
Wilson,Benjamin:.........359,361
Wilson,Birdv:................200
Wilson,Catherine:.184,258,420,421
Wilson,David:...48,73,100,252,315
:........................362,440
Wilson,Denny:................100
Wilson,Elizabeth:........100,246
Wilson,Ephraim K.:............35
Wilson,Ephraim King:.........341
Wilson,Ephraim:.46,49,100,131,246
:247,286,319,345,364,415,440,443
Wilson,Esther:...131,286,345,443
Wilson,George D.:........286,345
Wilson,George Dashiell:......415
Wilson,George:...59,96,99,120,131
:168,200,236,286,287,338,345,439
:............................440
Wilson,Henry:.....184,258,420,421
Wilson,Isaac:................111
Wilson,James:........99,100,362
Wilson,Jane:.............319,364
Wilson,John:...29,100,270,341,398
:............................439
Wilson,Leah Littleton:....69,280
Wilson,Leah:........164,254,273
Wilson,Levin:..73,292,317,362,441
Wilson,Mary:........270,398,439
Wilson,Polly:................320
Wilson,Prissy:...............442
Wilson,Richard:..............398
Wilson,Robert:...............270
Wilson,Sally:................420
Wilson,Samuel:.69,100,164,254,273
:............280,315,317,425
Wilson,Thomas:.29,100,270,332,341
:........................398,439
Wilson,William:..........258,438
Wimbro,Thomas:...............432
Wimbrow,Thomas:..............153
Winder,Charlotte A.H.:.......230

Winder,Charlotte:........361,386
Winder,Gertrude:...49,356,365,367
:............................441
Winder,Harriet:..............341
Winder,Harriett:.35,50,70,110,256
Winder,Henry:................230
Winder,Hetty W.:...320,356,365,367
:............................441
Winder,John:..109,232,245,246,318
:319,320,356,364,366,367,368,434
:....................435,441,442
Winder,Leah:.................442
Winder,Levin:..62,138,216,283,285
:304,313,319,320,356,365,367,423
:........................424,441
Winder,Nancy:................334
Winder,Peggy:................364
Winder,Rider H.:.............386
Winder,Rider Henry:..........230
Winder,Thomas J.:.35,50,70,256,341
Winder,Thomas Jones:.........365
Winder,Thomas:....110,320,427,434
Winder,William A.:...........334
Winder,William H.:.49,334,361,442
Winder,William Henry:.7,81,83,138
:....230,275,278,351,356,367,441
Winder,William:..2,3,4,7,10,44,45
:...48,50,73,81,83,91,92,117,133
:138,158,171,216,230,238,259,262
:275,278,285,304,313,317,318,319
:320,335,351,356,358,359,360,361
:364,365,367,368,373,385,396,407
:....412,423,424,425,441,442,443
Windsor,Ann:..................94
Windsor,Henry:................94
Windsor,James:.94,294,305,352,442
Windsor,Jesse:...............232
Windsor,John:.....94,136,175,362
Windsor,Lazarus:..............94
Windsor,Mary:.................94
Windsor,Phillip:.............232
Windsor,William:..............81
Wingate,John:............121,432
Wingate,Phillip:..121,254,333,432
Wingate,Thomas:..........182,432
Wingate,William:..............70
Winright,Ann:................411
Winright,Betty:..............315
Winright,Bridget:........119,307
Winright,Cannon:..132,217,218,315
:....................434,446,447
Winright,Charles:..16,181,319,320
:............................360
Winright,Eleanor:..40,145,189,411
:............................417

Winright,Elizabeth:...........335
Winright,Evans:............218,434
Winright,George:..........330,417
Winright,James:..40,51,143,145,189
:................315,411,446,447
Winright,Jane:.40,181,315,411,417
:...........................446
Winright,Jenny:................389
Winright,John:.....23,121,306,409
Winright,Levin:80,112,119,185,307
:....................357,411,442
Winright,Mary:.............218,249
Winright,Mezick:...............389
Winright,Nancy:40,315,389,411,417
:...........................446
Winright,Nelly:............315,446
Winright,Sally:................389
Winright,Sarah:.................16
Winright,Solomon:...56,72,112,119
:....185,189,255,307,315,373,446
Winright,Stephen:.132,211,217,218
:.......................249,434
Winright,William:...56,90,119,226
:................315,335,442,446
Wishart,William:..177,242,266,291
:...........................421
Wood,John:......................39
Wood,Thomas:...............15,407
Wood,William:..................39
Woodgate,William:......356,419,444
Wooten,Benjamin:...........214,219
Wooten,Edward:......91,214,218,219
Wooten,Hetty:.................210
Wooten,John:.......63,214,219,351
Wooten,Richard:.................9
Wooten,Sarah:..............91,214
Wooten,William Turner:..........9
Worthington,Samuel:...........163
Wright,Alice:.................340
Wright,Beauchamp A.:..........406
Wright,Belitha:....63,208,427,428
Wright,Benjamin:........16,65,302
Wright,Bloyce:........124,443,447
Wright,Boaz:..................153
Wright,Clement M.:............406
Wright,Delaney:........63,208,428
Wright,Easter:.................40
Wright,Edward:......15,27,273,430
Wright,Eliza:.................317
Wright,Elizabeth:.........359,385
Wright,Frances:...............287
Wright,George W.:.........306,324
Wright,Isaac K.:..........235,406
Wright,Isaac:.............362,436
Wright,Isaiah:............93,447

Wright,Jacob:...........16,65,302
Wright,Jeremiah:...14,273,327,440
Wright,John:...................97
Wright,Joseph:..16,65,302,314,338
Wright,Judith:................447
Wright,Levin:..40,292,306,314,324
:.......................338,385
Wright,Lydia:.......13,14,327,440
Wright,Mary Ann:...63,208,427,428
Wright,Mary:..................292
Wright,Methia:.........63,387,428
Wright,Sarah:.........124,443,447
Wright,Solomon:...124,284,385,447
Wright,Sophia:.............45,418
Wright,Stephen:.62,63,158,208,317
:....................387,427,428
Wright,Thomas:................262
Wright,William:40,124,284,287,292
:....314,319,359,385,414,443,447
Wright,Willin:........235,338,406
Wright,Zebulon:...........340,418
Wroten,John:...................66
Wroughton,Josiah:.............243
Wyeth,James:................29,30
Wyley,Jarrad:.168,219,416,432,448
Wyley,Martha:.................432
Young,Ann:................221,448
Young,George:.............141,357
Young,Jehu:...................298
Young,Jonathan:.......141,182,357
Young,Lawrence:.......220,221,298
Young,Mary:....................77
Young,Thomas:..................77
Young,William:........189,298,407

486

Other Heritage Books by Ruth T. Dryden:

Cemetery Records of Somerset County, Maryland

Cemetery Records of Worcester County, Maryland

Land Records of Somerset County, Maryland

Land Records of Wicomico County, Maryland

Land Records of Worcester County, Maryland

Maryland Mortality Schedule: 1850 and 1860

Parish of Somerset: Records of Somerset County, Maryland

Rent Rolls of Somerset County, Maryland, 1663–1723

Somerset County Will Books, 1748–1749

Somerset County Will Books, Liber EB1, 1788–1799

Somerset County Will Books, Liber WK, 1777–1788

Stepney Parish Records of Somerset County, Maryland

Worcester County, Maryland 1850 Census

Worcester County, Maryland Administration Bonds and Inventories, 1783–1790

Worcester County, Maryland Wills, Liber LPS, 1834–1851

Worcester Will Books, Liber JBR, 1799–1803

Worcester Will Books, Liber JBR, 1803–1806

Worcester Will Books, Liber JW, 1790–1799

Worcester Will Books, Liber JW4, 1769–1783

Worcester Will Books, Liber MH, 1806–1813

Worcester Will Books, Liber MH, 1813–1822

Worcester Will Books, Liber MH, 1822–1833